VISIONARIES

VISIO

1 - VIDENTES DE EZQUIOGA Evarista Galdós

2 - VIDENTES DE EZQUIOGA Benita Aguirre

3 - VIDENTES DE EZQUIOGA Cruz Lete

4 - VIDENTES DE EZQUIOGA Ramona Olazábal

NARIES

THE SPANISH REPUBLIC
AND THE REIGN OF CHRIST

WILLIAM A. CHRISTIAN JR.

UNIVERSITY OF CALIFORNIA PRESS

Berkeley
Los Angeles
London

Title page: Souvenir postcards of visionaries
at Ezkioga, 1931. Photos by Joaquín Sicart

The publication of this book was supported
by a generous subvention from the Program for
Cultural Cooperation Between Spain's Ministry
of Culture and United States' Universities

The publisher gratefully acknowledges the
contribution provided by the General Endowment
Fund of the Associates of the University of
California Press

University of California Press
Berkeley and Los Angeles, California
University of California Press
London, England

Library of Congress Cataloging-in-Publication Data

Christian, William A., 1944–
    Visionaries : the Spanish Republic and the
reign of Christ / William A. Christian, Jr.
        p.   cm.
    Includes bibliographical references and
indexes.
    ISBN 0-520-20040-3 (alk. paper)
    1. Mary, Blessed Virgin, Saint—Apparitions
and miracles—Spain—History—20th century.
    2. Mary, Blessed Virgin, Saint—Apparitions
and miracles—Spain—Ezquioga—History—20th
century. 3. Ezquioga (Spain)—Church history—
20th century. 4. Spain—History—Republic,
1931–1939. 5. Spain—Church history—20th
century. I. Title.
BT652.S7C57   1996
232.91'7'094609043—dc20   95-16729

Printed in the United States of America
1 2 3 4 5 6 7 8 9

The paper used in this publication meets the
minimum requirements of American National
Standard for Information Sciences—Permanence
of Paper for Printed Library Materials, ANSI
Z39.48-1984 ∞

CONTENTS

VISUAL EVIDENCE
AND MAPS

*If I do not give a source for the
item in its caption, it is from my
collection*

VISUAL EVIDENCE AND MAPS

CHRONOLOGY

1672–1675   Marguerite-Marie Alacoque at Paray-le-Monial receives promises of the reign of the Sacred Heart of Jesus

1733   Bernardo de Hoyos in Valladolid receives promises that the Sacred Heart will reign in Spain

1830   Catherine Labouré has vision of the Miraculous Medal in Paris

1846   Children have vision at La Salette

1858   Bernadette has first vision at Lourdes

1876   End of last Carlist War, beginning of constitutional monarchy in Spain

1903   Death of Gemma Galgani in Lucca

1904   First diocesan pilgrimage to Lourdes from Basque Country

1917   Three children have their best known visions at Fatima

1917–1920   Social and political unrest in Spain

1918   Stigmata of Padre Pio da Pietrelcina in Puglia

1919   Children first see the Christ of Limpias (Cantabria) move during Capuchin mission

1920	Children first see the Christ of Piedramillera (Navarra) move
1922	First falsification of writings of María Rafols, founder, Daughters of Charity of Santa Ana
1923–1930	Dictatorship of Primo de Rivera
1926	Stigmata of Thérèse Neumann in Bavaria
1931	*14 April.* Municipal elections lead to proclamation of the Second Republic; Alfonso XIII abdicates and leaves Spain
	23 April. Children have visions in Torralba de Aragón (Huesca)
	10–13 May. Anticlerical rioters burn religious houses in Madrid, Málaga, and other cities
	17 May. Government expels Mateo Múgica, bishop of Vitoria, for alleged political propaganda
	4 June. Children have visions in Mendigorría (Navarra)
	16 June. Government expels Cardinal Pedro Segura, primate of Spain
	18 June. Mendigorría townspeople ambush passing Republicans
	28 June. Elections to Constituent Cortes, political violence in Bergara
	29 or 30 June. Children have first visions at Ezkioga; nightly visions for rest of the year
	7 July. First notice of Ezkioga visions in the press
	12, 16, 18 July. People expect miracles, crowds of 50,000 persons

late July. Carmen Medina arrives at Ezkioga

1 August. Francisco Goicoechea allegedly levitates

10 August. Raymond de Rigné and Marie-Geneviève Thirouin arrive at Ezkioga

early August. Visions begin in Basque villages in Navarra, mainly by children

13 August. Antonio de la Villa denounces Ezkioga visions in Constituent Cortes

22 August. Government suspends rightist press and sends troops to the north

26 August. Children begin visions in Guadamur (Toledo)

2 October. María Naya finds Rafols prediction of visible miracles

14 October. Cortes approves separation of Church and State

15 October. Ramona Olazábal's public wounding; 20,000 present

16 October. 80,000 attend visions

17 October. Over 50,000 persons see "miracles" of girl from Ataun and others. Vicar general of diocese publicly repudiates Ramona's miracle

1–20 November. In *El Pueblo Vasco*, Rafael Picavea discredits the visions

13 November. Padre Burguera arrives at Ezkioga

17 November. The seer José Garmendia visits President Macià in Barcelona

13 December. First Aulina expedition from Barcelona at Ezkioga

27 December. Diocese forbids priests from going to the site

1932 *mid-January*. Vision crucifixions begin

29 January. Dissolution of Society of Jesus in Spain; María Naya finds Rafols prediction of the chastisement of Spanish cities

5 February. State decrees the removal of religious images from town halls in Gipuzkoa

20 April. Laburu's lecture against the visions in Vitoria (June 21 and 28 in San Sebastián)

10 August. General José Sanjurjo attempts coup in Sevilla from Medina family house

6 October. Believers install image in chapel

8 October–early December. Governor Jesús del Pozo confines seers and promoters

December. Visions at Beauraing, Belgium

1933 *January–March*. Visions at Banneux, Belgium

11 April. Mateo Múgica returns as bishop of Vitoria

May–December. Padre Burguera tests and eliminates seers

17 May. Beatification of Gemma Galgani in Rome

5 August. 300,000 persons at Beauraing for predicted miracle

	19 August. Bishop Múgica sends report on Ezkioga visions to the Holy Office
	10 September. Degrelle and Rex expedition at Ezkioga
	15 September. Bishop Múgica denies the supernatural character of visions and forbids seers to go to site
1934	*January.* Rigné publishes *Une Nouvelle Affaire Jeanne d'Arc*
	9 March. Múgica bans books on Ezkioga
	18 June. Holy Office issues decree against visions at Ezkioga; cult goes underground
fall 1934–spring 1936	Periodic arrests of Ezkioga believers by the Republic
1935	*March.* Burguera and Sedano de la Peña take the book *Los Hechos de Ezquioga* to Rome
18 July 1936–1 April 1939	Military uprising against the Second Republic; Spanish Civil War
January 1937–December 1941	Persecution of Ezkioga believers in Gipuzkoa by the Franco state
1945–1954	New visions, especially by children, throughout Spain, particularly after circulation of statues of the Virgin of Fatima
1952	Believers visit Bishop Font y Andreu of San Sebastián
1961–1965	Girls have visions at San Sebastián de Garabandal (Cantabria)
1981	Teenagers begin visions at Medjugorje

ACKNOWLEDGMENTS

When I started this work in earnest, in 1982, the visions at Ezkioga were within the range of useful memory. Some of those I thank below have died; others who talked to me have now forgotten not only what they knew but who I am. Eyes once bright are now weak. Every citation in the notes is a heartfelt thanks. I thank the following persons who helped me gain access to sources: Francisca Aguirre, Txemi Apaolaza, Gurutzi Arregi, Asier Astigarraga, Matilde Ayerbe, José Miguel de Barandiarán, Iñaki Bastarrika, Jesús Beraza, Josefa Bereciartu, Peter Brown, José María Busca Isusi, William A. Christian, Sr., Salvador Cardús (grandson) and Oriol Cardús Grau, Julio Caro Baroja, Leonor Castillo, Juan Celaya, Simone Duro, Jon Elorriaga, Francisco Ezcurdia, Cristina García Rodero, Angel de la Hoz, Luis Irurzun, Temma Kaplan, Rhys Isaac, William James, Marivi and Lorenzo Jayo, Lynzee Klingman, Manuel Lecuona, Ander Manterola, Andrés de Mañaricua, Andrea Marcos, José Martínez Julià, Francisco Mendiueta, Pío and Angeles Montoya, Antonio Navarro, Santiago Onaindia, Dionisio Oñatibia, Ignacio

Oñatibia, Jabier Otermin, Richard Pearce, Joan Prat, the widow of Fernand Remisch, Lourdes Rodes, Salvador Rodríguez Becerra, Josefina Romà, Antoni Sospedra Buyé, José Ignacio Tellechea Idigoras, Ignasi Terradas, Gail Ullman, and Laurence Wylie. Others requested anonymity but know who they are.

Libraries and archives: Archivo diocesano de Vitoria, A. González de Langarica; Archivo diocesano de San Sebastián, Andoni Eizaguirre; Archivo diocesano de Pamplona, J. Salas Tirapu; Seminario de Vitoria, Ignacio Oñatibia; Jesuit Province of Loyola, J. R. Eguillor; Hemeroteca Municipal de San Sebastián, Arantxa Arzamendi; Hemeroteca Municipal de Madrid; Biblioteca de la Provincia de Castilla, PP. Capuchinos, Madrid; Hemeroteca Municipal de Barcelona; all the staff of Instituto Labayru, Derio, who were extraordinarily attentive; Euzkalzaindia; Bibliotecas Municipales de Bilbao, Terrassa, Sabadell, and Reus; Editorial Auñamendi, especially Idoia Estornés Zubizarreta; Archivo Histórico de Navarra; Biblioteca Nacional, Madrid; Centro Nacional de Microfilm, Encarnación Ochoa; Bibliothèque Nationale, Paris; Bibliothèque Royale, Bruxelles; Library of Congress, especially Dolores Martin and Georgette Magassy Dorn; Wilson Center Library, especially Zed David; Getty Center Library, especially Lois White and Chris Jahnke; and the Basque Studies Center at the University of Nevada, Reno.

During much of this project I had the support of fellowships. My deepest gratitude to the John Simon Guggenheim Foundation, the U.S.-Spanish Cultural Committee, the Woodrow Wilson Center, the John D. and Catherine T. MacArthur Foundation, and the Getty Center for the History of Art and the Humanities.

The following readers commented on the entire manuscript: L.W. Bonbrake, Harvey Cox, Henk Driessen, James Lang, Kathryn Sklar, Richard Trexler, and two anonymous readers. Henk Driessen, James Lang, and particularly Richard Minear made especially careful readings. Others read particular chapters: Jodi Bilinkoff, William Callahan, Oriol and Josep Cardús, Eric Foner, Lynn Garafola, Judith Herman, Michael Holly, Willy Jansen, Gábor Klaniczáy, Aviad Kleinberg, Ander Manterola, Gaspar Martínez, Lourdes Rodes, and Tom Yager. Joseba Zulaika supported this project with head and heart from start to finish. *Biotz-biotzen lagun.*

My expert copy editor, Amanda Clark Frost, devoted considerable time and energy to making this book clear and coherent. Michelle Bonnice oversaw the book's production and helped with the hard choices among photographs. Randall Goodall designed the book and the jacket. In 1972 Stanley Holwitz saw to the publication of *Person and God in a Spanish Valley,* the engine in this long train of thought, and I am grateful for his support and advice in the final stages of this work. Josefa Martínez Berriel, Fatima Martínez Berriel, Josefa Berriel Jordán, and the rest of the clan cheerfully did my chores when I was away from home. This work is for Pepa and Palma with all my love. Just as the visions were a collective enterprise, so was this book. Thank you one and all.

On 29 June 1931 two young children in the Basque Country of northern Spain said they saw the Virgin Mary. That initial vision led to many others. Indeed, for many months visions took place on a nightly basis. In 1931 alone, about one million persons went to the apparitions on a hillside at Ezkioga and people began having visions in a score of other towns. The hundreds of seers at Ezkioga attracted the most observers for any visions in the Catholic world until the teenagers of Medjugorje in the 1980s.

This book is about two kinds of visionaries and their interrelations: the seers (*videntes* in Spanish, *ikusleak* in Basque) who had visions of Mary and the saints and the believers and promoters who had a vision for the future which they hoped Mary and the saints would confirm. Almost all are now dead, but they left behind words on paper, images in photographs, and memories in people who believed them. The protagonists included nuns, friars and priests, writers and photographers, military officers and civil servants, housemaids and aristocrats, farmers and textile manufacturers, and many, many children. Starting in 1931, they made a long, concerted attempt to convince a skeptical world that heavenly beings were appearing on the Iberian peninsula.

I have immersed myself in their lives, retraced their steps, hunted down their papers, attempted to reconstitute their world. When I began to write, the pleasure of telling their story mingled with regret that my time with them would soon be over. I am not one of them, as I never failed to tell their present-day survivors and successors. But while their efforts to arouse the world failed, the efforts of others like them in the past did not fail and most certainly have affected our world. How visions occur and who believes in them is everybody's business.

At this moment I am watching from my window exotic birds called hoopoes, sandy with black and white stripes, their crests flaring as they clash and play in the red-brown field of young, blue-green cabbages. They swerve, chatter in the air around each other, then separate to bob and feed in the shallow furrows. I have told stories of lives that begin before the visions, loop into them, intersect, and then loop out, each to a separate destination. In the first half of the book I tell the tales separately, building the picture of events layer on layer from the perspective of the different protagonists. For the people would not let me go. Through my immersion in this unusual world, their story has also become mine. This is not earthshaking history. It is small, intense, poignant, sometimes fierce, often funny. Its lasting lessons, I think, are about human nature itself. Like a novel, this book has a cast of characters, here listed as a separate index of persons at the end of the book. Unlike a novel, the story is a true one—at least as true as I can make it. For me, as I entered the story, Benita Aguirre, Padre Burguera, María Recalde, Mateo Múgica, and their contemporaries became quite familiar, a little larger than life. I hope readers too will get to know and enjoy them.

Readers seeking a narrative of the events can turn to four chapters: "Mary, the Republic, and the Basques," "Suppression by Church and State," "The Proliferation of Visions," and "Aftermath." Three other chapters about promoters and seers cover the events at Ezkioga through the lives of the principals.

The second part of the book uses the visions to detail the often secret ways that seers and clergy connected, the landscape seers imagined and constructed, and the trancelike states seers entered. The visions linked women with priests, the rural poor with the industrial wealthy, and the living with the dead. The events at Ezkioga show how much people welcome the chance to go beyond the world around them, see what the gods see, and know what only the gods can know.

José Donoso suggested that I stick with a few key characters and tell the events through them. But by then I knew too much about too many people. I had to tell what I knew to resolve my story as well as theirs. I regretted starting to write, but I have no regrets at coming to the end. The hoopoes have gone. Men are outside sending shafts of water curling down the furrows of cabbages, shouting instructions, opening and closing passages of dirt.

Tafira Baja, Gran Canaria
1 September 1994

1. INTRODUCTION

VISIONS OF THE divine are as old as humanity. They have continued in the postindustrial age. You may read about them in tomorrow's newspaper. The visions at Ezkioga in 1931 reflect a phase in the history of Western society and in the place of Catholic divinities in that society. Their story is also universal and perennial: it is the story of people who claim to speak with the gods and try to tell what they heard and saw and it is the story of other people who try to stop them.

Spanish Catholics used to deal with the divine not only as individuals but also as members of groups. Legally, citizens owed devotion to the town's patron saints. Members of guilds or professions had additional obligations to other saints. Typically, the Virgin Mary in a specific local avatar was the protector of a community for general problems, and some of her shrines, like Guadalupe and Montserrat, drew devotion from vast areas. Other saints were specialists for particular problems. People understood apparitions as one of the many ways that Mary and other saints bestowed protection and requested devotion.

In fifteenth-century Spain the visionaries that people believed tended to be men and children. The divine beings they saw generally offered ways for towns to avoid epidemic disease and often called on towns to revive older, dormant chapels in the countryside. Some of the visions harked back to stereotypic scenarios of "miraculous" discoveries of relics and to legends of similar discoveries of images. Two centuries earlier, theologians had condemned as pagan some of the motifs in the visions—Mary clothed in white light on a tree, a nocturnal procession of a woman accompanied by the dead. By the second decade of the sixteenth century the Inquisition had stifled these visions in central Spain. Local and devotional, the visions were no threat to doctrine, but both the church and the monarchy were afraid of heretics and freelance prophets.[1]

The Counter-Reformation served to focus devotion on Mary in the parish church rather than on specialist saints in dispersed chapels. A new set of lifelike images of Christ joined those of Mary as sources of help. In this period, the seventeenth and eighteenth centuries, Spanish Catholics found alternate miraculous events that did not threaten the church's control of revelation. In particular, towns turned to an ancient tradition of bleeding and sweating images. In these miracles without messages, everyone was a seer and the clergy controlled the meaning. Most of the three dozen or so Spanish cases of images that "came alive" in the Early Modern period were of Christ in some phase of the Passion. These events occurred particularly in years of crisis.[2] At the end of the eighteenth and the beginning of the nineteenth century bishops discouraged this kind of religiosity as superstitious.

Religious orders had their own images whose power was independent of place, like Our Lady of Mount Carmel. One such image, which the Jesuits in particular propagated, was the Sacred Heart of Jesus, based on the visions of the nun Marguerite-Marie Alacoque (1647–1690) in Paray-le-Monial, northwest of Lyon. She said that Jesus, with his heart exposed, promised that he would reign throughout the world. Devotions like Our Lady of Mount Carmel and the Sacred Heart came to have standardized images and the pope rewarded prayers to these devotions with indulgences. Communities often domesticated these general figures for local use, and some of these standard images became the focus of shrines in their own right, like Our Lady of Mount Carmel of Jerez and Paray-le-Monial itself. There was a constant tension between the Roman church, allied with religious orders, which stimulated devotions and holy figures that were inclusive and universal, and the local church, identified with nation, town, or village, which tended to fix a devotion and make it exclusive and local.

Toward the end of the nineteenth century, however, when Catholicism was on the defensive, the Vatican came to realize that the church should play to its strength. In southern Europe that strength lay in localized religion. By "crowning" Marian shrine images, the papacy associated them with the universal church. Rome also endorsed a new series of proclamations of Marian images as patrons of dioceses or provinces. And it regarded with increasing sympathy visions of Mary that led to the establishment of new shrines. For by the nineteenth century virtually every adult in the Western world knew that there were profoundly different ways to organize society and imagine what happened after death. The industrialization of Europe in the eighteenth and nineteenth centuries had separated large numbers of rural folk from local authority and belief and many migrants to cities had found alternatives to established religion in deism, spiritism, science, or the idea of progress.[3]

The continued strength of Catholicism in nineteenth-century France was an incentive for intellectuals to challenge the idea of the supernatural radically and intensively. As a result, French Catholics needed all the divine help they could get. Throughout the century they sought and received innumerable signs that God and, in particular, the Virgin Mary were with them. An efficient railway system and press ensured that regional devotions could reach national audiences. Secularization was a global problem, and the Vatican developed a global response to centralize and standardize devotion. France and Italy served as laboratories for devotional vaccines against moral diseases. Religious orders distributed these vaccines. Indeed, Our Lady of Lourdes became a new kind of general devotion, one with its origin in the laity. Replicas of the image entered parish churches worldwide.[4]

Visions took place throughout the nineteenth century in France.[5] Three particular French visions set important precedents for the events that are the subject of this book: those of Catherine Labouré in Paris in 1830, those of Mélanie Calvat and Maximin Giraud at La Salette in 1846, and those of Bernadette Soubirous at Lourdes in 1858. The people of Spain knew about these episodes from pious accounts.

According to these accounts, the Daughters of Charity delayed admitting Catherine Labouré, age twenty-four, until she learned to read and write. She had numerous visions, but the first in the series that made her famous occurred in July 1830, after she had been a novice three months. A spirit boy about five years old woke her and led her to the main altar of the novitiate, where she found the Virgin Mary seated. Mary wept violently, told of great disasters that would befall France and all of Europe, and said that Catherine, the Daughters of Charity, and the Vincentian Fathers would have grace in abundance. This was only days before the revolution of 1830, during which crowds attacked many churches and religious houses. Four months later, in November, Catherine saw Mary emerge resplendent from a dark cloud in the church. The Virgin bore a halo of words: "O Mary, conceived without sin, pray for us who come to you for help!" She held a small globe in her hands and lifted it up to heaven, where it disappeared. The Virgin then held out her hands and suddenly on each finger there were three rings covered with precious jewels giving off bright rays. Catherine saw the image revolve. On its back there was an M with a cross on top and below it the Sacred

Hearts of Jesus and Mary. She heard a voice say, "It is necessary to strike a medal that looks like this. All who wear it . . . will receive many favors, above all if they wear it around the neck." Mary insisted on the medals in successive appearances until finally Catherine's confessor, Jean Marie Aladel, ordered them made.

Labouré's visions were like those of other religious who received privileges for their orders. In this the Miraculous Medal was like the scapular of the Carmelites and the rosary of the Dominicans. The timing of Labouré's visions and the iconography—the Virgin had her foot on a serpent—pointed to the medal's assignment as a response to the devil and his works. Aladel emphasized the medal's efficacy for nonbelievers and Protestants as well as Catholics. The church publicized widely how the medal converted a Jew in Strasbourg in 1842. It worked apparently even if someone merely slipped it under a pillow. By 1842 people had bought 130,000 copies of Aladel's description of the visions and well over one hundred million medals.[6]

The pious accounts of the visions of La Salette were as follows: in 1846 in the French Alps near Grenoble, Mélanie and Maximin, fifteen and eleven years old, respectively, saw a lady in white. She warned of an imminent famine as a punishment from Christ and called for people not to work on Sundays and not to swear or eat meat on fast days. She also gave the children secrets. The waters there soon produced cures. And a military officer found a likeness of the face of Christ on a fragment of the rock on which the Virgin had sat. People began to go to the site in numbers. In 1851 the bishop of Grenoble decreed the visions worthy of belief and forbade any criticism of them. Subsequently, Mélanie released versions of her secret, which resembled medieval apocalyptic prophecies. The La Salette apparition was private. No one saw the children seeing the Virgin. And the seers did not claim to enter a trance state. In these ways too the La Salette visions were similar to medieval visions.[7]

The visions of fourteen-year-old Bernadette Soubirous of Lourdes marked a change. In 1858 Bernadette saw the Virgin about three dozen times over five months in the presence of crowds that reached thousands in number. She went with a lighted candle and prayed the rosary in public. The Virgin told her, she said, to return for fifteen days. Eventually over fifty persons had visions in and around the same cave. Bernadette's abstracted state while having visions convinced a skeptical doctor and through him other town worthies.

Prior to these nineteenth-century French cases, visions by rural laypersons had addressed broader geopolitical issues only occasionally.[8] Many people understood the visions at La Salette and Lourdes simply as signs to establish new shrines. But the secrets that Mélanie divulged addressed the division between Catholics and rationalists. And at Lourdes the Virgin reaffirmed the authority of the pope by confirming the dogma of the Immaculate Conception.

Although many churchmen were reluctant to accept children as carriers of messages from God, the French visions put these doubts by and large to rest. The crowds that converged on Lourdes by rail eventually made it one of the most popular shrines in Christendom. By the turn of the century the cures there became the great new argument not only for Bernadette's visions but for the Catholic religion and the supernatural in general. When in the First World War the bishop of Tarbes called on the Virgin to help France against Germany, even the Third Republic made peace with Lourdes.

How did these visions affect Iberia? In the nineteenth century Catholics in Spain, their church shorn and starved, needed a lift as much as those in France. Urban radicals and poor people afraid of cholera went on a rampage in the summer of 1835, killing seventy-eight male religious in Madrid and sacking religious houses throughout much of Spain. Liberal governments suppressed virtually all male religious orders and gradually sold off most church property. Spanish clerics began to look to the papacy for help and moral support. When the orders filtered back into Spain—first the female service orders, then the male ones—they brought new devotions from France and revived older general ones like the Sacred Heart of Jesus.[9]

The Daughters of Charity entered Spain in increasing numbers after 1850. Vincentians published Jean Marie Aladel's book on Catherine Labouré in Spanish in 1885. By 1922 there were twelve thousand members of the Association of the Miraculous Medal in Spain, mainly children in schools run by the Daughters of Charity. In May 1930 the primate of Spain, Cardinal Pedro Segura, held a national conference in Madrid celebrating the centenary of the visions. Five bishops led a procession including three floats of Labouré seeing the Virgin.[10]

Less than a year after the La Salette vision, people in Barcelona could buy pamphlets about it in Spanish and Catalan, and by 1860 they could buy manuals in Spanish for pilgrims. In 1883 Catholic militants in Barcelona formed the association of Our Lady of La Salette to combat both blasphemy and work on Sunday. They held dawn rosaries in the city streets. They eventually had to desist when crowds gathered to harass them and sing the Marseillaise. Spaniards who worried about the apocalypse knew Mélanie's prophecy. Eventually it intruded on the vision messages of Ezkioga.[11]

Lourdes became the spiritual touchstone of the times. There is no facet of the Ezkioga visions—the liturgy, the prayers, the new shrine, the chief promoters—that Lourdes did not influence. Lourdes was just across the Pyrenees. Devotion was intense in the Basque Country, Navarra, and Catalonia, all areas critical to this story. Prior to the Spanish Civil War in 1936 the Basque Country and Catalonia each provided over 30 percent of Spain's pilgrims to Lourdes. There had always been close ties across the mountains, and Basque, Navarrese, and Catalan cultural zones straddled the frontier. Basques considered Bernadette one of theirs, and Basque nationalists held pilgrimages with a political slant.

Spanish pilgrims saw that Lourdes was revitalizing Catholicism in France and began to hope for a Lourdes in Spain.[12] In the first two decades of the twentieth century Spanish visions that reached the press occurred mainly in the zone of devotion to Lourdes. In them people saw images of Christ move or agonize. This trend came to a climax at Limpias, a small town in Cantabria close to the Basque Country, precisely when World War I prevented travel to the shrine of Lourdes. In the period 1919–1926 the Christ in Agony at Limpias attracted over a quarter of a million pilgrims. The diocese of Santander modeled the Limpias pilgrimages on those of Lourdes. We can document at least forty-five pilgrimages and tens of thousands of pilgrims from the Basque Country and Navarra. About one in ten of the pilgrims saw the image move. The visions occurred in a period of high inflation, general strikes, and political turmoil. Some of those in power understood the visions as divine signs in favor of the nation. As at Limpias a year earlier, children and adults of a village in Navarra saw their crucifix move in 1920. These visions at Piedramillera lasted for more than a year, but the diocese took care to limit newspaper reports and people gradually stopped going there.

The visions at Limpias and Piedramillera were hybrids. Like the baroque miracles of the Early Modern period, they involved preexisting statues of Christ and did not include explicit messages. But like the medieval visions and those of Catherine Labouré and the children of La Salette and Lourdes, they were subjective experiences. That is, the crucifixes had no liquid on them and only some people saw them move. Spaniards appeared to be inching toward the full-fledged talking apparitions of the medieval past, which the French had already revived. The visions at Limpias and Piedramillera were important precedents for those of Ezkioga.[13]

By July 1931 Spaniards, and Basques in particular, had just begun to hear about the visions at Fatima in Portugal. Led by Lucia Dos Santos, born in 1907, children in a hamlet to the north of Lisbon had several visions from 1916 on; the most famous were those on the thirteenth day of six successive months in 1917. The Fatima visions took place during an anticlerical republican regime and they became a reaffirmation of Catholicism. In 1927 a Dominican magazine in the Basque Country began to publish accounts of cures at Fatima, which the author considered "a permanent challenge to materialist and rationalist criticism." In 1930 the magazine described the visions after the bishop of Leire in Portugal declared them worthy of credit. But Fatima did not gain popularity in Spain until the 1940s, after Lucia revealed messages that gave the apparitions an explicitly anticommunist slant.[14]

The visions at Ezkioga were the first large-scale apparitions of the old talking but invisible type in Spain since the sixteenth century. But they included the innovations of Lourdes: there were many seers, the seers had their visions in public view, and most of the seers entered some kind of altered state. We will see how the social and political situation of Spain and the Basque Country encouraged Catholics to believe the seers.

The reader should know something about nationalism in Spain, the Basque Country, and Catalonia. The less authoritarian and more democratic the central government, the less Spain coheres. At present, in the new freedom after the long dictatorship of Francisco Franco, in the Basque Country and Catalonia in particular, many people are careful to refer to Spain only as a state, not as a nation. When the majority of male voters brought in the Second Republic in April 1931, Spain was a mosaic of cultures that hundreds of years of royal rule had done little to homogenize. The regions with the strongest nationalist movements were those with the most international contacts: the Basques lived on both sides of the border with France and had a major trading partner in Great Britain; Catalonia, also on the border, traded with the Mediterranean countries and the Caribbean. These external contacts meant that some regional elites did not depend entirely on Madrid and resented its taxes, bureaucracy, and language. Eight years of centralized rule by General Miguel Primo de Rivera in the twenties had exacerbated these resentments. Even in regions with virtually no separatist sentiment in 1931, people had a strong sense that they were different culturally. The Navarrese, for instance, had a past that helped them maintain an identity distinct from that as Spaniards. Navarra was once an independent kingdom that spanned the Pyrenees. Those Navarrese who lived in a strip running across the north of the province spoke Basque, and in the distant past most of the region's inhabitants had been Basque-speaking. Most still had Basque family names and lived in towns with names of Basque origin.

As a mass phenomenon the apparitions at Ezkioga were a kind of dialogue between divinities and the anticlerical left—anarchists and socialists in the Basque coastal cities, socialist farmworkers in Navarra, republican railway officials and schoolteachers in rural areas, anticlerical poor in cities throughout Spain, and socialist and communist movements worldwide. In this aspect Ezkioga was similar to other modern apparitions. As over the years the enemy changed from Freemasons and liberals to communists, the messages seers conveyed changed to maintain the dialogue. But any analysis that reads the last two centuries of Marian visions as a clerical plot to thwart social progress is impoverished, as we shall see.[15] To be sure, visions are easy to manipulate for political purposes. But at Ezkioga people of all classes immediately put the seers to work for other practical and spiritual ends. Apparitions spark little interest without people's general hunger for access to the divine.

To ascribe visions to particular psychological needs—sexual drive, for example, or the search for parental affection—constitutes another kind of reduction. Of necessity observers base such theories on a very small and very skewed sample; the visionaries who become famous. It might well be that a given psychological profile simply makes seers more believable or more likely to persist in their visions. There will be visions as long as people believe in them, so to understand visions we must study the believers. Thus one set of lessons we can draw from the visions at Ezkioga has to do with context.

Other lessons are less bound to time and place. In religions people interact with the gods and with one another. This study is in part a window on how new religious worlds come to be. All innovation has to struggle against an established order that attempts to absorb or suppress it. Visions are intrinsically subversive; they go over the head of human to divine superiors. In this sense Ezkioga is a microcosm of the excitement and crosscurrents of every schism and heresy.

Another larger theme is the way people formulate their hopes. At Ezkioga people did so in various ways. One was a collective process of trial and error by which local elites, the press, and the general public selected and rewarded certain vision messages. Here it almost seems appropriate to speak of a collective consciousness. Particular groups also induced messages with a desired content by their questions. These processes illustrate the wider question that underlies this work: how society structures perception.

I wrote this book with the advantage of the work of others. And when I had completed the manuscript I read the book by David Blackbourn about the visions that started in Marpingen in the Saarland in 1876 and the books by Paolo Apolito about the visions that started in 1985 at Oliveto Citra in Campania. The visions at Marpingen, like those at Ezkioga, took place in a hostile state and in a diocese without a bishop. The visions at Oliveto Citra have had even more seers than those of Ezkioga. Apolito was present almost from the start and was able to observe many of the processes that I reconstruct from interviews and documents.

Church sympathy for visions has waxed and waned. It waxed in the mid to late nineteenth century (the model was La Salette and then Lourdes), the mid-1930s (the model was Lourdes), the late 1940s (the models were Fatima and Lourdes), and the 1970s and 1980s (the models were Fatima and Medjugorje). The needs of the church periodically overcome its suspicion of lay revelation, and particular popes have been more sympathetic than others. But there also exists a cyclical dynamic of discouragement that emerges when visions threaten church authority or become commonplace.

Since I began this study, most of the official place-names in the Basque Country and Catalonia have changed. I use the official place-names as of mid-1994. Many of these for Bizkaia, Gipuzkoa, and northern Navarra are different, usually only slightly, from the official names in 1931, but they were already in use among Basque speakers and in Basque-language publications at that time. I have respected the old spellings in direct quotations. In part 5 of the appendix I list the Basque places in this book whose names have changed. For the sake of simplicity I have left Vitoria (instead of Vitoria-Gasteiz), Mondragón (Arrasate-

Mondragón), and San Sebastián (Donostia-San Sebastián) in their Spanish forms.

I do not address the question essential for many believers: were the apparitions "true"? As I told my friends among the Ezkioga believers and in the diocese, I must stick to human history. By upbringing and nationality I am an outsider ill-equipped to tell Basques, Spaniards, and Catholics what is sacred and what is profane. In any case, I am quite unwilling to try.

EVENTS

DURING JULY and August 1931 at Ezkioga in northern Spain, scores of Basque seers had increasingly elaborate and explicit visions of the Virgin. The visions offered a way to mobilize the Basque community and focus their hopes. Watching Basque society define and tap this new power is like watching a kind of social x-ray or scanner. In the case of the Ezkioga visions, the scan highlights a struggle between competing views of the world. At a turning point in Basque and Spanish history, local leaders, the press, and the audience helped the visionaries to articulate general concerns.

THE REPUBLIC AND THE CATHOLIC NORTH

From 1874 to 1923 Spain was a constitutional monarchy in which the Liberal and Conservative oligarchic parties alternated in power. During this period parts of Catalonia and the Basque Country rapidly industrialized. As in much of Western Europe and North America, the labor movement in Spain reached a peak of strength at the conclusion of World War I. In the face of labor unrest and regionalist movements, General Miguel Primo de Rivera installed a military dictatorship, still under royal legitimacy, which lasted from 1923 to 1930. After the general stepped down, the municipal elections of April 1931 became a referendum on the monarchy itself. Republicans won in most major cities and proclaimed the Second Republic. King Alfonso XIII went into exile.

The fall of the monarchy jarred an entire order in which for centuries the relation of king to subjects had been the model for relations of God to persons. By extension it even shook the belief in God. It opened the door to changes in relations between women and men, workers and employers, laity and priests, and children and parents. Human relations are by nature imitative. The change to a republic led to changes in the ways people treated one another. Of course, the fall of the monarchy was effect as well as cause—the effect of gradual shifts in a whole host of social relations, particularly as a result of militant labor movements. Visions of Mary throughout Spain in the spring and summer of 1931 were short-term consequences of the change in the regime, but they also reflected more long-term changes.

On 23 April 1931, nine days after the advent of the Republic, children playing outside the church of Torralba de Aragón (Huesca) saw what they thought was the figure of the Virgin Mary pacing inside, and one girl heard the Virgin say, "Do not mistreat my son." Citizens took this to be a reference to a crucifix in the town hall which the anarchist minority had taken down and broken up. Catholic newspapers reported this vision throughout Spain.[1]

Two weeks later, from May 11 to 13, anticlerical vandals set fire to dozens of religious houses in Madrid and Andalusia. Banner headlines and photographs of gutted buildings and headless images left Spain's Catholics with little doubt about the will of the new republic to defend church property. In mid-May seminary professors in Vitoria, seat of the Basque diocese, concluded that they had no way to affect the policies of the government in Madrid and that instead they should concentrate on preserving the faith in the Basque Country. A priest who attended the gathering told me, "It was a fortress mentality . . . the attitude of us versus them." Further evidence of government hostility came with the expulsion from Spain of Bishop Mateo Múgica of Vitoria for agitating on his pastoral visits (May 17) and of Cardinal Pedro Segura, archbishop of Toledo and primate of Spain (June 16).[2]

In the Basque Country the superiors of urban religious communities asked for police protection. Their fears increased after a fire of suspicious origin at the Benedictine monastery of Lazkao on May 20. Strikes heightened the tension. In a general strike on May 26 and 27 fishermen, workers, women, and children from Pasaia marched on San Sebastián. Police gunfire killed six and wounded scores.

In June this tension found an outlet in religious visions in Mendigorría, a town of 1,300 inhabitants thirty kilometers southwest of Pamplona in the Spanish-speaking part of Navarra. In 1920 in the adjacent town of Mañeru children had had visions of a crucifix moving. Mendigorría, like Mañeru, was a devout town that produced many religious vocations. On 31 May 1931 the Daughters of Mary attended a mass with a general Communion and a sermon by a Capuchin from Sangüesa. In the afternoon, accompanied by the town band, they carried an image of the Virgin through Mendigorría.[3] On the evening of Thursday, June 4, the feast of Corpus Christi, the village priests were in confessionals preparing children for the Communions of the first Friday and the town band was playing in the square. The month of June was dedicated to the Sacred Heart of Jesus, and this image was on a table in the church. A girl went in and saw an unearthly woman in mourning clothes kneeling on a prayer stool before the Sacred Heart. Frightened, the girl told her friends outside. A group went in, saw the woman, and went to tell others. More girls, including younger ones, then went in, saw nothing, and started to pray the rosary. According to one of the children, the schoolmistress told them they should pray for Spain, because it was in a bad way. When the prayer leader reached the phrase in the Litany "Mater Amabilis," she said she saw the figure, and then many of the others girls cried out, "Look at her!" Some saw first a bright light on the little door of the tabernacle. Others saw only a brightness. Others, including the adults present, saw nothing. One adult told the girls to ask the Virgin what she wanted, but all they could get out was, "Madre mía." One girl fell over a chair when, she said, the Virgin called to her. And she saw the Virgin run onto a shelf between two altars. A seer, then nine years old, told me in 1988 that she saw the Sacred Heart tremble, then "a brightness; it seemed to us to be the Virgin of the Sorrows." At the time she felt a strong, sad feeling in her heart. She still thinks the vision was real, but she does not want me to use her name, lest her family think her loony.

Men in the church alerted the priests and rang the bells. After questioning the girls, the parish priest reported to the assembled town what they had said, assured them that he would inform the bishop, and led cheers for the Sacred Heart of Jesus, the Catholic religion, the Virgin, and the Jesuits. The church stayed open until midnight, a vortex of emotions.[4]

Two days later *El Pensamiento Navarro* of Pamplona broke the story with a letter from a villager to a relative in the city. Subsequently, the newspaper carried a more cautious version, which the clergy clearly influenced if not composed, leaving open the possibility of an "obsession" on the part of the girls. One seer told me a priest had offered them candy and told them to say that it was a lie, that otherwise they would have to go to jail; but the girls refused and swore they were telling the truth.[5]

In addition to at least twelve girls roughly nine to fourteen years old, there was a boy seer as well. Lucio, thirteen years old, was an "outsider" who had recently arrived in town. His mother was originally from Mendigorría and his father came from a village near Madrid. The boy worked as a cowherd and said—whether before or after June 4 is unclear—that the Virgin had also appeared to him in the countryside. On June 4 he was standing in line for confession and he too saw the Virgin as a mourning lady.

The next day the Vincentian Hilario Orzanco, director of the juvenile magazine *La Milagrosa y los Niños,* visited the house in Mendigorría of the Daughters of Charity. In his magazine he described the visions as a reward from the Virgin to the girls who had left the music in the square to pray for Spain before the altar of Mary. He pointed to their seeing the Virgin herself in sorrowful prayer before the Sacred Heart and the Eucharist as evidence that she was interceding for Spain and he held up her prayer as an example for his child readers, intimating that they too would have visions if they were good.

> To Her, then, we must address ourselves in these days of trial with a heart contrite for the sacrilege and horrible profanation of the Holy Eucharist and its churches. The profound sorrow of the Virgin, as seen in her mourning clothes and her weeping face, should make us turn inward and sweetly oblige us to atone through her for so many sins. You above all, boys and girls, subscribers to this magazine, you must dearly love the Miraculous Virgin. See how the Virgin answers the prayers of good children.[6]

Some of the Mendigorría children were subscribers to the magazine and would have read articles of a similar nature in earlier issues. As with the visions at Torralba a month earlier, those at Mendigorría did not draw many persons and had few consequences for the villagers or the seers, aside from heightening their piety and excitement.[7]

Incidents during the electoral campaign for the Constituent Cortes kept up a generalized fear in June 1931. On June 14 republicans at stations from Marcilla to Castejón assaulted a trainload of Catholic activists returning to Zaragoza from a demonstration in Pamplona. And in Mendigorría itself on the eighteenth, two weeks after the visions, villagers ambushed a busload of republicans with stones and staves. Police had to rescue two republicans marooned on a rooftop, and six others had to go to hospitals in Pamplona for treatment.[8]

An example of the way Catholics in the Basque Country reacted to all these disturbances was a cartoon on the front page of a Bilbao weekly the day before the election. The drawing shows a single Basque country youth with a club holding off a group of ill-clad urban riffraff carrying burning torches and heading for a rural chapel. The caption read "Not Here!!" An intemperate article railed against immigrant and local leftists.

> Here where little by little they have dirtied our land, where little by little they have invaded our home, where little by little they have undermined our tradition, our holy past, our mission, our honor, here, no! Those people, the accusers, the desecrators, the anarchists, cannot live together with us, because we are honorable people.

"Not Here!!" Electoral cartoon by Goiko. From Adelante *(Bilbao), 27 June 1931. Photo by García Muñoz from a copy in Euskaltzaindia, Bilbao*

In the elections rightist coalitions won handily in Gipuzkoa and Navarra. On that day in Bergara, fifteen kilometers from Ezkioga, electoral violence left several injured and one worker dead.[9]

It is no surprise that under these conditions on 29 June 1931, the day after the elections, a woman who had to stop her car because of a crowd on the highway near Ezkioga thought that some kind of political incident, or explosion, or assassination had taken place. But the crowd had gathered because a brother and a sister, ages seven and eleven, claimed to have seen the Virgin. The immediate and sustained interest in the Ezkioga visions showed that this was the right time and the right place for heaven to intervene in a big way.[10]

Ezkioga is a rural township of dispersed farms in the Goiherri, the uplands of the province of Gipuzkoa. In 1931 it had about 550 inhabitants. Almost all lived on farms and spoke Basque. The town hall, the parish church of Saint Michael, and a government school were in a cluster of houses up the hill from the highway linking Madrid and San Sebastián. Down on the road there were two other small groups of houses, together known as Santa Lucía. The western group, nearer the town of Zumarraga, included a church and a school. The father of the original seers operated a store-tavern in the eastern cluster, and many pilgrims stayed in the Ezpeleta fonda there. The visions occurred on the hillside above these buildings.

How had the Second Republic affected the people of Ezkioga? One of the changes that most pained believers was the removal of crucifixes from schools and government offices. From April 1931 until the end of 1932 the government removed the crucifixes gradually throughout Spain. Manuela Lasa Múgica was the interim schoolteacher in the Santa Lucía barrio of Ezkioga from 1929 to early 1931. She came from the village to the east, Ormaiztegi, and shared the beliefs of her pupils and their families. And so, like her predecessors, she opened the day with a prayer, led the rosary on Saturdays, and celebrated the month of May with flowers and prayers. She kept a statue of Mary and a crucifix in the classroom. But in early 1931 she had to make way for the official teacher, an outsider who did not speak Basque. The community received the woman coldly, and she needed Manuela's help to find lodging. The government instructed the teacher to remove religious images from the classroom, she obeyed, and Manuela remembers people commenting that it was a shame that the children could not celebrate the month of Mary. The Republic thus represented a change for the children of the Santa Lucía, including the two future seers, just as it did for the entire region. Perhaps more so, for the schoolchildren were virtually illiterate in Spanish. Manuela Lasa taught mostly in Basque to students who would leave school at an early age.[11]

In the Basque Country and much of the north of Spain priests and religious were an integral part of the rural and small town population. Many of them came from the more prosperous farms. They shared a common outlook with peasants and those who worked in the factories of the company towns. And all higher education was then still religious education. The universities of the region were its seminaries and novitiates in Vitoria, Pamplona, and Loyola.

This devout rural culture bore one hundred years of suspicion toward the violent anticlericalism of Spain's cities and Spain's progressive governments. The antagonism dated at least from the first Carlist War and its aftermath. In 1833 the deceased king's brother, Don Carlos, rebelled against the liberal monarchy. Carlos promised to restore local liberties and the power of the church and to rule Spain as a consensual monarch of a loose confederation of regions. The stronghold of the Carlists was Navarra and the Basque Country. Enough priests and religious threw in their lot with him that liberals identified religious in general as subversives. This was one reason for the killing of religious in

Madrid in 1835. The governments that sold off church property also sold off the peasants' common lands. In the Basque Country Carlist peasantry and the rural clergy repeatedly clashed with the commercial and working people of the cities.

The last of the three Carlist wars ended in 1876, but the party lived on, a utopian, agrarian anomaly in a Spain that was rapidly modernizing. In 1888 a branch of Carlists broke away. They called themselves Integrists and they stood for a patriarchal society in which right-wing Catholicism, rather than the Carlist dynasty, was the guiding force. More papist than the pope, their strength was in the small town gentry and clergy of Navarra and the Basque Country. Their special symbol was the Sacred Heart of Jesus, but this symbol was shared with other militant Catholics.

The Carlists in their two branches cared about Spain as a whole. Basque Carlists were allies of others in Catalonia, Valencia, Castile, and Andalusia. The literature of the time often refers to them as Traditionalists. After 1920 their chief competitors for the votes of the peasantry were Nationalists. Basque Nationalism originated in the devout commercial class of Bilbao and gradually spread to the countryside and Gipuzkoa. The men of Ezkioga generally voted for Carlists or Integrists until 1919, when almost half voted for a Nationalist candidate. During the Republic the Nationalists gained new force.[12]

Before the creation of the Second Republic the deputies representing the rural, Basque-speaking laity in the Cortes allied themselves with the monarchy; the governments of the monarchy by and large left the Basques and their traditions alone. But the Republic was different, and in the new parliament most Basque representatives were part of a small minority, which the Madrid press ridiculed as "cavemen" and "wild boars." The total lack of access to a government that rural Basques considered alien compounded their apprehension after the anti-clerical violence in the rest of Spain.

Furthermore, this devout society lived cheek by jowl with another enemy—enclaves of Spanish-speaking, largely immigrant republicans, socialists, and an-archo-syndicalists in the company towns, river cities, and coastal capitals. Factories near Ezkioga in Beasain, Zumarraga, Legazpi, and Tolosa offered evidence of the shift in the economic base of the region from the agriculture of dispersed farmhouses to industry. Parish priests took on the difficult task of combating new ideas and morality with religious sodalities, sermons, and revival missions. They saw the new republic tipping the scales in favor of the long-term, ongoing encroachment of modernism.

Some of the new factories were paper mills. The tenant farm of Ezkioga where the two children had gone for milk on the night of the first visions belonged to an entrepreneur who later refused to rebuild his tenants' house when it burned down; instead he planted pine trees for his paper mill in Legorreta. Farm families were under siege, not only from the new republic and its schoolteachers but also from industrial development. It can be no coincidence that the majority of the people who eventually had visions at Ezkioga were from the farms, not the towns or cities, of the Basque Country.[13]

The appearances of the Virgin seemed to provide a solution to the great crisis. The first words she uttered (not to the original seers from Ezkioga but to a seven-year-old girl from Ormaiztegi and a twenty-four-year-old carpenter from Ataun) were in Basque, asking them, "Errosarioa errezatzea egunero [Pray the rosary daily]."[14] And pray the rosary people did, at night, on a hillside, often in the rain, on their knees, with arms outstretched during the Litany, while the seers waited for the visions to occur. First hundreds prayed, then within a week thousands. On the nights of July 12, 16, and 18 and October 16, up to eighty thousand persons turned out expecting miracles. In the first month there were over a hundred seers, and the visions continued in public, outdoor form until the fall of 1933. Seers at Ezkioga came especially from Gipuzkoa and within Gipuzkoa from the upland Goiherri; others came from the Basque-speaking villages of Navarra, and a few from Bizkaia, Castille, Catalonia, and the French Basque region. The visions soon spread out from Ezkioga, carried home by these pilgrims who had become seers and imitated by persons who read of the visions in the national press. Few Basques over seventy-five today did not go to Ezkioga then. It is possible that more persons gathered on that hillside on July 18 and October 16 than had ever gathered in one place in the Basque Country before.

TAPPING AND DEFINING NEW POWER: THE PRESS AND LOCAL LEADERS

The atmosphere of rural Gipuzkoa and Navarra in June 1931 was like a cloud chamber with air so saturated that even slight radioactive emissions become visible to the naked eye. Two children whose own father did not believe them when they said they had seen the Virgin immediately attracted two to three hundred observers. In the following days, weeks, and months, in this atmosphere, other visions by other children and by adults, visions we would not normally hear about, left their marks. The impressions on these seers' minds held immense potential importance for the Catholics of the Basque Country, Spain, and Western Europe of 1931. These strong impressions are still available sixty years later in the form of memories and printed accounts.

The visions offered Catholics a source of new power or energy—power to know the future and to know the other world of heaven, hell, and purgatory, power that could heal, convert, and mobilize the faithful. The crowds that converged on Ezkioga even before the news came out in newspapers showed how much people wanted this knowledge and this intervention. Calling this power *new* implicitly accepts the local definition of what was happening, the

"The site of the apparitions." Crowd gathers on hillside, July 1931. Postcard sold by Vidal Castillo

truth of the divine appearances. But even believers would probably qualify the idea that the power was new, because for them it would be a new version of a power very old indeed, the everyday power of God among them.

At Ezkioga this power was manifest in an unusual but hardly unique way. The Ezkioga parish church had bas-reliefs of Saint Michael appearing at Monte Gargano. Many Basque shrines had legends of apparitions. Lourdes was nearby, and well over a hundred thousand Basques had gone there and experienced firsthand the spiritual fruits of Bernadette's visions. The vision sites of Limpias (about a hundred kilometers northwest) and Piedramillera (about fifty kilometers south) were even closer. And Basque children knew about the apparitions of Fatima. The Ezkioga visions occurred during a period of enthusiasm within Catholicism in which the devout, in the face of rationalism, had come to believe that the old power was closer at hand, certifiable miracles were fully possible, and the supernaturals were easier to see.[15]

This kind of power came from the conversion of potential to kinetic energy. The potential energy lay in the Basques' daily devotions, their normal attention

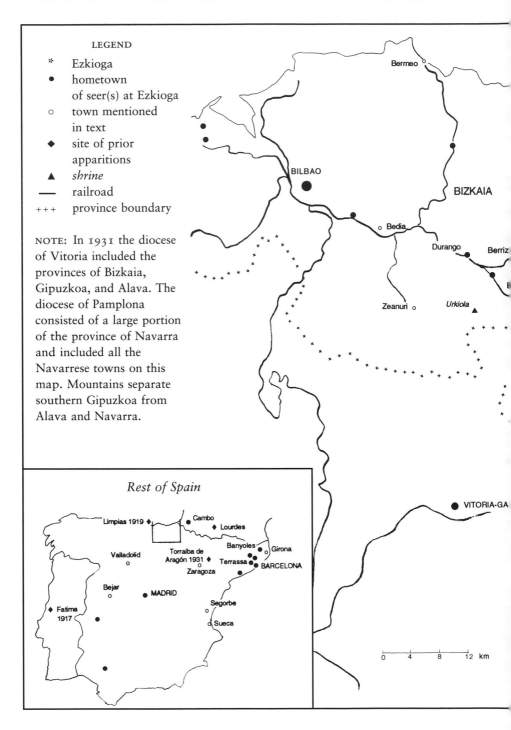

LEGEND

* Ezkioga
● hometown of seer(s) at Ezkioga
○ town mentioned in text
◆ site of prior apparitions
▲ *shrine*
— railroad
+++ province boundary

NOTE: In 1931 the diocese of Vitoria included the provinces of Bizkaia, Gipuzkoa, and Alava. The diocese of Pamplona consisted of a large portion of the province of Navarra and included all the Navarrese towns on this map. Mountains separate southern Gipuzkoa from Alava and Navarra.

Bermeo

BILBAO

BIZKAIA

Bedia

Durango Berriz

Zeanuri Urkiola ▲

VITORIA-GA

Rest of Spain

Limpias 1919 ◆ Cambo
◆ Lourdes
Valladolid Banyoles ○ Girona
Torralba de Aragón 1931 ◆ Terrassa
Zaragoza BARCELONA
Bejar
● MADRID
Segorbe
◆ Fatima 1917 ○ Sueca

0   4   8   12 km

Basque Country and Northwestern Navarra

to local, regional, and international saints. They deposited and invested this energy in daily rosaries, novenas, masses, prayers, and promises. They banked it through churches, shrines, monasteries, and convents. The church in its many representatives husbanded and administered it. The threat of the secular republic mobilized this accumulated devotional energy in the people of the north.

Tens of thousands of persons focused this power intensely on the seers. The seers were the protagonists, their stories and photographs in newspapers. Many of them seemed to feel in their bodies a tremendous force. Walter Starkie, an Irish Hispanist who wandered into Ezkioga and became for a few days in late July 1931 its one precious dispassionate witness, described a girl in vision as he held her:

> I could feel the strain reacting upon her: every now and then a powerful shock seemed to pass quivering through her and galvanize her into energy, and she would toss in my arms and try to jump forwards. At last she sank back limp and when I looked down at her white face moist with tears I saw that she was unconscious.[16]

As we will see, time and again beginning seers described blinding light and fell into apparent unconsciousness. The metaphor of great power was one that they themselves used. When they lost their senses, wept uncontrollably, or were blissful, they demonstrated this energy to observers.

How was this power tapped? Which visions made it into print and which are available only in memories? Who by controlling the distribution of news of the visions helped define their content? How did what the seers saw and heard come to address what their audience wanted to know?

The Basques and the Navarrese were more literate than most Spaniards. In 1931, 85 percent of Basques and Navarrese aged ten or older could read and write; the percentage was about the same for women as for men. The national average was 67 percent. Parents took elementary school seriously and teachers were important members of the community. This high rate of literacy ensured many avid readers for news of the Ezkioga visions.[17]

For most Spaniards the news came largely from the reporters of the rightist newspapers of San Sebastián and Pamplona. In addition, the small-town stringers of these papers occasionally went to Ezkioga with busloads of pilgrims. Only on two occasions in July did writers for the more skeptical *El Liberal* of Bilbao go to Ezkioga, and there were no such eyewitness reports in the republican *La Voz de Guipúzcoa.*

The Basque newspapers covering the visions were those who had supported the winning coalition of candidates for Gipuzkoa in the Constituent Cortes, the parliament in Madrid that would draw up a constitution. *La Constancia* was the newspaper of the Carlists and Integrists; its deputy was Julio Urquijo. Two priests had recently founded *El Día,* the newspaper that reported the visions in greatest detail. The Catholic press reprinted *El Día*'s stories throughout Spain. The newspaper was discreetly pro-Nationalist, with emphasis on news of the province of Gipuzkoa, and its deputy was the canon of Vitoria Antonio Pildain. The coalition candidates were selected in its offices. *Euzkadi* was the official organ of the Basque Nationalist Party, whose deputy was Jesús María de Leizaola. *El Pueblo Vasco* catered to the more worldly gentry of San Sebastián, and its deputy was its founder and owner, Rafael Picavea. The weekly *Argia*, which tended toward nationalism, went out to rural, Basque-speaking Gipuzkoa; it carried many reports on Ezkioga in 1931. News of the visions reached the public in these newspapers and their points of view affected the reporting. Even leftist newspapers depended on these sources.

While the newspapers reporting the visions were Catholic and broadly to the right, they did have some differences. The editor of *La Constancia*, Juan de Olazábal, was the national leader of the Integrists. In 1931 and 1932 this faction was in the process of rejoining the main Carlist party. The Integrists, "few but vociferous," had another organ in San Sebastián, the weekly *La Cruz*. The two factions were most powerful in Navarra, where they had two newspapers, the Carlist *La Tradición Navarra* and the Integrist *El Pensamiento Navarro*. In contrast to the readers of the Carlist and Integrist newspapers, the readers of *Euzkadi, El Día,* and *Argia* wanted an autonomous government that responded to the traditions, culture, and "race" of the Basques. For them the form of the Madrid government was immaterial, and they eventually allied themselves with the Republic and fought against the Carlists in the civil war of 1936–1939. But in 1931 the Basque Nationalist Party and the Carlists, the two main forces in the agricultural townships of the Goiherri and among the clergy of the diocese, stood together against the Republic. *El Pueblo Vasco,* whose Catholicism and Basque nationalism was somewhat more liberal, provided its readers with a more skeptical slant on the Ezkioga visions. While always respectful, its reporter occasionally pointed out inconsistencies and doubts. But in July 1931 its articles, some quite extensive, were largely factual.[18]

In July and early August 1931 the three San Sebastián Catholic daily newspapers each had an average of two articles daily on the visions, usually naming visionaries and describing what they had seen and heard. They also carried background articles on trances, levitation, and stigmata and on the German stigmatic Thérèse Neumann, the Italian stigmatic Padre Pio da Pietrelcina, and the visions at Lourdes, Fatima, and La Salette. Ezkioga was a big story; only the campaign for a Basque statute of autonomy surpassed it in column inches. These newspapers served as a filter. Some news passed, some did not.

Between the reporters and the seers there was another filter, that of an ad hoc commission of the two Ezkioga priests, Sinforoso Ibarguren and Juan Casares; a doctor from adjacent Zumarraga, Sabel Aranzadi; the Ezkioga health aide and the mayor and town secretary. The doctor examined those seers who came forward, and the priests asked questions that they eventually made into a printed form. By the end of July 1931 the commission had listened to well over a hundred persons, and because many persons had visions on more than one night, the total number of visions they heard about in that month was somewhere between three and five hundred. They sometimes allowed reporters to hear the seers and copy the transcripts. The doctor guided them toward the most convincing cases. The members of the commission encouraged some visionaries to return after future visions but dismissed others. The press and the commission tended to ignore adult women seers and heed adult men, comely adolescents, and those children who expressed themselves well (see questionnaire in appendix).

The seers themselves also participated in the filtering; some of them reserved what they saw for themselves or their families and did not declare their visions. This self-censorship particularly applied to the content of the visions. Seers were especially unlikely to declare unorthodox visions. For instance, one woman told others privately of seeing something like a witch in the sky. And a man from Zumarraga told me he saw a headless figure. He added, "Don't write that down; we all saw things there."[19]

Similarly, two girls about seven years old had visions of an irregular sort in Ormaiztegi in late August and early September 1931. The father of one of the girls, a furniture maker, wrote down what they saw. On August 31 the girls said that they saw a monkey by the stream near the workshop and that two days before in the same place they had seen a very ugly woman. They then saw the monkey turn into the same woman, whom they called a witch; the witch said she understood only Basque. Directed by the father, who saw nothing, they asked the witch in their imperfect Spanish why she had come and from where. She replied, in Basque syntax and Spanish vocabulary, that she had come from the seashore to kill them. Later she supposedly ran up to the workshop and tried to attack the religious images the father was restoring.

On September 1 the two children saw the witch in the stream with a girl in a low-cut dress, short skirt, painted face, and peroxided hair who said she was "Marichu, from San Sebastián, from La Concha [the central beach]." The father made the sign of the cross and the girl disappeared, leaving the old lady, who made a rough cross in response. Later, both appeared again, coming out of the water together. The next day the Virgin appeared to the children together with figures representing the devil and temptation. The girls also saw a procession of coffins of the village dead.

These visions are a mix of Basque folklore and contemporary religious motifs, with a dash of summer sin. "Marichu" was a kind of modern woman counter-image to the Daughters of Mary. The newspapers might never have reported the Ormaiztegi visions if the church had approved the apparitions of Ezkioga. The reporter did not reveal this unorthodox vision sequence until after the tide had turned against the apparitions in general.[20]

Such journalistic suppression seems to have been common in July, when the visions had great public respectability. Starkie provides an example from the village of Ataun of the kind of vision the newspapers did not report:

> I met a visionary of a more sinister kind who assured me with a wealth of detail that he had seen the Devil appear on the hill of Ezquioga . . . "I saw him appear above the trees—tall he was, with red hair, dressed in black, and he had long teeth like a wolf. I wanted to cry out with terror, but I made the sign of the Cross and the figure faded away slowly."[21]

Even mere spectators were aware that what others were seeing might not be holy but instead devilry or witchcraft. The word they used, *sorginkeriak*, literally "witch-stuff," reflected the ambiguous attitude toward the ancient subject, for it also had a looser meaning of "stuff and nonsense." Many priests preached that women should be *retirado* (indoors) after 9 P.M.; thus, the woman who appeared at night on the hill was *de mal retiro* and going against the priests, something the Virgin would not do. This widespread opinion, more common among men, was also an indirect criticism of the women who stayed out late praying on the hillside. As long as the visions were respectable in the summer of 1931, the press rarely put such criticism into print.[22]

A third kind of distortion or molding affected the orthodox visions when certain messages were emphasized over others. The allocation of attention was the business of every person who went to, talked about, or read about the visions. In a gradual collective selective process, the Catholics of the north focused on the messages they wanted to hear. We can follow this process day-to-day through the press.

The first visions of the first seers were of the Virgin (they had no doubt who it was) dressed as the Sorrowing Mother, the Dolorosa. The image appeared slightly above ground level, and the visions were at night. Sometimes the Virgin was happy, sometimes sad, but her emotions were the "content" of the visions. On July 4 others began having visions, and during the rest of July newspapers described over two hundred of the visions in which the Virgin's wishes became more explicit. Some visionaries told how the Virgin reacted to her surroundings, to the audience, or to the prayers. Some saw the Virgin as part of allegorical tableaux. Others saw her move her lips. And starting on July 7 still others heard her speak. Visions involving acts, such as cures or divine wounds, developed only in later months.[23]

The rosary, a fixture of the gatherings, began on the third day of the visions. During and after the rosary the audience engaged in a kind of collective blind dialogue with the holy figure through the seers: on the one hand, the prayers and Basque hymns; on the other, the seers communicating the Virgin's emotions and attitudes. The Virgin was alternately sad, weeping, sad then happy when she heard the prayers, and happy. She sometimes participated in the prayers and hymns, said good-bye, and even threw invisible flowers. Mute glances, reproachful looks, sweating, and an occasional smile had been the main—indeed the only—content of the miraculous movements of the crucifixes of Limpias and Piedramillera.

People also deduced Mary's emotions and mission from her dress, which was mainly that of a Dolorosa with a white robe and black cape (the commission took care to establish her apparel and how many stars there were in her crown), but sometimes she came as the Immaculate Conception, Our Lady of Aranzazu, Our Lady of the Rosary, or other avatars. Some seers saw one Mary after another in rapid succession.

The communication between the Virgin and the congregation was the central drama of the Ezkioga visions in the first month, but there were other vision motifs. Visions predicting a divine proof of the apparitions earned particular attention. From July 10 there were reports of an imminent miracle. Seers' predictions overlapped, so when one miracle did not occur, people's hopes shifted to another. A rumor circulated that a very holy nun—some said from Bilbao, others said from Pamplona—had predicted on her deathbed that in a corner of Gipuzkoa prodigious events would take place on July 12. On the day before that date the carpenter Francisco "Patxi" Goicoechea of Ataun had a vision in which the Virgin said that time would be up after seven days. People understood this statement variously to mean that the miracle would take place on the sixteenth or the eighteenth. On July 12 an article appeared in *El Día* drawing parallels between Ezkioga and Lourdes and raised hopes for a miracle in the form of a spectacular cure. On the fourteenth Patxi again referred to a time span (*un turno*) elapsing, and an eleven-year-old boy from Urretxu heard the Virgin say that she would say what she wanted on the eighteenth. On the twelfth and sixteenth of July there were massive audiences of hopeful pilgrims. The newspapers reported hundreds of seers on the twelfth, but on neither day was there a miracle of any kind. On the seventeenth the Zumarraga parish priest told a reporter he would rather talk the next day: "Let us see if tomorrow, Saturday, the Virgin wants to work a miracle; perhaps something startling and supernatural, as at Lourdes, will be a revelation for us all. Maybe a spring will suddenly appear, or a great snowfall."[24]

The Zumarraga priest's hopes in print set the stage for a day of record attendance on July 18, which the press estimated at eighty thousand persons. But the day before, Ramona Olazábal, age sixteen, was already setting up new expectations because the Virgin had told her that she would appear on the following days. No miracle occurred on the eighteenth. But Patxi heard the Virgin say she would work them in the future, and a girl heard her say that she would not show herself to everyone because people were bad; so hope for a miracle continued. On July 23 Ramona heard the Virgin affirm that she would work miracles in the future; on the next day there was a story that another nun, this one living, had announced great events in 1931; and on the following day a servant girl from Ormaiztegi announced that the Virgin "wanted to do miracles."[25]

When Starkie was in Ezkioga, around July 28, he found local people and outsiders in a kind of suspense, waiting for a sign. On July 30 the Virgin, ratifying what most persons had already concluded, declared through Ramona that "miracles were not appropriate yet."[26] By then the seers had worn out their audience, which declined to a few thousand persons and on some days to a few hundred, until Ramona herself became the miracle in mid-October.

VISIONS RELATING TO THE COLLECTIVE RELIGIOUS AND POLITICAL PREDICAMENT

The political-religious problems of 1931, which seem to have determined the immediate positive response to the visions, were not only pressing but also collective in nature, so help from the Virgin had to be collective as well. The Elgoibar correspondent in *El Día* of July 18 called for a message addressed to the Basques: "Let the Mother of Heaven make her decisions manifest, for we her sons in Gipuzkoa are prepared to carry them out." Already a month and a half before the visions began, *La Constancia* had laid out the collective plight:

> Difficult times, times of trial, sorrowful omens; disquieting doubts, bitter disillusions, anguished fright, ears and eyes that open to reality, at last.
> What is happening? What is going to happen?
> And in this disarray, with spirits cowed, the mind goes blank, confusion grows, and the already general malaise spreads.

The writer also proposed a solution: "We must turn our eyes to God and to our conscience and begin a crusade of prayer, fervent persevering prayer; and a crusade of penance and atonement." Three weeks before the visions started the Bergara correspondent of the same newspaper made a similar analysis:

> The simple and plain folk have understood that we are in the midst of a sea of dangers, that the hurricane wind tells us that we are two steps away from the most terrible storm, from which we will hardly be able to emerge without divine help; and in sacrifice they have gone to the feet of the Virgin to pray for Spain, the Basque Country, and for the town.

At Ezkioga the Basque people "turned their eyes to God" and went "to the feet of the Virgin" to pray for collective help in a way perhaps more literal than these writers expected but in a way they and others had already marked.[27]

The first hint that the visions would address this need came in the Bilbao republican paper *El Liberal* on July 10. The correspondent from Elgoibar reported:

> When on their return from Ezquioga these people arrive in town, they won't let you get by them. Some say they have seen the virgin [*sic*] with the Statute of Estella under her arm; others claim that what she has under her arm are the *fueros,* without a sword. They tell us, and they won't stop, that the aforesaid virgin has a complete wardrobe of outfits of different colors, and that at her side are two rose-colored angels. Is it possible that this occurs in the twentieth century, when Spanish newspapers cross the border and carry news of Spain to the rest of the world?

The *Liberal* correspondent may have made up the part about the Statute of Estella (the statute of autonomy that the rightist coalition supported) and the *fueros* (the traditional laws of the Basque Country and Navarra that the central government abrogated in the nineteenth century). But in any case the article pointed to political issues that the right as well as the left expected the visions to address.

On 8 July 1931, writing from his hometown of Ezkioga, Engracio de Aranzadi described the first visions and suggested what they could mean. Aranzadi was a successor to Sabino Arana as the ideologue of the Basque Nationalist Party, a frequent contributor to *Euzkadi,* and a relative of Antonio Pildain, the deputy in the Cortes and canon of Vitoria. Aranzadi's words carried great weight in the movement, and the apparitions were almost literally in his front yard. His article "La Aparición de Ezquioga" came out in *El Día* on July 11 and in *El Correo Catalán* a week later.

Aranzadi began by stating that the supernatural and the natural orders were particularly close in the Basque Country. For the Basques, he said, there was "harmony between spiritual and national activities, between religion and the race." Sabino Arana had founded the Nationalist party because of his "deep conviction that exoticism was here impiety," that is, that Basques were religious and impiety came from the outside. In the recent election the Basques alone had stood up to the Republicans and Socialists. While in the rest of Spain candidates on the right had played down their religion, in Navarra and Gipuzkoa the candidates had proudly proclaimed their Catholicism. As a result, only nine of twenty-three deputies in the Vasco-Navarra region were leftists and enemies of the church ("not Basque leftists, but leftist outsiders, encamped on Basque soil on the heights of Bilbao, Sestao, Barakaldo, Donostia, Irun, Iruña, and Gazteiz").

Aranzadi argued against Basques who favored an alliance with the Second Republic at the expense of their Catholic identity and he referred to the Nationalist cause as a religious crusade beneath the "two-crossed" Basque flag: "There is a great battle in preparation. For God and fatherland on one side, and against God and the fatherland on the other. . . . And to our aid heaven comes.

It seems to seek to invigorate our faith, which is attacked by alien impiety." He described the first visions, which began the day he arrived for a stay in Ezkioga, and concluded:

> May it not be that heaven seeks to comfort the spirit of Basques loyal to the faith of the race? May it not be that heaven seeks to strengthen the people, ever faithful to their religious convictions, in the face of imminent developments? Is it so strange, given the path we believers have taken, that to the calls of a race, of a nationality which with its blood has sealed the sincerity of its faith, a response should come from above with the help that we seek?

Aranzadi expressed the belief of many Nationalists that Mary supported the Basques against the Republic. For instance, the pro-Nationalist weekly *Argia*'s first article on the apparitions concluded, "God has great good will toward the Basque people." And in the next issue the Zarautz correspondent described how going to pray at Ezkioga had the effect of increasing Basque Nationalist fervor: "At this mountain the lukewarm get hot, and the hot get all fired up for Euskadi to be free and live in Her love." Throughout the month the visions of certain seers, particularly Patxi Goicoechea, himself a Nationalist, confirmed Aranzadi's diagnosis of heaven's intentions. The Virgin was preparing the Basques for a civil war.[28]

On July 14 Patxi saw the Virgin with a severe expression bless the four cardinal points with a sword. Leftist newspapers, which until then had made fun of the visions, quickly asked the government to intervene. Rightist papers countered that the visions were harmless and that it was natural that the Virgin, who as the Sorrowing Mother had a sword through her heart, should use the sword to make a blessing. On July 16 Patxi saw an angel give the Virgin a sword. The Virgin, holding a Christ with a bloody face, wept.[29]

Allegories of justice and vengeance continued on successive days. On July 17 a nineteen-year-old girl from Pasaia also saw the Virgin with a sword and a man saw the Virgin threaten him with her hand. Patxi began to reveal matters that reporters decided not to print: "The youth from Ataun told us many more things that we prefer not to mention, as they might be wrongly interpreted"; "Francisco Goicoechea made revelations of great importance which will be reserved for the time being." At the end of the month Patxi "specified certain revelations" that a writer did not "consider prudent to reveal."[30]

But the press described ever more explicit tableaux. On July 18 the Virgin blessed the audience with a sword, which she then gave to the attending angels. The next day the republican *Voz de Guipúzcoa* denounced "the manipulation of a hallucination" as part of a "rightist-separatist" plot and the provocation of "hatred and civil war." And a republican deputy warned in *El Liberal* of Madrid that Ezkioga was the product of clergy "ready to hitch up their cassocks, shoulder their guns, and take to the hills." On July 25 an assiduous seer, an eleven-year-old boy from Urretxu, saw angels with swords that were bloody, and on July 28 so did Patxi.[31] Starkie was present at this vision and heard Patxi describe it to the priests. He revealed what the press suppressed, that Patxi said openly that

> there would be Civil War in the Basque country between the Catholics
> and the non-Catholics. At first the Catholics would suffer severely and lose
> many men, but ultimately they would triumph with the help of twenty-
> five angels of Our Lady.

Starkie also described the mood of monarchist pilgrims expecting momentarily an uprising in Navarra against the Republic. They encouraged, supported, and chauffeured selected seers. The theme of imminent war became a permanent part of the visions. On August 6 or 7 Juana Ibarguren of Azpeitia saw the Dolorosa with sword in hand, a river of blood, and Saint Michael the Archangel with a squad of angels running quickly along the mountaintops, as if fending off some invisible enemy.[32]

Carlist as well as Nationalist newspapers reported the tableaux of celestial wars. Engracio de Aranzadi notwithstanding, Basque autonomy was less an issue in the press reports on the visions than the mobilization of Spaniards in general. For the newspapers of Pamplona and *La Constancia* of San Sebastián, the upcoming battle was not to secede from Spain but rather to reconquer it. Indeed, as early as the morning of July 9, a rumor circulated to the effect that the Virgin had said to the child seers, "Save Spain." In mid-July the vision sessions included applause, shouts of "Long live Catholic Spain!" and possible monarchical vivas.

We know of these shouts because of the outrage they provoked in the Basque Nationalist *Euzkadi*. A priest writing on July 15 knew it was a "complete lie" that the Virgin would say to save Spain, and a week later a correspondent complained bitterly:

> "Viva España la católica! Viva la católica España!" They should keep these
> shouts and vivas to themselves. Why didn't they go and put out the fires
> in the convents they burned in Madrid and Seville? . . . [T]he ones who burned
> the convents were Spaniards, although many of those inside were Basques.

Because of the turn toward the salvation of Spain by some seers, some of the audience, or the prayer leaders, most *Euzkadi* reporting was cool and reserved from mid-July.[33]

Simultaneously, Carlists throughout Spain became more interested. On July 24 a writer in *La Constancia* asserted that the visions had produced a sensation in the entire nation and he hoped for church approval, as at Lourdes and Fatima. The same day an article in the Vitoria Carlist paper *Heraldo Alavés* also emphasized Spain. This paper was the Catholic daily of the diocesan seat and, with the church hierarchy reticent about the visions, *Heraldo* had ignored the story almost completely. One of the only exceptions was this article, "Ama Virgiña [Virgin Mother]," by the Catholic writer and labor organizer María de Echarri.[34]

Echarri's piece was the equivalent for Spanish Catholics of that of Aranzadi for Basque Nationalists, a kind of ideological blueprint for the visions. She herself had twice witnessed the movement of the eyes of the Christ of Limpias and thought Our Lady of Lourdes had converted her brother on his deathbed, so she was attentive to supernatural events.

> Some ask why that sword in her hand. God has his mysteries. But some suspect also that God's justice is suspended over the guilty, prevaricating fatherland, over the land that was known as that of María Santísima, over the earth where the Virgin of Pilar came in mortal flesh, over Spain, which she considered one of her most cherished prizes. And that this justice the Lord has held back and placed in the hands of the most holy Virgin, so she will spare us from it if we know how to make reparation, do penance, expiate. . . . [The devotion manifest at the visions] gives one's heart hope for a day when the dark clouds that now hang over Spain, the tempest that now blows against our holy religion, the hurricane of cold terrifying secularism that today threatens the faith of Spanish children, will have dissipated.

The seer children from Mendigorría were brought to Ezkioga with the banner "Mater Amabilis, Salva a España." And some of the Basque seers pleaded to the Virgin to save Spain from impiety.[35]

On August 13 the deputy Antonio de la Villa, a journalist from Extremadura, denounced the political drift of the visions in the Constituent Cortes, charging a conspiracy. The cover of the anticlerical magazine *La Traca* reflected his analysis. Most deputies in the Cortes did not take him seriously, but by attributing political significance to the visions, de la Villa had much in common with the ideologues of the Basque press and with some of the seers. His speech produced no action against Ezkioga. But the government was already aware both of Carlist paramilitary organizations and of contacts between Basque Nationalists and monarchist military officers. On August 22 it shut down all rightist newspapers in the north and sent troops on exercise through the countryside.[36]

THE VISIONS AND THE YOUNGER GENERATION

The apparitions at Ezkioga evoked an enthusiastic response in the rural devout and the urban gentry in July 1931 because everyone recognized immediately, even before there was any explicit idea of their content, the visions' potential for resolving a crisis in competing ideologies.[37] While this crisis came to a head with the proclamation of the Second Republic, the burning of religious houses, the elections of the Cortes, and the Basque autonomy movement, its long-term cause was the change from agriculture to industry and tourism.

Cover of anticlerical La Traca (Valencia), 29 August 1931: "Long live the Virgin Mary! Death to the current regime! Long live the king and the monarchy and Segura the Cardinal, the undefeated general of our brotherhood!" Courtesy Hemeroteca Municipal de Madrid

The Basque ethnographers of the time, who were rural clergymen dedicated to preserving "traditional Catholic ambience," presented the conflict as a struggle between rural agriculture and urban industry. In truth, small-town factory owners like Patricio Echeverría of Legazpi or Juan José Echezarreta of Legorreta (who owned the Ezkioga apparition field) were themselves of farm origin, shared these values, and counted on them to ensure their company towns a dependable workforce from the younger sons of the farms. Industrialists, it is claimed, subsidized *La Constancia* and kept up the fight for traditional Basque and Navarrese legal and fiscal privileges. Doubtless they financed much of Nationalist party activity as well. But whether Carlists, Integrists, or Nationalists promoted this patriarchal ideology (against, respectively, Liberals, Freemasons and Jews, and outsiders), all knew Catholic rural culture was threatened, and the diocese of Vitoria had long since geared up to defend it. Devout Basques judged the apparitions in this context.[38]

Most churchmen considered industrial urban society lost to atheism or liberalism. But they hoped they could yet contain the corrosive effects of these new ways of life on rural society. Carlists had been denouncing city life for one hundred years, but the success of Basque coastal resorts at the turn of the century caused additional confusion in rural areas and more defensive measures on the part of rural elites. In 1924, writing about his hometown of Ataun, the Basque ethnographer José Miguel de Barandiarán described the deleterious effects of contact with the cities.

> Hence, many of the young people of Ataun spend part of their lives in more or less close contact with the base, tavern-going mobs of the cities and see the ostentation and show of the "fine" and "elegant" public that to-day makes up a large effeminate caste of little brains, but which is in the forefront of style and is the prime expression of a thoughtless and sensual outlook ever more dominant in the big cities.

In the cities, he wrote with uncharacteristic luridness, "the flower of youth wilts in sumptuous orgies and . . . lewd old men paint their faces and dye their white hair."[39]

San Sebastián, in particular, with its fashionable beachfront, provoked rural antagonism, which can be seen in the Ormaiztegi vision of "Marichu" from La Concha arm-in-arm with a witch. In San Sebastián at the beginning of the Second Republic there was an upsurge of sexually explicit literature. Even the republican newspaper called for "liberty in laws, but morality in customs." Some saw this immorality as the result of a breakdown of parental authority. Consider one priest's analysis of the reasons for the relatively low church attendance in the factory town of Eibar.

> There is a total absence of family life: in Eibar paternal authority barely exists; "democracy and equality" have reached the intimacy of the home where people go their separate ways—more like a boardinghouse than a home. The house serves only to satisfy physical needs; apart from this all go out to the street, the bar, the café, the political club, or the movies, and this every day, in turbid promiscuity of sexes until very late at night, with dire consequences for morality and religiosity.

The clergy saw this kind of city life as a threat to the souls of rural youth.[40]

At first glance the challenges to authority in the countryside seem trivial and incidental. For they had less to do with strikes and revolts than with family and community matters like deference, social control, and gender. Examples include couples' close-dancing (a threat to parental control of courtship); women's wearing more revealing clothes, riding bicycles, or staying out later at night (threats to the authority of husbands or parents); lack of deference to the priest as measured in public reverences or greetings; and lack of deference to God and

El toque del "Angelus", rezado por las Misiones,
interrumpe las faenas campesinas.

Daughters of Mary in tableau at Vitoria, February 1932: "The Angelus prayer for
the missions interrupts farm work." From Iluminare, *20 February 1932, p. 57.*
Courtesy Instituto Labayru, Derio

the Virgin Mary with the abandonment of the family rosary or prayers at
daybreak, noon, and nightfall at the ringing of the Angelus. Barandiarán's
students and collaborators focused on the erosion of traditional practices in a
1924 survey. His clerical correspondents considered issues like close-dancing as
threats to religion and to an entire way of life.

The initial reports about the Ezkioga visions show the children, returning at
nightfall with milk from a farm, kneeling to pray at the ringing of the Angelus
bells. Validating traditional piety, those children immediately became emblems
of the Basque heartland. At this time one could see well-off girls in Vitoria dressed
as farmworkers and praying the Angelus in a tableau. The Virgin thus appeared
as a reward to those who kept the faith.[41]

By the same token, small matters under local dispute could also be the basis
for rejecting the visions in general or particular seers. Should women be out at
night? Many men decided the visions were not real because they set an example
of immorality. Similarly, an argument against the truth of the visions of Ramona
Olazábal was that she liked to dance; indeed, she did so on some of the same days
she had visions. We may suppose that this level of discernment often escaped the

urban newspaper reporters and on this basis local people disqualified some visionaries who had passed muster with the local commission and the press. In San Sebastián one might know, at most, if someone went to church or not. Rural folk cut finer distinctions—whether one prayed on one knee or two, confessed weekly, on major feast days, or annually, and touched one's beret or took it all the way off when greeting a priest. Local people soon knew how devout seers had been prior to their visions and whether their behavior had subsequently improved.[42]

The erosion of devotional practices and respect for authority was taking place above all in the younger generation, particularly among males working in factories or on military service and among females who went to work, at ages fifteen to seventeen, as servants away from home. By 1924 an Oñati member of the youth sodality of San Luis Gonzaga read the republican *Voz de Guipúzcoa* in his workshop and a girl in Ataun could prefer expulsion from the Daughters of Mary to giving up her strolls with her boyfriend, transgressions unthinkable a few years earlier. A young freethinker who had worked as a waiter in Paris lived three doors from the first seers.[43] Girls on bicycles were also breaking the rules. An older lady in Zumarraga told me that when as a girl she rode past on a bicycle, a priest called out that he hoped she would not have the nerve to go to Communion the next day. One of her friends recalled Don Andrés Olaechea, one of the priests who led the rosary at Ezkioga, crossing the town square where a girl was riding a bicycle and muttering "Sinvergüenza, sinvergüenza, sinvergüenza, sinvergüenza [hussy, hussy, hussy, hussy]" until he was out of sight. To such women Dolores Nieto, the first girl to ride a bicycle, was a social hero.[44]

And of course the dancing issue was generational. In June 1931 in Markina (Bizkaia), for example, the town authorities fined girls who danced closely in the modern fashion (*el valseo* or *agarrado*). The citations referred to the girls as "delinquents" for violating collective community vows. The diocesan bulletin describes how on 29 March 1931 Jesuits giving a mission led one such vow.

> To the final service, held in the village square on the afternoon of Palm Sunday, Ceánuri came out en masse, 2,500 persons, with many more from the surrounding villages. It was there that P. Goicoechea, grasping the holy crucifix of the mission prior to the papal blessing, was able to ask that all, with their arms in the form of a cross, give their word to dance the *agarrado* no more and to preserve in pure form the traditional custom of being indoors when the Angelus is rung, and other customs that had been observed until now, and which are now seen as in danger because of the constant pressure of outsiders.[45]

One of the major battles fought by Liberals, and later Republicans and Socialists, was to relax attitudes toward sex and the body. Their correspondents chronicled the struggle in villages between the youth in favor of close-dancing and the clergy and town councils in favor of the traditional (*suelto*) varieties. In Ormaiztegi one of the issues in the changeover from an older to a younger town council in 1932 was pressure from the parish priest against close-dancing at town fiestas.[46]

Rural cinemas posed a particular challenge to the old ways, both in the movies they showed and the opportunities they offered couples for privacy. Around 1930 the diocese of Vitoria had tried and failed to stop Juan José Echezarreta, the owner of the Ezkioga apparition site, from opening a cinema in Ordizia. After the films on Sundays, youths from the surrounding villages stayed on for dances.[47]

On these issues peer pressure was the first line of defense for the church and the older generation. The main vehicle for this pressure was the Daughters of Mary, a pious association, or sodality, for girls. In some towns the priests who directed the sodality made girls who danced the *agarrado* wear a purple ribbon when receiving Communion. After the girl's third offense they expelled her and confiscated her medal, as they expelled those who walked alone with boys. Morality was the responsibility of the girls, not the boys. The church had less leverage over the boys; few of them belonged to the male sodality of San Luis Gonzaga.[48]

Given this generational conflict, the press and the general public quickly accorded adolescent and young adult seers prominence at Ezkioga. These seers were the good examples. Some, like Patxi, who started out mocking or skeptical, were even exemplary converts. By the same token, some of the divine messages most successful with the press and the public were those that spoke to these skirmishes in the war against modern ideas and religious laxity. The first message, "Pray the rosary daily," would have been superfluous in earlier times. But already by 1924 only the more devout households, particularly on the isolated farms, were saying the prayers. Commentators in *Argia* and the magazine *Aránzazu* suggested that the Virgin appeared in order to restore the rosary.[49]

And, of course, the physical presence of the Virgin, Saint Michael, and other saints at Ezkioga itself confirmed most overtly heaven's direct links to the Basques and the Spaniards. It was especially for this purpose people wanted a miracle that would demonstrate the truth of the apparitions and, by extension, of the divinity. Eventually the visions persisted in spite of the bishop's denunciation and the result was the undermining of church authority. At that point, the diocese as well as the government (the Republic and later the government of Francisco Franco as well) persecuted the visionaries and believers. But such was not the case in the summer of 1931, when priests stepped right in to lead the rosaries, direct the crowds, examine the visionaries, and even escort them from their home villages. In July, at least, there seemed to be an unbroken line from the divine to the Basque faithful, abetted by enthusiastic clergy, that served to confirm a way of life seriously in question. To the extent that the visions contradicted this way of life, people did not believe them.

The more political messages from visionaries responded to the most grave and immediate source of the threat to Basque lines of authority, the Madrid government of the Republic. Unlike the monarchy, which even with Liberal governments maintained a certain divine connection and an alliance with local power, the secular Second Republic of 1931 was totally outside the lines of authority that ran from God to bishop to parish priest to male head of household, with ancillary lines for civil and industrial authorities. The standing Sacred Hearts of Jesus in prominent urban locations and the enthroned ones that Spain's Catholics had in the previous decades consecrated in parish churches, town halls, factories, and households served as storage batteries along the way. With the burning of convents and the expulsion of the bishop of Vitoria and the primate of Spain, the Republic seemed bent on disrupting these lines and dismantling these structures.

The Second Republic was not just an external enemy. There was a danger that the youth of the Basque Nationalist movement might pass to the pro-Republican Acción Nacionalista camp. Engracio de Aranzadi feared they would defect in his 8 July 1931 article. A fifth of the voters in Ezkioga had supported the Republican coalition. It was entirely conceivable that Basque youths might see the Republic as a defender of freedom of ideas and of a less restrictive sense of morality and as an ally against excesses of paternal, clerical, municipal, industrial, or male authority. The Republic was thus also an internal enemy that aggravated the division of generations. Even in rural Gipuzkoa Starkie came across heated arguments in taverns between republicans and rightist Catholics. When he played his fiddle in nearby, equally Catholic, Castile in the summer of 1931, both in Burgos and in remote villages young girls shouted out for him to play the Marseillaise, the anthem of liberty.[50]

The Catholics of the north, and in particular the Basques, perceived that their society and culture, once unified, was divided and under a violent attack from without which accentuated its internal divisions. This perception determined in part the way Basque Catholics tapped, defined, and interpreted the new devotional power generated by the visions of Ezkioga.

Taken as a whole, the many newspaper reports and analyses about the visions are quite revealing. A "fast" medium like daily newspapers, radio, or television (as opposed to the "slow" media of pamphlets, books, and letters of, say, late-fifteenth-century Italian visions) is a forum for the tacit negotiation between what is really on the minds of individuals, what material is all right to distribute, and what people want to hear. Note that from at least the fourteenth century in Europe few socially significant visions have been single events; rather, they have continued and developed over time, sometimes years, allowing for feedback even from slow media. While word of mouth was no doubt the most effective way of spreading enthusiasm for both ancient and modern visions, the daily articles on the visions ensured for Gipuzkoa a homogeneous core of knowledge.[51]

The seers of Ezkioga were well aware of the importance of the press. Many of them made friends with reporters and wanted the press to tell their story. The seers' visions no doubt converged in part because they read about each other's experiences. Moreover, information could be quickly spread by word of mouth throughout the region. In 1931 Gipuzkoa had one of the most extensive telephone systems in all of Spain; indeed, there was a telephone office at the base of the apparition hill. The hope for a miracle created a network of friends and believers who could alert the entire region within hours.[52]

Most of the repeat seers were children or youths, who had an unparalleled chance for fame in the Basque Country, fame of the kind only the best improvisational poets, dancers, jai alai players, weight lifters, or log-splitters could hope for. And the seers were more than famous—they were important, they were part of a critical historical moment: Mary's direct intervention in their nation.

These visionaries gained power so surprisingly because they could express the diffuse yearning for miraculous change or, if you will, serve as lightning rods for the divine. In such a complex situation it is difficult to speak of individual responsibility. All who were present and hoping for apparitions had a hand in negotiating their content. On 8 July 1931, when by all reports the Virgin was simply appearing as Dolorosa, Engracio de Aranzadi publicly surmised that she was preparing the Basques for an imminent battle. Eventually the visions confirmed his expectations because many others, including some of the seers, shared them.

In part, the onlookers' concerns reached the seers in questions for the Virgin. A reporter stated that Patxi "directed at the apparition interminable questions, which were suggested to him by those around him." A skeptic observed that "many who question [Patxi in vision] themselves provide the answer, and others draw from the seer the desired response." Even believers in the visions would agree that when the Virgin responded to questions put to her, her messages thereby addressed and reflected the preoccupations of the questioners.[53]

For students of other places and times, the first summer of the Ezkioga visions may suggest the importance of the context in which "prophets" and charismatic leaders formulate and gradually fix their messages. In the Basque visions and movements, individual seers responded to general anxieties and hopes with what they said were God's instructions, but it seems clear that the messages were as much a consensual product of the desires of followers and the wider society as of the leaders, the prophets, or the saints. We will therefore pay as much attention to the audience—the Greek chorus, the hagiographer, the message takers, and the message transmitters—as to the visionaries themselves.

3. PROMOTERS AND SEERS I: ANTONIO AMUNDARAIN AND CARMEN MEDINA

MARY'S SORROWFUL opposition to the Second Republic was the central interest of believers and seers at the Ezkioga visions in the summer of 1931. Press and public nudged along the evolving political message in a collective fashion. Simultaneously, another process, less collective, ensured that the seers produced messages for particular constituencies. Socially powerful organizers sought divine backing for various programs. After the summer of 1931 their projects absorbed much of the seers' attention.

In early August 1931, in the absence of a confirming miracle, the people of San Sebastián and Bilbao and their newspapers got over their first, sharp interest in the visions. Reporters tired of the same seers and the same messages. In any event the seers lost their forum. For the government, fearing a rightist military uprising, suspended most newspapers in the north on August 22. *El Día,* which printed the most about Ezkioga, only came out again at the end of October.[1] By then the tide had turned against the visions. After early August there was little detailed reporting of the visions and visionaries. This decline in publicity coincided with the Radical Socialist Antonio de la Villa's attack on the visions in parliament and military exercises in the area. For whatever reason, the visionaries subsequently shied away from overt political messages.

Diaries, letters, books, and circulars by literate believers are our main sources for the following months and years. They show the extent to which the visions, like those at Limpias a decade earlier, served as a sounding board for movements and new devotions within Spanish Catholicism. This is not surprising. Catholics came to Ezkioga from all of Spain and southern France, many of them with prior agendas. A large number of visionaries continued to provide messages of great variety. Many seers were open to suggestion. Highly literate emissaries from the urban world of devotional politics latched onto particular rural visionaries or were actively sought out by them. This kind of symbiosis points us toward the mystical side of these Catholic movements and to principles governing alliances across boundaries of class, gender, age, and culture.[2]

The next three chapters recount the principal alliances of promoters and seers. Pressure from the increasingly hostile diocese, counsel from spiritual directors, and rivalry among seers and among promoters affected these alliances. Seers attempted to convince observers. Observers had to decide whom to believe. Or, if observers believed in several, they had to decide who had the most important messages. Those believers who sought to influence or to gain inside information from seers had to win them in some way. Believers drove the most convincing seers to the site, gave them gifts, and spread their vision messages. Over time, as these seers gained an ample public, they tended to address issues that were more general—at first political and later apocalyptic. Coming from the most convincing seers, such dramatic messages more easily passed the severe scrutiny they provoked. At the other end of the spectrum, the less theatrical, less convincing visionaries nonetheless each had a band of followers (called a *cuadrilla*) which principally included persons who had known the seer previously—friends, family members, and neighbors—and who therefore trusted the seer. These less virtuosic visionaries spent more time attending to the spiritual and practical needs of constituents with less ideological interests.

As the popularity of the visions as a whole rose or fell, individual seers might move from one mode of response to another. A number of seers, when they started, addressed personal questions. When they became more popular, they supplied a more general public with news about political developments and the Last Judgment. If the visions then lost favor and only die-hard supporters remained, the seers responded once again to believers' personal needs.

Such relationships between seers and critical believers have affected the lives and work of virtually all Catholic mystics who achieved fame, for what is at stake is fame itself. Promoters are critically important for seers whose access to literate, urban culture can only be achieved through others. We know the nobleman

Francis of Assisi primarily through the eyes of those around him. We depend even more on chroniclers and promoters to learn about the day laborer Marcelina Mendívil of Zegama. As we look at particular learned believers and their contacts with particular seers, we gradually become aware of a far more general process by which the parties creatively combine suggestion and inspiration. As they court and separate, promoters like Antonio Amundarain, Carmen Medina, Manuel Irurita, Magdalena Aulina, Padre Burguera, Raymond de Rigné and their seers show us one way societies create new religious meaning.[3]

ANTONIO AMUNDARAIN

The first, crucial link between visionaries and influential believers was between the girl from Ezkioga who was the first seer and the parish priest of Zumarraga, Antonio Amundarain Garmendia. Apparitions with a broad public appeal can be halted with ease only at the very start. The parish priest, usually the first authority to deal with the matter, is of utmost importance. If he is indecisive or reacts positively, the visions can build up momentum before newspapers and diocesan officials notice them. So it was fortunate for the Ezkioga visions that the girl seer found her way to Amundarain, a clergyman influential in the diocese and fascinated by mystical experiences. The parish priest of Ezkioga and the curate in charge of Santa Lucía were far less famous and far more hardheaded.[4]

Amundarain heard about the Ezkioga visions from the woman who brought him milk. Antonia Etxezarreta, then twenty-three years old, had found out from Primitiva Aramburu, who brought milk from the farmhouse nearest the site of the visions. Primitiva had heard about them from her sister Felipa, who had been with the girl and her brother when they had their first vision.* Antonia was a curious, lettered woman who contributed reports in Basque to *Argia*. She stopped by the school in Santa Lucía to talk to the seer girl and then took her with mule and milk to Zumarraga. At the rectory she presented the girl to a curate she trusted and liked. He was inclined to dismiss the matter, but it was Amundarain who was in charge. The next day, July 2, when Antonia brought the milk, Amundarain had her tell him what had happened and that evening he went to observe the visions.[5]

Amundarain's past and character are vital to this tale. They explain why he did not dismiss the visions but instead nursed them into a mass phenomenon in the first week. A priest with intense energy and drive, Amundarain was a born organizer who was also a photographer, musician, and author of religious dramas. In Zumarraga he supervised six clergymen and three houses of nuns. He

---

*As in the case of other seers who are or who may be alive at the time of this writing, I do not refer to the original brother and sister by name.

EL SIERVO DE DIOS
Rvdo. Sr. D. Antonio Amundarain Garmendia
Fundador de la ‹Alianza en Jesús por María›
(26 Abril 1885 - 19 Abril 1954)

Left: *Antonia Etxezarreta, the milkmaid who connected the first seer with Antonio Amundarain. Photo ca. 1931. Courtesy Antonia Etxezarreta.* Right: *Antonio Amundarain Garmendia, 1948*

came from the rural town of Elduain, and his father had been a Carlist soldier in the Carlist War half a century earlier. Amundarain's mother had bad memories of the Liberal household in which she had worked in San Sebastián, and her son had no yearning for the easy life of the city. One of his brothers was a Franciscan missionary in South America, a nephew became a priest, and two nieces were nuns. Amundarain himself was a Carlist-Integrist. He received *La Constancia, La Gaceta del Norte,* and *Euzkadi.* Occasionally he contributed to *Argia* and *La Constancia.* He considered *La Voz de Guipúzcoa* sinful. He read standing up so as not to enjoy the activity too much or waste time.[6]

Amundarain's first post had been as chaplain to the Mercedarian Sisters of Charity in Zumarraga from 1911 to 1919 and directing female religious remained his true calling. In San Sebastián, where from 1919 to 1929 he was a curate, he served as confessor to several communities of nuns.[7] There in 1925 he founded the Alliance in Jesus through Mary (La Alianza en Jesús por Maria), a lay order in which young women and older teenage girls took temporary vows of chastity and poverty, followed a rigorous dress code, and helped in parishes. By 1929 there were 207 Alliance members (*Aliadas*) in twenty chapters in Gipuzkoa, Alava, Bilbao, and Madrid. By then an eighth of the young women had gone on to become nuns. The Mercedarian Sisters came to know the Aliadas well; numerous Aliadas joined the order and the sisters helped to set up Aliada centers in the towns where they had houses.[8]

In the next two years the lay order quintupled in size, spreading to most Spanish regions. In the Basque Country Aliadas were established mainly in the provincial capitals, but there were centers in six other towns, including Zumarraga. Each section had a local spiritual director, so in 1931 Amundarain had a network of priests with whom he was in close contact. At that time the Basque Aliadas were largely from *kaleak,* the town centers. In the eyes of the farm people they were "señoritas [young ladies]," and I have the impression that in more rural areas many were sisters of priests. For all of the Aliadas Amundarain was a charismatic figure.[9]

With this order Amundarain worked to preserve women from corrupt modern society, especially its sexual side. And he tried to ensure that these women at least would not make modern society more corrupt. Some women have told me that in those years in the confessional he concentrated heavily on the sins of impurity. And in this sense the Alianza was an extreme expression of a reigning preoccupation.[10] Members kept close count of their rosaries, Our Fathers, masses, novenas, and mortifications, and Amundarain reported the totals in the journal *Lilium inter Spinas.* While the idea of an order of devout laywomen working in the world was unusual for the 1920s, it was not new in Spain. Prior to the Council of Trent women known as *beatas* had taken temporary vows and many had led lives in contact with the world. In 1926, however, Amundarain's concept of a lay institute was new again. Two years later, in 1928, José María Eserivá y Balaguer founded another lay institute, Opus Dei.

Even for his time, Amundarain's religion was stern and rigorous. This was the Catholicism of the amulets of the Sacred Heart of Jesus which read, "Detente Enemigo [Stop Enemy]." This was a Catholicism wounded and angered by the anticlericalism in much of Spain. Yet this was also a Catholicism bound to the profane world it opposed. In San Sebastián in 1921 Amundarain instituted weekly prayer meetings on Friday afternoons during the summer as atonement for the sins on the nearby beach, and this session became a fixture of the Aliadas. The Aliadas themselves were a defense against the enemy of God. As Amundarain wrote in early 1931, the Alianza was an army of virgins, "of victim souls, a host of love, an oasis of purity, a legion of chaste Judiths and valiant Jeannes d'Arc." Their goal was to "placate" and "discharge the wrath of God" in the face of "irreligion, libertinism, immorality, corruption," and "pillage, anarchy, atheism, and destruction." All this took place, he wrote, on "the eve of a worldwide cataclysm."[11]

Mateo Múgica, bishop of Vitoria, shared this strict Catholicism. We see him posed in photographs with the Aliadas. The strategy of Múgica, Amundarain, and many of their peers was essentially defensive. They retreated to the high ground of rural religiosity and the protected zones of the upper class and defended them tooth and nail from the surrounding world. They considered the urban working class almost irredeemably lost. For Amundarain only supernatural help could soften the hardened heart and regain those lost to the church.

To maintain and deepen the faith of practicing Catholics, Amundarain placed great value in the spiritual exercises of Ignacio de Loyola. These were a directed series of prayers and meditations with vivid use of the imagination to draw people out of the everyday world and focus their minds and emotions on the life, passion, and resurrection of Christ. He himself performed the exercises annually. In 1928 he organized them for 700 girls in San Sebastián. When he went to Zumarraga in 1930, he held them first for 300 teenage girls, then for 150 boys, and in early 1931 for adult men and women. No parish priest in the diocese made more energetic use of the exercises at this time; at least no one else published the statistics in the diocesan bulletin. When Amundarain brought parishioners to the Ezkioga visions, they were well prepared in spiritual imagination.[12]

Amundarain also promoted local shrines. A devotee of the Virgin of Aranzazu and a leader of pilgrimages to Lourdes, in Zumarraga he composed a hymn to the local devotion of Our Lady of Antigua and began an annual novena at her ancient shrine above the town. In June 1931 he dedicated the novena to atonement for the burning of religious houses, and an Aliada present remembers him saying when they came to the Litany, "Now, with great devotion, put your arms in the form of the cross." He also started an annual mountaintop rosary on May 1 at the iron cross of Beloki above the town; nine meters tall, the cross was lit on the nights of special feasts.[13]

Amundarain's collaborator and biographer, Antonio María Pérez Ormazábal, referred to him as "excessively credulous—as credulous as he was pious." In the 1920s in San Sebastián, says Pérez Ormazábal, Amundarain was "the paladin of all the movements of a spiritual and supernatural nature that emerged at the time." When the Mercedarians completed their convent chapel in 1929 under his supervision, they installed a bust of the Christ of Limpias. In early 1931 he published in the Alianza journal excerpts of a message from a French mystic nun. In 1932 we find Amundarain passing out the first Spanish pamphlet about the apparitions of Fatima. And he was a devotee of Madre María Rafols of Zaragoza and gave his nephew a picture of her as a talisman in the Civil War.[14]

I learned much about Amundarain from this nephew, Juan María, who grew up with Amundarain in Zumarraga. Juan María's sister Teresa was an Aliada and Amundarain's favorite. Juan María was one of the last weavers of wicker furniture in Gipuzkoa, and I talked with him as he worked in a cool, dark loft in the old quarter of San Sebastián. There he sang "Izar bat [A Star]," a hymn composed for the Ezkioga visions. That year a church commission considering the beatification of his uncle had interviewed him for three days. One sticking point for the commission was precisely Antonio Amundarain's enthusiasm for the visions.[15]

Other priests, family members, friends, and the people of Zumarraga describe Amundarain as righteous, rigid, discreet, and extremely pious. He traveled throughout the diocese to give sermons and was famous as an effective confessor. By 1931 he was a leader among the clergy who knew how to act with energy and authority. In the absence of Bishop Múgica, known to be his friend, he organized and supervised the Ezkioga visions in the first months. His presence gave the visions a credibility and legitimacy they would otherwise have lacked.

We can follow much of Amundarain's involvement at Ezkioga in the press. He took the first seers to find the exact spot where the Virgin appeared, led the rosary, managed the news that reached the crowd, confided to a reporter his hope for a miracle, and retained the children's declarations in written form. On July 28, a month after the first visions, he instructed the public, through the newspapers, how to behave at the site, as if the Ezkioga hillside was his parish church. This note provoked a public rebuke from the diocese. Thereafter Amundarain kept a lower profile and let his subordinates lead the vision prayers.[16]

In correspondence and in the Alianza journal Amundarain revealed some of his more private thoughts and hopes about the visions. On July 6 he wrote to María Ozores, head of the Aliadas in Vitoria: "Soon you will all find out about alarming prodigies that we are witnessing here these days. Tell the sisters to pray a lot . . ." To an ally in Vitoria he wrote on July 25: "The Ezquioga affair is something sublime, the most solemn act of atonement that Spain now offers to God. The Virgin cannot abandon us." On September 13 he took three hundred Aliadas to Ezkioga in a heavy rain "to pray for the Alianza . . . the church . . . the bishop in exile, for our poor Spain, and for everyone." "Two little virgins in ecstasy" had visions while the Aliadas prayed and sang. One seer told the Aliadas afterward:

> The Virgin was down close. I have never seen her so low, almost touching
> the ground and in the midst of the Sisters. She wore her black mantle
> very loose, and let her white interior tunic be seen, tied at the waist with
> a white cord, and showing the tips of her bare feet, and with a very pleas-
> ant and happy expression on her lovely face, and with a very sweet voice
> she spoke . . . and said that *she was very pleased with the Alianza, and that
> the Sisters have much, much confidence in her, and her powerful protec-
> tion will guard the Obra.*

It is possible that one of these seers was Ramona Olazábal, but by September a number of seers delivered this kind of tailor-made message.[17]

Amundarain believed the first seers. He then turned to others, like Ramona. Why was he so soon distracted? Let us look at the seers.

The First Seers

The sister was born in 1920, the brother in 1924. (In this account they shall remain anonymous.) When they had their first vision she was eleven and he was seven years old. Their father had a small roadside bar and they lived upstairs with their four brothers and sisters. The girl was quiet and introverted. The Irish traveler Walter Starkie wrote, "I have rarely seen such a tragic expression on a child's face. She looked as if she had already borne the brunt of a whole life's sorrow." When Starkie was at Ezkioga at the end of July, he noted that "she had stopped seeing the Virgin, and she shut herself up in her room and refused to play with the other children." In all, the girl had sixteen visions. She never fell into a trance when doing so, she remained impassive, and her pulse did not vary. She never heard the Virgin speak.[18]

Her brother was more lively. Starkie described him as mischievous and impudent. Newspapers reported him as "unruly," "brusque," "alert," "smart," and "simpático." After the visions were discredited, they called him "impertinent," "bold," "brazen," and "wild." The Ezkioga parish priest wrote, "The boy is pure rebellion." According to some reports he did not speak Spanish. A San Sebastián writer commented at the beginning of August: "He is a terrible rebel, and by now he is used to the vision and does not attribute it the least importance, and he is sick of being questioned."[19]

The boy rarely fell into anything like a trance. He would simply stop playing, extend his arms and pray during his vision, then go back to playing. He might climb trees as people prayed on the hillside or run off into the woods when people wanted to talk to him. His visions occurred in various places, especially in apple trees behind his house. He did not hear the Virgin speak. By early September he had had thirty-one visions and believers claimed that he continued having them daily for at least two years. In early 1934 he had them during family prayers at night. By then he went to school in Zumarraga.[20]

An older neighbor followed the events closely from 1931 to the present. She told me that this family "was very simple, the simplest family around here, so modest and humble. They never liked to stand out. A family always unassuming."[21] And despite snide allusions to the contrary in the press, the family and seers profited little if at all from the visions. Older Ezkioga residents distinguish the sister and brother from the later, more famous seers and emphasize the children's innocence and lack of ulterior motives. They feel that older seers "messed it up." But people hungry for answers to religious and political questions and aching personal problems could hardly rest happy with the sister and brother, especially while other, more theatrical and more attractive seers were delivering the desired goods.

For others were hearing messages from the Virgin and providing answers to the public. The voluble seers, not the silent ones, led Amundarain and many others to expect a great miracle in mid-October. Two seers in particular convinced him. One was an Aliada from San Sebastián who had had visions at Ezkioga. She had another on about 6 October 1931. In "a pleasant conversation," the Virgin told her, as Amundarain reported to a colleague,

> that within a few days there will be a prodigy (in this she coincides with the visionary of Ataun) and three times She insisted to her that all the Sisters be that day at Ezquioga, and each one with her emblem on display; that the Alianza has been called to save many souls in the world.[22]

An even better reason to expect a portent on October 15 was a semiprivate prophecy by Ramona Olazábal.

Ramona Olazábal, the Girl with the Bleeding Hands

Ramona Olazábal was fifteen when she had her first vision on July 16 at Ezkioga. Born and raised on an isolated farm in Beizama, about twenty kilometers away, she was one of nine surviving children. Before the visions she stood out for her vivacity and her fine dancing more than her piety. At age nine she had gone to live with her sister in Hernani, and by age thirteen she was working in aristocratic households in San Sebastián. When she began to have visions in July 1931 she had spent much time away from the farm and had had some contact with the upper classes.[23]

Like other visionaries in July, Ramona wanted to know if there would be a miracle and when it would be. By the end of the month, she was "one of the best known seers," for newspapers had reported nine of her visions. At the beginning of September a Catalan pilgrim wrote that "her prayer consists of an insistent clamor for pardon and mercy for everyone" and that of the seers she was "the only one who sees the Virgin as happy."[24]

About this time Ramona stopped working and moved to Zumarraga, closer to the vision site. There she stayed with her cousin Juan Bautista Otaegui, one of Amundarain's curates, who boarded in the house of Amundarain's brother. She had many followers and for some she provided special messages. Amundarain's niece, the Aliada Teresa, often accompanied Ramona shopping, for Ramona had money from believers. Ramona gave a sealed letter to Otaegui saying that on October 15 the Virgin would give her a rosary. Amundarain took the prediction seriously, no doubt because it coincided with the visions of the San Sebastián Aliada. Ramona sent a similar letter to a prominent family in San Sebastián. And on October 13 and 14 she told many people to bring handkerchiefs, for the Virgin was going to wound her.[25]

On October 14 Amundarain wrote to the Aliada leader María Ozores in Vitoria: "It seems the Virgin is calling you here; we are in historic days, and we have to give heaven strength." He assigned Ozores and another Aliada to stay with Ramona the next day and search her before she went up the hill. Amundarain had a family lunch to celebrate the saint's day of his mother, and then he, his brother, and his nephew went to the apparition site.[26]

After the Aliadas searched her, Ramona went into an outhouse before going up the hillside. Fifteen to twenty thousand persons, the largest crowd since July 18, had been attracted by the predictions she and Patxi Goicoechea had made about a miracle. Ramona emerged at about 5:15 P.M. with her close friend, a girl from Ataun who was also a seer. When Ramona neared the fenced area for visionaries, she lifted her hands. Blood spurted from the backs of both. "Odola! Odola! [Blood! Blood!]" shouted the crowd. Men carried Ramona into the enclosure, and there a doctor found a rosary twisted around the belt of her dress. In an atmosphere of awe and anguish men carried her downhill seated in a chair, like an image in a procession. All the time people collected her blood on their handkerchiefs. Alerted by phone, pilgrims poured in from all over the Basque Country well into the night.[27]

The Aliadas Amundarain had detailed to observe Ramona were totally convinced. When María Angeles Montoya arrived at her home in Alegia, she told her brother Pío that a miracle had happened. Pío, a priest who was co-founder of El Día, immediately called Justo de Echeguren, the vicar general of the diocese and an intimate family friend. Pío emphasized that unless Echeguren investigated Ramona's wounding at once there would be no stopping the matter.[28]

The next morning Echeguren arrived by train at Zumarraga, where he met Montoya, Amundarain, and Julián Ayestarán, a priest who worked with Amundarain on the Aliadas and whose sister had watched Ramona the day before. Amundarain reported what had happened and spoke favorably about the innocence of the original seers. Echeguren was skeptical about the miracle, but the fact that María Angeles Montoya, who was like a niece to him, believed in it gave him pause. So he immediately formed an ecclesiastical tribunal consisting of himself, Montoya, and Ayestarán to interview witnesses.[29]

Before starting the proceedings, Echeguren had in hand the letter that Ramona had given her cousin Otaegui. He also talked to a man whom Ramona had told to bring a handkerchief and to her friend from Ataun, whom Ramona had told she would receive stigmata. He then asked Ramona whether she had told anyone about what would happen. She denied three times that she told anyone, and Echeguren became so angry that he broke his pencil. He confronted her with the conflicting evidence, including the letter, and she admitted that she had indeed told people and named still others. He told her she had been lying and sent her off.

Crowd at Ezkioga, mid-October 1931

At that point a man from Lezo asked to speak to Echeguren in private. He said that the day before he had been next to Ramona when, stunned by seeing the blood coming out of her hands, he had lowered his eyes in awe and seen to his surprise a razor blade on the ground. He had come back to look for it. To settle the matter, Echeguren asked Montoya to find two doctors, one Catholic and the other, if possible, a non-Catholic, to examine Ramona's wounds. Montoya called in Doroteo Ciaurruz, later the Basque Nationalist mayor of Tolosa, and Luis Azcue from the same city and both examined Ramona that afternoon. That night they reported to Echeguren at Montoya's house that they thought Ramona had inflicted the wounds on herself, most probably with a razor blade. Echeguren immediately drew up a note for the press that said there was positive evidence of natural, not supernatural, causes for Ramona's wounds.

At some time in the fall of 1931 Echeguren instructed priests not to lead the rosary at the site and, according to one source, reprimanded Amundarain for his involvement in the apparitions. On November 4 Amundarain sadly wrote to María Ozores:

> Ezquioga continues to wind down. New prophecies of something extraordinary, new dates, new preparations, new failures. I continue to believe in a

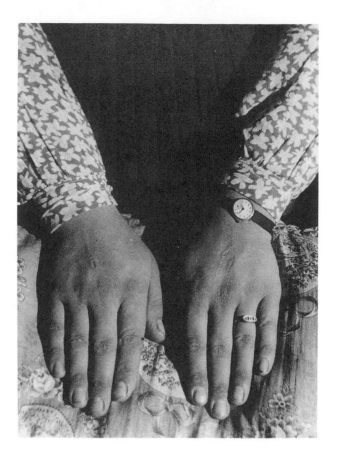

powerful, extraordinary intervention and presence in these mountains of Our Mother, but among the seers there is a lot to be purged.[30]

I find no more reports of Amundarain at Ezkioga. But he continued to hear the effects of the visions in the confessional. On December 14 a group of Catalan believers visited him. One of them wrote:

> The parish priest of Zumárraga spoke to us of the beautiful spiritual fruit harvested at Ezquioga. There have been countless general confessions, he told us, and they still continue. Even today, he added, there were some in this church. Even men eighty years old have wanted to make a general confession.

He said he believed 80 percent of the seers, but that Freemasons had become involved to discredit the apparitions. By this time both he and Otaegui had broken with Ramona.[31]

A year later, on 16 December 1932, due to stress and ill health, Amundarain resigned as parish priest to devote himself fully to the Alianza, which he did for the rest of his life. But he did not renounce his hopes for Marian apparitions or his hopes for the role the Aliadas would play. In his copy of a book of prophecies published in 1932, the following passage from the prophecy of Madeleine Porsat is underlined and "¿Alianza?" written in the margin:

The church is preparing everything for the glorious coming of Mary. . . . It forms a guard of honor to go out and meet the angels that come with her.

The arch of triumph has been erected. The hour is not distant.

It is she herself in person, but she has her precursors, holy women and apostles, who will heal the wounds of the body and the sins of the heart.[32]

Antonio Amundarain was prudent in public about the visions. As far as I know, he had little personal contact with the seers, but his sharp attention, foresight, and careful use of the media were critical to the pace and momentum of the visions. Many people thought he was acting on behalf of the diocese. *El Pueblo Vasco* reported that "it was [Amundarain] who was charged by Vitoria to gather testimony of the events." If this was the case, Amundarain's role would have been unofficial. Such a procedure was not unusual. Both at Limpias and at Piedramillera bishops instructed the parish priests to take down testimony of seers as if at their own initiative. When Amundarain issued the note on July 28 referring to the commission of priests and doctors as "official," the vicar general immediately issued a denial, disavowing any diocesan connection. Given the vicar general's subsequent total skepticism, it would seem that Amundarain was on thin ice from the start. But at least in some matters he seems to have worked for Echeguren. That Amundarain had matters in hand probably contributed to the diocese's relaxed attitude in the first months.[33]

CARMEN MEDINA Y GARVEY

Amundarain's cool distance contrasts with the active engagement of most of the other key believers at Ezkioga, including the second leader to arrive on the scene, Carmen Medina y Garvey, whose close contacts with seers—including Lolita Núñez, the girl from Ataun, Patxi Goicoechea, and Evarista Galdós—lasted for at least three years.

At the Casa de Pilatos in Seville I learned about Carmen from her nephew, Rafael Medina y Vilallonga, the former mayor of the city.[34] He estimated that Carmen was about sixty years old in 1931. One of the ten children of the marquis of Esquivel and Dolores Garvey, she was very wealthy, for she inherited land from her father and money from the sherry fortune of her bachelor uncle, José Garvey. She became a nun in the convent of the Irlandesas in Seville, which she helped to restore with her money. She later left this convent and founded another of her own, but the new convent apparently did not survive.

Carmen Medina at the base of the Ezkioga hill before an automobile with diplo-matic plates and the stand of the photographer Joaquín Sicart, 1932 or 1933. Photo by Joaquín Sicart

Two of Carmen's sisters became nuns and a sister-in-law entered a convent when widowed. Carmen's sister María Josefa and her brother Luis married, respectively, the son and daughter of the couple, Rafaela Ibarra and José Vila-llonga. In 1894 Rafaela Ibarra founded an order, the Instituto de los Santos Angeles Custodios, dedicated to the care of young women in danger of becoming prostitutes. Indeed, Rafaela has been beatified, and when I asked to speak to the family about a relative involved in religious visions, they thought I referred to her. José Vilallonga was the founder in Bilbao of Spain's biggest iron works. In the early twentieth century the alliance of Andalusian aristocrats with Basque in-dustrialists was not unusual. The women of both families in this particular alliance had enduring religious interests and a social conscience. Carmen had other powerful relations, including the leader of the monarchist Unión Patriótica, who was the minister of public works under Primo de Rivera.

Carmen Medina's nephew and niece remember her as loving, high-spirited, and generous, but they were somewhat wary of talking about her, for they also thought her a little unstable and feared her enthusiasms might reflect badly on the family. It was my understanding, although this was left rather vague, that she herself had had visions at some time in her life. The family, I gathered, thought of her as a beloved, credulous eccentric. They remember, for instance, when she announced to her nieces in San Sebastián that on a certain day a tidal wave would wipe out the city. She had learned this from a male seer, who had it from the Virgin. When the tidal wave failed to materialize, she went back to the seer, who told her (and she told her nieces) that when he saw the Virgin again, he noticed a tail sticking out from under her mantle and recognized the devil in disguise.[35]

In late July Walter Starkie found Medina already ensconced in an Ezkioga fonda with two female companions.

> Doña Carmen, in the intervals of putting Gargantuan morsels into her mouth, pontificated about everything. She apostrophized the girls who were serving the dinner; she abused the cook; she asked for the priests; she criticized the behavior of some of the young people at the religious service: her resonant voice echoed and reechoed through the house. I tried to crouch in my corner, but I knew that sooner or later I should be dragged within her sphere of influence and become a butt for her inquisitive questioning.
> . . . she was one of those imperious women who declare their views but never wait for an answer. Such people's whole life is so rooted in assertion, that they only hear their own voices. Destiny fortunately deafens them to any other sound.[36]

Medina assumed that Starkie was a pious Irish pilgrim, so she made no secret of her politics. She told him the Republic was a force of Satan.

> Though [Carmen Medina] was a daily communicant and spent a great deal of the day in prayer, she was a very active and practical woman, and directed many organizations connected with the church and the exiled monarchy. . . . The Basque province and Navarra, in her opinion, would rise before long in defence of their religion. In my own mind I felt quite convinced that she was doing her best to use the Ezquioga apparitions as a political lever. . . . "Our Lady is appearing in order to inspire people to defend their religion. And I tell you that in many cases she is appearing, holding a sword dripping with blood."[37]

Starkie saw a kind side as well. Carmen Medina was generous with the poor and spoke easily to everyone she met. But:

> she was a fighter . . . she should have been fighting Moors at Granada and raising the Silver Cross above the minarets of the Prophet. . . . She longed for battle, and I saw her nostrils dilate like those of a war-horse when she described how civil war might come in a few weeks, with the Basques as the leaders of the revindication of the Church of Rome.

Carmen's family had a tradition of rebellion against liberal governments. Her paternal grandfather was a Carlist general. Her father, Francisco, and an uncle participated in the Carlist rebellion of 1873 and as a result her family spent two years in exile in Portugal. From "Casa Blanca," the home in Seville of Carmen's widowed sister, General José Sanjurjo attempted to launch a monarchist coup in August 1932. One of Carmen's nephews was an active participant, and one of her brothers had to take refuge in France.[38]

María Dolores (Lolita) Núñez

Doña Carmen knew the original child seers and introduced them to Starkie, but by that time her interest, like that of Amundarain, had shifted to those who could provide messages. Her first great interest was in María Dolores Núñez, known as Lolita. Medina took Starkie in her car to pick up the eighteen-year-old seer and take her to the vision site.

Núñez was educated and refined; according to Starkie, she and her family were "poor members of the bourgeois class" who lived in a small second-floor apartment on the main street of Tolosa. By the time Starkie met her at the end of July, she had had seven visions and her name had appeared in print a dozen times. Her blurry and poignant photograph in *El Pueblo Vasco* was the first of a seer in vision. She would cry out to the Virgin to save Spain—it was probably this aspect that attracted Carmen Medina—and afterward she would report the Virgin's reaction.

The visions exhausted Lolita, but the excitement prevented her from sleeping at night. She told a reporter, "There is no human force that could resist so much magnificence and splendor. One feels a thousand times more blinded than when one looks at the sun." Her mother and older sister worried for her and opposed her visits to the site. One night in the room where the seers recovered Lolita declared, "Our Lady has told me that I must come here the next seven days, and I must depart from here and sing for joy in the streets." Starkie was disenchanted when Lolita came down to dinner afterward: "She had dwindled again to the fair typist with a good dose of coquettishness and pose" who confided that she had a boyfriend who knew nothing about the visions. Starkie played his violin for her that night and left early the next morning. Lolita's name appeared no more in the press after July 31; no one made postcards of her. If she returned the seven times the Virgin requested, I find no record, nor, alas, do I know if she sang in the streets. Her name meant nothing to the old-time believers left in Tolosa in the 1980s.[39]

Lolita was one of several seers that Carmen promoted among friends and relatives. At Ezkioga Starkie met Medina's elderly cousin, the duke of T'serclaes. The duke was a fixture of the San Sebastián summer set and Mateo Múgica used to stay in his house on the Calle Serrano on his trips to Madrid. Carmen's sister María, the duchess of Tárifa, went to pray for her husband, and one seer, after consulting the Virgin, assured the duchess that he would recover. A sister-in-law, the countess of Campo Rey, was at Ezkioga in December.[40]

María Dolores Núñez, 12 July 1931, the night of her first vision. From El Pueblo Vasco, *14 July 1931. Courtesy Hemeroteca Municipal, San Sebastián*

Carmen is almost certainly the grand dame a visitor described in early August as "the confidante of the most interesting seers" who assured visitors that the great miracle would come soon. She took particular interest in two seers from Ataun, both of whom learned "secrets" from the Virgin and claimed knowledge of the timing and content of the upcoming miracle.[41]

Ramona's Friend, the Girl from Ataun

By early October a girl seer, age eighteen, from Ataun had become inseparable from Ramona. Like Ramona, she too was from a farm and had worked as servant to a prominent family in Ordizia. Her hands were those of a señorita, and there is a photograph of her sitting at a Singer sewing machine. Her visions had started on July 12, four days before those of Ramona. They were quite detailed and received wide publicity. The Virgin first spoke to her, she said, on July 16. At the end of the month she was seeing the Virgin several times daily.[42]

In August she gave a special blessing from the Virgin to a Catalan cleric who had singled her out of the mass of seers. She claimed to have a vision every time she went to the hillside; by September 27 she had had them on forty-one days. Like Ramona she was conspicuously good-natured and felt no call to the cloisters.[43]

This girl, Ramona, and an unnamed Tolosa seer helped one another when in trance. They stayed together on the morning of October 15. When Ramona's hands started to bleed, the Ataun girl was probably the seer who announced to the crowd, "The Virgin has cut her with swords and now places a rosary around her waist!" The next morning as the public pressed to kiss Ramona's hands, she, the Tolosa seer, and Ramona talked to reporters together.[44]

At that time a family from Bilbao was pampering both the Ataun girl and Ramona. Julio de Lecue was a stockbroker and his brother José was a painter and sculptor. They had nieces the age of Ramona and her friend. José in particular was close to Ramona, and in mid-October she began to dictate to him what she saw in her visions.[45] On the morning of Ramona's miracle José de Lecue refused to leave her side, which prevented an effective search by the Aliadas. He was one of the two men who carried Ramona down the hill in a chair. On the days after the miracle some reporters briefly suspected him of having made the wounds on her hands. Another suspect was a confidence man and pickpocket who had allegedly boasted how he could arrange a miracle at Ezkioga.[46]

On October 16 after the diocesan inquiry into Ramona's wounds, attention shifted to the girl from Ataun. Over sixty thousand persons had gathered on the hillside, and for the first time the seers used a stage Patxi Goicoechea had been building with lumber and manpower from the owner of the land. Only family members, priests, and reporters could go with the seers on the stage. The seers lined up in late afternoon, and many fell into trance. A medal of the Daughters of Mary on a blue ribbon appeared in the Ataun girl's hands, as if out of nowhere, and shortly thereafter another appeared in the hands of a seven-year-old girl from Ormaiztegi.[47]

On Saturday, October 17, yet more people came, most of them unaware of the vicar general's finding about Ramona. The Ataun girl suddenly lifted one of her hands, which had a little scratch, and said that the Baby Jesus had left the mark with a dagger. We see her the next day in a proud pose with Ramona, both of them discreetly displaying their bandages from a window of the fonda. Shortly after this high point, Carmen Medina began to look after the Ataun girl.[48]

Ramona Olazábal and the girl from Ataun, 18 October 1931. Photo by Raymond de Rigné, all rights reserved

Francisco (Patxi) Goicoechea, the Convert

Carmen Medina also took an interest in Francisco Goicoechea, known as Patxi or "the lad from Ataun." At the end of July Medina told Starkie that Patxi (pronounced Patchi) had become a veritable Saint John of the Cross in his piety. His parents were tenant farmers and he was a carpenter on construction jobs. His first vision occurred on 7 July 1931, as he was making fun of the visions of others. His deep trances became a highlight of the vision evenings. Stern young men from Ataun generally went with him; they would carry him semiconscious down to the recovery room. He became the central figure in the apparitions from early July and was, in the words of the industrialist and deputy Rafael Picavea, "the most famous youth in the entire region."[49]

We have seen that it was Patxi, a Basque Nationalist, who came out and said that the Virgin called for the overthrow of the Republic. He took the initiative in other ways as well. He put up a wooden cross at the site in August, the stage in October, and stations of the cross the following February. Patxi repeatedly predicted miracles, including ones for July 16 and mid-October. The Ataun girl and Evarista Galdós from Gabiria normally supported him.[50]

Patxi made a large and varied number of friends. He allegedly had the use of the automobiles of a devout Bilbao heiress, Pilar Arratia, and the Traditionalist physician Benigno Oreja Elósegui, brother of a deputy in the Cortes.[51] Because of his prestige, believers took him to observe the visions of little girls in the riverbed by Ormaiztegi, which he judged diabolical, and those of children in Navarra. Carmen Medina took him to Toledo at the beginning of October so he could attend the visions of children in the village of Guadamur.[52]

By November Patxi had tried to pass on divine messages to the Basque deputies Jesús Leizaola, Marcelino Oreja, and José Antonio Aguirre. When he heard that Patxi had a message for him, Leizaola replied, "Message from the Virgin? I know her too. If she has something important she wants me to know, she will give it to me herself." In early December it had become clear that the vicar general of Vitoria rejected all the Ezkioga visions, and Patxi, Carmen Medina, and the other believers could only hope that the exiled bishop felt differently. Rumor had it that on December 14 Patxi had given Bishop Mateo Múgica, by then in the village of La Puye near Poitiers, a sealed letter that said the miracle would take place on December 26.[53]

I am not certain that Patxi went to France, but in any case he passed on the Virgin's instructions for Carmen Medina to take a group of seers to see the bishop. Medina went with Ramona Olazábal, the girl from Ataun, the child Benita Aguirre, Evarista Galdós, and a fifth seer on December 19. Bishop Múgica spoke to each seer separately for half an hour and allegedly told Carmen Medina that, whatever the origin of the visions, he did not think the seers were knowingly lying.[54]

Francisco Goicoechea (second from left) and friends at Ataun, October 1931.
Photo by Raymond de Rigné, all rights reserved

For the people of Ataun Goicoechea was "Patxi Santu [Holy Patxi]." They remember lines of cars parked in front of his farm and people kissing his hand and leaving presents. The nickname probably came after his apotheosis on 1 August 1931, when newspapers reported that he had levitated. After that he received large numbers of letters. In the summer of 1931 or 1932 Carmen Medina organized a bus excursion to Ezkioga for her many nieces and nephews living or vacationing in San Sebastián; they also went to Ataun, where Patxi obligingly entered into a trance. When they asked what the Virgin had said, one of Patxi's friends said she wanted them to leave the bus in Ataun for the use of the village.[55]

Patxi was a complex individual, and those who knew him offer conflicting testimony. Some say he drank a lot; others say he did not. They agree that he attended church, both before and after the visions, and that for a while during the visions he went to church daily. He was tall and handsome and spoke Basque better than Spanish. With some reporters he was camera shy and defensive, especially when there were questions that implied his vision state might have a component of mental illness or epilepsy. Some remember him as messianic. In the projected reconquest of Spain, they recall, he was going to be the captain. Like some of the other more dramatic seers, he asked to die for his sins to save the world: "Mother, mother, do not weep, kill me, but forgive the rest, for they know not what they do."[56]

Patxi had his cuadrilla, a friend who answered his mail, and a schoolteacher who took down his messages. He also had the support of priests, at first from his parish, then from elsewhere. Therefore he did not need the kind of patronage that the younger or poorer seers did. From the end of August 1931 and continuing through early 1933 at least, he usually went to Ezkioga on Tuesday, Thursday, and Saturday nights with his friends. By the beginning of 1932 he was no longer the center of attention, and by May 1933 his nocturnal visions were almost furtive, his small band quite separate from the daytime seers. Formerly he arrived in a chauffeured car; now he came and went on bicycle after work.[57]

I do not know whether the subsequent absence of news about Patxi was the result of his rejection by others or his own self-exclusion. Perhaps the Carlist-Integrist believers, who predominated after 1931, rejected him for his nationalism. Or perhaps he was burned by bad publicity. His public downfall began with that of Ramona. As Catholic newspapers began to feel freer to print negative information, they pointed out that Patxi had made many false predictions. Rafael Picavea in *El Pueblo Vasco* exposed Patxi's inconsistencies. And when Patxi protested, Picavea ridiculed him for social climbing with Carmen Medina. As Patxi, Ramona, and the girl from Ataun fell from grace, the other seers also began to turn on them. Benita Aguirre reported that the Virgin had told her that the decline of a seer named F (almost certainly Patxi) should be an object lesson for seers, that they should shun worldly honors: "They spoiled him, and now what is left for him?"[58]

The diocese early identified Patxi as a troublemaker. In August 1931 he refused to remove the cross he had put up on the hillside. And on December 26 Bishop Múgica of Vitoria sent his fiscal, or magistrate, to take testimony in Ormaiztegi that Patxi predicted a miracle for that day. Patxi had convinced Carmen Medina, who had imprudently spread the word. Patxi lost further credibility when he predicted a miracle for January. His clerical support in Ataun dropped away. He probably made his nocturnal visits to Ezkioga in late 1932 and 1933 in spite of explicit, personal diocesan orders not to go. Like most prominent seers, he also had trouble with the Republic, and in October 1932 the governor sent him for observation to the Mondragón mental hospital.[59]

We catch a final glimpse of Patxi's complexity when on 15 March 1935 he appeared as a witness in a traffic case in San Sebastián. There reporters learned that the government had indicted him for taking part in the October 1934 uprising. Socialists had led the rebellion and took over much of the province of Asturias. In the Basque Country the more radical nationalists participated by trying to organize a general strike. When a reporter asked Patxi about his involvement in the rebellion, he complained, "If I had known that they brought me here to bother me with questions about my private life, I would not have come. Whose business is it that I am the fellow involved with Ezquioga and at the same time an advanced republican?"[60]

I do not know how Carmen Medina's friendship with Patxi ended. Surely his crossover from the revolutionary right to the revolutionary left would have alienated her had they maintained contact. Her family remembers that Carmen dropped one youthful male seer when he told her that he and she should get married, by order of the Virgin.

Evarista Galdós

A final seer in whom Carmen Medina took special interest was Evarista Galdós y Eguiguren. Evarista was seventeen years old when she began to have visions in early July 1931. She came from a farm in Gabiria, not far from the vision site, and when the visions started she was in service in the home of a journalist in San Sebastián. The press described her visions in early July but did not mention her again until the fall. By that time she had had over thirty visions and went to Ezkioga on Thursdays and Sundays, presumably her days off from work.[61]

The believers heeded Evarista more from mid-October. On October 18 and 19 the Jesuit José Antonio Laburu filmed her and Ramona having visions.[62] On October 19 she told a reporter that both she and Patxi knew when the big miracle would be and that it would be soon. She predicted a miracle for the next day, which attracted a large crowd that was duly disappointed; with the seer girl from Ataun she predicted another for November 1 between 4:00 and 4:15 P.M. On December 4 she claimed to receive from heaven a medal on a ribbon like those others received previously. She announced this event in advance to a sympathetic priest and had herself searched beforehand. By this time she was important enough for Carmen Medina to take her to the bishop in France.[63]

On 17 January 1932 Evarista, Ramona, the Ataun seer, and six other girls from the district attended the spiritual exercises offered by the Reparadora nuns in San Sebastián. Carmen Medina may have paid for them. Her family patronized this elite order, whose first house in Spain was in Seville. Carmen's sister Dolores had founded the houses in San Sebastián and Madrid. Antonio Amundarain might have suggested the exercises; he had been the confessor of the Reparadoras in San Sebastián, and the Aliadas went for exercises there. Whoever was responsible probably also had a hand in the spiritual exercises at Loyola for male youths who were seers and converts. The Reparadoras based their rules on those of the Jesuits, and the Jesuits worked closely with them. Like the exercises of the Jesuits, those of the Reparadoras emphasized atonement, in which "a detailed contemplation of the scenes of the Passion . . . poses the question of acting and

suffering for Christ in return." Immediately subsequent to these exercises Evarista and other seers began to have visions in which they experienced the crucifixion.[64]

In 1932 Evarista and Ramona stayed for a time in Azkoitia in the house of a wealthy woman, who paid a driver to take them back and forth to Ezkioga daily. But the two seers had a bad falling-out. Only the concerted efforts of José de Lecue, the Bilbao artist, and Patxi in a meeting in Bilbao in April led them to make peace. In the fall of 1932 and early 1933 a young male convert recorded Evarista's visions. This friendship cost Evarista some of her more prudish followers. She lived for most of 1933 in Irun. There she convinced a priest after having a vision in his house, and he started taking down her messages. Many of these visions had to do with the adventures of the believing community. She saw specific churchmen conspiring against the visions, other seers having their final visions, the hostile clergy changing their minds and believing, and other mystics making prophecies.[65]

In January 1934 Carmen Medina spirited Evarista off to Madrid. There Medina hoped to set up a refuge from the coming revolution for a "high dignitary," who was in all likelihood the papal nuncio, Federico Tedeschini.[66]

Carmen Medina was in the class of grandees, enjoying powerful ecclesiastical, political, social, and financial connections. She was untouchable, even unmentionable. When the diocesan investigator went to Ormaiztegi to document Patxi's false prediction, his investigation included Medina, but he nonetheless accepted her hospitality and ate with her. The bishop and vicar general had no qualms about attacking other key figures openly, but they steered clear of Medina. Even in private correspondence Ezkioga believers mention her circumspectly. Only a complete outsider, Walter Starkie, could be frank about her.[67]

The most overtly political of the Ezkioga patrons, Carmen Medina needed no one to tell her a civil war was imminent, and she knew which side she was on. Nor did the other patrons have any doubt about their sympathies. But they considered politics a distant second to religion. Amundarain is a case in point: what was foremost for him was the saving of souls and the spiritual mission of his new order in the unfolding divine plan. In the June 1931 issue of *Lilium inter Spinas* he put politics in its place:

> Say it, dear Sisters. Hail Jesus in our hearts and in those of all others as well! Hail Jesus in those who love us and those who persecute us! Hail Jesus in those who rule and those who obey! Hail Jesus in the Republic, in its governments, and its laws! Hail Jesus in the Church, in its ministers, and in its faithful! Hail Jesus in the heavens, on earth, and in the depths! Hail Jesus now and forever, Amen, Amen![68]

4. PROMOTERS AND SEERS II: THE CATALANS

FROM DECEMBER 1931 through October 1932 Catalan believers in the Virgin of Ezkioga played a central part in the visions. Like Antonio Amundarain and Carmen Medina, many brought prior commitments. Some believed the bogus prophecies a nun in Zaragoza was concocting. Others were militants from the movement of a charismatic preacher. Many followed the spiritual directions of a mystic from a small town in Girona.

The immediate interest of the Catalan Catholic bourgeoisie in the apparitions is not surprising. Like Basques and Navarrese, Catalans were especially receptive to new visions because of their proximity to France. In the 1850s Catalans had been attracted to the visions of La Salette; by 1910 they were sending hospital trains on large and regular pilgrimages to Lourdes; and in the years 1919 and 1920 they sent three diocesan pilgrimages to Limpias. Of the Spanish press outside the Basque Country, two Barcelona newspapers gave Ezkioga the best coverage: the Catalanist and centrist *El Matí* and the Carlist *El Correo Catalán*. In 1931 *El Correo Catalán* carried several firsthand reports by priests; this interest reflected that of the bishop of Barcelona, Manuel Irurita Almándoz.[1]

THE BISHOP OF BARCELONA AND THE NUN FROM ZARAGOZA

Manuel Irurita paid close attention to Ezkioga in part because he was from nearby Navarra and returned every summer to the Valle de Baztán. But perhaps more important was that he, like Antonio Amundarain, had a taste for the marvelous. He was born just over the border from France, and of all bishops up to the Civil War, he was the one who went to Lourdes most frequently.[2]

Irurita was not shy about recounting a strange experience of his own. In 1927, when he was a canon in Valencia, he took the wrong train, an express instead of a local, on his way to preach at a Carmelite convent. He prayed for help to Thérèse de Lisieux, and the train jerked to a halt at the station for the convent. When he got off, he asked the engineer what had happened. The engineer said he had seen a nun standing on the tracks. None of the people on the platform had seen her.[3]

Incognito, dressed as a layman, Irurita visited Ezkioga at least four times in 1931. He made his first visit with the priest from Alegia, Pío Montoya, and this may have been around July 21, when Irurita was in Navarra on vacation. His visit on July 31, in the company of Antonio Amundarain, was his third. By then he had had occasion to speak with one of six seers from his native Baztán who had traveled together to Ezkioga; he was impressed with the seer.[4]

In the aftermath of Ramona Olazábal's wounding Irurita returned to Ezkioga. We see him in photographs kneeling next to Ramona.[5] Irurita's last visit to Ezkioga was an open secret and helped to maintain the respectability of the visions at a time when the diocese of Vitoria was turning against them. Pilgrims could buy a souvenir postcard showing Ramona, the Virgin, and Irurita. Irurita subsequently delegated a layman from Barcelona to observe the Ezkioga visions and report back to him. The Barcelona diocesan censor approved articles in favor of the visions for Catholic newspapers as late as the summer of 1932, and at the end of that year Irurita was still saying in private that he believed in the visions.

Irurita's prior entanglement in the spurious prophecies of Madre Rafols deepened his interest in Ezkioga. For some time the Sisters of Charity of Saint Anne had been campaigning to canonize their founder, María Rafols y Bruna. The pseudo-Rafols story is a fascinating example of religious politics and merits study.

Rafols was born in 1781 near Vilafranca del Penedès in the province of Barcelona.[6] She founded her order in Zaragoza, but it remained small until 1894, when Pabla Bescós became the superior. Bescós obtained approval for the order from Rome and before her death in 1929 organized over sixty new houses, some

Manuel Irurita, bishop of Barcelona, in civilian clothes watches Ramona Olazá-bal in vision, 19 or 20 October 1931. Photo by J. Juanes. Courtesy Arxiu Salvador Cardús i Florensa, Terrassa

in South America. In 1932 there were 2,500 religious in 130 houses. As the order grew, its leaders moved to honor their founder. Bescós held meetings in homage to Madre Rafols in Zaragoza and Vilafranca, commissioned a biography, and began gathering documents.[7]

In the 1920s Madre Bescós's niece, María Naya Bescós, was a teacher of novices. Perhaps out of a sense of proprietary connection with the order and its history, she began to falsify documents to fill in and illustrate the life of the founder. She made her forgeries with care, using period paper. Her procedure was to observe or provoke contemporary events and have the Sacred Heart of Jesus predict them to Madre Rafols a century earlier. Then she would "discover" the prophecies. For instance, when Naya and the acting superior Felisa Guerri went to purchase the Rafols homestead on 31 August 1924, Naya pointed to a crucifix and identified it as belonging to Madre Rafols. Supposedly the crucifix was fixed to the wall, but Naya was able to remove it with ease, as if she herself had some supernatural power. Later she doctored a prophecy (and discovered it on 2 January 1931) to confirm that the crucifix belonged to Madre Rafols and to

Souvenir postcard of apparitions at Ezkioga: The Sorrowing Mary, Ramona Olazábal, and Manuel Irurita, bishop of Barcelona, October 1931. Photo by J. Juanes

consecrate its removal as miraculous. This crucifix—El Santo Cristo de la Pureza y Desconsuelo—became an important relic.

María Naya "found" forged letters and spiritual writings in 1922 and between 1926 and 1932. She confirmed her own special role in 1930 by putting into a message from Jesus that the documents would be discovered by "one of [Rafols's] daughters much beloved by my Heart." The prophecies implied that the church would canonize her aunt Pabla as well. On 15 November 1929 workers digging the foundations for a convent at the Rafols homestead found a second crucifix, allegedly with fresh blood on it. In January 1931 Naya located a prophecy about this crucifix—El Santo Cristo Desamparado—and in October 1931 another about its discovery.

Irurita was named bishop of Barcelona in March 1930 and Vilafranca del Penedès fell within his diocese. On 30 April 1931 he laid the cornerstone for the complex of buildings at Vilafranca. From September 14 through 16 he displayed in his episcopal chapel the crucifix that had "bled" as public atonement for Spain's sins. For long periods he himself held the image for the faithful to kiss. This provoked scenes of religious enthusiasm unusual in Barcelona under the Second Republic. Barcelona Catholic newspapers printed the tales of the miraculous discovery of the crucifixes, and a Barcelona cathedral canon put out a pamphlet. A Zaragoza manufacturer sold copies of El Cristo Desamparado nationwide. Of course, these were trying times for Catholicism and Irurita was acutely aware that the church was no longer one of the powers in control of the nation. In this context a bleeding crucifix meant something special, as did the appearance of the Sorrowing Mother in the Basque hills.[8]

A canon of Zaragoza, Santiago Guallar Poza, was in charge of the Rafols cause. The diocesan tribunal, the first stage in the beatification process, began in July 1926 and finished in February 1927. In 1931 Guallar published a biography of Rafols with the materials he had gathered. That year he was one of eight priests elected to the Constituent Cortes in Madrid. I do not know whether Guallar was aware of the forgeries. But in 1931 politics was on everyone's mind, and Naya began to compose prophecies with a political slant. On 2 October 1931, when the Cortes was about to discuss separating church and state, Naya uncovered a text that included a vision by Rafols of the Sacred Heart predicting visible miracles. And on 29 January 1932, the day the government dissolved the Jesuit order in Spain, Naya found a political prophecy that foretold a chastisement and explained that sacrilege, the removal of the crucifixes, and the expulsion of the Jesuits was the work of the Masons and God's punishment of Spain for female indecency.

The Vatican checked these more political texts and permitted their publication (although the names of the cities God would chastise and the names of living persons were excised). The last prophecy caused a special stir, and Pius XI gave Felisa Guerri and María Naya a second audience. They had already visited him in February 1931 to show the crucifixes. The political prophecies gave the Rafols cult an enormously expanded audience. The texts, in booklets introduced by the Navarrese Jesuit Demetrio Zurbitu, went out by the tens of thousands in early 1932. What started as a pious fraud to make a saint turned into a rally to toughen Spanish Catholics against the secular Second Republic.[9]

A commission of experts appointed by the diocese of Zaragoza decided unanimously in January 1934 that the documents were forgeries, but their finding, since it was part of the beatification process, was kept secret. Clergy who openly questioned the documents included the French Benedictine Aimé Lambert; the preacher Francisco de Paula Vallet; the Dominican Luis Urbano, even more scornful of the Ezkioga visions than he had been of those of Limpias and Piedramillera; and the liturgical scholar Josep Tarré. In the Basque Country Canon Antonio Pildain spoke against the revelations in the cathedral of Vitoria in 1933, and in 1941 Manuel Lecuona, a Basque folklorist from Oiartzun and a former professor at the seminary in Vitoria, published proof of plagiarism.[10]

After the case reached Rome, in 1943 another panel of experts, including the Catalan Franciscan Josep Pou i Martí, was also unanimously negative. They based their finding on anachronisms, the use of metal pens, the use of the same batch of paper over what was ostensibly a span of forty years, the handwriting, and the outright copying of contemporary literature. The Vatican closed the case, but discreetly, never informing the general public of the fraud. María Naya lost her position with the novices and the order had to withdraw the crucifixes from veneration. But people still read the old books and pamphlets, as well as an occasional new book. Naya, who died in 1966, never spoke on the subject, never admitted her role, and never revealed who, if anyone, worked with her.[11]

María Naya hoodwinked Irurita into the Rafols deception by flattery and co-optation, just as she hoodwinked certain Jesuits and even Pius XI. In the message she found 2 January 1931, the last before the messages turned political, Naya had Jesus tell Rafols that "a holy prelate very zealous in the salvation of souls and devoted to his Divine Heart would help my Sisters with his advice and with the other means that [Jesus] would provide him in order to put into practice all the plans of his Divine Heart."[12] Irurita's support was important for the beatification, for Rafols had been born in his diocese. His support was also essential for the new convent and shrine at the homestead site. His personal promotion of the Rafols shrine and the crucifixes demonstrated his total identification with the prelate in the prophecy. Later, to erase any doubt, Naya inserted in the message of 2 October 1931 a reference to the "Lord Bishop who in those years [1931–1940] governs this diocese of Barcelona."[13]

The belief that he had a providential role to play in Spain's dramatic days sharpened Irurita's interest in the Ezkioga visions. He quickly noticed the convergence of the Basque vision messages and the Rafols prophecies. In the fall of 1931 both predicted visible public supernatural events and by that time both emphasized not Euskadi but Spain. In the Rafols message of 2 October 1931, when the Ezkioga multitudes expected miracles, the Sacred Heart of Jesus said he would, if he had to, save Spain from the devil. He would do so, he said, "with the help of portentous miracles that many people will see with their own eyes; and my Most Holy Mother will communicate to them what they must do to placate and make amends to my eternal Father." A Catalan correspondent wrote to Ramona about Irurita's attitude toward this vision:

> I know that some time ago our Bishop warned your Vicar General to act very carefully since the revelations of the Sacred Heart to M. Rafols ultimately support the cause of Ezquioga. I do not know how he took it. Do not speak of this as it is a sensitive matter.[14]

The Rafols document of January 1932 warned of a chastisement of Spain which would precede a new age.

> This writing will be found when the hour of my Reign in Spain approaches; but before that I will see that it is purified of all of its filth. . . . [M]y Eternal father will be forced, if they do not reform after this merciful warning, to destroy entire cities.[15]

Since October 1931 Ezkioga seers had been speaking about chastisements on a grand scale, including the destruction of three Spanish cities. The new Rafols revelation also pointed to a solution—prayer with arms in the form of a cross—that had been in use daily at Ezkioga for seven months by the time Naya produced the message: "The most powerful weapon to win the victory will be the reform of customs and public prayer. The faithful should gather and do petitionary processions and other devotions with their arms in the form of a cross." The Terrassa writer Salvador Cardús noted this similarity immediately and attempted in vain to point it out in the press.[16]

The convergence was not casual. By the time of the last two forgeries, María Naya was clearly aware of what the Ezkioga seers were saying. She and others in the order would have heard from Irurita himself about the visions. And groups of Catalan pilgrims stopped to see her on their way to Ezkioga. One of the group leaders recounted a visit to Zaragoza as follows:

> Hermana Naya explained to us the details of her wonderful finds and how she would hear an interior voice that told her to pick up a certain key [to a cabinet or closet], and where and which ones were the writings she was looking for. And then, without our asking her, she expressed her conviction that the Ezkioga matter was certain, that an interior voice affirmed it, although she added prudently that there might exist a small proportion of exaggeration or fiction. And to a question by D. Luis Palà she answered that the interior voice that affirmed to her the reality of the Ezkioga matter was the same, exactly the same, as that which made her pick up a key and find the writings of Madre María Rafols.

In 1932 Naya produced yet another document that confirmed the Ezkioga visions more explicitly. On June 25 she told Ezkioga seers who visited her of a great new revelation, still secret. And on July 12 an Ezkioga enthusiast knew from a Jesuit friend that "in Rome there is another document of Madre Rafols and that this one is even clearer about Ezquioga. It seems that it will not be made public because it specifies many things and even events of great importance." While these visits and those of high churchmen to Hermana Naya were no doubt in good faith, they bring to mind Leonardo Sciascia's tale *Il Consiglio d'Egitto*, in which a Sicilian monk lets it be known he has discovered a manuscript of a Moslem history of Sicily and the nobles of the land pay him court and give him presents, hoping to get their families and landholdings mentioned.[17]

Naya and the pseudo-Rafols prophecies in return influenced the Ezkioga visions. When pictures of Rafols began to appear in the souvenir stands at the bottom of the hill, seers began to recognize her. On 1 October 1931 Benita Aguirre had a vision of a nun and later, when given a picture by a Catalan believer, claimed to recognize the nun as Rafols. The visionaries saw Madre Rafols particularly in the spring of 1932, when they were reading booklets and articles about the prophecies.[18]

In early 1932 the Ezkioga seers had another source of news of the Rafols prophecies, this one close at hand. A priest using the pseudonym Bartolomé de Andueza had written an article about Rafols for *La Constancia* in 1925. Starting in late February 1932 and ending in late June 1932 he published a series entitled "The Stupendous Prophecies of Madre María Rafols." Andueza seems to have known Irurita. He reported that the bishop had given a woman dying with tuberculosis a picture of Madre Rafols; when the picture touched the woman, it cured her. Referring to the prelate in the Rafols prophecy, Andueza wrote, "Both to you and to me, there comes to mind the very fervent Dr. Irurita, the present bishop of Barcelona."[19]

In an article in early March 1932 Andueza, aware of the latest developments at Ezkioga, detailed the parallels between the Ezkioga visions and the Rafols prophecies, suggesting that the Ezkioga seers and believers were those the Sacred Heart referred to as "just, pure, and chaste souls." And he suggested that the visions and visible miracles the seers expected at Ezkioga were those the Sacred Heart had predicted to Rafols.[20]

Andueza had begun the series to spread the news about Rafols to the Basques. When he mentioned a pamphlet about the Rafols crosses, the Librería Ignaciana in San Sebastián sold all 100 copies of the pamphlet in one hour and 1,000 that week. Andueza obtained excerpts of the second political prophecy from sources at the Vatican. He published them on 10 April 1932, scooping the rest of the country by a month. That issue sold out immediately, with copies going to Barcelona and Zaragoza. When in late May a pamphlet arrived in San Sebastián with the last prophecies, it too sold briskly, 1,500 copies by June 2. One gentleman bought 200 to distribute to friends, and some parish priests purchased as many as 50. For Spain's distressed Catholics the Rafols prophecies, like the Ezkioga visions, were a godsend.[21]

In early May 1932 a prominent doctor drove Andueza with two other priests to Zaragoza. There they saw the holy crucifixes and the site of the document discoveries and spoke to Hermana Naya. Andueza's account of the trip inspired other visits, both from the upper class of San Sebastián and Bilbao ("very prestigious priests, doctors, lawyers, dukes, counts, marquises") and from the community of Ezkioga seers and believers.[22]

In the end the proponents of the Rafols prophecies had to repudiate the connection with Ezkioga because of the church's rejection of the visions. Domingo de Arrese published a triumphant series of newspaper articles at the height of the Civil War. In them he showed how Madre Rafols had predicted Franco's victory and the reign of the Sacred Heart in Spain for 1940. His book had at least two editions after the war ended. By then the diocese and the Vatican had rejected the Ezkioga visions, so Arrese took care from the start to separate them from Rafols, a clear instance of the pot calling the kettle black: "The case is totally different. Here [with the Rafols revelations] there are no spectacular apparitions, no stigmatizations in which fraud is a possibility."[23]

THE TERRASSA CONNECTION

Other movements of religious enthusiasm in Catalonia found echo and support at Ezkioga. Rafael García Cascón, a wool dealer from Bejar who lived in Terrassa and had access to Bishop Irurita, made one of the first links. According to his daughter and others who knew him, García Cascón was a man of enormous enthusiasms and restless energy. Throughout his long life he dedicated as much time and money to religious excitement as he did to wool.[24]

In Terrassa García Cascón married Vicenta Marcet, daughter and sister of textile moguls. Her uncle, Antonio María Marcet, abbot of the Benedictine monastery of Montserrat, was one of the spiritual leaders of Catalonia. Catholics in Terrassa were proud of their devotion to the Virgin of Montserrat; the devotion explains in part their interest in the visions at Ezkioga.[25]

Like many militant Catholics worried by Catalonia's social and political plight, García Cascón was active in the Parish Exercises movement of the Jesuit Francisco de Paula Vallet. In the mid-1920s, in an effort to win back lost souls and head off a civil war, el Pare Vallet held hundreds of spiritual exercises for laymen of all social classes. For four or five years Vallet was the most famous preacher in Catalonia; his sermons, some of them broadcast on radio, were blunt and entertaining. Wherever he held missions he set up "Perseverance" chapters to prolong their spiritual effect, thus forming an extensive, self-financed network of laymen. In 1925 García Cascón asked Vallet to give exercises in Terrassa. Subsequently, he was one of Vallet's chief financial backers; he even paid for a trip to the Holy Land for Vallet and two disciples.[26]

Vallet's Parish Exercises movement quickly grew large and powerful. Working largely in Catalan, it spread across diocesan boundaries. And Vallet himself was totally in charge. The Jesuits knew they could not control him. The church hierarchy, especially Cardinal Francesc de Asis Vidal i Barraquer, archbishop of Tarragona, distrusted Vallet's charisma and was afraid he would increase political tensions. And the dictatorship of Miguel Primo de Rivera was intransigent when it came to regional nationalism. Vallet first had to leave the Jesuits, then hand over his movement to diocesan and Jesuit control, and finally go into ecclesiastical exile, initially to Uruguay in 1929.

With Vallet in Uruguay, García Cascón went to Ezkioga with his family on 29 August 1931. There he met several of the main seers—the original brother and sister, the girl from Ataun, Patxi Goicoechea, Ramona Olazábal, Juana

Ibarguren, a boy seer from Zumarraga, and Benita Aguirre. A month later García Cascón wrote Vallet from Terrassa about the apparitions and linked them to the inactivity of the Parish Exercises: "Little is being done here. Everything is sort of paralyzed. It is a good thing that God steps in to make up for our weaknesses."[27]

García Cascón's most trusted employee was Salvador Cardús. At the time of his employer's letter to Vallet, Cardús was at Ezkioga. This trip began Cardús's long, intense involvement with the Basque visionaries. And thanks to his meticulous archive and his extensive correspondence with the seers, Cardús became one of the great recorders of the entire Ezkioga phenomenon.

The life of this extraordinarily sensitive man encapsulated the political and social tensions of Terrassa and Catalonia at the beginning of the century. For at least eleven years, from 1899 to 1910, his father, Josep, was a weaver in the textile mill of Miquel Marcet. After Salvador's birth in 1900, his mother nursed, along with him, one of the sons of the mill owner. Marcet was implacably pious. He had the Sacred Heart of Jesus enthroned in the workplace and printed on his receipts and he pressured his employees to attend special spiritual exercises. But the weaver Josep Cardús attended the exercises only once and dared to send two of his children to a non-Catholic free school. In 1910 he was the only employee who was a union member. In November of that year a famous freethinking philanthropist and republican politician died in Terrassa, and Catholics and non-Catholics turned out for the civil funeral. Josep Cardús and many other mill workers attended. At this time an adjacent factory was in the midst of a long strike and Marcet feared the weaver might bring the strike to his factory. The mill owner therefore used attendance at the funeral as a pretext to lay Cardús off as a regular employee. A week later the weaver committed suicide, hanging himself prominently from the Vallparadis bridge. At a time of anticlerical and revolutionary fervor, his death became a cause célèbre.[28]

Salvador's mother was pregnant and miscarried when her husband committed suicide. Salvador, aged ten, had to leave school and work in a mill; when he was twelve a carding machine mangled his hand. After four years working in a pharmacy by day and studying by night, he became the assistant to García Cascón, whose wife was the niece of the pious mill owner who had fired Salvador's father, causing his suicide. Extremely devout, Salvador worried about his father's going to hell. Like so many of those who went to Ezkioga, he needed specific news from heaven.

The Ezkioga seers had convinced García Cascón that a great miracle was imminent. And García Cascón sent Cardús to find out when it would be. When Cardús arrived on October 3, he found a crowd of about ten thousand persons in prayer. The Terrassa pilgrims with him made special contact with Ramona Olazábal, her friend from Ataun, and Evarista Galdós. Cardús made a generic request for his family, and Ramona said that when she asked on his behalf, the

Salvador Cardús i Florensa and his wife, Rosa Grau, Terrassa, October 1924. Courtesy Arxiu Salvador Cardús i Florensa, Terrassa

Virgin smiled in response. Cardús returned to Ezkioga a few days later with the sole purpose of asking about his father. After her afternoon vision Ramona assured him his father was in heaven. Cardús was so happy he wanted to cry. Ramona shared his emotion and sealed a bond with this timid young father of three which lasted for several years.[29]

Patxi was then finishing his wooden deck at the vision site and Cardús heard the rumor that the great miracle would take place when the deck was ready. Cardús therefore called his employer to come quickly. García Cascón asked him to stay on and report back. On the night of October 13 Ramona told Cardús in confidence that he should stay until October 15. For then there would take place not the great miracle but a "little" miracle, an advertisement, as it were, for the big one. Cardús learned from the Ezkioga schoolmistress that Ramona had told her that the miracle would consist of receiving something in her hands. The same teacher had learned from Patxi that the government would learn nothing from the miracles and would imprison him and that there would be a brief holy war in which the Basques saved Spain.[30]

On the fifteenth Cardús was present when Ramona's hands bled. That night he could neither eat nor sleep. His friend Ramona, he felt sure, was a saint. Early the next morning he wept in the Zumarraga church: "I was praying with all my soul for the salvation of Catalonia." "So many Catalans," he wrote in his diary, "are coming to Ezquioga and praying fervently and asking the seers to pray for Catalonia, that I have no doubt that the most holy Virgin will listen to their appeals." Cardús asked Ramona if García Cascón should come, and she said "Yes, tell him to come." On that afternoon, October 16, a caravan of private cars carrying about 150 persons left Terrassa for Ezkioga. It arrived the next day, as did sixty thousand other pilgrims, in time to see the minor miracle of the scratch on the hand of the girl from Ataun. Cardús talked to two men from Terrassa who said they saw rosaries hanging in the air before the seer.[31]

When Cardús prepared to leave on October 18 after visions at which up to eighty thousand persons were present, García Cascón introduced him to a short, stocky man from Legazpi, José Garmendia.

THE BLACKSMITH AND THE PRESIDENT OF CATALONIA

José Garmendia worked in the small foundry of Joaquín Bereciartu in Legazpi. Like many seers, he would have led a life of total obscurity except for the apparitions. Born in Segura in 1893 of an unwed mother, he was thirty-eight years old when he had his first visions at the end of July 1931. The press paid him little heed except to make light of a vision of his mother in purgatory. He was a figure of fun for his neighbors (his heavy drinking did not help), so he convinced few of his experiences. As García Cascón wrote, "He is such a humble man that in his own town no one believes him." In the 1980s few people in Legazpi remembered him by his given name. His nickname was "Belmonte," some said because Belmonte was his favorite bullfighter, others because of the little backward steps, like those of the bullfighter, he would take in his visions. But the Ezkioga believers elsewhere remembered him warmly. A single man, he had few if any local relatives, and in photographs from 1932 he poses with Catalans or with a baker and a real-estate broker from San Sebastián. He seems to have found his family in the community of visionaries. His visions typically included a struggle between good and evil, with the devil acting as a major protagonist.[32]

When García Cascón met him in mid-October 1931, Garmendia, overshadowed by attractive and convincing youths and children, was still one of the "invisible" seers. But he convinced García Cascón immediately when he said the Virgin had given him a special message to deliver to an important Catalan figure.

This news pleased Cardús and the others from Terrassa but did not surprise them. "It was not strange that the Virgin should have a certain partiality for Catalonia," García Cascón wrote to Vallet, "precisely because so many Catalans had come to this miraculous mountain to pray on behalf of our land."[33] Cardús and the others from Terrassa guessed correctly that the "important figure" in question was the president of the autonomous region of Catalonia, Francesc Macià. García Cascón paid Garmendia's train fare to Barcelona, and on October 23 Cardús accompanied the seer to the office of the president. On being told it was a matter involving the Virgin of Ezkioga, Macià received Garmendia and Cardús at once, then Cardús withdrew, leaving the two to talk alone for fifteen minutes.

Garmendia was exhilarated afterward. According to him, Macià had listened with interest as on behalf of the Virgin Garmendia revealed some intimate personal details, warned that life was short, and assured him that he and his sister, a nun, would go to heaven. As Garmendia told it, Macià requested an image of

Francesc Macià, president of the autonomous government of Catalonia, at Montserrat the day after José Garmendia's visit. Macià is with his granddaughter and Abbot Marcet, 24 October 1931. Courtesy Arxiu Salvador Cardús i Florensa, Terrassa

the Virgin as she appeared in Ezkioga and asked what he could do. Garmendia asked him to help obtain permission for a chapel on the vision site. Garmendia had wanted a chapel virtually from his first visions in late July. So Macià wrote a note, "Autorizo la construcción de la capilla, Francesc Macià," which Garmendia showed to Cardús. The next day Macià, his wife, daughter, and granddaughter went to Montserrat to open an art exhibit and there he told Abbot Marcet about Garmendia's visit.[34]

Garmendia returned to Barcelona on November 14. José María Boada, a wealthy member of the Vallet movement, knew about the previous visit and invited Garmendia back to Barcelona. García Cascón accompanied the seer to Montserrat. There the abbot told them that Macià had spoken at length about Garmendia's first visit, repeating over and over, "I don't know what the Virgin wants me to do." Garmendia quickly observed, "Well, that is what I am here to tell him, what the Virgin wants him to do."

Three days later Macià and his wife received Garmendia in their house, and Macià reportedly asked the seer if the Virgin was happy with him. Garmendia pleased him by answering that she was indeed. Garmendia said he had gone to Madrid the previous month and the Virgin was not so happy with the prime minister, Manuel Azaña, who had refused to receive him. Macià allegedly asked, "So he is worse than I am?" And Garmendia said yes, the Virgin had told him that Azaña would receive the punishment he deserved.[35]

Garmendia made other visits on behalf of the Virgin. On November 23 he went to see Justo de Echeguren, the Vitoria vicar general, who treated him abruptly. On December 6, this time with García Cascón and Boada, he went back. Echeguren was firm about the matter of Ramona's wounds, and the next day Garmendia claimed the Virgin told him, when he asked her to bless Echeguren, that "the apostles of her son were betraying both her son and her, and they will have to suffer for it later." García Cascón sent the bad news to Echeguren along with prayers for enlightenment.[36]

Cardús and his employer kept in touch with Garmendia at least through 1934. Garmendia could barely write, so he dictated his letters. In June 1933 he said he was having fewer visions, only "when the Most Holy Virgin wants me to give some special message." But that fall he was again having visions daily, at home, in bed, outside, or in church. Garmendia did not always convince the Terrassa believers. But for García Cascón and Cardús, he remained a good friend and a valuable connection to heaven.[37]

BENITA AGUIRRE

During García Cascón's stay at Ezkioga in late October he made another key contact for the Catalans, the child seer Benita Aguirre. Her visions had begun on July 12, two weeks after the first ones at the site. Aged nine, she was the fourth of eight surviving children of Bernarda Odria and Francisco Aguirre, a foreman at the tool foundry in Legazpi. Like many of the seers in the first weeks, Benita sometimes went to Ezkioga with her parish priest. In her vision she saw her stillborn baby brother as an angel near the Virgin. For two weeks she saw but did not hear the Virgin, who on occasion carried a handkerchief embroidered with words. On July 21 *El Día* introduced her to the public with a summary of her visions, including the Zumarraga doctor Sabel Aranzadi's clinical report:

> Benita Aguirre y Odria, born in Legazpi, age nine, with height appropriate for her age, thin, with a pale face, of the neurotic kind; her second teeth are coming in; four years ago she suffered a horizontal nystagmus in one eye, which later disappeared; a year or two ago she suffered a generalized contraction in her entire body which lasted only briefly; she is trusting, not shy, good humored, correctly educated, and she explains herself fluently.[38]

On July 27 Benita began to hear the Virgin speak. A reporter described her at this time in a characteristic pose:

> It is as though she were sleeping, with a smile and with her mouth open, as if marveling. Her eyes look up. Her mother suggests she say some things to the Virgin, and the girl does so without losing her attitude, which is half-surprised and half-joyful.[39]

By then observers were singling Benita out as particularly impressive, and she was having visions of a certain complexity. Her vision of August 6 was her sixteenth. The Barcelona Carlist newspaper printed the account she gave to the priests at Ezkioga:

> First there appeared in the firmament a hole, then a great brightness came out of it, which when it came above the cross [at the vision site] became concentrated at the feet of the Virgin, who appeared with a black cape and a white bib. The child was dressed in white. Shortly afterward two angels came down with baskets of flowers and arranged themselves at the

feet of the Virgin, one on each side. Shortly after that a man came down with a blue cape crossing from his right shoulder to his left dressed in white. Benita asked spontaneously without anyone prompting her who the man was, and the Virgin replied, "Saint Joseph."

Then Saint Joseph placed himself above the Virgin's head with his hands as one sees in images, but without the lily. Then two white crosses appeared. Then Saint Joseph disappeared. All the people disappeared in the hole in the firmament. The Virgin also disappeared, as did, a little later, the two crosses. The angels circled around and also disappeared.

Note: when the crosses appeared, the angels withdrew so as to leave the crosses placed where they had been.

When the apparition began I asked it, "Ama Maria guk ser egitea nai dezu [Mother Mary, what do you want us to do for you]?" and she replied, "Errezatzea [Pray]."

The Virgin smiled the entire time.

Benita asked for a blessing, and the Virgin shifted the Child from one arm to the other and gave a blessing.[40]

About the same time a Catalan priest heard Benita recount the following exchange: "My Mother, when will I enter a convent?" "When you are a little older."

About ten days later a canon from Lleida described her as sharp and lively (*vivaracha*), and contrasted her correct use of Spanish with that of Patxi. Benita described for him her twenty-sixth vision.

Yesterday [August 16] I saw the Most Holy Virgin with the backs of her hands cut and bloody. She appeared with two swords, one through her heart and the other, with a bloody point, in her left hand. In her right hand she carried a bloody handkerchief. She was dressed in black and wore a crown, which had some long things that gave off light. To her right was Jesus Christ nailed to a cross. When I asked why she had so much blood and if it was for our sins, she answered, "Yes."[41]

As we have seen, active swordplay was common in the visions at the beginning of August. The heavy emphasis on blood is reminiscent of some of the visions of the Italian mystic Gemma Galgani. Benita's vision prefigured all the imagery for Ramona Olazábal's miracle in October: the bloody backs of hands, the bleeding swords, even the bloody handkerchiefs.

That evening the canon of Lleida Juan Bautista Altisent was next to Benita as she had another vision and he asked her questions while she was rapt. About three hundred persons were present. She saw a variant of her vision the previous night. Six angels carried the bloody swords. Benita moved her lips pronouncing unintelligible words, as if conversing with an invisible person. Altisent asked her what she was saying and hearing, and she said that the Virgin told her she could not tell anyone. Throughout the vision, which lasted a half hour, Benita's mother, at the canon's instructions, lifted her up so that everyone could "admire the transformation of that little angelic face." At the end the girl stretched out her arms as if trying to catch something going away and said, "Agur Ama [Farewell, Mother]," sadly, three times, "each time with more emotion and reaching out with her little hands as far as she could." Altisent said he had never felt such a strong emotion in his life. Benita told him that Our Holy Mother had been close to everyone, but especially close to him. The child returned to her normal state and dried her tears.[42]

Benita's visions after the first couple of weeks moved almost all who saw them. Even a reporter from *El Liberal* said they made him sad. In 1932 a priest from Barcelona, who was doubtful about much he saw, still wrote of Benita, "Truly it is impossible that a child of nine years could learn to act like that theatrically. The greatest actress after a brilliant career could not do it better. That is admirable." However he could not be sure whether the vision was the work of God or the devil.[43]

María de los Angeles de Delás from Barcelona heard Benita cry out a wrenching, "Mother, Mother, why are you so sad?" The girl leaned on the woman on the way down the hillside, and Delás noted the tears in her eyes. Like each of these contributors to *El Correo Catalán,* Delás went away feeling especially connected to the Virgin by personal contact with Benita Aguirre.

> After speaking to the child I gave her a kiss, asking her to offer it on my behalf to the Most Holy Virgin, something I saw made her happy, and so we became friends. After that we smiled at each other when our glances crossed, and the next day she would accept the stool I offered for her to sit next to me during the third Rosary.

Here we glimpse the delicate courtship of glances, smiles, and favors constantly at work between the seers and the believers, in this case between a child seer and a believer with notebook in hand.[44]

At this time—the beginning of September—Rafael García Cascón first met Benita. On his return after Ramona's miracle in late October, his friendship with Benita deepened; he would pick her up, take her to lunch in Zumarraga, drive her to the vision site, and drive her home. He also invited her and her parents to a family gathering at the Hotel Urola in Zumarraga on his saint's day. On his last day Benita had supper and stayed over at the hotel, something he considered "another special favor of the Virgin."[45]

One day on the way to Ezkioga García Cascón asked Benita to ask the Virgin whether she was pleased with the work of Vallet and if so to bless him and his disciples. Garmendia overheard the request, and he asked the Virgin about Vallet as well. As García Cascón wrote Vallet, both seers separately said "that the Virgin had said that she was very pleased with what you have done in Catalonia and in South America and that if you continue this way you will have immense glory,

Rafael García Cascón holds a rapt Benita Aguirre on the vision deck, late October 1931. Courtesy Lourdes Rodes Bagant

and that the Virgin had given her blessing for you and your companions." García Cascón also reported what the Virgin told certain seers about himself and other Catalans:

> The Virgin has said that she is very happy for what we have done for Garmendia and that we will be reminded of this. Imagine how pleased this made us, even though we did so little, but the Most Holy Virgin is most grateful.
>
> We also know that the Virgin has said that those who have come from far away, making a great sacrifice and believing in her apparitions, will go to heaven without going through purgatory, and that of these there will be many. From Catalonia have come many people, perhaps more than from anywhere else, taking distance into account.

Benita wrote to García Cascón after his return to Terrassa that the Virgin had told her he should come back as soon as he could. Although only nine, Benita was hardly a passive protégée.[46]

In November García Cascón visited Bishop Irurita to relate his experiences at Ezkioga and tell him about the contact with the Catalonian president, Macià. By then there was great interest in Catalonia. In the fall of 1931 the press carried notices of excursions from Badalona, Calella, l'Espluga Calba, Lleida, Mollerussa, Mataró, Palamós, Reus, Sabadell (at least three trips), Tona (at least two), Torelló, Terrassa (two), and Vic (four). The followers of Vallet, however, organized the most sustained contacts with the visionaries. All Vallet did, far away in Uruguay, was to reprint in the magazine of his movement a newspaper article and a letter from García Cascón. More influential in this respect was Magdalena Aulina of Banyoles.[47]

MAGDALENA AULINA, THE MYSTIC FROM BANYOLES

The Vallet followers in Barcelona met in their social center, a downtown mansion known as the Casal Donya Dorotea. There García Cascón lectured on Ezkioga and there early in the previous year another industrialist had brought Magdalena Aulina i Saurina to tell of her miraculous cure and to speak about her new religious society.[48]

Developing religious orders drawn into the Ezkioga orbit got a boost of religious enthusiasm. But all came to regret the connection. Magdalena Aulina's institute obtained approval from Rome with great difficulty in 1962, and her successors in the Señoritas Operarias Parroquiales find it difficult to speak about the inspiration of Gemma Galgani and the trips to Ezkioga. They wished me to make clear that the institute existed before the visions at Ezkioga and was quite independent of them.

Magdalena Aulina was born in 1897, the daughter of a wood and coal dealer in the market and summer resort town of Banyoles (Girona). From an early age Magdalena had accompanied her sister, later to become a cloistered Carmelite, in works of charity among the poor. In 1916 she organized a Month of Mary for the children in her neighborhood and later a parish catechism group. By this time she was sure that she had a religious vocation. In part she was inspired by Gemma Galgani, a young woman from Lucca who died at age twenty-five in 1903 after a life dense with mystical phenomena. In 1912 Magdalena read Gemma's biography. In 1921 at age twenty-four Magdalena recovered from a heart condition after a novena to Gemma. This cure confirmed in her mind her spiritual link with the saintly Italian.[49]

The early twentieth century was an era of well-publicized miraculous cures at Lourdes. Very early on, the Barcelona pilgrimages prepared clinical dossiers to present to the Lourdes medical commission in case a cure should occur, and the *Annales* of Lourdes record several cures of Catalans. Those cured became living proof of the Virgin's power and indeed of the existence of God in a doubting world. Miracles invested those cured with charisma. Aulina's cure

Magdalena Aulina with nephew of Gemma Galgani at the Banyoles "Pontifical Fiesta," at which the first stone was laid for a monumental fountain to Galgani, 1934

brought her respectful visitors and she told them about Gemma Galgani's help. Banyoles was the headquarters of diocesan parish missioners, and they too spread the word.[50]

The year after Magdalena's cure, in 1922, with the aid of industrialists who were summer residents, she founded a kind of social house in Banyoles for women workers. In 1926 she helped to build a church in her neighborhood and organized a literacy program. She assisted Vallet when he gave parish exercises in Banyoles, and it is possible that he had her in mind to form an order of nuns to assist his movement.[51]

Aulina had plans of her own, however, and more than enough contacts to put them into practice. At a meeting of Catholic social workers in 1929 at

Montserrat, she met Montserrat Boada, a member of a wealthy Barcelona family with influence in the Vatican. Through the Boadas and similar families, Aulina found support in exactly the same social stratum as Vallet had. When in early 1930 she told Vallet's supporters at the Casal about her spiritual link to Gemma Galgani, she made a deep impression. Shortly afterward José María Boada praised Gemma in the group's magazine, concluding, "Let us let her lead us sweetly through the paths of life."[52]

Gemma Galgani seemed to speak through Aulina, who acted more like a spirit medium than a seer. For instance, Cardús was present once at Banyoles when Gemma spoke through Aulina of the future of the institute. Thus, to follow Gemma was in effect to follow Aulina; through Aulina, believers sought Gemma's help in matters both ethereal and mundane.[53]

By 1931 some unmarried young women lived with Aulina in Banyoles full-time, and three of them took the first private vows of chastity, poverty, and obedience in 1933. On weekends entire families of supporters would come to stay in Magdalena's house, the houses of relatives, hotels, and rented quarters. The supporters were typically doctors, industrialists, and lawyers from Barcelona, Girona (where the group had a clinic), Reus, Terrassa, Sabadell, and Tarragona. Visitors would remark on the sumptuousness of the religious services, with massed choristers in robes and much incense; every Sunday seemed a high feast. Those privileged to dine with Aulina might see her go in and out of trance at the table, as Cardús did, or even watch her in struggle with the devil.

José María Boada helped to persuade Aulina to send regular "expeditions" to Ezkioga. When he heard the praise that seers like Benita passed on from the Virgin about Pare Vallet, he went to Ezkioga to obtain more details. It may be that the seers led Boada to think that he himself had a divine mission; on December 9 Garmendia claimed to see the Virgin on his arm. After Boada reported back to Aulina and Aulina consulted Gemma's spirit, the Casal Donya Dorotea expeditions began on 12 December 1931. Two weeks previously the pope had read in Rome the official proclamation of Gemma's heroic virtues, a stage in the process of beatification, so there was a spate of articles about Gemma in the press which doubtless increased the fervor of Aulina's followers.[54]

Bartolomé de Andueza, the Rafols enthusiast, was aware of the role of Aulina and Gemma in the trips. In March 1932 he wrote in *La Constancia* of

> the very devout expeditions of Catalans that arrive at Ezquioga weekly to do penance under the patronage of the angelic Gemma Galgani. They were suggested to their organizers by a soul in Barcelona living an extraordinary life who emulates the Italian virgin and has "inherited her spirit."[55]

There were eventually twenty-five trips of twenty-four to thirty persons. All included a lay "director" who led prayers (often Boada) and a technical manager, Luis Palà of the Casal. And, despite the prohibitions of the diocese of Vitoria,

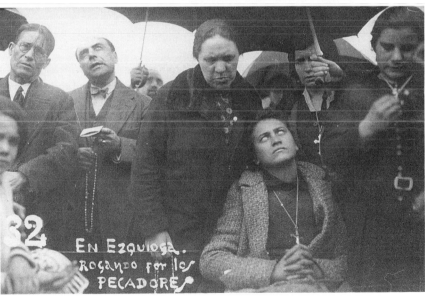

Top: *The sixth Catalan expedition to Ezkioga, 8 March 1932; the politician and writer Mariano Bordas holds a hat.* Bottom: *José María Boada, with eyes upturned, leads prayers for sinners, winter 1932. Photos by Joaquín Sicart*

there was a priest on most trips. Arturo Rodes Buxados, who went four times, acted on his own as a chronicler. Cardús and García Cascón were not core members of the group, although both for a time became devoted to Aulina-Gemma and both spent periods at the Banyoles complex. The trip took a day and a half each way, and the pilgrims spent four days at the site, staying at the Hotel Urola in Zumarraga. They maintained files of cures and visions and, following the practices of the Parish Exercises movement, posed for group photographs as a public witness of their commitment as Catholics.[56]

The trip members often prayed for as many as eight hours on the hillside, and some evenings for two hours more in the hotel. To outsiders their effusive piety seemed showy. The Piarist priest Marc Lliró of Barcelona watched Boada and Palà lead prayers at Ezkioga and later wrote disapprovingly: "Piety is not ridiculous, or tiresome, or exaggerated, or different from a peaceful normality. At Ezkioga it seemed to me . . . I found these kinds of false piety."[57] Aulina's mysticism spilled over to her followers in other ways. Many of them perceived a perfume on the bus trips and at other significant moments in their daily lives. Often a majority of passengers perceived the scent simultaneously, and to avoid confusion women did not wear perfume or cologne. They understood the scent as a sign of approval from Gemma. For these pilgrims Providence charged every moment of the trip and there was no place for chance. At least a dozen of the six hundred or so expedition members had visions at Ezkioga. Others were converted or cured.[58]

From the start these pilgrims cultivated the seers García Cascón and Boada had come to trust. They would pick them up in the morning and take them to the vision site. There they would have a private vision session. After lunch at the hotel, they would return the seers to the site for late afternoon prayers and then they would take them home. Often seers would also have visions on the bus. The seers quickly incorporated Gemma, as they had Madre Rafols, into their visual repertoire. At the end of October 1931 a Catalan assured the teenage seer Cruz Lete that if he said a novena and promoted devotion to Gemma, she in turn would set things straight at Ezkioga (presumably restore the credibility of the seers, damaged by the Ramona episode). When Lete finished the novena on November 17, he began to see Gemma Galgani in his visions. The Catalans worked to convince the seers that, as Cardús wrote in a letter, "Everything, everything, Ezkioga, Madre Rafols, and Gemma, are all the same thing."[59]

The seers nourished the sense of Providence in these pilgrims. Evarista Galdós predicted that certain of them would have visions, told others they would smell the scent of Gemma, and revealed to a young man his secrets. José Garmendia picked out the only doubter in one group, interceded with the Virgin to remove the devil from one Catalan's visions, and divined the secret prayers of a young Catalan male. On three occasions he pointed out trip members who would be seers.

Garmendia's greatest success was with García Cascón's servant of six years, Carmen Visa de Dios, who went on the trip from 20 to 22 June 1932. Garmendia privately told two trip members that Visa would be a seer and all the members then signed his sealed prediction. The next day while Garmendia was having his vision, Visa had hers. She was a widow, age forty-seven, from Torrente de Cinca (Huesca). Her visions at Ezkioga were of Christ Crucified and the Sorrowing Mother, and for most of the return trip she saw Gemma Galgani hovering like a bird outside or on the hood of the bus. When the pilgrims offered Gemma prayers, Visa saw her nod in response, and as she saw Gemma say farewell on the outskirts of Barcelona, many members said they smelled the Gemma scent.[60]

Benita Aguirre, like Garmendia, interceded for Catalans with the Virgin. From the start she was the group's favorite seer, both because of earlier publicity and because of her message about Pare Vallet. Of the six sessions on the hillside of the first trip, Benita was the central figure in five. Right away the pilgrims invited her to visit Barcelona.

Like previous Catalan observers, the chroniclers of this trip admired her stance in vision. On the afternoon of December 15, as on earlier occasions, the Catalans had given her objects for the Virgin to bless. She laid out the crucifixes in front of her on the vision deck and draped the rosaries on her arms. According to a youth who was present, she then fell face forward and sat up again,

> leaning slightly backward, resting in the arms of my friends, her head slightly raised, her eyes fixed on a point high up, but not so fixed that they did not move somewhat or blink occasionally. She speaks with the apparition; she smiles, suffers, sobs, but without tears, asks forgiveness with a sad and tender voice. Then she bends and takes one by one the objects lined in front of her, and each time raising her arm, presents them to the apparition to kiss and bless them. I have a crucifix about a palm long I bought there that Benita held in her hands that afternoon. It was kissed by the Virgin, Gemma (whom she saw again today), and the angels. I also have three red rosaries. The medals on the safety pin I wear were kissed by the Virgin and Gemma. All this as said by Benita.

The youth describing the trip had already stocked up on blessed objects at the two sessions with Benita he attended the previous day. In the morning he had obtained blessings for "three men's rosaries, twenty medals, a miniature image of the Virgin the nuns at Llivia gave me, and a small crucifix that belonged to my mother," all kissed by the Virgin and Gemma. In the afternoon he had "five black rosaries, with smaller beads" kissed by the Virgin, Gemma, and the baby Jesus. He wrote his aunt, "I'll send you some of each." He paid little heed to grand messages of chastisements and miracles scheduled for an indefinite future. As at Limpias a dozen years before, pilgrims were interested in the here-and-now, in resolving spiritual problems and obtaining holy souvenirs.[61]

Benita Aguirre raising object to be blessed for Catalans, ca. 28 February 1932. Photo by Joaquín Sicart

In mid-March Benita went to Barcelona in the group bus and stayed for three days. The group received her enthusiastically at the Casal. And Magdalena Aulina, it seems, enrolled her as a "Servidora de María" in the Obra. At Montserrat the dark Madonna did not impress her. Her Virgin, she said, did not look like that! She stayed with the Rodes family, and Lourdes Rodes, age nineteen, gave Benita her oversize four-foot doll.[62]

Lourdes Rodes finally got to go to Ezkioga from April 29 to May 4, and there, as Benita's father sheltered them from the rain with an umbrella, she supported Benita in vision. The experience was a spiritual one Lourdes remembered vividly over sixty years later:

> Benita was looking upward and speaking in Basque while a man translated and my father took notes. I was filled with an intimate feeling of peace and tranquillity, like a ray of sunlight that warmed me. When the vision went away that feeling stopped. I was left very deeply moved and wanted to cry with happiness.[63]

Later, when Benita could no longer stay in Legazpi, Catalonia proved to be a second home, for she won the hearts of its pilgrims. A clerical observer of an expedition wrote in early October 1932, "I felt sorry for these people who, it seemed to me, believed more in Benita than in the mysteries of the faith."[64]

Benita Aguirre in vision next to Arturo Rodes with his notebook, 14 December 1931. Courtesy Lourdes Rodes Bagant

MARÍA RECALDE FROM DURANGO

María Recalde was another seer the Catalans favored. She was born into a poor rural family in Zenarruza (Bizkaia) in 1894. María could read but could write only her name. She lived in Durango, a clergy-centered town of five thousand. There none of the twenty-six parish priests, none of the Jesuits in the school, and only a handful of the nuns in the five houses believed in her visions. Recalde was one of the few married women to become famous as a seer at Ezkioga. She had had nine children, three stillborn. It was because her first child was born out of wedlock that many local people summarily dismissed her visions.

María's first vision took place on 9 August 1931, just after the intensive newspaper coverage ended. Like Garmendia, Recalde was "invisible" to the press. Only once did a newspaper mention her, although by December 13 she had already had 139 visions. (Counting seems to have been part of the religious ethos; the seers kept score of their visions the same way the Aliadas counted their rosaries and mortifications.) She became well known only after church opposition depleted the ranks of seers and believers.[65] She continued to go to Ezkioga for several years. Whether at Ezkioga, at home, or elsewhere, she had visions until her death in 1950. In the 1980s the older generation throughout eastern Bizkaia and the uplands of Gipuzkoa remembered her as a seer.

María Recalde with cornerstone of chapel, spring 1932. Photo by Joaquín Sicart

María Recalde is a particularly engaging character in the Ezkioga story. She had a powerful vitality and combativeness as well as a preternatural shrewdness. She allegedly faced down the judge who interrogated her. She was also warm-hearted and generous. In many photographs she can be seen caring for other seers in vision. She was one of the seers about whom I knew the least until the day her granddaughter Mariví Jayo came to visit me in Las Palmas. Mariví brought with her a tape recording of her father talking about his mother and Ezkioga. Like many families of visionaries, the Jayos had felt the shame of being known as the family of an Ezkioga seer. It was a relief for Lorenzo Jayo to talk about his mother to me when we met subsequently.[66]

María's husband was a market gardener supplying milk and fresh vegetables to Durango. María, her son told me, "wore the pants in the family." When in early August 1931 she began to have visions at Ezkioga and took the train there every afternoon, the family adjusted. With her visions María gained the following of important commercial and manufacturing families in Bilbao and Elorrio, including Manuel and Luisa Arriola, who owned the Artiach cookie company, the Abaytuas, who were stockbrokers, and Matilde Uribe, whose husband owned a steel mill. Like other seers with loyal believers, María supplied these families with news from heaven, some of it obviously convincing. She also developed a following among the rural believers of the Goiherri, the Gipuzkoan uplands; they stood by her until her death.

Starting in November 1931 Recalde and Benita Aguirre began to take people aside and tell them their secret sins as signs from heaven that they should confess, repent, and make their peace with God. The sole newspaper article about Recalde told how she converted one of the souvenir stand operators, Vidal Castillo, by revealing his past sins. This kind of vision became general among the more sociable seers, but it remained Recalde's specialty.[67]

Recalde made each of her devotees feel special. For Arturo Rodes she was "the seer most favored by heaven with extraordinary confidences." He was impressed that, like many seers, she knew the date of her death and yet remained calm. He also respected her imperturbability in the face of mockery and slander. Recalde had singled him out; she saw in heaven his two children and four godchildren who were deceased and she promised all would meet him when he died. Similarly, she said the Virgin particularly liked a crucifix that Cardús carried. Another time Recalde picked out from the items Cardús gave her to be blessed a devotional card of Gemma Galgani that included a relic, telling him, "Gemma loves you dearly and considers you her brother." For Cardús, who considered Gemma his spiritual director, this was powerful medicine. Similarly, Recalde in vision informed García Cascón that a crucifix he carried was especially sacred. On his return he installed it in a place of honor in his house, and his visionary servant saw it sweat blood, like the bleeding crucifix of Madre Rafols.[68]

María Recalde made the connection with García Cascón and the Catalans during his stays in October 1931. In November she told him that she had seen the Virgin with Madre Rafols and Gemma Galgani together early that month and that the Virgin had said that trips would come with devotees of Gemma from a place where they love Gemma a lot. For this reason García Cascón and his friends thought of María Recalde as a kind of godmother to the Catalan expeditions. María's son winces when he recalls the buses week after week filling the narrow streets of Durango, when the pilgrims came to pick up his mother.[69] On 8 May 1932 she had a vision in which the Virgin told her where to look for jewels and an image buried in the church of Santa Ana of Barcelona 266 years earlier. And on May 23 she saw not only Gemma Galgani but Magdalena Aulina as well. Two weeks later she went back with a Catalan trip to Barcelona. There she visited Montserrat and the shrine to the souls in purgatory at Tibadabo. On her return to Ezkioga, she claimed, the Sacred Heart of Jesus asked for her hand and, with the Virgin and Gemma Galgani looking on and smiling, pierced it, giving her great joy. Jesus told her that she had much to suffer for Catalonia.[70]

The Sacred Heart of Jesus piercing María Recalde's hand on behalf of Catalonia points to an ethos of female sacrifice that the Catalan devotees of Rafols and Gemma shared with the Basque seers. Francisco de Paula Vallet had come to believe that, with civil war inevitable, his parish exercises were preparing martyrs, men who would die at the hands of other men. Among Aulina's followers there was a different but complementary program for women. God would take their lives directly. The religiosity of Gemma Galgani, as expressed in the letters and vision texts that Aulina's disciples studied, had as a central premise that people could choose to be victims and stand in for the sins of others. Like Christ, Gemma and Magdalena suffered wounds, the torments of the devil, and illnesses on behalf of the human race. In a key passage from her letters that Cardús cited in his diary, Gemma said Jesus told her:

> I have a need for victims, but strong victims to calm the holy and just wrath of my heavenly Father. I need souls to come forward whose sufferings, tribulations, and discomforts make up for the malice and ingratitude of sinners. Oh, if I could only get everyone to understand how indignant my celestial Father is with the world! Nothing is now able to contain his wrath. He is preparing a horrible chastisement against the human race![71]

For Gemma, Aulina, and doubtless many cloistered religious of their day, their willing sacrifice averted a chastisement. As José María Boada described Gemma in 1930, "It pleased Jesus to find in her a true image of his own passion; thus the blessed servant was able to fulfill her sharp desire to make herself like Jesus and suffer for Him."[72]

This taste for pain and sacrifice was much in the air. The printed picture of Thérèse de Lisieux in the Ezkioga souvenir stands bore the motto, "Suffering, together with love, is the only thing to be desired in this vale of tears." The mysterious nun known as Sulamitis wrote about "victims of love." At the turn of the century Cardinal Salvador Casañas of Barcelona cultivated "victim souls of Jesus."[73] And Antonio Amundarain used victim terminology throughout the literature of the Alianza. It was also an idiom of the Passionists, whose holy friar, Gabriele dell'Addolorata, appeared to Gemma and served as her spiritual guide. So too it was part of the language of the Reparadora nuns, to whose house Evarista, Ramona, and the seer from Ataun went for spiritual exercises. In this economy of substitute pain, it was largely Spain's Catholic women who chose to suffer.

The willing suffering of women had a certain logic, for it was a commonplace in more traditional circles that the indecency of modern female dress and behavior was the root cause of the nation's problems. A woman columnist in Navarra argued that low necklines on the dresses of liberal Catholics explained why the Christ was suffering at Limpias in 1919. The theme reappears in the last "revelation" of the Sacred Heart to María Naya:

> Many are the offenses that I have received and that I will receive, above all from women with their *shameless* dresses, their nakedness, their frivolity and perverse intentions, by which they will achieve the demoralization of families and of men, and in large part this will arouse the Justice of my Eternal Father, who will be obliged to chastise mankind.[74]

Bartolomé de Andueza, the priest and writer who linked Rafols with Ezkioga, did not beat around the bush when he glossed this message in *La Constancia*. Women were to blame and how!

> The indecent fashions of women are the great sin of the twentieth century.
>
> With what offending stigmas are marked an enormous number of Catholic women who, ignoring the voice of the Pope, bishops, preachers, and confessors, have paraded through the streets, plazas, paseos, and *beaches* their nudity and the shamelessness of the dissolute pagan women of ancient Rome, the sewer for all the aberrations and the lowest and most repugnant moral turpitude.
>
> You women who have worshiped fashion, you are the cause of the travail that our Nation now laments. The Divine Heart of Jesus says so solemnly. I am not one to hide the truth. You women are the reason for the dissolution of the Jesuits, for the removal of crucifixes, for the horrible sacrileges that have been done, for all the savage persecution, in short, that this poor Spanish nation has endured.[75]

This perception that women were corrupting contemporary society was common. Amado de Cristo Burguera, who will loom large in this story, attributed many of the ills of the times to a pagan renaissance. Prime examples were women athletes, women in cabarets, and women in film, all indecently glorified in illustrated magazines. He believed that "the decadence and the ruin of nations is in direct relation to the cultivation and the idealization of femininity." As soon as a civilization presented total nudity in paintings and statues, he said, the society began to go downhill. He detected in modern society an exaltation of woman "in all her profound vacuity, her great puerility, and her immense vanity (Forgive me, ladies)."[76] If women were to blame, then women should do the redeeming and the proxy suffering. Andueza suggested that the penances done by Ezkioga seers

Left: *The problem: Carmen Girón Camino, described in the caption as "Miss República and, even better, Miss Spain." Cover of* Crónica, *12 July 1931 (detail). Courtesy Hemeroteca Municipal de Madrid.* Right: *The solution: Marcelina Mendívil in vision, ca. 1932. Photo by Joaquín Sicart*

and believers were those that the Sacred Heart had called for through Madre Rafols.

This expiatory ethic was typical of contemporary mystic exemplars like the French, Italian, and German stigmatics Marie Julie Jahenny, Pio da Pietrelcina, Thérèse Neumann, and the French holy child Guy de Fontgalland. It contrasted with the ethic of active saints doing good in the world, whether by conquering infidels, converting heathens, or performing social work. Examples would be Jeanne d'Arc, Ignacio de Loyola, Francisco Javier, Vincent de Paul, Giovanni Bosco, Albert Schweitzer, or Mohandas Gandhi. Patxi as captain of the reconquest better fit this active model. By and large the former model was intended for women, the latter for men.

But throughout Catholic Europe women were also enrolling in unprecedented numbers in religious orders that enabled them to lead active, socially useful lives while remaining relatively independent of men. While Carmen Medina's two sisters were Reparadoras, cloistered nuns who did atonement for the sins of the world through prayer, her in-law Rafaela Ibarra was one of the many women for whom sanctity involved activity in the world. In Gipuzkoa houses of active nuns like the Daughters of Charity outnumbered those of contemplatives three to one.[77]

Nevertheless, the holy mode that caught the imagination of the Basque seers by the winter of 1932 was that of passive sacrifice. Often using language similar to that we find in Gemma's writings, they too began to describe themselves as victims. Both Ramona's attempted miracle with bloody hands and the spiritual exercises with the Reparadoras pointed the seers toward one obvious physical expression of the victim stance, the mimic crucifixions that began in January 1932. This mystic fad reached its climax on Good Friday. On that day dozens of seers, children, men, and women, writhed on the Ezkioga stage in simultaneous agony, feeling imaginary nails being driven through their hands and feet and lances piercing their sides. Previously, through Lent, seer after seer had led groups of followers up the hillside reciting the stations of the cross, with seers experiencing them as if they were Christ.

Benita explained the new development in a letter to García Cascón in February:

> I suppose you know already how we are crucified, suffering a lot; we have to suffer still more. But this is nothing. In order to save a soul one can do much more. One day when they were crucifying me, the Virgin told me that I was suffering for a sinner in my village, and since then she does not tell me who it is for, but I know it is for the sinners.[78]

For the seers the concept of sinner changed subtly over time. In July of 1931 sinners were clearly those who burned convents, read *La Voz de Guipúzcoa*, wore low-cut dresses, or danced the foxtrot—in short, sinners as Catholics in general defined them. But as the diocese turned against the visions the definition of sinner seems to have broadened. The term *conversion* among Catalans generally meant the "conversion" of those members who were practicing Catholics but who did not believe in or who were unsure about the visions at Ezkioga. The new canon of belief was not just in the Virgin Mary in general but in this Mary in particular. Those who truly believed in this Mary would go straight to heaven. The crucifixions suffered by the seers in the winter of 1932 were not only atonement for the anticlericals who expelled the Jesuits and removed crucifixes from schools but also for clerics like the priests of Ezkioga who kept the vision stage under critical surveillance.

The Ezkioga seers also used the atonement idiom to explain the travails of their followers. A seer, probably Evarista Galdós, informed a young man from Reus that his nine-year-old sister, who was ill, was "the expiatory victim for the conversion of the family, and that before [the sister] died, her father would convert." Arturo Rodes states that the seer foretold the date of the little sister's death. The Catalan pilgrims did not find this calculus strange since they were fully caught up in its logic already. When the husband of a Catalan woman died, she feared he would go to hell because he had been lax. So she offered her children in exchange for her husband's soul. Soon after, her eldest daughter died.[79]

After Ramona's exposure the church and the press turned against the seers and fewer spectators came. The whole notion of what it was to be a seer changed. In the previous summer the seers were carrying with them the hopes and dreams of the vast majority of Basque and Spanish Catholics. Benita Aguirre was the most important and well-known person in Legazpi. It was exciting just to be her sister. But by the winter of 1932 the tide was turning. People were beginning to wonder, snicker, and point. And for the seers and their families life in these small, pious villages became a holy nightmare. The vision crucifixions in part reflected this crucifixion by public opinion.

To persist with visions was difficult. In mid-April 1932 Salvador Cardús summed up the point of view of the believers, by then a small, harassed minority: "Seer is now synonymous with hero, and a hero with a high ideal, an ideal of continuous pain and suffering here on earth from which happiness will not begin until heaven."[80] The presence of Gemma's followers week after week between mid-December 1931 and October 1932 became a major incentive for the seers close to them. Of necessity the seers shifted their points of human reference from their hometowns and their region to the dwindling community of believers.

The logical limit of the seers' sacrifices was that they would really die, not just die on stage. By the end of the first months some seers while in vision would ask to die. In October Evarista announced that a male seer would suffer five wounds, like Christ. Ramona had said that she would die after the miracles and that the Virgin would carry her to heaven. Not all the deaths the seers imagined were those of passive victims of God. On 25 January 1932 shortly after her spiritual exercises, Ramona believed a rumor that she would die the next day in mortal sin. All night she searched her conscience in vain. The next morning she went to confess, fully prepared to die, but the Virgin appeared to her and consoled her. Similarly Evarista told the Catalans that she, María Recalde, and other seers would die assassinated on the vision platform.[81]

In his *Basque Oral Literature* (1936) the folklorist Manuel Lecuona recounted an incident during Lent of 1932 which almost included a messianic sacrifice inspired by the events at Ezkioga. In the mountains of his town, Oiartzun, there was a group of charcoalers. Since they could not go to mass on Sundays, they would listen to a man famous for his memory sing religious verses written by the nineteenth-century poet Xenpelar.

> One day the carter for the group, who had taken a load of charcoal down to the village, was surprised on his return to the mountain to find the charcoal pyre abandoned and totally aflame. When he voiced his surprise, they berated him, "Forget about the charcoal. Don't you know that the end of the world is at hand, and that this man has to die this afternoon?" One of

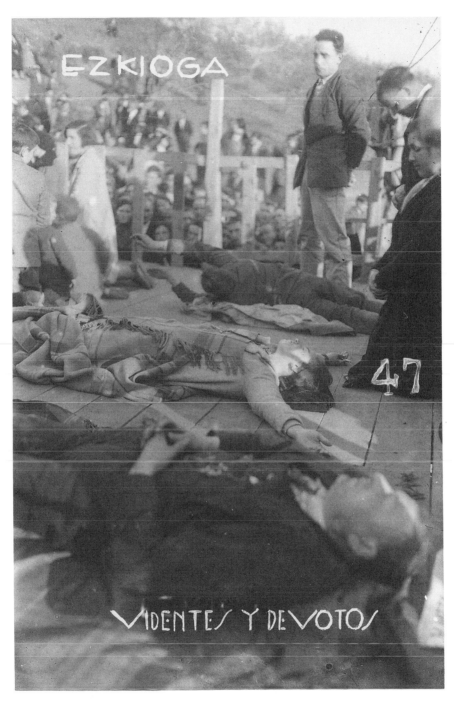

Seers in crucifixion on vision deck, Good Friday 1932. Photo by Joaquín Sicart

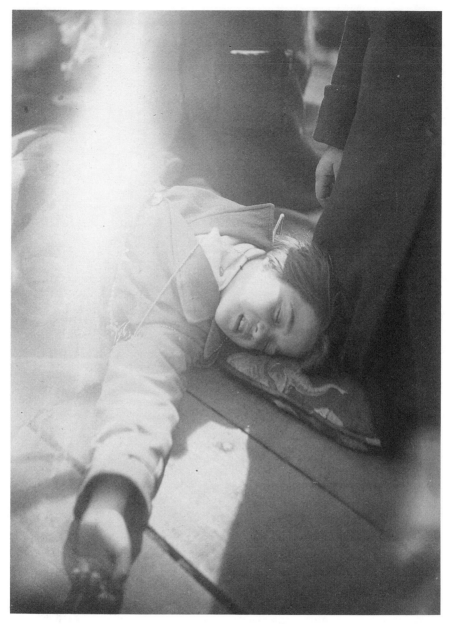

Benita Aguirre in exhaustion after crucifixion, Lent 1932. Photo by Raymond de Rigné, all rights reserved

the men considered himself the Messiah, and that afternoon his two companions were going to crucify him.[82]

In these first years two seers did die, both of tuberculosis. The first was the teenager María Celaya, who had visions both at Ezkioga and in her home village in Navarra starting on 16 October 1931. She died 23 September 1932. Cruz Lete Sarasola of Itsasondo had visions at Ezkioga from late October 1931 to February 1932, when he entered the order of Brothers Hospitallers. He died devoutly on 30 October 1933. For seers and believers both Celaya and Lete died in willing sacrifice for the sins of others, victims for the visions.

EL PARE VALLET AT EZKIOGA

Shortly after the visionary crucifixions on Good Friday and shortly before people read about the Rafols prophecy of chastisement, Ezkioga's suffering seers had a surprise visitor. Francisco de Paula Vallet had come to realize that his project was being sidetracked and he returned from Uruguay to investigate. From García Cascón and other followers, Vallet had heard about the trips to Ezkioga, the "grace" obtained on the visits, and the growing influence of Magdalena Aulina. Whereas in the fall of 1931 he was receptive to the Ezkioga visions, his doubts about the path the Barcelona Casal group was taking increased over the winter. In early April 1932 Vallet made an unannounced visit. At once three close followers drove with him to Ezkioga so he could see for himself what was going on there. On the way they stopped in Zaragoza, where he talked with Hermana Naya. She did not impress him. At Ezkioga he watched several of the seers from the base of the hill and he questioned them when they came down.[83]

Vallet talked at greatest length to Benita and her parents. They had heard much about him from the Catalans and were quite upset when he tried to persuade them that the visions were the work of the devil. In Legazpi that night Benita and her parents spent the night praying to the Virgin and asking for a sign. The next morning Vallet appeared at their house, begging forgiveness for the way he had spoken the night before and asking insistently for Benita to intercede for him with the Virgin. He came away, I am told, convinced that the older seers, whom he fooled with captious questions, were not having divine visions. But the original boy visionary as well as Benita impressed him.[84]

Back in Barcelona Vallet worked hard against Ezkioga and attempted to win back his followers. For erstwhile admirers like García Cascón, Cardús, Boada, and Arturo Rodes, who trusted the Ezkioga seers and Aulina-Gemma, there was little choice. They lost their faith in his discernment and seriousness. At Ezkioga the visionaries were finely tuned to events in this important circle of followers far away. On 10 April 1932 Garmendia asked the Virgin about Vallet and said that she replied, "He has saved many souls, but because of him, many will be lost." The next day he asked whether Vallet would change his mind, but the Virgin allegedly pointed out Lucifer to him and said, "This one will control him."[85]

Despite Vallet's attempts to reconcile his followers with the diocese, he gained no ground with Cardinal Vidal i Barraquer of Tarragona. And Bishop Irurita refused him permission to remain in the diocese. In 1934 Vallet left for France. There he established his order under the aegis of the bishop of Valence. Vallet remained firmly opposed to Ezkioga and to the Rafols prophecies. Alone of the opponents of María Naya's forgeries, Vallet recognized her debt to the Basque visionaries, noting in the prophecies "some vague statements taken from the predictions of the Ezquioga people, which she thought were true."[86]

Magdalena Aulina and Francisco de Paula Vallet, the would-be founders of two orders, were in fact competing for the same followers. One family epitomizes that struggle. Bartolomeu Terradas had been an active member and financial backer of Vallet's movement in the 1920s and he was president of the Casal in 1930. His son Joan went with Vallet to the Holy Land in 1928 and later to Uruguay. The father drove Vallet and son Joan to Ezkioga on 6 April 1932. But by April 10, because of Vallet's stance on the visions, Terradas had removed his son from Vallet's order. Eventually the son attended the Barcelona diocesan seminary. The father dedicated the rest of his life and money to Magdalena Aulina. The son eventually rejoined Vallet and became his chief disciple. Another son, Miguel, also a priest, became a chaplain to Aulina's order.[87]

EZKIOGA, EUSKADI, AND CATALUNYA

Many Basques believed that the Virgin chose to appear at Ezkioga to reward and strengthen Basque nationalism. But nowhere in the letters and diaries of Catalan believers is there any interest in or comment on the relation of the Virgin to the Basques, even though they sometimes took the trouble to learn the Basque hymns, and some spelled Ezkioga the Basque way with a *k*. The Catalans had no sense that they, from another nation, were intruding on a privileged relationship between Mary and the Basques, and they certainly had no sense that the Virgin was appearing for the Basques in particular.

Implicit in the Catalans' many references to the Virgin and Catalonia was the notion that the Virgin's message was not set. The Catalans assumed that they could change and bend it. They knew that she was appearing for all humanity or at least for Europe and that they could affect by prayer, penance, and sacrifice her influence over Christ, miracles, punishments, and the future in general. The Catalans went to Ezkioga representing their nation, as proxies for the Catholics there, even for the entire population.

This understanding that the Virgin's message was contingent on human response was general. The seers said as much. Benita declared in April 1932, "If the Catalans had not gone to Ezquioga, the inhabitants of Barcelona would now be in heaven, hell, or purgatory, because Barcelona would have been leveled." This too was the attitude of Antonio Amundarain when he wrote that the Ezkioga rosary "must find in heaven an almost omnipotent echo." Although believers came to expect a chastisement, they assumed that through prayer people could affect when and whom it would strike.[88]

The seers the Catalans chose to listen to were those who could provide the kind of messages that the Catalans would want to hear. García Cascón's selection in early September seems to have left out Patxi, the seer most oriented to the Basques. García Cascón could not have extensive, intimate contact with other seers whom he could not understand. He chose two kinds: those like Benita, whose messages were oriented more toward Spain, and those like María Recalde, who were eager and able to address the needs of particular people. Some of the most adaptable seers were not selected by García Cascón but rather selected him. Patxi, whose messages were for the Basque deputies in the Constituent Cortes, had no need for Catalan intermediaries. Garmendia, whose scope was wider and included Macià, did.

Thousands of pilgrims went to Ezkioga from Catalonia and the Basques welcomed the Catalans as brothers and sisters. Cardús described a Terrassa bus arriving in a town where a Nationalist festival was in progress; the Basques performed a special dance in their honor, receiving them and sending them on their way with "Visca Catalunya! [Long Live Catalonia!]" The Catalans replied, "Gora Euzkadi! [Up with Euzkadi!]"[89] However much they were interested in Madre Rafols's messages for Spain as a whole, the Catalans on the Aulina trips wanted to attract the Virgin's favor for Catalonia. Cardús wrote to the brother of the owner of the vision site:

> Catalonia will be saved, and the words of our great bishop Torras y Bages will find full confirmation, "Catalonia will exist if it is Catholic." . . . We may take more or less time, but in the end the victory will be ours, and Euskadi and Catalonia will continue like good brothers on the same path.[90]

The Catalans took no interest in the visions in Toledo in late August. When Carmen Medina took Patxi there he rather sniffed at the whole thing. Both for Basque and Catalan Catholics strong regional identities made it logical to pray to and give homage to a Virgin who appeared in order to reproach and punish the atheist Republic at the Center.

There was, however, a difference between urban Catalan and rural Basque pilgrims. For the Catalans a trip to Ezkioga was one from a land of apostasy to a land of faith. Canon Altisent of Lleida wrote in September 1931, "Ezquioga is putting the Catholics of other regions of Spain in contact with the noble integrity and deeply rooted faith of the Basque people, at present so admired in the world." When he and his companions visited Loyola, they worried that some day the rabble might burn it down. In the spirit of the "Not Here!" cartoon, their Basque guide reassured them, "Have no fear, they will not get in here, unless it is over the dead bodies of all the sons of this Catholic land." Just as Catholics from all over secular France refreshed themselves at Lourdes, where every night tens of thousands of believers created an infectious mood of piety, so the Catalans refreshed and renewed their faith in the massed fervor of Ezkioga's hymns and rosaries.[91]

The members of Vallet's movement were particularly heartened to find so many Basque men at Ezkioga—about half of adult spectators by my count from crowd photographs. In Catalonia male Catholics were in short supply. Indeed, the entire thrust of Vallet's movement was to convert lukewarm male Catholics into militant visible witnesses. Of the exercises Vallet gave in Catalonia, all but three or four were for men.

The way the Catholics of the two regions experienced the threat from the Republic was quite different. Rural Basques thought of the anticlericalism they read about—thefts from churches, the burning of religious houses, and assassinations of clergy as well as the removal of crucifixes from schools, the separation of church and state, and the dissolution of the Jesuits—as external, things that happened on the outside or policies that came from the outside. They received divine messages to defend the mountain heights of Euskadi from the invaders or to follow the angelic host and retake Spain. They redefined the enemy within—Basque republicans and socialists—as foreign. In the summer of 1931 apprehensive landowners from southern Spain also considered the conservative Basque Country a safe haven.

In Catalonia church and monastery burnings in the nineteenth century and in 1909 had accustomed Catholics to the idea of internal, Catalan anticlericals. Catholics there knew their own language was a vehicle just as appropriate for blasphemy as for prayer, for the scurrilous *L'Esquella de la Torraxa* as well as the pious *El Matí*. They knew from experience that impiety was part of the body politic in Catalonia, indeed, in the 1930s a major part. As Cardús wrote Ramona, "At present our land is like a volcano, and some day this volcano will erupt, and I do not know what will happen in Catalonia. God forgive us for the offenses he has received from our land, which cannot be imagined."[92] The communities of Terrassa, Sabadell, Badalona, and Mataró, which early sent contingents to Ezkioga, were mill towns in the very crater of the volcano, with strong anarchist or socialist movements. There Catholic men were outnumbered, visible, and vulnerable.

Vallet himself had organized many of the males through exercises; he always had a clear awareness of the upcoming contest. Whereas for the rural Basques the notion of a religious civil war was thrust upon them on 11–13 May 1931, the days when crowds burned and sacked religious houses in Madrid and other cities to the south, the people of Catalonia's industrial towns and cities had been experiencing a civil war of sorts—sporadic worker uprisings, anarchist killings, and state terror—for over twenty years. Vallet saw conversion as the only hope. He and other activist Catholics considered recourse to prophecies, apparitions, and mystics like Magdalena Aulina an abandonment of the struggle.[93]

But for Cardús and many the veterans of Vallet's movement, the prayers at Ezkioga were a continuation of, not a break from, what they had learned in spiritual exercises:

> I had done closed exercises twice and one series with the great apostle Padre Vallet. But even though I always gained good spiritual benefit I can say that the best exercises I have done are those I have done in Ezquioga, and what I say goes as well for many of the Exercise friends who have been to Ezquioga.[94]

The active involvement of the Catalans at Ezkioga proper ended with the government crackdown of October 1932. Thereafter García Cascón and José María Boada visited their visionary friends in jail and interceded for them at the mental hospital, but they sent no more expeditions. The decision was made by Aulina-Gemma. The seers, by then dependent on the trips, wrote wistfully on their Virgin's behalf declaring that the Catalans would return or ought to. Their friends wrote back expressions of support but also of reproach.

> All of us would come, but you well know that it is Gemma who is in charge, and if the director does not order us to go, or rather, says that this is not the right time, what can we do? . . . You well know that the expeditions do not come because of the quarrels and the disgusting hatred that for a considerable time now have been evident even out on the hillside.[95]

The quarrels and hatreds involved not only the seers but also their patrons. With Antonio Amundarain and Carmen Medina on the sidelines, the most important promoters were Raymond de Rigné and Amado de Cristo Burguera y Serrano. Both thrived on conflict.

5. PROMOTERS AND SEERS III: MONSIEUR RIGNÉ AND PADRE BURGUERA

ANTONIO AMUNDARAIN always kept his distance from the visionaries. Although Carmen Medina became close to some seers, she did not stay at Ezkioga for long periods. García Cascón, Cardús, and Magdalena Aulina lived in distant Catalonia. But Monsieur Rigné and Padre Burguera moved right in and became social landmarks. Both were obsessive. Their grand obsession with the visions of Ezkioga consumed the remainder of their lives.

Self-appointed impresarios like the promoters at Ezkioga exist all around us, and those working on a more grand scale have left their mark around the world and throughout history. William James wrote about such persons, "[They] do not remain mere critics and understanders with their intellect. Their ideas possess them, and they inflict them, for better or worse, upon their companions or their age."[1] At Ezkioga we observe these passionate characters at work in unusual circumstances. When they went there to confirm their ideas, they came up against canny and inspired rural seers—the canniest and most inspired of a cast of hundreds. The interests of the seers and the patrons did not exactly coincide, but each needed the other. Seers, of course, have left their mark on the world as well. These two rare metals made complex, unstable, alloys that we can watch solidify and break down.

My aim is to probe the dynamics of such relations. For although these metals are rare, when they combine, the effects on human history can be explosive. Someone with a line to the gods together with a virtuosic organizer who knows the right questions can do more than just change the world; on occasion they have even been able to reconfigure heaven.

MONSIEUR RIGNÉ

When Raymond de Rigné and Marie-Geneviève Thirouin arrived at Ezkioga on 10 August 1931, he was forty-seven and she was thirty-six. The Irish Hispanist Walter Starkie had just left, Antonio Amundarain and Carmen Medina were both involved with seers, and the Catalans were reading about Ezkioga in their newspapers. Rigné came to the visions like a moth to a flame on a dark night.[2]

Rigné inherited his enthusiasm for seers from his father, Raymond de la Ville, a general who dedicated his retirement to investments and literature. When de la Ville rashly invested in Andalusian railroads, the fall of the peseta drove him in distress to a spirit medium. She so convinced him with her insight on Spain's geography and political economy that he came to consult her on family matters as well. His son too turned to female visionaries in time of trouble and made a similarly ruinous investment of time and energy in Spain.[3]

Rigné's father had made no secret of his Catholicism and felt that his career had suffered because of it. Rigné *fils* himself lost his faith as an adolescent but regained it at age fifteen, thereafter becoming a believer on his own terms. He enjoyed conflict with the church hierarchy. Until his death in 1956 he skirmished in particular against rigorist and "morose" Catholicism. In 1910 he published a defense of Huysmans's *La Foule de Lourdes*. Rigné, like Huysmans, disliked Catholic sexual morality, and in 1917 he began to publish fiction about purity, prurience, nudism, and beauty. His aim was to unite Greco-Roman aesthetics with Christianity, so he chose for the name of his personal press "La Renaissance Universelle."[4]

In 1921 Rigné laid out a grandiose plan for a set of novels that would deal with people's souls. Entitled *Le Cité Vivant,* it would be a kind of spiritual sequel to the work of Balzac. (Everything he did was grandiose—one of the nicknames the Basque Ezkioguistas gave him was "Le Maréchal.") The eccentric books in his scheme mixed fact with fantasy. They were written supposedly by his own characters, who had fancy names like Jean d'Arvil and Supplicien Costèceque. In all he published a dozen books and drew most if not all of the illustrations.[5]

In 1911 Rigné married a Protestant woman, with whom he had six children, and he thereafter advocated the merging of Christian faiths. He described his wife as his "most precious collaborator" and his work and life as "a religious experience."[6] But in 1927 his marriage fell apart. The self-published books, which went unnoticed, were a continuous financial drain. And the inheritance his father had promised disappeared in the investment program managed by spirits. According to the autobiographical novel *Mariage Nul,* when Rigné was away on one of his many trips, his wife left him, taking the children, and over the next two years obtained a civil divorce.

In 1929 under the stress of this separation Rigné visited the German stigmatic Thérèse Neumann. In trance she told him to keep on writing and to pray, not to look for a job and not to try to force his family's return. That year he advertised for a literary collaborator and secretary and in Marie-Geneviève Thirouin, a devout and romantic poet, he found a soul mate for the remainder of his life. According to *Mariage Nul,* she was the great-granddaughter of a novelist and one of four daughters of an army colonel. Before meeting Rigné she had published a book of poetry and some theater sketches. The new couple considered it a sign that they had witnessed the same miracle cure at Lourdes in 1910. Since they could not marry in a religious ceremony, they invented one of their own and exchanged vows at Notre-Dame de Paris in 1930. Rigné told the people of Ezkioga that he chose his first wife himself but that the Virgin chose the second one for him.[7]

Rigné had an acute sense of chivalry that he deployed first in defense of Joris Karl Huysmans and later in defense of Alfred Dreyfus. In the late 1920s he focused on Jeanne d'Arc and wrote about her in a way both serious and playful. He claimed that after praying on the tomb of Cardinal Stanislas Touchet (who maneuvered Jeanne d'Arc's canonization in 1920), he "discovered" (or was divinely inspired to compose) a manuscript journal of Pierre Cauchon, the bishop who prosecuted Jeanne. This journal explained and filled in the major gaps in the historical record. Rigné's books on Jeanne, which he published in 1928 and 1929, combined his distaste for theologians (Jeanne's rehabilitation proved them mistaken) and his trust in visionaries.[8]

Rigné had an especially deep affinity for Jeanne d'Arc. For she had lived simultaneously on two planes, with humans and with spirits. Rigné saw himself in the same light. He held that God inspired great writers with knowledge: "The mystical life is the basic element of our existence as writers." As he wrote, he was "present at events that really occurred, in the prescience of the divine."[9] Rigné was aware of the difficulty his readers had in separating fact from fiction. But because the "fiction" part in his mind came from the divine and thus was just as true as the "fact," the difference between the two was perhaps not entirely clear to him. His multiple identities, each with a separate point of view, blurred the line between reality and fantasy.[10]

Jeanne d'Arc's mixture of reality and inspiration no doubt enhanced her appeal for Rigné. In an analogous way he could attribute failure as a writer to disbelief in his inspirational powers or to the challenges that he posed to staid morality or established ideas. Such challenges were at the heart of his enterprise. As he wrote in 1921, neatly equating his vocation as a gadfly to that of his military forebears, "It is easier to go to death on the field of battle than to go against public opinion." Jeanne d'Arc's glory became his as well, and he appointed himself "Secretary General to the International Committee for the Centenary of Jehanne d'Arc."[11]

At the time of the Ezkioga visions of 1931 Rigné was still smarting from the pain of his failed marriage and the indignity of his common-law remarriage. In *Mariage Nul* he and Thirouin recounted his experience in order to show how the civil marriage required in France, because it could end in civil divorce, vitiated the parallel Catholic one. In this way they justified publicly their own new "mystical" marriage and challenged the system that prevented their obtaining an annulment. The newlyweds also wrote the futuristic "Encyclical on Conjugal Morality." The putative author was one of Rigné's characters, a converted Protestant who became Pope Innocent XIV. They deemphasized the negative aspects of original sin and proposed a Christian education in the positive aspects of the body, a delight in conjugal sex, and contraception when the couple could support no further children or when childbirth would threaten the life of the spouse. Rigné proclaimed himself "a convinced believer and a thinker truly free before God." He and Thirouin saw themselves as freelance Catholic activists subordinate only to the pope or—if opposed by the pope—subordinate only to God. Except for the issue of birth control, the arguments of this joint work were much like Rigné's before they met.[12]

On 9 August 1931 Rigné and Thirouin went to Lourdes so the Virgin would bless their union. At the grotto Rigné claimed verbal approval from the Virgin Mary for a lifetime mission against civil marriages for Catholics. According to him, the Virgin instructed them to enter Spain the next day and make their way to Ezkioga.[13] There Rigné sought the same kind of certainty that his father found in spirit mediums and that he himself had known with Thérèse Neumann and Our Lady of Lourdes. He was known in various dioceses as a nuisance, and he had estranged first his parents and siblings and then his own children. As human props to his edifice gave way, Rigné found heavenly props to replace them.[14]

Rigné quickly decided that the Basque visions were genuine and that part of his mission from Lourdes was to publicize them. Through an interpreter the girl from Ataun told the couple from the Virgin that they should keep on their course and pray a lot and that they would have two children. The couple went to France to get photographic equipment, eager to document for the world the visions that provided them with moral passports.[15]

By September 6 they were back. On that day they met Ramona Olazábal. Rigné was proud that Ramona trusted him from their first meeting. Two days later she said the Virgin blessed sealed envelopes of his improvised marriage

Ramona Olazábal with Marie-Geneviève Thirouin and Raymond de Rigné, October 1931. Courtesy Lourdes Rodes Bagant

certificate and contract. He had suggested to Ramona that she try to have her vision at noon, permitting daylight photographs. Over the next four years he took hundreds of pictures of more than eighty visionaries. He considered the mystical and aesthetic appearance of the seers in the photos irrefutable proof of the apparitions.[16]

Rigné met Carmen Medina at Ezkioga, but he disapproved of her monarchist plotting. He got along better with a freethinking waiter who had worked in Paris and could translate for him. During the winter of 1931–1932 Rigné and his wife moved to Ormaiztegi, first to an inn and eventually to an apartment. Their landlord was José Olaizola, a conservative republican who became mayor of the village. That year Olaizola married Manuela Lasa, the former schoolteacher of Ezkioga. This educated young couple, skeptical of the visions and bemused by them, provided Rigné and Thirouin with company and French conversation. Rigné left debtors behind in France (more than likely he owed child support), and he wanted to safeguard his camera, typewriter, phonograph, record collection, and period furniture. Residence in Spain gave him extra protection, and his friendship with local officials like Olaizola stood him in good stead in his numerous scrapes with the government.

Monsieur Rigné was memorable for all who knew him. The priest Daniel Ayerbe remembered him as "a demented person of intellectual standing," more vehement even than Ayerbe's own father, Juan Bautista Ayerbe. Manuela Lasa remembers him as "a fanatic." "Nos zarandeó a todos"—"He was always pushing us around. Why was he so sure about the visions?" she wondered. But he and Thirouin nonetheless delighted Lasa. They left her, "enchantée, très enchantée."[17] Rigné's flamboyance, his letters to the editor, his extensive correspondence with the diocese, at first collaborative then openly hostile, made him conspicuous. He was an easy target for those who needed to explain the persistence of the seers. Vallet even suspected him of hypnotizing them. But within the believer community there was little such suspicion, for Rigné's lack of Spanish or Basque impeded his influence on messages for the general public.

Rigné's arrival on the scene in the early fall of 1931 coincided with the rise of Ramona. After he took his first photographs of her he left once more, but someone alerted him that a miracle would occur in mid-October. He returned and recorded the critical days from October 13 to 18 in which first Ramona and then other seers experienced "miracles." He was one of the last persons to see her before she went up the hill on her fateful mission. And he and his wife were present on October 17 when Ramona's friend from Ataun received a scratch on the hand from the baby Jesus; he immortalized their triumph with photos.

When the vicar general proclaimed the miracle a fraud, Rigné became indignant and began to collect statements from witnesses. In line with his concept of assisted history, he asked seers to ask the Virgin to reconstruct the events. They then narrated to him in vision what happened. On 28 October 1931 he and his wife published the results in *El Pueblo Vasco*. In early December Ramona, who must have been grateful for this defense, heard the Virgin say that she blessed the couple's marriage every single day.[18]

Rigné himself took copies of his photographs to the exiled Bishop Múgica in La Puye on November 6 and he sent others to the vicar general Echeguren in Vitoria. He had no fear of writing to the diocese or talking to local priests. He was apparently capable of putting the bishop enough at ease that Múgica mimicked a folk dance for him. This kind of aplomb contrasts with the awe of the rural visionaries, who when they met with church officials would normally take along upper-class companions.[19]

As a result of Carmen Medina's visits to Bishop Múgica, the diocesan investigator was in Ormaiztegi on 26 December 1931. Rigné testified that Patxi had made, then retracted, an announcement of a miracle for that day. He was unaware that he himself was a target. A servant in the Ormaiztegi inn had noticed that he occasionally got up in the night to drink water or snack, breaking the fast, although he and his wife were daily communicants in the parish church; and no one saw them in confession.[20]

About this time in late December, Rigné received a boost from José Garmendia, who learned that the Virgin would help Rigné to write a book about the apparitions. Garmendia reported that all those who helped to spread the truth about the Virgin would go to heaven and that Rigné would have enemies but should not fear them. "The book" became a major theme in the visions relating to Rigné. Here was a clear symbiosis. The seers needed social respect. Rigné needed to know that his mission was divine and that he was doing it well. At one point he even asked a seer to ask the Virgin to find him a publisher. The awareness that Rigné and Thirouin were "liburuak eskribitzen dituenak [people who wrote books]," as the Ataun girl heard the Virgin say in August 1931, could not be far from the minds of the seers when around the couple. This knowledge gave Rigné and Thirouin a kind of leverage that Carmen Medina lacked. By then the seers had learned the power of the printed word and had tasted the addictive nectar of fame.[21]

In 1932 Rigné and Thirouin received more encouragement from Evarista and Ramona. After Ramona's visions ended on August 15, the couple continued to visit her at her sister's house in Tolosa. But in late 1932 they fell out with Evarista, who was gravitating into the orbit of the rival author, Padre Burguera.[22]

Ramona was the only seer about whom Rigné wrote anything substantial. In December 1932, in the wake of the government crackdown on the visions, he distributed a four-page leaflet in Spanish that attacked the vicar general and named those who had observed Ramona's wounding. Echeguren sent a priest to cross-check Rigné's "sworn" witnesses. While some held to the substance of their statements, all said they had not sworn anything, and Echeguren used this discrepancy against Rigné, threatening to tell the press if he distributed the leaflet further.[23]

By April 1933 Rigné had completed a draft of the book on Ramona; in January 1934 he issued it in French under a pseudonym as *Une Nouvelle Affaire Jeanne d'Arc*. In it he drew parallels between Ramona and Jeanne and between the theologians who condemned Jeanne and the diocese of Vitoria. Just as Jeanne was right to obey her voices rather than the bishop of Beauvais, so Rigné was right to submit his book to the Virgin rather than to the bishop of Vitoria. Rigné "served God first, exactly like Jeanne d'Arc." In late 1933 the prospect of this book brought him the full and terrible scrutiny of Bishop Mateo Múgica.[24]

Rigné's interest in the vision messages was limited. Like other spectators he was caught up in the tantalizing wait for miracles, and because he was one of the only literate believers permanently on location, he issued periodic summons to the Catalans to attend divine events. But the prophetic visions did not interest him. In mid-1933 he added to his manuscript on Ramona a chapter about the

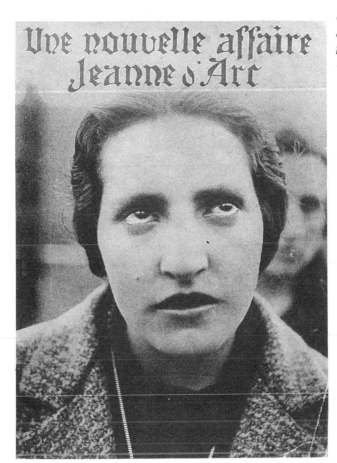

upcoming chastisement, which he related to La Salette, Madre Rafols, and older prophecies. But his addition was almost an afterthought, one more vindication of Ramona (and thereby of his own marriage).[25]

Nor was Rigné's interest in the visions political. He was hostile to the monarchists, and he leaned neither to the Carlists nor the Basque Nationalists. He saw no reason, he told the civil governor of Gipuzkoa in late 1932, why a shrine at Ezkioga should be incompatible with the Republic. In fact, he thought that the Republic could promote the visions in order to win over the Catholic peasantry. In this he was consistent. In 1921 he had written that there was absolute truth in religion but not in politics.[26]

What attracted Rigné to the seers was more visceral: he identified with them as underdogs in a contest with church and state. In visionaries like Ramona he found a pure cause for his skill as a writer, artist, and photographer. With the seers and believers who accepted his marriage and his mission, he was all heart.

He and Marie-Geneviève maintained close ties with several local families for decades: they gave wedding presents, wrote to sons in the army, and remembered the dead. Among these families Rigné and Thirouin found a quiet refuge. But Rigné could not resist a fight. He seemed only able to gain the recognition he yearned for as a writer or artist by creating enemies and provoking their responses.[27]

PADRE BURGUERA

Raymond de Rigné was not the only person who thought he had a divine mission to chronicle the apparitions. In late October 1931 a sometime-Franciscan made his first appearance. He, even more than Rigné, became a central figure in the affair and the bête noire of diocesan authorities. Like the other promoters, he brought his own philosophical casserole to the great spiritual potluck that the visions had become.

Amado de Cristo Burguera y Serrano was born in 1872 into a Carlist family in the agricultural market town of Sueca, Valencia. At age sixteen he entered the seminary in Valencia; three years later he joined the Franciscan order. By then he was already gathering material for what would be his first work, a seven-volume encyclopedia of the Eucharist, which he published with family money in 1906, when he was thirty-three years old. Thereafter Burguera returned to Valencia and Sueca, supposedly because of chronic laryngitis, and the diocese allowed him to live apart from his order. He served as diocesan censor of books and in 1910 and 1911 published moral evaluations of eleven thousand plays and works of literature in four volumes.

From 1917 to 1925 Burguera wrote biographies of two Sueca women (one of them had been the family seamstress) whom he chose to dub "Venerable" and "Servant of God." In these credulous books the holy women revealed the future, saw images weep and show emotion, played with the baby Jesus, heard the Child reveal private sins, and suffered from the devil's interference. Burguera later found these features at Ezkioga, where he considered unmasking the devil one of his major tasks.[28]

As the official chronicler of Sueca, Burguera wrote a two-volume town history. This work too reflected his intense, passionate nature. Like nearby Gandía and Cullera, Sueca has the feel of a Renaissance city-state, a nation unto itself that creates deep loyalties in its citizens and sharp rivalries with its neighbors. Burguera was a product of this environment, an extreme form of Iberian sociocentrism. His successor as chronicler, Fermín Cortés, told me that local people had considered Burguera slightly unbalanced but nonetheless sincere and of pure and good faith. Burguera, he said, wrote from vital necessity. While normally good-natured and entertaining, Burguera was extremely excitable on matters of religion and brooked no contradiction. Never one to avoid a battle,

El R. P. Amado de C. Burguera y Serrano

he took on local spiritist healers in his sermons. He offered them a prize of one thousand pesetas if they could demonstrate one genuine cure. Cortés thought Burguera was the kind of person whom in earlier times the Inquisition would have burned at the stake.[29]

As we might expect from someone who undertook a magnum opus on the Eucharist, Burguera was not reluctant to apply his vigor or to invest his self-importance in matters beyond local history. Poor health seems to have been a pretext not only to avoid the direct supervision of superiors but also to see the world. In 1914 Burguera went for his health to Lourdes, to Paris, and finally to Paray-le-Monial, where he knew there was an institute for Eucharistic studies. Its director was the elderly Baron Alexis de Sarachaga, a half-Russian, half-Basque retired diplomat who had converted from a frivolous liberalism to a devout integrism. Beginning in 1873 Sarachaga spent a fortune on apologetic publications, a museum to the Eucharist for pilgrims, and an association for the Social Reign of Jesus Christ, all at the Paray-le-Monial shrine to the Sacred Heart.[30]

If Burguera thought that a one-man encyclopedia was impressive, he was unprepared for the baron's scheme, which was to show that the entire history of natural and human creation was a preparation for the Social Reign of the Sacred Heart. Burguera (here "we") described Sarachaga in words similar to those used by others to describe himself: "We thought, as we listened, that we were hearing a lecture from a man who was a little nutty, but we were intrigued by so much knowledge, however strange, and we were convinced, finally, that our intellectual equipment was no match for that of Sarachaga."

By the time the baron died in 1918 he had produced twenty-eight volumes of studies, mostly "scientific" and archaeological, as part of the project for universal knowledge. When Burguera and Sarachaga met in 1914, Sarachaga was casting about for ways to generate more of an impact. Few persons seem to have heard about, much less taken seriously, his "École Bardique" or his "Instruction Supérieure Diplomatique" ("according to the rules and disciplines of the Sacred Heart"). Sarachaga found a willing disciple when he told Burguera the visit was providential and asked him to hold a "Chair of Eucharistic Pomp" in Spain. Burguera needed little encouragement to sense that he had a mission. He felt that the esoteric Ars Magna of the thirteenth-century savant from Mallorca, Ramon Llull, would appeal to Sarachaga. It did, and the baron encouraged Burguera to use the work to seek out a universal sacred language.[31]

As a result of this unusual stimulation, Burguera decided after the death of Sarachaga to write the projected universal divine history himself. He published the first two volumes in 1932. They are most curious (*disparatados*, Spaniards would call them). Burguera identifies a sacred ur-language linking, for instance, Chinese with Berber, and he asserts that Catalan-Valencian-Mallorcan is not a Romance but an Iberian language, like Basque. He claims the words in Llull's glossary were used in the Garden of Eden. He identifies a kind of sacred world geography of four prototypic natural features—"the pyramid," "the boat," "the crater-grail," and "the sphinx"—which he calls "telluric symbol-signs." And he shows great interest in the lost continent of Atlantis. Much of this work Burguera derived from Sarachaga's fanciful research, but some came from his own studies and visits to museums throughout Europe and in the Holy Land. There are similarities with the later pop archaeology of Eric von Dániken and Jorge María Rivero San José. Yet in this long and strange work there are also moments of beauty, as when Burguera goes into detail about the number of plant and animal species in the world and then points to the complexity and perfection of each. And the overall plan, while crude, has a distant resemblance to that of the French philosopher Teilhard de Chardin.[32]

Burguera connected this project to a school, Studium Catholicum, which he founded in one of his family's orange groves outside Sueca. He designed it as a day school similar to those of the contemporary reformer Padre Andrés Manjón. It was also to train catechists. With so much of Spain falling away from Catholicism, Amundarain, Aulina, and Burguera's future adversary, Echeguren, had all given time and thought to catechism for adults. Topped by a statue of the Sacred Heart of Jesus, the building was completed in 1931, hardly an auspicious year. Three days after the burning of religious houses (11 May 1931), Burguera gave an intemperate sermon against the Republic and the town authorities temporarily banished him.[33]

At the request of an acquaintance, this curious, intense, authoritarian, opinionated, and credulous man went to Ezkioga. He arrived on 13 November 1931, after attendance had fallen off in the wake of the Ramona fiasco. He met Iñaki Jaca, a boy seer, Patxi, Ramona, and a young girl seer from Ormaiztegi and he learned about José Garmendia's visit to Francesc Macià in Barcelona. He quickly classed the seers he observed by their type of trance and evaluated their visions as divine, diabolical, or human. His learning impressed the local doctor, Sabel Aranzadi, who asked him to sit for two days on the commission examining the seers.[34]

Burguera received several "proofs" of the apparitions. Two took place in the village of Bakaiku (then Bacaicoa) in Navarra. There on November 17 he observed eight children, first in the schoolhouse and then down by the river, who saw the Infant Jesus of Prague. Burguera's prior study of the Infant Jesus in Sueca must have quickened his interest. When the children were running and playing, not in trance, one of them came up to Padre Amado and said, "It was my mother who carried your suitcase in l'Espluga de Francolí." Burguera was astonished, for the boy referred to an incident that took place thirteen years earlier and that he had never been able to fathom.[35]

According to what his disciple Juan Castells told me in Sueca, Burguera had gone to take the baths at l'Espluga in Tarragona. He arrived by train in the evening and found no way to get to his lodgings. The station manager advised him to go back to Barcelona, for thieves made it unsafe to go into town on foot. A woman turned up to ask him if he wanted to go to town, but he was abrupt with her, telling her it was none of her business. He was about to take a train back to Barcelona when the woman returned, asked him again if he wanted to go to town, picked up his bag, and set off walking fast. He followed. It was raining, but it seems neither she nor he got wet. The woman left him at the hotel saying, "Remember me to God." The desk clerk assured him that there was no woman like that in the town. The episode, rather like Manuel Irurita's mysterious train stop, had troubled Burguera, and other priests he consulted had not been able to explain it. So when the child seer told him that it had been the child's (spiritual) mother, Burguera recognized a sign to believe in the visions.

Burguera often retold the second proof in Bakaiku. There he observed María Celaya in trance, and on November 19 he accompanied her to Ezkioga, where she had visions as well. When he saw her again at Bakaiku on November 22, she revealed to him that eight days earlier there had been an attempt to break into and burn down his Studium Catholicum in Sueca but that the vandals had been repelled by the Sacred Heart of Jesus. Burguera quickly returned to Sueca to see what had happened. Indeed, he said, he found hatchet marks on the door and the mark of flames. It appeared to him that the flames had come at the vandals from inside, from the Sacred Heart.[36]

Burguera's first stay in Ezkioga and Navarra did not make much of an impression on the seers or their more prominent followers. At that point he was just one more curious cleric. The second volume of his universal divine history had already passed ecclesiastical review, so he smuggled into it sixteen pages on the apparitions. He did so in a chapter on the beauty of God's art in creation, emphasizing the beauty the seers saw in the face of the Virgin Mary. He noted approvingly that two child seers had visions in which the child Jesus and the Virgin referred to the "official dishonoring of God" by the Constituent Cortes. But he snorted at the deputy Antonio de la Villa's idea that "the miracles of Ezquioga were a way of rallying the forces of the Traditionalists and the Basque-Navarrese Nationalists to rise up against the Republic." Rather, he saw the apparitions in the longer perspective. The evil, he pointed out, "was not just of this century, but also in all of the previous ones. We have reached a point in which science, art, history, literature, and social development are all Satanized."[37]

The multivolume opus itself, so long in the writing, was still Burguera's main preoccupation in 1931; it took him a while to assimilate what he had seen in Ezkioga and adjust his enterprise to the virtually unlimited scope for knowledge of the divine that the many seers offered. At any rate, he did not return to Ezkioga until 27 June 1932, but when he did, he was ready to write a defense of the visions as a work on its own. Over time he came to consider Ezkioga the climax of world history, the logical crowning point of all his previous endeavors, and the means by which God would once and for all reunite the human and the divine.

In the long run Burguera planned to write "a big book, well-documented and carefully verified," on the apparitions. In the short run he wanted to write a rebuttal of the Jesuit José Antonio Laburu's lectures discrediting the visionaries (see chapter 6). On his arrival in Ezkioga Burguera immediately started evaluating the seers, separating "the dross (not much and naturally occurring) from the gold." An expedition of Catalans was in Ezkioga on the day of his arrival, and either that week or the next they showed him the manuscript defense of the visions by the wealthy Carlist politician Mariano Bordas Flaquer. On very short acquaintance, they asked Burguera to write a prologue. Within three weeks the diocese of Segorbe had approved the booklet and the prologue.[38]

Pilar Ciordia in vision, probably 13 July 1932. Photo by Joaquín Sicart

A visit with Burguera became a fixture of the Catalans' weekly tours. He would tell them the latest messages, explain the different kinds of trances, and place the visions in a wider context. On July 17 he told them that four days earlier he had been working on his book when he heard that three schoolgirls on an excursion from Pamplona were in trance on the vision deck. Twice he went out to examine and test the seers and speak to the entire group about the mercy of the Mother of God. After many hours the visions ended and a nun came to say that two of the seers had messages for him. The first was Pilar Ciordia, a woman who lived at a Pamplona convent school. She claimed that she had been present in spirit when Burguera had delivered the sermon in Sueca that had caused his banishment and that the Virgin had then pointed him out as her (the Virgin's) defender in Ezkioga. Ciordia said she had recognized him at once when he got up on the vision deck. Burguera believed her.

Burguera also believed the second seer, Gloria Viñals, a student at a different school in Pamplona. She claimed that in February of 1932 she too had had a vision of Burguera in Sueca in which the Virgin had also pointed him out as her defender in Ezkioga. Viñals's proof was that the Virgin told her that once she had carried him through the air to a lodging house, which Burguera again must have taken to refer to the episode in l'Espluga de Francolí. These seers persuaded Burguera that the Virgin wanted the "big book" he planned to write about Ezkioga. Note here a cumulative process. Burguera believed the visionaries essentially because they said the Virgin had chosen him to lead others to believe the visionaries. The Catalans believed Burguera in turn because he said that the seers said that the Virgin said the Catalans had been specially chosen to be told to believe the visions or to tell others about them.[39]

As the chronicler authorized by the Virgin of Ezkioga, Burguera needed the texts of the messages of the seers. In 1932 few of the thousands of vision texts had circulated. He had no chance to obtain the messages in the notebooks and printed questionnaires of the informal commission; by 1932 the parish priest of Ezkioga, firmly opposed to the visions, held this material closely. But he could obtain some of the messages seers wrote in their own notebooks or dictated to friends and confessors. Burguera obtained the messages of the Pamplona seers when they were in Ezkioga or when he went to see them in Navarra. Sympathetic priests provided him with the messages of Evarista Galdós, Martín Ayerbe, and Marcelina Mendívil. And his friendship with the Catalans gained him access to their favorite seers, Benita Aguirre, José Garmendia, and María Recalde. With Recalde a priest from Valladolid, Baudilio Sedano de la Peña, was especially helpful.

Baudilio Sedano de la Peña and Cruz Lete

I went to see Don Baudilio in 1982 at the instance of the family with whom he had boarded at Ezkioga. A short, chubby man with a dirty worn cassock, unctuous and jovial, but with darting eyes, he was then seventy-six years old. He lived in Valladolid in a squalid apartment above a convent of Franciscan nuns, for whom he served as chaplain. As we talked, the smells of the pastries and cookies they baked drifted up from the kitchens below. I later learned of his extreme secretiveness about the large portion of time he gave to visions and visionaries and that only the name of that one Basque family (which, like many others I talked to, wishes to remain anonymous) would have got me in the door. As it was, on my repeated visits from Madrid he let me into his confidence only gradually and partially. He loaned me first some prints and then the glass plates of photographs of visionaries, but it transpired later that they were not in fact his. I never got to see his store of documents and he eventually gave me copies of the Burguera book only at exorbitant cost. Nevertheless, he did let me look at a typewritten memoir of his involvement with the Ezkioga visionaries and Padre Burguera.[40]

Baudilio Sedano de la Peña and Vidal Castillo (wearing glasses) with seers and believers, including a stockbroker and his wife from Bilbao, winter 1931–1932. Photo by José Martínez

Sedano was born in a village of the province of Burgos in 1906 and trained as a priest and a contralto for cathedral choirs. His first post was in Sigüenza and his second was in the cathedral of Valladolid, where he was also chaplain of the convent. In 1931 he read newspaper reports of the visions. With money he had won after buying a lottery ticket with Ezkioga in mind, he went there at the end of July.

Like Burguera, he felt he had particular proof that the apparitions were true. He saw Benita Aguirre after a vision run down the hill, pick a man out of the crowd, and give him a private message. Sedano kept an eye on the man, who prayed on the hillside with tears streaming down his face. When Sedano approached him, the man said he was from Tenerife and that there was no way Benita could have known him, yet she had revealed secrets about the state of his soul. For the first year or so Sedano went to Ezkioga every two weeks and stayed about four days. He did so with utmost discretion, fearing reprisals from his diocese or protests from the priests at Ezkioga. He took down María Recalde's messages as early as September and arranged for her to save them for him. María's son remembers that he came to Durango about once a month.[41]

Sedano also provided Burguera with the messages from the seer many people considered the most convincing, Cruz Lete Sarasola of Itsasondo. Lete studied first at a grammar school in Ordizia and then at a normal school in Pamplona. He was thus one of the most educated seers, and the solid reputation of his family enhanced his credibility. When he was home in the summer or fall of 1931, he went to the apparition site out of curiosity and began to have visions. He told Sedano that the Virgin instructed him not to resume his studies in Pamplona and above all not to return to the apartment of the freethinking family where he had been boarding. At the insistence of his parents, he did go back to Pamplona, but when he was going up to the flat, the Virgin appeared to him and he fell down the stairs. When he tried to study, he found that all he could see in his books was blank pages. He said that in his first vision at Ezkioga after his return, the Virgin asked him jokingly, "Did you study a lot?"

Tall, thin, and austere, Lete was a striking seer. Many of his visions were of Christ and he often settled into Christlike stances. A Catalan referred to him in vision as having "an angelic tenderness." And Sedano said that "just hearing him pray the seven Hail Marys of the Sorrows of the Holy Virgin gave you such a feeling of sadness that it was obvious that it did not come from him but that he was seeing something extraordinary that could only be the Holy Virgin." Like others, Lete said the Virgin had told him that he would die soon. A Basque sheepman recalled Lete's private messages from the Virgin to those around him: "Some people would laugh, but he got them serious and weeping."[42]

In the fall of 1931 Lete had a vision of the Virgin in which she pointed out a heavenly friar as Juan de Dios, the founder of the Brothers Hospitallers, and asked Lete whether he wanted to join the order. He did, and she instructed him to write the superior of the house in Ciempozuelos near Madrid. Lete and some of his friends were admitted. They are said to have participated in spiritual exercises with the Jesuits at Loyola before leaving. Lete's last vision at Ezkioga, of Roman soldiers crucifying him, may reflect the visual imagination of the exercises (see text in appendix).[43]

Sedano had been taking down Lete's visions and was present at this one. He accompanied Lete as far as Valladolid, where he put him up for a night. In Sedano's chapel Lete said in vision that many who believed in the apparitions would later disavow them. He went on to Madrid, reappearing in the Ezkioga story only a year and a half later when his edifying death (he died confidently singing a hymn) provided the believers with their first saint.[44]

Burguera was frustrated in his attempts to gain documents from other seers, including some of the most famous ones. Their refusal placed him in a quandary—how could those who saw the Virgin not cooperate with someone the Virgin herself had chosen? Ramona Olazábal's spiritual director was the curate of Beizama, Francisco Otaño, and he retained her vision texts in case there was an official inquiry. Allegedly on the Virgin's orders, Ramona kept Otaño's role

Cruz Lete in vision,
6 February 1932.
Photo by Joaquín
Sicart

Nº 1. Ezquioga: Cruz Lete en éxtasis.
6. Febrero 1932.

secret and gave messages to no one else. Because she would not cooperate with him, Burguera judged her visions diabolical. But he left her the option of changing her mind.[45]

In the summer and fall of 1932 most of the believers recognized Burguera as their expert defender. Free from the supervision of a religious order and without a fixed post in Valencia, he was less vulnerable than other believing priests. Thus he was active in the planning of the chapel at the vision site and he contacted the sculptor who made the image of the Virgin. With the chapel complete and the arrival of the image imminent, the spirits of the believers revived. In honor of the Virgin's birthday, a female seer claimed that the Virgin wanted Burguera to run a kind of festive contest of three theological questions. The Virgin would provide a prize. On September 4, after all had performed the stations of the cross, Burguera read out the questions to about three hundred persons on the vision deck. Four days later three thousand persons came to hear the replies. For three hours seers and believers proposed their answers. No one guessed what the seer wanted to hear, so, she said, the prize was hers. This strange episode exemplifies Burguera's two sides: on the one hand, the authoritarian leader of thousands of docile believers, a master of sacred ceremonies; on the other, an innocent subject to the most flimsy of visionary claims.[46]

Burguera and Rigné were similar in a number of ways. Both wrote and paid to publish numerous books. Both had independent wealth, although Rigné seems to have started out with more. Both sought in vain recognition and respect. Both had been to Lourdes and had a great openness toward extraordinary manifestations of the supernatural. And both were about to come head to head with church and state.

But there were contrasts as well. Rigné was an advocate for chaste nudity, while Burguera considered nudism the ultimate sign of Satan's dominion. While both were the stuff of heretics, Burguera, like Calvin, also was the stuff of the inquisitor general. Both were constitutionally incapable of taking orders, but in Burguera's case it was because he preferred to give them, whereas Rigné was too playful or obstreperous for hierarchy in any form. Burguera saw himself as a grand spiritual director who distinguished the good from the bad, the sacred from the profane, the just from the unjust. Rigné was constantly challenging these categories and taking pokes at the classifiers.

Like the other patrons, Rigné and Burguera were in such close symbiosis with seers that without them some seers would not have maintained—in some cases would not have gained—their fame. And wittingly or not, each guided the seers into pronouncements of a certain nature and away from other themes and other directions. They connected the rural seers to the wider literate society. But they filtered and bent the light that passed through them. This distortion became especially evident as the diocese closed in on seers and patrons alike.

6. SUPPRESSION BY CHURCH AND STATE

OVER THE FIRST year the vicar general marked his distance from the visions and successfully turned public opinion against them. Then the governor investigated promoters for conspiracy and dispatched some seers to a mental hospital. Finally the bishop decreed the visions devoid of supernatural content. Government persecution brought the believers together. Diocesan persecution split them apart. Relations between promoters, between seers, and between promoters and seers were strained to the breaking point. Visions of the devil and accusations that visions were diabolical mirrored these strains. The bishop eventually singled out the two most visible promoters, Raymond de Rigné and Padre Amado de Cristo Burguera, for special treatment.

THE VICAR GENERAL

The visions at Ezkioga took place at a time when the church in Spain in general and in the Basque Country in particular was on the defensive. Visions began after the expulsion of the bishop and the burning of churches and convents. They reached a peak during the discussions leading to the separation of church and state in October 1931. And they flared up again in the spring of 1932 as the government removed crucifixes from public buildings and disbanded the Jesuits. The church's vulnerability during this period may help explain why the hierarchy tolerated the visions for so long and why ultimately it suppressed them with such vigor.

While the bishop of Vitoria was in exile, the vicar general took charge of the running of the diocese. Elderly priests remember Justo de Echeguren for his rectitude and tell me he was an *Integrista* with friendly contact with the Basque nationalists. Some emphasize his diligence and activity, others his humaneness, studiousness, and intelligence.[1] He allowed Antonio Amundarain to organize the visions at Ezkioga for the first few months, as long as Amundarain did not say where he obtained his authority. Waiting to see what would happen, Echeguren did not stop priests from leading the rosaries at the ceremonies or Catholic newspapers from reporting the visions in detail. He had regular channels for making his wishes known to the Catholic press, and *El Día,* the newspaper of his protégé, gave the visions the most coverage of all.[2]

Much of this news was favorable. In July, August, and September 1931 the Catholic press throughout Spain liked the outpouring of piety at the visions. Leftist newspapers did not make an issue of the matter. When the deputy Antonio de la Villa protested in the Cortes, Manuel Azaña, then minister of war, thought him vulgar, and other deputies, including the philosopher Miguel de Unamuno, thought him ridiculous. The minister of the interior pointed out that the French republic tolerated Lourdes and an entire district lived off the popularity of the site. The political slant of the visions in late July did not reach the press, so they did not embarrass the diocese.[3]

Echeguren maintained one consistent policy—he deprived the vision prayers of the legitimacy that external Christian symbols would have provided—but otherwise he underestimated the depth of public interest and the potential of the visions for disruption. When his friend and protégé Pío Montoya called him urgently on the evening of Ramona Olazábal's wounding, Echeguren refused to go to Ezkioga because he had to adjudicate a marriage annulment proceeding. Only Montoya's excited insistence brought him on the morning train. At Ezkioga he dealt with Ramona expeditiously and decisively, but by his own admission he had come with his mind open to the possibility that here at last was the confirming miracle.

As a result of Echeguren's press release against Ramona, *El Día* stopped reporting on the visions and Rafael Picavea thereafter prepared his entertaining articles for *El Pueblo Vasco.* About this time the vicar general forbade priests to lead the rosaries and ordered the seer Patxi Goicoechea to take down the vision stage. But not until Carmen Medina and the seers went to see the exiled Bishop Múgica in France in mid-December 1931 did the vicar general and the bishop choose to go on the offensive. By then Rigné had published his defense of Ramona and had shown Múgica photographs, and Catalan gentry had accompanied José Garmendia to see the vicar general in Vitoria. There was lobbying as well from Bishop Irurita of Barcelona. The leaders of the diocese of Vitoria now realized that the seers would not stay home and their supporters would not stay quiet.[4]

When Patxi announced a miracle for December 26, the bishop sent his *fiscal* to Ormaiztegi to expose and discredit the seers in general. Such predictions, coming in a series of relays, had been maintaining the hopes of believers from the start of the visions. José María de Sertucha took testimony from Carmen Medina, Rigné, Ramona, Evarista, and Patxi about the prediction. By then Patxi had amended the date to a month later. The day after the Sertucha mission the vicar general prohibited all priests from going to the vision site. He asked the Jesuit Padre Laburu to reason with an industrialist in Bilbao, Manuel Arriola, who supported the visions. The industrialist promised to stop going to Ezkioga if the miracle did not occur in January.[5]

The Jesuit Expert, José Antonio Laburu

Forty-eight years old, José Antonio Laburu was then at the height of his popularity as one of Spain's most eloquent preachers. He was also a kind of popular scientist whose specialties in 1931 were "psychology, psychobiology, and characterology." He gave lectures to audiences in the thousands, with simultaneous radio broadcasts, on subjects that ranged from morality on the beaches to the psychology of fighting bulls. His oratory was "eminently popular, attractive, full of overwhelming conviction, within reach of the illiterate worker as well as the university professor." He taught biology at the Jesuit school in Oña (Burgos) and traveled widely the rest of the year. In 1930 many of his thirty-seven lectures were in Chile, Argentina, and Uruguay, to audiences top-heavy with university, government, and military leaders. His psychology leaned more to the Germanic than the French, but he was dismissive of Freud and occasionally cited Pierre Janet. In the ecclesiastical firmament, he was a very bright star. Oña was close to Vitoria and Laburu had fluid relations with the diocese. In Holy Week of 1930, according to the diocesan bulletin, his spiritual exercises in San Sebastián "were the sole topic of conversation in cafés and workshops, factories, and offices."[6]

Apparently Laburu's natural curiosity led him to try to capture the experience of the visionaries on film, perhaps as material for his lectures. He first went to Ezkioga with a priest from San Sebastián on 17 and 18 October 1931, just after Ramona's wounding, when he filmed Ramona and Evarista Galdós. Evarista, he said, obligingly rescheduled her visions to midafternoon so there would be enough light.[7] He returned to Ezkioga around January 4 to show the films to the seers and their friends. On the next day he filmed some more, in part at the request of the seers. This time he included Benita Aguirre, who also rescheduled her visions for him. Skeptical from the start and perhaps inspired by the photographs of religious hysterics in books by Janet and other French psychologists, he intended to compare the seers to mental patients. Seers and believers considered his presence a good sign. They still hoped for a favorable verdict. After all, Bishop Múgica had treated Rigné, Carmen Medina, and the sample seers gently; and even the vicar general's delegate Sertucha had been convivial while drawing up his affidavits.[8]

In the first months of 1932 activity picked up at the apparition site. The nonstop stations of the cross proved attractive not only to the Catalans but also to the Basque and Navarrese. The removal of crucifixes from public buildings helped focus attention on the living crucifixes at Ezkioga. The Rafols prophecies fed this enthusiasm. Echeguren needed a master stroke, so he asked Laburu to give a series of public lectures critical of the visions. At the beginning of April he sent Laburu the evidence he had against content of the visions and the seers' conduct. Since much of this was rumor and some of it actionable, Echeguren specified what Laburu could mention but not print and which names he could use. Laburu himself gathered more information from the seers' former employers or skeptics in the Bilbao and San Sebastián bourgeoisie, to whom he had easy access.[9]

The Vitoria vicar general hoped that Laburu's first lecture, in the seminary in Vitoria, would serve to disenchant those professors, parish priests, and seminarians who believed in or were confused about the visions and persuade influential laypersons then providing moral and logistical support to the seers. Echeguren posted the parish priest of Ezkioga at the door to keep the seers out.[10]

Both in its debut on April 20 and in repeat performances at the Teatro Victoria Eugenia in San Sebastián on 21 and 28 June 1932 Laburu's lecture against the "mental contagion" at Ezkioga was a devastating success.[11] With daunting theological and psychological vocabulary, Laburu laid out the characteristics of true visions, citing Thomas Aquinas and Teresa de Avila, and showed how those at Ezkioga did not measure up. Rather, he said, they were purely natural, if unusual, mental processes. He went down a list of aspects that disqualified the visions:

1. The seers' certainty about when their visions would occur. They had a special stage and they could have their visions virtually at will. He cited in particular the behavior of Ramona, Evarista, and Benita from the time when he made his films.
2. The childishness of what the seers asked about and saw. He cited their asking whether the duke of Tárifa would survive an operation and whether

various relatives were in purgatory. He mentioned visions in inappropriate places, visions of persons in hell or heaven or still alive, visions of the devil making faces at Benita through a bus window, visions of the Virgin walking through a house in Ormaiztegi and blessing the rooms, and visions of divine figures with the wrong attributes (Jesús Elcoro allegedly described the Virgin Mary with a Sacred Heart of Jesus pierced with a sword). And he referred to "the alleged delivery of medals, ribbons, rosaries, without any purpose other than the gift of these objects to 'seers' whose spiritual life was an open question."[12]

3. The falsity of what the apparition was supposed to have said. His examples: the Virgin said she would not forgive those who did not believe in Ezkioga, whereas the church did not require belief even of "approved" apparitions; a seer saw someone in purgatory who was actually alive; and a seer said that Carmen Medina's brother-in-law would survive, though he did not.

4. The behavior of the seers before and after the visions. Here Laburu referred, at least in his unpublished text, to the reputation of Patxi and Garmendia as drinkers; to Ramona's dancing soon after her wounding; to the seers' showing off in gestures, photographs, and on film; to boasts as to the length of time in trance; to female seers being alone behind closed doors with male seers or believers; and to male seers kissing female believers.

5. Obvious frauds: Ramona's wounds and rosary; a false report in a Catalan newspaper.

6. "The total absence in the 'seers' of supernatural behavior, whether in (1) humility; (2) recollection; (3) prayer; (4) penance; or (5) obedience; and their distinguishing themselves by overt exhibitionism, utilitarianism, and dissipation."[13] He also remarked on a kind of habitual dullness (*abobamiento*) on the part of several seers caused by their repeated trances.

7. "The enormous emotional pressure on the seers to have visions." Here he mentioned as examples: that believers gave slickers, shoes, stockings, and wool socks to Ramona and Evarista; that Carmen Medina took the girl from Ataun to live with her; that believers admired or praised the seers as if holy and asked them to pray for people; that believers kissed Patxi; that believers offered Patxi the use of automobiles; and that the seers gave the general impression of being on holiday.

Finally, in a kind of catchall category, Laburu cited the refusal of the seers to remove the cross and the stage; the scheduling of apparitions of the Virgin at ten o'clock at night or later, "an hour at which it has been the prudent and traditional custom of the church to suggest that young women should be in their houses" (what can happen at these gatherings, he added darkly, is obvious); and the repeated announcements of extraordinary events for all to see, none of which had occurred.[14]

Although the Jesuit referred favorably to the public display of faith at Ez-kioga, he warned that people could not deduce from this piety that the visions were supernatural. He distinguished "a true faith, solidly reasoned and cemented, a faith instructed and conscious," from "faith of pure emotionality or family tradition [held by] sentimental and mawkish persons who confuse secondary and unimportant things with what is essential and basic in dogma." After reviewing diocesan policy in regard to Ezkioga, he emphasized that the diocese had made no formal inquiry because there was no trace of the supernatural to investigate. Finally he showed his films of the seers and compared them with a film of patients in insane asylums.[15]

Laburu stayed at the seminary in Vitoria and made himself available to answer individual questions or doubts of the professors and seminarians. One professor had brought back a blood-soaked handkerchief from Ramona's wounding. The seminarians were divided. Attitudes of the clergy in the zone around Ezkioga ranged from tenacious opposition to tacit approval.

But Laburu convinced many. Francisco Ezcurdia was then a seminarian and had been a frequent observer of the visions. The Rignés lived in his parents' boardinghouse in Ormaiztegi in the winter of 1931–1932. He had been especially puzzled by the case of an acquaintance, a cattle dealer from Santa Lucía whom María Recalde repeatedly tried to see. The man did all he could to avoid her, but she finally caught up with him and told him a secret about himself. The event so changed the dealer that thereafter he received Communion daily. Through his teacher José Miguel de Barandiarán, Ezcurdia asked Laburu how this knowledge of conscience was possible. Laburu's commonsense response was that there were other, natural ways, such as gossip, to find out people's sins. Ramona's spiritual director also had a chance to consult Laburu personally. He too was convinced by the Jesuit, if only temporarily. Another priest who was a seminarian at the time told me that although he personally found Laburu's talk superficial and pseudo-scientific, it convinced the other students.[16]

Laburu's impact went far beyond the seminary. Major regional newspapers repeated his main points. So did local periodicals in areas where there were supporters of the visions, like a Basque-language weekly in Bizkaia and the parish bulletin of Terrassa in Catalonia. *El Matí*, at first enthusiastic about Ezkioga, by then opposed it. Even *El Correo Catalán* summarized the talk. It was clear that Laburu spoke for the diocese, and his lecture permitted priests and laypersons opposed to the visions to speak out. And the lecture changed the minds of many believers, like the priest of Sant Andreu, in Barcelona, who in his parish hall spoke first in favor of the visions in December 1931 and then, on the basis of Laburu's lecture, against them six months later.[17]

Among Ezkioga enthusiasts the lecture provoked consternation, disillusion-ment, and anger. For those whom the visions touched in a personal way or who felt that they were witnesses to miracles, Laburu's arguments were thin stuff.

Only greater miracles could have persuaded them to disavow the seers. The rector of Pasai Donibane warned Laburu not to give the lectures in San Sebastián.

> You have no right to come and play the Vitoria phonograph record as if we the priests of Gipuzkoa could not demand more respect for matters related to the Mother of God. . . . If your reverence wants to preach in a theater, preach against the terrible torments that in hell await those who adore the flesh, but let Most Holy Mary appear to whomever she wishes at Ezkioga, although she did not appear to your reverence who went to Ezkioga with a movie camera.

Never shy about writing anyone, Rigné asked Laburu to study the problem with greater care, rebutted specific points regarding Ramona and Evarista, and informed the Jesuit that "the Most Holy Virgin spoke to me herself at Lourdes last August 9, the feast day of the saintly Curé d'Ars for whom I have a special devotion. She entrusted me with a certain mission and now I know why." In the same vein a Catalan pharmacist informed Laburu of an Ezkioga spring that allegedly went cloudy when an unbelieving soldier approached it. In sizzling terms an art restorer from Vitoria denounced "official science and the pedantry of this collection of dolts with pretensions of wisdom who monopolize the diffusion of knowledge they do not possess." He blamed Laburu and the diocese for not orienting the seers from the beginning and then making fun of them for being disoriented.[18]

Ezkioga believers were not the only ones upset by the speech. The novelist Pío Baroja's sister had gone to Ezkioga from Bera and returned impressed with the piety. Baroja thought it ridiculous that Laburu should adduce proofs against the seers, and he said so in a short book, *Los visionarios:* "The exact measurement of a miracle is sort of thickheaded. The only ones who would think of that are these poor Jesuits we have now, who are pedantry personified." His nephew later wrote, "Everyone knew that my uncle did not believe in miracles; but in that case, as in others, what irritated him was the pseudo-positivism of those who denied them, not the denial in itself."[19]

After the first talk in San Sebastián, the Ezkioga parish priest, Sinforoso de Ibarguren, wrote to Laburu that he had stirred up a hornet's nest.

> You must surely be tired of having hot ears, as they say; this is inevitable after the storm you have raised with your talk. The Ezquioguistas are of course infuriated. Even the farm folk have heard about the lecture and comment on it. And the Catalans tear into you on every occasion. They would skin you alive.

Ibarguren ended with a thought about the long-term consequences: "Church authority comes out of all this badly shaken. Great damage is being done; how will it be repaired?"[20]

Cover of pamphlet by Mariano Bordas Flaquer defending apparitions, published October 1932

Because Laburu was so effective, believers scrambled to find a priest to counter his arguments in public. Some asked a learned Carmelite, Rainaldo de San Justo, which worried the vicar general enough for him to contact the Carmelite provincial in Bilbao. The provincial reported that Padre Rainaldo said he would not speak unless his superiors in the order and the diocese asked him to. With the diocese thus on the alert, the rebuttal could come only in print. Mariano Bordas Flaquer was one of the leaders of the weekly Catalan trips. A lawyer, former member of parliament, and former assistant mayor of Barcelona, Bordas had led a pilgrimage to Limpias in 1920. In June 1932 he prepared a series of articles refuting Laburu. The diocese of Barcelona approved the series for *El Correo Catalán,* but for some reason the newspaper did not publish the articles. Burguera added a preface that gave Bordas some theological legitimacy, but *The Truth about Ezkioga* did not come out as a pamphlet until October 1932.[21]

Bordas distinguished seers who were true, naming ten Basques and the Catalan seers in the weekly groups, and others who, he admitted, were not. But he denied that the great majority of seers asked childish questions or had visions at any set time. He explained the vision messages containing errors in dogma as misunderstandings on the part of seers or mistakes in copying. He accused Laburu of slandering the seers but said that in any case their behavior before and after the visions was irrelevant to the truth of the visions themselves. He argued that even if there were seers who said someone alive was in purgatory, this would not disqualify the others.

As proofs for the visions he gave the seers' clairvoyance, their knowledge of unconfessed sins, and their conversions of sinners. He adduced three instances of the seers' preternatural knowledge: a seer's answer of a Catalan youth's unspoken question about the fate of his mother; Benita Aguirre's and María Recalde's knowledge of the pious death in Extremadura of a Catalan's relative; and María Recalde's reply in vision to an unread, carefully folded, query.

As their popularity and even their respectability melted away, the seers reacted in their own way against the lectures. Already before the first lecture, Garmendia had worried about its effect. According to a visitor, in the week after the Laburu talk the only people around Ezkioga who believed in the visions were Joaquín Sicart the photographer, the Zumarraga hotel owners, the taxi drivers, and some of the inhabitants of the Santa Lucía hamlet. Benita Aguirre wrote plaintively that in her town of Legazpi "no one believes; almost all have grown cold."[22]

María Recalde told her Catalan friends that two weeks after his lecture in Vitoria Laburu called her to a convent in Durango and reproved her for sending him a disrespectful letter. Feeling divinely inspired, she allegedly rebuked him for making Christ suffer on the cross during his talk, and what she said led Laburu to renounce the lectures planned for San Sebastián. Since he subsequently gave them, the account is of dubious accuracy. But it captures the depth of the seers' distress.[23]

After Laburu spoke in San Sebastián, the Virgin supposedly told one seer that he was a sinner and another that in the end he would change his mind. Subsequent rumor among seers and believers had it that Laburu had a cancer of the tongue as punishment, that he wanted to retract what he had said and to study Ezkioga seriously. In visions in 1933 Benita Aguirre and Pilar Ciordia said the Virgin gave messages for Laburu to mend his ways and help Padre Burguera with the book. But this was all wishful thinking.[24]

THE GOVERNOR

Seers and believers now worked with a new urgency to dignify their holy place. The vicar general denied permission repeatedly for a chapel, and the

Chapel virtually completed for the first anniversary of the apparitions, 1932. Photo by Joaquín Sicart

lectures showed that he had made up his mind. So finally, following José Garmendia's inspirations, Juan José Echezarreta started building the chapel anyway. Vigilant to the point of obsession, the Ezkioga pastor notified the diocese at once, and in an official note on June 10 the vicar general prohibited the chapel. Echezarreta pushed ahead and by the end of the month the chapel was virtually complete. Garmendia also described the image in detail; an artist sketched it in his presence, and a sculptor in Valencia, José María Ponsoda, prepared the image. Again Echezarreta footed the bill. The parish priest must have been suspicious about the large pedestal, often wreathed in flowers, waiting in the structure.[25]

In September 1932 it became clear that the next offensive against the seers would come from the government. In August General José Sanjurjo had led an attempt to overthrow the Second Republic from Seville. Sanjurjo was surprised when the uprising fizzled from lack of support, which he had expected in particular from Navarra and the north. This was the rebellion that Carmen Medina was sure the Virgin of Ezkioga was announcing in 1931. At that time, when the visions were drawing tens of thousands of spectators, the government had not been worried or at least had not acted. Paradoxically, when the Republic did crack down in 1932, there were far fewer spectators and the visions were much less of a threat. There was no longer the kind of chemistry among newspapers, seers, and social anxiety that a year before had turned seers into political subversives. The difference in the government's reaction may lie in its greater insecurity after the coup attempt or, more simply, in the personality of the new governor.[26]

Pedro del Pozo Rodríguez came to Gipuzkoa as governor on 20 August 1932 from Avila, where he had been governor since the creation of the Second Republic. Spanish *governadores civiles,* like prefects in France, are above all in charge of public order and police. During the Republic they were generally young, well-educated members of political parties in the government. Those in the provinces of the north, where the majority of citizens opposed the Republic and the political landscape was as complicated and rugged as the physical one, were men in the confidence of key members of the cabinet. *La Voz de Guipúzcoa* noted that del Pozo was "bound by ties of close personal and political friendship with [the prime minister] Señor Azaña" and that Azaña had personally briefed him.[27]

Just one month later del Pozo served notice in the press on the Ezkioga seers and believers, who had been gathering in greater numbers at the new chapel:

MORE MIRACLES AT EZQUIOGA?
Word has reached the governor's office that there is a renewal at Ezquioga of reactionary religious movements, using as a pretext apparitions recently discredited by an official of the church.

It is surprising after the presidential visit to Guipúzcoa, a visit that was a triumph without precedent, after the approval of the Statute of Catalonia and a renewed governmental interest in coming to terms with the Basque Country, that once more the name of Ezquioga should be heard from the lips of deceivers who with the pretext of the alleged apparitions are undertaking a political campaign.

The governor is ready to act in this matter and will tolerate no more "miracles." Our enemies must play fair. They cannot be allowed to play politics with religious images that deserve their total respect. Seeking to maintain the faith, in fact they destroy and undermine it with their maneuvers.

"As long as I am in this post," Señor del Pozo told us, "I will not tolerate this kind of politics disguised as religion."

Very severe measures will be taken.[28]

On October 1, ten days after this warning, the Bordas and Burguera booklet on Ezkioga came out, and on October 6 or 7 Echezarreta installed the new image of the Virgin on its pedestal to "ardent tears, continuous prayers, pious hymns, and fervent applause." All of the slow accretions of liturgical respectability had come to this climax, an image in a shrine, complete with a Way of the Cross on its approach, a holy spring, and a photographer standing by at the foot of the hill.[29]

The final straw for del Pozo was an incident on a train from Zumarraga to San Sebastián on the afternoon of October 8. Tomás Imaz and two other believers, brothers who owned a bakery in San Sebastián, were returning to the city with the seer Marcelina Eraso. As they prayed out loud, Marcelina fell into a vision. At least one of the passengers began complaining vociferously that Imaz was exploiting the seer, and in San Sebastián police hauled off the little group for disturbing the peace. Dr. José Bago, the head of medicine for the government in the province and a republican hero, examined Eraso and sent her for observation to the provincial mental hospital. The governor reprimanded Imaz and fined him five hundred pesetas.[30]

The following afternoon Governor del Pozo stopped at Ezkioga to see for himself what was going on. There was quite a crowd, and when Echezarreta came forward, del Pozo ordered him to remove the image by daybreak, to forbid entry to the site, and to take down the souvenir stands. If he did not, the government would dynamite the chapel. Perhaps not understanding the fine points of the matter, del Pozo told him to put the outlaw image in the parish church. He suggested that if Echezarreta wanted to be altruistic he could offer the property for a school. The photographer from Terrassa, Joaquín Sicart, his livelihood in immediate danger, alerted the Catalan supporters.[31]

Echezarreta agreed to remove the image, but he had not counted on the opposition of the believers, who swore to defend it. When he returned with workers from his paper mill, there was a tense standoff. Echezarreta paused to pray part of a rosary so as not to offend the Virgin, whereupon the believers declared they would pray fifty rosaries for the Virgin to strike dead the first to touch her. The workmen then refused to help. Burguera intervened to calm things down and persuaded Echezarreta not to remove anything; rather he should let the governor do it. The standoff around the image continued from October 10 to 13 with round-the-clock prayers and visions. Del Pozo insisted not only that Echezarreta take the statue away but also that he raze the chapel and wall off the site. Four seers told Echezarreta from the Virgin that he should not give in. Civil guards protected the workers as they dismantled the stands at the foot of the hill.[32]

José Garmendia defended his image and temple as best he could by visiting President Francesc Macià once more in Catalonia. He arrived in Barcelona on October 12, and that evening, in the private chapel of a wealthy believer, he asked the Virgin whether the image was still at the Ezkioga site. He said she refused to tell him in order to spare his feelings. The next day believers drove Garmendia and Salvador Cardús to Macià's country home at Vallmanya in the province of

Lleida. There Garmendia and Macià spoke for about fifteen minutes in the patio. According to Garmendia, Macià said that he preferred not to approach the prime minister, Manuel Azaña, who was a republican of the "red" variety but would speak instead to the president of the Republic, Niceto Alcalá-Zamora, "who always goes to mass," and ask him to intervene "to leave you in peace." Garmendia gave him a photograph of the image and the Bordas pamphlet. That night at Ezkioga about thirty believers and seers stayed with the image. Many but not all present thought they saw the image weep, and at three in the morning they sent for Burguera. He too saw the weeping and drew up an affidavit that those present signed.[33]

Cardús arrived the next day just after workmen had removed the statue from the chapel. He just had time to kiss the images of the surrounding angels before the workers took them away. Citing the diocesan ban on objects associated with the visions, Sinforoso de Ibarguren had refused to let the image into the parish church, so the workers had carried it to the nearest farm. They did so reverently, on their knees, praying the rosary to the tears of the onlookers. Shortly afterward, they sawed down the great cross that Patxi had erected a year before, and it broke into pieces as it fell. Many of the several hundred persons present gathered splinters as relics. For the seers and believers, who so often had simulated crucifixion or acted out the stations of the cross, the Passion was taking place yet again at Ezkioga. They saw Echezarreta as a coward and Ibarguren as Judas. Cardús described the fall of the cross with the words of Christ: "Consummatum est, it is finished." Many seers had visions and all of them wept. The believers held continuous rosaries, some fearing divine punishment, others pleading for the Virgin to make herself visible. "In the meantime the blows of the hammers and chisels that began to demolish the building cut into people's hearts." That evening the mayor of Ezkioga announced on behalf of the governor that as of the next day all seers who had visions in public would be jailed. After dinner Cardús returned to find the image adorned with flowers and lit by a multitude of candles. Believers prayed before it in the rain.[34]

On October 15, the feast of Teresa de Avila and the anniversary of Ramona's wounds, Salvador Cardús was surprised to encounter his spiritual director, Magdalena Aulina herself. She had come incognito as "María Boada," and with her were José María, Tomás, and Carmen Boada and Ignasi Llanza. Together in the rain they watched the workers remove the iron grille from the chapel. Around noon, on orders from the governor, the workers stopped. Burguera speculated that Macià's intercession with the government had had some effect, but it could also have been the result of the meeting in San Sebastián of Echezarreta, the mayor and town secretary of Ezkioga, and the governor. Nevertheless, civil guards prevented people from going up the hill. Sometime during the day Echezarreta had his workers take the image in a wheelbarrow down to a house on the road and install it in what had been Burguera's room.[35]

The Boada party invited Cardús, Garmendia, and Burguera to lunch in Zumarraga. There Burguera told them that his superior, the archbishop of Valencia, Prudencio Melo y Alcalde, had ordered him to go home. He was not obeying. According to Cardús,

> P. Burguera also revealed his contacts in regard to the events at Ezkioga with the papal nuncio, who several times has expressed interest in them, even though he had said he could not intervene in the internal affairs of the diocese. The nuncio had a note given to P. Burguera to pass on with this significant message for Ramona Olazábal, dated 25 July 1932. *"Tell Ramona from me to suffer with patience everything that Our Lord God sends her, and if she is innocent He will help her and she will triumph over all."*[36]

On their return to Ezkioga, the party found believers and onlookers had arrived by car and bus and were milling about on the road. The houses along the road were full of believers praying and in almost every one a seer was having visions. A few defied the ban on outdoor visions. The original boy seer had his at the back door, facing the nearby apple trees. Evarista Galdós had hers under apple trees near the road and told Cardús that the Virgin told her to tell Burguera not to worry, that she (the Virgin) would watch over him. To the others she said, "Don't forget that the Virgin has said that there would be martyrs here!" Benita excitedly told José María Boada that she would write him from jail and that the Virgin had told her, "This is the hour of my soldiers." Even though she had met Magdalena Aulina in Barcelona, Benita did not see through the disguise; she even asked to be remembered to her. The guards heard that Patxi had had an outdoor vision and they tried to find him, but he escaped through a house to the hills. Then they tried in vain to locate Evarista, whom Cardús found huddling in a bus, "like a dove waiting to be sacrificed." That evening Burguera and his family were praying before the image and again saw that it seemed to weep, although there was no liquid on it. Burguera pronounced that here was not one miracle, an image weeping, but as many miracles as people who were seeing the image weep, for separate miracles were affecting the eyes of each.[37]

To round out this eventful day, around midnight Cardús went with Garmendia to the foot of the hill. Garmendia had had a vision in the afternoon and expected another. Since the houses were all closed for the night, they prayed by the road. Garmendia saw Gemma Galgani and the Virgin. He said the Virgin told him she was happy they had come out so late. As Cardús said good-bye to Garmendia on the dark road, a car went by and they heard one occupant say to another, "Poor man, what a shame!" It was the son of Garmendia's employer in Legazpi.[38]

The next day the Catalan party, including Magdalena Aulina in disguise, stopped to say good-bye to Burguera and Cardús. They said the rosary, and

Garmendia entered into a lengthy trance in which he described the Virgin, Gemma Galgani, and the devil, who threatened him. Aulina almost gave herself away by pointing and saying, "Look! Our Mother!" After the rosary, pilgrims arrived from Pamplona with a letter from Pilar Ciordia, who claimed that the previous day the Virgin had said to tell Burguera that she was at his side. Burguera pointed out to the visitors that Evarista had said the same thing and that seers regularly coincided in this way. The Boada party left an observer but took Cardús, our witness, back with them to Barcelona.[39]

The governor opened a judicial inquiry on October 11. Because of the Gipuzkoa newspaper strike, we catch only glimpses of the witnesses. Echezarreta testified on October 14 and October 18. Garmendia, Patxi, the child Conchita Mateos from Beasain, and María Luisa of Zaldibia appeared on October 21. Patxi had a vision before the magistrate, who sent all these seers to the mental hospital. Burguera wrote Cardús theatrically about the catacombs and of "repeating the early days of the church" and forwarded a letter from Garmendia asking further help from Macià.[40]

Over the next week the magistrate called Ignacio Galdós, Evarista, Benita, Recalde, Rosario Gurruchaga, and Vicente Gurruchaga. When seers took the train for San Sebastián, small groups of believers greeted them at many stations with flowers. On October 28 del Pozo appointed a trusted republican and fellow Freemason, Alfonso Rodríguez Dranguet, as special magistrate. By then the case centered principally on Burguera and other organizers for "fraud and sedition." This judge saw witnesses for about a month and finally remanded the case to the court in Azpeitia. Believers estimated that thirty to forty persons testified in all.[41]

Burguera compiled a list of the magistrates' questions and noted the following themes: how the Virgin looked; how the visions took place; how the visions related to the Republic and if and when anyone sang the royalist anthem, "Marcha Real"; what Padre Burguera's role was; whether the seers gained any benefit from the visions; how the seers and believers organized their meetings and who were the ringleaders; whether they disobeyed church authority; and what the Catalans were up to.

The magistrate and the governor did not know what to do with seers who talked back, fell into swoons, and were ready for the worst. The telling and retelling of the dialogues, however improved or apocryphal, gave the seers an aura of martyrdom. The girls and women enjoyed going beyond the passive role of victims of God to become, like the men, active witnesses against iniquity. The believers appreciated this shift, which was in keeping with the well-publicized imprisonment of women for holding religious processions and returning crucifixes to schools.[42]

The authorities released several seers after questioning them. The judge questioned Evarista on October 26. She claimed later that the Virgin told her what to answer. When the judge asked her whether she had seen a devil, she said she had. When he asked whether the devil was naked or clothed, she allegedly said, "He was dressed like you." After more questions he let her go. A young woman from rural Urrestilla, Rosario Gurruchaga, seems to have had a fit. After ten minutes only the neighbor who accompanied her was able to unclasp Rosario's hands by touching them with a crucifix. The judge did not commit Rosario either. Benita was euphoric before she went. She wrote García Cascón, "Thank God we are not crazy; knowing this I am ready to go anywhere, as if on a social call. I am so happy I cannot explain it." The magistrate quizzed her on general knowledge, such as the capital of France, and sent her home too.[43]

On November 25 Ramona's spiritual director went with her to San Sebastián. This was Ramona's second appearance, and the priest relayed some of the exchanges to Cardús.

> Ramona told me that the judge asked her if she sees the Virgin. She said she did. [He asked] at what distance she saw it, was it within shooting range? I think at that moment Ramona had some kind of divine inspiration. She replied that yes, that she saw it close enough to fire on a civil guard, but it was the Virgin. The curious thing about this is that the man who asked this question some days before the Republic was established in Spain killed a civil guard in a riot in San Sebastián.[44]

The Catalans heard that when the judge asked María Recalde if she had lost any weight on her repeated trips to Ezkioga, she said she had. Portly like her, the judge said that maybe he too should go. She told him it would do him good—his body would lose weight and his soul would gain it. Allegedly via a vision on October 22 Recalde was sure that Justo de Echeguren was behind the government offensive.

> Judge: What did the Virgin tell you about the Republic?
>
> Recalde: She told us nothing.
>
> J: But she must have said that now we are worse than before.
>
> R: No. Before you acted against the clergy; now it is the clergy that has gotten you to act against us.
>
> J: Who told you that?
>
> R: I have my sources.
>
> J: Well, the vicar general told me he would not tell anybody.

In Burguera's account she went on to say that she laughed at her accusers, that she feared her heavenly judge, not the earthly one. She spent a night in a holding cell and went on to the mental home.[45]

Burguera, the big fish, was called to San Sebastián on November 3 along with José Joaquín Azpiazu, the justice of the peace in whose house he was staying.

Burguera claims that the court typist told him that three priests from around Ezkioga had already been there to testify against him. The governor held Burguera responsible for the resurgence of the visions in the summer of 1932 and thought he had "manipulated people who were mentally ill in order to maintain the fiction of the visions." He said Burguera had "created more seers, held clandestine meetings, and organized apparitions, in some cases where the Marcha Real was played during the visions." He therefore jailed Burguera, releasing him seven nights later on condition that he leave Gipuzkoa. By that time the press had held Burguera up to ridicule. *El Socialista* of Madrid printed a satirical poem "The Last Miracle-Worker," which referred to "Padre Amado," who first lost his license to say mass "because he wanted to do miracles on his own without the permission of the holy mother church" and then was "thrown in the clink" for conspiring against the government.[46]

Shortly after the governor released Burguera, the mental hospital released the seers, virtually all with a clean bill of health. Recalde had visions there, convincing some of the nuns who were nurses. Catalans from the Aulina group had gone to intercede with the staff. Del Pozo fined five prominent believers a thousand pesetas each, substantial sums. He told the press he had received a letter from Navarra saying that a female seer saw devils dragging his soul into hell. After he was transferred to the province of Cádiz on December 7 the government left the seers alone. Civil guards stopped patrolling the site in late November because the towns could not pay them.[47]

Like Recalde, the other seers and believers were convinced the diocese was behind the government's actions, something Bishop Múgica vigorously denied. A more elaborate theory was that the diocese sponsored the Laburu lectures in exchange for the bishop's return from France. Múgica entered Spain on 13 May 1932 through the intercession of Cardinal-archbishop Vidal i Barraquer and of the nuncio with Prime Minister Azaña. But he could not go back to his diocese of Vitoria for a year, and it is unlikely that Ezkioga, after 1931 a negligible threat to public order, had anything to do with his return.[48]

PADRE BURGUERA IN CHARGE

Burguera's imprisonment consecrated him as the defender of the seers. Benita had a vision that he would be a martyr, Patxi said the Virgin had a crown for him, and Garmendia said the Virgin called Burguera "your apostle." When he got out of jail, Burguera seems to have concentrated on finishing his book, and he went at once to Barcelona for copies of the Catalans' documents of cures and predictions. A month later, in mid-December 1932, he took his manuscript to a bishop he thought would be sympathetic, probably Luis Amigó of Segorbe. On 1 April 1933 he found out that the diocese would not give him permission to publish, and a month later the seers had visions that he should print the book anyway.[49]

All this time he was away from Ezkioga, but he did not forget his flock of seers and believers. He wrote many individually; he also sent an apostolic letter to the group. Assuming his position by divine right, he reproved the seers for denigrating one another, urged humility, and told them not to let themselves be photographed. The devil, he warned, was always ready to disturb their friendships and imitate true visions. He urged them to check against the devil by asking the apparition to repeat a pious phrase, by examining their own feelings after a vision, by vetting messages through other seers in trance, by consulting with their personal spiritual director, and by clearing messages for the general public with him, their "general director." He warned that if they did not behave well, God would take away their gift, and he closed commending them to "Gemma, the efficacious protector of our work" (see text in appendix).

The Mission of Juan Bautista Ayerbe

In Burguera's absence a new defender came forward. Juan Bautista Ayerbe Irastorza was the secretary of the small town of Urnieta, forty kilometers northeast of Ezkioga. There his brother Juan José was the parish priest. Previously, while town secretary of Segura, Ayerbe had rescued the municipal archive and published a book of local history. In August 1919 he visited Limpias and he wrote about those visions in national newspapers.[50]

From his enormous output of mimeographed, dittoed, and typewritten semi-public letters and leaflets, it seems Ayerbe started circulating news of the Ezkioga visions in December 1932. He was led to believe in his own divine mission by Patxi.

> On Saturday, the third of this month of December [1932], the seer Francisco Goicoechea went up the apparition mountain at four in the afternoon. During his ecstasy, which lasted about forty minutes, he received four messages. The third of these was for a J. B. A., who lived near San Sebastián, who thereby satisfied a wish made to the Holy Virgin on the same day at ten in the morning without contact with the seer. The message has a close connection with these notes.[51]

It took courage and commitment to defend this cause when many seers were in the mental hospital and Burguera himself was just out of jail.

A visiting expert helped confirm Ayerbe's belief in the visions. In mid-December 1932 Father Thomas Matyschok, "Professor of Psychic Sciences" from Germany, told him that the ecstasies of Conchita Mateos of Beasain were supernatural. That month Ayerbe wrote his first pamphlet, "The Marvelous

Juan Bautista Ayerbe, ca. 1930. Courtesy Matilde Ayerbe

Apparitions of the Most Holy Virgin in Ezkioga," and distributed two hundred dittoed copies in January.

Conchita Mateos was the twelve-year-old daughter of a worker in a Beasain factory. Ayerbe wrote, "She is the seer with whom I have most contact and whom I like the best because of her angelic manner and a prudence truly unusual in a girl her age." She was the youngest seer sent to the insane asylum. The real-estate agent Tomás Imaz took down some of her vision messages in December 1932 and subsequently Ayerbe went weekly to visions in her house in Beasain. About twenty persons generally attended these visions. She also had them in Ayerbe's house in Urnieta, where the Virgin showed a special partiality for Ayerbe's family. Ayerbe also distributed the vision messages of Luis Irurzun of Navarra, Esperanza Aranda, an older woman who then had most of her visions in San Sebastián, and others to believers in Terrassa, Barcelona, Madrid, and San Sebastián.[52]

His children grew up in a house where the presence of rapt visionaries was normal. According to his son Daniel, Ayerbe was devoted to anyone who was a believer. "He would not leave you alone, bringing you one thing after another until he overwhelmed you. But if you did not take an interest, you were public enemy number one." As Ayerbe wrote García Cascón, "I cannot disguise my sincere love for all who share my fervor for the apparitions. Maybe it is because there are so few of us or because we are so persecuted. . . . Is it because we imitate to some extent the first Christians of the catacombs?"[53]

In spite of his "obsessive," "fanatical" (the words are his son's) activity in favor of the visions, an activity that lasted the rest of his life, Ayerbe never took sides among the seers or the leaders and was relatively modest. He did not want to threaten the careers of his brothers, so he usually remained just inside the limits of what might bring a public rebuke from the diocese. Because of the priests in his family, however, he was able to get away with more than others. He did not have a personal agenda for the visions, like Rigné, or a political one, like Carmen Medina; he was simply a scribe. Although he was an Integrist, his involvement in the visions stemmed from an interest in the politics not of Spain but of heaven—the broader designs that God held out for humanity. He wanted Ezkioga, as he had wanted Limpias, to be the Spanish Lourdes, but this time he went deeper and circulated messages about chastisements and Antichrists.

Ayerbe kept in touch with Pedro Balda, town secretary of Iraneta (Navarra), who served as the seer Luis Irurzun's scribe. In the rural north town secretaries were professionals with typewriters and time to use them. As the representatives of literate bureaucracy in rural villages, Ayerbe and Balda provided the seers with some local credibility. But their influence in the wider society was slight. On that level people like Medina, Burguera, and Rigné had more impact.

Away from Ezkioga in the winter and spring of 1933, Burguera worried about bad news he heard about the seers. From March 25 to 27 he accompanied a small group to Lourdes. At the grotto he felt that the Virgin confirmed his mission again. For when he asked the Virgin through a female seer in his group whether they might stay longer, the Virgin purportedly answered, "Tell the Padre that his duty is to go at once to Ezquioga, and when he has the Ezquioga matter all fixed up as at Lourdes, then he may come here."[54]

Burguera no doubt knew that in mid-March 1933 one of the teenage seers had given birth to a child. Believers explained away the pregnancy by rape and dignified the birth by claiming it occurred without pain during a vision. But for the general public the pregnancy was a disgrace that affected the apparitions as a whole.[55] The scandal, which roused the many people in the region who had become skeptical, showed up in the broadsides of verses which are a Basque tradition. In October and November 1931 both the famous bertsolari (oral versifiers) José Manuel Lujanbio Retegi ("Txirrita") and his relative from Ordizia, Patxi Erauskin Errota, had published verses in praise of the seers Ramona and Patxi. Now José Urdanpilleta responded with two sheets. No doubt the most effective was the unsigned, scurrilous "The Great Miracle of the Virgin of Ezquioga," in which he identified by village two girls who had become pregnant and one boy who, he said, was as licentious as a ram and had even corrupted two nuns. Urdanpilleta had at least one public verse debate on the subject with Txirrita, and old-timers still remember lines from the argument. The Albiztur enthusiast Luistar published verses in support of the seers in 1931; but Laburu persuaded him to change his mind and in 1933 he published a long verse sequence against the seers. For Luistar and Urdanpilleta the great issue was immorality. Txirrita had claimed the visions were true because they led to conversion; these poets claimed the visions were false because they led to sin.[56]

Prior to clearing up the scandals, Burguera had to recover his dignity. He attempted to do so in a four-page printed encomium signed by Ayerbe. It called for serious study of the Ezkioga visions and presented Burguera as "extraordinarily expert in the theological and ascetic-mystic matters so necessary for clarifying and resolving the apparitions . . . very well known by the intellectual elite of the Catholic world . . . armed with stunning erudition and perspicacity . . . with an apostolic zeal and an iron will." It described the Studium Catholicum, listed Burguera's published and unpublished works, and reproduced the entry for Burguera in the main Spanish encyclopedia ("a wise theologian").[57]

The scandals, following the attacks by the church and the Republic, convinced Burguera that he had to do some serious "weeding" of the seers. His perplexity because some seers refused him their vision messages grew to a conviction that the devil was at work. After a month taking counsel with the Virgin in the visions of Ciordia, Benita, Aranda, and Garmendia, Burguera called a general meeting of seers. There he tried to rein in those who had taken advantage of their special status to lead freer lives. He told the girls who had found lodgings in order to be close to the vision site to go home, and he forbade seers to go on any more excursions.

Burguera claimed that some of the seers disobeyed him and started a "schism" because they did not want to give up their newfound liberty. In fact, any unity was in his own mind. He himself wrote that by this time there were three kinds of seers, the docile and obedient ones (obedient to him, that is), the untutored and credulous ones (by which I think he refers to the more rural, less classy or attractive seers, including those who spoke only Basque and trusted other, Basque-speaking leaders like Tomás Imaz and Juan Bautista Ayerbe), and the crafty and proud ones (he meant in particular Ramona and Patxi), who enjoyed the limelight and let no one direct them. As he began to do his weeding, the seers he rejected came out openly against him.[58]

By now Burguera made no move without divine authority from trusted visionaries. He first tested the seers in vision by burning them on the hand with

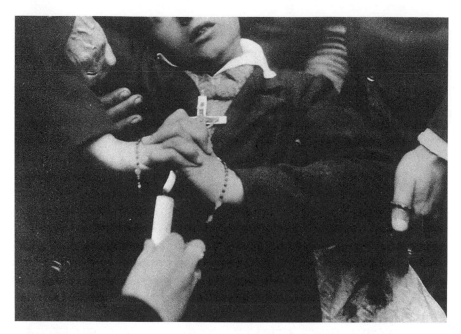

Padre Burguera, probably, tests with a candle a boy seer in vision, mid-1933 (detail). Photo by Raymond de Rigné, all rights reserved. Courtesy Arxiu Salvador Cardús i Florensa, Terrassa

the flame of a candle. Those passed who did not react and felt no pain after the vision. For him this did not mean automatically that the visions were divine, but it did mean that the seers were worthy of further study.[59] When he tested Esperanza Aranda on 5 May 1933 in San Sebastián, two believing priests were witnesses. The flame burned "skin, flesh, and cartilage, causing a blister and a wound." Aranda did not react and her pulse remained steady. Lorenzo Jayo was present when Burguera tested his mother, María Recalde, at Ezkioga and remembers vividly the fat in her finger melting and a wound forming. A French writer saw the badly burned hand of José Garmendia. Rigné photographed Burguera burning with a candle the clasped hands of a boy in trance. In Albiztur he did the tests in the home of the parish priest. By July 14 sixteen seers had passed; others took the test later.[60]

These tests coincided with a new diocesan offensive. Starting in May 1933, less than a month after his return to Vitoria, Bishop Múgica instructed parish priests to obtain signed statements from the prominent seers, including Benita, Evarista, Ramona, and Gloria Viñals. The seers should retract their visions and vow not to go to the hillside. Benita signed that she would not go but added that she did so on the Virgin's instruction. She continued to have visions at home and when her parish priest found out and she refused to declare her visions diabolical or illusory, he excluded her from the church. Accompanied by prominent Bilbao believers, her parents went to the bishop to protest, but Múgica went a step further and denied the child all the sacraments. Most other seers agreed to suspend their trips to the site, but few if any retracted the visions.

The combined pressure from Burguera to prove some visions "false" and from the bishop to force seers to retract the visions sent many seers into a kind of tailspin. They desperately sought divine messages that would please Burguera and affirm his authority. Garmendia, for instance, told him that the Virgin had said that all seers should obey Burguera and that whenever she had a message for Burguera, she would appear to Garmendia as long as necessary.[61]

By the end of May Burguera's most trusted seers began to help by specifying the number of "true" seers who remained. Then, supposedly repeating what the Virgin told them, they began to finger the false ones. Pilar Ciordia declared that Conchita Mateos's visions were diabolical and that others should not go to the house. Burguera broke the bad news to the family, and Conchita agreed to a fire test. She passed and delivered a message: Burguera did well to test seers and those who disobeyed were not true seers. But Burguera nevertheless excluded her because of others he trusted more.[62]

The accusing continued, as in a witch-hunt. On June 3 Benita heard the Virgin say that Burguera should remove all reference to Patxi from the book because of the things he made up ("sus mixtificaciones"). Two days later Benita learned from the Virgin that of nine true seers only four would remain. The three others she had in mind would have been Evarista, whose visions she was explicitly confirming, Pilar Ciordia, who came from Pamplona to stay at her house from time to time, and her friend María Recalde. These four gradually eliminated others. On June 29 Burguera informed the Bilbao supporter Sebastián López de Lerena that his protégée Gloria Viñals was no longer a true seer. Burguera based this judgment on a vision by Evarista in Irun. On the same day Evarista and Garmendia declared that Burguera should remove from the book those who did not obey him.[63]

Seers had more spectacular visions under the stress of denouncing their friends. On July 14 Burguera and others watched an eight-hour Passion trance of Pilar and Evarista. The seers had announced the event twelve days in advance; lying on the floor they described the devil in the form of a great serpent encircling and strangling them. As they went through the motions of the Passion and were attacked by twelve devils (whose tortures with giant needles must have been reminiscent of Burguera's tests), they narrated their experience through a running dialogue with the Virgin. The Virgin took part in the crucifying. The ordeal was a sign for the upcoming chastisement of the sinful people in "packed theaters and movie houses and crowded beaches" who did not believe the apparitions. The Virgin was most bitter about the disobedient ex-seers who had once believed but then after falling into evil company abandoned her. But Pilar and Evarista were obedient. "No Mother, we wish to be very good. Rather than stop seeing thee, we prefer a thousand deaths."[64]

The core seers heard the Virgin say where to print the book and warned Burguera not to open certain letters, for the diocese wanted to pack him off to Valencia. Burguera was present in Navarra when Evarista in Basque and Pilar in Spanish both claimed to see eight devils drag the vicar general (yet again) to hell.[65]

Burguera also felt the pressure, for the seers confirmed that the devil was out to stop him. Benita Aguirre, who had taken refuge with believers in Girona when denied Communion in Legazpi, wrote that in a vision she had seen him writing his book with good angels on one side and bad angels on the other. She and Evarista had seen a false Ezkioga book held by the devil, whom Evarista saw disguised as Gemma Galgani. Because the devil might interfere with his revisions, Burguera had to check his proofs and arguments with seers.[66]

On 16 July 1933 Burguera, Garmendia, and Baudilio Sedano were in the hallway of the Hotel Urola in Zumarraga on their way to lunch. An uncouth man came in and warned Burguera he should "stop persecuting at Ezkioga." Burguera told the hotel owner to call the police because of the threat, but the man had disappeared (mysteriously, Burguera thought). The man could well have been a relative or follower of one of the seers whom Burguera was busy repudiating, but Burguera was convinced that he had seen the devil in human form, something María Recalde confirmed in a vision two days later.[67]

The conflict between Burguera's seers and those he excluded came to a head a week later when on the apparition hillside Benita Aguirre's father read a warning from the Virgin that those who disobeyed Padre Burguera would suffer terrible divine punishment. The rumor was out that Burguera had asked as a special grace that only the seers who cooperated with him could see the Virgin. That would have simplified his job of discernment considerably. The first to react was Rigné, who on July 25 printed an open letter warning the seers that priests in rebellion against the church were misleading them. Instead, he said that they should consider Bishop Múgica Christ's representative and pray that he change his mind. The true history of the apparitions, he wrote, could only come from a canonical inquiry. Rigné was convinced that the seers who refused to obey Burguera were the most trustworthy.[68]

Sebastián López de Lerena, an electrical engineer from Bizkaia who was perhaps the most balanced and realistic of the opinion leaders among the believers, wrote a stinging letter to Burguera denouncing his errors, his self-appointed authority over the seers, his improper trials by fire, not approved by theologians, and his attempt to blackmail seers into giving him their vision messages for his book under threat of declaring them nonseers. Above all López de Lerena charged that Burguera had unwittingly suggested many of the visions. He blamed the padre for dividing believers when more than ever they needed to stand together. These attacks increased Burguera's testiness. In the ensuing days he had a falling out with José Garmendia. Two weeks later Pilar Ciordia told him that he had just avoided an ambush on his way from Zumarraga to Benita's house.[69]

While the seers and their leaders were squabbling, Bishop Múgica of Vitoria was preparing a dossier against the Ezkioga apparitions. On 19 August 1933 he sent the Holy Office an extensive account in Latin of the visions. In mid-September he published in the diocesan bulletin "On the Alleged Supernatural-ness of What Is Going On at Ezquioga." In this circular he denied the visions any supernatural content and prohibited Catholics from retaining any pictures, pho-tographs, images, hymns, leaflets, books, or mimeo material relating to the visions. Further, he instructed parish priests to notify seers in the presence of two witnesses that they could not go to the sites of visions on penalty of being denied Holy Communion, and he requested the remaining believers to avoid vision sites or conclaves.

After repeating in summary form many of Laburu's arguments, Múgica dwelt at greater length on the blatant disobedience of the seers and "their self-appointed protectors, panegyrists, and publicists." He attacked Burguera by name as

in open rebellion without permission from his Bishop and without Ours, violating the prohibition imposed on priests personally delivered to him on several occasions, arrogating to himself the position, which no one has given him, of spiritual director of the "seers." For his obstinacy and contu-macy We are obliged to denounce and publicly rebuke his scandalous con-duct.[70]

I suspect that Múgica had not counted on publishing this strong stand as soon as he did. But on September 8 and 9 he faced a new promoter who might radically expand the audience for the visions.[71]

The International Challenge: Léon Degrelle

The challenge came from Léon Degrelle, an energetic Catholic militant al-ready well known in his Belgian homeland. As a student at Louvain, Degrelle had supported the French rightist Charles Maurras, and he was famous for anti-communist pranks. He was also active in the Catholic Action movement, and in 1929 he had gone to Mexico, where he spent several months with the Cristero Catholic rebels. After he graduated in 1931 he revitalized the Catholic Action publishing house, Éditions Rex. In the fall of 1933 Rex was in financial diffi-culties, which Degrelle alleviated partially by promoting and profiting from the new apparitions in Belgium.[72]

The first of a series of Belgian visions began at Beauraing in an artificial grotto to the Virgin of Lourdes on 29 November 1932. There, before a total audience of 150,000 persons, five children, aged nine to fifteen, had visions until 3 January 1933. Then from January 15 to March 2 an eleven-year-old girl had eight visions at Banneux. At Beauraing there was a new seer in the summer of 1933, an adult male who was supposedly cured on June 11 and who had visions in June, July, and August, drawing a crowd of 300,000 on August 5. Subsequently individuals had visions in Onkerzele and Etichove in Flemish Belgium as well as at other sites.[73]

News of the Beauraing visions reached San Sebastián in mid-December 1932 as "An Ezquioga in Belgium." Even foreign Catholic commentators observed that the Belgian "epidemic of heavenly communications" was like "occurrences of a somewhat similar nature at Ezquioga." Supporters of the Belgian visions preferred to compare them with those at Lourdes. The Walloon dioceses of Belgium had some of the highest rates of attendance and some of the greatest numbers of Lourdes pilgrimages outside of France. In this they were similar to the dioceses of Vitoria and Barcelona. There were other similarities. Like the Basque Country, Belgium was peopled by two groups with different languages. Both had highly devout rural areas cheek by jowl with industrial development. And for Spanish Catholics hoping to recapture the allegiance of the working class, Belgium was a model to follow.[74]

The Ezkioga believers had shown immediate interest in Beauraing. In June 1933 the photographer Joaquín Sicart printed a sheet that compared the two sets of visions. He pointed to the numerical superiority of Ezkioga in terms of visionaries and visions and contrasted the publicity and the sympathetic diocesan attitude in Belgium to the paltry number of pamphlets and the harassment of seers in Spain.[75]

As soon as Degrelle read about the visions in Beauraing, which lay close to his hometown in the Ardennes, he left for the site. As at Ezkioga, so at Beauraing: in the absence of an official inquiry the local doctor played a central role in evaluating the visionaries and served as a liaison with the press. Degrelle persuaded him to write a quick description and published it while the visions were still in progress. The pamphlet sold phenomenally both in Belgium and in France. As apparitions unfurled across the land, Degrelle published at least six other pamphlets on visions at Beauraing, Banneux, and other sites.[76]

Articles in the French photo magazine *VU* may have alerted Degrelle to the potential of the Ezkioga visions. In any case, at the beginning of September 1933 he showed up with a team of writers. His group observed a seer in Tolosa and visited Gloria Viñals in Bilbao. She surprised them by telling of a set of visions in Belgium they did not know about. Luis Irurzun cooperated with a vision that confirmed the authenticity of the Belgian apparitions. On the night of September 9 the group put up a cross where that of Patxi had been cut down. Some of the

Las apariciones de la Stma. Virgen en BELGICA y en EZQUIOGA

DATOS COMPARATIVOS

Del 29 de Noviembre de 1932 al 3 de Enero de 1933, la Stma. Virgen se apareció unas 33 veces a cinco niños en Beauraing (Bélgica).

De Enero a Marzo se ha aparecido por 6 veces en Baneux (Bélgica a la niña Mariete Becó, y el 25 de Mayo se colocó la primera piedra de la creación de una capilla, bendiciéndola el Excmo. Sr. Obispo.

A raiz de dichas apariciones se han publicado unos 50 libros, y han salido dos revistas.

El 30 de Junio de 1931 se apareció la Stma. Virgen en Ezquioga a dos niños, y desde aquella fecha no ha dejado de aparecerse ni un solo día a multitud de personas de todas las edades, lo mismo a hombres que a mujeres, siendo los niños los más favorecidos.

Se han publicado tres folletos.

TOTAL EN BELGICA:

Videntes	6
Apariciones	39
Libros	50
Revistas	2
Capillas con todas las de la ley	1

EN EZQUIOGA:

Videntes más de cien
Apariciones, sólo a un vidente cerca de tres mil.
Libros, 3 folletitos
Revistas, ninguna.

Lo que no pueden escribir en Bélgica es una persecución tan despiadada como la que están sufriendo los videntes de la Stma. Virgen de Ezquioga, la cual contribuye a hermosear y a embellecer la historia que se haga de las apariciones.

Ezquioga 30 de Junio de 1933

Pidan el mensaje de la Stma. Virgen a sus devotos de Ezquioga en la tienda

SICART
Colección de 20 fotografías
a 6 pesetas contra reembolso

Ampliaciones fotográficas. SICART es el que más barato las hace

---

local Ezkioga believers at once wrote the bishop, asking him to allow the cross to remain and informing him proudly that the Belgians were in Ezkioga "gathering ample information about the apparitions which they will distribute throughout Europe."[77] Múgica's pastoral letter forestalled Degrelle, who had time to issue only photographs of four seers in his magazine *Soirées* with a note announcing a major series of articles. He never published the series.[78]

The bishop's circular placed the Ezkioga visions out of bounds for ordinary people. By having it read in all parish churches on September 17 and 24 and once again in the month of October, Múgica ensured that no Catholic in his diocese failed to hear about it. The circular made official the discredit from Laburu's talk, from the governmental offensive, and from slanderous verses. Many believers did as they were told and handed in postcards, leaflets, books, and other memorabilia. Others gave their souvenirs and vision material to friends in neighboring dioceses to keep. On October 12 when Luis Irurzun had a vision on the hillside, only twenty-two persons were there to watch.[79]

The bishop's decree stunned the vision community. It was Múgica's first public act against the visions since his return to the diocese. Rigné was dismayed at the blanket dismissal of all seers and believers and at what seemed to be a reference to himself, though he felt Burguera got what he deserved. He and his wife went to mass in another town so they would not have to hear it read in front of their neighbors.[80]

As Laburu had done after his talk, Múgica attempted after his decree to silence particular visionaries. On 18 September 1933 when he was in Durango he called María Recalde to the church of Santa María; three priests were present. I have only her version of events—that he tried to get her not to go to the vision hillside or to meet with believers, under denial of Holy Communion, and that he was particularly interested in Padre Burguera and her written vision messages. She told him that just as the apostles had to shed their blood to spread belief in Christ, so the seers were ready to shed theirs for Ezkioga. Similarly, the parish priest of Legazpi confronted Pilar Ciordia, who was staying at Benita's house. Her replies, at least as Burguera reported them, were just as spunky. Other parish priests notified prominent believers to stay away from the site.[81]

The seers looked once more to the Virgin for a response. Luis Irurzun heard her say that this was a test, that the seers should obey the bishop and pray and that the truth would triumph. Luis believed that the bishop's edict did not apply to Navarrese, so he himself continued to go to Ezkioga, one of the few who did so. In the long run, he said, "The writings that go against the apparition are like wet paper that falls apart and the ink washes away. That will happen with this document." The child Martín Ayerbe reported that Múgica would change his mind eventually. Another seer said this about-face would happen in November, when everyone would go to Ezkioga and the catastrophe would finally occur. But Pilar and Benita were less sanguine and heard the Virgin say the bishop would be punished.[82]

Those who had no hope that Múgica would alter his opinion could imagine his replacement by a bishop favorable to the visions. Such rumors circulated among Basque believers in mid-November 1933. Someone, probably Carmen Medina, took Evarista Galdós to Granada sometime late that year to see the auxiliary bishop there, Lino Rodrigo Ruesca. Rodrigo reputedly had visited the north, spoken to seers, and believed in the visions. Evarista hoped he would be named bishop of Vitoria.[83]

A shift of bishops would have had to come from the nuncio, Federico Tedeschini, and from Rome. Medina told Ezkioga believers in the summer of 1932 that Tedeschini thought the Ezkioga visions were "from heaven." Rumor had it that Evarista had helped to cure him after an automobile accident on 23 August 1933 in Miranda del Ebro. Tedeschini spent almost a month recuperating in San Sebastián in the clinic of Benigno Oreja, who was or had been a believer himself. At that point Carmen Medina lent the nuncio Evarista's crucifix, one of many that Ezkioga seers and believers claimed had given off blood. According to Carmen, the nuncio kept it next to his bed.[84]

We can only speculate what Tedeschini really thought about the Ezkioga visions. He was working to achieve a modus vivendi with the Republic and as such was diametrically opposed to the Integrists who were die-hard supporters of Ezkioga in 1933. The aristocratic, sociable, and extraordinarily flexible nuncio may have been using Medina to put pressure on Ezkioga publicists to hand over their writings and may have misled Medina about his sympathies. What we know for certain is that some Ezkioga promoters considered him an ally.[85]

Burguera, on the contrary, was sure that the nuncio was part of a plot to suppress the book. Burguera pinned his hopes instead on Pius XI, to whom he and five seers sent a petition. But on 21 December 1933 Cardinal Donato Sbarreti, secretary of the Holy Office, wrote Múgica that, after examining the dossier from Vitoria in August and the circular of September, the Vatican approved the bishop's decisions.

After parish priests read the bishop's attack on him three times from every pulpit, Burguera went into hiding. He depended almost daily on visions to guide him through the last details of his book and to help him publish it. Pilar Ciordia, who appears to have cultivated his paranoia, warned him on 10 October 1933 of impending danger, and he fled from the Hotel Urola in Zumarraga to Legazpi. There he learned from Benita and Recalde that Baudilio Sedano would find a printer for the book in Valladolid and that the believers would pay for publication.[86]

Fernand Remisch and L'Enigme d'Ezkioga

Bishop Múgica's fears of foreign interest in the visions were justified. In late 1933 the Belgian Fernand Remisch, a young man drawn to apparitions and mystical events, published a new periodical exclusively about Ezkioga. Remisch was born about 1903 in Arlon, Belgium, the son of a white-collar railway worker and a devoutly Catholic mother. He worked for the steel firm Aciéries de Longwy, first in Longwy, then in Brussels, then in Lyon. It was on a trip with his superiors in the firm that he became interested in Lourdes. He thereafter stopped there whenever in the vicinity, and once he cured his legs of near-paralysis in the holy baths. Lourdes was the impulse for a lifelong spiritual quest that took him all over Europe. Remisch visited the German mystic Thérèse Neumann in 1927, wrote about her, and remained devoted to her until her death. He also became deeply interested in the Belgian visions and wrote for Annales de Beauraing et Banneux. In 1933 he published a short book on Beauraing in which he criticized the gathering of evidence and compared the visions to those of Neumann. Because

L'ENIGME D'EZKIOGA

Librairie		Rédacteur en Chef :		Imprimerie :
93, rue de Molenbeek,		F. D·ROLA,		COLIN
Bruxelles II.		23, rue Kolois, Bruxelles II		Vieux-Condé, (France).

Le Saint Office et Ezkioga | Un Saint (1) d'Ezkioga :
Cruz de Lete

Front page, second issue of L'Enigme d'Ezkioga, *February 1934 (detail)*

he did not want to compromise his business career, he signed his writings with a pseudonym, F. Dorola.[87]

Raymond de Rigné was in touch with Remisch and his companion Ennemond Boniface in July of 1933 and no doubt encouraged them to visit Ezkioga. Remisch first went on August 13 and again the same month with Boniface. He wrote favorable articles for a Luxembourg newspaper and the *Annales de Beauraing*. But once Múgica had condemned the Ezkioga visions, it was not politic to write about them in a journal promoting the Belgian ones. Remisch chose to issue a separate journal in newspaper format, *L'Enigme d'Ezkioga*.[88]

The journal appeared at quarterly intervals from December 1933 until the start of the Spanish Civil War, eleven issues in all. Remisch printed Múgica's circular, a summary of the visions, and articles by the abbé Daniel Goens, the theologian Gustave Thibon, and several French doctors. There was also news, not always accurate, of events in Spain and the diocese of Vitoria, reviews of articles and books on Ezkioga, and notices of similar events elsewhere, including stigmatics and "bleeding" crucifixes.[89]

Remisch's tactic was to argue for scientific study. His widow told me he had church permission to read books on the Index. The journal did not have the imprimatur. Judging from letters to the editor, its readers were in Belgium, Holland, Luxembourg, and the northeast of France. Spanish readers included Burguera, Luis Irurzun, and even the parish priest of Ezkioga, evidently keeping an eye on the opposition. Rigné at first advertised his photographs in it, but later broke off contact. The journal included photographs and articles about seers Burguera had rejected, so he too declined to collaborate.[90]

The Bishop and the Books

Even more threatening than this journal for Múgica were the books that Rigné and Burguera had announced. The first book published after Múgica's circular was G. L. Boué's short guide in French, *Miracles and Prodigies of Ezkioga*. Boué, who lived in Tarbes, drew most of his information from souvenir booklets and Ayerbe's tracts. He had already published a book on Madre Rafols.

In January 1934 Rigné published anonymously *A New Jeanne d'Arc Affair*. In an accompanying flyer he explained that the work did not require church permission, and he cited the more relaxed attitude of the Belgian bishops toward visions, vision shrines, and vision publications. He ended with a bold challenge to Múgica: "Obedience to the laws of the holy Roman Church: YES, ALWAYS! To human error and misjudgment: NO, NEVER!"[91]

Rigné and Múgica had similar personalities. Both were mercurial, alternately choleric and charming, but Múgica totally lacked Rigné's sense of humor, and they had radically different ideas. Rigné's defense of sensuality put him squarely at odds with the prudish, grim views of Múgica and Amundarain. Rigné was a vain literary peacock strutting provocatively in an austere Basque churchyard. Luckily for him, there is no hint that the diocese ever saw his more daring books. But first Justo de Echeguren and then Mateo Múgica came to consider him a personal enemy. He brazenly defied diocesan authority in its rural heartland—all the time attending church and receiving Communion. He was waving a red flag before bulls.

Múgica seems to have judged that the most expedient way to neutralize Rigné was to discredit his character. The bishop had heard rumors from Ormaiztegi about Rigné's marriage. He also saw the result of an informal ecclesiastical inquiry. A "learned and worthy" Paris religious, possibly one who had spiritual dealings with Thirouin when she was a tertiary, wrote that Rigné had published books that were "strange," especially on the subject of marriage, that the person with him was probably not his wife, and that they claimed a "'mystical' betrothal." When Múgica then wrote to church officials in Paris in December 1933 asking about Rigné, he received a sizzling indictment:

> With an extreme audacity and an appearance of exaggerated piety and faith, this character is capable of the most hateful calumnies and the most fraudulent deeds. He spitefully attacked Mgr. Baudrillart with calumnious accusations when *Jeanne d'Arc* was published. He uses blackmail. In brief, one must mistrust him and keep him as much at a distance as possible.[92]

Múgica had two diocesan officials armed with this information visit Rigné on 23 January 1934. They asked for the death certificate of Rigné's first wife and the proof of his canonical marriage to Thirouin. According to Rigné, they also wanted him to retract in the diocesan bulletin his previous writings. They told him that Múgica had a decree from the Holy Office that would permit him to excommunicate all who persisted with the Ezkioga affair. In turn Rigné warned them that according to the visionaries God would punish them with violent deaths. Rigné failed to deliver the documents and on 6 February 1934 the diocese notified him that he that he could no longer receive Communion. He responded by denouncing to the diocesan prosecutor both Justo de Echeguren and Juan Thalamas Landibar, the priest who had spoken with him, for disobedience to the Holy Office and for blackmail.[93]

At the same time Rigné marshaled all the vision messages he could to back up his marriage. In March 1934 he went to Pamplona looking for the seer Gloria Viñals. He thought that the bishop there, Tomás Muniz y Pablos, was following Gloria's visions, and he wrote asking for a message Gloria had received about his marriage. He also made a desperate, unsuccessful effort to see the nuncio in Madrid.

Meanwhile Múgica put out the news of Rigné's irregular union. To Muniz y Pablos, who had inquired just who this Rigné was, Múgica sent copies of the reports from Paris and this summary of Rigné's activities at Ezkioga.

> At first he made a lot of money taking photographs of "seers" and selling them for a good price and publicizing Ezquioga in illustrated magazines in Belgium and Paris. He is the one who sustains Ezquioga by having foreigners come here, since now, with few exceptions, others do not.

Múgica revealed that he was about to condemn Rigné's book and ended his letter: "This Frenchman wants to disturb the peace of a very devout village, receiving Communion there with gestures, announcements, and displays of a piety that he does not have or know about." Some Catalan notables went to persuade Múgica to change his mind on the visions; Múgica told them too about Rigné's marriage. They then went to Rigné and asked him to leave Ezkioga. They also told Salvador Cardús, who wrote to the curate in Beizama so that he could warn Ramona. The best Rigné could do under these circumstances was to explain his situation to close friends. He told them he had indeed obtained an annulment of his first marriage, not in Paris, where Múgica had blocked him and he had enemies, but elsewhere in France. He would not tell Múgica where lest Múgica have the annulment reversed.[94]

Together with a pamphlet on Cruz Lete, the Boué and Rigné books led Múgica to issue a circular on 9 March 1934 in which he prohibited the three works and ordered people to hand copies over to their parish priests. He dedicated five pages to answering Rigné's version of fact and canon law. Múgica emphasized that there had never been any discrepancy between him and Justo de Echeguren on how to treat the visions, defended the investigation of Ramona, backed up Laburu, and denied that the diocese and the government were in collusion. In a follow-up circular he reminded priests to refuse seers Holy Communion if they persisted in going to the apparition site or other vision meetings. He pursued his inquiries about Rigné, made a pastoral visit to Legazpi and Zumarraga, and solicited help from Rome.[95]

On 13 June 1934 the Holy Office settled the matter by issuing a decree that "declared the alleged apparitions and revelations of the Holy Virgin Mary in the place called Ezquioga devoid of all supernatural character and prohibited ipso jure three books about them." Pius XI backed the decree on June 14. On July 2 Múgica published it as a special number of his diocesan bulletin. He forbade any Catholic to go to the vision site. And he prohibited "as superstitious" any "acts of private cult which, based on the false supposition of supernaturalness, some people have been holding in spite of our circular of 7 September 1933 and the individual warnings that we have given to them, in some cases repeatedly." He sent these decrees to all parish priests to read at mass.[96]

Burguera lost the race to publish his book before the Vatican acted. The seers had encouraged him for more than a year, allegedly at the Virgin's behest. In November 1933 Baudilio Sedano found a printer in Valladolid, a devout widow who not only promised to be discreet (she did not let her Jesuit son know about it) but also took the job on credit. And he collected money from believers. One worker in Bilbao, whom María Recalde had converted, donated his life savings of a thousand pesetas.[97]

Burguera's decision to publish without church permission lost him the support of the Catalans, who had done their best to talk him out of it. He had already decided that their seer, Magdalena Aulina, was not a true one; and Magdalena Aulina in turn had expressed her doubts about him. Cardús found it difficult to speak ill of anyone, but he wrote Ayerbe that he regretted Burguera's impetuosity and pride, "which will only get him into trouble and endanger the cause he defends. . . . I always kept my distance from him and was somewhat suspicious."[98] In the meantime Burguera continued to anathematize seers and alienate their supporters. By December 1933 Benita Aguirre and María Recalde were his only visionary guides. He had ruled that even Pilar and Evarista had ceased to have true visions.

In February and March 1934 Burguera was with Benita Aguirre in Girona and Lleida. There on four occasions he and others claimed to have seen crucifixes bleed, as Benita had predicted. In and around Ezkioga the rash of bleeding crucifixes had begun in 1933. Witnesses agreed there was actual blood on the images; how it got there was another question. The appearance of blood on crucifixes was in fact a European phenomenon that included a case that a bishop approved in Asti, in Italy, and numerous instances in Belgium and France. For the Ezkioga seers the bleeding crucifixes, which included photographs and lithographs of the Christ of Limpias, served as a kind of supernatural counterpoint to their travails. The bleeding was one more escalation in the effort to maintain the allegiance of believers and convert the doubters.[99]

There were other innovations. In 1933 a seer who had visions in Tolosa began to receive in vision what she claimed was a mystical Communion in the form of a host-shaped object on her tongue. This happened to her not only in Tolosa but also in Limpias, Itsasondo, and Ordizia before believers and devout visitors like the Rex group, the superior of the Carmelite house in San Sebastián, and pious photographers. The latter sold postcards and published portraits of the phenomenon. Later she distributed water scented with violets, which Gemma Galgani supposedly provided during the night.[100]

During the months of April, May, and June 1934 Burguera and Benita Aguirre lived in a flat that Baudilio Sedano had found in Valladolid and they went over the proofs of the book. Before Burguera returned each set, Benita would fall into a vision. Through her the Virgin would pass on the final text and edit or remove questionable material. Burguera considered that the book had the imprimatur of the Virgin Mary herself. By then he and Sedano were totally subject to the girl's guidance.[101]

The eight-hundred-page book, *The Events at Ezquioga in the Light of Reason and Faith,* was published in June 1934, the very month Rome declared the visions not supernatural. In October Baudilio Sedano took the copies in a truck to Elorrio, near Durango, where the believer Matilde Uribe stored them in her mansion. Burguera and Sedano went to Rome in March 1935 to plead their case. Cardinal Segura supported them and obtained an audience for them with Cardinal Sbarreti of the Holy Office. But Sbaretti gave them short shrift.

In the meantime, Rigné and Thirouin retreated to France after the book on Ramona was banned. But by the end of 1934 they were back. The Basque Country was then under martial law and Rigné's conspicuous activity put all the Ezquioguistas at risk. One of them wrote him a jocular warning through a mutual friend:

> In the meantime, as always, serenity and energy! Without imprudence. Do not fail to preach the latter to Dr. Arvil, because if he insists in his senseless "offensives," which are really just vanity and literary ambition, he may end up getting denounced by us as the promoter of all the rebellion.[102]

Eventually on 19 July 1935 the military governor expelled Rigné from Spain. In his last months he had caused incidents in the Santa Lucía church by seeking Communion and then denouncing the priests who denied it to him.

Rigné wrote to his friends in 1936 from Orléans that he and Marie-Geneviève were living in poverty, preparing a play about Jeanne d'Arc, and working on a scheme of mutual credit that would abolish money in Europe. He had nothing further to do with Ezkioga, he said. But in fact in March 1936 he had disguised his prohibited book with a new cover and title, *Open Sky above the Abyss.* In spite of the couple's troubles, they ended the preface with an exuberant flourish:[103]

> In spite of our initials [the first book was signed with the initials B. M.] Mgr. Múgica has accused us of maintaining "ignobly" our anonymity. No

doubt he judges the anonymity of *The Imitation of Christ* "ignoble." But we have nothing to hide, quite on the contrary. And before the Universal Church, we now accuse Mgr. Múgica of having betrayed all his duties in the Ezquioga affair. We sign proudly,

Bénédicte de Marsay   25 March 1936

PROMOTERS AND SEERS

The promoters brought a trajectory and momentum to the visions. The seers confirmed the trajectories and renewed the momentum. A decade earlier at Limpias religious leaders and publicists had found in the mute glances of the Christ of Agony similar support for their organizations, their campaigns, and their devotions. At Ezkioga the promoters had words, not just gestures, to work with. We will see how the same process worked with some members of religious orders and with simple laypersons with practical or spiritual problems.

People like Padre Burguera, Antonio Amundarain, and Carmen Medina had strong, preset ideas about how the earth and the heavens were configured. Their notions served as templates for the malleable products of the visionaries. The seers in trance provided what the promoters wanted to hear and became, wittingly or not, their mouthpieces. Armed with this divine authority, the promoters presented their schemes ever more convincingly. In turn, they elicited divine backing in yet other seers.

Organizers with simpler needs, like Salvador Cardús, Raymond de Rigné, or Juan Bautista Ayerbe, who were wrestling with personal spiritual problems or who enjoyed the trances as aesthetic or cathartic experiences, felt no need to exert authority over the seers. On the contrary, they found themselves dependent on the seers, their only means of obtaining divine blessing, love, forgiveness, or knowledge. In turn seers gained access to a broader audience from all the organizers. Patrons and seers found complex, mutual satisfaction.

In the first month of the visions the newspapers and the public rewarded seers who addressed the threat from the secular Republic to the Basques and their religion. Hence there was early interest in the visions by Basque Nationalist ideologues, priests, and party organs. In contrast, not one of the major promoters had any interest in the visions as a Basque phenomenon. Their interests were either more particular or more universal and in some cases both. All of them were aware of the ongoing class warfare and the prospect of a nationwide civil war.

For many believers, as we will see, the Virgin of Ezkioga announced punishment on an apocalyptic, worldwide scale. The chastisement would transcend the place and occasion of Spain with its class warfare and moral turpitude to change the course of time itself. But most of the organizers had smaller, secondary hopes for the visions—Amundarain for the Aliadas and the role they would play in maintaining an island of purity in the morass of modern indecency; Carmen

Medina for the return of a government she liked; Rigné for peace of mind and the beauty of harmony between body and spirit; Magdalena Aulina for her new institution and the glory of Gemma Galgani; and Cardús for the profound satisfaction of a life suffused with significance.

All of these promoters—at once patrons and clients—and among them especially Rigné and Ayerbe, were caught up also in a stubborn support for the seers as cultural underdogs. The promoters formed close relationships with children, teenagers, and women from poor rural families, some of whom spoke little Spanish. The refusal of the wider world and the church to believe the seers helped to confirm for these promoters the validity of the visions. The organizers had the power of money and experience in the wider world; the seers had the power of divine privilege. Some seers stopped giving messages to certain promoters and some promoters stopped helping certain seers. But Ayerbe with Conchita Mateos and Esperanza Aranda, Burguera with Benita, and Rigné with some seer families in Zumarraga remained friends for decades.

The removal of the visions from the arena of mass media and regional politics was easy for the diocese of Vitoria. The vicar general's note discrediting Ramona's "miracle" did the job. The newspapers, already skeptical, took their cue and dismantled the prestige of the star seers. The Jesuit José Antonio Laburu then convinced many waverers among clergy and bourgeoisie with his critical lectures.

But the small knots of believers, intense, secretive, and nourished with constant grace by a particular seer, were tightly knit. These cuadrillas bothered the local clergy, for whom they were tiny rival sects with independent revelation. They did not bother the bishop all that much at first. The diocese merely denied these groups public use of liturgical symbols. The groups became dangerous for the diocese only when they had access to the media—when they linked up to one of the promoters. With proper publicity the news of the visions could get back into the newspapers or become news elsewhere in Spain, Europe, or Latin America, the purview of other, possibly more sympathetic bishops. Therefore the friendships between seers and publicists were of extreme concern to the diocesan leaders. The repeated attacks in Sunday masses across the Basque Country as well as sporadic government crackdowns led to a collective historical repression. For the people of Euskadi the visions and the hopes and the enthusiasm they provoked in 1931 became an embarrassment and Ezkioga became taboo.

7. THE PROLIFERATION OF VISIONS

MANY IF NOT most of the great vision sequences in modern Europe have provoked waves of replication. Visions in the Papal States and at La Salette, Lourdes, Marpingen, Knock, Fatima, Limpias, Beauraing, and Siracusa each produced a skein of similar events. Those at Medjugorje especially, because of televised publicity, elicited hundreds if not thousands of other visions. In all these cases there seems to be a chain reaction. Visions that gain public attention spark others that provoke yet others, until the media becomes jaded and stops reporting them and the pent-up emotional energy of consumers is exhausted. A careful look at the emergence of subsequent visions as news of Ezkioga spread reveals processes that may also be at work in the transmission, particularly by children, of other complex paranormal constructs like airborne witches or, more recently, Satanic baby killers.

Seers at Ezkioga came from all the areas that sent pilgrims, including the neighboring provinces of Alava, Navarra, and Bizkaia. But newspapers mentioned many of these seers only once, their visions often being weak

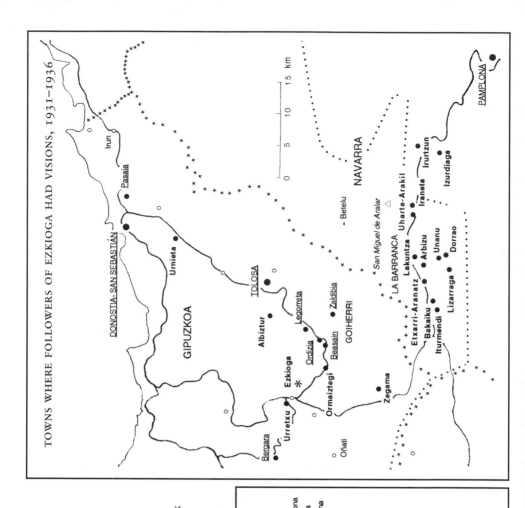

TOWNS WHERE FOLLOWERS OF EZKIOGA HAD VISIONS, 1931–1936

LEGEND

*	Ezkioga
●	**public visions**
●	regular clandestine visions, 1931–1936
○	occasional clandestine visions, 1931–1936
△	*shrine*
■	town
—	railroad
⋯	southern limit of area in which children speak Basque, 1931
+++	province boundary

VISIONS ELSEWHERE IN SPAIN, JULY–DECEMBER 1931

and vague. There were invisible barriers that excluded many and favored the regular Gipuzkoan crowd at Ezkioga. The language of the ceremonies and the visions was predominantly Basque, which left out the Castilian speakers of Alava and most of Navarra. There was no regular public transport from Navarra. There were trains from Bizkaia to Zumarraga, but Bizkaians spoke a different dialect and had a quite separate identity that made the provincial boundary a cultural frontier. With few exceptions the better known seers, those with habitual "strong" visions, came from the southern, highland, half of Gipuzkoa, the Goiherri, where villages or towns sent buses daily or weekly to Ezkioga through the fall of 1931. Each of these seers came with an entourage, or cuadrilla, of relatives, friends, neighbors, and converts.[1]

Visions spread out from Ezkioga in three ways: newspapers reported the events throughout Spain, pilgrim seers returned from Ezkioga to their home villages, and later seers abandoned Ezkioga because of church edicts. In all there were dozens of mini-Ezkiogas. They took place out of the public eye, almost totally unrecorded. The only way to find out about them was through the hazy memories of participants fifty years later. In several towns people were reluctant to speak of the visions, as the child seers were now adult neighbors. I can only hope that those towns where people did talk to me are representative of the others. In any case, the reader will have to forgive me if I am imprecise with dates and discreet about names.

VISIONS SPREAD OR BROUGHT TO LIGHT BY NEWS

While the visions were in part behavior that was learned, they were also behavior that was permitted and rewarded. Some people already knew how to have visions but had done so only in private. The publicity Ezkioga received allowed people to share their religious experiences and showed them uses for their contacts with another plane of reality. It was not necessary for all such people to go to Ezkioga; it was sometimes enough that they knew of the free-for-all inspiration by word of mouth, by radio, or by newspaper. The effect of the sensational news was a sensitizing to the subject throughout Spain in seers, potential seers, and the media alike. This effect worked quickly, often at considerable distance. Within weeks of the first reports in July 1931, the press was noting visions in many other places.

Bachicabo, a hamlet in Alava, was one of the first places to reproduce the visions. Located in the valley of Valdegovia on the border with Burgos, it was beyond the zone from which buses took people to Ezkioga. The first to see the Virgin there was the fourteen-year-old son of an emigrant to Sestao, a Bilbao industrial suburb; the boy was back in the village for the summer. On about 2 August 1931 he was tending oxen a kilometer from the village near a spring called Petrás, where the villagers often stopped on their annual pilgrimage to the shrine of Nuestra Señora de Angosto. In a cavity of a large boulder he saw a flower, and when he went to touch it, the Virgin Mary appeared in its place.

The villagers did not heed the boy, but a group of them paused before the boulder on the evening of August 6 on their way to the fiesta of San Salvador in Espejo. One of them, Ignacio, aged about twenty-two, went to the rock, put his hand in the cavity, and said, "Aquí no hay Virgen ni hostias!" This was a blasphemous way of saying that the Virgin was not there. But then he shouted that she was indeed there and lay down, weeping, on the ground. His friends wrapped him in a blanket.

A woman and a man who had been present described that moment to me with great gusto and a certain amount of jocular hindsight.[2] They themselves saw nothing but took the matter seriously. That evening the boy from Sestao, accompanied by the Bachicabo sexton Timoteo, recounted his original vision to the parish priest in Espejo. The priest was skeptical: "You must have heard about the people seeing apparitions in Ezkioga." Nevertheless, the fiesta was interrupted as everybody, including the priest, went to the boulder and said the rosary.

As in the rest of the nuclear villages in northern Spain, the people of Bachicabo were used to doing things together and in combination with neighboring communities. They had common land they used for pasture and commons they shared with other villages; they helped one another with harvests; they shared shrines with other villages; and, of course, they prayed together in mass and in the rosary. Whether they themselves or the boy from Sestao had heard of the Virgin of Ezkioga, as is likely, or not, there were precedents in their own local geography for divine visions. They knew that the Virgin de Angosto was supposed to have appeared in ancient times to the shepherd Cecilio and that in a nearby village an image of San Lorenzo was supposed to have returned by itself to its mountain site at night.

What the Bachicabo villagers decided to do was similar to what the people at Ezkioga had done. Every night for at least three months they gathered to say the rosary, led by a youth, while several seers, all of them males, had visions of the "Virgen de Petrás." For the first month they met at the original vision site. Bachicabo had 170 inhabitants (in 1983 there were only twelve families), and at night after supper the village would empty out. One woman I talked to felt so impelled to go that she would leave her fifteen-day-old baby behind alone. People came from the surrounding villages, Barrio, Tobalina, Salcedo, Salinas de Añana, Espejo, and even from the town of Miranda del Ebro. Later, in September, they held the evening prayer sessions in the village itself, and the Virgin appeared to seers in various houses. In late October people were collecting money (probably to build a chapel), but by the winter the visions were over.[3]

People in Bachicabo most enjoy recalling the funny incidents: the night a seer in trance said, "Boost me up into the pine tree, for I am going to throw myself down" (they did; he did not); how one seer's announcement, "The Virgin of Petrás is arriving now, wearing sandals," tended to coincide with the flash of headlights on a distant highway; the time they went to the site and found a crudely lettered sign that read, "By the intercession of the Virgin, the spring water of Petrás make you powerfully hungry"; the night a male seer asked the Virgin how she was going to punish those who had spoken ill of him, provoking a lady to have a fit and scream, "O Virgen Santísima, no, for we are all sinners!"; the night a shoemaker from Espejo ordered spectators to come down from the pine trees where they were perched; the time a seer had a vision that everybody had to harvest Eusebio's potatoes (they did). They also recall the night that the seer Ignacio's father announced in the Petrás pine grove, "My son has sent me to say that the Virgin has said that this is more sacred than the church." And they remember that the local priests were against the visions.

Nevertheless people recall that they were fully caught up in the events at the time. One of the women said, "If you did not go to the rosary and to see what happened, it seemed you were lacking something. . . . It was not something fun, because what they said there was so—I don't know, so serious. . . . Sometimes it was frightening because of what some of them said they saw."

The seers obviously knew what was going on elsewhere in Spain. One night Ignacio said, "Good evening. The Virgin of Petrás has left for Toledo." And everyone had to wait until she returned, when they said another rosary. We can date this moment with some precision, for in Guadamur, Toledo, children began to have visions at the end of August. The news was in the national press starting 29 August 1931 and in the press of Alava on September 2. Toledo had already shown a marked interest in Ezkioga, and the Catholic newspaper there had published more on the apparitions than any other periodical of the Spanish interior.[4]

Some Catholics in the province of Toledo had reason to welcome heaven's hand. For instance, they read about class rebellion when socialist farmworkers almost succeeded in throwing the mayor from a balcony of a town hall. They read as well about shootings and stabbings in the meeting of a town council; about riots to protest arrests—in one town of a man who made fun of the mayor and in another of a man who struck a private guard; and about invasions of private estates to cut down trees and to poach.[5]

In the wake of the events at Ezkioga people of all persuasions were alert to the idea of supernatural help. On August 18 a republican newspaper reported that a fortune-teller was predicting "great unrest in the future of Spain."[6] And the following day another newspaper, in all likelihood unaware that visions were going on in several other places already, ran a cartoon on the front page suggesting that sleepy villages needed a miracle, "as in Ezquioga," to attract summer visitors.

On August 19 *El Debate* presented a short report about a series of visions that had started a week earlier in the Toledo village of Rielves. The article revealed a community divided into Catholics and socialists, believing women and disbelieving men.[7]

[Dateline Toledo, August 18] We are informed from the village of Rielves that during the night of the eleventh the thirteen-year-old girl Teófila, when she was seated at the door of her house, saw a glow issuing from the window bars of the house of Don Lucio Pérez. She called her mother, Celestina, who said that it was the Virgin Mary with a white mantle.

On the fourteenth Marcelino, the father of the girl, saw a resplendence in the same place and called his wife, saying, "This is what you saw." She answered that it was, indeed, the Virgin, although this time more beautiful, with her outline more clear, with a white mantle and a black blouse. Celestina Parra, the mother of the girl, says she is willing to give her testimony under oath.

On the night of the fifteenth, the vision appeared on the facade of the house of Justo Pérez Díaz and was seen by the girl Amparo, who called her uncle, Agapito Centellas, and her aunt. Agapito was so moved that he knelt and took off his cap, crying, "What do you want, Most Holy Virgin?" but he received no reply. Justo Pérez Díaz also saw her. He is a person who is not a believer and says it was without doubt the bust of an image. Two socialists who were on their way home saw the vision on the window bars of the house of Isidoro Morales. "Look there on those bars," said one of them, moved, and the other replied, "It is the Virgin!" Both told their wives when they arrived home.

The placement of this report on an inside page, the absence of a follow-up report, perhaps even the explicitness with which the article addressed the issue of unbelievers, all indicate to me that what happened in Rielves was something Catholic newspapers would not normally have printed. Given the anxieties of the times, the social strife, and awareness of the events at Ezkioga, however, the story made it over the threshold of acceptance—but even then the paper reported it as an anecdote. The vague, ghostlike luminous sightings by villagers on the bars of various windows were not the stuff of Lourdes. The visions at Bachicabo never made it even that far. Both were episodes that under normal circumstances would have gone unreported; the bigger news from Ezkioga "smoked them out," as it were. We saw how similar visions in Torralba de Aragón in April and Mendigorría in May ended quickly. That the visions at Rielves and Bachicabo were believed and reported was a result of the same tense religious and political climate that nurtured the visions of the Ezkioga children.

The subsequent visions at Guadamur were more successful in attracting attention and respect. Toledo's Catholic newspaper, *El Castellano,* reported them fully. The diocese of Toledo, then running on collegial leadership after the expulsion of Cardinal Segura, permitted these reports. Both sets of visions that were permitted major publicity during the Republic were in dioceses where the bishops were in exile.

There was a connection. Two deputies from Toledo, Dimas Madariaga and Ramón Molina, a canon in the Toledo cathedral, went to Ezkioga on 16 August 1931. This was three days after Antonio de la Villa's attack on the visions in the Cortes, and the Toledans went in order to rebut him. Molina described the visions in *El Castellano* a week later. Another canon of Toledo, Gregorio del Solar, was at Ezkioga for a longer period, until mid-October, dressed in a threadbare cassock and deeply involved in the visions, to the point of learning Basque. Del Solar became convinced at Ezkioga that he was destined for martyrdom. Another canon, the dean of the cathedral, José Polo Benito, who was an unsuccessful candidate in the elections for the Cortes, wrote that the Ezkioga visions and those of Guadamur were "God's offensive."[8]

On August 26, two days after Molina's article describing the visions of Benita Aguirre, two daughters of the Guadamur physician came back from their evening paseo saying that they had seen the Virgen de la Soledad in an olive grove near the town. The next evening at the same time a boy said he had had to stop his bicycle on the road near the grove to avoid hitting the Virgin. That night up to five hundred persons gathered at the site. Thirty of them claimed they had seen the figure, slightly raised above the ground. In addition to children, a doctor, town councillors, and young farmworkers were among the seers. This news was published first in nearby Toledo and then in Madrid.[9]

As a result of the publicity attendance at the visions surged. On the night of August 28, one thousand people went from the adjacent villages and Toledo and on the night of September 2 seven thousand. By then seers included not only adults and children from Guadamur but outsiders from a wide range of surrounding towns, including a "señorita" aged twenty-four from Madrid, where photographs of many of the seers appeared in an illustrated newspaper. On September 1 a speaker mentioned these visions in the Cortes.[10]

The archdiocese of Toledo took the events seriously, and on September 2 after the rosary the boys choir of the cathedral performed in the village. Apparently the left read the visions in political terms, for groups of youths in Toledo's main square harassed the city's pilgrims. While the visions at Ezkioga and Bachicabo occurred in a largely sympathetic environment, those of New Castile faced active hostility and ridicule.[11]

The Guadamur visions or the reports of them in turn sparked others or other reports. Republican newspapers delighted in locating new visions. On about August 28 in Sigüenza the head of the telegraph office and his family saw the Virgin on the tower of the cathedral. And on about September 4 in Guadalajara many people gathered near the church of San Gil because children were seeing the Virgin on an arch at the entrance. Apparently unbeknownst to the outside

En el lugar de las supuestas apariciones se congregan diariamente numerosas personas, llegadas de muchos puntos de la comarca, que a la hora del crepúsculo rezan el rosario

Guadamur, province of Toledo, August 1931: above, *girl seers (photo by Vilaseca);* below, *rosary begins at dusk (photo by Contreras). From* Ahora, *5 September 1931, p. 16. Courtesy Hemeroteca Municipal de Madrid*

world, there had been some local visions going on in Orgiva (Granada) since April. Following the publicity about Ezkioga, a local leftist newspaper brought these visions to light and the Madrid leftist press followed suit. The press claimed that the visions took place in a cave, that an entrance fee was charged, and that there were sightings of "Saint Joseph, Saint Roch with his dog, Curro Cuchares, Primo de Rivera, Saint John Nepomucene, Juana la Loca, Saint Exuperio, Nebuchadnezzar, and Attila's horse." Madrid newspapers published cartoons making fun of the rash of visions.[12]

By this point the visions must have been an embarrassment for churchmen even in Toledo. As at Ezkioga, so at Guadamur: different seers saw different apparitions and there were too many visionaries to control. Although the parish

—¡Vayan pasando, señores! ¡Espectáculo de moda, sólo por dos pesetas!   —¡Que va a empezar!   —¡Aparición de la auténtica Virgen, garantizada contra imitaciones y falsificaciones!

"Summer Theater": "Step right in folks and see the latest, only two pesetas"; "It's about to start"; "Apparition of the authentic Virgin, guaranteed against imitations and falsifications." From El Liberal *(Madrid), 6 September 1931. Courtesy Hemeroteca Municipal de Madrid*

priest defended his seers, *El Castellano* stopped its daily reports on September 11, and the visions slowly decreased. When I went to Guadamur in 1975, oldsters treated the matter diffidently; the younger generation did not know about it.[13]

VISIONS SPREAD BY CONTACT: THE ROLE OF CHILDREN

By mid-August 1931, about the same time that the news of Ezkioga began to show its effects throughout Spain, a more local kind of spread was occurring. Returning pilgrims and seers took home the Ezkioga liturgy, emotion, and access to the divine. In adjoining Navarra the same kind of replication spread the visions from village to village. These villages were located in a band between one and two hours' travel from Ezkioga, from which the new shrine was accessible but inconvenient. Seers from the Ezkioga area who worked as servants elsewhere and especially children from elsewhere who had visions at Ezkioga were key vectors in this spread because they could not get to the main site frequently.

The only substantive article on the Ezkioga visions in a Basque republican newspaper, *El Liberal* of Bilbao, revealed that other visions were taking place in Iturmendi, Bakaiku, and other towns of Navarra south of the Goiherri.[14] The Barranca is the broad, high valley of the Arakil river, with high mountains to the north and south. Its inhabitants do not live dispersed in farmhouses, as in most of the Basque Country, but rather clustered in tight villages, as in Alava to the west. But unlike the people of Alava, those of the Barranca speak Basque, and in particular the dialect of their neighbors in Gipuzkoa. As in much of Pyrenean

Spain and France, the house is the major unit of identity. People belong to a given house and are identified by their house names. The houses are passed on through impartible inheritance, and noninheriting children who marry have to seek their fortunes elsewhere. In 1931 the wealthier households included servants and farm laborers.

From the Barranca two roads wind down into Gipuzkoa: the main highway from Vitoria to San Sebastián, which passes through Altsasu and enters Gipuzkoa at Zegama, and a smaller road from Arbizu through the mountains to Ataun. These roads and countless trails have served traditionally as conduits for frequent contact. Sheep from the mountains of Navarra came down to winter in the milder climes of Gipuzkoa; young women from the Barranca found homes in the convents of the river towns and young men jobs in the factories. The high valley is less than an hour from Ezkioga by car, bus, or truck. But its people—mostly farmers and shepherds, apart from workers in an industrial enclave around Altsasu—were more isolated and poorer, cut off linguistically from the prosperous cities of Estella and Pamplona to the south or Vitoria to the west. They were also devout, and in the first decades of the century the towns received frequent missions, given particularly by the Capuchins in Altsasu.

In the first weeks of the visions the road through Ataun brought constant bus- and truckloads of Navarrese pilgrims to Ezkioga. José Miguel de Barandiarán, the Basque ethnographer from Ataun, remembered them passing in front of his house and once stopping nearby because a girl from Navarra said she was seeing the infant Jesus on a rock in the river.[15] In July Navarrese seers at Ezkioga included a man from Lekunberri (on July 15) and on July 16 a boy from Errotz (near Izurdiaga) and a girl from Arbizu. And when the canon Juan B. Altisent stopped in Arbizu to ask directions, he was told that several children of the village had been lucky enough to see the Virgin.[16]

In June 1984 I drove to the Barranca to search for memories of what had happened fifty years before. In some towns the atmosphere was tense. The district has been a stronghold of Herri Batasuna, the political party supporting the ETA fighters who from 1968 have kept up a campaign of violence to force Basque separation from Spain. The day before I arrived a demonstration in Etxarri-Aranatz had left one man dead. In Arbizu my guide was Francisco Mendiueta Araña, expert in accordion, harmonica, singing, and whistling. He remembered the truck that came at dusk to take people down to Ezkioga. People were packed into it like upright candles in a box; many were carsick.

The visions in Arbizu started at Ansota, about one and a half kilometers north of the town center, in higher pastureland belonging to the township. The first seers were girls, who were tending cows, but boys had visions too. The visions would start in the late afternoon and go into the night, when the townspeople came and everyone would say the rosary. When I asked Francisco Mendiueta, eight years old at the time of the visions, whether before then anyone had ever seen witches, he said yes, that with his father at the same place he had seen fireballs on Mount Aitzkorri. The visions at Ansota lasted about a month and then shifted to a new site, still to the north of town, on the road at a place named Baldasoro, where there was a garage and a large ash tree. Finally, they moved to a walnut tree at the east end of the village. There people prayed with great faith at an altar put up against the Zubaldi house, and one after another the seers would keel back into trance. The visions continued for a couple of months and then petered out. Of the seers Francisco could name four girls and two boys aged seven to twelve, the children of farmers and masons, but he said there were more. A priest native to the village did not believe and said it was witch-stuff and a lie.

It was hard for Francisco and his friends to remember what the seer children saw, apart from the Virgin and the village dead in heaven and hell. What most surprised them was that their pals could perform little miracles. They remember one boy in vision, who somehow knew that Francisco and a friend, out of sight, were rattling a heavy metal ring and called out, "Paco and Blas will go to hell!" And particularly they remembered the seer children, when the visions were over, holding out invisible candy given them by heavenly beings, then eating it. They heard the crinkle of the candies being unwrapped but saw nothing.[17]

These stories, like those from Bachicabo, are at once delightful, like home-made fairy tales, and moving. They reveal children and young people who found an opening and accepted an unprecedented gift of authority and usefulness in the village arena. In these backwaters the stakes were less titanic than at Ezkioga, where rural children and adults were eventually negotiating with the gods for the future of the nation and humanity before an audience of thousands. Here the miracles and stakes were often on a smaller scale, involving bread-and-butter questions of daily life among neighbors.

Francisco Mendiueta took me to Torrano (now Dorrao), where we ended up in the large dark house of Felipe Rezano and Felisa Lizarraga. They first went to the visions in other villages and then were intimately involved in those of Dorrao, still believed in them, and talked about them directly, simply, and without complexes. But they said these events were something they had largely forgotten.[18]

The main seer in Dorrao was Inés Igoa, who was about seventeen years old in 1931. Inés would fall into trance during the rosary in her house or outdoors with most of the small village present. She narrated what she was seeing in her trance ("ahora ha salido no-sé-qué"), including, they remember, the Virgin and the Heavenly Father, and she would tell them things "as in a sermon." As for the content of the sermons, they recalled only that she foretold a civil war with the death of many sons. On the whole, they preferred the predictions of Inés to those of the Jehovah's Witnesses.

The only other Dorrao seer was Felisa's brother, José, then twenty years old, but he did not have his visions in a trancelike state, and for Felipe, at least, they

Las cinco videntes sobre el tablado, en Echarri-Aranaz. La primera ha caído en catalepsia.

"The five seers on the stage, at Echarri-Aranaz. The first has fallen in catalepsy."
Photo by Carlos Juaristi published in Diario de Navarra, *25 October 1931. Courtesy Hemeroteca Municipal de Madrid*

carried less authority. Felipe was one of five youths chosen by the Virgin through Inés as "angels" to help organize the visions. One of their jobs was to cut pine trees, bring them to the village, and set up an altar for the visions. He was a little embarrassed about his being an angel—"How do I know if it was true or not? We said, this cannot be true because we are the worst in the village. What do we know?"

As children Felipe and Felisa both wanted to have visions and went to various sites trying to see. But neither could. At most, they remembered their friends noticing stars that were especially bright. One imagines children, teenagers, and adults peering intently into the heavens at night. Felisa's father and grandfather were great devotees of the Virgin. They took Felisa, who would have been only nine or ten, to Ezkioga three times after the visions in Dorrao had begun.

By a year after her first vision Inés's messages, as reported by Padre Burguera, were quite sophisticated and included references to Freemasonry, Christ the King, the reign of Jesus and Mary in Spain, and a chastisement. Inés also suffered the crucifixion. She was well aware of the government offensive in the fall of 1932.[19]

At Iturmendi the seers were two boys, aged nine and ten, the sons of farmers. They had their visions on the flat threshing ground called Martinikorena, on the edge of the village, where there were some walnut trees. They too would fall into vision during a rosary at which much of the village was present. In Iturmendi the parish priest forbade an outdoor altar. By identifying some of the village dead in hell these boys caused deep rifts in the town. Not everyone believed their visions, and "some wise guy made a jack-o'-lantern out of a sugar beet with a candle inside and put it in the cemetery." People remember that the visions lasted two or three months.[20]

At Etxarri-Aranatz a number of seers were having visions by early October. Victoriano Juaristi, president of the Colegio de Médicos of Pamplona, a distinguished psychiatrist and man of letters, was sent there by the bishop of Pamplona when the visions had already built up momentum. On 25 October 1931 he published a critical article in *Diario de Navarra*. Juaristi's son Carlos, also a doctor, took photographs, and his photos of Etxarri-Aranatz and Unanu, however dark and blurred, are the only, precious, visual evidence I could find of a brief period in the Barranca in the last half of 1931 in which every night children took control.[21] Victoriano Juaristi described five or six girls of Etxarri-Aranatz on a low stage separated from the onlookers by barbed wire. During the rosary, "they fell back on their backs one after another, like dolls in a carnival shooting gallery." When Carlos Juaristi fired a magnesium flash, the villagers screamed, apparently thinking the devil was about to appear, and then roughed him up. One man exclaimed, "Coño! Pues eso se avisa" or, approximately, "Shoot! Give us some warning."

In Etxarri-Aranatz I spoke with José Maiza Auzmendi, an old believer who had gone on foot to Ezkioga and to other towns in the Barranca to witness the visions. In his town the visions took place on the south side of the highway to Altsasu, before an altar of sorts. After two or three months people gradually stopped going, and the child seers ordered a cross to be placed there. When the parish priest refused to permit a cross, Maiza's father, father-in-law, and uncle put a cross up in the village cemetery. On the whole, the attitude of the village priests was neutral, he said. The anecdotes townspeople recall confirm the local flavor of the visions. One girl seer relayed news that Serafina, a woman who had died young, was in some difficulty in the afterlife because of an unkept promise. An older woman had been dubbed "Santa Rita" for the saint she was always seeing. And one night the Holy Family appeared with a spirit donkey, and children and adults followed them with lighted candles and lanterns.[22]

The visions in Bakaiku began by the river and the train tracks, where there were poplar trees. According to *El Liberal* this was in mid-August.

> At Bacaicoa the infant Jesus appeared and spoke to a villager who made doughnuts [*churros*]; but the man could not reveal what he heard as it was a secret. Nevertheless he says he has it all written down in a sealed envelope. The doughnut man made a penitential promise not to speak at all and to go for several days to the apparition site barefoot and with his head hanging down.[23]

The writer observed that children were usually playing at the place the infant Jesus appeared, and he commented cynically that the doughnut business was doing very well. He said the Virgin was seen in "another nearby village" walking in a poplar grove along the banks of the river.

The visions were still in full force on 17 November 1931 when Padre Burguera arrived. He was particularly impressed with María Celaya, who kept a notebook entitled "Las Apariciones de Bacaicoa," starting with her first vision on October 16. Burguera accompanied her to Ezkioga and observed her again in her home village. In all he named eleven seers there: a woman aged 58; girls aged 17, 12, 11, 11, 10, 9, 9, 8, and 5; and a boy aged 8. These children included two sets of siblings.[24]

According to Burguera the visions had begun with two eight-year-old children, a boy and a girl, playing by the river. There they met a strange child and gathered mulberries with him. The child told them that he was named Jesus, his mother was named Mary, and they should go to Ezkioga where his mother was waiting for them. They noticed that his hands, unlike theirs, did not become stained by the berries and that he walked on the water of the river. A wealthy female relative duly took the children by car to Ezkioga, about thirty kilometers away, and there they saw the Virgin, who confirmed their vision by the river and gave them secrets. More children went to the river site and had visions of Mary and the child Jesus, whom they referred to as the Infant Jesus of Prague, after the Carmelite devotion popular in the zone.[25]

At Bakaiku the visions received a boost from some of the village elite, including the wife of the civil engineer and politician Wenceslao Goizueta, and the schoolteacher, Francisca Setoáin. When Burguera went to the school, eight children went into trance for him. He referred to the teacher as a "tireless apostle." Perhaps in the vision messages there is an echo of her interest, for the first two seers said that the Virgin told them the visions were for the people of Spain, "who honored God so much and now officially dishonor him." Messages like this should alert us to the bias of oral testimony based on memory. No doubt local people are much more likely to retain anecdotes anchored in kinship and place and less likely to remember messages of political or theological importance. By contrast, the written reports of ideologues like Burguera would likely leave out the more local meanings. These seers were speaking simultaneously to both levels.[26]

The seers also ran into opposition, especially from some of the men of the village, which María Celaya described in her notebook. For a while their visions attracted spectators from a wide radius, but as more villages had their own seers, with messages more specific to their neighbors and problems, fewer people went to Bakaiku.[27]

People I talked to remembered the Lizarraga visions beginning after those of Bakaiku. Lizarraga-ergoien was on an excitement route, the road from Lezaun and the Estella region of Navarra, which sent many busloads of pilgrims to Ezkioga in the months of July and August 1931. Such routes became corridors of enthusiasm. Francisco Argandoña, who as a boy went from Lezaun, said that after an outdoor rosary all the children, agreeing with whoever spoke first, saw the saints arrive from over the mountains. The night he was there, the procession began with Saint Joseph, centered on the infant Jesus, and ended with Saint Adrian on a white horse. The next morning he was taken to a girl who said she played with the infant Jesus whenever she wanted to and who handed him an invisible baby Jesus so small it could fit in the palm of her hand.[28]

By late November, as at Ezkioga, the visions had taken a turn for the macabre and apocalyptic. Burguera saw twelve seers from seven households: a woman aged 21; girls aged 12, 12, 11, 11, 10, 9, and 4; and four boys, all of them younger brothers of girl seers, aged 13, 8, 7, and 6. Another observer put the number of seers at more than thirty and wrote:

> The seers seemed to be petrified, first supplicating with their eyes upward and their hands joined, then horrified by what they were seeing in their terrible and tragic vision, sometimes giving screams of fear for the catastrophe that they saw coming in the war and other chastisements that would occur in the world.

As in the other villages, the seers had an altar on the threshing ground and an enclosure for their visions, and adults brought chairs and benches to sit on. Some visions were right out in the road. One boy had a vision on top of a delivery van; when it drove off, the boy fell off but was unhurt.[29]

The Lizarraga seers said the devil attacked them. According to the psychiatrist Victoriano Juaristi, adult seers saw Saint Michael struggling and tried to help him by hitting the devil with a candlestick. Seers said that on the highway the devil tried to get them to throw off the many rosaries, medals, and crucifixes they were wearing for the divine to bless. Burguera himself at least twice gave his rosary to the seers to hold when they were seeing the infant Jesus. A town official eventually forbade the visions. One household with four child seers resisted and the matter ended in a lawsuit. This family was still holding visions at home in the fall of 1933.

From Lizarraga the visions spread to adjacent Dorrao and then down the road to Unanu. While people in Unanu refused to speak of the visions in 1984, they were open with Juaristi in October 1931. He left a striking account and a valuable photograph that shows an altar decked with pine boughs like that of Dorrao.

> We are at the foot of the pointed peak of San Donato, which looks like a gigantic altar. And above the green and black floor of the valley, next to the cliff base, there is a circle of weak, reddish light, which has drawn to it about fifty persons who are kneeling. In the middle of the circle there are four children and an equal number of women, kneeling as well, facing the base of the cliff, whence the light comes. An elderly man, thin and erect, recites with a dry, firm, clear voice a litany that the women answer; then he gets up and leads them in a hymn.
>
> The light is hidden in the boughs of some high bushes, formed into a strange kind of multicolored oven shape; it seems to be some kind of altar. Suddenly, one of the girls opens her arms out like a cross, throws her head back, arcs her body, and goes stiff, the moonlight bathing her pale face, her eyes, as if dead, staring unblinking into the infinite. Immediately a boy, younger, and another boy fall into a similar cataleptic state, and two women with white coifs hold them. The prayers continue without interruption.
>
> We are filled with awe, spectators in the dark at a rite like that which must have been the moon cult of the ancient Vascones.
>
> The children come back to life, first the older girl, then the others. The girl says she has seen the Virgin with a blue mantle and a silver crown, barefoot and with golden rays in her hands, and the Virgin told her . . . that we should go and have supper! The spell is broken and we mix with the spectators, who get up. Some friendly words in Basque serve to relieve their fear and distrust, and the children (the youngest is barely four years old) answer our questions as any children would, their mothers filling out their replies.
>
> The girl is lively and communicative, and she is aware of the authority she wields among her kind. Always "by order of the Virgin," she says how much they have to pray, and who has to do it; she orders that the Daughters of Mary spend Sunday making paper flowers and that people come in the evening. She recounts struggles between Saint Michael, dressed in gold with his flashing sword, and a blackened, horned devil. To a request for more details, she says that the devil wears a black jacket, goes without pants,

Apariciones en la Barranca

El altar y los orantes en Unanua.

and uses a staff. She describes macabre processions, identifying the dead of the town as they go past. Behind the dead walks a young idiot girl who used to work with a hatchet; she carries it in the funeral procession as well and limps because she wounded herself with it trying to open the gates of heaven. She blesses *pacharanes,* or bilberries, so that the sick can eat them and get well.

Time and again she falls into a new fit, followed by the other children. Then we are able to observe them as doctors and notice all the signs of a neurosis.

The parish priest, whom we visit, is an educated man with common sense who gives us interesting information and is happy that we doctors have intervened to set right something he always thought was pathological and harmful to true faith. But his counsel and his sermons along these lines have fallen on deaf ears. The seer girl has "her" church; she wants nothing to do with the "other," or with the priest. And the mothers consider themselves happy for the "celestial" favor that their children have received.[30]

Juaristi presented visions as neurotic and pathological. In Pamplona he was something of a liberal, a black sheep who did not attend church and who the bishop knew in advance would not sympathize with the phenomena. In his article Juaristi pointed out that waves of hysterical behavior were common in all times and that in the past the seers would have been accused of witchcraft. Yet his observations do not appear to have been skewed, for the setting and the social dynamic he described are similar to what we know about in other villages.

Like José Antonio Laburu's lectures, Juaristi's article bore the authority of science. Pedro Balda, the Iraneta town secretary and scribe for another seer, described for a friend its impact on the Barranca:

> Finally a doctor declared that it was not ecstasy but instead a sickness called "neurosis," and that it had occurred in a similar form in Germany before the European war. It did not take much for people to lose the fervor of the first days, and many who were believers in the supernatural [aspect of the visions] became enemies of the mysterious phenomena. . . . If they fed them well, some said, the neurosis would disappear immediately. Others said that with a good beating every day, they would stop having visions at once. Most said that it was a "farce." That is why most of the believers withdrew from attending what had attracted the attention of so many thousands.[31]

There were visions in two other Barranca villages, Lakuntza and Iraneta. In Lakuntza a seventeen-year-old Bakaiku youth who worked in the lock factory told people about the visions in Bakaiku and led them down the railroad line to the regular site there. When he got there, he claimed to see the Virgin in the poplars by the river.

Two boys, sons of farmers, claimed to see the Virgin in Lakuntza in an oak tree near the railroad tracks, on the road to the mountain, and on a door-latch in the village. According to one witness, the people of the town attended for a while, but on one night when the boys announced a vision at two in the morning in the pouring rain, an elderly man announced that he was going to stay home, dry and in bed; that seemed to put things in perspective and no one went.

Lakuntza seems to have turned against the visions rather quickly, perhaps because of its factory workers but in part because of Blas Alegría, a priest born in the village. He was outspoken against the visions, maintaining that "the Virgin is in heaven, and she does not leave it." The man I spoke to most in Lakuntza had another reason for not believing. He was twenty-nine in 1931 and worked in the factory with the seer from Bakaiku. He kept pressing the boy, who finally told him, "Well, when a lot of people go, I say that I see because they pay me; but when just a few people go, I don't see and I go home."[32]

Six kilometers east of Lakuntza lies Iraneta. This is the Barranca town in which the visions lasted the longest, primarily because of the special alliance between a seer, Luis Irurzun, and the town secretary, Pedro Balda. I talked to Balda in the old-age home in Alkotz and to Irurzun in San Sebastián. Balda, born in 1894 in Iraneta, where there were about sixty houses, was the eldest of seven siblings in a poor family without land. His father was a pastry and chocolate maker and his mother took in laundry, made bread in people's houses, and did agricultural labor. Before her marriage, Balda's mother cleaned and decorated the church for a parish priest who belonged to Luis Irurzun's "house." The priest took an interest in young Pedro Balda, made him an altar boy, and taught him to sing the mass in Latin. Starting when he was ten years old Pedro worked as a farm laborer, and he barely learned to read and write until his military service, during which he studied and rose to be a sergeant. In 1923 he became the town secretary.

Balda took a keen interest in all matters religious and went to Ezkioga on 18 July 1931, one of the big days. Then, when the visions started in the Barranca, he visited several sites, particularly Lizarraga. His self-education, rare in a town secretary, gave him perhaps a more independent frame of mind and left him closer to the people. Similarly, his informal training in the church, like that of many sextons, demystified for him the opinions of the clergy. He paid little heed to the first seer in Iraneta, a girl about eight years old named Inocencia who saw the Virgin in late September and told people to pray the rosary. Others began to have visions at the outdoor site, including a disbelieving adult relative of the girl, María Arratibel, who saw Saint Michael the Archangel. On September 29 another woman, Juana Huarte, aged thirty, also saw the Virgin and Saint Michael, whose shrine on Mount Aralar dominates the Barranca.[33]

Luis Irurzun, a youth aged eighteen, from a prosperous house, was not one of the persons who went to the visions. He liked to dance and play the accordion, which stricter members of the community considered "the devil's bellows." On October 12, when the Ezkioga visions were attracting large crowds and the Cortes was debating the separation of church and state, Luis was on his way with seven or eight youths to the fiestas of Lekunberri to see traveling puppeteers. They stopped briefly at the vision site in a field by the road, where a rosary was getting started. Luis was smoking, and a woman named Petra pulled the cigarette from his mouth, saying, "When you pray, do it right." Luis started to smoke again and suddenly lost consciousness.

Balda had been at the visions in Lizarraga that afternoon, and he claimed to me that the seer Nicasia Lacunza, aged twenty-one, had told him that Luis would have visions. On his return Balda heard what happened, and he found Luis at home in a stupor. The next day Luis had a vision of the Virgin with twelve stars around her and thereafter at three in the afternoon he had daily visions. As a friend and favored client of Luis's house, Balda was affected profoundly.

There were other new seers, including a contemporary of Luis's.[34] Balda remembered the two marching in unison as soldiers of the archangel. I wondered how much Balda himself, as a significant member of the audience and the only one keeping a record, helped to elicit bellicose visions. He had been reprimanded by the governor of Navarra because at the first town council meeting after the Republic was declared he had said, "We are in mourning." When recalling the visions, he emphasized the predictions of war.

Luis had a flair unmatched in the Barranca. He was capable of delivering sermons while in trance for up to two hours in a voice that could be heard across the fields. In spite of other new seers, he was indisputably the central figure. He claimed not only to know future events but also to read people's consciences and thereby provoke conversions. As he put it to me, "I had a grace to be able to look at someone and to know what was wrong with him—sickness and sins and everything."

Balda's family frequently drove Luis to Ezkioga, and his visions there and in Pamplona, Bilbao, and throughout Gipuzkoa spread his fame. Joaquín Sicart sold his photograph. Carmen Medina and Juan Bautista Ayerbe befriended him, and for a time Padre Burguera was his spiritual director. Luis was friendly with several seers, including Patxi, whom Carmen Medina took to Iraneta.

According to Luis, about a month after his visions started, in mid-November 1931, all the seers received orders from the governor of Navarra to submit to a medical examination. Then, at the height of his popularity, Luis went to Juaristi's clinic in Pamplona. In 1983 he told me that after twenty-five days the doctor confessed that medical science could not help and asked for his intercession with the Virgin. Luis also said that in Pamplona his companion from Iraneta, an atheist, tried to take him to a brothel, but when he saw the women inside he fell down the stairs unconscious.

Luis's visions continued on his return. He told me that at that point every day there were eight or ten buses of spectators, some of them from Pamplona, as well as those who came on foot. His fame increased because of a kind of miracle announced by Saint Michael in one of Luis's visions three days in advance. During the Litany on 8 December 1931 in the church packed with spectators, Luis's hands and shirt were suddenly covered with blood. Luis announced solemnly that the blood was "the tears of the Virgin." Marcelo Garciarena, the parish priest, who had no truck with the visions, snapped, "Shut up, fool." Still apparently in vision, Luis announced that the Virgin wanted him carried home, with the Salve to be sung along the way. As they carried him singing, Balda remembers that a woman came out of her house, furious, and said, "Throw him on the fire. That'll

Luis Irurzun at home, late 1931 or early 1932; on the ribbon at the left are the words "Blessed is She who appears" and on the altar is a card of a Rafols crucifix. Photo by Carlos Juaristi

wake him up!" Balda saved the shirt as a relic and eventually Padre Burguera collected it.[35]

Most town councils in the Barranca had opposed the Republic in April 1931. By the end of 1932, however, many of them had town councillors who defined themselves as republicans.[36] The modus vivendi with the Republic worked against the visions. The church also came down against the visions, and most people in Iraneta sided with the parish priest. Some people found incongruities in the content of the visions. At first most spectators were from Iraneta and Ihabar, and one Iraneta woman stopped believing when in vision Luis said, "The Virgin has said that the girls from Ihabar should sing a hymn." The Iraneta woman saw no reason why the Virgin should single out the girls from Ihabar.[37]

Nevertheless, Luis's visions survived the longest in public of all those in Navarra. In March 1932 Governor Bandrés called him to Pamplona and told him he would have no more visions, which earned the seer a headline and, doubtless, more followers. Irurzun told me he assured the governor that he was having visions at 3 P.M. every day and offered to return at that time, but the governor declined (in panic, Luis thought). He said the governor threatened him with jail but in fact did nothing, and Luis went home. At this point the Navarrese were still going to Ezkioga itself, some in buses from Pamplona and others on foot from the Barranca, praying out loud as they went. When the governor ordered the last outdoor vision stages and altars in the province dismantled, Iraneta was one of the holdouts. In October 1932 Luis was still having visions, and seers and their families from other places went to see and have visions with him. An occasional bus brought spectators from the city.[38]

In March 1933 Bishop Muniz y Pablos of Pamplona sent a circular to the priests of the valleys of Arakil and Burunda that forbade attendance at the visions and denied that they had any supernatural character.[39] José Maiza remembered being mocked in Lakuntza and Arbizu when he would walk to Iraneta from Etxarri-Aranatz. And the two families who were the last to go from Arbizu had to do so secretly, so much had public opinion there changed.

In May 1933 Raymond de Rigné brought J. A. Ducrot, a journalist from the French photo magazine VU, to Iraneta. By then Luis gave vision sermons in his house. Ducrot saw Luis fall backward "as if hit on the chin," for a while maintain a praying posture, eyes closed, but then begin to preach like a seasoned orator. "His voice, resonant, swells, takes on a poignant tone. Little by little he gets more deeply involved, and he lives what he describes." Luis then acted out a battle between Saint Michael and the devil, "like a tempest that shook the house." It ended as suddenly as it began. Luis answered Ducrot's questions, and from Luis's instructions the reporter made a sketch of the devil and Saint Michael. Luis told him that in the great chastisement "the sword of Saint Michael would kill people at the rate of two million every five minutes, and the earth would be almost depopulated in several hours." Luis's story constituted most of the third and concluding installment of Ducrot's report on Ezkioga. The cover showed Luis just as he had fallen to the floor, held by Pedro Balda and two other young men.[40]

Five months later there were only twenty-two spectators, and in May 1934 people attended from only four households.[41] Attendance was even sparser when Maritxu Erlanz arrived as the new schoolmistress, probably in 1935, and Pedro Balda took her to a secret session. By that time it was considered sinful to attend and Maritxu had to be careful not to be seen. The visions were no longer held daily. Only five men were present: three from Iraneta, one from Lakuntza, and the vision promoter Tomás Imaz. They said the rosary and the Litany and then Luis gave a cry in Basque and fell down. He was propped up with a pillow, his face began to sweat, and he delivered a long, disjointed, sermonlike speech in

Luis Irurzun on floor of his house, ca. 1933

Spanish. He told of the call-up of conscripts, of a coming war, and of bodies in roadside ditches, with an admixture of biblical material. The highlight for Maritxu was that he seemed briefly to levitate, but her overall impression was a certain lack of spontaneity, a feeling that the vision was prepared, and she did not return. She told me that comparing Pedro Balda's version of Luis's sermon with what Luis actually said, it seemed that Balda was dressing up the language and adding things. Balda confirmed to me that in his enthusiasm he had interpolated material in the texts and that for that reason they should not be published.[42]

Balda's interpolations raise the difficult question of how to reconstruct what any of these visionaries said or what they wanted to say. Almost inevitably we are restricted to describing the multiple mirrors—the hopes and anxieties of the listeners—that distorted the messages. For instance, Balda included in his wide correspondence poems of his own, such as the one he vigorously recited to me at age ninety, composed in 1933 or 1934. I translate the last quatrains:

The right and the left laugh	Derechas e izquierdas se ríen
at the Holy Apparition.	de la Santa Aparición,
If they keep it up	si persisten en su empeño
they will be sent to hell.	tendrán la condenación.
What sorrow! What bitterness!	¡Qué tristezas! ¡Qué amarguras!
will some day be felt	algún día se han de ver
when God casts his sword	cuando Dios lance la espada
and shakes the world.	que al mundo haga mover.
"That day is not far off"	"El día no está lejano"
the seers are saying,	van diciendo los videntes
and at the divine warnings	y de los avisos divinos
the people are laughing.	se van riendo las gentes.
The laughter will cease	Las risas se acabarán
when the great fright comes,	cuando llegue el gran espanto
and all the happiness	y todas las alegrías
will change into tears.	se convirtirán en llanto.
For our enemies	Para nuestros enemigos
that day will be horrible;	será espantoso ese día;
it will be a day of fulfillment	será día de ventura
for the sons of Mary.	para los hijos de María.
Hear the voice of Christ	Escuchad la voz de Cristo
who will come to reign soon,	que pronto vendrá a reinar
for if Christ did not come	que si Cristo no viniera,
the world would be ruined.[43]	el mundo se iba a arruinar.

Although Pedro Balda refined the written messages, it is clear that Luis not only took people aside to tell them (whether correctly or not) their private sins but also announced that certain people, like the male schoolteacher, would die. Pedro Balda wrote the vicar general Justo de Echeguren in Vitoria and over a back fence informed a priest in Iraneta that seers had foreseen their untimely end. These announcements were not well received, and many villagers came to look at Luis askance.

For what Luis and others were doing was risky. People knew they had visions of and struggles with the devil. If their predictions turned out to be accurate, the question could be posed: Did they act or speak with the devil's help? The fear of malevolence that led to accusations of witchcraft three hundred years earlier was still alive in the twentieth century. Rural folk were alert to the power of curses and of quasi-religious rituals to maim and kill. Once the church denounced the visions, not a few people, like the parish priest of Arbizu, judged them to be sorcery and shunned the seers. If the seers were wrong in their predictions, they could be labeled charlatans. The psychiatrist Juaristi opened yet another line of explanation: mental illness. In the long run his diagnosis may have helped to relieve seers of opprobrium, but in the short run it tended to isolate them, for Juaristi described the illness as contagious.[44]

There were other mini-Ezkiogas in the near vicinity. One sequence of visions took place in a pair of villages to the east of the Barranca, Izurdiaga and Irurtzun. According to one source, the Izurdiaga visions began on 11 October 1931, that is, at the height of those in the Barranca. At the beginning of December a priest, Marcelo Celigueta, reported to the vicar general of Pamplona on behalf of the pastor of Izurdiaga, his brother Patricio. For more than a month there had been three seers in Izurdiaga, two girls aged seven and ten and a boy aged eleven. Watched by about thirty children and ten adults, they were having visions every day during prayers to the Blessed Sacrament. The schoolmistress led these prayers in the church prior to the evening rosary. Perhaps because one of the girls was his niece, the parish priest was sympathetic.[45]

The youngest girl had been to Ezkioga. There the Virgin had said that she would make herself visible whenever the girl prayed a Hail Mary. Then the three children had visions on a hillside in Irurtzun for several days, attracting a thousand spectators. The littlest girl said the Virgin had given her a picture of the Sacred Heart of Jesus, which she gave to her schoolmistress to keep. The Virgin said there that those who kissed the little girl's hand or received the blessing of the other girl could receive Communion the following day. Like seers of the Barranca and at Ezkioga, the children saw an apocalyptic battle between devils and Saint Michael. There had been Irurtzun children who had had visions as well, but their parents had treated them harshly. The Izurdiaga seers learned from the Virgin that those parents would be punished. By December the Irurtzun outdoor visions had ended.

The sessions in the Izurdiaga church were similar to those in the rest of the Barranca. When the children first began their prayers, they would fall into "ecstasies" (Marcelo Celigueta's word) lasting up to an hour. They would offer flowers to the Virgin and at the end of the session distribute the flowers by name to the persons that the Virgin indicated, even if they did not know them. They did so on their knees and without removing their gaze from the Virgin.

Marcelo described other aspects of the visions as well.

> Other times, after having put on behalf of the Virgin much fear into some child who was not praying or who was distracted, they would mark out with the petals of the flowers a kind of cloud that when they returned to their normal senses they explain is the perimeter of the aura, like that of the sun, around the Virgin; and within this they mark out another circle, like that which a person occupies when standing, and they do not let anyone go there or step there during the apparition.

> They are given rosaries and medals so that at the end, when the children say the word "Bendición," the Virgin blesses them several times, or perhaps blesses several people in particular. And as the Virgin does it, the children once or several times make a perfect cross in blessing. Normally the rosaries in question are already blessed by a priest. One day they gave a rosary like the others to the girl when she was in ecstasy, and she rejected only this one. A priest, who had the authority to do so, made the sign of the cross and blessed it; and they gave it to the girl and she was not sure whether to accept it. She finally took it, and without waking up from her ecstatic sleep or whatever, she gave it by name to the girl it belonged to. After the session they asked her, "Why did you not accept the rosary the first time and then accept it later?" "Because the Virgin did not want it because it was not blessed." "And why later?" "Because it had been blessed." "Then who blessed it?" "I don't know, but the Virgin said it was now blessed."

> During the ecstasy, their eyes are always fixed on something; their retinas are motionless in spite of the sharp glare of a light put before them, and when their bodies are pricked they feel nothing. The first days they appeared to be frightened and wept because the Sorrowing Virgin wept, and later they are seen smiling because she does not weep. You can see them speaking to the Virgin and answering. A person close to them can follow the conversation. Then they say something like, "Virgen Santísima, Save Spain," and after finishing, they say that the Virgin will save Spain.

> Asked on someone's request if certain persons have been saved, of almost all they say yes—of one they said that he needed two Rosaries for his soul. A woman asked that the Virgin give the name of one of the souls that was *saved*. "That question should not be asked; [the woman] knows the name." Another time they asked where three (deceased) persons were, and the children understood, as with the previous woman. The response, that "the ones who are dead are in heaven, but do not ask about the other one because you know he is alive and in what village he lives," was true.

Celigueta also wrote that the children in vision used flower petals to make on the altar a perfect design of a monstrance and a decorative host with a cross in the center. And he said that "most persons present noted an intense fragrance of lily [*azucena*]." When asked, the children said it was the scent of the Virgin. Other days they played on their knees with the infant Jesus and their flowers. Sometimes the devil wanted to take the flowers away. "Not for you, ugly; these are for the Virgin," and they would chase him away with the sign of the cross, making fun of him.

Marcelo Celigueta was dubious about much of what he described, which he called "the dark side of the picture." He singled out the time the children claimed to have gone to heaven.

> One day they wanted to go to heaven with the Virgin, and helped by those present, they got up on the altar, respecting the sepulcher, and there they stood forming a tight group, kissing each other. They were asked how they had done this, even though they were in ecstasy. "Because the Virgin had taken them to heaven"—where they said they had been, and the little one added, "I was so happy in heaven that I did not want to come down!"

Many aspects impressed Celigueta: the way the children in trance seemed to know names and persons and who was dead and who still alive, the physiological aspects of their states, the artistic beauty and exactness of their floral decorations (these especially impressed Balda when he visited), and their consistency—in spite of frequent and separate questioning they did not seem to contradict themselves or one another.

Again evident in this report is the immediate political relevance of the visions. At Izurdiaga the Virgin told the children that all persons who entered the church should dip their hands in the holy water and repeat:

Sacred Heart of Jesus, Save Spain
Virgin of El Pilar, Save Spain.
Sacred Heart of Jesus, in you I trust.
Virgin of El Pilar, in you I trust.

Both Juaristi and Bishop Muniz y Pablos of Pamplona spoke of the political moment as a major factor contributing both to the visions and belief in them. In his 1933 circular the bishop wrote,

> Historically, in times of serious social strife like the one we are experiencing, it is common that these seers appear and multiply, and there are usually two causes attributed to this: the first is the anguish and disorientation normal in simple souls who, not finding an easy solution either in the human order or in the ordinary paths of divine providence, aspire and believe to find it in the supernatural, in God acting directly on society and not through intermediate causes; the second cause is that the spirit of evil himself suggests these aspirations, whether so that people will relax in the hope of extraordinary solutions and not work diligently to solve things on

their own; or to stifle the faith, as they stifle it in those persons who believe in these visions and prophecies and then see that they do not come true.[46]

In Izurdiaga, as in Bakaiku, the schoolteacher encouraged the visions. Pedro Balda remembered that she tried to get reports into newspapers and even spoke to the bishop. She seems to have relayed to her charges adult issues. Six months before the visions began, she got the boys and girls to write the director of a mission magazine. Their letters convey the mix of adult and child-like elements which made all the children's visions possible and attractive.

Izurdiaga, 31 March 1931

As soon as our new schoolmistress told us how to rescue the soul of an unbeliever, we gladly deprived ourselves of treats in order to contribute to save souls. We drew lots, and it fell to me to send you this letter, and I want [the pagan child] to be called Francisco Javier. Later we will send you used stamps. I ask for your blessing for all the boys of this school, without forgetting our schoolmistress, and kiss your holy scapular in the name of all of us.

Francisco Satrústegui

Izurdiaga, 6 May 1931

We, the girls of this school, who will not let the boys outdo us, have saved by not buying sweets the 10 pesetas needed to baptize a little Chinese girl, and we send them very gladly. Since we collected the money in the month of May, we wish to offer a rose to the Virgin to make very holy, and we want her to bear the name Rosa María, and Soledad for that is the name of the girl to whom it fell to write the present letter. On Ascension Day we will receive into our hearts for the first time the Baby Jesus, and we will beseech him to make us missionaries so we can save many souls. Pray, Father, so we will be conceded this grace. Bless us all, without forgetting our dear schoolmistress, and kiss your scapular in the name of all of us.

Soledad Antolín[47]

These letters are little different from those of children in other schools in the magazine. But they share aspects with the subsequent visions: the children joining in a common sacrifice for the conversion of others; the role of the schoolteacher as a facilitator; the motif of the Eucharist; and the awareness of issues far beyond school and village. On 9 and 12 December 1931, at the height of their visions, these schoolchildren sent more money. One of the letters was signed by a twelve-year-old girl who was a visionary both at Izurdiaga and Ezkioga. The money was "to rescue a little pagan girl from the power of the devil" and have her named María Pilar. In a similar letter on behalf of the schoolchildren of Piedramillera dated 26 April 1931, twelve days after the Second Republic was proclaimed, Lidia Gastón sent money for a "paganito" to be named Nicasio, "who is the patron saint of our village and to whom we fervently pray to intercede very extraordinarily in favor of our Spain, now in bitter and difficult straits." Magazines such as these and schoolteachers brought the children into the bigger picture.[48]

The Izurdiaga seers were still having visions a year later on 11 September 1932 when Padre Burguera saw them in a chapel in a private home in Pamplona. There he marveled that the girl claimed to know that a certain flower came from a convent of nuns who were disbelievers. He describes the seers, much like those who followed Bernadette at Lourdes, running around on their knees unusually fast with their eyes fixed on a flower that they considered the Virgin as Burguera carried it from room to room and hid it from them. They subsequently underwent vision crucifixions, their vision lasting four hours in all. Sessions like these were held in these years in Pamplona convents, the *asilo* of the cathedral, and private houses, including the home of the parents of the Carlist leader Jaime del Burgo. There is no evidence that politicians in any way provoked the visions, but there can be little doubt that in Navarra the climate was propitious.[49]

Finally, there were also little Ezkiogas in Gipuzkoa. One set of visions occurred simultaneously with the visions in Navarra in the fall of 1931 and indeed may have been a kind of replication of the Navarrese visions. At a house named Kaminpe, close to a road into Urretxu, child seers from the house itself and from Urretxu and Zumarraga gathered with parents and neighbors. The seers included siblings from three different families for a total of at least nine children, four boys and five girls, aged four to thirteen. Almost all of them had had visions at Ezkioga.

A woman who went as a spectator recalled that the seers distributed roses blessed by the Virgin. People lit large numbers of candles and the children fell down into a vision state and later chased the Virgin, who once hid from them under the sink. Once many people went up a nearby mountain when the children announced visions there; those attending included an invalid wrapped in blankets and riding in an ox cart and parents carrying sick or handicapped children.

One argument against the visions here was that the children who were seers later led lives just like the others—seer girls even rode bicycles, for instance. As a child aged seven or eight, my informant did not treat the visions of her playmates with the same importance that the grown-ups did. As in the Barranca, where the children sometimes played with holy dolls, it seems adults were taking seriously what for children had a component of fancy or play. But in any case the Kaminpe visions were a neighborhood affair; they did not attain in Urretxu the status of those in Navarra, which drew entire villages—and sometimes polarized them—for weeks or months. Presumably for the seer families it was simpler to go to Kaminpe than walk to Ezkioga, but later several children resumed visions at the main Ezkioga site.[50]

Twenty-five kilometers from Ezkioga by road in the hills above Tolosa, Albiztur was a more durable satellite. In 1931, as today, it was a rural township with just a few houses near its church at the bottom of the valley and with farms on the mountainsides. The pious pastor, Gregorio Aracama, had prepared Albiztur's children and adults well to believe the Ezkioga visions. Deeply devoted to Mary, he dedicated his first sermon to her when he arrived in 1921 and put something about her in each sermon until he left in the late 1950s. Aracama asked parents to add the name María to the names of girls and boys he baptized, promoted Mary's month in May, and organized the sodality of San Luis Gonzaga for boys and the Daughters of Mary for girls. Before the visions, Aracama had led his parish in pilgrimage to Lourdes and had told and retold the Lourdes story in sermons. His sense of duty was so strict that when he heard a report of minor misconduct on the part of a girl, he was capable of going to her home to tell her parents. This alienated him from some families.

It was Aracama who arranged for a bus to take his parishioners to Ezkioga, and he went every Sunday. People from Albiztur went as early as 8 July 1931. An Albiztur girl, eight years old, had visions there on July 15; a second, thirteen years old, two days later; a third, fifteen years old and a sister of the first, on July 25; and a fourth, nine years old, on August 15. What they saw was retold in loving, enthusiastic detail in the Albiztur column of *Argia* by the local correspondent, "Luistar" (Juan Múgica Iturrioz), poet, barber, maker of espadrilles, and sexton. Like the priest of Izurdiaga, he too was the uncle of a seer. In his 2 August 1931 column he compared one of the girls to Bernadette. In subsequent visions, they saw the Virgin of Lourdes, Bernadette, and Bernadette's sheep.[51]

Three of the girls were from farms; the father of another worked in a pharmacy in Tolosa. There were, however, child seers of poorer people in the village. One of these, a girl whose father had only two cows and who worked in the quarry, first began to have visions in Albiztur proper. At the time, I think early 1932, she was caring for the baby of another family. She began to fall into vision by the road near the center of the village, and the woman who cared for the church went and prayed with her, attracting other followers. One day the schoolmaster chased them away, and they moved to the covered area of the church porch. Gradually more girls—only girls—began to have visions there, including three of those who had had visions at Ezkioga. Villagers can name ten, aged six to thirteen, who were seers. In this group were two leaders, an older one whose visions started late and especially the young one, the eight-year-old who had been the first to see at Ezkioga.

As elsewhere, the believers brought flowers that the seers redistributed in vision. The girls also saw the souls of the village dead and found out what prayers or masses they needed. Believers thought the girls could read unspoken thoughts and answer unspoken prayers, and I have talked to persons who were led to repent their sins in the sessions. People from neighboring towns went to

Les petites filles d'Albiztur ont construit à flanc de montagne un petit oratoire devant lequel elles viennent prier. L'appareil photographique les fait rire.   PHOTO J. A. DUCROT

see the children, but the sessions never reached the newspapers. The parish priest prayed discreetly at a distance, but afterward the girls went to his office and dictated what they had seen. These sessions coincided with outrage in the town over the removal of the image of the Sacred Heart from the exterior of the town hall.[52]

Luistar, the sexton, was a Basque Nationalist. He was devoted to the Virgin of Lourdes, but not to the "Castilian" Virgen del Pilar. He went to Ezkioga fifty-three times starting on 8 July 1931. His last trip was on 30 June 1932, before the arguments of Laburu converted him from the visions' chief supporter to their chief opponent in *Argia*. The town as a whole split for and against the visions (the split eventually coincided roughly with the split between Carlists and Basque Nationalists), and little by little the girl seers and their families became isolated. "They thought we were fools," one steadfast believer told me.[53]

In May 1933 the vision sessions on the church porch were still going on, with about thirty persons gathering at dusk to say the rosary and accompany the seers. By then the girls also held afternoon sessions at a little makeshift chapel their families had set up on the hillside above the village, at a site called Partileku. They posed there for J. A. Ducrot, the French photojournalist from the magazine *VU*. The bishop inevitably found out about the visions and threatened to deprive Aracama of his parish. So sometime in 1933 the girls stopped holding the sessions in public. At least one girl continued in the intimacy of her family until 1940.[54]

Each public mini-Ezkioga, like the "pre-Ezkiogas" of Torralba de Aragón and Mendigorría, had original aspects. In Albiztur all the seers were girls, in Bachicabo all were boys or young men, but in most places there were both boys and girls. In some places it appears that one seer led the others but that the leader might be older or younger. In some places local elites were sympathetic, and where there was a favorable priest or schoolteacher, the visions lasted longer. In some places, like Dorrao, Unanu, and Bachicabo, the Virgin insisted on worship outside the church. Certain divine beings, like Saint Rita, showed up more in one place than another. The Sorrowing Mary was common to many places, but Mary's avatars varied. Saint Michael and the Infant Jesus of Prague appeared more in the Barranca, where such devotions were strong.

There were also innovations in places. Invisible candy wrappers, the naming of five angels, a vision boulder, a Virgin who played hide-and-seek, visions as sermons, apparitions on house facades, and visionary flower designs were special twists that made each sequence of visions unique. And of course what made each unique was that the seers were members of the local population seeing divinities who had chosen that particular place and landscape.

Except for some sites of "unsuccessful" visions—the ones that drew no following—all these locations are rural. But the "successful" vision sites are well placed. Just as the visions of Ezkioga were just off a main highway, within a long walk of Zumarraga's three train stations, so the village vision sites were on or near main roads, many of them in or near village centers. Those in inconvenient places, like the Fuente Petrás of Bachicabo or the mountainside above Arbizu and Lakuntza, soon shifted.

As we will see for Ezkioga, however, the sites tended to incorporate emblematic elements of the landscape: a pine tree and a spring at Bachicabo; olive trees at Guadamur; a cave and spring at Orgiva; first a sacred mountain at Arbizu, then a walnut tree; pine trees at Dorrao and Unanu; a river and poplar trees at Bakaiku and Lakuntza; walnut trees at Iturmendi; a mountainside at Irurtzun, Albiztur, and above Kaminpe. When the visions were forced indoors the flowers remained as a link to the land.

The visions that were exclusively "urban," or architectural, as at Torralba, Mendigorría, Rielves, Guadalajara, and Sigüenza, were the most fleeting, perhaps in part because there was too much church and social control. The governor and the bishop of Palencia quickly checked a girl who in November 1931 tried to move her visions from the outskirts of the capital to a city church. In the provincial capital where public visions would have had the best chance, Pamplona, the bishop was too close for comfort. Conversely, in the cities of the north coast—Irun, San Sebastián, Bilbao, in all of which there were habitual seers—the hostile secular Republic was too close. In Tolosa sometime around 1933 two middle-aged women of humble extraction were able to attract people to visions outside the town in a big meadow, where they placed a picture of the Virgin on a tree. But those visions lasted only briefly.[55]

Almost all visions produced a reversal of power, with initiative and control in the hands of children or unmarried youths. And although this reversal coincided with an ancient southern European pattern, it may have had a particular significance for the period: the fear that the youth would lose their faith. By the same token, this fear may have provoked the marked increase in religious imagery directed at the young by missioners, parish priests, lay catechists, and schoolteachers. In the process, young and old alike became aware of the enhanced status of children in the distribution of religious power. Only in such an unusual ambience could a priest or schoolteacher have tolerated the kissing of child seers' hands, a youth seer's appointment of "angels," the use of a child seer's blessing to forgive sins, or the child's provision of sacred berries for healing. By obeying the minors, people were obeying and humbling themselves before the divinities for whom the minors spoke.

At Ezkioga, at center stage, as far as we know no one gave orders to harvest another's potatoes. The mini-Ezkiogas, however, were more domestic versions, like local-access cable studios rather than national networks. But within vision cuadrillas at Ezkioga, the same precise allotment of grace and favor took place, with flowers going to X and not Y and private messages delivered to certain persons in the knots of believers. The local seers of Navarra and Gipuzkoa were largely in synchrony with changes in vision motifs at the Ezkioga center. As at Ezkioga, struggles of Saint Michael and the devil occurred in the summer and early fall of 1931, seer crucifixions started in the winter of 1932, and seers' crucifixes "bled" in 1932 or 1933. There was clearly enough contact between the different groups to keep everyone up to date.

VISIONS SPREAD BY PERSECUTION

As the dioceses of Vitoria and Pamplona moved step by step toward denunciation of the visions, it became increasingly difficult to hold sessions in public. And in any case as the audience shrank large outdoor venues were unnecessary. Those surviving became restricted, private séances, many with seers who had retreated to their hometowns or to safe havens protected by sympathetic priests.

In May 1933 the only public, outdoor vision site left was at Albiztur, and its days were numbered:

> While it is true that only small, isolated, furtive groups now go to Ezkioga, and although the protagonists of this affair try to be forgotten by the authorities, one should not conclude that everything is back in order. Far from it, for now it is at home, in a little group, that the seers have their ecstasies. With their holy place ruined, they have dispersed, gone to ground,

but they have hived off. In every valley, there have thus formed little clusters of believers who keep the faith, in spite of persecution and defections. One by one the church denies them the sacraments and excommunicates pitilessly even little children.[56]

Sometimes only the seer and the family held sessions, but in the years 1932 to 1936 in the cities of Bilbao, San Sebastián, and Pamplona and in the towns and villages of Astigarraga, Legazpi, Legorreta, Ordizia, Ormaiztegi, Pasaia, Urnieta, Zaldibia, and Zegama there were regular secret meetings for persons outside the immediate family.

The visions of Ezkioga aroused exceptional interest in the large rural townships to the southeast, in the mountains on the Navarrese border. Zaldibia and Zegama were devout Carlist breeding grounds for priests. Both showed early interest in the visions, and photographs of seers at Ezkioga show people from these townships as close, attentive spectators. Farm families from Zaldibia told me of rushing through the day to finish their chores early in order to be able to get to Ezkioga for the evening rosary. There was equal interest in the village center, where believers held all-night rosary sessions.

The earliest seers from Zaldibia were two teenage girls. María Luisa was a foster child on a small farm. She was not believed in her house and eventually had to take refuge elsewhere. Inés worked as a servant in Ordizia and eventually became a nun. Neither achieved the fame of the seers from Ataun. By July 1933 a married farm woman, age thirty-four, Cándida Zunzunegui, had begun to have visions, first at Ezkioga, then elsewhere, including the Echezarreta house in Legorreta, a shop in Ordizia, and her farm. I think it was to her that the schoolteacher of Zaldibia referred in *La Voz de Guipúzcoa* on 11 November 1933:

> A NEW LOURDES OR A NEW EZQUIOGA?
> The apparitions of the Virgin increase daily. Recently she seems to have begun appearing in Belgium, according to a Madrid weekly.
> The Virgin is also being seen here. Here too there is a female seer who sees her. She was left unemployed at Ezquioga by church decree, but it seems she has found in her home village a place where she can continue to exercise the same "profession."
> There is no lack of people. Some day we are going to wake up and find ourselves not in Zaldivia, but in a new Lourdes, among the noisy sirens of buses arriving full of people.

The teacher, apparently not a Basque, was answered a month later by the Zaldibia correspondent of *El Pueblo Vasco,* who wrote, "The Basques have been losing their culture ever since teachers like him have come to colonize us." In Zaldibia the visions were associated with Basqueness.[57]

Zaldibia believers faced the stiffest opposition in the diocese. The parish

Cándida Zunzunegui of Zaldibia in vision, 1933. Photo by Joaquín Sicart

priest Martín Elorza was the cousin of Bishop Mateo Múgica of Vitoria and he took the matter personally. In 1984 I spoke to an elderly priest in Zaldibia who knew Elorza well. On the wall was a panoramic photograph of a huge diocesan pilgrimage to Lourdes led by Múgica and including Elorza. Elorza was a stern man. His sympathies were with Hitler, whose picture he had on the wall of his study and whose ideas on racism he defended with vigor. But the day he read Pius XI's declaration on Danzig, he tore the picture in two, saying, "I have been wrong." Because he was so strict with himself, he demanded the same obedience from his parishioners and tirelessly preached against Ezkioga. The priest said Elorza lost ten years of his life because of the Ezkioguistas.

The Zaldibia believers were the most combative and stubborn of all. When the governor in 1932 and Bishop Múgica in 1933 prohibited seers from going to the vision site, the Zaldibia followers accompanied the few seers who went, especially Cándida, Juliana Ulacia of Tolosa, and a girl from nearby Gainza. Even Burguera could not dissuade them. They told me how they would go on foot from Zaldibia in small groups of four or five and sneak in among the apple trees after the guards had passed. People whistled or laughed at them on the way. Sometime after July 1934 Elorza began to deny Communion to those who went. The believers told me that he sent a nephew and four or five Zaldibia seminarians to Ezkioga to take the names of those who turned up there.[58]

When the Zaldibia believers went to take Communion in the church Elorza would refuse to give them the host in a ritual of authority and disobedience acted out at every Sunday mass for a decade. When they stepped up to receive communion, Elorza or his assistants would say, in front of everyone,

"Do you go to Ezkioga? I say this to you before Christ."

"Yes. I go to Ezkioga to pray."

"Well, I will not give you Communion."

"Well, somebody else will."

At least a dozen persons were denied Communion in Zaldibia for up to twelve years, although not all had the courage or stubbornness to present themselves and be refused regularly.[59]

At least one Zaldibia cuadrilla was arrested. In late January 1935 Gipuzkoa was under martial law in the wake of the October Socialist uprising and all unauthorized gatherings were illegal. The military commandant announced that he would jail all those participating in "the reappearance of new activities in Ezquioga," since the diocese had explicitly forbidden them. The next month *La Voz de Guipúzcoa* reported, "The Civil Guard informed the governor that a clandestine religious meeting, possibly 'Ezquiogan' in nature, had been discovered in the house of the mayor of Zaldivia. The matter has passed to the jurisdiction of the military." Apparently the civil guards merely took down the names of those present. The matter cannot have troubled the military commander seriously; he set modest fines of fifty pesetas. When the Zaldibia believers asked through a seer whether they should pay the fines, the Virgin said no. The government insisted and the Zaldibia town council finally paid for them.[60]

The believers told me that during the Civil War Martín Elorza had the group arrested again. Civil guards went to the regular Sunday session at Cándida's farm and took the whole group to Zumarraga, Bergara, and finally the Ondarreta prison in San Sebastián. Legend has it that Cándida in vision was so heavy the guards could not budge her until she came to her senses. There was also a political angle. From at least 1933 the town was bitterly divided between Carlists and Basque Nationalists. The two groups competed in public piety and the result was a kind of devotional spiral. When Franco's troops occupied Gipuzkoa, the Carlists turned in the vision group as separatists. The Carlists had been irked by seers who would stand up in town council meetings and announce what the Virgin wanted done.[61]

The cuadrilla arrested had five women and six men, ranging in age from about thirty to about sixty. Four were relatives belonging to three farmsteads. They included a young man, unmarried, in his late twenties, his aunt and her son, and a third male cousin. In addition, there was an older male neighbor of the youth, Cándida and her husband, a man and a woman from an Ordizia store, and a man and a woman from the Zaldibia village proper. In jail, where they were held for not paying still larger fines, they felt quite out of place with the political prisoners. A farmer whose brother was jailed told me,

> There they said, "But how can this be? How did you people come to be here?"
>
> "As Catholics."
>
> "What do you mean, Catholics? These other people are Communists, or Modern, or Anarchists. How can they denounce people for praying? Don't you have anyone on your side, anyone who will speak up for you and clear this up?"
>
> "We have no pull anywhere."

Nine were freed when the government confiscated property to cover the fines; three others, who had no property in their own names, remained incarcerated for sixteen months until their case came up. The wife of one prisoner died while he was in prison and he was not allowed to go to the funeral. They say that when the judge released them, he said those who denounced them should have been the ones in jail.

In Zaldibia the lines between believers and nonbelievers remained drawn until the late 1940s at least, and the conflict worsened when a new seer moved in. For Martín Elorza, the seers' defiance of his authority—including back talk in front of the congregation and visions in the waiting room of the rectory— was intolerable. With the word straight from heaven seers felt no qualms about confronting the priest. And according to them, he, in his anger and rigidity, slandered them publicly and even fell into heresy, as when he said, they claimed, that in the celestial hierarchy the Virgin Mary was lower than the worst priest.

Fifty years later the older Zaldibia clergy and the old-time believers were still traumatized although generally at peace. They all agreed that Elorza's rigor had been counterproductive. A believer put it this way,

> Faith, yes, it is good. But a faith that is persecuted has more strength, be-
> cause love takes on more firmness. And when the enemy attacks, there is a

reaction, "Well, no; it is this way, and it has to be this way." Little by little they began to let us do what we wanted, and little by little we left off going to Ezkioga. We still go, but less.

Said the priest, "We made abundant mistakes. It has been demonstrated that in the towns and villages where there was the most repression, the believers stayed the strongest. The more we hit them, the more they resisted. By violence it could not be done, for these are delicate matters."[62]

Denied Communion in Zaldibia and Legorreta, many seers and believers went to Ordizia, where the parish priest was more lenient. Ordizia was a market center for the Urola valley farmers and was less industrial than neighboring Beasain. Rural seers and believers had two kinds of ties to Ordizia: they were clients of its merchants and they were servants. In March 1934 there were restricted vision sessions in the house of the branch bank director, whose servant was a seer from Zaldibia, and in the flat of relatives of another seer. But most frequently the believers met in a small room behind a grocery store run by a fervent believer, Juana Usabiaga; they called the room "El Rinconcito" (the nook). The secret sessions there on market day, Wednesday, were already taking place in early 1933 and went on for at least twenty years. Believers and seers attended from as far away as San Sebastián, Oñati, and the Barranca.[63]

On the wall of El Rinconcito there was a picture of the Christ of Limpias taken from a box of candles. When the journalist Ducrot visited in May 1933, he was assured by the proprietress that it had bled in prayer sessions six times since the beginning of the year. Ducrot saw dried blood on the image. When he asked why it was not kept behind glass, she said that through a female seer the Virgin had forbidden it. A picture of the image was on sale at Ezkioga, and in 1982 I talked to a believer in Zaldibia who still kept fragments of the blood.[64]

People in Zaldibia described a typical vision session.

[Male believer:] In a vision you have to pray a rosary of fifteen mysteries, the stations of the cross and all those things. Then we get messages or errands, the person who has the visions explains them—you have to do this or that, and then [the divine figure] blesses the crucifixes that people bring and flowers, too. And the seer then hands out the flowers, giving explanations, to each person by name, although the seer had never seen the person before. And they passed on the messages—for the wife, for the children, for the good or the bad they had done.

[Female believer:] And those flowers would generally be good for healing. My father had bad eyes. And the seer said, "Here are some roses; sprinkle them with water from Ezkioga, and go with them to your father." It healed his eyes. We would be happy to get those flowers.

Always when the seer was in vision we lit candles or wax. When [the divine figure] began to appear, they would say that it said, "Make light for me, even if it is just matches." And so we always had candles or wax handy.[65]

An Ormaiztegi woman whose mother went regularly to Ordizia attended once herself. She remembered especially the pain of kneeling. The believers would enter at nine in the evening and leave at six in the morning. Some stayed on their knees all night.[66] In these sessions the divine figure, or, if you will, the seer, became a spiritual director. No longer confessing with the parish priest, these believers felt themselves to be under direct divine scrutiny, judgment, and penance. Through the seer the believer was a member of an intensely scrupulous community where every doubt about the past and the future could be answered.

In 1946 Dionisio Oñatibia, doctor in Urretxu, and Juan María Galarraga, assistant priest there, went to one of these sessions out of curiosity. Oñatibia told me that about twenty-five persons were present, men and women. After a large number of rosaries and stations of the cross, two seers, a man and a woman, went into a lengthy and "photogenic" (the doctor's word) trance state and announced that Ignacio de Loyola was celebrating mass. The seers would narrate the mass, step by step, "Now he is going to read the Gospel, everybody stand up." And the seers and believers received Communion; that is, they extended their tongues as if receiving the sacrament, though he and the priest saw no host. When the seers were in trance, Oñatibia took their pulse and observed their pupils; both were normal. At a given moment their hands appeared bloody (like those of Luis Irurzun at Iraneta). Unimpressed by the blood, Oñatibia was impressed by the prayers: "They prayed tirelessly. It was remarkable. Prayer, patience, and penance, that was the watchword." When the session was ending a woman stood up and called out in Basque the motto of Saint Michael the Archangel, "Nor Kristo bezelakoa, Nor Kristo bezelakorik" (There is no one like Christ, no one else like Christ). Sometimes at the end a stuffed pigeon, as the Holy Spirit, was passed around and kissed.[67]

The Ordizia store became a clearinghouse for messages, prophecies, and dates of the chastisement. The town also was the point of departure for the peripatetic vision sessions of Tomás Imaz which kept different cuadrillas in touch.

Tomás Imaz and the Vision Trips

Tomás Imaz Lete, a thin bald man in his early fifties, first came to the public eye when he was arrested and fined for making a scene with Marcelina Eraso on the train. By then, October 1932, he had been a leader in the vision community for at least seven months. The believers nicknamed him "Tximue" because of a certain chimpanzee-like quality to his face and ears; they heard rumors that he was connected to high church officials. Imaz was a real-estate broker based in San Sebastián. While he was not a publicist, he was very much an organizer, and he was one of the few believers to follow his convictions to their logical consequence. If indeed the world as everyone knew it was going to come to an end, and soon, with a great chastisement and a great miracle, there was no point in

Tomás Imaz, on left, with José Garmendia in vision at Ezkioga, winter 1931–1932. Photo by José Martínez

selling real estate. So he liquidated his assets and slowly spent his funds on the seers and the believers.

Starting in June 1932 Imaz rented buses and invited seers on pilgrimages. He took several trips to Zaragoza to speak to Hermana Naya, venerate the Rafols crucifixes, and pray for Spain to the Virgen del Pilar. The French author G. L. Boué met the seers, including José Garmendia and Benita Aguirre, on their return from a trip on 25 June 1932 in which Benita had visions of the Virgin and Gemma Galgani. José Garmendia's declarations on these expeditions would have confirmed Burguera's worst fears about uncontrolled seers and uncensored messages:

BLOOD OF THE DEVIL
Declaration and vision on this day taking place on the fifth pilgrimage organized by D. Tomás Imaz with seers of Ezquioga to the Santo Cristo Desamparado of the Venerable Madre Rafols in Zaragoza.

Zaragoza, 22 September 1932

On the way, after passing Tudela in the bus, the Most Holy Virgin made me aware that although she had forbidden the devil from bothering us pilgrims on this trip, he had come close to the bus, and Saint Michael had wounded the brazen devil with his sword on the right side of the neck, and from that wound fell two great drops of blood that stained the outside of the windshield of the bus; and when the infernal dragon returned again later, Saint Michael hit him again, and blood spattered the hood of the bus. All these bloodstains remained very visible for two days, as all the pilgrims present have been able to confirm.

The seer

José Garmendia

Tomás Imaz; Jesús Imaz, priest; Rosario Gurruchaga; María Luisa;
José Antonio Múgica; Juana Múgica; Martín Berrondo; José Azaldegui;
Marcelina Eraso; Vicente Gurruchaga; Francisco Otaño, priest.[68]

Here we have another rare glimpse of a clandestine group. Besides Garmendia there are at least five second-rank seers, the two (unrelated) Gurruchagas, María Luisa of Zaldibia, and Marcelina Eraso. Juana Múgica was a believer from Zaldibia, and José Antonio Múgica was the baker from San Sebastián detained two weeks later with Tomás Imaz and Marcelina on the train. The baker and his brother frequently accompanied Garmendia, and Marcelina stayed at their house in San Sebastián. Jesús Imaz Ayerbe had been a missionary overseas; he had moved to San Sebastián in 1928, where he was the chaplain to a community of nuns. On 18 July 1931 he had been cured of a chronic stomach ailment at Ezkioga. Otaño we know as Ramona Olazábal's spiritual director. Martín Berrondo and José Azaldegui were believers. So we have a gathering of seers and believers, priests and laypersons, urbanites and rural folk, men and women. There was a mix of class as well. The real-estate man and the retired missionary were listening intently to farm girls and barely literate factory workers. As for the blood of the devil, it is no coincidence that it was seen on a trip to see the crucifix of Madre Rafols; that crucifix was supposed to have been found with blood on it. Believers proudly showed the stains on the bus to townspeople in Ordizia.[69]

Since Tomás Imaz spoke Basque, he could connect better with the rural seers than Burguera or the Catalans could. At the vision sessions he frequently led the rosary. His special protégées in 1932 were Esperanza Aranda and Conchita Mateos, in addition to José Garmendia. He introduced Juan Bautista Ayerbe to them and accompanied him to their séances. Tomás's belief in the apocalypse made him fearless in defying the government, the church, Burguera, and social convention. Burguera concluded that Imaz was doing the work of the devil. José Garmendia eventually had a revelation that "the seers who go with I[maz] are betraying her and us."[70]

Imaz's trips were a way to avoid parish, diocesan, or governmental control. He took seers to places like a sympathetic convent in Alava where, with discretion, they could have visions in peace. Later he was reduced to leading pilgrimages on foot to Aralar or Urkiola. And when his last money was gone and the world had not yet come to an end, he lived on the charity of the believers.[71]

The shrine of San Miguel de Aralar is near the peak of Mount Aralar between the Barranca and Gipuzkoa. For the seers and followers this isolated site was always a safe haven, and with or without Imaz they made numerous trips there, even when it was snowbound. At that time San Miguel de Aralar was the great shrine of Basque Navarra. In an annual ritual of great emotional impact its thaumaturgic image of Saint Michael was carried from town to town in the province; this veneration stitched together the fabric of Navarrese identity. In each town the image would be met with a procession and would be carried to the parish church and to the houses of invalids. In Iraneta devotion to Saint Michael was "*terrible*," according to the town secretary, Pedro Balda, who described annual fiestas during which the town council went to the shrine on foot. As a youth, Balda himself carried the image down from the shrine and from Iraneta to Irurtzun. In Betelu too there was "a blind faith in the Saint Michael of the Basques." On the Gipuzkoan side of Aralar there was also devotion, if not so thoroughly programmed. The parish church of Ezkioga, dedicated to Saint Michael, has a sixteenth-century plateresque reredos with reliefs of the apparition of Saint Michael at Monte Gargano. In Ataun people made promises to the saint and used ribbon measurements from Aralar for healing. In Oñati a youth dressed as Saint Michael, complete with sword, walked in the Corpus Christi procession, as did boys in Good Friday processions in Andoain and in Azkoitia.[72]

People thought of Saint Michael as a precursor of the end of time, a warrior captain against the enemies of the church. At Ezkioga the photographer Joaquín Sicart distributed a picture of the saint with these words: "This image, approved by His Holiness Pius IX in 1877, represents the Archangel Saint Michael, sent by the holy spirit to remove the obstacles to the reign of the Sacred Heart."

Saint Michael's shrine at Aralar was a symbol for all Catholics of the region. When he was bishop of Pamplona Mateo Múgica wrote a stirring pastoral letter in praise of the saint. It opened with Apocalypse 12, verses 7 and 8: "And there was a great battle in the sky: Michael and his angels fought against the dragon, and the great dragon was slain, that ancient serpent, who is called the devil." In the letter the bishop discussed the cult of angels and the apparitions of Saint Michael in Italy, in Normandy, and in Navarra. (In the year 707 the saint was said to have appeared to a noble warrior living on Mount Aralar as a hermit in penance for having slain his wife.) Bishop Múgica's predecessor had revived the shrine's brotherhood and Múgica himself had built a road, brought electricity, and planned an illuminated cross for the remote site. He had seen the thousands of Navarrese and Gipuzkoans who gathered at the shrine on May 8, September 29, the last Sunday in August, and the first Sunday in September. He concluded the pastoral letter with an intemperate attack on blasphemers, adulterers, those who work on Sundays, young libertines who attend theaters, movie houses, and dance halls, overtolerant parents, indecently dressed girls (those with bare arms and short skirts), makers of short skirts, drunkards, skinflints, thieves, exploiters

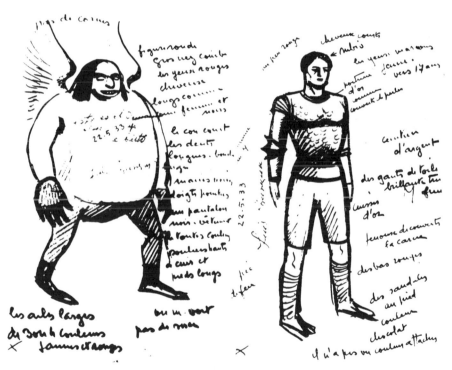

Saint Michael: top left, *patron saint of Ezkioga parish church (photo by Joaquín Sicart);* top center, *boy saint Michael from Good Friday procession, Andoain, 1915 (from* Anuario de Eusko-Folklore, *1924, courtesy Fundación Barandiarán);* top right, *holy card sold at Ezkioga, ca. 1932 (printed by Daniel Torrent, Barcelona);* bottom, *the devil and Saint Michael as seen by Luis Irurzun and drawn by J. A. Ducrot (from* VU, *30 August 1933, all rights reserved)*

of workers and the poor, gossips, proud and worldly people, spiritists who worship the devil, as well as apostates, heretics, schismatics, and sectarians. On all of these he called down Saint Michael's sword.

Writing in *El Pensamiento Navarro* on 17 July 1931 a cathedral canon equated Michael of Aralar's struggle with the dragon and that of Catholics with the Second Republic. In doing so he anticipated by one week the visions of Patxi and others. For the canon Saint Michael of Aralar was

> the shrine of our beliefs and the bastion of our traditions, whence resounds the old triumphant cry, "There is no one like God!" whose echo, rolling from peak to peak and spreading from valley to valley, has gotten the sacred militia of your brave men on their feet, ready to struggle fearlessly with the dragon until they slay it or cast it, defeated, in its cave.[73]

For conservative Basque Nationalists too Aralar was a rallying point. Luis Arana Goiri, the brother of the founder of the Nationalist party, had Saint Michael named the patron saint of the party. In August 1931 party ideologue Engracio de Aranzadi wrote that the shrine was "the point of vital union of all Basques" and he warned people not to abandon "their invincible Chieftain, the Angel of Aralar, at a time when the race needs the help of all its members in order not to succumb before the number, power, and hatred of its eternal enemies." The great advantage of Michael of Aralar as party patron saint was his attraction for the Navarrese, doubtful members of a greater Euskadi.[74]

The visions of Saint Michael battling dragons and devils in the sky at Ezkioga pointed to Aralar as a place of contact between the celestial and regional landscapes. Michael figured prominently in the visions of the seers from both slopes of Aralar, those from Ataun and those from the Barranca. In the visions Michael was the Virgin's great auxiliary, and when the great miracle was to occur, it was he who would explain it and later carry out the chastisement. So when vision meetings were forbidden at Ezkioga, Aralar became a logical alternative for Tomás Imaz and the seers.

There were other private vision places. In February 1933 police arrested the inhabitants of a flat in Bilbao because people were going there to see a miraculous Christ. By 1934 there were also regular meetings of believers in San Sebastián. And two male seers held sessions in the house of José María López de Lerena in Portugalete the first Fridays of every month. In Oñati women from town and farms said the rosary in a chapel of the parish church of San Miguel and embroidered a banner with the Virgin of Aranzazu and Saint Michael. Thus they prepared for the day of the great miracle, when they would come into the open and show their colors.[75]

In Ormaiztegi a wealthy lady held prayer sessions almost continually in her large house; she had a chapel-like prayer room with an altar and stations of the cross. Seers, two of them young women servants, would go into trance. On special holy days the dozen or so believers might hold a procession in the walled garden and sing hymns. Those attending included shopkeepers from Urretxu and Zumarraga. Persons involved in this circle describe a closed, intense world where every illness was treated with holy water from Ezkioga and every death lit by candles that had previously been lighted and blessed during visions. Some families were divided, and believers had to pray extra hard and have extra masses said so nonbelieving relatives would not go to hell. The sick offered their illness to God as sacrifices, and some who died were considered saints and intercessors in heaven. The believers contributed money and jewels for liturgical ornaments and a chalice for the shrine planned for Ezkioga. The host died in 1966.

Zegama was another center of support for the Ezkioga visions. This large township had a big new Carlist community center, complete with movie theater and bar. Relics and a statue of the Carlist general Zumalcarregui were in the parish church, where the boys in catechism class could put on the general's beret and the best one got to touch the relics. The religious activity of children was highly organized, both informally in fiestas and by the church in sodalities.[76]

In 1924 a priest reported that only ten persons did not go to church at all, but he was alert to the railroad, the paper mill, and the alcohol factory as threats to community morality. The women were devout, but most men were indifferent. The clergy worked hard to counter the inroads of modernity: from 1918 to 1924 almost every house enthroned the Sacred Heart of Jesus. In this effort the clergy could bank on Zegama's strong Marian traditions, which included an overnight pilgrimage on Pentecost Sunday over the mountains to Our Lady of Aranzazu.[77]

In 1931 several of the many diocesan priests born in Zegama supported the visions. One of them, the parish priest, took down the messages of Zegama seers Marcelina Mendívil and the eight-year-old boy Martín Ayerbe. Burguera was much impressed by the boy's visions of dead children: "He gives minute details about them to their families, which is why these families and others who know about the prodigies believe him."

Martín Ayerbe had visions both in Zegama and at Ezkioga, where his picture was sold on postcards. Like the other seers, he saw not only the Virgin, but also Christ, Saint Michael, other angels, and Saint Paul (walking among the people with sword in hand, a crown on his head, in white clothes and white shoes). The parish priest was intrigued by Martín's visions of a book the Virgin was reading that the devil wanted to destroy; he assumed it was the one Burguera was writing. The boy's vision on 17 October 1931 shows one way the visions could spread among children. He told a farm girl, aged twelve, from

Zumarraga that the Virgin had appeared over her head and instructed him to tell her to pray six Hail Marys on her return and to go every day to Ezkioga, where she too would see the Virgin.

In January 1933 when Martín was in vision in catechism class in a chapel, he saw a crucifix in a corner bleeding. According to Burguera, the other children and persons who came in, including two priests, saw the blood too. On Martín's advice, the parish priest notified Bishop Múgica, not yet in the diocese, instead of Echeguren, the vicar general. When the French photojournalist Ducrot went there in May 1933, other children as well were having regular visions before an altar in the chapel.[78]

Finally there was a vision substation in the mountains of Urnieta coordinated by the town secretary, Juan Bautista Ayerbe. In 1933 and 1934 Conchita Mateos, Esperanza Aranda, the servant Asunción Balboa, and others sporadically held sessions in houses there. Gradually Ayerbe became more daring. The first news came from the local stringer of *El Pueblo Vasco* on 1 December 1934, under the leader "Another Ezquioga?"

> It seems that part of the stream of tourists has been diverted to this town. We are assured that several persons frequently go to a certain place between the hermitage of Azcorte and Mount Buruntza, among them several from this town, and even that some go up barefoot. The visions take place not only at this site but also in two or three houses in town.

The correspondent added details the next day, reporting that the seers were adults, that some were from San Sebastián, that people went daily from Urnieta, and that after the visions the believers gathered to talk about them at a nearby farm, where the farmer was one of the seers. Few households in Urnieta were involved actively, but the correspondent named Juan Bautista Ayerbe and "Señor Imaz" of San Sebastián. Ayerbe denied the charge, and an angry lady visited the newspaper office in San Sebastián and said in broken Spanish, "Do not mess with the apparitions. Leave us in peace. We will follow the Virgin anywhere."[79] Clearly there was more than visions at stake, for three days later an explicitly political diatribe against the correspondent appeared in *La Constancia*. The author, I think Ayerbe himself, admitted only that the farmer and his friends were praying the rosary and doing the stations of the cross at the chapel. With the kind of vehemence that can best be aroused in small towns, he pointed out that the *Pueblo Vasco* correspondent was a Basque Nationalist and attributed his derision of the devotional practices to politics. By then Basque Nationalists had become allies of the Republic, and he tried to attribute their opposition to the visions to anticlericalism.[80]

The correspondent replied that in Nationalist homes throughout Urnieta, rural and urban, people still prayed the rosary and that monarchists like Ayerbe did not have a corner on Catholicism. He alluded to two years of visions in Ayerbe's home and cited a brief exchange that gives a sense of how difficult it was for persons going about their daily lives to contend with others who believed that the end of time was at hand.

> Not long ago an assiduous male devotee of Ezquioga went up [toward Mount Buruntza] with a lady, and when they came to a farm and saw that its inhabitants were quietly eating their afternoon meal, they snapped, "What are you doing eating? The Virgin is appearing up there."[81]

With martial law in force, all meetings required government permission. Ayerbe recklessly continued the sessions, and civil guards surprised a group praying at the chapel of the Santa Cruz de Azkorte. Three persons were fined. When the military commandant consulted with the diocese, the archpriest of the zone asked him to ban all meetings in the chapel. At Urnieta the Republic thus came to an understanding with the church to suppress visions, and this under-standing was applied in Zaldibia.[82]

Only a week later Ayerbe reconvened his group in Tolosa, where on 23 December 1934 the poor seer Asunción Balboa talked over the crackdown with the Sorrowing Mother. The Virgin told her the Basque Nationalists were to blame and would be punished and warned that bad men would throw bombs into convents. The unusually explicit politics of this cuadrilla comes out in Balboa's conversation with Jesus, who told her that King Alfonso would soon come back to reign in Spain. She also saw Thérèse de Lisieux, Gemma Galgani, and Our Lady of Mount Carmel, who said that because of the group's prayers twenty-five souls would leave purgatory the next Saturday. There was still time for many private messages for individuals.[83]

Starting then in 1932 Gipuzkoa had a number of groups that maintained their own parallel Catholic rituals, firm in the knowledge that a civil war would occur and that sooner or later there would be a great chastisement. Each cua-drilla met in secret, but everyone in the zone knew that such groups existed. As far as I can tell, apart from some intransigent priests, few people felt moved to do anything about them. One exception was a potter from Zegama who stood up on the vision stage at Ezkioga and shouted, "I believe in Christ but not in this nonsense!" After all, the majority of Catholics in the Basque uplands were hopeful at first that the visions were true, and huge numbers had been devout and enthusiastic spectators. Later, instead of denouncing the seers and the be-lievers, people either tolerated or laughed at their delusions, often with grudging admiration for their piety.[84]

I was told stories about the believers which, true or not, demonstrate how some of their contemporaries dismissed them. Women in Zumarraga told me about a couple from Zaldibia who were convinced by visions, their own or others', to reenact the flight of Mary and Joseph to Egypt. They borrowed a child and set off walking with a donkey. When they reached Valencia and found they would have to cross an ocean, they turned back. In Legorreta, I was told, a great fear swept the town one election day when a man came down the steep moun-tainside above the town with a blazing pine torch, and people were convinced Saint Michael the Archangel had finally descended to separate the just from the unbelievers.[85]

But what nonbelievers, whether indignant, mocking, or tolerant, all seemed to ignore was the zest of the believers. Paradoxically, while having visions of dire events in their closed secret cells, the believers were having a wonderful time, creating pockets of social space full of goodwill and good humor. For them their rosaries, their hymns, and their vision messages were a taste of heaven on earth. In these groups the mixing of unrelated men and women, of wealthy and poor, of merchants and farmers, of San Sebastián sophisticates and rural Basque speakers, of adults and children, led to a kind of exhilaration that comes with the breaking of taboo and convention. Rural women were suddenly on an equal footing with educated urban men, who served as their secretaries.

These people now recall their arrests as heroic. One day in October of 1937 or 1938 Juliana Ulacia and her group were caught at Ezkioga, put in a truck, and detained in a vacant house in Zumarraga.

[Woman:] How we prayed and sang! [laughs] From morning to night!

[Brother:] From that empty house they wanted to make it to heaven! [laughs]

[Woman:] Then they brought us to testify. Even the guards had to laugh. They didn't know what to do. We did nothing but pray and sing. But they had their job to do. We spent eight days like that; then when they got tired of our praying and singing, they gave us food and said, "All right, you can go home now."[86]

The old-time believers, their faces alight with pleasure, remembered these groups with great fondness.

VISIONS AND ACCUSATIONS OF WITCHCRAFT

In the 1930s many people drew comparisons between the Ezkioga apparitions and the great Basque witchcraft epidemic of 1608–1617. Cultural ecology may have facilitated the spread of the two phenomena.

The witchcraft accusations started near the border as a direct result of prosecutions nearby in France. The more the Spanish Inquisition got involved, the more witches were accused, mainly by children, until the entire zone of mountain Navarra, Gipuzkoa, and eastern Alava was sensitized to the pattern and the fear.

The accusations featured fear and suspicion; the visions, at least at first, featured hope and enthusiasm. The beings seen in the visions were generally good and beneficent, not maleficent, as in the accusations. Whereas the witchcraft scare was a chain reaction of ill will, the visions at first were a chain reaction of benevolence and grace, toward individuals, families, towns, regions, and nations. In both situations the proximate paradigms were French, from the Labourd region for witchcraft and from Lourdes for the apparitions, but both built on older local traditions as well. And both ended with an ecclesiastically imposed silence.

Children and teenagers played important roles in both sequences of events, testifying to the persistence both of their lack of power and their reputation for innocence. In 1611 people accused witches of corrupting children. When the enlightened inquisitor Salazar traveled around undoing the damage, he found that 1,384 of 1,802 persons whom he allowed to retract witchcraft accusations or confessions were children, girls under twelve or boys under fourteen. In 1931 children were considered more likely to have visions because of their moral innocence. In both sequences adults granted children an unusual credibility. In 1611 the adults projected onto children their fears and in 1931 their hopes. The children themselves quickly took advantage of the new opportunities that high-culture witchcraft (in 1611) and Lourdes-type vision prophecy (in 1931) accorded them. By providing the reports that adults wanted to hear, they temporarily reversed the order and hierarchy of their little societies. In 1611 the children verified that they were victims of the devil, who defiled them, or of witches, who sucked their blood. In 1931 children proclaimed themselves God's messengers and God's willing victims. The spread of the phenomena in both cases was helped by the flexible nature of children and their more fluid notions of reality.

The children's accounts of strange experiences were especially convincing because they made contact with the spirits in an altered state: in the case of witchcraft, as far as we know, a fictional or dreamed one; in the case of most seers, a real one (although one that was uncommon). In both sequences the new powers were double-edged. Witches might be agents of the devil, but there were teenagers like Pedro de los Reyes of Oiartzun who had a divine gift for unmasking witches. Some of my less educated informants accused various Ezkioga seers of having powers from the devil, not from God, and considered those seers witches.[87]

Promoters helped the spread of both epidemics; in the case of witchcraft local elites and learned inquisitors pressed people to confess and with their edicts and questions standardized the patterns of belief; in the case of the visions, informed enthusiasts convoked the seers and parents, and parish priests and schoolteachers communicated to seers their own hopes and anxieties. In both cases, servants, children, and the less privileged elements of society gained a temporary advantage.

Witchcraft accusations and visions spread with equal ease through dispersed farms and grouped settlements, but both developments seem to have done better in the countryside than in the cities, in the uplands than in the lowlands. And the events had their greatest effect in the areas of Basque language. The visions in Spanish-speaking Bachicabo and Mendigorría did not spread. Those in the Barranca reached their southern and eastern limits at the first Spanish-speaking villages. The cultural isolation of rural Basque speakers may have left them with fewer defenses against and fewer inhibitions about the spirit world and sheltered them from critical alternatives.

Finally, both proliferations may have had common roots in a landscape people already considered sacred. Witches were supposed to meet in caves. Ancient spirits called *sorguiñak* were supposed to live in caves as well, whence the Basque word *sorguin* for witch. In Bakaiku and Lakuntza children had visions along or in rivers, and rivers were one of the dwelling places of attractive but dangerous spirits known as *lamiak*. And many seers saw beings coming from mountains, both at Ezkioga and in the Barranca, mountains associated with powerful spirits, whether local gods like Mari, who could send hail and lightning as punishment, or Christian spirits like Saint Michael. But these deep cultural roots are much easier to postulate than to demonstrate; and not once did they appear explicitly in my oral, manuscript, or printed sources. I suspect them because of the intense pressure in contemporary Basque society to provide a primordial local origin for cultural phenomena.[88]

PATTERNS

8. RELIGIOUS PROFESSIONALS

SELECTIVE MEMORY is no doubt essential to the human condition. The only way we can see ourselves as coherent is to revise history continually. Some clerical historians reorder the past by silencing the role of clergy in movements they judge unorthodox. In recent times this tendency has coincided with the search by lay historians of religion for truly nonclerical, "popular," or even "pagan" traditions. But except when the clergy is of a different caste or race, we are unlikely to find sharp divergence between their thinking and that of the laity. This is particularly so in Catholic areas like the rural north of Spain which produced their own clergy and even exported them. It is not surprising that some priests and religious abetted the seers of Ezkioga.

VOCATIONS

In 1931 there were about 2,050 diocesan priests born in the diocese of Vitoria and by my estimate about 2,700 other male religious and 5,500 female religious born there. Some Basque families regularly produced clergy and religious for generations. Consider, for instance, the family of David Esnal, a priest living in San Sebastián who in 1932 and 1933 was in guarded contact with Patxi Goicoechea. Esnal's brother was a Franciscan and his sister was a Franciscan Conceptionist in a convent in Villasana de Mena (Burgos). His brother Roque had married a woman who had a cousin who was a Franciscan Conceptionist in the same convent. Of Roque's eight children, two sons were diocesan priests and one a Franciscan and a daughter was a Franciscan Conceptionist known for her holiness. In two generations, Esnal's and the next, seven out of twelve persons became diocesan priests, nuns, and male religious.[1]

Families with many vocations were at least moderately well-off, for prior to the end of the nineteenth century the regular orders required dowries and it could be expensive to educate a secular priest. Laypersons in these clans—the nieces and nephews, brothers and sisters, or mothers and fathers of priests or religious—came to have an easy familiarity with the profession. Such persons were less easily cowed by their parish priest or bishop. They knew the inside gossip, the politics of appointments at the diocesan, national, and Vatican levels, and the currents of opinion within the church. They took full advantage of the alternatives in liturgy and moral theology which different priests and religious orders had to offer. Individuals like Carmen Medina, José María Boada, and Pilar Arratia who had the resources and the inclination to found orders and restore church buildings had direct social access to archbishops, cardinals, nuncios, and the Roman Curia.

Not only clans but entire towns became famous as nurseries for the clergy. Some places specialized in male or female religious of a given order, others were more diversified; some specialized in diocesan clergy. In 1935 Zeanuri, a mountain town in Bizkaia with 2,500 inhabitants, was proud to be the birthplace of 53 living priests and seminarians, 106 male religious, and 109 female religious.[2]

A survey of clergy in the diocese of Vitoria in 1960 (by then essentially the province of Alava) showed that some towns producing many religious did so irregularly. These vocations seem to have corresponded to the efforts of particular priests or recruiters. Members of religious orders have described to me friars who came to their village, gave talks at the school, and convinced whole sets of friends to join the order. The route to a vocation could also be through a parish *preceptoría*. This was a school, generally free, that often prepared children for the orders or seminaries favored by the particular priest who ran that school. From 1902 until his death in 1961 Bruno Lezaun of Abárzuza (Navarra) stimulated through his schools around a thousand vocations.[3]

But other towns, presumably those like Zeanuri in which vocations became a family matter, maintained their role over several generations. If we compare vocations by size of town of origin, the diocesan priests of Vitoria in 1931 came far less from the industrial areas around Bilbao, San Sebastián, Eibar, and Irun and the fishing towns along the coast and more from the agricultural and pastoral uplands.

When we look at the towns within the immediate zone of the Ezkioga visions which for their size produced the most priests, we find those towns that stayed faithful to the Virgin of Ezkioga the longest: Zegama (23 priests from a population of 2,119), Albiztur (8 priests from a population of 805), and Ataun as well as Itsaso, Ormaiztegi, Legorreta, and Ordizia.[4]

Ataun, the home of two prominent Ezkioga seers, had 2,424 inhabitants in 1931. Thanks to a careful count of its vocations we know that in that year it was the birthplace of 26 living diocesan priests, 60 nuns, and 37 male religious, that is, about four times as many male and female religious as secular priests. In 1931 Ataun had approximately four hundred households. About one in six had a living member who was a priest or religious, as follows:[5]

TOTAL VOCATIONS

63 houses with 1 vocation	63
6 houses with 2 vocations	12
4 houses with 3 vocations	12
4 houses with 4 vocations	16
4 houses with 5 vocations	20

Vocations in Ataun often occurred in family clusters. One in three individuals with a vocation had a sibling with a vocation. About one in five had an uncle or aunt or niece or nephew on their father's side with a vocation. We do not know how many had relatives through mothers, but there were probably as many as through fathers. This would mean that a majority of Ataun's religious or clergy had a close family relative in religion.[6]

The houses with the most vocations were on the whole the more prosperous farms. Several of their families, like Arín and Tellería, had produced religious and priests regularly in previous centuries. The rise of active orders and the endowment of scholarships at seminaries at the end of the nineteenth century opened up clerical careers to more people, and it was from the 1890s that the boom in vocations in Ataun occurred. The great revolution came not in the secular clergy but in the religious orders. Prior to this period, the religious from Ataun were concentrated more in contemplative orders, particularly Benedictine monks and Cistercian Bernarda nuns. As more orders returned to Spain at the end of the century, entrance became easier and vocations of religious jumped to a high level in 1890–1909 and increased 50 percent more in 1910–1929.[7]

There was now room in the secular and regular clergy for the wealthy and the humble, the intellectual and the worker. In 1931 Ataun natives were seminary professors, pastors of large and prosperous parishes, directors of schools, and mother superiors. Others were coadjutants, a Jesuit tailor, a Passionist convent cook, and Benedictine, Capuchin, and Franciscan lay brothers. Among the nuns there were teachers and nurses but also cooks, ironers, cleaning women, and other lifelong menials. The orders people chose were generally

Grupo de la procesión misional de Guernica.

Guernika'n, Mixio-jaietan.

Children of Gernika dressed as Native Americans for mission procession, 1930.
From Nuestro Misionero, *January 1930. Courtesy Instituto Labayru, Derio*

those with houses closest to Ataun. Youths often entered the same order as their aunts, uncles, or siblings (five brothers from Orlaza-aundia became Benedictines, four sisters from Lauspelz became Daughters of Charity and their brother joined the Vincentians), and there were families whose tradition was to provide secular priests.

The religious orders did not keep the youths of Ataun close to home. First, they sent them to a novitiate, the most distant of which were in Paris and Madrid. Then they assigned them according to their particular calling and the order's needs. In 1931 only those who had become secular priests or contemplative nuns or monks were likely to return to the diocese. The active male religious were often found working abroad, particularly in Latin America, and the active nuns mainly elsewhere in Spain. In all, half of Ataun's vocations were posted out of the diocese; one out of five was out of Spain.

If these figures hold for the diocese as a whole, they should give us pause. The period 1918–1930 was a golden age of missionary propaganda, particularly in the north. The heartland of conservative Catholic Spain was not a closed, ingrown society but one with intimate family links throughout the world. In

La Misionera, rodeada de sus chinitos.

Children dressed as Chinese for mission pageant in Vitoria, 1932. From Iluminare, 20 February 1932, p. 56. Courtesy Instituto Labayru, Derio

1931 there were natives of Ataun in China, Jerusalem, the United States, many countries in Latin America, and France in an ecclesiastical version of the great worldwide diaspora of European peasants at the opening of the century. Through letters and rare visits these religious kept in touch with their relatives at home.[8]

We have seen that interest in missions extended even to children, who participated in the conversion of heathens through monthly magazines and dressed in elaborate costumes for annual mission pageants. In some of her visions Benita Aguirre heard the Virgin ask her to pray for the conversion of the Chinese. Some of the same families contributing alms and promises to the Ezkioga vision network had brothers, sisters, uncles, and aunts who were missionaries.[9]

For women especially missionary work offered the possibility of holy adventure in wild contrast to life on the farm or in an urban apartment. Teresa de Avila dreamed as a child of becoming a missionary. From around 1910 Basque and Navarrese women could fulfill these age-old fantasies. María Recalde was from Berriz, where a new missionary order of nuns had been founded in her lifetime; the founder, Margarita María López de Maturana (d. 1934), was a

ÁNGELES DE LAS MISIONES

Women missionaries: masthead of magazine from Mercedarians of Berriz, 1932. Courtesy Instituto Labayru, Derio

candidate for beatification. Some of the Mercedarian Sisters of Charity trained in Zumarraga went overseas, and there was a new house for female missionaries in Astigarraga as well. These orders depended on alms and new vocations to keep up their mission work, so they kept the Basque public well informed of their activities. The result was a region in which not just families—Esnals or Ayerbes—but entire towns had a proprietary interest in the church.[10]

The importance of locally born clergy becomes obvious in towns that produced many religious. There virtually everyone was either related to or neighbor to the family of a priest or other religious. Resistance to diocesan policy on Ezkioga was strongest in towns like Zegama, Ataun, Itsaso, and Ormaiztegi precisely because in such an intensely devout rural society only priests or religious, or those who enjoyed their support, could resist the hierarchy. In the townships that produced many vocations, a kind of kin-based ecclesiastical culture was strong enough to allow some people to make up their own minds.

Sometimes more important than the village parish priest were the sons or daughters of the village who were priests or religious elsewhere but who returned to the village for visits to their families. Among both kinds of priests, those most friendly and open had the most influence in public opinion about the visions. José Domingo Campos, the pastor of Ormaiztegi, was a native of the village but never let on how he felt. "Nunca se supo [We never knew]," some of his most assiduous parishioners told me. When parishes were deeply divided, such priests found it prudent not to express personal opinions or give sermons on the subject; they often limited themselves to reading diocesan decrees. Priests or religious who came from the village but practiced elsewhere might be less hesitant to speak their minds.

THE PARISH CLERGY

I know of no diocesan priest who had visions at Ezkioga, but in the first months of the summer of 1931 many priests expressed pride in their seers, accompanied them to the vision site, stood with them as they saw what they saw, and debriefed them afterward. There were also those who held back from the start. Consider the six priests in Zumarraga. Two did not let their sympathies show. Antonio Amundarain and Andrés Olaechea were enthusiastic organizers and participants. Juan Bautista Otaegui sometimes led the rosary at the vision site in July 1931 and until the fiasco in October believed his cousin Ramona Olazábal. Miguel Lasa, the most approachable and best loved curate in Zumarraga, openly opposed the visions. He was the son of a charcoal-maker in Ataun, and it was to him that the Ezkioga milkmaid had taken the first girl seer. He spoke out against Patxi's theatrical trances: "The Virgin does not come to scare people." He warned at once that Ramona's wounds could have been faked. And in 1932 he instructed parishioners not to participate in the stations of the cross at Ezkioga.[11]

In March 1932 Juan Casares, the curate of Ezkioga in charge of Santa Lucía, sent a letter to Justo de Echeguren, the vicar general, who at that time was actively planning with Padre Laburu the talks that would discredit the visions. The letter is evidence of division among local priests. It seems that the curate of nearby Itsaso had been boasting that the vicar general had called him in and approved of his stance (in Casares's words a stance "of credulity and encouragement") toward the seers. In the Itsaso annex of Alegia down the road from Ezkioga seers and believers could be sure of a friendly ear in confession. Obviously peeved, Casares asked if the Ezkioga priests should change their policy:

Pray let us know if we ought to favor and promote these apparitions, in which case we will avoid the animosity of the people who, emboldened by this priest and a few others, have got to the point of making our lives almost impossible and our ministry unfruitful, and we will avoid as well letters complaining about us being sent to you, although in any case if my conduct has not been as it should be, you may shift me somewhere else, in which case you could count of course on my obedience.

Perhaps the vicar general was using the Itsaso priest as an unwitting informant or perhaps he was trying to provide some kind of church outlet for the pilgrims. In any case, his task as the head of a deeply divided and at times strong-headed clergy was complicated, and one can understand why he let Laburu do the convincing.[12]

To understand fully how the clergy made up their minds about Ezkioga, we need to know about their internal, informal groupings. The clergy and seminarians were divided, largely along linguistic lines, between those who cultivated a Basque identity and those who cultivated a Spanish identity. Many of the more cultured younger priests with Basque leanings, inside and outside the seminary, looked to the teachers José Miguel de Barandiarán and Manuel Lecuona as their leaders. One of these younger priests was Sinforoso de Ibarguren, the pastor of Ezkioga, who participated in the Eusko-Folklore Society. From the very start Barandiarán and Lecuona, as they told me separately, felt that despite their curiosity about the visions as a human phenomenon they as priests should not encourage or validate them by going to the site. In all the years of visions, they never did. A young member of their group did go and wrote one of the only negative articles published about the visions in the summer of 1931. Yet other priests with Basque Nationalist sympathies were swept up by the same hope for a divine sign in favor of the race which moved the Nationalist writer Engracio de Aranzadi and the newspapers *Euzkadi, Argia,* and *El Día.*[13]

But even in July Basque Nationalist clergymen were not the key actors. The organizers of the prayers seem to have been José Ramón Echezarreta, the brother of the owner of the field, who had been in Latin America, and above all, the Zumarraga parish priest Antonio Amundarain and the local directors of the Aliadas. Particularly enthusiastic in this respect was the assistant priest of Zumaia, Julián Azpiroz. But when the bishop forbade priests to go to the site, Amundarain and his group obeyed, regardless of their private sympathies. After Echeguren's verdict against Ramona, most of the Basque Nationalist clergy turned against the visions. Those who stuck with the seers were Carlists, especially Integrist Carlists. By 1934, except for one group of believers in Zaldibia, the Ezkioga visions, to the extent that they were politically defined, were an affair of the pro-Spanish right.[14]

Zegama in particular was a stronghold of clerical sympathy for the visions. Of the twenty-three priests in the diocese native to Zegama, at least seven were at some point enthusiastic supporters. Foremost among them was the parish priest, José Andrés Oyarbide Berástegui (b. 1868), who worked with Padre Burguera, took down the Zegama vision messages, and forbade the seers there to tell the Ezkioga priest what they saw. His sister Romana often accompanied the child seer Martín Ayerbe to Ezkioga. In Zegama Oyarbide was assisted by a brother, and another curate was also a believer.[15]

From the same generation was José Antonio Larrea Ormazábal (b. 1869), Benita Aguirre's parish priest in Legazpi. At first he accompanied her to Ezkioga and took her statements; later he turned sharply against the visions. Francisco Aguirre Aguirre (b. 1873) was a curate in Irun. Like Juan Bautista Ayerbe, he provided a link to the earlier visions at Limpias. He had been on a pilgrimage there in June 1919, and after his return to Irun he recovered from a chronic limp after praying to the Christ and putting its picture to his leg. In the summer of 1931 he and his sister went several times to Ezkioga from Irun by train. On 8 September 1931 while he was saying mass, the Virgin told him to tell the vicar general that it was she who was appearing at Ezkioga, that she wanted a church built there, and that a miracle would take place soon. Aguirre went to Vitoria the next day but was unable to see the vicar general. In May 1933 Evarista Galdós had visions in Aguirre's house which convinced him to take down her messages for Padre Burguera.[16]

Gregorio Aracama Aguirre (b. 1884), the pastor of Albiztur, was Francisco Aguirre's cousin. At the start of the visions Aracama's nephew, Juan José Aracama Ozcoidi (b. 1909), was a seminarian. In 1933 he became curate of Urrestilla, where he believed in and assisted the seer Rosario Gurruchaga. Two other believing priests from Zegama, Doroteo Irízar Garralda (b. 1875), director of the Ave María School in Bilbao, and Isidro Ormazábal Lasa (b. 1889), parish priest of Orendain, saw and were convinced by Ramona's bloodletting.[17]

Soledad de la Torre and the Priest-Children

Several of these priests from Zegama were prestigious older rectors. Some had had experience with a local mystic prior to the events at Ezkioga. For in the mountains bordering Navarra and Gipuzkoa an extraordinary woman held influence over diocesan priests. She was Soledad de la Torre Ricaurte (1885–1933), the founder in Betelu (Navarra) of the Missionary Sisters of the Holy Eucharist and its ancillary movement, La Obra de los Sacerdotes Niños, the Society of Priests as Children. Like the visions at Ezkioga, La Madre Soledad has been expunged from history. Much like Magdalena Aulina, she encroached on male territory, extending the time-honored role of conventual mystic consultant to include overt tutelage of priests.

My first clue to her role was a Basque-baiting pamphlet by the priest Juan Tusquets. In February 1937, soon after San Sebastián had been taken by Franco's troops and Ezkioga believers imprisoned there, Tusquets delivered a lecture entitled "Freemasonry and Separatism." In his talk he referred in passing to "meetings of a spiritist nature in order to mislead and discredit the Catholic faith, like those of Ezquioga and Betelu, organized by the Basque Nationalists and visited by groups of Catalans." To him such meetings were part of a general decline in moral order, manifest as well in the Masons, the Rotary Club, and Jehovah's Witnesses.[18]

In Betelu and Pamplona I learned about Madre Soledad and why some clergy would have thought her subversive. Born in Colombia into a well-to-do family, at age thirty Soledad was moved to go to Spain, where she arrived in 1915 a kind of missionary in reverse, from New World to Old and from women to men. She had been encouraged by her Jesuit confessor, and through him other Jesuits arranged for her to use a large house in Betelu. Betelu was a prosperous Navarrese village that like Ormaiztegi and Banyoles was a genteel summer resort. She eventually obtained permission from the Augustinian bishop of Pamplona, José López y Mendoza, to found her missionary order; the bishop in turn obtained Benedict XV's oral permission.[19]

Madre Soledad brought two women from Bogotá and found others locally to be missionaries. She recruited other women as lay auxiliaries. Her aims were "to restore an evangelical life, glorify the humanity of Christ, and popularize the Eucharist that the Lord wants for the sanctification of souls" (in the house in Betelu the Eucharist was always exposed), but in particular she sought "to sanctify priests." Several associations to sanctify clergy had been founded from 1850 on, and in 1908 Pius X had specifically called for more such associations. Madre Soledad's innovation was to work toward this goal through an order of women.[20]

In Betelu she set up a school for the children of the rural elite and she offered adult literacy classes on Sundays for servants and country folk. According to women who attended her school, she was quick, good-hearted, and holy. "She had something special, a gift; she solved your problem as if she was a confessor." Betelu is in a Basque-speaking area, and although all the teaching was in Spanish, she diligently acquired Basque. Villagers remembered that she subsisted on fruit and milk.[21]

Madre Soledad gathered around her a number of priests who supported her order, and she created for them an association based on the concept of childlike innocence. She published its rules in 1920. At its head was an "Older Brother" and a governing council named by the bishop. The diocesan examiners who approved the rules remarked on the novelty of her idea, noting that the priests who joined would lead a kind of monastic life while in the world.[22] According to her manual, *El Libro de las Casitas* (The Book of the Playhouses, or Dollhouses), printed in 1921, the Sacerdotes Niños were supposed to be as open and as generous as very young boys. In the manual she uses diminutives in speaking to the priests and refers to supernatural beings or sentiments as if they were characters in children's books, like Da. Pánfaga (Mrs. Bread-eater). The Niños had to flagellate themselves six days a week and do other simple exercises:

> Stay five minutes in a little corner of your room, very still, without moving, and as if you have in your arms the baby Jesus, and kiss it five times. . . .
>
> Imagine that the Virgin arrives, takes the little boy by the hand, and takes him to a garden; there he enjoys seeing the most beautiful flowers (the virtues of the Virgin). Noticing that he wants them, she picks him some, makes him a bouquet, and gives them to him. Do this for five minutes.

For special penances she prescribed praying with arms outstretched, lying prostrate on the floor, eating only half a dessert and offering the rest to the child Jesus, contemplating the stations of the cross, writing the Lord a letter about one's dominant passion and then burning it, "speaking for three minutes with the Virgin in child talk," offering a bouquet of "posies" to Jesus, or visiting for five minutes the Lord in his playhouse and speaking to him in child talk.[23]

In all Madre Soledad's work she applied the spirituality of female contemplatives to adult males living in the world. But implicit in this program was the priests' personal belief in her spirituality, since in the role of little boys they accepted her as a kind of mother. A prerequisite for joining the association was "to destroy oneself, renouncing in a certain way one's own personality and abandoning oneself totally in the hands of God." A discipline of puerility may have been particularly attractive for rural Basque and Navarrese clergy as a kind of relief from their inordinate social and political power. We glimpse this power in the rare republican newspaper reports from these villages, which refer obliquely to the excessive influence of the *jauntxos* (literally *señoritos*, but figuratively "honchos") in all aspects of daily life. Humility in Madre Soledad's association balanced a heavy diet of daily authority.[24]

What bishop approved such a constitution? At the end of a long career, at the age of seventy-two López y Mendoza was just then firmly suppressing all public reference to the miraculous Christ of Piedramillera. But by the same token he very much had a mind of his own. Like other bishops of his time, he took refuge in convents when he needed a break, in particular with the Augustinian nuns of Aldaz, ten kilometers from Betelu. He was also interested in the theme of holy childhood. In 1919 he exhorted each parish to take up collections and enroll children in the missionary club, Obra de la Santa Infancia. Madre Soledad's school and literacy program would have appealed to his sympathies for Catholic social action as well.[25]

From the diocese of Navarra Madre Soledad's most important recruits were two cathedral canons, Bienvenido Solabre and Nestor Zubeldia; they served as the diocesan examiners for the rules. From 1922 to 1924 Zubeldia was rector of the diocesan seminary. There he hung maxims of Madre Soledad on the walls, exposing entire cohorts of priests to the Niño idea. Other adherents included priests in the neighboring villages of Almándoz, Errazkin, Betelu, and Gaintza and a few from as far away as Tudela, Granada, and La Coruña.[26]

Betelu is just five kilometers from the border of Gipuzkoa, and some Gipuzkoan priests became Niños. They included Gregorio Aracama of Albiztur, possibly some priests from Zegama, and Juan Sesé of Tolosa. Manuel Aranzabe y Ormachea, a wealthy priest from Lizartza, was a strong supporter; the nuns cared for his sister, who was mentally ill.

The priest-children considered that Madre Soledad had the gift of reading their consciences, and she gave them sermonlike lectures. In the mid-1920s, when the Gipuzkoan priest Pío Montoya was a seminarian, Juan Sesé took him, his sister, and their father to see her. They were favorably impressed and remember her as a small woman, very modest, who spoke much and brilliantly and referred to human pride as "Señora Chatarra [Mrs. Junk]." The townspeople of Betelu understood that Francis Xavier appeared to her in ecstasy and recall that the village was sometimes crowded with visitors.[27]

By 1919 her fame as a "saint" had spread widely, for several bishops had inquired about her to the nuncio, and he wrote López y Mendoza. It may have been then that she and the bishop of Pamplona decided that the wisest course was to institute her order for nuns and her association for priests as diocesan congregations. This the bishop did on 5 March 1920, pending Vatican approval. López y Mendoza protected her until he died in 1923. His successor in Pamplona, Mateo Múgica, did not like what he heard. The unusual submission of male priests to a female had led to unfounded rumors of sexual license.[28] The same rumors later circulated about the group of Magdalena Aulina, which also associated males and females.

The Holy Office condemned the *Book of the Playhouses* and the rules of the institute and dissolved the association of priests as children altogether. On 23 February 1925, following the orders of the Vatican Congregation of Religious, Múgica severely restricted the freedom and power of the women in Betelu. The erstwhile *Misionarias* were to be strictly contemplative *Adoratrices* who renewed their vows annually. They could found no more houses. Their goals could have nothing to do with clergy, "only the sanctification of souls in general," and the Niños could visit them no longer. The auxiliary laywomen could continue provisionally, but only if they had no contact with the priests and were not members of the convent.[29]

Madre Soledad immediately went to Rome. There, accompanied by the superior general of the Augustinian order, Eustasio Esteban, she appealed to Cardinal Laurenti, the prefect of the Congregation of Religious. She protested that "if the Holy Church does not permit us to have as our object the greater sanctification of priests, we humbly request our secularization." She told him she would appeal to the pope if necessary to avoid being cloistered. According to her, Cardinal Laurenti allowed her to continue "the practices of the past"—I assume she meant her contact with priests—as long as the rules nowhere mentioned the sanctification of clergy.

Not surprisingly, when Madre Soledad returned to Navarra Mateo Múgica rejected this Mediterranean solution of doing one thing and saying another, so the entire community petitioned the Congregation of Religious to return to secular life. By 1928, when Múgica was transferred to Vitoria, Rome had not replied and the community remained in a kind of limbo. In her explanation of the situation to the new bishop, Tomás Muniz y Pablos, Madre Soledad listed nine professed nuns, two novices, and a postulant.[30]

In spite of Muniz y Pablos's visit in 1929, neither he nor the Vatican acted; the nuns remained contemplative. Theoretically at least, their priest followers could not maintain any contact with them, although the auxiliaries continued to operate the school. In fact, given Cardinal Laurenti's verbal consent to Soledad's mission, she continued to have contact, direct or indirect, with the priests. Women who lived near the convent and who attended the school remembered that even after the nuns were cloistered, Soledad de la Torre addressed the priests from behind bars on Thursdays. We may assume that contact with laywomen was even easier.[31]

In July 1931 Madre Soledad and the nuns were living under this ambiguous, provisional regime. Gregorio Aracama of Albiztur sent two of his sisters to ask if he should go to Ezkioga. Her response was, "Go to Ezkioga and pray a lot." This attitude confirmed his interest, that of his parishioners, and, we may presume, that of other Niños with whom he was in contact. And the fervor and mystical enthusiasm of the first years of her movement must have made other people in the area receptive to the Ezkioga visions.[32]

Soledad de la Torre died on the feast of the Immaculate Conception, 8 December 1933. Her believers considered the date a portent, but thereafter the convent gradually disintegrated.[33] *La Constancia* published a front-page obituary signed "A Priest," and three weeks after Madre Soledad died, two women from Segura presented the article to Conchita Mateos in vision. Conchita murmured, "Now you are better off, but your daughters must be sad," and said she saw the nun with a white habit and a crown of stars next to the Virgin.[34] Similarly, Esperanza Aranda claimed that when she held up a picture of Madre Soledad during a vision in 1949, Our Lady said the nun was then a saint in the choir of virgins. Esperanza had experienced more than her share of ostracism and ridicule and asked the Virgin how Madre Soledad could have been so slandered in her lifetime. Aranda said the Virgin replied, "Do not place your trust in men; they are like a hollow reed that even the wind can break." Juan Bautista Ayerbe, who recorded the vision, noted that Soledad de la Torre's "marvelous writings have now been collected to be sent to Rome."[35]

FEMALE RELIGIOUS

Madre Soledad's attempt to assume formal authority over parish priests was daring and ultimately fatal for her order, but the authority itself was ancient. Priestly consulting with female mystics has a long history in Mediterranean Catholicism, and indeed in pre-Christian times, as at Delphi and Dodona.[36] When the Ezkioga visions began, it was natural to compare what the lay seers were saying with what the "professional" nun seers like Madre Soledad said, for convents were by design platforms for contact with God.

It was easy to pin divine rumors on anonymous nuns, like the one who on her deathbed predicted prodigious events for 12 July 1931. On July 24 *La Constancia* cited another unnamed nun in support of Ezkioga:

> An illustrious religious who occupies a high post in his order told us that a nun who leads an extraordinary life whom he knows and talks to has announced for this year great appearances of María Santísima. Would she be referring to Ezquioga?

A mimeographed letter that circulated among believers in 1933 referred to a nun "directed by one of the highest eminences of the church" as "a very holy soul with a very elevated spiritual life" and "a fervent devotee of the Holy Christ of Limpias and his prodigies; she is very old and burdened with crosses." In spite of the verdict against Ezkioga by the bishop of Vitoria she counseled patience and happiness, saying, "All God's works need persecution; otherwise they would not be true, and by it they gain strength."[37]

In many convents there were nuns thought to be especially spiritual. One nun in Zarautz was thought to predict deaths accurately; she was also called in when houses were bewitched. In Aldaz there was a visionary Augustinian nun who could see a picture of the Christ of Limpias respond to her prayers or feelings.[38] In female orders male religious already had mystical guides when they needed them. The tradition of consulting holy people governed the response of male and female religious to the visions at Ezkioga. They did not question whether such visions were possible but rather how well the visions fit the criteria with which they judged their own mystics.

The census of December 1930 found 5,450 female and 2,251 male religious in the Basque Country, about half of them in Gipuzkoa. The number in the province had increased greatly when religious took refuge there after the separation of church and state in France in 1905. The number of nuns continued to increase between 1910 and 1930. Since the beginning of the century Gipuzkoa, Alava, and Navarra had been first, second, and third among Spanish provinces in the number of religious as a percentage of total inhabitants.[39]

About one in four houses of female religious in Gipuzkoa and Bizkaia were contemplative. This proportion declined as the active orders, particularly in San Sebastián and Bilbao, took on more tasks in hospitals, social services, and schools.[40] Male and female religious helped to ease the dislocation caused by an economy that was shifting from agriculture to industry. Since many of the active orders were French, they kept the Basques abreast of the latest developments in French piety, including the great apparitions.

Religious orders establish a rule, a way of life, and a set of devotions that make each order an extended family different from other orders. Some orders, like the Capuchins, regularly transferred members from house to house, creating a certain homogeneity within the order in each province. Cloistered religious might spend all their adult lives in the same small group; these houses, rather than the orders they belonged to, were the group that determined belief or disbelief in the visions. Orders varied widely in the source of their members, whether rural or urban, wealthy or peasant; these factors could predispose them in favor of or against the messages of the largely peasant seers. All of the orders in July 1931 were uneasy in a nation that had turned against its religious.

The orders most active in the vicinity of Ezkioga had propagated many of the devotions that showed up in the apparitions, thereby laying the groundwork for the public's acceptance of the messages. Ezkioga seers saw religious in their visions and attempted to win over religious houses to the cause. The laity watched closely for the reactions of the religious to the apparitions.

Cloistered religious were a major, long-term constituency for the visionaries, especially the female seers. In 1930 there were at least thirty convents of contemplative nuns in the Basque Country, particularly of Franciscans of various types, Augustinians, and Carmelites. And Basque women entered convents in the rest of Spain as well. These little societies developed their own criteria on matters supernatural; at times they felt little bound by the church hierarchy. Nuns might be enclosed, but they could write the seers with questions and requests for the divine. Convents of believers transmitted news of Ezkioga to their clerical and lay friends and benefactors. Some houses in Pamplona were intensely interested; Tomás Imaz, the San Sebastián broker, took seers to the Cistercian convent at Narvaja in Alava for visions, and in Oñati "those inside the convent knew more about the visions than those outside."[41]

Maria Maddalena Marcucci

Passionist nuns shared the key devotions of the visions. According to their rule, the Sorrowing Mother was the heavenly superior of all their convents. At Ezkioga the Passion as experienced by the Virgin was the dominant visual metaphor.

The most prominent Passionist nun in Spain was the Italian Maria Giuseppina Teresa Marcucci, in religion known as Maria Maddalena de Gesú Sacramentato. From 1928 to 1935 she was superior of the house in Bilbao-Deusto. She had known Gemma Galgani of Lucca by sight, as she herself was from a village near Lucca. Many thought Maria Maddalena was a holy woman, and she herself had revelations and visions. Starting in 1928 her writings were published by her director, Juan González Arintero, the Dominican expert on spirituality, and his successors in the magazine *Vida Sobrenatural*. In her letters and autobiography we see a woman in close, obedient contact with Dominican guides.

In a letter dated 15 October 1931 Maria Maddalena referred to the visions at Ezkioga: "The apparitions of the Most Holy Virgin of the Sorrows seem intended to show us the sufferings and anguish of the Heart of Jesus. Some souls believe they have seen him as the Nazarene, carrying the cross." Marcucci attributed Christ's anguish to Spain's rejection of him and worried about what she could do to protect her community.[42]

Marcucci met Evarista Galdós in early 1932 and afterward wrote her from Deusto with requests to the Virgin to intensify the Passionist vocations of the community, to cure a sick nun, and to take Marcucci herself directly to heaven when she died. Her initial contact with Evarista may have come through male Passionists in Gabiria or Irun. But it could also have come by way of Magdalena Aulina. In February of 1933 Salvador Cardús understood that Aulina was directing Marcucci spiritually. Marcucci came from the same pious environment as Gemma Galgani and knew about the surprising supernatural events that Gemma described. It was fitting that she should believe both the visions of Ezkioga and Magdalena Aulina.[43]

This independent abbess was accustomed to receiving spiritual help from other women as well as from male guides, just as she gave such help to women in her convents and readers of her writings. In her letters Marcucci refers to holy women in the different convents in which she lives and others in her order whose inspirations, revelations, or visions guided her and others in the order. Women and men who felt as she did that they received particular communications from the divine formed a community of mutual support. A permanent, hidden, conventual mystical network thus underlay the more spectacular lay visions known as apparitions.[44]

The Franciscan nuns of Santa Isabel in Mondragón were firm believers in Ezkioga. Magdalena Aulina was said to have served as spiritual director to their superior, who had in the house a saintly lay sister. The priest Baudilio Sedano de la Peña encouraged belief in the visions among the same nuns in Valladolid and brought Cruz Lete to speak to them. One nun had visions of her own, and the house was divided for decades between those who believed in her and Ezkioga and those who did not. She warned the latter that they would go to hell.[45]

The seers Pilar Ciordia, Gloria Viñals, and others attempted to sway houses by having visions inside them, a kind of home delivery of grace. One young woman reported that the Virgin told her, "I want you to be the tutelary angels of the religious communities. Get them to pray, because many, not all, need it." But it was not always easy to convince those whose chaplains or spiritual guides did not believe. Evarista Galdós is said to have converted one convent when she discovered in a vision that one of the sisters had a bad foot. And Benita Aguirre said she had private messages from the Virgin for certain cloistered religious

> about internal practices that made them marvel, such as that [the Virgin] was very happy with a rosary that they prayed secretly as it is prayed at Ezkioga, or that they should not stop praying the three Hail Marys before

the Litany, or that, as in former times, they leave the keys with an image of the Virgin, for she would protect them.

In Pamplona a girl from Izurdiaga saw the Virgin threaten a community of nuns for not believing. When the tide turned against the visions, clergy made every effort to "deconvert" believing houses. Padre Burguera complained of "instances of communities where a Father cast the spiritual exercises he was leading so that when he finished, the religious ended up not believing anything [about Ezkioga]."[46]

Several Ezkioga seers eventually became cloistered nuns. One of the small dramas in the vision dialogues was whether and when the seers, including the girl from Ataun, Ramona Olazábal, and Benita Aguirre, would enter convents. In January 1942 Conchita Mateos claimed she received her vocation after seeing a nun who had recently died in a Franciscan convent in a town of Castile. The spirit nun dictated a letter for Conchita to send to the mother superior saying that Conchita had her same playful nature and would take her place. This unusual reference letter was successful, and Conchita and twelve other girls from five families of believers entered the convent, where she continued to have visions.[47]

The order of active female religious with the most communities in the diocese, over sixty houses in 1930, was the first female active institute, the Daughters of Charity of Saint Vincent de Paul. Its members, who took temporary vows renewed every three years, were in charge of the old-age home and the parish schools in Urretxu as well as hospitals in Tolosa and Beasain. In the province of Gipuzkoa alone they staffed at least thirty institutions.[48]

Given the large number of active women religious in the region, they seem remarkably little involved in the visions. Their activity and freedom to circulate, however, gave them access to moments and places where the supernatural and the "world" coincided. In the fall of 1931 a Daughter of Charity who was a nurse in the Tolosa hospital was present when doctors diagnosed Marcelina Eraso's sister as having an incurable cancer. The nurse asked Marcelina to ask the Virgin to intercede and later signed a document describing the cure. One seer, Esperanza Aranda, worked in San Sebastián in La Gota de Leche, an establishment run by the Daughters of Charity which provided milk for babies and pregnant mothers. Aranda held some of her visions with nuns present and once pointed out in a vision a Daughter of Charity who had just died in Urretxu.[49]

The women in the Daughters of Charity led lives of a certain independence. An example is Sor Antonia Garayalde Mendizábal, who died at age seventy-eight in Beasain in 1932. Born in nearby Altzo, she entered the order in 1849 and worked in a home for abandoned children in Córdoba before going to Beasain in 1896 to head the clinic. Garayalde visited the sick in their homes and cared single-handed for the ill of the nearby village of Garín when it was struck with typhoid fever in 1896. She also set up a nursery school, which at one point had three hundred children, promoted the cult of souls in purgatory, took care of the cemetery, and prepared the corpse of virtually every person who died in Beasain. Sisters like Garayalde took on the work formerly done by women for their extended kin; these sisters were especially needed in factory towns like Beasain where immigrants had left their grandmothers, aunts, and sisters behind.[50]

In Elorrio the mother superior of the community at the old-age home and clinic was a faith healer. When the doctor's guild complained to the bishop and he passed the complaint on to the Spanish headquarters of the order in Madrid, the order tried to transfer the nun, but the people of Elorrio protested so much that the order backed down. The hands-on miracles of this nun, however, were quite different from the holiness of the saint-as-victim, like Gemma Galgani, which the seers of Ezkioga came to embrace. Sor Antonia Garayalde touched the bodies of the living and the dead in Beasain; the Ezkioga seers were intermediaries with the spirits in the other world.[51]

We can see the contrast in contemplative and active stances as reflected in religious devotions. In the first years of the century the Daughters of Charity began to circulate little images of the Miraculous Mary. Groups of thirty households, known as "choirs," pooled money to buy them and passed these boxed images of a powerful Mary daily from one house to another. The people would always light a candle or oil lamp before the image, and the boxes had a slot for alms for masses for deceased members, the costs of the Association of the Miraculous Medal, or the local poor. Images like these of different devotions circulated (and still do) throughout Catholic Europe. The Passionists circulated ones of their saints, as did the Carmelites the Infant Jesus of Prague, Our Lady of Mount Carmel, and Thérèse de Lisieux. Some orders supplied printed prayers with the image. In this period the Miraculous Mary was fresh and exciting. In Beasain Sor Antonia established no less than twenty-four *coros* covering 720 families. In some places the devotion took on a life of its own.[52]

Not surprisingly, from the start at Ezkioga this Mary was in a sort of competition with La Dolorosa as the preeminent divine figure. The Beasain chauffeur Ignacio Aguado saw the Miraculous Mary on July 8, and for a while others saw her as well. A Daughter of Charity was present when the Bilbao engraver Jesús Elcoro saw La Milagrosa on July 30.

> [Elcoro] tries to explain the stance that the Virgin took in her appearance, and begins to hold out his arms the way the image of the Miraculous Mary does. The crowded conditions do not permit this, and a Sister of Charity says, with extraordinary excitement, "The Miraculous Mary! It's the Miraculous Mary! Isn't it true? Make room, let him put his arms the way he has seen the sweet Virgin."
>
> And as if conjured by the outburst of faith of the little nun, the youth has an apparition again. The nun says to him, "Tell the Virgin that we

Cover of home visit manual of the Miraculous Mary, published by Vincentians in Madrid, ca. 1926

La Visita Domiciliaria de la Virgen Milagrosa

love her a lot, and that we come to make up for the many offenses against her in Spain."[53]

Eventually La Dolorosa emerged as the dominant symbol of the visions, a symbol oriented more toward contrition and penance. It was more suited to contemplative and Passion-oriented orders, like the Passionists, Capuchins, Carmelites, and Reparadoras. La Milagrosa, like Our Lady of Lourdes and the Sacred Heart of Jesus, was a more active, optimistic image appropriate for orders involved in good works or healing.

Nuns might be believers or disbelievers, supplicants or sister seers of the visionaries. Male religious could also be spiritual directors to the seers or expert examiners of visions. Some clergymen, like Padre Burguera himself, thus had a professional as well as a personal interest in the apparitions.

From their junior seminary just over the hill in Gabiria, Passionist professors and students could hear the hymn singing and prayers at Ezkioga and they were inevitably embroiled. The Passionist order, founded in Italy in the eighteenth century, had established its first house in Spain in Bilbao in 1880. In 1931 the north was still its stronghold. In the first weeks of general excitement at Ezkioga the Passionists were "almost all in favor." Some individuals converted at Ezkioga went to confess at the Passionist seminary. On 1 August 1931 two fathers were said to have seen one of Patxi's "levitations." The seers tapped into Passionist interests with visions of the Passionist Gabriele dell'Addolorata and the would-be Passionist, Gemma Galgani. The Ezkioga farmer Ignacio Galdós had a vision of a Passionist preaching to more than four thousand people; in the vision a star fell from the sky until it was by the side of the preacher, who distributed parts among the crowd. Two-thirds of the people disappeared into the darkness, while the remainder, brilliantly lit, fell to their knees; the Passionist blessed them with his cross.[54]

The initial enthusiasm of the Passionists is understandable given their devotional aesthetic. Passionists had accompanied their sodalities to the visions of the Christ in Anguish at Limpias, a kind of throwback to the Baroque devotions of Holy Week that declined in the north in the nineteenth century. This kind of devotion had revived in part because of parish missions. In their missions the Passionists set up outdoor stages. A parish priest in Navarra commented on their "special method":

> preaching from a stage or platform in an appropriate place and giving a brief talk on one aspect of the Passion of Our Saviour after the principal sermons; they did the apparition or entrance of the Most Holy Virgin, the descent from the Cross, and the procession of the holy burial.

The visions at Ezkioga also had as their central metaphor the Passions of Christ and the Virgin, and Patxi's similar stages at Ezkioga served the same purpose, the provocation of remorse by a kind of sacred theater. The order's magazine, *El Pasionario,* carried almost no news of the apparitions, but issues published before the visions started included depictions of the Passion in poses much like those later struck by the Ezkioga seers and descriptions of the mystic life of the German stigmatic Thérèse Neumann. The magazine was read in the villages and towns around Ezkioga.[55]

After the exposé of Ramona's miracle, most of the Passionists turned against the visions. Indeed, some, like Basilio Iraola, a friend of the Ezkioga pastor, were opposed from the start. But a few remained firm in their belief. I spoke in 1982 to Brother Rafael Beloqui, who said he had been to the visions thirty-nine times, primarily because he enjoyed the praying so much. In June 1933 a certain Padre Marcelino, based in Villanañe (Alava) and Deusto, was thrown from a horse when returning from a remote village where he had celebrated mass. A rural doctor told him he was in critical condition, and after his condition worsened he said he saw the Virgin who told him he would recover. He attributed the cure to the Virgin of Ezkioga. Rumors like this and one that a Passionist had seen Gemma and San Gabriele at the site gave the believers hope that the order would be on their side.[56]

In the first flush of enthusiasm in the summer of 1931 Franciscans, Capuchins, Claretians, and Dominicans went to the vision site and published their impressions, which varied from noncommittal to guardedly enthusiastic. And as with the Passionists, so with the other orders: after early enthusiasm for the visions they eventually followed the diocese into opposition. Only a few individuals persisted.

The Franciscans carried the most weight in Gipuzkoa, with houses in Zarautz, Oñati, and Aranzazu. The believers and friars I talked to agreed that the Franciscans came to oppose the visions strongly; believers attributed this to a fear of competition. A man in Tolosa claimed Aranzazu was the place Bishop Múgica met to plot against the visions. Another rumor had it that a Franciscan outspoken in his opposition to the visions had fallen to his death while directing the construction of the church of Our Lady of Lourdes in San Sebastián.[57] The Franciscans were from the same kinds of families as the seers and believers, so their opposition was especially hard to bear. Indeed, of all the religious I visited, it was among Franciscans at Aranzazu that I found most sympathy—not for the seers, but for the believers. When the seer Martín Ayerbe of Zegama became a religious, he joined this community.

In the 1920s about thirty thousand pilgrims went to Aranzazu each year. This was a relatively small number for that period, especially compared to the crowds at Ezkioga. But Aranzazu was the major Marian shrine in the province and one to which many of the believers in Ezkioga were devoted. They recognized the apparition of the Virgin in Aranzazu as a local precedent, and when the Ezkioga site was declared out-of-bounds, some believers went to Aranzazu to meet and pray.[58]

In 1919 Capuchin preaching had sparked the visions in Limpias. The Capuchins had six houses in the wider vision region but none close to Ezkioga. Some of the friars involved with Limpias took an initial interest in Ezkioga, but many became convinced that the visions at Ezkioga were a plot to embarrass Catholics.

Pedro Balda, the town secretary of Iraneta, told me that he and Luis Irurzun went to Pamplona in an attempt to leave the notebooks of Luis's messages with Balda's uncle, a Capuchin. Luis went into a vision, with Balda's uncle in prayer alongside him, but as he came out of it the superior arrived and gave him a kick. Balda and Luis decamped with the notebooks and Capuchin alms-gatherers spread the word that Luis had been booted out of the house.[59]

Dominicans went to Ezkioga from Montesclaros in Cantabria and nearby Bergara and reported for *El Santísimo Rosario,* the magazine that first publicized Fatima in Spain. But not all Dominicans were receptive. Luis Urbano, the man who single-handedly discredited the visions at Limpias and Piedramillera in 1919 and 1920, published in his magazine *Rosas y Espinas* the first negative article about Ezkioga written by a religious. In this period Dominicans in Salamanca, Madrid, and Pamplona had a kind of rival to Ezkioga: the divine messages relating to Amor Misericordioso, Jesus of Merciful Love, received by Marie-Thérèse Desandais (1877–1943). The abbess of a convent of Dreux-Vouvant in the Vendée, Desandais published her revelations under the pseudonym P. M. Sulamitis. González Arintero, the Dominican who published Maria Maddalena Marcucci, first came across Desandais's writings in 1922. He dedicated much of the last seven years of his life and the pages of his journal to spreading them. In the late 1920s a wealthy laywoman in Madrid, Juana Moreno de Lacasa, financed the publication of the messages in pamphlet form by the hundreds of thousands. In San Sebastián the count of Villafranca de Gaytán de Ayala persuaded a number of bishops to allow leaflets to be inserted in diocesan bulletins. And Dominicans spread the devotion with lectures and a special magazine and by installing paintings of the Merciful Christ in their house in Madrid in 1926 and in Pamplona in 1932. The Ezkioga seer Jesús Elcoro, given to seeing nuns, claimed to see Sulamitis with the Virgin.[60]

The messages of Merciful Love posed fewer problems for the church than those of Ezkioga. Very little of their content was bound by time and place. They were the product of a single visionary who could be silenced at any time; they came through a respectable journal and enjoyed ecclesiastical permission. They were not propositions to the hierarchy from the lay public, much less from poor rural children, housemaids, farmers, and workers. Inspired females could be heard only if cloistered and directed. It helped to disguise their identity. Most readers did not know that J. Pastor (Marcucci) and P. M. Sulamitis (Desandais) were women. The Merciful Love messages too were quite different from those of Ezkioga, emphasizing the mercy of God as good father, not the anger and chastisement of God offended. In 1931, when events seemed to be going against Catholics and Catholicism in Spain, the idea of a chastisement was perhaps more in line with contemporary developments. Merciful Love had less appeal to the Basque public than darker calls for penance, atonement, and sacrifice.

"I am Merciful Love!" holy card, ca. 1932

Two orders with influence in the area, the Benedictines and the Jesuits, kept their distance from the visions. At the Benedictine monastery of Lazkao, eight kilometers from Ezkioga, most monks strongly opposed the visions and told their confessants not to go.[61] The Jesuits did not report the visions in their magazines even in the first months. The elite male order in Spain, they educated Spain's elite. They were largely an urban order and were less likely to be related to the seers at Ezkioga. I know of few direct Jesuit links even to believers.

But even before Laburu got involved, the Jesuits could hardly ignore what was happening. Their great shrine at Loyola was only twenty kilometers away, and the confessionals periodically filled with people from the vision sessions. Pilgrims to Ezkioga from other parts of the country and abroad made detours to see Loyola and inevitably commented to the fathers about the visions. Nonetheless, in the summer and fall of 1931 the Jesuits were keeping a low profile. In May Jesuit houses had been burned down in Madrid and elsewhere, and they knew most republicans thought the order should be dissolved. Antonio de la Villa accused them in the Cortes of promoting the Ezkioga visions, the accusation itself a cause for prudence.[62]

Examples of Jesuits speaking even guardedly in favor of Ezkioga were thus rare. A Jesuit at Loyola told two French visitors from Tarbes that the purpose of the visions at Ezkioga and Guadamur was not to set up a shrine like Lourdes but to warn of impending persecution and to revive the faith of Spaniards. Salvador Cardús of Terrassa corresponded with a Jesuit in India who was interested in Ezkioga and Madre Rafols, but even this distant friend requested great discretion lest "someone else, with indiscreet zeal, might later go around saying to people, 'A Jesuit said this,' and many times it turns out that what was said with the best of intentions is not interpreted in the same way."[63]

Believers resented the Franciscans but held no grudge against the Jesuits, despite Laburu's hand in their defeat. A Jesuit from Betelu was the key person distributing the prophecies of Madre Rafols. And the ex-Jesuit Francisco Vallet had prepared the followers of Magdalena Aulina. Male seers went to the Jesuits for spiritual exercises. Even the Ezkioga souvenir shops of Vidal Castillo had a Jesuit connection: they were owned by the Irazu family, who ran the stands at Loyola and Limpias. So however much the Jesuits tried to keep their distance from Ezkioga, they formed in fact a part of the context that nurtured the visions.

Hence we find visions in which the seers protest the expulsion of the Jesuits, settle into stances that seem to replicate those of Ignacio de Loyola in paintings or in the wax statue at Loyola, and report seeing Loyola himself giving Communion. And, as in the case of the Benedictines, believers occasionally came across a Jesuit they considered sympathetic. Nuns from Bilbao persuaded one Jesuit to go see Gloria Viñals when he was in Pamplona, and López de Lerena alleged that he subsequently had a vision of his own in the cathedral. After the war the Jesuit confessor of a seer from Azkoitia introduced him to another Jesuit in a high position in the Vatican. But the believers I talked to knew of no member of the order who worked actively or spoke out publicly for their cause, and the documents I have read mention no Jesuit other than Laburu who actually went to Ezkioga.[64]

Carmelites took more interest. Since the time of Teresa de Avila and Juan de la Cruz, the Discalced Carmelites considered visions, revelations, and investigation of such phenomena as their particular expertise. And although Basque and Navarrese Carmelites were standoffish on the whole about Ezkioga, some individuals were sympathetic. The order drew on rural and small-town Basques to supply missions in South America and India. Children participated in this effort through *La Obra Máxima,* based in San Sebastián.[65]

Believers placed their hopes for a convincing public rebuttal of Padre Laburu on the Carmelite Rainaldo de San Justo, for two decades a professor in Rome. I talked to his nephews, the well-known Nationalist clergymen Domingo and Alberto de Onaindía. He told them that one little element of truth in an apparition was enough to give it great significance.[66] In Pamplona Padre Valeriano de Santa Teresa, known for processions of children in honor of the Infant Jesus of Prague, supported confessants who had attended vision sessions. And at Altzo before the Civil War Padre Mamerto, a simple man from Bizkaia, a naturalist, friend of animals, and healer, was a firm believer in the visions and was not afraid to proselytize for them.[67]

The Carmelite who took the task of testing seers most seriously was Doroteo de la Sagrada Familia, born Isidro Barrutia in Eskoriatza, another enthusiast of the cult of the Infant Jesus. From 1933 until 1936 he was the superior of the Carmelite house in San Sebastián. Shortly after Bishop Múgica's edict against the visions, Padre Doroteo attended one of the visions of a seer in Tolosa. He knew Juan Bautista Ayerbe and let him know he was Patxi's spiritual director. When I mentioned Doroteo's involvement to his brethren, they said it was in character. He may have been the Carmelite who made Ramona swear that her messages were true and one of those López de Lerena and others mentioned as having tested the seers.

> Many religious, especially Carmelites, submitted the seers to mystical tests, such as having them end their visions by mental command from their spiritual superiors, and they assured us that the phenomenon that occurred in the seers was, without a doubt, of a supernatural character.[68]

Burguera's volumes on God and art were printed by the Carmelites of Valencia, and when he went to Rome in 1934 he carried a letter of introduction to the general of the order.[69]

The Carmelite Luis de Santa Teresita was the brother of a child seer from Ormaiztegi. His parents believed deeply in the visions, and the Catalan supporters often stopped at their house. He was studying for the priesthood when the visions started and was ordained in 1933. He eventually was named a bishop in Colombia and died there in 1965. Two of his sisters became nuns. Brothers of other seers became Jesuits, Dominicans, and Franciscans. Before and after the visions, seers, believers, and the religious professionals around them were often related to one another.[70]

A few sympathetic members of the clergy can have a disproportionate effect on a religious movement stigmatized as unorthodox. In the seers' search for confessors and spiritual directors they were in a buyer's market. There were priests in their own towns and villages, priests in surrounding towns, priests in rural religious houses, and finally priests in the cities and neighboring dioceses. These clergymen offered a broad spectrum of attitudes toward the visions, and any of them could dispense sacraments and absolution. So it was relatively easy for seers to find sympathetic clergy and religious. At the beginning of 1933, in spite of the Laburu lectures, Juan Bautista Ayerbe knew personally ten priests who were open believers and another twenty who believed in private.[71]

Bishops could not control what the laity, clergy, and religious did in private. Múgica could make rules and decrees, but in the protected secrecy of the confessional information and grace could flow in both directions. In selected female houses the Ezkioga female seers found curiosity and goodwill as well as a clientele for spiritual services. Some priests and members of orders found support for their devotional agendas in the visions. But others had practical, personal uses for direct contact with the divine. In the intimate communities of cloistered nuns in particular these two modes of belief coincided, the interests of the order and the interests of a specific set of human friends, living and dead. Some houses became unanimous centers of belief.

There could be many reasons for persons in religion to support the visions, if discreetly. But there were few reasons to oppose them actively and vocally. Such opposition would earn the enmity of fervent believers, who in Gipuzkoa and the Barranca were virtually everywhere. Clergy opposed to the visions were generally more than happy to leave the task of discrediting them to the vicar general, the bishop, and Laburu. The Dominican Luis Urbano and the Carmelite Bruno de Sainte Marie, sharply opposed to the visions, were safely distant in Valencia and Paris. Republican ridicule was insubstantial. In Gipuzkoa only the layman Rafael Picavea took up the thankless task of examining the visions critically. Even Laburu did not publish his lectures in anything like their entirety. Only in Tolosa, Legorreta, Zaldibia, Legazpi, and Ezkioga itself did parish priests rigorously enforce diocesan orders to deny Communion to seers and believers.

It is not difficult to be enthusiastic about alleged religious visions or miracles. As long as the seers seem to act in good faith it is more difficult to work up a strong head of indignation against them. For six months El Día, a newspaper administered by priests, described the visions in detail. But after the diocese spoke against the visions, El Día fell silent. Thereafter it provided almost no new information or analysis of the phenomenon. If the apparitions were not "true," how could they have come about? After Laburu's talks, Bishop Múgica's circulars alone answered the articles and books in favor of the visions. As in other spheres of public life in Spain, enforcement of rules was left to the authorities.

THE KINDS OF SEERS
PEOPLE HEEDED

HE VISIONS at Ezkioga occurred in a society whose members believed that certain kinds of people were closer to the sacred than others and thus more likely to have visions. These biases affected the seers' acceptance or rejection by the community. They also set limits on our knowledge. We may assume that those whom society penalized rather than rewarded for having visions reported them less. Ecstatic religion surely has systematic relations with the social order, but we can know of these relations only through social facts. Secret, private, and unrecognized seers evade us.[1]

In the first months of summer 1931, when the Ezkioga visions were respectable, stereotypes and prejudices determined which seers people recognized. For instance, the priests, doctors, and town officials of the informal commission at Ezkioga made a special effort to obtain the statements of adult male seers; these authorities were all males and they seem to have trusted the male visionaries most. The Zumarraga priest Antonio Amundarain declared in mid-July 1931,

> We have, gathered by us and examined by doctors and priests, about sixty cases. Of these about half are rejected immediately after a very summary examination, either because of the physical condition of the declarers or because of the state of their nerves, etc. There are others, however, who interest us intensely, as they offer an extraordinary sense of reality.[2]

According to a Catalan pilgrim, the Zumarraga doctor was the first hurdle: "Dr. [Sabel] Aranzadi (who is quite strict) examines the psychic state of each alleged seer, and only after he decides that a case offers certain guarantees is it considered by the office." Aranzadi himself told a reporter the men especially interested him.

> Thus for instance we see healthy and strong men profoundly affected who return time and time again to Ezquioga because they continue to be troubled when they go back to their homes and cannot bring themselves to think that what they have seen so clearly could be a hallucination. The trouble is that these men, precisely because of the emotion that takes hold of them, are the persons least willing to come to the first-aid room [to make statements] so as not to encourage what they consider a morbid curiosity.[3]

Others on the commission shared this attitude: "In general little attention is paid to the statements of the women (Pardon, fair sex) [sic]. The statements of tough, strong men, like those of children, give one pause and are profoundly troubling." Newspaper reporters usually selected certain seers to feature from those the commission interviewed, and they shared the commission's respect for men. In spite of the virtual absence of repeat male visionaries in the first month, newspapers printed photographs of seven of the twenty-three adult men, as opposed to none of the sixteen women seers they reported. Those photographed included a farmer, three cattle merchants, a chauffeur, and a taxi driver. Reporters played on the religious indifference of the male seers, especially the San Sebastián taxi driver. The Irish observer Walter Starkie was told that the driver had been "a drunken dissolute sot" and was now "a model of holiness." Subsequent literature dwelt similarly on the conversions of two or three workers who were anarchists and socialists from Bilbao. But adult men were a small minority of the seers. They were newsworthy because they were exceptions and because they gave the visions dignity.[4]

Patxi Goicoechea was one of the few male "youths" with multiple visions, and from July 8 until mid-October press and public paid him exceptional attention. Although he had already been a practicing Catholic and a "man of order," the press presented him as a model of conversion. In analogous fashion, the highlight of parish missions was the Communion of hitherto lukewarm men on the last dramatic day.

Throughout Spanish history until very recently authorities have consistently discounted the visions of adult married women. The attention women received at Ezkioga was no different. Only in its later, disrespectable phase did any mothers come into prominence. Reporters named many women as seers but generally did not describe their visions in detail. The following account, for 18 July 1931, is an exception that reveals the underlying attitude:

A woman at our side with a tearful voice says [to the Virgin], "Mother, mother, why have you been scaring us for so many days?" Can this poor woman be aware of what she is saying? Later she says [again, to the Virgin], "You have come very late tonight; what do you want?" Frankly, it would never have occurred to us that this woman could see the Virgin Mother. . . . Every firefly brings forth two or three cries from women.

We may assume that many of the women seers had repeat visions that the press ignored.[5]

There seems, however, to have been a reverse discrimination, a certain partiality for young and unmarried women. Teenage girls from urban Tolosa and Pasaia and from farms in Azpeitia, Gabiria, Ataun, Bergara, Beizama, and Ormaiztegi, some of them servants in town houses, were regular seers at Ezkioga from the second week. By covering them extensively the newspapers encouraged and rewarded them for their visions.[6]

Why did people consider young women particularly credible as seers? During the first half of the century in the Basque Country much religious effort had as its goal the control of females, particularly unmarried ones, and thereby the salvation of men as well. For girls this control centered on the Daughters of Mary, which placed them in a quasi-sacred role in the parish. In revival missions the Daughters of Mary received Communion after the children, by this measure becoming the group second closest to God. The missioners knew they could count on adolescent girls for piety and enthusiasm. The Jesuits, the Daughters of Charity, and the secular clergy all promoted the sodality. The first chapters in Gipuzkoa were in Azkoitia and Azpeitia in 1860; by 1930 there were one hundred chapters. Catholics mobilized this sodality in the crisis of 1931. The assembly of 1,500 Daughters of Mary at the shrine of Itziar in early May was a kind of public witness of support of the exiled bishop. And in Bergara on May 31 the monthly Communion of the group coincided with municipal elections; in this tense atmosphere the clergy paraded 350 girls through the streets, showing the flag. *La Constancia* reported the sortie with the headline, "The Fine Example Set by the Daughters of Mary."[7]

A measure of the effectiveness of the church's control of girls is that even anticlerical skeptics took the purity of the teenage seers for granted. The republican schoolmaster of Ezkioga wrote to a Madrid newspaper, "All the hysterical señoritas are confirming the famous apparitions; we say give them a good boyfriend and they will be cured of their neurasthenia." One kind of "miracle" at Ezkioga in the autumn of 1931 consisted of medals, seemingly from the sky, falling to girls in vision. The medals were those of the Daughters of Mary, badges of heavenly approval and certificates of good conduct for visionaries.[8]

Those present at the visions have pointed out to me that beauty enhanced credibility. Patxi Goicoechea was held to be quite dashing. Walter Starkie himself was smitten with Lolita Núñez. Photographs of seers in vision show that some quite ordinary faces took on a special attractiveness when rapt, and spectators likened the young girl seers to young saints. A Catalan compared one girl seer to Gemma Galgani, and photographs of the seers resemble Gemma in pose and facial expression. Others besides Raymond de Rigné compared seers to Jeanne d'Arc, whose resistance to foreign rule had a special resonance for Basque nationalists. The adolescent girls stood ultimately for the Virgin herself, whom one seer described as "very young" in one vision and "age nineteen or twenty" in another.[9]

Children were another sacred category. Up to 21 August 1931 newspapers reported, in addition to the original two seers, ninety-two separate visions of nine girl and eight boy visionaries aged three to fourteen. The percentage of child seers, especially girls, who had two or more visions reported in the newspapers is quite high, indicating that children persisted in visions and that the press was interested in them. The children most involved, after the original seers from Ezkioga, came from the adjacent towns of Ormaiztegi, Zumarraga, and Urretxu and the slightly more distant towns of Legazpi and Albiztur. Parents and sometimes parish priests accompanied them to the site. While 80 percent of the regular teenagers were from farms, children with visions were more likely to be from village centers or towns; many spoke Spanish. Their more sophisticated backgrounds may have helped them receive and produce vision messages with political overtones.

People expected young children at Ezkioga to see something. A brother and sister from Estella in Navarra agreed to believe in the visions if, on an excursion, their younger brother, aged seven, saw the Virgin. The sister remembers continually inquiring, "Have you seen anything yet?" as the boy peered into the darkness and replied dispiritedly, "No . . . no . . ." In mid-July 1931 a thirteen-year-old boy from San Sebastián went to Ezkioga with his father and his young cousin from Legazpi. The cousin pointed out a spot in the trees where he saw the Virgin on July 8. The city boy then had his first vision in the same place. He moved in with the Legazpi relatives and went to Ezkioga daily, and his picture was in *El Día* on July 21. Once children started having visions, it was hard for them to stop. The seven-year-old girl from Ormaiztegi who first heard the Virgin speak had visions from July 6 to July 10; the next day the child did not want to go to the site, but believers came and bundled her into a taxi. The deputy Antonio de la Villa protested in the Cortes against school excursions to Ezkioga because of the unhealthy pressure to have visions.[10]

Several persons who went to Ezkioga in these first months of 1931 told me they were impressed especially by visions of very young children or infants. Children have been models for the devotional behavior of adults since the Gospels. At the time of the visions, parishes often organized skits or processions, with children as angels or saints; some parents dressed their children as angels with wings for First Communion; in some areas adults considered children privileged intercessors for the dead. The boy Guy de Fontgalland was a new model for a holy child in France.[11]

Children also played prominent parts in village missions. Hear a priest describe one in Navarra in 1920:

> On the second day the Communion of the children was followed by the consecration of all of them to the Sacred Heart. This was a tender and moving ceremony, during which I saw many fervent tears quietly falling, not being foreign to this holy weakness he who writes this. The ceremony was a very powerful way to rend completely the hearts of parents and other adults present.

Children as angels on mission day at Lasarte, 1930. The girl in the center is the Miraculous Mary. From Nuestro Misionero, *January 1930. Courtesy Instituto Labayru, Derio*

Grupo del Día misional de Lasarte.

Lasarte'ko Mixio-jaiak.

Similarly, in a secular context in Spanish-speaking Navarra, I have seen reticent, suspicious parents won over to an interest in Basque culture by witnessing their own young children performing folk dances and singing the Basque soldier song. A cultural group from Bilbao prepared the children with one afternoon's rehearsal.[12]

What made children important as visionaries was their alleged lack of guile and their supposed ignorance of the wider world. A man from Lezaun remembers being the only child in Lizarraga who did not see the saints arrive in the sky. As a result, his own mother considered him, age seven, "incrédulo [lacking in faith]." His mother had taken him so he would have a vision, for at the time in Lizarraga people simply assumed that all young children would see. The Catholic press placed great emphasis on the spontaneity of the first children's visions, and Antonio Amundarain took pains to refute the idea that they had heard in the Eskioga school about the visions at Torralba de Aragón.[13]

Nevertheless, articles about the child seers at Fatima, La Salette, and Lourdes must have contributed to the number of child seers at and around Ezkioga. Consider the girls of Ea in Bizkaia, for instance. In April 1931 ten of these girls,

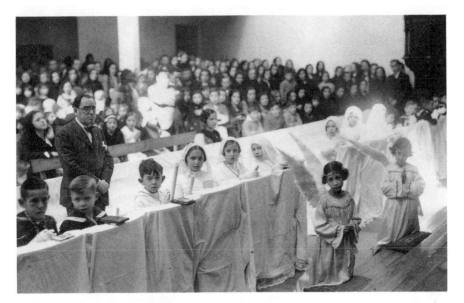

Children as angels for First Communion at Piarists in Pamplona, 1934. Collection of Ramón Goñi Nagore, Basque Studies Program, University of Nevada, Reno

who look from a group photograph to be between eight and fourteen years old, saved their pocket money and sent it to *La Obra Máxima* to baptize a pagan girl whom they wanted to name María Fátima "because the recent apparition of the Virgin to three little Portuguese shepherds enchanted us." We have seen that Bernadette was especially important for girls from Albiztur. The child seers in general are good examples of a kind of circular validation: when children reproduce material from adults, they enhance or consecrate it.[14]

As potential visionaries children had skills that most adults had forgotten. Children throughout the Catholic world play "church" just as they play "doctor," "teacher," and "house." The historian José Ignacio Tellechea, who like a seasoned bloodhound put me on the track of many documents and witnesses for this study, writes in his autobiography about his childhood games. He remembers at age eight in 1936 confessing and saying mass for his pals on a makeshift altar in the Navarrese village of Ituren. The children held processions, prayed, and sang hymns in the attic, where an image of the Infant Jesus of Prague (his mother signed him up in the sodality right after he was born in 1928) presided over the ceremonies. Tellechea writes that his play church was "immensely serious." Here are all the ingredients of the child visions in the Barranca, not far away in time and space.[15]

The step from game to vision is short. The children of La Salette were erecting a play altar of flowers when their visions began. Two vision sequences in Spain in 1961 began when the religious game children were playing took on a life of its own: at Garabandal (Cantabria) they were imagining the devil and the guardian angel; at Villaesteva (Lugo) they were playing mass.[16] Children having visions were often deadly serious. But in presenting their visions and organizing the spectators they applied the skills they developed in play. All children know how to imagine, how to intensify emotion, and how to abstract themselves from those around them. It seems that one reason the Ezkioga visions multiplied was that in a region suddenly alert to divine help, the adults were eager to join the game. Schoolteachers, village priests, and parents were willing to take children and children's claims seriously. Young children had an unusual mandate to play, and play was rampant.

It was not chance that children started off the Ezkioga vision sequence. Adults would not have been credible. Ten days before the visions of the two original seers, Santa Lucía schoolchildren, a respected farmer from Ezkioga allegedly had an accident with his oxcart loaded with logs; the Virgin appeared, saving the oxen and his son, who had been on the cart, from falling down an embankment. The man, Ignacio Galdós, told the story at home and in the tavern, but nobody believed him. In late July he showed the site of the accident to the Valladolid priest Baudilio Sedano and wept in gratitude that finally somebody cared. Galdós later became an assiduous and well-respected seer, attending the visions from August on. But even so the press paid him little heed. As an uneducated, pious peasant, his visions were less newsworthy than those of more distinguished or less devout men. Men served as confirming witnesses and as exemplary converts, but it seems that adult men were not acceptable, at Ezkioga or in most of the other twentieth-century Spanish visions, as initiators of a vision sequence.[17]

THE KINDS OF PEOPLE WHO WERE SEERS

We have seen how clergy and press tended to promote some men, teenage girls, and child seers and to exclude adult women. As the church and urban arbiters of culture gradually relinquished control of the visions, some kinds of seers became more "visible." From all my newspaper, printed, photographic, manuscript, and oral sources I compiled a list of about 250 persons who had visions in Ezkioga proper, the rest of the Basque Country, and Navarra from 29 June 1931 until the Civil War in 1936.[18] Of the seers I identified, about 50 had no visions at Ezkioga. Most of these were children who had visions only in their home villages.

The remaining 200 or so persons, those with visions at Ezkioga proper, fall into two groups. One group comprises those (40 male and 28 female) who turned up in the press only once, about whom subsequently we hear no more. Most of these had their visions in July 1931, and it is among these early seers that reporters seemed to have skewed their reports to emphasize older males. We may assume that there were many more casual seers on the days of mass attendance like July

12, July 16–18, July 25 and 26, and October 15–20, when reporters referred to other, unnamed seers; it is likely that women predominated among the unnamed.

For July 1931 I know of about 100 seers in all, many identified only by gender and town. My sources are almost exclusively the press. From August through December, when there are letters, diaries, and photos but fewer newspaper reports, I know of 37 new seers, many of them children and teenagers who visited Ezkioga from the Barranca, Albiztur, Zegama, and Urretxu. After the vicar general's note in October that discredited Ramona's wounds, turning the tide against the visions as a whole, there was no longer the stimulus of thousands of people praying together and singing Basque hymns which earlier produced seers out of spectators.

From 1932 to 1936 I found 39 additional seers at Ezkioga, almost exclusively in the writings, photographs, and memories of believers. Here there was no bias against women, but these sources mention few casual seers (the 3 named were women on the Catalan trips). The regular seers in this period were well known, since literate believers were busy chronicling the events. We can thus safely say that from 1931 until the Civil War children and women predominated, that they were largely poor by national standards, and that as the visions lost public respectability the proportions of children, women, and the poor increased.[19]

Sixty percent of the seers I know were female. This proportion was roughly the same for children, youth, and adults. For the repeat seers at Ezkioga proper, the proportion of female seers ranged from two out of three (67 percent) in the first month to four out of five (80 percent) of the new seers in the last years.

Children aged fourteen and under accounted for 40 percent of the seers at Ezkioga proper and 70 percent of the seers whose only visions we know about took place away from Ezkioga. After July they accounted for about half of the new seers at Ezkioga. Children—Benita Aguirre foremost among them—retained prominence until the Civil War.

Youths (*jóvenes*, *mozos*, or *mozas*, terms that seem to refer approximately to the age range 15 to 25) accounted for about 40 percent of the seers in the first month and less as time went on. Ramona, Patxi, Evarista Galdós, and Cruz Lete worked actively to organize and promote the visions. Unmarried and with few family responsibilities, they were able to find the time to build reputations and create a following at the visions.

Adults—whom I define as those over twenty-five years old, about when youths began to marry—comprised only about 33 percent of the seers overall. As we have seen, for the first month the newspapers inflated this number by including casual seers who were men. Only at the end of July 1931 did three men emerge as habitual seers. They were all of humble background: the farmers Ignacio Galdós of Ezkioga and León Zabaleta of Oñati and the foundry worker José Garmendia of Legazpi. Thereafter there were only two more male seers and they were prominent after the Civil War. Among the habitual adult seers, then,

UNOS CUANTOS DEVOTOS

Spectators at Ezkioga, Lent 1932. Photo by Joaquín Sicart

women were the great majority. The audience, however, was mixed: crowd photographs show men and women in equal numbers.[20]

Women, youths, and children, in comparison with adult men, have in common a lack of power. What we know about the backgrounds of the seers confirms that on the whole they were persons with little public power in society. Those who became "regulars" tended not to be well-off or well educated. I was able to place about 75 percent of the seers at Ezkioga roughly on a social scale. Some were "distinguished"—the kind of people the press referred to as Don, Doña, Señor, Señora, Señorita, or Señorito. Such deference was never gratuitous and referred exclusively to those, including children, with a high rank. One in six seers (about 16 percent) at Ezkioga overall fit this category, but only about one in ten in this group admitted to more than one vision and none admitted to many. The newspapers featured these seers because they provided credibility to the visions as a whole. Similarly, distinguished seers were highlights in the literature about the Christ of Limpias. One of the reasons the diocese of Pamplona did not make public the visions at Piedramillera was precisely because none of the seers was a Don.

At Ezkioga, in fact, there was not much "society" to boast about. No priests or doctors admitted to having visions. One nun from Barcelona did tell about a vision, but only to her fellow pilgrims. The absence of priests was troubling for the seers, and Evarista claimed that some clerics had visions and kept mum about it: "The Virgin told me that here in Zumarraga there is one who has seen her and there are two in Navarra." A Madrid lawyer was a seer, as was a diplomat, the director of an electric company, and the son of a bank manager from Zarautz; but each reported a vision only once. A few of the summer people had visions, as did some upper-class Catalans in 1932, mostly notably a woman from a prominent landed family of Vic. The upper-class child seers included Iñaki Jaca, the son of a manufacturer of wicker furniture in Zumarraga and the boy from San Sebastián on vacation in Legazpi. But these were exceptions as well. In retrospect, the most famous "distinguished" seer was Haydée de Aguirre, a young woman who later became well known as a fiery speaker at mass meetings for the Basque Nationalist party. She said she saw one or more rosaries in the air above the hands of a little girl.[21]

A big step down on the social scale were people from the trades in the market towns—cattle and pig dealers, a draughtsman, the child of a furniture restorer. From this level there were about twenty seers; only three—Lolita Núñez, Jesús Elcoro of Bergara and Bilbao, and Cruz Lete—became seers of renown. Others from Ormaiztegi, Beasain, and Zarautz had visions for shorter periods.

But the seers well represented the peasant families of Gipuzkoa, or at least the farm women and children; the rural folk who went to the visions would have recognized in them their own kind. Fully half of the seers I know at Ezkioga were from farming families or families of artisans—blacksmiths, rope-makers, and woodworkers—who directly served the farm communities.

Servants, like Ramona Olazábal, were in this class. In the early decades of the twentieth century service in the homes of the wealthy or the shorthanded was part of the life cycle of rural women in Gipuzkoa, who learned domestic skills that would serve them in married life. The mother of the first two seers had worked in the home of some rural bakers of Urretxu before she married. Service was also a recourse when running a farm was no longer an option. The seer Juliana Ulacia grew up on a farm her parents rented in Beizama, but when in 1932 her father died in an accident, her mother took a job as a servant in Tolosa. Juliana began to have visions a year later, when she was thirty-three.[22]

Seers also included a few urban workers or members of their families. Most were from the company towns around Ezkioga and had farm backgrounds. Included here are four chauffeurs (*mecánicos*), servants of the wealthy. Like the "distinguished" male seers, they had their visions once and dropped out of the picture. Whereas female servants, as we will see below, had incentives to keep on having visions, male servants and industrial workers had reason in the ridicule and political distrust of their fellows to stop having them.

Finally some seers came from Gipuzkoa's underclass of temporary labor, the poorest of the rural poor, the homeless kind who subsequently died in hospices or had to be taken in by believers. I know of eight of these seers. While the very rich quickly shied off, the very poor, the downwardly mobile, and the unconnected stuck to the visions. Such persons through their visions found a spiritual shelter and a caring community. But by no means were they the norm.[23]

Certain kinds of people in Gipuzkoa were less likely to be seers, or at least they were less likely to reveal visions: adult men, male and female factory workers, men and women dependent on fishing, merchants, priests, the liberal professionals, town dwellers (especially "distinguished" ones), and nuns. By and large the visionaries we know about were rural and Basque by birth. Out of one hundred Ezkioga seers resident in Gipuzkoa and Bizkaia whose surnames I know, only ten might not have been Basque in origin.[24]

CONTACT BETWEEN SOCIAL CLASSES

While there were no "distinguished" regular seers, we have seen the interest the visions aroused in the wealthy and the aristocratic. Many summer visitors to San Sebastián, Zarautz, and the watering spots of Zestoa and Ormaiztegi went to Ezkioga. As a member of the gentry wrote in the Madrid monarchist daily in August 1931, "Going to Ezquioga this year is the unavoidable duty of every good vacationer, as it was to go to Limpias in 1919." Bilbao industrialists and stockbrokers, their wives and friends, also went. These people shared with the rural Catholics a deep anxiety about the Second Republic, and some were equally hopeful that God would step in.

On the Ezkioga hillside the well-off prayed side by side with the poor, an anomaly not lost on observers of all stripes. *La Constancia*'s correspondent from Tolosa wrote on July 15 that pilgrims to Ezkioga were "numerous in all classes and conditions in this city, from the best known to the most humble." The same newspaper returned to the theme:

> One of the most distinctive aspects of this constant pilgrimage is the mixing of people of all social classes. Indeed, next to the local and summer aristocracy, which gives such an extraordinary contingent of devotees to Ezquioga, go the most modest people, who willingly make the financial sacrifice that the trip entails.

Rural folk noticed the mix as well. The *Argia* correspondent from Matxinbenta argued that the presence of the rich proved the seriousness of the visions: "Those who say this is the stuff of witches or the foolishness of farmers should go to Ezkioga to say the holy rosary, and there they will see if all those cars belong to farmers or people from towns, and when they see rich folk kneeling in the mud they will know who has faith."

Outsiders too found the mixing remarkable, as did the canon and deputy from Toledo, Ramón Molina. A decade earlier, Catholic commentators found similar relief from the class struggle at Limpias.[25]

Social hierarchy was as rigid and economic differences as sharp in rural Gipuzkoa as in the industrial towns and cities. Apart from the gap between nobles and nonnobles and between those with degrees and liberal professions and those without them, there were steep gradients separating wealthy from poorer farmers and those with access to land from the rootless. Religious houses reproduced these differences. They distinguished between fathers and lay brothers, mothers and lay sisters, the former educated and fulfilling the sacerdotal, teaching, and healing tasks, the latter uneducated and limited to the menial maintenance tasks. And in the diocese there were major differences between priests after years in the priesthood. Benita Aguirre heard the Virgin address these differences: "During the chastisement the rich will be poor and the poor will be better off than before, but nobody will be rich."[26]

The extremes met in the arena of domestic service. Antonio Amundarain's mother, who married a Carlist soldier, served before her marriage in the Liberal household of a San Sebastián shopkeeper. During the Carlist bombardment of the city in the 1870s a grenade hit her employers' balcony and she heard them say, "The Carlist pigs, full of cider and beans!" Her grandson felt the slur like a whiplash more than one hundred years later; for him it epitomized the gulf between the devout agricultural countryside and the mercantile city. We find the same resentment in Pilar Ciordia's vision of the vicar general's untimely death and abrupt removal to hell. She asked rhetorically, "What good to you are so many servants, being driven so much in automobiles? Poor thing, what good is it to have a rich family, if you cannot take anything with you?"[27]

Whereas the servants were the poor in the houses of the rich, priests and doctors were the rich (or at least the learned) most likely to enter the houses of the poor. Benita in her visions learned from Jesus that doctors who charged too much and priests who did not believe in the visions would die in the chastisement.[28] Doctors and priests served as go-betweens. The doctor from Tolosa who examined Ramona's wounds had assisted at her birth. The local Zumarraga doctor, Sabel Aranzadi, was the ideal intermediary between the seers and the press; he was at ease with both, for he grew up on a nearby farm, as did the Ezkioga priest, Sinforoso de Ibarguren. Another doctor provided Laburu with inside information on seers and their work experience in San Sebastián. When the milkmaid, herself an intermediary between the farm and town folk, wanted to spread the news of the initial visions, she went to a priest from her social class, Miguel Lasa. Doctors, priests, and servants were links between the classes; they introduced seers to believers and to the press.

The intensity of the visionary experience fused disparate elements—at least temporarily—into unusual compounds: women and men, mistresses and servants, children and adults, peasants and urbanites, priests and confessants. Previously, well-determined patterns had connected the different elements. Potentially, every farm girl was an urban servant, every wealthy person a master.

Farm families paid rent to urban and noble landlords, sold milk to town families, sold pigs, lambs, and calves to town dealers, and bought from town stores and bread trucks. Children and adults, men and women, all knew the patterns and the degrees of deference.

They also knew the system was changing, that workers could make a decent living in the new factories and bright children could find a career in the church. They saw how entrepreneurs, originally canny farmers, could gain economic leeway in the changing society and, like Juan José Echezarreta of Legorreta and Patricio Echevarría of Legazpi, build industrial empires in a lifetime. And they had learned that younger sons could make their fortunes in Latin America and return to live in leisure in new chalets.

In any case, the wealthy and the poor, the socially prominent and the anonymous, interacted. The rural and urban elites were visible in their summer places, on the beaches, and at their rural "palaces," like one near the foot of the Ezkioga hill. Women of modest means who took turns as servants saw the wealthy from inside these houses. Just as in the preindustrial rural South in the United States there was a certain familiarity between blacks and whites, so in Gipuzkoa wealthier and poorer families made alliances and knew each other well. Walter Starkie noticed the ease with which Carmen Medina interacted with the people around Ezkioga: "She stopped to speak to every peasant she met and later in the day she visited sick women of the parish and gave money for the poor."[29]

Juan Ignacio Tellechea in his autobiography alludes to the friendship between his modest family and a wealthy one. In 1910, at age twenty, his mother, who was from Zumarraga and then unmarried, started sewing for the family of the owner of a large textile factory in Vilabona. On occasion the family would invite her to eat with them or take her to the theater in San Sebastián. The relation lasted all her life. She made christening gowns, wedding dresses, even shrouds, for five generations of the family. Over the years she formed a close bond that she passed on, when she married, to her own children. The lifelong confidante of the mother, she was also close to the children. And when her own son José Ignacio lay critically ill in the hospital of San Sebastián seventy years later, her employer's children were among his visitors. When one of the employer's daughters became a Carmelite, Tellechea's mother made her habits. In turn, the nun became Tellechea's spiritual godmother when he became a priest. She organized her convent to pray for him in his illness.[30]

Benita Aguirre's large family had a series of connections with those more wealthy. Patricio Echevarría of Legazpi chose Benita's father as foreman of a production line at his tool works and helped him acquire a large old house. Benita's eldest sister, Bitori, described the visit of a wealthy woman who knew her parents well, perhaps from earlier employment, and carried Bitori off, then age twelve, as a maid with the promise of taking her for the first time to the beach.

A third wealthy family, the Garayaldes of Tolosa, later befriended the Aguirres during the visions and provided a refuge from the press in their home.

When the subordinate members of these alliances had visions they gained new options. They did not necessarily gain the options in current relationships (with fathers, landlords, employers, politicians, parish priests, shopkeepers, doctors) in their daily lives. These partners may not have been believers. But for farm girl visionaries there were aristocratic ladies who took them on as servants because of the visions; for children there were adults who served as temporary adoptive parents; for confessants there were priests who wanted to hear more about the other world.

The system of connection up and down the social scale could be played in both directions, and prior to the visions some families were better at playing it than others. Of course, under normal circumstances, those higher in society had the most options. Patricio Echevarría chose which man he wanted as foreman. Benita's father could do little more than say yes or no. Workers, servants, and confessants were not a scarce resource in an economy that counted on over-population. But as in Spain today people from any level of society could initiate the process of establishing chains of long-term contacts up and down the social structure, and the links could be extraordinarily durable. For what was at stake was a trust that transcended class or personal short-term interest—a moral bond that would ensure that a transaction would not go sour, that a maid would not steal, that a worker would not go on strike, that a client would pay for goods he bought on credit. In such a system a person with a complaint could go to other members of the family or to the intermediaries through whom the contacts were made. Obligations to kin served as bonds for economic transactions. The visions at Ezkioga took place in a rural society in which economic bonds were moral bonds, even in the local factories. It was a society well aware of the alternative— the more purely economic vertical connections between workers and employers in Bilbao, Irun, San Sebastián, and Madrid. In these places workers needed the countervailing horizontal bonds of socialism or anarchism for protection.

The groups of Basque farm neighbors who as a matter of course worked together in material and spiritual matters turned up in the cuadrillas of the rural seers. And the long-term help that the Virgin at Ezkioga offered reaffirmed this kind of long-term cooperation of rural folk at the same level. The Virgin ordered the people of Bachicabo to harvest Eusebio's potatoes, as they would normally do when a neighbor was sick or injured.

The Virgin's attitude reaffirmed as well the long-term bonds of patronage that had grown up between the wealthy and the rural poor. The seers replicated this kind of bond with the major promoters. Benita's family moved easily between the Echevarrías, Bitori's employer, Padre Burguera, and the Catalans. But in these new relationships there was no longer such an imbalance of options. Benita's father may have had few choices economically, but Benita herself, once people understood that God had chosen her, could select from among all the promoters, reporters, and photographers. Even the boss's family took a lively interest in her visions.

The women who had visions at Ezkioga worked in the houses of persons who could patronize the visions. We know of seers who were ex-servants (Ramona Olazábal) and servants (Evarista Galdós and the Ataun girl). We know of seers who began having visions while servants of believers (Carmen Visa), seers whom believers took on as servants because of the visions (Evarista Galdós and the Ataun girl, both by Carmen Medina; at least one seer by Isabel Arcelus in Ormaiztegi; and Luis Irurzun as aide-de-camp in the Civil War), and seers who made believers out of their masters by having visions in the houses where they worked (the case of servant-seers in Tolosa, Ordizia, San Sebastián, and Madrid). We know of visions by the chauffeurs of a lady from Eibar, of the duke of Infantado, and of the owner of the apparition site.

The same spiritual adventure joined servant, mistress, and sometimes master in a new way. In Tolosa a sister of a servant held visions and there would appear on her tongue a white wafer, seemingly out of nowhere, all in the house of believing masters. A Portugalete family held regular vision sessions with two servants, a man and a woman, as seers. Anna Pou had visions in the house of her masters near Vic in the winter of 1933. In Barcelona some of the same people who went to Ezkioga were followers of the washerwoman Enriqueta Tomás, whose messages appeared written on her arms. For all of them the story of Gemma Galgani must have had a special resonance. She too was a kind of servant, experiencing visions and reenactments of the Passion in a house where she helped with the laundry and the ironing.[31]

The visions inevitably affected the relations of seeing servants and believing masters. In his lecture denouncing the visions Laburu used the fact that Carmen Medina and the girl from Ataun ate together as evidence against the visions. We saw that a male visionary told Carmen Medina that the Virgin had said they should marry. A servant seer prominent in Spain in the 1980s went from serving meals to her masters to being served meals by them.

Servants are trained cultural mediators. In order to serve they have to learn the idiom of their masters and be sensitive to their needs and inclinations. The messages the servant seers of Ezkioga received from the divine at the same time transcended and resolved their bicultural way of life, providing for them, their families and communities, and their masters' families and class a common enterprise. Masters sometimes treated servants as ignorant and innocent boys and girls, which made the servants' visions more believable for their masters.

The cultural historian David Sabean has written that "the position of anyone in a hierarchy of the exercise of power is not simple, and there are satisfactions and deprivations at all levels."[32] Some of the seers seem to have taken pleasure in getting their wealthy, powerful, or prominent believers to do things for them.

Benita Aguirre came to control Padre Burguera's life almost absolutely. María Recalde at the drop of a suggestion got Luisa Arriola to drive to Burgos. Patxi got Carmen Medina to take him to Toledo. And for a while seers throughout the region got their parish priests to act as their secretaries.

But as Sabean suggests, there could be a converse pleasure. In the visions I have studied, the powerful and sophisticated refresh themselves by shedding power and placing it, however symbolically, in the hands of the less powerful. What interests me is not so much the sudden intoxication that the less powerful experience when they have new options. After all, that transformation we understand intuitively because it is part of the process of growing up. What interests me more is the refreshment that the powerful experience when they withdraw from control, which is more counterintuitive. In some ways child seers could become like adults because certain adults joyfully became like children, like the Priest-Niños. The ultimate model for this relinquishment of power was Christ in the Passion.

The unseemly mixing of social classes as a result of the visions at Ezkioga provided one way for opponents, like Laburu, to discredit the seers and the apparitions. When referring to Patxi's connections with Carmen Medina and her like, Rafael Picavea played on its unnatural aspect: "They take you back and forth in automobiles. Marquises and duchesses, sisters or consorts visit you. Aristocrat? Come on, Patxi, be reasonable. I like you better as a regular lad at the Basque social club."[33]

But there was a deep logic in the mingling. Patxi was an anomaly, a peasant among aristocrats as well as a young man who was devout. Whether by inspiration or nudging, he was able to reach the edge of the possible and voice the unspeakable, the unpublishable: the call for a holy war to reclaim the state from the unholy republicans. His vision was a "hidden transcript," a scenario that many people already feared and many hoped for. He could voice the scenario only because conditions were extreme, because he was a Basque country lad, and because of the charisma he had accumulated in his spectacular trances. I doubt that the general public would have accepted the message as divine had it come from a priest or an upper-class seer.[34]

The mixing of classes itself was clearly an incentive both for seers and believers. The visions provided a way to overcome barriers that kept people apart. Although the class struggle was not as burning an issue in rural Gipuzkoa as in Catalan textile towns, the visions at Ezkioga, like the movements of Father Vallet and Magdalena Aulina, were attractive in part because they provided one way to transcend social tensions. In Gipuzkoa the gap the visions bridged was that between rural farm families and the urban elite. This bridge was achieved at a time when both urban Nationalists and Integrists idealized rural life for its cultural traditions and intense faith. For years the Catalans had been singing wishfully in the Parish Exercises hymns with words like:

> We are brothers! both rich and poor
> Away with strife and bitterness!
> We are brothers! With good works
> Let us unite our hearts.

At Ezkioga they saw their ideals in action.[35]

Many of these elements come together in María Recalde's account of her meeting with Padre Laburu in Durango. She claimed that she reminded him of his errant youth and his own conversion by a woman as humble and miserable as she, and this allusion supposedly made Laburu burst into tears. At least in the retelling, Recalde challenged hierarchies of gender, class, and respectability by using her position as underdog. For the bourgeois Catalan and Bilbao supporters, the Ezkioga visions in general and the Recalde/Laburu story in particular resonated with the old traditions of apparitions to the powerless and the despised. Believers saw Laburu, as they had seen Justo de Echeguren before him, as obstructing a divine will that made no distinctions based on gender, wealth, or education. But Laburu too, so this story went, could be touched, just as he had been converted (in the story) by a poor woman, perhaps a nurse or a servant.[36]

The Ezkioga visions suggest the hidden potential of intimate contact between social classes throughout the hierarchically organized Spain of the 1930s. The left labeled and identified social class as an issue. But it was the right that through religion forged an interclass alliance of the devout peasantry, the regional bourgeoisie, and the monarchist aristocracy. It is typical of these inspired interclass movements that the seers or mystics are from the better-off peasantry and either have been or subsequently come to be servants in the households of the powerful. In their visions and divine messages they formulated a worldview and agenda that spoke to the world they came from and the world they were coming to know. Part of the excitement, even exhilaration, of the movements came from a catalysis of social classes. A parallel would be the exhilaration and energy released in the American civil rights movement of the 1960s when blacks and whites worked together. Historians have underestimated the popular Catholic support for the military uprising of July 1936 that started Spain's Civil War. That support increased throughout the 1930s. In this critical period a religious mobilization cut across the lines of social class to defend the old society under attack with a preview of the coming reign of Christ.

10. THE VISION STATES

A VARIETY OF uncommon physical states helped the Ezkioga seers to break the bonds of social class, gender, and age and enabled the seers to speak the unspeakable and express the inexpressible. The *videntes* (in Spanish) or *ikusleak* (in Basque) (those who can see, seers) saw things that the mass of spectators did not, whether blinding light, the Virgin, saints, Christ, the devil, or heavenly tableaux. Over time many of them also became "hearers" of divine messages, and some of them felt the divine touch. Often during the visions, believing spectators smelled heavenly perfumes.

I located references to the physical states of seers in about four hundred visions. This material reveals patterns for individual seers and a slowly evolving general model of how to have visions and what kinds of things to see. It reveals as well the attitudes toward unusual physical states of those who chronicled them and of the doctors and priests who diagnosed them. We are thus led to the highly polarized debate as to whether atypical states of consciousness are evidence for the supernatural. Positivist psychologists, spiritists, and followers of Catholic mystics quickly incorporated the visions at Ezkioga into this ongoing argument.[1]

People thought of visions and ecstasies as experiences that happened to saints, occasionally to religious in convents, but rarely to ordinary people like Bernadette or the children at Fatima; visions were definitely not a part of daily life. Devout laypersons may occasionally have had ecstasies. The contemporary poet Orixe described a repeated childhood experience in Huici (Navarra) when his grandmother would fall into a daze as he read to her the Way of the Cross on the balcony. Her eyes turned up and she seemed not to breathe. But none of the scores of elderly persons I talked to in the course of my research had experienced such a mystical encounter before the visions began at Ezkioga. One visionary about seventy-five told me he had known no seers before the events started. His only ideas about visions or ecstasies came from sermons about saints.

> They would say here when friars came or in sermons that in such and such a place people talked with God, and that even today there are people who talk with God and so on. But we could not understand it. It is so hard to grasp. It is easy to say. But who speaks with God?

Yet there may be more in the way of a local tradition than I discovered. Trancelike states occurred in religious of both sexes; moreover, rural Basques read deeply in religious literature and many had kin in convents. In 1877 the Prophet of Durango, who proclaimed himself Saint Joseph, had visions of angels in his attic.[2]

In a number of places in Spain and Europe laypeople regularly enter into some unusual physical state. Shrines like El Corpiño (Pontevedra) attract persons who are afraid they are possessed. In southern Italy and Sardinia persons who think spiders have bit them perform a kind of curative dance. At the feasts of the Madonna dell'Arco near Naples and Santa Rosalia in Palermo pilgrims arrive in abstracted states. And at Echternach in Luxembourg pilgrims until recently entered a kind of trance through dancing. But in Europe in the early twentieth century the altered states that the church tolerated were isolated from everyday society; they took place behind convent walls or in remote cultural pockets. Only a few revered laypersons, like the German mystic Thérèse Neumann, bore witness to ecstasy, if at great physical cost.[3]

Yet a collective memory of trances in apparitions persisted throughout Europe and was maintained in shrines, legends, sermons, and prints. For the Basques Lourdes was the most obvious example. And it seems that the Ezkioga seers and organizers leaned first on Lourdes as a model for a liturgy, for an etiquette of how to act, and for physical symptoms of ecstasy.

THE ROLE OF THE LITURGY: PRIESTS, SEERS, AND AUDIENCE

Starting on the third day of visions, in July 1931, a kind of liturgy provided a context and meaning for the events at Ezkioga. Within this context seers came forward in a variety of physical conditions, ranging from the unaltered, everyday state of the first girl, to the deep trances of Patxi, to what appeared to be total unconsciousness in others. The seers appear to have learned from one another and from those who paid attention to them, so over time their physical states converged. As the number and quality of the spectators waxed and waned and the liturgy evolved, so did the vision states.

As we have seen, the priest Antonio Amundarain of Zumarraga improvised the liturgy. He got the first seers to hold candles (like Bernadette at Lourdes) and recite after him the rosary in a small procession to the vision site on the Ezkioga hillside, and he had the onlookers recite the Litany with arms outstretched. The time of the seers' first vision—about 8:30 in the evening—determined the time for these prayers. What quickly evolved was a kind of orthodox ceremony, led by at least two priests, at an unorthodox time (after dark) and in an unorthodox place (a semiwooded hillside). Apart from the late hour, all of the other elements were fairly predictable. From the fifteenth century, at least, on the rare occasions when people had visions in the countryside, the townspeople would go there in procession. And no one thought it strange to say the rosary, for the words "Hail Mary, full of grace . . . Holy Mary, Mother of God, pray for us sinners" were quite appropriate.[4]

Doubtless Amundarain called on his experience at Lourdes. In the diocesan pilgrimage the year before "the zealous parish priest of Zumarraga, don Antonio Amundarain, recited the Rosary, alternating in our two national languages. The fifth mystery was prayed by all with arms outstretched in the form of a cross, with the bishop setting an example." As at the apparitions at Ezkioga a year later, the Basque hymn of farewell, "Agur Jesusen Ama [Goodbye, Mother of Jesus]," followed this rosary at Lourdes and many present wept.[5]

The Zumarraga clergy organized the vision scenario in the first months. On July 7 they separated the two original child seers, praying a rosary simultaneously with each to check whether they were separately seeing the same thing; subsequently the priests confirmed the simultaneous vision to the crowd. After the visions were over and the children appeared to the crowd in a window, people applauded and wanted them to speak. So Amundarain recounted the details of the first week of visions and had the children recite three Hail Marys. On the next night his assistant Juan Bautista Otaegui led the rosary, and during the second mystery the prayers halted as Amundarain gave a running account of what the girl said she was seeing. During the Litany another girl interrupted the prayers, crying out "Mother, what do you want?" from the shoulders of her father.

> It is not easy to describe the emotional jolts of faith that people felt in that impressive crowd of men and women. What sad groans! What humble words! What distress! What trembling! What tears of joy! . . . Hearts of

stone would have softened in that touching moment. How could one fail to weep in that happy moment of love?[6]

Amundarain thereafter extended and fine-tuned the liturgy. On July 11 after the rosary and the Litany, a priest directed the crowd in the singing of a Salve. On July 12 after the five mysteries of the rosary, Amundarain asked the crowd (by then 25,000) to sing "Egizu zuk Maria [Pray for us, Mary]," One writer described this mission hymn as "the dear melody that our mothers put in each of our souls to invoke in times of importance the Mother of Heaven with the clean confidence of children." After the Litany Amundarain added seven Hail Marys in honor of the Seven Sorrows of the Virgin. He was applying time-proven techniques of parish missions to arouse repentance in the vision sessions. As on other nights, the seers punctuated the prayers with cries. *La Constancia* confirmed that the effect was "simple and grandiose, with an emotion that makes the soul swoon. If only for the benefits of this public fervor, one should go to Ezquioga."[7]

The ceremony enhanced the visions and the number of seers increased dramatically. After noting that on July 12 about one hundred persons had visions, the somewhat skeptical reporter of *El Pueblo Vasco* warned that the mood had become contagious.

> Of the thousands and thousands of persons who come to Ezquioga, there are many whose temperaments, already excited by what they hear and read, are in a state of extraordinary impressionability that disposes them to a fit or a fainting spell as, in the midst of that impressive religious expectation, the almost fixed hour approaches people consider propitious for the apparition. So while these special circumstances continue, there will always be half a dozen persons who fall into trance and assure they have seen the apparition. But it is possible that there are also those who out of vanity or by imitation assure the same thing and even talk about it with a disorienting seriousness or with a suspicious good humor.[8]

Soon the crowd became a vibrant, collaborative chorus for the visions and a source of new seers. The group prayers became a kind of clock. Seers began their visions "during the second mystery," "at the start of the fourth mystery," "during the fourth mystery," "at the second Hail Mary of the fifth mystery," "at the beginning of the Litany," or "after all the prayers were over, when people were beginning to leave." And the seers or the holy figures they saw began to intervene in the ceremony and direct the crowd. On July 8 the ceremony was over by 9:45 P.M.; four nights later it lasted until 11 P.M. because more seers interrupted the prayers. When a woman from Azpeitia continued to see the Virgin after the rosary on July 13, the priests led extra prayers and she reported that "the Virgin's face was happier, and [the Virgin] went down on her knees."

The next night a twelve-year-old boy who saw a panoply of holy figures—the Virgin, the Sacred Heart of Jesus, two angels, some male religious—noticed that a heavenly nun was saying the rosary with the people. What began with children seeing the Virgin as a distant divine figure became in two weeks a kind of joint mission session. Earthly and heavenly participants met at a junction of the two realms.[9]

El Pueblo Vasco again warned how easily these conditions could give rise to visions.

> The ambience could not be more propitious for suggestion, and so, admitting, of course, the possibility of the supernatural, we should read these reports with great reserve, above all taking into account the age and condition of those who claim to have participated in these visions.

On the next day, July 16, people expected a miracle. *El Día*'s description of the atmosphere confirmed this warning:

> The voice of the priest who led the prayers reached distinctly the entire field. A vast murmur replied religiously. . . . The moment was one of intense emotion, and not only religious emotion, but the expectation of the unknown, and an expression of anxiety or fear could be seen on many faces. The cry would go up. Where would it be? Everyone looked at his neighbor, and no one was sure of himself.[10]

On the eighteenth of July, another day of expected miracle, seers periodically cut into the priests' prayers, and when these were over, few in the enormous crowd departed.

> Everywhere there started up prayers of isolated groups, men and women on their knees with their arms in the form of a cross praying devoutly without anyone allowing the least lack of respect. Gestures and partial movements [of individuals] throughout the crowd indicated that the mysterious phenomenon was under way.[11]

By then the sessions of prayers and hymns began after the priests had demanded quiet and continued in what one newspaper called a "sepulchral silence." The seers interrupted the service during and after the prayers. A schoolteacher described the spontaneous part on July 19:

> And here the marvelous, the eminently simple and moving part began: "Ayes" and isolated shouts here and there: strangled cries, loving questions to "Mother! Mother!" some serene and ingenuous, others anguished and with an indescribable tone of voice—wails, fainting, tears, pressing appeals for forgiveness and grace; alteration of the calm and silence around the seers.[12]

We saw that some of this "alteration of calm and silence" involved applause, enthusiastic shouts, and vivas to the Virgin, to Christ, to Catholic Spain, and probably to Euskadi, to Christ the King, and to Alfonso XIII.

Walter Starkie, the Irish Hispanist, described the mix of liturgy and visions:

> The Litany in contrast to the rosary was recited in Latin, and right from the start I felt that curious sensation of collective excitement . . . as if the devotional excitement of those thousands and thousands of people had enveloped me and lifted my soul out of my body. Suddenly I heard a cry piercing through the buzzing rhythm of the Litany.[13]

The visions and the prayers, the cries and the buzzing rhythms, created a single dramatic structure. On July 21, for example, the original girl seer saw the Virgin open her arms during the rosary and she saw her wave when the crowd sang farewell with "Agur Jesusen Ama [Good-bye, Mother of Jesus]." And a boy saw the Virgin pray the rosary with the crowd, passing the beads through her fingers, and he saw her smile and move her lips as if singing.[14]

This boy seer began to have visions a quarter of an hour before the official prayers, and other seers imitated this kind of excursion from the liturgical perimeter. On July 23 a fifteen-year-old farm girl from Ormaiztegi also saw the Virgin before the prayers. She described the Virgin following the movements of the crowd in prayer and kneeling on a kind of stairway when the Litany began. The ceremony Amundarain had set up to contain the visions had been outflanked, and the visions thereafter often preceded the official program and almost always continued after it.[15]

Amundarain thought of the prayers he led as collective atonement for the burning of religious houses in May. María de Echarri confirmed that the prayers addressed the hostile climate for Catholics in Spain:

> No prayer against the Liberals precedes or follows the rosary. They pray, for sure, fervently and with many tears, for Spain, for the nation that is more loved when it is more humiliated and disgraced. They pray for those who persecute Christ; they ask for mercy for those blind with hatred, so they can see, repent, and be saved. In the prayers there is not a whit of anger or indignation. Mercy and forgiveness are the feelings expressed.[16]

But as we have seen the seers even more than the priests keyed the visions to the particular circumstances of Basque and Spanish Catholics, expressing on behalf of the Virgin what the priests would not have dared to say in public. The familiar prayers and hymns of the liturgy set a general tone of penance; the vision messages that erupted during the ceremony provided specifics.

At 5 P.M. on July 24 an Ormaiztegi teenager seer was the first to see the Virgin in daylight. Her vision was a relief to Amundarain, for many people had voiced unease at the nighttime appearances. Four days later Amundarain started the night session earlier, at 6:30 P.M. Nevertheless, most of the seers did not have visions until nightfall, about two hours later.

> Shortly after the rosary had ended, and with still some daylight left, a movement of suspense of the entire crowd lets us know that one of the phenomena that everyone is awaiting with feverish anguish has occurred. The light gets dimmer and dimmer until the hillside is completely dark. It is at this time that the cases of vision occur in greatest number. . . . No one is capable of describing the emotion one feels at this time.[17]

The priests decided that if the visions were going to continue and masses of spectators remain in the dark, a liturgy the clergy led was better than freelance prayers in small groups. So in spite of the new daylight rosary, priests led others into the night. The original rosary had five mysteries in Basque and a Litany in Latin. Later people prayed the expanded version of three parts and fifteen mysteries. By August 18, because of the numerous pilgrims from San Sebastián, Navarra, and Catalonia, one five-mystery section was in Spanish. This formal service generally ended around 8:30 or 9 P.M., but at least on some nights there were rosaries as late as the visions lasted.[18]

Up to the time of Ramona's wounding in mid-October, the seers continued to orchestrate the prayers, interrupting the official liturgy and expanding into the periods before and after it. A visitor described Benita Aguirre in the rain of July 27, "with a powerful and angelic voice, crying out repeatedly, 'Egizu zuk Maria gugatik erregu [Pray for us, Mary]' (the first line of the hymn), leading the immense multitude to get down on their knees and sing hymns to Mary and say repeatedly the Litany and the Salve." Another wrote on July 30 that a girl from Bergara asked the Virgin, "'Do you want us to pray?'" The girl then "asks us to pray and all of us prayed fervently seven Hail Marys." On August 16 during the liturgy a young girl from Albiztur told the crowd the Virgin wanted them to pray the rosary with more seriousness and sing the Salve better.[19]

In late July the hope for a great miracle waned and attendance declined from tens of thousands to under five thousand nightly. People began to come with a different attitude. No longer potential seers, they became spectators. No longer nervous, fearful, and excited at the prospect of becoming seers themselves, many came just to see the famous in action. At the end of July Walter Starkie wrote, "Poor Dolores, for many of those good people you are like Francisco Goicoechea—a purveyor of nightly stunts, and you act as a thriller for them." In early September a writer in *El Liberal* of Bilbao observed: "For several weeks now, people who go to Ezquioga no longer think they will see the Virgin; they go to see the seers, the ones who do not miss a day."[20]

This shift in spectator attitudes had various causes. After two or three weeks the visions lost their novelty. Attendance from the immediate Basque hinterland declined, and visitors from farther away, less sensitive to the local mood, were

People watching seers in vision on stage, 27 December 1931. Photo by José Martínez

less likely to be seers. Starting in mid-July the press had begun to point to the unusual nature of the trances of some seers, like Patxi. In October Patxi put up the stage so that people could see the seers better. The platform was especially necessary when it became evident that miracles—trances, stigmata, or falling ribbons or medals—would happen to the seers themselves, not to the assembled crowd or the world at large. Priests led the nonstop rosaries from October 15 to October 20 from the stage, near the seers in a row, each seer in front of a helper. The seers were still facing the cross and holy trees where they saw the divine, but the people now faced the seers, not the cross or the trees. Many people had their backs to the Virgin.

After the end of October the cold and the rain and the negative press reduced the audience; at times all the spectators could fit on the stage with the seers. On a more informal basis, priests continued to lead rosaries, but Amundarain no longer organized them. When on December 26 the vicar general forbade priests to go up to the site, the prayers were led by seers, laypersons, or believing priests from other dioceses. Separate seers in vision led their cuadrillas up the hillside following the stations of the cross. Catalan pilgrim groups had their own prayer directors. But only during Holy Week 1932 and in September of that year did attendance climb once more into the thousands, with the kind of massed prayers so powerful in stimulating visions and moving hearts.

With a smaller audience, the seers could attend to the needs of those around them. Over the summer believers began to give the seers large numbers of medals, rosaries, and crucifixes to be blessed. A Catalan woman described Ramona Olazábal in early September:

> One day, before the prayers began, one of those present gave this girl his rosary so she would have it in her hands during the ecstasy. She accepted it with signs of pleasure, but the idea spread and they did not stop calling her, each handing over to her a rosary. . . . When the rosary began, she stopped, knelt devoutly, and the ecstasy came very quickly. Afterward I asked her, "Did the Most Holy Virgin bless them?" "Yes, She blessed them," she replied.[21]

On the left, bent over by the weight of an invisible cross and kept from falling by two men, a seer who is an elderly farm woman acts out the stations of the cross in vision, May 1933. This seer will distribute as divine tokens the roses the woman in the foreground carries. From VU, *23 August 1933. Photo by J. A. Ducrot, all rights reserved*

Photographs from the fall of 1931 and the spring of 1932 show the visionaries draped with devotional paraphernalia. As in the Barranca, most visions featured a moment when the Virgin would bless these objects. People who had connected medals with the holy trees now gave them to the seers to hold. The seers themselves had become the center of attention and a focus of miracles.

The believers took great pleasure in these divine tokens. A vision by Ignacio Galdós in November 1931 of angels receiving medals from the Virgin reflects the relation of believers to seers.

> In her right hand the Virgin held silver rosaries, and in the other, many gold medals, which, raising her hand, she offered to all of us. The medals were all different, and I recognized only one, of Saint Anthony. Eight angels appear, and all kiss the scapular of the Most Holy Virgin, and then she puts a medal around the neck of each, and the angels, in their enthusiasm, like children, show them to each other and then soon disappear.[22]

Catalans watch Benita Aguirre hold a crucifix for a boy to kiss, winter 1932. Photo by Joaquín Sicart

Medals and rosaries by this time had become a kind of medium of exchange that bound believers and seers together. In some cases, on instructions from the Virgin, the seers gave their own crucifixes, medals, or rosaries as gifts to believers; then the believers would buy others and give them in return.[23] Visions included the obeisance of angels, who formed a kind of court for the Virgin, bowing, kneeling, and receiving orders. Similarly, believers kissed seers' hands, whether those of Ramona after the wounding or those of Benita when she returned their rosaries.

We have also seen the flower become a divine symbol. Away from Ezkioga, some children in trance saw the Virgin in a flower or had visions of flowers or rewarded spectators with flowers. This distribution of flowers, easier in small groups, became common in the Ezkioga visions in 1932; thus blessed flowers, like blessed rosaries, were something that pilgrims took home as personalized talismans from the Virgin.[24]

Another way to distribute grace was to press a crucifix to the lips of observers on the Virgin's command. From December 1931 seers in vision offered crucifixes to certain persons or invited certain individuals to come forward, giving them a crucifix to kiss. Seers gave some believers the crucifix to kiss for an especially long time and ignored others altogether.

By distributing divine approval, the seers set up a kind of hierarchy of grace among the spectators. In the case of the Catalan expeditions, this new hierarchy sometimes reversed the order of the group. The factory worker José Garmendia and the humble farm woman María Recalde picked out the servants and the poorer members of the group not only for special favors but for notice as future seers. To be sure, they also singled out those who were chroniclers, like Salvador Cardús, Arturo Rodes, and Rafael García Cascón. Those they skipped were generally the few doubters or cynics in the expedition or onlookers obviously skeptical of or entertained by the events. In the Catalan groups these were the persons for whose "conversion" to Ezkioga members prayed. The later liturgies then, like those of the visions in villages away from Ezkioga, incorporated into the relations between seers and spectators a kind of theater of grace. Promotion, inclusion, conversion, or exclusion provided the tension in the plot.[25]

VISION STATES: HOW OTHERS SAW THEM

In about half of the Spanish lay medieval visions that we can document village priests or civil authorities instructed seers to return to the divine figure and request a proof. Some of the proofs they brought back were signs on their bodies or on those of other townspeople: a hand fixed as a cross; a mouth that would not open; wounds from a divine beating; sudden blindness; the prediction of imminent death from the plague of a seer or villager. We saw an echo of these signs when the judge could not undo Rosario Gurruchaga's hands, when Cándida Zunzunegui became supernaturally heavy after the police arrived, when Ramona and Luis had blood on their hands, and when the seers foresaw their own death.

In medieval accounts the physical state of the seer while having visions was not an issue. Only when laypeople began to doubt visions at the beginning of the sixteenth century do we read of a seer's claim to *trasponerse*, to be "transported so that she did not know or think she was in this world but rather the other." The authorities did not ask witnesses about these states, and indeed, most visions we know about took place without witnesses.[26]

By the time of the Ezkioga events, however, the new model of public trance-like visions applied, based presumably on Lourdes and ultimately on conventual mysticism. No longer did lay seers shuttle back and forth between the saint and the community after private visions. While their first vision might be private, they took along witnesses in subsequent sessions, and their state of consciousness while in vision was relevant to the process of validation. An altered state served as a sign. For inexperienced observers such a state might be proof that the visions were true. For seasoned clerics it might simply indicate that a seer was not consciously faking. In any case, the old idea that contact with the divine left some kind of effect on the body resurfaced. Ezkioga believers refer to this state as being "en visión." Reporters from Basque newspapers, careful about prejudging the visions, generally avoided the word *éxstasis,* associated with sainthood, and only occasionally used the more neutral word *trance.*

Since at least the turn of the seventeenth century, when the Italian physician Paolo Zacchia described some religious visions as symptoms of mental illness, doctors took part in deciding whether visions were authentic.[27] For some altered states might indicate not an ecstasy resulting from contact with the divine but another physical or mental condition. Animal magnetism, catatonia, epilepsy, hypnotism, hysteria, intoxication, mania, neurosis, obsession, somnambulism (which associated a trance with a dream state), and suggestion were diagnoses that experts offered at one time or another for seers at Ezkioga. Amundarain wanted to rule out alternatives like these, so in the first days he brought in the local doctor, Sabel Aranzadi. As with the doctors of the Bureau de Constatations at Lourdes in regard to miracles, Aranzadi's job at Ezkioga was to eliminate natural alternatives to ecstasy. His presence gave the commission the legitimacy of science.

Aranzadi and other doctors took the pulses of the original brother and sister in vision and found them normal and steady. But since these children did not seem to experience any altered state, either during or after their visions, what they saw rather than what they felt was newsworthy. One of the reasons the public abandoned them rather quickly was the sheer simplicity of their experience. Rafael Picavea wrote of the boy, "The new seers have eclipsed him. He neither suffers moving faints nor falls into truculent pathological dreams."[28]

The newspapers spent more time on those who showed more physical symptoms. The first of these was the chauffeur Ignacio Aguado, one of four successive youthful males who were skeptical about the visions and were then struck with visions themselves. When Aguado saw the Virgin during the rosary on July 4, he had been laughing and joking with friends. He felt something like a faint and fell down for about a minute. To observers he seemed unconscious, but as he described it, "I fell to the earth, but I did not lose my senses [*el sentido*] and I continued to see the image." He had to be carried into a house and then driven back to Beasain. By one account he made a confession and became a churchgoer. The big play the press gave Aguado, side by side with the initial account of the child seers, indicates his critical role in supporting them. *El Pueblo Vasco* even inserted a cameo photograph of Aguado alongside one of the original seers' family. For most readers his conversion was part of the first account of the visions they read.[29]

Patxi Goicoechea of Ataun was next. He fell down on July 7, after the regular prayers were over and he had made a joke about the Virgin. He had bounded to a rise on the hillside and pointed her out with a shout. On the advice of someone nearby, he asked the Virgin three times what she wanted, and she said they should say the rosary. Those around him did so. Reporters described him then as keeping his eyes open but losing consciousness (*sin sentido, kordegabeta*), as fainting (*desvanecido*), as having a fit (*pasmo*) or a rapture (*arrobamiento*), or as remaining ecstatic (*extático*). His friends carried him down the hill. Like Aguado, he said, "I fell down in a faint but I did not lose consciousness; as I went down the hill in their arms she continued before me." By this time there was a first-aid room, and the doctors there found Patxi's heart working well. Like Aguado, he was shaken and someone had to drive him home. He did not recover fully until late that night, and for four days he did not eat, hardly slept, and was sad.[30]

In early July there were other seers experiencing trancelike states, but at first the press was interested not so much in the seers' partial loss of senses, which served as a kind of proof, but rather in their fall to the ground and the physical aftereffects. On July 8, the day after Patxi's vision, it was the turn of Xanti, a youth from Gabiria. He was allegedly stunned in mid-blasphemy as he raised his wineskin (or, in another account, as he rolled a cigarette). He had said there was no saint, male or female, who could knock him down, presumably referring to what happened to Aguado and Patxi. Three days later Aurelio Cabezón, an eighteen-year-old newspaper photographer who had been bantering with teenage girls during the prayers, suffered a similar shock. By his own account he saw the Virgin coming toward him, he gave a shout, and he fell to the ground unconscious. There doctors found his pulse racing. He regained consciousness in about half an hour. Afterward he was pallid, faint, thoughtful, preoccupied, and distracted. When he returned to take photographs on July 18, he had another vision during the rosary and was spooked again as the Virgin seemed to be coming toward him. He let out "a terrifying cry that echoed across the entire hillside" before falling unconscious.[31]

This kind of initial "conversion by reaction," something like that of Saul on the road to Damascus, also occurred to a factory worker from Beasain. He allegedly said he would shoot his pistol at the Virgin if she appeared, and he promptly fell back into the arms of the church organist. It also happened to a taxi driver from San Sebastián, who allegedly made fun of the visions and fell backward and began to weep. It happened as well to Ignacio in Bachicabo in August, to a youth aged twenty-four named Nicanor Patiño, who made fun of the apparitions in Guadamur on August 29, and to Luis Irurzun in Iraneta in October. In 1920 a youth from Los Arcos had experienced the same reaction when he threw a coin at the Christ of Piedramillera. Under the pressure of the events, some of the most adamantly opposed, the most skeptical, were paradoxically those closest to belief. For Catholic newspapers these cases provided perfect object lessons for the Republic—they emphasized how divine power reduced proud men to weaklings. Therefore journalists emphasized not the altered state or the vision itself but the physical and psychological defeat.[32]

Attention to working men with "conversions by reaction": top, *reporters and chauffeur Ignacio Aguado in Legorreta, 9 July 1931 (photo by Pascual Marín, courtesy Fototeka Kutxa, Archivo Fotográfico, Caja Gipuzkoa, Donostia-San Sebastián);* bottom, *priest and doctor with farm laborer Nicanor Patiño at Guadamur, 1931 (from* Ahora, *5 September 1931, courtesy Hemeroteca Municipal de Madrid)*

As these males were achieving special prominence, women and children were also fainting right and left (the words used included *deliquio, desmayo, desvanecimiento, síncope, pérdida de conocimiento*). Again, the final faint and aftershock seemed to be the determinative reaction, the evidence that the vision was real. For example, an eighteen-year-old female from Zestoa gave a great scream when she saw the Virgin on July 14 ("I could not hold it in"). She was not able to sleep the next night and was in an acute state of nervousness the next day.[33]

But *El Día*'s reporter was early in discerning a difference between genders. After interviewing a farmer still terrified the day after his vision, he wrote, "But not in all cases does the apparition have this upsetting effect, which seems to be more common among the men, who fall into faints or are semicataleptic." He mentioned two young women, Evarista Galdós and Juana Ibarguren, who "saw the apparition and far from being frightened ran after her, wanting to get closer and find out for themselves if the apparition was flesh and blood."[34] Other descriptions of Benita Aguirre, Lolita Núñez, Ramona Olazábal, and the original sibling seers show that at least some women and girls welcomed the visions rather than feared them. This too was a pattern in the testimony at Piedramillera in 1920, where a woman saw the Christ smile each time she entered the church. The implication in these accounts seems to be that the women and children were more comfortable with the divine, while men were uneasy because of unconfessed sins and unresolved doubts.

We may question whether a pattern emerged at all at Ezkioga or at Piedramillera. An unconscious selection by reporters and priests may in fact have prejudiced their reports. After the initial conversion reactions in July, the priests and doctors fished for more conversion reactions with their printed questionnaire: "What did you think about what was going on at Ezquioga with the visions? What mood were you in when you came to Ezquioga—devotion? diversion? or to make fun?" From Elgoibar a newspaper correspondent wrote that on July 16 four young men in their twenties had had visions. The note described an aftershock for one of them, who could not sleep that night and had to stay home the next day because he felt "abnormal and nervous." Of the other three it said nothing; presumably they slept well and went happily to work. Conversely, the press did not report some of the more traumatic visions of women because they considered the women hysterical. So our sources may be working from a script similar to the one used a decade before to describe those who saw crucifixes move.[35]

The stories of men converted by visions affected the debate on women's suffrage in the Constituent Cortes in Madrid. When the republican priest Basilio Alvarez and the republican pathologist Roberto Novoa Santos argued that women were hysterics subject to the whims of the uterus, the feminist Clara Campoamor countered that all the seers at Ezkioga and Guadamur were hysterical men. Newspapers on the Catholic right cultivated one misconception, that only men had deep visions at Ezkioga, to show that irreligious men felt guilty. Campoamor used this misconception to refute another, that women were biologically irrational, born of the positivist left.[36]

When the miracles of July 12, 16, and 18 failed to materialize, public attention shifted to Patxi. His visions were a prolonged spectacle of conversion (weeks after his first vision he would still cry out that he had been bad and he asked the Virgin to forgive him), and he was leading the way with exciting political messages and predictions of miracles.[37] He attracted attention in yet another way: in vision he appeared wholly insensitive to pain. When seeing visions he could talk, hear, and see those around him, but he could not, it seems, feel. As a result he became a kind of exhibit A, like a fakir. His local doctor from Ataun sometimes accompanied him to Ezkioga and other doctors and priests came to examine him in vision. They took his pulse, stuck him with needles and other sharp objects (including, by Bilbao doctors in 1932, a lancet under the nail of his big toe), burned him with a cigarette lighter, tested his pupillary reflex (he had none), and attempted with lights to provoke blinking (in vain). Occasionally he was excited and had what seemed to be convulsions, and once on his return to Ataun his doctor had to give him morphine to calm him. But he seems to have settled into a routine of visions on certain nights at certain moments of the rosary. Doctors described him in vision as catatonic or semicataleptic but in his normal life, out of vision, as sane and well.[38]

This intense scrutiny culminated on August 1 when Patxi supposedly levitated. He declared that the Virgin had insisted, in spite of his objections, that he be elevated for seventy seconds. Although a day later the newspapers backpedaled and said that Patxi's friends simply felt his body become weightless, the idea stuck. Levitating was the stuff of the saints of cloisters, and Patxi became "Patxi Santu." A long and favorable article in *Pensamiento Navarro* on August 4 entitled "Apparitions? A Trip to Ezquioga" totally ignored the Virgin or her messages and dealt instead with Patxi and his strange vision states.[39]

The first step in any examination by the doctors was to take the seer's pulse. Almost any result was evidence for the truth of the visions for persons disposed to believe. For instance, doctors thought it exceptional when seers went through what were obviously highly moving visions with no change in pulse. The canon Juan Bautista Altisent of Lleida wrote of a boy seer: "I take the pulse of this child while he speaks to me, and it is completely normal. This is precisely, in the opinion of the doctors, the most remarkable thing of all: that in spite of the psychic state of the seer, his pulse keeps completely steady." Conversely, doctors thought it remarkable that Goicoechea's pulse ran so fast after a vision on July 11. Dr. Aranzadi told a reporter: "His pulse rate was fantastic. I was going to draw some of his blood because I feared his veins would burst." For this doctor Patxi's state of arousal demonstrated sincerity.[40]

Later, when doctors found some seers' pulses to be so slow during visions as to be imperceptible, they considered this phenomenon remarkable too. A professor from the Institut Catholique de Louvain in late August examined a teenage girl, probably Evarista, in vision. He listened to her heart and lungs, took her pulse, and examined her eyelid reflexes. He judged that the heart was beating irregularly, so he brought her out of her vision as a hypnotist would. A San Sebastián doctor examining Evarista in March 1932 found that her heart went three minutes without beating and considered her survival proof that the visions were supernatural. When believers tried to sum up the evidence of pulse rates during visions, they could not agree on a pattern. One Catalan doctor said the pulses tended to be normal, another maintained that they tended to be slow, weak, and sometimes even temporarily absent, and Burguera held that they were largely normal, although those of nervous persons tended to be fast.

As these examples show, doctors tried to apply science to these seers' states, but they had little experience and few standards. Thus they fell back on their inclinations, and since those who went to Ezkioga were more likely to be sympathetic, their findings tended to be favorable. The seers came to recognize doctors as allies. In vision Evarista turned to the San Sebastián doctor, saying, "The Virgin is very pleased by these scientific observations designed to illustrate and propagate the events at Ezquioga." Conversely, what the Jesuit Laburu saw of Evarista and other seers merely confirmed his prior skepticism. In the notes for his Vitoria lecture he wrote, "In any hypnotist or spiritist session, one can find identical phenomena. These things are common and very well known in suggestive phenomena."[41]

From late July observers stuck seers with pins and burned them—some on the neck, others on the face and on the arms. Baudilio Sedano recounted that when he stuck Benita Aguirre with a long pin, she turned and smiled benignly. A skeptical French doctor did the same to a fifteen-year-old boy. In these instances, the seers showed no sign of pain. Observers tested children in Navarra in similar ways.[42]

The pupils of the eyes of many seers, like those of Patxi, did not contract when exposed to light. And both skeptical and sympathetic observers mention seers who, like Patxi, did not blink during visions.[43] Starting in late July doctors and priests held a cloth or some other object in front of the seers to test whether the visions were "subjective" (if they continued) or "objective" (if they ceased). The objects blocked visions of some seers but not of others. Again, no one seemed to know what this information meant. In retrospect, one fact seems clear: the seers were in a variety of physical states.[44]

Another proof used to validate the apparitions was the change of expression on seers' faces. A reporter for *El Pueblo Vasco* noted, "The great transformation in their faces . . . impressed us vividly, leading us to exclaim, 'Something is going on here!'" Both believing and skeptical spectators singled out the same seers, by no coincidence those whom Raymond de Rigné, Joaquín Sicart, and José Martínez from Santander later photographed the most. Canon Altisent wrote of Benita Aguirre:

> The child has a normal kind of face, but at the moment of the apparition the face is so transformed as to become exquisite, something that cannot be described. Then I thought that if Murillo were alive now he would go there to seek the model for the faces of the angels in his inspired canvases.

Similarly, a Catalan woman wrote that Benita seemed "like one of the angels she is contemplating." Salvador Cardús saw the transformation in Ramona as "a reflection of the beauty of the Mother of God" on the seer's face, with "a sweet smile that could only be the Virgin's."[45]

People also singled out Cruz Lete ("one of those whose face is transformed most angelically") and Evarista Galdós, whose expression was "incredible if she were not really seeing something extraordinary." The skeptical French doctor Émile Pascal also noted the change in Evarista's face.

> Little by little her face lights up, she smiles and seems to be seeing a marvelous spectacle. For a half hour her features reflect expressions that are really very beautiful: beatitude, joy, piety, happiness, etc., one after another with an unheard-of intensity. Without exaggerating, one thinks when seeing her of the Saint Teresa in ecstasy by Bernini in the church of Santa Maria in Rome. . . . Monsieur de Rigné has obtained some remarkable pictures of her . . . but they give only a poor idea of the intensity and beauty of this ecstatic's expressions. Remember that Bernadette at Lourdes in her visions was as though transfigured. Just seeing her was enough to convince certain witnesses.[46]

But not all faces were beatific in visions. Some, like Patxi's, alternated between ecstasy and a thick, sleepy look: "During the phenomenon he has two phases, one of apparent ecstasy and another of sopor. When he returns from the latter to the former, Dr. Aranzadi exclaims, 'Look, look what an enormous difference in the lines of his face!'" Others did not look right at all. Several observers I talked to disbelieved the visions precisely because of the faces, presumably the faces not photographed. In Ormaiztegi a priest's sister said, "What faces! They had fear on their faces. If they were seeing the Virgin would they look that way? I cannot conceive it." Two elderly sisters from Ordizia said the seers in trance had "disfigured faces."[47]

People saw other changes in the faces. Even skeptical observers noticed a sheen (brillo) on the face of Luis Irurzun. And occasionally people remarked a special light like an aura or halo. The mother of Antonio Durán, a young lawyer from Cáceres, saw his face "illuminated, as if some kind of light emerged from his features." Arturo Rodes described the original boy seer from Ezkioga as if

Evarista Galdós in vision, 11 March 1932. Photo by Joaquín Sicart

alight: "It was pitch-black and he seemed to shine like an angel that was adoring the divinity."[48]

A pilgrim from Catalonia noted as physical signs of the sincerity of a seer from Sevilla, Consuelo Luébanos, the bruises on her cheek from her fall into trance. But the absence of bruises from falls could be still another reason to believe. Two Catalans saw none on Benita Aguirre's face despite her fall, and they generalized, "Even heavy men like Garmendia, whose solid body falls hard and loud against the ground, have never received any injury as a result of such spectacular spills." All of these observations sharpened the public's awareness that many of the seers were in a special state while having visions.[49]

During the summer of 1931 medical interest in the matter was intense. Within a week of the first report there were several doctors present, including the famous Fernando Asuero of San Sebastián. When seers collapsed on the hillside, a doctor was generally available. Doctors accompanied some seers from their villages; periodically groups of doctors examined the seers together. As the vision states became news in themselves, so did the doctors, including two from Hendaye and the professor from Louvain. This medical interest reflected the importance of doctors at Lourdes and was characteristic of most other nineteenth- and twentieth-century apparition sequences. Rumor had it that Manuel Azaña, then minister of war, had sent Gregorio Marañón, the nation's greatest medical authority, to diagnose the visions on July 22. Patxi, by then well aware of his own exotic properties, said he would like to meet the doctor.[50]

The most active among the many doctors on the Catalan trips were Miguel Balari, a homeopath who had previously studied the Barcelona mystic Enriqueta Tomás, and Manuel Bofill Pascual of the Clínica San Narciso in Girona, Magdalena Aulina's personal physician and public defender. The close-knit Basque medical establishment kept its distance, and persons with cures they attributed to the visions could not obtain medical certificates. Not one Basque doctor was a public supporter, much less a seer. At most, some were involved collaterally.[51]

At first the vision states intrigued the Zumarraga doctor Sabel Aranzadi enough that he pointed reporters to the most "interesting cases." He eventually ended by supplying some of the most telling negative evidence. Yet he was never absolutely sure that the visions were false. In later years he told his friends that in spite of all he knew he could not bring himself to throw away the bloodstained bandages of Ramona Olazábal. The president of the medical association of Gipuzkoa, the ophthalmologist Miguel Vidaur, helped Padre Laburu. But neither Vidaur nor Aranzadi took a public stand.[52]

We have seen how in Navarra the psychiatrist Victoriano Juaristi, a kind of regional version of Gregorio Marañón, turned public opinion against the visions in the Barranca. In San Sebastián the only doctor publicly opposed was José Bago, who remanded the seers to the insane asylum. Politics rather than a personal knowledge of the visions seems to have moved him. As far as I know, the pathologist and deputy in the Cortes Roberto Novoa Santos did not go to observe the Ezkioga seers, but his assistant, José María Iza, was at Ezkioga on 17 October 1931. Not surprisingly his diagnosis was that "all have the muscular rigidity, the lack of reflexes, and certain peculiarities in the pupil and the nostrils that indicate the cataleptic state characteristic of hysterics."[53]

There was always the possibility that some of the seers were mentally ill, a danger to society and in need of treatment. In 1934 a doctor in Soria published the case history of a male patient and seer whose first vision—he saw the Miraculous Mary surrounded by lights—was in 1929. The Virgin told him to "Love charity and you will see the Father of the Poor." He gave his money away, spent some time with the Vincentian Fathers in Guadalajara, then went off preaching on his own in the Alcarria, Córdoba, and Granada. People called him "the crazy friar." Local authorities took him to a mental hospital in Córdoba, where among other claims he said he had become an automobile driver by order of the Virgin. She chose him to transport the column of Our Lady of Pilar to the village of Villaseca in Soria, where the Last Judgment would be held. He also asserted that one day he would be pope.

This patient was ill in more painful and dysfunctional ways as well, and the doctor concluded that he was insane and a danger to society, with symptoms including weak-mindedness, schizophrenia, and paranoia. But he also pointed out that

> there are many mentally ill persons like M. G. whom we come across in daily life, who work and have a social life, individuals who, if they run along in a rut without difficulties and without coming across obstacles that require a healthy mind to overcome, get into trouble only when they run afoul of laws and legal codes.[54]

Doctors, reporters, or the general public diagnosed none of the Ezkioga seers as obviously crazy. When studying the unusual and varied vision states, the doctors were observing persons who had every appearance of being mentally healthy, so they focused more on the phenomenon than its bearers. Even Laburu recognized the similarities of the trances at Ezkioga to those other nonpathological contexts produced and he steered well clear of their physical properties in his lectures. When he showed the film of mental patients after a film of the seers, he did so, I think, simply to sway the audience; in the text of his lecture he never suggested that the seers were mentally disturbed.

Whether they believed in the visions or not, those who went to Ezkioga did not think the seers' unusual behavior was the result of mental instability. Some considered rather that the seers' actions embodied the reigning social and political instability (what the count of Romanones, referring to Ezkioga, called "the religious hypertension that the Basque people have reached"). For the believers the dramatic states of the seers reflected the extreme reactions of the divine beings to the plight of Spain.[55]

Thérèse Neumann: The Model for the Evaluators

The holy person who came to mind most when commentators searched for comparisons was the German mystic Thérèse Neumann of Konnersreuth in Bavaria. After a series of physical disablements and cures, in 1926 when she was age twenty-eight she began to have every Friday an extended sequence of visions of episodes of Christ's Passion. During the visions she seemed to weep tears of blood and had the marks of the stigmata on her hands, feet, and left side. Between episodes, in a trancelike state, she might answer consultations of pilgrims. Starting in September 1927, she claimed, she took no food but Holy Communion. The Sunday after Ramona's wounding, somebody distributed at Ezkioga large num-

Drawing of Thérèse Neumann in vision. From El Pasionario, *before March 1931*

bers of an article on Neumann from the Madrid daily *Informaciones*. The Basque press that reported on Ezkioga carried lengthy stories about the German stigmatic and had in fact already done so before the visions. *El Pasionario* had been running a series of articles on her for more than a year when the visions started. Those looking for divine signs found that Ezkioga and Thérèse Neumann were part of a divine offensive against materialism and atheism.[56]

News of this mystic reached Spanish newspapers in September 1927. Some clerical commentators warned against gullibility, referring to the recent cases of Claire Ferchaud and Padre Pio. Ferchaud's vision at Loublande during World War I found favor in the French church, but the Holy Office intervened and in March 1920 condemned the visions unequivocally. Padre Pio da Pietrelcina, an Italian Capuchin, experienced the stigmata in 1918. By 1920 leaves from a rose-bush in his monastery and letters with his signature were used in healing in Spain. Spaniards visited him and wrote him for advice. The Holy Office issued five decrees against him starting in 1923, the latest in May 1931. Neumann convinced others, like a Capuchin who had been an early promoter of Padre Pio.[57] By the start of the Ezkioga visions Editorial Litúrgica Española in Barcelona had published three books on Neumann. In 1931 she was at the height of her popularity, living proof of the truth of Catholicism, receiving three hundred letters a day.[58] Reports about her fit into an ancient tradition of fasting laywomen who serve as intermediaries for humans with the dead and with heaven, a tradition that continues to the present day in Spain.[59]

Some of the enthusiasts for Ezkioga had been to see Neumann. The Bilbao religious philanthropist Pilar Arratia found the visionary crucifixions at Ezkioga in January 1932 similar to those of the stigmatic, except they were without blood. The noted Basque clergyman and philologist Resurrección María de Azkue visited Neumann in September 1928 and on his return gave lectures about her; he seems to have been a discreet sympathizer of the Ezkioga visions. Neumann enthusiasts like Raymond de Rigné, Fernand Remisch, Ennemond Boniface, and Gustave Thibon spread news of Ezkioga in Belgium and France.[60]

Father Thomas Matyschok, a professor of Psychic Sciences in Germany, gave lectures on Neumann in Pamplona in August 1932 and in San Sebastián in December. His experience with Neumann qualified him as an expert, so Juan Bautista Ayerbe took him to evaluate Conchita Mateos in vision. Matyschok found in the child the five key qualities he observed in Neumann: (1) she fell into ecstasy suddenly; (2) she was not aware in sight, sound, or intellect of what was happening around her; (3) she remembered faithfully and precisely what happened in the ecstasy; (4) she was insensible to fire, pricks, blows, and the like, and (5) she did not blink or move her eyes when struck by a powerful electric beam.[61]

Like Soledad de la Torre, Padre Pio, and other "living saints," Neumann was used as an oracle and a prophet. She seems to have worked in synergy with other sources of religious enthusiasm. I do not know if visitors asked Neumann about Ezkioga, but she did answer questions about Spain. Matyschok said that she told him that the Limpias visions were true and that it was the Christ of Limpias that she saw in her visions. Similarly, she told a priest from Zaragoza in September 1935 that she had heard of Madre Rafols's prophecies and that "a young man," whom the priest retrospectively identified with Francisco Franco, was working firmly for Christ in Spain.[62]

People also used Neumann as a counterexample. Rafael Picavea sought to discredit the Ezkioga visions by describing "morbid" phenomena in which self-suggestion played a large part. He cited evidence that Neumann ate secretly and deceived herself as well as others in order to show that Ramona and other seers were equally open to self-deception.[63]

Starting in the mid-nineteenth century, as psychology became more prominent, even among Catholics there was a kind of open season on religious ecstasy. A diagnosis of hysteria for Teresa de Avila was a major issue in Spanish publications appearing around her third centenary.[64] The pathologist Roberto Novoa Santos proposed angina as Teresa's divine wounding. These were offshoots of an enormous French literature that sought natural explanations for trances, raptures, miracle cures, and stigmata. Orthodox Catholic psychologists spent much of their time refuting the new studies or denying their applicability to true visions.[65] Those defending Thérèse Neumann had to show how different she was from the mentally ill stigmatic studied by Janet in *De l'angoisse à l'extase*, or from

Louise Lateau, the most famous stigmatic of the previous generation.[66] The Jesuit Juan Mir y Noguera charged that many of those challenging Catholic mysticism were Jews: "Yes, Jews who, not satisfied by making themselves lords of wealth, politics, and the press, scale the bastion of science to work more thoroughly their iniquity." The challenge had reached Spain. "Rationalism has infected not a few doctors in the peninsula, and the number of enemies of miracles and divine mysticism is still growing."[67]

As far as I know, only one psychologist made a serious effort to examine the Ezkioga seers with "rationalist" theories in mind. The French doctor Émile Pascal was at Ezkioga sometime in early 1932 and two years later he published his attempt to "deoccultize" the apparitions, first in a specialized journal and then in a book entitled *Hallucinations or Miracles? The Apparitions of Ezquioga and Beauraing.*[68]

Pascal proposed that at Ezkioga the first seers' visions were based on stories about other apparitions and that the visions spread by imitative suggestion. As other instances he cited the Jansenist visionaries in the cemetery of Saint-Medard, an epidemic of possession at Morzine in the 1860s, the contagious effects of mesmerism, and American revival meetings. Similarly, the psychiatrist Victoriano Juaristi from Pamplona considered the Navarrese child visions an epidemic of neurosis like similar contagions in schools, hamlets, and entire regions; and the deputy and journalist Rafael Picavea compared the spread of visions to psychological contagion among women factory workers and to the seventeenth-century witch craze.[69]

What interested Pascal especially was the psychic state of the seers. He suggested that the seers were

> plunged into a light subconscious state, with a tendency toward a fixed idea. More precisely, the seers are plunged in a low-grade somnambulism, with all their spontaneous attention concentrated on the vision, as with a hypnotized subject under the influence of an intense suggestion. We would call this a light state. For there is missing here one of the characteristics of a deep somnambulism: amnesia upon awakening.

He pointed out the similarity of these seers to persons he had observed under the influence of certain drugs or light hypnosis: all were at least partially aware of what was going on and could remember their experience later. In this kind of half-trance they had contact with the external world and could answer questions from those around them: "The normal consciousness of the ecstatic is present, like a kind of spectator, at the apparitions provoked in the subconscious by the suggestions of the ambience."[70]

Padre Burguera objected to suggestion as an explanation. He pointed out that many people went to Ezkioga wanting visions but did not have them, while others who were merely curious or even skeptical did. Pascal countered with the psychological axiom that "instead of evoking the expression of the subconscious, voluntary and conscious attention paralyzes it and blocks its development," which is why those who wanted visions often did not get them. But, Pascal argued, "fear that the subconscious might erupt and the attempt to prevent it from doing so will often evoke it in sensitive persons," a process that would seem to apply to unwilling visionaries like our young male converts.[71]

Pascal could not avoid Raymond de Rigné, who insisted that Ramona Olazábal's stigmata were not fraudulent. But Pascal held that even if not fraudulent they could be the result of "the intense action of the spirit on the body." He referred to the opinions of Michel de Montaigne and Giordano Bruno that the stigmata of Francis of Assisi were caused by imagination. In a fine demonstration of the single-minded determination of his times to undermine mysticism, Pascal detailed the many as yet unsuccessful efforts by hypnotists and psychologists starting in 1853 to cause stigmata by suggestion.[72]

Pascal agreed with Laburu that the visions at Ezkioga were the effect of suggestion. But Laburu thought there were other, true apparitions. So Pascal tried to show how Laburu's objections to Ezkioga applied equally well to the visions of Bernadette and the other children that followed her at Lourdes. It was in this broader debate over the truth of mystical states and apparitions in general that Catholics and non-Catholics interpreted the vision states of Ezkioga.

VISION STATES: HOW THE SEERS' EXPERIENCE EVOLVED

Over time the way the seers had visions changed. As a rule, seers progressed from lesser to greater states of dissociation, from less definite to more definite perceptions, and from less to more sensory involvement.

In the first month men, women, and some children tended to collapse physically after the visions, and observers paid little attention to the vision state itself. Recovery took from a few minutes to a few hours, but it took less time as seers had more visions. The seers obviously tended to find the first visions more traumatic. As time passed their attitude changed from respect, awe, or fear to confidence.

By the time the first Magdalena Aulina trip arrived from Catalonia in December 1931, most of the noisier, more theatrical aspects of the visions had disappeared. At Ezkioga in mid-May 1932 Miguel Balari summed up the trances as he knew them: "So this absence of the senses comes to an end, without a convulsion, without any sign of hysteria or anything that could be remotely said to be spectacular or noisy." Pascal remarked on this change: "At times, especially toward the beginning, there were sometimes nervous fits. . . . But these great agitations are more and more rare. The calm and deep ecstasy is what is most frequently seen."[73]

When Juan Bautista Ayerbe described the general pattern of vision behavior at the end of 1932, he pointed out other changes as well.

At first there were visions that were not ecstasies, just exterior visions. Some seers continued communicating with those around them, whom they continued to see, hear, and answer. Later the seers in ecstasy as a rule neither see, hear, nor have the least relation to what is around them.

Nevertheless, they move and retain their intellectual faculties. During the ecstasies the seers move, pray, speak with the Most Holy Virgin and the saints who appear, reason perfectly well, pose the questions they have been asked to pose, receive and later remember the replies obtained from the Holy Virgin, at times unexpected and surprising.[74]

This change may have come about partly because Patxi was so famous. As observers came to consider insensibility essential to a true vision, they made more and more tests, culminating in Burguera's cull by flame in the spring of 1933. The original seers never fell into trance and made no pretense of being in an altered state. I do not know whether Burguera or anyone else applied fire to them. People later paid more attention to seers who were in unusual and dissociated states.

In the evolved kind of vision, instead of collapsing into a faint when the vision was over, the seers collapsed when it began, as here with Benita Aguirre:

At once, and without transition, as if struck by lightning, the child falls face first, as if some invisible force had thrown her face against the ground. . . . These falls reminded the observer of the way the Apostles fell back when confronted by the resplendent cloud on Mount Tabor and the way the soldiers fell who had gone to capture Jesus at Gethsemane.[75]

When the seers surfaced from this new version of abstraction, they did so quickly: "They return to their normal state as rapidly as they entered into ecstasy, remaining from this moment on completely calm without the need that epileptics have to recover during minutes, hours, or days." More jaundiced observers noted incongruous behavior immediately after the vision ended. It will be remembered that Luis Irurzun was struck down and converted after he insisted on smoking when watching a vision. Two years later he had yet to kick the habit and was lighting up right after coming out of his vision:

And this young fellow who had been undergoing for three hours this totally exhausting physical exercise [a pantomime of Saint Michael's combat with the devil], this wild man who I expected to collapse in complete prostration, comes to his senses, takes a cigarette out of his pocket, and lights it. And what's more, he is in that instant perfectly calm, as if he had not got out of bed since the night before.[76]

Within the vision many seers experienced a progress, noted by the anthropologist Clara Gallini in the visions of Bernadette, from vagueness to concreteness in what they perceive. Often visions began simply with a bright light somewhere which developed gradually, evolved, and opened up to produce a humanlike figure, most often the Virgin. This process could take place in one vision, in every vision, or in a series of visions. The commission may have helped along this process of definition with its questions.[77]

Light was essential to the visions, as most took place at night. Blinding light characterized the nocturnal visions in the late fourteenth and early fifteenth century but not the later daytime visions in Castile and Catalonia. By the time the priests at Ezkioga drew up their *Hoja interrogatorio* (see appendix), they paid special attention to light: "How does the vision first appear—the image, the brightness, or both at the same time? Is the brightness in the form of a frame [*cuadro*], oval, or a chapel or altar? Does it light up the Virgin only, or the atmosphere? Is the light intense or faint?"

As at Mendigorría, light was all some people saw—in trees, as a cross, or simply in a blinding flash. Luis Irurzun described to me his first vision in Iraneta as a great light that made him think he was about to die. But usually the visions of light heralded the arrival of the Virgin. Many seers referred to this preliminary light simply as a great resplendence, but several described the light first taking form. A Catalan woman reported that Ramona told her in early September: "I see the Most Holy Virgin in a brightness [*claridad*], but a brightness that opens up (and she joined her hands and opened them to express herself better) and inside it is the Most Holy Virgin of the Sorrows." Similarly, an elderly rural seer explained to me that he would see something like a cloud, which would open to allow the Virgin to emerge surrounded by light. Something like this kind of nimbus of light was a general pattern for the seers in early September 1931: "The Virgin is always seen as if inside a very bright cloud, brighter than the sun they claim, and suddenly it opens and the Virgin appears in the middle, crowned with beautiful stars."[78]

For Evarista Galdós a circle or hoop of light provided a space for her first, quick, glimpse of the Virgin. She saw

> a light in the form of a halo that got bigger and bigger. But I could see
> the tips and the trunks of the trees, so it would have had a radius of about
> four meters. But I could not distinguish anything where the light was. In
> the middle of that brightness, I saw a lady dressed in mourning. . . . I could
> not make out her face, as the apparition was momentary, and what's more,
> it seemed as if she had a curtain of cloud in front of her.

The light itself seems to have continued after this glimpse and to have changed in response to the crowd's behavior: "I saw the light for about five minutes. When the people would begin to shout, it would go higher away, and when they were praying attentively, it got closer."[79]

Similarly, a woman from Beizama who worked for a family that moved around Spain saw a "grandiose circle of light that was opening wider and stretching so that inside it I saw heaven [or the sky]." In the center, which "I call heaven [*cielo*] and I do not know how to explain," she saw an elaborate scene including a dove, an old man, Christ embracing a cross, and the Virgin as a queen with two angels. In one of Benita Aguirre's visions the splendor emerged from a hole that opened in the sky and into which the Virgin, the Christ child, and angels with baskets of flowers eventually disappeared.[80]

Resplendence accompanied the Virgin, whether in the form of points of light or light surrounding or wrapping her entire body. One seer saw the light as emanating from her hands. And Santos Bustos, age thirteen, took a second look and saw a light shining from the Virgin's stomach:

> He sees again the apparition, vision, or image of the Virgin, but with greater brilliance and clarity, observing, in addition to what he saw at first, that toward the middle of the body (he points to the upper abdomen) she had something shining that is not like a lamp [*lámpara*] but that gave off a very intense light that his eyes could not resist, for they were blinded, and he was again frightened so that he turned his head aside and did not wish to turn it back.[81]

Beams of divine light seem to have been one means by which the Virgin could arrive and leave. When Evarista Galdós claimed to receive a medal of the Daughters of Mary from on high, it too descended in a light-way: "I saw a light, and in its midst came down a blue ribbon with a medal at the bottom."[82]

Perhaps prompted by the priests, the seers remarked on the light's intensity. Several said it was brighter than the sun. This intensity sometimes increased as the Virgin emerged or, in one case, as people prayed more. Few mention its color. An elderly seer told me that for him it was more yellow than the sun. For another seer it was reddish. Patxi claimed to see it with the Basque colors, red, white and green. But for most it was whitish.[83]

Some were visibly troubled by the brilliance they saw and they turned their heads away. Pascal, there in early 1932, wrote, "We note that at the end of the ecstasy all declare to have been lit up by 'great light' that blinded them. They all make the same gesture, wiping their eyes with a handkerchief." Seers claimed they could not understand how others could not see it. Patxi pleaded for the crowd to be given a glimpse, "Ama Ama, argitasun pixkabat emaiezu [Mother, Mother, give them a little brightness] . . . let them see your silhouette at least." The end of the vision was the end of the light. One seer said the Virgin disappeared leaving a kind of flame; another described the aftermath sadly as "all black, all black."[84]

Mary healing the wounds of Spain: "Her heart is still beating." "Lord I have sinned against thee." "Love my Vicar. Obey the Commandments. Detest blasphemy." Holy card sent by Ramona to Cardús, 10 March 1932. Card by Industrial Fotográfica, Valencia. Courtesy Arxiu Salvador Cardús i Florensa, Terrassa

For some seers, including the original siblings, the divine figure they saw never spoke. Receiving a message under these circumstances was difficult but not impossible. One recourse was that of a ribbon in the sky with letters on it. People carried similar devotional ribbons in processions, left them at shrines, and placed them on wreathes with messages for the dead. Two boys from Zumarraga said they saw a ribbon that read "I ask one thing of you." At Iraneta a youth saw Saint Michael with a waistband with gold letters reading "Defending the Fatherland." Benita Aguirre said she saw the Virgin with handkerchiefs that read

"Peace on Earth" and "Glory in Heaven." One of her visions with a label, "The Most Holy Virgin healing the wounds of Spain," corresponds to a holy card the seers knew.[85]

A more common solution was the careful scrutiny of the Virgin's silent reactions—smiles, tears, hand gestures—to the seer's questions and the crowd's prayers. The questionnaire asked seers if the Virgin communicated by gesture, and indeed there were entire dramatic scenes silently acted out in heaven. These were pantomimes more characteristic of Italian visions in which the actors were the Virgin, Saint Michael, angels, Joseph, the Christ child, other saints, and the dead. Seers recounted scenes one after another; some scenes were stills, like postcards, others were in motion, like silent films. On 5 August 1931 an eight-year-old girl from Albiztur described this sequence in the space of a half-hour:

1. The Virgin of Lourdes on a rock, with Bernadette kneeling before her, and up the mountain the Virgin as the Milagrosa.
2. Jesus, his heart with a great brilliance.
3. The dove, casting a great light from on high on the cross there.
4. I. H. S. These letters on the cross.
5. Bernadette, surrounded by many lambs.
6. Bernadette going out from a house surrounded by many lambs and doves. There is a cross there, and before it, in its center a host . . . Bernadette and the lambs kneel down.
7. A half of a host on the cross.
8. Four crosses above and below three hearts surrounded by stars.
9. Jesus dressed in white and the Virgin Mother as the Immaculate Conception in a starry robe.
10. A ray of light shining up from below, lighting very clearly the face of the Virgin.[86]

The cross, which Patxi had recently put up, was part of scenes 3, 4, and 7. It gave those hearing this running commentary something to look at. Three avatars of the Virgin appeared, two of them simultaneously, in scene 1. Note also in scene 1 a vision by Bernadette; we can imagine a kind of infinite regression in this vision of a seer having a vision. Such a regression corresponds to the historical awareness of seers of the visions of their predecessors.

At first Ramona Olazábal saw biblical scenes—the child Jesus lost in the temple, Jesus in the midst of a flock of doves, or Jesus as the good shepherd next to some bleating lambs. Later the scenes became more complex and active, like a frightened angel finding refuge under the mantle of the Virgin and then running happily to play with the others. Or two angels who descended from heaven, one with a rose, the other with a chalice; the first dried the tears of blood of the Virgin with petals and put the petals in the chalice, which both angels then covered and took back up to heaven.[87]

Some of the scenes seem especially cinematic. Those of Patxi could be grandiose with military overtones. Ayerbe reported this one:

> The Virgin Mary appears to one side, and in the center is a very white dove that gives off more light than ten thousand suns together, and that turns into a white horse. Then Saint Michael appears and does homage to the Virgin, kneeling before her and sticking his sword in the ground. He mounts the white horse and leads thousands and thousands of angels who maneuver following his orders. Again he kneels before the Virgin. The horse turns back into a dove with brilliant light that disappears. And the Virgin says farewell to the seer making the sign of the cross on his chest with the sword she holds in her hand, saying, "Agur Jesus-Jesusekin, Good-bye, Jesus be with you."

Other scenes resembled choreographed sequences from the films of Busby Berkeley or Esther Williams. Evarista Galdós saw Madre Ráfols coming down a long stairway from heaven. When she arrived, "She went to the middle of a circumference formed by many angels and knelt before the Virgin. In another vision she came with twenty-four angels, each with a spray of flowers."[88]

With tableaux it was possible to communicate horrible warnings as well. We remember the warring angels with bloody swords of late July 1931. On 15 April 1932 Evarista Galdós described moving *cuadros*—pictures or scenes of the chastisement:

> One cuadro is full of blood, which is dripping. Another is full of dead people, some of them very black, several of whom I know. A third shows men at the moment of the chastisement, some asking for a confessor, others, for mercy from heaven. Finally, the last has fire falling in a terrifying way.

Two days later: "One of the cuadros was the rain of an enormous number of snakes, which when they reached the earth rolled around the necks of people, making many bleed."[89]

The messages became explicit when the scenes included speech. In visions of Ignacio Galdós saints explained the tableaux. On 11 November 1931, for instance, he saw the Virgin. Then twelve angels appeared with gray and white flags and little white books in their hands, singing in a language he did not know. Then he saw a golden door surrounded by fifty golden stars; then Saint Peter with keys around his neck. Galdós asked what the door was and reported that the Virgin and Saint Peter told him it was for "all of us who were here." The holy figures entered, then the Virgin came out and blessed everyone. Then the vision ended. Ramona also asked what her scenes meant and heard the Virgin or Jesus reply with one-line summaries like those on holy cards: "Those maligned will be consoled by their consciences." "You will have no nourishment for your souls if you do not eat my food." "Receive the body of Christ, for he will purify your thoughts."[90]

The banners, pantomimes, and tableaux vivants show that some seers had trouble adding sound, or maybe additional senses, to what they saw. For seers in other places the barrier seems to have been to sight; individuals heard words, but only after a series of such experiences did they see visions. This sequence sometimes happens to those who claim contact with the dead. In any case, the process is cumulative. Once the breakthrough to sound or sight occurs, the more complete communication continues; the visions do not revert to the less complete type.

As the seers added senses, what they perceived also became more precise. Vague and diffuse lines became sharp. Images acquired faces. Faces took on well-defined features, and the features took on emotions. In some ways the process was similar to that of getting to know someone—first seeing the person, perhaps repeatedly, and only later making verbal contact. But there were differences, for nearly all of the seers who heard nothing from the Virgin continually asked her what she wanted, and to some she did not reply. This was no normal acquaintance; the Virgin knew how to keep her distance.

Most seers, if they did not hear words at first, heard them within days of starting their visions. But some took longer. A boy from Zumarraga whose visions began on July 5 did not hear the Virgin speak until his birthday on December 13, when he made a petition for a special blessing for a Catalan lady and received an answer. Evarista Galdós had thirty visions over four months before she heard the Virgin. When she finally heard the Virgin speak, Evarista became more abstracted from the spectators around her. "Until that day I was aware of those who were around me, and what they said, but that day I lost my senses completely, since the Virgin appeared with great light, and I saw nothing but her."[91]

The number of seers declined at the end of July, and the decline in attendance meant that the seers could see one another more easily. Thereafter vision poses and states seem to have become more homogeneous, so some observers began to make blanket statements about trances as a whole. These patterns and this convergence were both the result of the attention of doctors, who rewarded by their attention the seers most insensible, and of priests, who got some seers worrying about the devil.[92]

The Devil and Gemma Galgani

Padre Burguera thought few if any of the seers were faking their visions and few vision states were pathological in nature. He thought the problem was the devil. In 1932 he instructed seers to be wary of the origin of their visions and to test verbally the figures they saw. He also instructed them to examine their own feelings. Citing ancient doctrine, he wrote:

> [The apparition] is good, in general, when it serves or tends to the glory of God, when it sanctifies and saves humans, and when it leaves in the soul of the seer a residue of perfect peace, joy in the Holy Spirit, and great stimulus to advance on the road to Christian perfection. When it leaves trouble in the soul it is diabolical.[93]

In the questionnaire the local clergy sought the same information. They asked, "During the events, did you feel happiness, sadness, terror, or awe? Afterward?"

The traditional Catholic rules governing investigation of spirits worked against the more spectacular fits and frights. The French writer Gaëtan Bernoville, who was present in mid-October, found three "zones" at Ezkioga. A zone of "theater and fraud," in which he included some of the stigmatizations; a zone of "hallucination, neurosis, and hysteria of a mystic nature"; and finally a zone of "veracity, sincerity, simplicity, and piety." He spelled out his criteria for separating the last two zones:

> Fainting spells, cataleptic states, the convulsions into which certain seers are plunged, do not enjoy, we know, the favor of theologians expert in miracles. The impression produced on the observer by certain states of ecstasy at Ezkioga is sorrowful, disagreeable, surrounded with an aura of ominous melancholy.

He singled out favorably the two children who had started everything, "who have never, to my knowledge, been victims of fainting spells or unquiet states of the nervous system."[94]

We have seen that in late 1931 some visionaries began to suffer the pains of the Passion in trance, just when more and more of them were placing more emphasis on a chastisement than on a miracle. The start of this trend was the wounding of Ramona, and it represented the logical outcome of public attention shifting from the divine figures to the seers. Rather than describing the Virgin's suffering, as in the first months, the seers suffered themselves. After Lent in 1932 some teenage and young women acted out Passions lasting up to twenty-four hours for select observers in private houses. Here the model appears to have been Gemma Galgani. I do not know how much the local Passionists had promoted her story. Already before the visions people in the zone around Ezkioga contributed alms for her beatification. Some seers claimed to have heard of her first from the Catalans in August 1931.

Germano de San Estanislao's biography of Gemma and his texts of her letters and ecstasies came out in Spanish in Barcelona in 1912 and 1914.[95] His first-person account demonstrated in an ordinary person the Catholic physics and metaphysics—levitations, visions, physical appearances of the devil, stigmata—

which refuted the rationalists. Gemma used as models Gabriele dell'Addolorata and Marguerite Marie Alacoque. The painful but nonbleeding Passions of Ezkioga seers like Evarista Galdós and Pilar Ciordia, complete with flagellation and an unusual concentration of images of blood, resemble Gemma's Thursday-night Passions.

The model of Gemma as a substitute Christ may have helped change the passive trances of the seers into active, dramatic performances. With a greatly diminished audience and virtually no coverage by the press, the seers became holy people for their private followers more than charismatic guides for the nation or prayer leaders for the multitudes. In her last years Gemma was a kind of living saint who in ecstasy relayed to Christ and the Virgin the prayers and requests of those who came to her for help.[96] The Ezkioga seers would have recognized her as a precursor; they expected an early death, like hers. Burguera tested the Ezkioga seers by flame and needle as priests had tested Gemma. Gemma's spiritual director told her how to test for tricks by the devil, and Burguera repeated these instructions. The seers who had Gemma-style visions said they saw the devil as well as the Virgin in their visions.

CONCLUSION

In spite of general patterns in content and behavior each seer had idiosyncrasies. Some were rigid in trance, others relaxed; some were alternately rigid and relaxed. Some fell forward, others backward; others did not fall at all. Some kept their eyes open, others kept them closed. Some were placid and beautiful, others tortured and frightened. Some eventually could have visions anywhere, some only at Ezkioga, and a few only in their home village or at home. The vast majority fell into a quietness, but Luis Irurzun, in contrast, sometimes launched into intense movement, like the fourteenth- and fifteenth-century "athletes of God." As Rigné put it, "The truth is that God can vary infinitely the kinds of his manifestations."[97]

Whatever form the vision state took, it was the entry into that state and the passage into another realm that gave the seers a new and unusual power. Affluent urbanites pampered, chauffeured, and listened to them. Children in trance could get whole crowds of adults, including the priests, the moral leaders of their region, to obey them. And children and farm people could govern the crowds' emotions much as a mission preacher might, making them weep out of sympathy, wail for their sins, and cry out for the nation.

These strange states enabled children to govern their immediate superiors, bring their parents day after day to the visions, and summon their parish priests and doctors. At Ezkioga a four-year-old seer from France was able to get his mother and his uncle to eat grass, as Bernadette had done at Lourdes on the Virgin's orders. In subsequent sequences of apparitions the pattern of testing their power continued as child seers made unusual demands on adults. One day in 1947 a ten-year-old girl at Cuevas de Vinromà (Castellón) gathered in vain several hundred thousand persons on the outskirts of town, including the lame, the halt, and the blind from half of Spain, hoping for miracle cures; and in 1954 two girl seers of Ibdes (Zaragoza) set up camp in a hut outside town, had their meals brought out to them, and tended sheep contributed by the villagers, until, on the Virgin's orders, they donated the flock to a home for the aged in Calatayud.[98]

But most important these children and farm people achieved free public speech. Just as spirit mediums provided a voice for women in nineteenth-century America to tell large audiences their deepest ideals, so the trances at Ezkioga provided the young, the dispossessed, and females a place in the public arena usually reserved for adult men. The vision state protected this speech. In spite of dozens of false predictions that mobilized hundreds of thousands of people, led some to give away their money, and in a few cases brought the seers new clothes, free travel, and easy lives, no court ever tried seers for fraud.[99]

There were suspicions about some seers, in addition to Ramona. Several older priests I interviewed thought that one of the most prominent male seers was acting in bad faith. And I heard that two female seers with spectacular trances had admitted in confession that none of their visions were true. One confessed on her deathbed and the other gave permission for her confessor to spread the word without naming her. But the idea of lies and willful fraud I found only among the clergy, not among the press or the laity.

More than the divine messages, the strange physical states themselves were the ultimate argument for the truth of the apparitions. When in September 1933 Bishop Múgica condemned the visions, the Integrist weekly *La Cruz* was disappointed. The newspaper had believed Ramona's miracle and had argued against the governor's offensive. It reported none of the diocesan moves against the seers and nothing of Laburu's lectures. In a front-page article on September 24, *La Cruz* finally gave in: "El Señor Obispo has spoken on Ezquioga. And definitively. Obedience has more merit when it is difficult." But two weeks later *La Cruz* ran a dialogue between a believer in Ezkioga, Martín, and a disbeliever, reserving the most attractive arguments for the believer, who was still impressed by the extraordinary, unexplainable vision states:

> I saw them with my own eyes—the way they lost consciousness [*konortea galtze ura*], the way they were staring fixedly up as if they were dead, without hearing anything, the way they stayed there a long time without being aware of anything. All this—if the Virgin Mary or some other celestial being was not involved, how could it have happened?[100]

His opponent could only reply vaguely that there were other ways to explain such phenomena.

The need to dismiss the trances inevitably led to shorthand "explanations," much as folk wisdom had it that the Christ of Limpias had a mechanism that enabled it to weep (in fact, people claimed to see the image move, but no one saw it weep). The most common way of labeling and dismissing the vision states at the time was to call them vaguely "witch-stuff." Some reached for scientific terms. A Terrassa couple reported: "It is all hypnotism, just as we thought before we went." And a priest wrote Salvador Cardús that the cause was "illusionism and autosuggestion." When disbelievers speak now of what they saw, they still give pseudoexplanations: "cosas de histerismo [hysterical things]" said a hotel owner in Zarautz, "ataques epilépticos [epileptic attacks]" claimed a merchant in Ormaiztegi and a doctor, "espiritismo y teatro [spiritism and theater]" argued people in Durango. An educated woman from Beasain told me that she thought the trances were

> the result of some kind of injection or some drug or something. . . . I remember that they would go into [one of the houses near the apparition site] and people would say, "O there they go, yes, now they're going to prepare them." But we didn't know if they really gave them a shot or if they just gave them breakfast.[101]

Others simply wonder about the strange behavior. An elderly priest from Oiartzun recalled a boy, probably the original seer, "playing with two stones in front of me, and suddenly [the priest looked up at the sky], "Ama . . . bai ama . . . bai ama [Mother . . . yes mother . . . yes mother]."[102]

I have tried not to mix my understanding of what was going on with the understanding of the people of the thirties. I prefer the neutral term *vision state* to the usual suspects like apparition, trance, ecstasy, hysteria, dissociation, possession, or shamanism. Theological, anthropological, psychological, psychiatric, and social neuroscience understandings of these phenomena as well as the vocabulary change rapidly. What people understood in the 1930s and the words they used then are primary material. Different kinds of readers should be free to understand them as they like. Virtually every label for these phenomena has an analytic and ideological load. Labels commit the discussion to a discipline and then within a discipline to one side or another in what for many specialists is a passionate, ongoing ideological war. The different written forms of the Basque language pose similar problems for nonpartisans. The mere act of writing a place-name (Ezquioga, Ezkioga, or Ezkio) or even naming the language (vasco, euskera, gipuzkoano) can immediately alienate some readers.

My reticence is also born of ignorance. There is an enormous literature in books, journals, and symposia on trance, ecstasy, dissociation, and altered states. Much is highly technical and forbidding. But the following ideas inevitably influenced my presentation.

In cultures throughout the world socially acceptable entry into the vision state is the rule rather than the exception. All humans can enter into such a state. By the mid-nineteenth century there were scholars who recognized that trance or ecstasy was a feature of most religions.[103] I have treated the vision states at Ezkioga on the whole as "genuine," that is, not a product of conscious deceit or what people normally consider illness.

Some classes of people, or people in certain phases of the life cycle, enter these states more easily than others. Scholars have selected as candidates, whether reasonably or not, near-pubescent girls, women in general, those under stress, those deprived of calcium, those deprived of light, those whose diet contains ergot, and those who have something to gain in prestige, attention, or goods. We have seen that at Ezkioga women and children predominated. Among the children there were more girls than boys. There were more seers at some ages than at others. We cannot know how much social censorship and self-censorship affected these figures.

Broad cultural patterns may help determine just who feels free to declare visions and whom people believe. Spanish Catholics of the early twentieth century understood that some stages in the lives of females and males were more conducive to holiness, and they believed some kinds of seers more than others. There were particular sociopolitical reasons why visions and conversions would be welcome from young men. For reasons of obvious self-interest, in the Basque Country of the 1930s some groups, like children, would want to have visions and others, like adult men, would not. In short, social attitudes powerfully affect which visions we come to know about.

A variety of techniques can facilitate the entrance into the vision state: meditative, pharmacological, or outside stimuli like music, rhythms, lights, or hypnotic suggestion. Psychologists of the period knew these techniques; Émile Pascal was an expert. At Ezkioga the rosary, the hymns, and in particular the rhythmic choral stimulus and response of the Litany may have helped to prompt visions.[104]

There was also a kind of learning through imitation among seers. At Ezkioga new seers had visions while observing the visions of their predecessors. Not all who tried succeeded, but children especially found it natural to try. A woman who was a child at the time in Urretxu told me: "Boom. They would be saying the rosary, boom, suddenly one would fall, boom, suddenly another. They fell down. . . . It had an effect on me, it scared me and all. I remember that we played at falling into a position like that. But we couldn't get it right."[105] In her case the imitation was conscious, but recent studies on the contagion of moods through facial expressions indicates the extent to which humans are intimately linked consciously or unconsciously to those in proximity. There may be other yet undiscovered modes of connection between bodies—through pheromones, for instance—which facilitate imitation and contagion of emotions. At Ezkioga imitation of some kind was clearly at work from seer to seer, from seer to spectator, and from spectator to spectator.

The vision state can also become habitual. As a seer gets used to the experience, the nervous system adjusts and the behavior changes. Scholars describe these adjustments as "tuning" and "sensitization." Observers noticed such changes at Ezkioga. The seers calmed down as their visions continued and their perceptions became sharper, including more of the senses. With habituation the seers also gained greater control. While the first visions seem to have been involuntary, sometimes even against the seer's will, as time passed the more practiced seers could have trances whenever they wanted. Seers from a set of visions elsewhere in Spain in the 1960s explained to a diocesan commission how they could enter deep trance at will and gave an on-the-spot demonstration. Ezkioga seers entered trances at will in the offices of the judge and the governor in San Sebastián. One of Laburu's arguments against the visions was precisely the seers' control of their visions. The seers explained their ability as a divine gift.

This habituation may also have had pleasurable qualities. Apart from spiritual and social rewards (presents, respect, transcendence of class, gender, or age discrimination), I wonder if there was some biochemical addiction at Ezkioga. Children would drag their parents to the site, with trips up to an hour each way on foot in the rain on muddy paths. Some seers persisted with regular visions for years, sometimes in most unpleasant conditions. Patxi, for instance, kept going to the site three times a week at night into 1933, rain or snow, although the press pilloried him and most of the believers ignored him. Luis Irurzun seemed to become as addicted to visions as he was to smoking. And the first boy also continued having visions for more than two years, although totally shy about public attention. Whether there was a seer present or not, the rosary seems to have had an exhilarating, restorative effect for the old-time believers.

That there was a variety of vision states at Ezkioga was patent for all to see. At Ezkioga the external differences seemed to fall into groups that occurred in sequence: the distressed conversion by reaction of July 1931; the quiet, passive visions in a second phase in late 1931; and the active, performative trances of 1932. But there were also individual styles that connoisseurs learned to expect and appreciate as they would those of artists.

The seer in vision does not necessarily experience a radical break between the "normal" and the "altered" state. In spite of major variants in terms of insensibility or reflexes, almost all Ezkioga seers were partially conscious and partially rapt, able to communicate and mediate between their inner world and those around them in the outer one. Teresa de Avila would have recognized this state, for she wrote, "Although a few times I lose my senses . . . normally they are disturbed, and although I can do nothing with myself, I do not cease to understand and hear exterior things, like something far away."[106] It is evident from the Ezkioga visions that this halfway state was ideal for mixing the voluntary and the involuntary, for satisfying the needs of others as well as expressing the divine or inner world's imperatives.

The many Ezkioga visions I have studied were never totally unpredictable. While it is probable that the scribes would have rejected any truly unusual visions, it could be that there was little truly unusual to record. It could be that the visions derived from elements in the seers' memories. The phenomenon of déjà vu is perception experienced as memory because of a short-circuit in the brain. The Ezkioga visions may have been the converse: memories that the force of fear or desire recombined and seers experienced as perception. The halfway vision state could have facilitated such a short-circuit. Of course, the devout had no reason to expect any truly innovative or unusual content in visions; for them apparitions were a way to gain access to a supernatural world they already knew a lot about. As Willa Cather had Bishop Lamy explain: "One might almost say that an apparition is human vision corrected by divine love. . . . [F]or a moment our eyes can see and our ears can hear what is there about us always."[107]

Vision states will have a greater impact in societies where visions are less frequent. The visions at Ezkioga occurred in an unusual environment as far as world societies go, one in which people did not normally see others having visions. The whole appeal of apparitions in the special form they developed in nineteenth-century France depended on the general public's understanding of apparitions as unusual, critical events, special divine interventions to change the course of human destiny. Since seeing persons transported was also exceptional, the public associated the two. The exceptionalness of the vision states became proof of divine intervention. We can measure the impact of deep trances in the West by the inordinate attention doctors and social scientists have accorded them.

11. SACRED LANDSCAPES

SHRINES, VISIONS, AND THE LANDSCAPE IN SPAIN

I N SPAIN, as in the rest of Mediterranean Europe, the sacred is part of the landscape. About half of the 360 or so district and regional shrines in Spain are on hills or mountains; about one out of five has an important relation to trees or shrubs, and the same proportion has a relation to springs and to caves. Indeed, many have two or more of these natural features as a significant part of their sacred ecology. Shrines to Mary relate much more to trees than do those of other saints or of Christ.[1]

The legends of rural shrines often involve tension between town and landscape. The divine will repeatedly foils attempts by clergy and civil authorities to capture images (as if they were relics) and take them to the parish church. Images return mysteriously to their place of origin; shrine building materials move at night; a half-constructed shrine collapses if it is not in the right place. In these stories the saint virtually drags the human group out into the countryside. Half-wild animals and marginal humans like shepherds and children serve as intermediaries. The humans come to know the healing powers of water and dirt and the sacred talismans of leaves, twigs, and stones.

Both in the late medieval period and in the twentieth century documented visions, like undocumented legends, feature these elements of the landscape. Nineteenth-century folklorists tended to see in this continuity an atavistic paganism. Such an understanding has given some historians the idea that true Christianity only got under way in Europe in 1545 when the Council of Trent reorganized the religion under parish and diocesan control. Perhaps they would reconsider this conclusion if they knew what their twentieth-century Catholic neighbors still practice. But if Christianity is simply the common religious beliefs and activities of Christians, it is unreasonable to regard such practices as pagan.[2]

HILLS, TREES, AND WATER AT EZKIOGA

An examination of how people incorporated a hillside, trees, and water into the visions at Ezkioga will help make this point clear. Starting with the visions the Ezkioga site was sacred for some people, not sacred for others, and of undecided status for still others. Visionaries, believers, chroniclers, and photographers seemed collectively to develop the shrine and its setting.

From newspaper reports, the private papers of believers, and photographs for the first three years of visions at Ezkioga we have an almost week-by-week record of how seers and believers discovered aspects of the place to be sacred. We can watch their attention shift from one element in the landscape to another. In a process of wishful remembering, they adjusted the story of the apparition to fit the sacred landscape as they revised it.

According to a woman who as a child was with the original seers, the brother and sister first saw the Virgin "up the mountain" or "in the sky." They might well have continued with visions looking up at the sky from the bottom of the hill, for only when the priest Antonio Amundarain took them up the hill did they identify a particular place. A devotee of the Virgin at Lourdes, Aranzazu, and the chapel of La Antigua on the mountain above Zumarraga, Amundarain made sure to identify the place.[3]

This siting was not easy. The first report relating the visions to the landscape placed them in brambles between two apple trees, and someone even drew a souvenir postcard of this scene.[4] But there were days when the priest had to lead the children to various points on the hill before they saw anything. Other seers took up the idea of two trees, but most of the earliest reports mentioned no trees at all; indeed for years afterward there were visions of the Virgin and other heavenly figures moving over the landscape—from higher to lower on the slope, from the oak grove over the meadow to the apple trees, or simply across the sky.

When early newspaper reports did mention trees, they might place the Virgin between, above, or directly on them. On 11 July 1931, when there had already been many seers, the city youth Aurelio Cabezón jokingly asked some girls, "Do you really think the Virgin is going to put herself on top of that tree?" But then he himself saw four or five lights above the tree, which disappeared, leaving "on the background of the clear sky, the image of a woman . . . and then the figure moved, walking in the air ten meters toward the top of the mountain." The next day two different seers saw the Virgin with a new attribute—flowers. The flowers are pictured on the apple orchard postcard and we have seen that they became a kind of attribute of the Virgin. Sometimes seers saw the Virgin throw flowers to the multitudes.[5]

But as more people became seers and had visions more complex, they reached a consensus on location that provided a center for the hillside arena. Already on July 7 the first newspaper report mentioned "the site of the apparition." From then on the vision was in "the accustomed place." While this expression might refer broadly to the entire hillside with its mix of fields, meadows, orchard, and woods, the context always pointed to a particular spot. Photographs taken in mid-July placed the "site" of the visions to the left of the meadow, near the edge of the woods. A caption on July 15 read, "According to those who assure us that they have seen it, the apparition is located over the trees that appear at the left of the photograph."

On the night of July 16, when up to forty thousand people were present, a reporter wrote that "[the girl seer] is taken to a spot in front of the trees where, according to her, the first apparition took place." A Bilbao paper published a daytime photo of the seers praying there, with the label "the place of the apparition." Note how the press and perhaps even the children had merged the downhill position of the children at the first apparition and the new, uphill site in front of trees. The trees in this picture may be the same ones that provided the focus for the visions for the rest of the first year. The children are looking at a frame, like one for a large picture, at the base of the trees, presumably over the blackberry bushes where the visions at first seemed to occur.[6]

But what happened on July 16? Led to this by now official place, the girl saw nothing and wandered "from one end of the hillside to another, hunting out the most propitious places and fleeing the crowds. She could be seen looking in all directions at all points in the horizon," until she finally had her vision. Although this description left the phenomenon as amorphous and unfixed as it really seems to have been, the newspaper also used the phrase "the site of the apparitions" and put a cross on a photograph that gave readers a focus and a center, however illusory.[7]

The Bilbao reporter first identified the site as "a little group of oaks." Like all reporters, he had obtained an account of the first vision, which, although it correctly placed the children downhill, placed the Virgin in the trees. He said one particular oak was important, and when on the second day the children tried to get to the Virgin, "the vision disappeared in a very bright flash of gold as they touched the tree." Here again the past had been reworked, for he made no mention of apple trees or brambles. The oak was the key, he emphasized: "That's what we said, an oak, a young oak. But on this oak . . ."—echoing the biblical phrase "But on this rock I shall build my church." When he was at the site on July 15 there was already barbed wire around the trees. A Franciscan from the shrine of Aranzazu who visited the site the next day found that indeed people had singled out one oak and put some kind of mark (*contraseña*), presumably religious, on it. Many of its leaves had disappeared. "It is, they told us, the tree around which the vision generally occurs."[8]

The arbitrariness of choosing these particular trees and surrounding them with barbed wire was not lost on another journalist:

> There are three little trees there surrounded for the last few days with barbed wire, because popular devotion, it is not known why, chose to locate the apparition there, despite the fact that, according to the seers, the apparitions occur practically everywhere.[9]

But it was not "popular devotion," a phrase as vague in 1931 as it is now, that chose to locate the apparition, for the press and Amundarain contributed to this choice. If by "popular" the writer meant "unlettered," "primitive," or even "lay" the word was incorrect. Whoever put up the barbed wire could not have done so without the acquiescence of Amundarain, noted churchman, writer, and spiritual director.

Indeed, only twelve days after the visions had started and before the barbed wire was up, Amundarain sent a letter to the regional press which in essence said that people should act at the site as if it were holy: "The apparition site has begun now to be regarded with veneration and the greatest respect; it has become a place of prayer, of recollection, of greater faith and piety." For Amundarain the prayers and hymns that he and other priests led had created a sacred space. I take it that he refers to the hillside in general. He sought to reinforce this piety and warned against immodest dress in women and indecorous behavior in men. A Franciscan at Ezkioga on July 16 also remarked on the churchlike nature of the proceedings and the atmosphere.

> We had not gone to a shrine; but the place itself had been converted into a living shrine, with no walls but the surrounding mountains, and with no roof but the immaculate vault of heaven. The prayer, which issued from fervent hearts, dissipated in the underbrush and then was lost in space.

In short, on the hillside people soon adopted a churchlike, or more exactly a shrinelike, attitude. On the night of July 18 an old man told villagers, "Boys, take off your hats, because it's like we're in church here." I think the absence of walls and a roof to enclose the space and enforce the piety heightened the emotion.[10]

Not all attending the visions felt this piety, and the public needed periodic reminders. Hence an *Argia* correspondent wrote in mid-August, "We should be as serious as if we were in church and speak only when absolutely necessary." And Amundarain had to demand, once more, piety and respect: "From the beginning people have noted at the site of the apparitions (and everyone agrees on this) something very difficult to explain, which somehow turns them inward, deeply moves them, and powerfully invites piety." Had everyone agreed, his note calling for piety and respect would not have been necessary. He implied that the "something very difficult to explain" was not just a product of the prayers of those present but was intrinsic to the place, or the result of the divine presence, or both. By then the place was special.[11]

Given this specialness and the requisite decorum, we might think of the group of trees as an altar and bank of images in a church. Just as Christ was present in the consecrated hosts, the monstrance, and the tabernacle, so Mary was present in the trees—especially, people said, somewhere between two and four meters up on the slim trunks. As happened later in the Barranca, believers set up an altarlike bench and decorated the trees, like an altar, with flowers or religious paraphernalia. The simile was in the minds of the priests, who asked in their questionnaire if the lights seen around the Virgin were in the form of a chapel or an altar.

Although there had been articles in the Basque press about the apparitions of Fatima (where the Virgin appeared on a scraggly holm oak), the shrine in the back of most people's minds was that of Lourdes. On July 12 the seer María Inza from Oñati saw "the personification of the Virgin of Lourdes." Amundarain betrayed his model when he suggested for the July 18 miracle "something startling and supernatural, as at Lourdes . . . maybe a spring of water." The Lourdes landscape centered on a cave and a spring, and Amundarain hoped for one of these features at Ezkioga. The basic model was some sort of church connected to the landscape, and in this broad sense traditional Spanish shrines were models too, shrines like that of Our Lady of Aranzazu, the patroness of Gipuzkoa, where a shepherd supposedly found the image of the Virgin and a cowbell on a hawthorn tree.[12]

If we extend the analogy, the enclosure around the trees (the owner replaced the barbed wire by wooden fencing in early August) would be the equivalent of the presbytery, the area for officiants in churches. And indeed at Ezkioga this space was for the priests, but also for the visionaries, who often superseded the clergy. An elderly priest recalled for me his entrance into this special precinct. It was 15 October 1931. Men had just carried Ramona, with blood streaming from her hands, inside the fence and laid her on a bench. By then aristocratic ladies like Carmen Medina had taken charge of the site. When the gate was open the priest, Pedro Agote, slipped behind Ramona into what he referred to as the "sancta sanctorum." He was observing the various visionaries when a woman came to him and said:

"You cannot be here."

"Why can't I be here?"

"Because this is a holy place."

"And how do you know it is a holy place?"

"You mean to say that with all these people praying, looking on, you don't understand clearly that this place is sacred?"

Fifty years later Agote was still indignant. For it was the role and duty of the church, and the men of the church, in particular, to decide which places were sacred and which were not. The church had not made a decision and he personally was dubious. Furthermore, priests had every right to be in sacred places, like the presbytery, and women generally did not. For the woman, however, the presence of the Virgin while the seers were in ecstasy far outweighed any priestly privilege. The fact that thirty thousand people were there, respecting the precinct and implicitly backing up the woman's claim, meant nothing to the priest.[13]

The visionaries and believing clergy wanted to remove the ambiguity and transform the site into a legitimate, consecrated shrine as soon as possible. On July 22, for instance, a girl seer saw a basilica complete with towers, bells, and two doves. And a rich duke supposedly promised to finance the building should the church approve. The basilica, some said, would enclose the trees (now people referred to four trees). One seer saw the Virgin moving across the landscape, "searching for a place for a church."[14]

In the meantime, the four trees were semiofficial. Pilgrims kissed the important one, festooned it with flowers, and removed bark and leaves as sacred souvenirs. Women told the Irish Hispanist Walter Starkie that the four oaks symbolized the four Basque provinces. Patxi said the Virgin told him to put up a cross and decorate it with flowers at the site of the four trees. Photographs from around 5 August 1931 show him on a ladder installing a crossbar on one of the trees with the site owner's workmen. Local priests are looking on (and reporting every move to the diocese).[15]

With flowers at the top like a maypole, the cross was a great success with the seers. They began immediately to see Mary on or above it. By mid-August Patxi Goicoechea had hung on it an open wooden box with a picture of the Sorrowing Mother inside. Justo de Echeguren, the vicar general in Vitoria, ordered Patxi to remove the picture. The youth refused, so the Ezkioga priests themselves took it down toward the end of the month. They let the cross remain, but only grudgingly, for as La Croix of Paris pointed out, "no exterior sign of cult can be tolerated before a canonical inquiry makes a pronouncement."[16]

Francisco Goicoechea converts a tree into a cross, ca. 5 August 1931. Courtesy Archivo Diocesano de Vitoria

The cross with the shorn and debarked trees remained the center of attention. A Catalan pilgrim in early September described the original visionary boy from Ezkioga patiently accepting rosaries and medals given to him from outside the sacred precinct and touching them to each of the trees next to the cross. In front of the cross and trees Patxi built a nine-by-seven-meter stage for the visionaries. The landowner supplied the lumber and workmen.[17]

The stage was half-completed when on October 15 Ramona Olazábal's hands spouted blood, and people carried away on handkerchiefs this new material token to all corners of the Basque Country. A San Sebastián reporter described a priest who cut out a bloodstained splinter from a tree on which Ramona had leaned and he commented disapprovingly:

> At the beginning in Ezquioga there was a truly beautiful climate of faith that profoundly moved all who were present, but soon after came the breaking of boughs from trees, and now the soaking of blood in handkerchiefs. This amounts to superstition in persons who by their social position have been trained to control themselves better.

The same correspondent had complained at the end of July that "some people break boughs off the trees to have a souvenir or to keep the branch as a relic. It is a little sad to see the short distance for some people between faith and superstition."[18]

Much of the clergy did not share this writer's attitude, and the writer was mistaken in judging attention to bark, leaf, or blood as rustic or lower-class piety. The respected Catholic magazine of Barcelona *La Hormiga de Oro* captioned a photograph of the four oaks: "Bushes around four oaks without bark or branches. Who would not carry off some splinters to keep and venerate as relics?" Priests owned and supervised *El Día*, in which a contributor wrote, "I have taken home leaves from those small oaks."[19] For many priests it was quite all right to collect sacred tokens from Ezkioga. We have seen that a priest from Markina, a teacher in the Vitoria seminary, and even Dr. Sabel Aranzadi collected Ramona's blood. The distinction that the journalist made between educated and uneducated did not hold. For what was acceptable or not, orthodox or unorthodox in this matter was in dispute.

In the 1930s the Basque Country was more advanced in understanding its own folk customs than the rest of Spain. José Miguel de Barandiarán, a Basque ethnographer and professor at the seminary in Vitoria, had studied in Cologne, attended conferences all over Europe, and was the driving force behind the Basque folklore society. Work like his had sensitized the educated public to ancient traditions, of which the Ezkioga visions might be part. But even among the informed, there was disagreement as to whether the visions were a bad or a good thing. The Navarrese psychiatrist Victoriano Juaristi, for whom the outdoor night visions smacked of "the cult of the moon of the ancient Vascones," warned that if a stop were not put to the visions, they could degenerate into witches' covens. Conversely, for Federico Santander, the monarchist ex-mayor of Valladolid and director of the newspaper *El Norte de Castilla,* the mythic, folkloric aspect of the visions enhanced them. He emphasized that the Virgin generally came out of the woods, which "acquire a mysterious power to intimidate" at night. He was moved that "today like yesterday and as always, in the full twentieth century as in the Middle Ages, to the echo of the romance of the little Virgin and the shepherd, thousands of persons burning in the same flame of desire should go to the woods at night to see if they can see a shadow." While he was inclined not to believe the visions, he argued that there was no intrinsic reason why they could not be true.[20]

In Lent of 1932, when people began to return to Ezkioga in significant numbers, Marcelina Mendívil from Zegama announced that the Virgin would mark out a Way of the Cross. By this time the owner of the hill had made a transverse path to permit easier access to the four trees with the cross; along this route Marcelina in vision acted out the stations, falling at the places where Jesus fell on his way to Calvary. Patxi put up crosses the following day. An observer wrote, "With these emblems we discover that the Virgin desires this mountain to be considered a place of prayer and penance. . . . No one dares to do anything that would be out of keeping with a holy place. Speaking should be as quiet and brief as possible."[21]

The new Way of the Cross helped bring back the crowds. Supposedly obeying Mary, different visionaries led the stations of the cross at different hours for nine days in a row. Patxi started the novena at midnight. There were groups going up the hill in prayer at virtually all hours. Finally under diocesan pressure Patxi removed the crosses in early April.[22]

The next attempt to make this hillside a place of Catholic cult was in May 1932. From the first month of the apparitions visionaries had seen a shrine on the hill, and those who went to see the bishop described it to him. While the diocese could not legally keep a building from being constructed, it could refuse to consecrate it. The vicar general had refused permission repeatedly for a chapel before José Garmendia saw the Virgin herself mark out the site. On May 2, after a seven-minute trance, Garmendia climbed down from the stage, strode about six meters uphill from the cross and the trees, knelt, made the sign of a cross on the earth, and kissed it. Then he drove in stakes as markers. He explained to the Catalans present that the Virgin wanted her image to be worshiped in a chapel there: "[The Virgin] herself went walking to that precise spot; there she paused a few moments, and then disappeared."

"I don't have to say," one man present wrote, "how all of us, moved, kissed that spot, which from that moment on was sacred for us." Evarista Galdós, who was on the stage, confirmed the location. When she came out of vision fifteen minutes later, she too went and kissed it. The pilgrims immediately gathered earth there, "more as a relic than as a souvenir." But not all were sure that they should keep it. They asked Evarista to ask the Virgin, and the Virgin told her, "Yes, yes, they should keep it."[23]

At this point the vision definitively came to ground. The children first saw it in the sky, then they and others saw it above, but close to, trees and brambles. Gradually most seers came to see the vision halfway down the trees and then around the cross as well. But by the spring of 1932 the trees were dead or dying. The Virgin, or Garmendia and Evarista, then chose a new place on the ground for a home. The owner of the land was present at Garmendia's vision and on May 30 laid the cornerstone for the chapel in a formal ceremony, with souvenirs in the foundations and many seers present. Despite diocesan notices on church doors forbidding construction, he continued the work.[24]

In the meantime María Recalde announced that she had seen the shrine with two spouts of fresh water, and then she somehow found a new spring. The believers channeled this water to issue directly behind the pedestal in the chapel. As work on the chapel progressed, the center of the weekly commemorative photographs of the Catalan pilgrims shifted from the trees and the cross. When

Catalan group and seers, ca. 26 June 1932: center shifts from trees and cross to chapel under construction. Photo by Joaquín Sicart

the chapel was finished the trees were out of the picture altogether: image pedestal and fountain had taken over.[25]

On June 27 the Ezkioga priest, Sinforoso de Ibarguren, wrote Padre Laburu, "From the spring within the temple they are drinking water, as at the miraculous fountain at Lourdes; everyone thinks it is just fine. What won't some of them believe?" Three days later, on the anniversary of the first vision, the landowner inaugurated the chapel and the fountain, leading about one hundred persons in the rosary. Afterward at the bottom of the hill a Navarrese visionary told him the Virgin had told her that "the water was blessed by her and her Son and would have great value as time went on." That summer the water supposedly cured the landowner's wife of stomach cancer.[26]

Throughout the summer of 1932 the chapel drew pilgrims. After October 7, when the large image of the Virgin made to Garmendia's specifications arrived, the shrine became an immediate target for the government. The statue did not last in the chapel for more than a week. The image moving in exile from house to house became the center of devotion, superseding the landscape of the holy hill. When Léon Degrelle erected a cross a year later, it only lasted eight days. In 1934 the bishop finally forbade believers to go to the site. They prepared architectural plans for a basilica in 1935, but all for naught.[27]

Neighbors at Ezkioga say that the owner took the chapel down before the Civil War. For a while the statue was in Legorreta; there are rumors that a priest in Madrid or nuns in Valencia are keeping it until the church approves the visions. In the attic of an Ezkioga farmhouse lies a seven-foot segment of a wooden cross. Now there is a small concrete one near the site of the trees, and a wall set in the hillside serves as a backdrop for religious pictures and a white wooden cross. In 1973 believers following instructions of Luis Irurzun put up a large picture of the Virgin of Perpetual Help.[28] Believers still meet regularly on the hillside and still carry off bottles of water from the sacred spring. There is a spigot in the wall.

MODELS FOR THE LANDSCAPE AT EZKIOGA

What lessons can we draw from the relation of seers and believers to the Ezkioga terrain? What were their criteria for selecting natural features for the newly sacred landscape?

In a collective process people added incrementally the elements of nature that enhanced the shrine. In this process they modified the terrain itself—removing trees, cutting a path, digging a foundation, channeling a spring—to suit the needs of the humans and the divine. And as the shrine evolved they provided it with attributes both similar enough to those of other shrines so as to be recognizable and different enough so as to be attractive.

Oaks have special significance for some Basques. Perhaps for this reason the oaks supplanted the blackberry bushes and apple trees as the vision site. The most immediate models for the idea of the Virgin on a tree may have been the shrine of Aranzazu and the visions at Fatima. Patxi converted one tree into a cross and decorated its top with flowers. In some of the Spanish visions in the fifteenth century Mary holds a cross, and in one she sticks it in the ground. Surely in the late Middle Ages as in 1931 the wooden crosses were viewed in part as civilized trees connecting heaven and earth. One blatant attempt to assimilate the Ezkioga story to older legends was a newspaper account of the children having their first vision when driving the cows home for milk; this report made the children shepherds and brought domestic animals into the picture. The effort was unsuccessful (others did not repeat this version), doubtless because the known facts were too much against it—the family had no cows. In a sense the shift from trees to a spring recapitulates the ascendance of the new shrine at Lourdes over the traditional Basque shrines like Aranzazu. At Ezkioga the suggestion and selection of natural elements came in myriad visions. The fittest configuration survived.[29]

But while people tended to assimilate Ezkioga to existing shrines and symbols there was an innovative force at work as well. For instance, the image of the Sorrowing Mother, which was represented in the Ezkioga parish church in a black robe, appeared in the chapel at the vision site in a white robe. When the diocese demanded the removal of the new statue from the chapel in the fall of 1932, the bishop offered to donate a statue of the normal Sorrowing Mother to the nearest parish church. The seers, however, disdainfully rejected the offer, insisting that the diocese's statue would not have the right dress and would not be in the place where the Virgin wanted it, where new grace was at work through trees, water, and earth.[30] So while the Ezkioga shrine would be like other shrines, it would also have to be different. Mary appeared on a tree as at many other places, but not the same kind of tree—not a hawthorn, as at Aranzazu, but an oak. It happens that in all of Spain there is no district shrine with an image associated with an oak tree. Of course, the very name of the shrine, the Virgin of Ezkioga, ensured distinctiveness.

Another clear lesson is that the episode of Ezkioga involved no "pagan" wallowing in nature, no reversion to moon cult. The visionaries wanted diocesan acceptance, civil recognition, and a church as soon as possible. They pushed continually for the crosses, images, and altars of parish Catholicism. The diocese's strict control of these symbols left the believers with the natural ones. But Catholicism had long since absorbed the natural symbols of hills, trees, and water from previous religions. In 1931 these elements were as orthodox as church bells and the relics of saints. Fixing on them was evidence of orthodox learned behavior, not instinct and above all not some kind of paganism, whether ancient Basque or the ersatz version inspired by the writings of the historian Margaret Murray. The chief architects of the sacred landscape were the landowner Juan José Echeźarreta and the seer Patxi Goicoechea. Both were close to priests and doubtless priests counseled them—Echezarreta's brother José Ramón and the priests and religious of Ataun and San Sebastián. In Mediterranean Europe the sacred landscape is mainstream Catholicism. The apparitions at La Salette, Lourdes, and Fatima ratified and celebrated this sacred landscape. But Catholics could find such reverence as well in the Bible: Mount Sinai, Mount Carmel, Mount Tabor, the hill at Calvary, the tree of knowledge, the tree of Jesse, the burning bush, Abraham's oak at Mamre, and the spring that issued when Moses struck a stone with his rod.[31]

The biblical scenario most related to the visions at Ezkioga was the hill of Calvary. The Sorrowing Mother, the cross on the hillside, the stations, the visionary crucifixions during Lent, all point toward the Passion. In this replication the nearby towns or the inhabited world would be the equivalent of Jerusalem, joined to the apparition site by the Way of the Cross. Such replications spread throughout the Mediterranean in the sixteenth century. The pious added the processional routes of Holy Week, stations of the cross, and *Sacro Monti* to their landscape as aids to exercises that provoked sympathy and contrition.[32] The exercise of the stations of the cross was a high point of every Basque pilgrimage to Lourdes. Visionaries and key lay believers at Ezkioga pushed for the Calvary-like elements, amalgamating them with other elements like trees and springs whose models would have been shrines like Aranzazu and Lourdes.

We can see what the acceptable vision sites in the landscape had in common from comparison with those locations rejected, ridiculed, or doubted in interviews, documents, or newspapers. At first there was some doubt about the trees themselves as a suitable site for the appearance of the Virgin. Two of the mockers thought it silly to think of the Virgin Mary on a tree—until they saw her there themselves. But in 1931 most Catholics accepted this placement. A woman I interviewed ridiculed a neighbor who saw the Virgin on the lid of a stew pot. And children saw Mary in several places that witnesses considered implausible: in Urretxu under a sink in a box of sand used for washing pots and pans; on the outside door-latch of a house in Lakuntza; in a road in Albiztur. Marcelina Eraso was interned for her vision on a train, and Laburu found it ludicrous that the Virgin might appear in a bus or a taxi. These places were deemed too mundane and domestic. Such reactions were echoed in the ridicule that greeted the report of the appearance of the face of Christ on a refrigerator door in Tennessee in 1986; a local skeptic commented, "When the good Lord comes, it won't be on a major appliance."

Two other aspects of the visions that people questioned may also help to define what was believable for sacred sites. In the first months the visions occurred at night, when women were supposed to be indoors. We have seen that many men rejected the Ezkioga apparitions for this reason. The implication was that if real visions were taking place, then it was not Mary, but perhaps a witch or the devil disguised as Mary. The psychiatrist Victoriano Juaristi referred to the demonic qualities of the night by mentioning moon worship and covens. Day and night can affect places. Just as there are places, so there are times more appropriate to sacredness in a given culture. In the Basque Country of the 1930s many people considered nighttime inappropriate for outdoor sacred ceremony, despite the torchlight processions at Lourdes.

Another aspect that immediately disqualified the visions in the eyes of some observers was their access to a special kind of space—the places where people go after they are dead. As we will see, many visionaries and their families were interested in precisely this kind of space. Night was a particularly appropriate time for contact with the dead, for this was the time when the dead were believed to circulate as ghosts. For most of the clergy, to see the dead in hell or heaven was like trespassing, and this issue divided them cleanly from laypersons.

What seemed to be needed to frame these visions was a space that was accessible to humans yet out of the normal sphere. This space had to be appropriate for meetings with beings from another realm, but from another realm that overlay and interpenetrated this one. The locations of Spanish shrines and vision sites were not unknown to country folk, but these natural sites were less known than houses, churches, kitchen sinks, and trains. Otherness, otherworldliness, nonhumanness, semiwildness, connection with the sky or with the underground have been common features of "successful" vision and shrine sites in Spain and Western Europe. Perhaps as spaces that are less domesticated, they are more appropriate for spontaneous, and less tamed, manifestations of grace.

While hardly a reversion to paganism, apparitions in the countryside were in a certain sense a reversion to the time prior to the Catholic Reformation. Then the land around settlements had more sacred meaning.[33] Recourse to lay visionaries at La Salette, Lourdes, and Fatima reversed two centuries of emphasis on the parish church. We should not be surprised that parish clergy and dioceses were suspicious.

It is significant that in the nineteenth and twentieth centuries the key actors in this reversion were often children. In spite of the emphasis on the parish in modern Catholicism, the sacred landscape retained force for the laity in the form of legends and landmarks associated with semiabandoned chapels. The visions in France and Portugal revitalized these traditions and seem especially to have captured the imagination of children. Those who at Ezkioga and in the Barranca insisted on rosaries in front of tree-altars, not in the parish churches, were like the visionary children of the Drôme in 1848–1849 who, following the example of La Salette, led adults out to mass prayers on remote mountainsides. These children seemed to serve as repositories of the culture's prior practices.[34]

At Ezkioga the added elements of visions at night and visions of the dead accentuated the otherness of the visions—for many observers too much so. These elements pushed the visions beyond the acceptable otherness of the divine world into the suspect otherness of supernatural forces that by 1931 people had come to define as evil. But it should be clear by now that within the limits of the acceptable otherness, Catholics all over Europe have continued to find harmony in their religion, their church, their sacred figures, and the landscape. This was the case a thousand years ago; it is the case today.

MANY OF THOSE who went to Ezkioga did so for personal reasons
that had little to do with the fall
of the monarchy, Basque nationalism,
or new religious movements. They
sought spiritual refreshment, forgiveness, good health, or news of deceased
loved ones. They went to the visions,
as to Aranzazu or Lourdes, with matters to raise in the divine presence.

Petitioners at Ezkioga had an advantage over those at normal shrines:
they might well receive an immediate
response. In this respect a trip to Ezkioga was like a visit to an ancient
oracle, or a contemporary spiritist séance, or a session of inspired advice
from Thérèse Neumann or Padre Pio.
The immense, ongoing panoply of connections between the devout and the
divine involved both human and divine
intermediaries—persons praying for
other persons to souls in purgatory and
to saints who might in turn be intercessors with other saints and finally
with God. People concentrated their
affection on certain saints and asked
for help at certain sacred beacons in
the landscape. In this slowly changing,
blinking network, vision sequences like

those at Ezkioga were like a steady lightning bolt, a shortcut to heavenly grace and heavenly news, a highway of light to the sky.

From the start seers and onlookers tried to obtain divine help for particular persons—a boy seer aged eleven for a crippled friend; Patxi Goicoechea for his brother whose eyes were bad; and Lolita Núñez for a woman from Burgos whose daughter was dying of tuberculosis. When the Virgin gave an eighteen-year-old servant in Zarautz one wish, she asked for her brother, injured in an airplane crash, to be healed. The Irish traveler Walter Starkie witnessed "a whole host of blind men with their long sticks."[1]

To understand how people used the new power for personal problems, we must put aside the notion that individuals sought help or salvation primarily for themselves. People generally went to Ezkioga in groups of family, friends, or neighbors, as they would have gone to other shrines or other spectacles. And by the nature of Mediterranean society they approached the divinity, as they would approach any person of significance, as members of a group with intense interest in one another's welfare.

When I observed the efforts of family members, close friends, and neighbors to help a very sick child in the Canary Islands, I found dozens of people intervening on the child's behalf. They spoke to God, Mary, the saints, doctors, nurses, and hospital administrators, both directly and through colleagues, friends, friends of friends, and relatives of friends. A given chain of intermediaries was sometimes four or five persons long. Similarly, in the Basque Country the large size of rural families and the necessary close cooperation among neighbors ensured that in times of need country people generally could count on an active network of mutual aid and affection. The historian Juan Ignacio Tellechea's account of people who intervened on his behalf during a critical illness in the 1980s demonstrates that such networks of mutual support function even in urban society. We may expect that at Ezkioga people made prayers more for others— relatives, friends, third persons—than for themselves.[2]

For members of these large, dense networks, getting access to the seers at Ezkioga was a critical task. The anthropologist Elizabeth Claverie has described with sensitivity the many strategies used by visitors to Medjugorje to locate seers and pass their concerns to the Virgin.[3] What she describes accords with what I know of Ezkioga and with what I have seen in the last three decades at apparition sites throughout Spain. In these places persons close to seers—family members, friends, divinely appointed "apostles," trusted priests—play a vital role, for they have the ear of those who have the ear of the Virgin, who in turn has the ear of God. In these places the private nature of the contacts—a fleeting conversation, a visit to the seer's home, a word passed through a third person—makes it difficult to trace requests and responses, to know who gets what in exchange for what. These exchanges are as hard to follow as the unrecorded, often unspoken, traffic in political favors.

The Barcelona priest Martín Elías described his own experience at Ezkioga in the first week of August 1931, when the seers with smaller audiences were beginning to find more time for supplicants. On his third day the visions had still not entirely convinced him: "I must confess that many worries, scruples, and difficulties bother me, doubts that I solve as I can, or remain to be resolved. I look for a proof." He decided to work though the girl from Ataun: "As the praying of the rosary had not yet begun, I call the seer. 'A favor. Ask the Virgin for a special blessing for me.' Those around me protest, claiming that the blessing should be for everyone, with one in particular for me." The seer said she would make the request, and during her trance Elías had a mystical experience.

> I went off about twenty paces from the site, with a group of workers, and we began the rosary. [The seer] was in ecstasy. We prayed the Litany and sud-denly I was as if blind, my entire being invaded by a consuming fire that moved me profoundly, leaving me afterward a well-being and a taste of heaven. For a few instants I thought I was going to fall over on the workers. I have no doubt at all. The request had been made, the special blessing con-ceded. Now I remember it with joy. Truly, something special happened at Ezquioga.[4]

The French doctor Émile Pascal described believers writing letters to the Virgin and placing them in the hands of seers; after a certain time the seers reported the Madonna's response. Believers who could not make their requests personally could send them by mail. In late August 1931 Patxi Goicoechea's volunteer secretary in Ataun read many letters: "But we cannot answer all of them. We reply to three or four every day. Most of them contain curious questions; others are to ask Goicoechea to pray to the Virgin for such and such a person or such and such a need."[5]

We get an idea of the content of these oral and written requests from the diary and correspondence of the Catalan believer Salvador Cardús. Friends and rel-atives gave him numerous messages to forward to the seers and the Virgin. Since he kept almost all the letters he received and rough copies of the vast majority he sent, we generally know who made requests and for whom, and how the seers responded.[6] By extrapolation we can estimate the seers' overall traffic.

As editor of Terrassa's Catholic weekly and a veteran of its Parish Exercises, Cardús was well acquainted with the members of Terrassa's industrial and intellectual elite on the town's first bus trip to Ezkioga. By the afternoon of the first day the Terrassa pilgrims had overcome their shyness and were approaching receptive seers with requests. After one of the youths asked Ramona Olazábal to ask the Virgin for a "grace" for the group's members, Ramona subsequently told him "the Virgin had said that she was very pleased with those who had come from Terrassa, that she would help them a lot, and that she had given them a special blessing."

At least four of the trip members had gone with pressing problems. Two brothers brought a letter for the Virgin from a sister bedridden with a heart condition; a couple came to find help for a young son seemingly deaf, dumb, and insane, with destructive behavior we might today call autistic. One of the brothers spoke to Ramona, who passed the letter on to the Virgin, who allegedly replied that the matter was settled. The couple approached Evarista Galdós, who told them after her vision that the Virgin told her that their son would get better little by little and that they should say the rosary in his presence and make a novena to Our Lady of the Sorrows. The pilgrims sent news of the promised cures by telegram to Terrassa, where it was published in the main newspaper.[7] Given these results, other trip members brought up additional, perhaps not so pressing, problems. The trip organizer asked a boy for the conversion of a certain person, and another trip member made a similar plea for someone else. The boy said the Virgin responded that one of the two would convert over time but for the other she wept tears of blood.

On the last day the requests came in fast. Cardús had scruples about asking anything for himself, but he realized how much his wife would want him to. So he asked through the Ataun girl for the cure of his chronic asthma. The seer received so many more petitions that Cardús thought twice and told her to ignore what he had said. One of the other petitions was from a Terrassa woman who asked whether her father, who had died suddenly, was in heaven; she was relieved to learn that he was. Later, on the hillside, one of the four Terrassa priests on the trip told Cardús it was too bad he was missing his chance. The priest called Ramona over, and she encouraged Cardús to ask for a cure. The Virgin smiled at Cardús's petition, according to Ramona, who explained that "even if the Virgin did not say anything, it might mean that you will be cured."[8]

Cardús reported a total of seven specific requests over two days from the group of twenty-five from Terrassa, and he implied there were others. By this rough yardstick, at least one in three persons made personal petitions to the seers at Ezkioga. Cardús estimated that there were between ten and twelve thousand persons there on Sunday, 4 October 1931, and no account of the visions between the beginning of September and mid-October mentions more than fifteen seers on any given night. I calculate that each seer daily had to consider about two hundred requests. The demand on their time must have been staggering. No wonder that when Cardús got a chance to speak to a famous seer in private he held it a matter of providence. Perhaps as Catalan gentry the Terrassa group received special treatment from the seers, but local Basque pilgrims would have had similar problems and the seers must have been hard put to listen, remember who had asked for what, and report answers.[9]

We may presume that such consulting comprised much of the regular seers' day-to-day activity, that wherever they were during the day before their visions they would be accumulating requests and reporting on the Virgin's responses.

Indeed, such demand would itself go a long way toward making visions habitual. The implications for the sense of importance and social usefulness of the farm people, children, and servants who made up the bulk of the seers can hardly be overestimated. In the long, supple strands of delayed reciprocity that formed and still form the unseen moral fabric of Iberian society, these actors were building up stockpiles of favors: suddenly, unexpectedly, astoundingly. The fibers in the society converged on them, as if they were bishops, factory owners, or grandparents of huge clans. Given the seers' similar social demand, it is no wonder that some of them felt qualified to address the bishop, the deputies in the Cortes, the head of the Catalan government, and Prime Minister Azaña. They had become *important* overnight.

The seers were important not as persons with "clout," kindness, or wisdom but as simple brokers or intermediaries. In the same way female spiritists of the mid-nineteenth century had achieved fame not ostensibly for what they themselves had to say but as passive mediums for the messages of goodwill, social justice, goodness of life in nature, or happiness in the bye-and-bye that their spirit guides proclaimed. But the fact remains that in the seers' patient attention night after night, in some cases for several years, to the spiritual and physical needs of their supplicants, they performed hundreds, even thousands of small acts of mercy and consolation.

On Salvador Cardús's second trip, from 11 to 18 October 1931, he strengthened his bond with Ramona Olazábal, finding through her that his father was in heaven and that he himself would be saved and was "good, very good."[10] He witnessed her wounding and found further proof of her visions in her responses to the petitions of other pilgrims from Terrassa. On his return to Barcelona he became equally close to José Garmendia during the adventure with the Catalan president, Francesc Macià.

By the end of October about two hundred fifty people from Terrassa had visited Ezkioga.[11] In the following twelve months others went by car or train or on the Gemma trips. For all of them the friendship of Cardús with the two seers was common knowledge; a dedicated proselytizer, he made known the cures, conversions, and other proofs of the visions. People who could not go to Ezkioga came to him, to his wife, and to their close friends with problems for him to relay to the seers.

The forty or so petitions in Cardús's diary and letters fall into four roughly equal groups: those initiated by him; those made directly to the seers by others; those initiated by others and routed through him; and those originating in third parties and relayed to him by those close to him (by his wife, by a fellow wool salesman, by a Piarist priest in Tàrrega, and by a sister-in-law of his employer). There is even one instance of intercession at fourth remove: from an unknown person to a nun who had been his wife's teacher, to his wife, to him, to be forwarded to a seer and then to the Virgin.[12]

In these chains of contacts Cardús sometimes did not know the person or the reason for the petition he was passing on; sometimes he knew the person or the reason but did not mention either to the seers. This lack of clarity made the seers' job more difficult. When Cardús sent unexplained petitions for two unidentified persons to Garmendia, the seer replied crisply that "the Most Holy Virgin Mary Mother of all human beings had stated that in the matter of questions it is necessary to state clearly the subject."[13]

From October 1931 until the end of 1934 Cardús made petitions or relayed those of others to five seers (the number of petitions is in parentheses): José Garmendia (18); Ramona Olazábal (11); Benita Aguirre (2); Magdalena Aulina (2); the girl from Ataun (1). He reported direct petitions of his friends to María Recalde and Evarista Galdós as well. His heavy use of particular seers was typical of other intermediaries. The Catalan wool dealer Rafael García Cascón sent petitions he received to Benita Aguirre, and the Urnieta town secretary Juan Bautista Ayerbe was a conduit for Conchita Mateos and Esperanza Aranda.

The language of the petitions and the debt that Cardús and his wife Rosa Grau acknowledged in his letters to the seers for addressing the petitions shows they were like secular favors:

> If you have the opportunity I would be ever so grateful if you could . . . Thank you a thousand times.

> A friend from Sabadell well respected also by Señor García asks me to pray to the Virgin for ——— . . . if you could ask her I would be truly grateful.

> Although I do not know you personally, I take the liberty of asking that you intercede with the Holy Virgin for someone very dear to me. I will be very grateful.

> I will thank you a lot, a whole lot.

> I do not know how to thank you for your attentions to my mother and especially for your interest in having her next to you during your vision. I have taken all this as one more example of the feelings you have for us, which to be sure, Ramona, we will never be able adequately to repay.

> Thank you for what you tell me the Most Holy Virgin said about the sick persons I told you about and especially for your great trouble in helping me, for which I am very grateful and will be always at your service however I can.

This last phrase marked Cardús's long-term debt to Garmendia for saving the lives or souls of his friends.[14]

This gratitude accrued to Cardús and his wife from each of their petitioners:

> Since your husband is in direct contact with the seers of Ezquioga I will beseech you to send this little note to the one you are closest to, entreating

him to present my petition to the Virgin. A thousand thanks in advance. . . .
You know that I, most devoted to you in Christ, am grateful.[15]

Cardús thus came to have a position in Terrassa similar to that of the seers he was writing to in Gipuzkoa. For although he was an educated, lettered man, he too was of humble origin. His father had worked in the factories whose owners came to Cardús for spiritual favors. Like the servant and child seers at Ezkioga, Cardús lived in two worlds and this experience deepened his sympathy for the seers and his understanding of them.

These written requests to seers were in addition to oral petitions from their immediate audience. Different seers were better or worse at keeping up with their mail. While Ramona Olazábal was conscientious about oral petitions, she was only a fair correspondent, and Cardús and his wife shifted their mail orders to José Garmendia. Although he was functionally illiterate, Garmendia found a series of scribes to write down his responses. In spite of her youth, Benita (age nine) wrote down her visions when she went home each day and answered her mail herself.[16]

Over time the personal petitions took on increasing importance for the seers and their enthusiasts. By mid-November 1931 the spectators rarely numbered more than a few thousand and on many days there were fewer than a hundred. To these pilgrims the seers could give their full attention and would find out for them from the Virgin whatever they could. For some mail requests in the late spring of 1932 Garmendia describes even making a special trip to the apparition site. By then it was this bread-and-butter work of petitions and divinations that kept some of the seers and some of their followers going. And as earthshaking miracles did not take place, Cardús and others began to consider the personal services of the seers, the conversions that they predicted, and the cures they announced as the main evidence for the apparitions as a whole. For a couple of cures he tried to get certificates from doctors.

Garmendia too took more interest in his responses to the petitions as prophecies and asked Cardús for documents and letters to show that the Virgin had read consciences or foretold the future accurately. Even though, Garmendia said, he "knew everything already from the Virgin," he still asked for the outcomes of the cures he predicted. In January 1933 he wrote that Mary and the Baby Jesus had said that any worthy petition made through him would be granted:

DECLARATION OF THE SEER JOSÉ GARMENDIA
ABOUT HIS VISION OF 8 DECEMBER 1933 AT EZKIOGA

The Most Holy Virgin appeared to me as always with the Baby Jesus on her arm, and she told me that her Divine Son conceded to me as with the saints the following privilege:

That to everyone who asks by thought and not by word or writing, by my mediation, some grace or favor, it will be granted, so long as it be for the greater glory of God. The Baby Jesus confirmed this and added that I was his disciple.

The Most Holy Virgin also said: that this year there would be great political and social upheavals, for there would be wars and revolutions.

The Seer, José Garmendia.

A request: We would like to thank everyone who obtains any grace by the mediation of the above seer to communicate it either to the seer himself or to him who writes this, for "the Most Holy Virgin said that until now Garmendia has been very criticized and looked down on, but from now on he will be very well known and appreciated."

This was too much even for the credulous García Cascón, who advised Garmendia "not to tell anyone since it will do you much harm." And Cardús thought that "Garmendia might be the victim of a ploy of the devil to discredit the apparitions." But Cardús did not doubt Garmendia's good faith and kept passing on requests to him.[17]

Cardús made, forwarded, or witnessed 17 petitions for cures, 7 for the verification of other apparitions, 6 for conversions, 4 for blessings, 3 for information on the afterlife of dead relatives, and 6 that remain unspecified. The most dramatic case of sickness, one that lasted throughout the period of Cardús's interest, was the boy with symptoms of autism. The parents approached the Virgin of Ezkioga through both Garmendia and Evarista; later they approached the spirit of Gemma Galgani through Magdalena Aulina. Despite what Evarista said, the child did not get better. The girl with a heart condition took seven months to get better, and when she did improve, her family was saying a novena to Madre Rafols. She sent alms and a notice of the favor to the pious magazine of the Sisters of Charity of Saint Anne. This made Cardús indignant, for he was sure that the Virgin of Ezkioga had played a part in the cure ("As if the Virgin could not have done the cure by means of Madre Rafols!").[18]

In other cases of illness the Virgin's answers were more ambiguous: "It is taken care of." "He should bear with saintly patience the calamities and she will keep him company and he should pray every day seven Hail Marys for the Seven Sorrows and she will visit him some day." "She gave her blessing." "Let him remember her and be very devoted to her and she too will remember him." At times seers merely said they had prayed to the Virgin for the sick person. Believers took even the mute blessings and ambiguous phrases as positive signs.

Three events provoked requests for clarification or verification of possible divine interventions. One father wanted to know if his young child, who was behaving unusually, had seen some kind of apparition or had had a vision. None of the three seers consulted provided an answer, but the third one, Benita Aguirre, put the matter to rest by writing: "The Most Holy Virgin did not answer anything about the child since it is not appropriate to answer." The second was the result of rumors of visions near Sant Llorenç Savall, in the mountains north of Sabadell.

When a group went to Ezkioga in April 1932, Cardús and the group leader asked three different seers—Ramona, Evarista, and Recalde—separately whether the visions were true. In no case did the seers come back with an answer. Cardús and another couple went to the town afterward and found a shepherd who had seen in the mountains what looked like busts of a male and a female saint. The shepherd said a couple of other people had glimpsed them. He concluded, "Signs from the heaven, travails on earth."[19]

Only one request for clarification brought a definite answer. The request came from a Catalan couple who were firm believers in Ezkioga. The night after they had returned from Ezkioga, they were driving from Barcelona to Terrassa. They watched a strange light follow their car and at the outskirts of Terrassa shoot off toward Montserrat. Later, at Ezkioga, they told Benita Aguirre they had seen something unusual and asked what it was. Benita said the Virgin had shown her the light and that it meant the Virgin was with them.[20] It is surprising Cardús did not make even more of these requests for verification. By 1933 Padre Burguera was spending most of his time in Ezkioga putting questions about some seers to others in his effort to separate the true from the false. And Cardús himself was busy following up stories of visionaries in Catalonia. These included Madre Rafols's relative Teresa Puig-Ràfols in Vilafranca del Penedès, Anna Pou i Prat in Tona, and Magdalena Aulina in Banyoles.

In towns like Terrassa and Sabadell with many families divided between Catholics and unbelievers, requests for conversions were not surprising. Through Ramona the Virgin asserted that a young man on the trip, unconvinced by the visions and skeptical in general, had converted. Cardús later learned the youth had indeed changed his ways. Atheism became an issue when people asked for blessings. A young woman who was the sole support of her aged parents and younger siblings and who had had to leave her job when she took ill, went to Cardús to get help from the Virgin of Ezkioga. Garmendia wrote back that the Virgin had not answered "but gave her blessing weeping bitterly and told me to tell that family that it is not enough to say they believe in God and the Virgin with the tongue, for they have to believe in their hearts." Cardús noted that while they were not practicing Catholics, at least they were not unbelievers. But he added a marginal note saying that, after all, the girl's father had died refusing the sacraments.[21]

Requests about the afterlife of relatives arose from the same divided families as the requests for conversions. For many people in industrial Catalonia, it was not at all clear that their loved ones had met requirements for paradise. But here the Ezkioga seers gave unequivocal answers, which no one could disprove. All three persons about whom Cardús forwarded requests were, according to the seers, in heaven.

The petitions as a whole bear out the general principle that people made requests more for others than for themselves, at a ratio of about 2:1. Those for whom people made petitions included the dead, unbelievers, and children. The petitions themselves—requests for help put to a factory worker by a captain of industry, to a farm boy by a lawyer, to a servant girl by a grande dame—are testimony to the language and system of spiritual exchange these very different people shared. The people differed culturally—from farm to urban, Basque to Catalan, functionally illiterate to educated—as well as socially. They shared a language of interpersonal exchange, of favor and of thanks, and the knowledge of a joint religious system. In that system the wealthy and the powerful were as helpless as the poor before the power of God and the mercy of the Virgin. Through the vision state, a newfound key to an ancient mystery, these rural seers could obtain precious information denied their social superiors. And for the first time in their lives in the wider society the lines of persuasion and of thanks went to them and they provided the favors and the help.

13. THE LIVING AND THE DEAD

THE HOUSEHOLD DEAD

ROM THE FIRST days at Ezkioga the dead appeared in the visions. Those who appeared were almost always close family members, whether of the seer, of those around the seer, or of people in the seer's town. Rarely were the dead unidentified. In spiritist sessions the dead of other nations, races, or religions turned up, but at Ezkioga the deceased were those for whom the seers or their followers were responsible.

As with the visions as a whole, so with visions of the dead: more than two-thirds of the seers were women and girls. But the dead persons the female seers saw were likely to be males. As in other religious matters, women or girls were representing their families when dealing with the other world. Slightly more than half of the dead relatives seen were brothers, sisters, spouses, or children of the seers; so they were seeing those who had died relatively young, not parents or older relatives. Eventually the seers progressed from reporting on the dead to interceding for them. And after Ezkioga became an underground cult, some of the seers helped the dead to heaven as a profession.[1]

For the first two months of the visions the seers tended to see their own dead, especially those who had died prematurely. On July 18 a gentleman from Madrid saw next to the Virgin his only child, killed in a railroad accident. On July 30 a girl from Bergara, aged fourteen, learned that her father and little brothers and sisters were in heaven and she would join them there. On the same day Benita Aguirre saw her baby sister as an angel, and the next day José Garmendia followed the trend, learning that his mother was in purgatory and needed two masses to get to heaven. In August a seven-year-old boy from Zumarraga saw his baby brother in heaven and a teenage girl from Albiztur saw her brother carrying the flag of his sodality at the foot of a crucifix. The youth had died recently from a fall from a moving truck when he was returning from a meeting of the San Luis Gonzaga sodality.[2]

At the end of August, as the crowds dwindled and individual seers were reduced to helping their own loyal followers, the visionaries began to see the dead of others. During her first vision at Ezkioga María Agueda Antonia Aguirre, aged forty, a poor farm woman living in Bidegoyan, had been cured after being partially crippled for four years. The Virgin instructed her to say the rosary daily and go to Ezkioga every week. She did so with a stable group of friends and neighbors. Her third vision, on August 31, included the dead:

> When reciting the second rosary, she saw an intense brightness between the trees of the woods on the left side and the tree that holds the cross. In the midst of this brightness appeared the Most Holy Virgin in a black mantle and a white tunic with her hands crossed in front of her. At her feet there appeared three little angels and three more were above her head. She is sure that of the three little angels who were at the feet of the Virgin, two were her own deceased children and the third was a two-month-old girl who died eight years ago on a farm near hers. These three children were looking at the Most Holy Virgin. Their robes were the same as the angel costumes in which they had been buried.[3]

She returned on September 15 and identified the other three angels as well.

> At the feet of the Virgin were the three angels she saw August 31, and above the Virgin's head three more angels whom this time she recognized. She is sure that they were three children who were her relatives, one six years old, another six months old, and the third two months old. These too wore the same angel clothes in which they had been shriven. At the feet of the Virgin she saw as well, dressed as San Luis Gonzaga, a son of Señor Lasquibar of Albiztur, who died twenty-two years ago at age twenty-three.[4]

The dead were just one element of María Agueda's visions. Like other seers she also saw the crucified Jesus and Saint Michael and other angels with swords.

María Agueda Antonia Aguirre in vision at Ezkioga, 1932. Photo by Joaquín Sicart

She worried about the political situation in Spain, and the Virgin said she would appear in many places and work signs that all would experience. The dead were not the highlights. Rather, seeing them seemed to show that the partition between earth and heaven was down. It was no great surprise to María that her young children were there; she had shrouded them as angels because she knew that they would inevitably go there, baptized as they were and below the age of sin. The important news of the visions of the dead was that the Virgin stood with the living as well as the dead in the seer's family, clan, cuadrilla, locality, and nation.

María Agueda reported no contact with the children—it was enough to have recognized them with the Virgin. She would have known already that they were interceding for her. As the church bells tolled when they were dying, she would

have recited the Bidegoyan prayer: "If for any sin committed in this world you find yourself suffering in purgatory, let the beloved Jesus receive you now free of suffering, and when we ourselves are in need, be our intercessor."[5]

Young Lasquibar was the deceased son of the wealthy town secretary of Albiztur (the seer's place of birth). He was not the only dead person a visionary saw dressed as San Luis Gonzaga. About the same time, in one of a series of visions in and around the town of Ormaiztegi, seven-year-old Matilde saw her grandfather like the saint in a black habit, a surplice, and a clerical hat, holding a crucifix. That is how the family had laid him out in 1900. The grandfather was but one of the dead Matilde and a friend identified for those around them.

> [The girls] say they see a very wide road. In the center is the Virgin. On both sides there are long lines of dead persons. Those on the right are already in heaven; those on the left, in hell. The girls read the name on each coffin. Among them are many from Ormáiztegui, some of them recently deceased, but others who died many years ago, before the girls could have known them. . . . Finally the angels take to heaven the dead on the right and those on the left disappear in flames as if in a great hole that opens in the earth.[6]

The file of coffins with identifiable dead going off to hell reflects both what children might surmise about the Last Judgment and what they knew for sure about Ormaiztegi. The town had both church people and a Republican minority; the Republicans had a social center, sent articles to *La Voz de Guipúzcoa,* and complained about the power of the parish priest. Beatriz of Unanu also identified the dead of her town as they went by in procession.[7]

Just which dead the seers saw seemed to depend on their listeners. In Navarra, where children performed before neighbors, news of the town dead was a central feature of the visions. The names of the dead meant something to everyone present. The visions were a devout nightly spectacle for the townspeople, for whom the children narrated a kind of heavenly theater of the town dead. A boy in Arbizu exclaimed in surprise when he saw the deceased wife of a neighbor up in the sky, "Coño, aquí está la Bárbara! [Hey, here's Barbara!]"

In contrast, at Ezkioga each vision cuadrilla would be surrounded by onlookers who did not know the core people or one another. The seers might see the dead they knew, those of the core followers. But they generally did not see the dead of onlookers, whom they would not have recognized; instead, they heard about them from the Virgin. The Catalan Salvador Cardús described how a woman from Terrassa learned that her father was in heaven. The seer was the girl from Ataun.

> The wife of my friend Joan, who was there on Monday, October 5, told the seer to ask the Virgin about the fate of her father, who had died almost instantly and for whom they were worried. The seer went down to the road after the rosary and waited until she saw the woman, to whom she said that the Virgin had told her that her father had been saved. And she added, speaking to the couple, "The Virgin told me to tell you that she is very pleased with the life that you lead, and that you should continue the same way."

Six days later Cardús heard from Ramona Olazábal that his father too was in heaven. In both cases the fate of the dead, unlike the fate of the child angels, was seriously in doubt, and this news gained the seers loyal followers. There must have been pressure on others to provide similar information.[8]

The members of the first Gemma trip in mid-December 1931 also made these requests.

> Some ask [the Virgin through José Garmendia in trance] about dead persons. Sometimes she makes no response, other times she smiles, and sometimes she weeps. One man asked about a dead person. The Virgin wept as her only response. When the man asked Garmendia what her reply was, Garmendia could not bring himself to disappoint him. "The Virgin said nothing and simply gave a blessing." He did not say the whole truth, and he had a scruple about it, so in another vision he asked Mary, in his simple and rustic manner, "Did I sin, Mother?" She told him no, since he had done it out of charity.[9]

By 1932 the Catalans' habitual seers—Benita Aguirre, María Recalde, and José Garmendia—were helping the dead to heaven by specifying which devotional acts the survivors should perform. Benita would often ask for masses. When I asked her brother if any money came into the house because of the visions, he said none at all, except that occasionally Benita would ask her mother to solicit money for a mass for a given soul in purgatory, saying, "So-and-so is suffering in purgatory and asks that you order a mass."[10]

Benita would see the souls ascend. A French journalist described the audience response to one such vision:

> Often the pilgrims want to know the fate of the soul of a deceased person. They exclaim when in a collection of yellowed pictures [by this time the Catalans routinely brought photographs of deceased relatives to help the seers with their identifications] a little girl picks out one, saying she recognizes someone she had noticed in the flames of purgatory. Little Benita astounded in this way a group of Catalan pilgrims by specifying exactly how many days one of their dead relatives had been awaiting pardon. The relative had been dead 72 days, and the date was easy to verify. Those present said the Our Father that he needed to enjoy eternal peace, and the seer made his entire family break out in transports of joy when she guaranteed that she had seen the deceased go up to paradise in her séance.[11]

On 17 May 1932 during a vision with eight or ten believers, Benita

> suddenly said loudly, "Pray three Hail Marys for each of the souls who are about to leave purgatory." With utmost devotion those present prayed what the seer had ordered, and she exclaimed, "They are entering heaven." One of them was the Cura Santa Cruz, well known in the region, a combatant in the Carlist Wars who died in Latin America as a tremendous and exemplary missionary.

This was no run-of-the mill soul. Manuel Ignacio Santa Cruz y Loidi was a local Carlist hero and a nationwide symbol for clerical involvement in reactionary rebellion.[12]

For the Ezkioga defender Mariano Bordas, Benita Aguirre's vision of a particular soul entering heaven was proof for the apparitions as a whole. At Ezkioga in April 1932 the Terrassa wool merchant Rafael García Cascón had learned that one of two relatives in Extremadura had died, but he did not know which. He told Benita and Recalde, and later at the vision site while the two seers were in vision, he asked for an Our Father for the deceased. After the prayer

> the little seer transformed her face in an expression of angelic happiness and spoke in Basque that her countrymen, especially her mother, trans-lated; apparently the Virgin told her that the deceased had died at 4:00 A.M. and that at that very moment (it was 5:30 P.M.) [the Virgin] had taken Mar-celino out of purgatory. The girl saw an angel put a halo on his head and saw him enter heaven dressed in the habit of Saint Francis and belted with a Franciscan cord. A little later during the vision of the girl Marcelino ap-peared again, and Benita said that Marcelino thanked Señor García Cascón and all who accompanied him in the Our Father.

María Recalde backed up Benita, saying the Virgin had told her the soul had entered heaven at the moment of the Lord's Prayer.[13]

HEAVEN, THE BELIEVERS' REWARD

When believers and seers themselves died, other seers saw them in purgatory or heaven. In September 1932 those around Benita asked her to ask the Virgin if the seer María Celaya, who was gravely ill, would recover. Benita seemed to see María in purgatory.

> I saw the seer but only her head. Her face was very disfigured, and she seemed to be suffering a lot. I do not know where she was, since the place was so dark. After the vision, which was about six o'clock in the evening, they told me that she had died that morning.[14]

José Garmendia reported that the servant seer Carmen Visa, who died two weeks after María Celaya, spent only a few moments in purgatory before going to heaven.

In January 1934 Martín Ayerbe learned that the sister of the parish priest of Zegama was in heaven. Three weeks later Conchita Mateos in vision spoke to the dead woman, before about twenty people in Beasain. Juan Bautista Ayerbe described how Conchita made the connection.

> Next, and with *the desire* I had not mentioned to anyone, not anyone, to know if the late Ramona Oyarbide, a very fervent devotee of the Holy Ap-

paritions of Ezkioga who died in Cegama last January 21, was in heaven, I gave the girl a death card I had received from the parish priest of that village, the brother of the deceased. The girl, without opening the card, became very excited, "Is that Ramona? You must be better there than here! You left this earth, for you were so sad, and now you are in delight for eternity! How many times would you say, 'When will I be in heaven?' Well, now you are in the heaven you so desired. There you are together with Gemma and Mama [*Amatxo*, referring to Mary]." (When the vision was over the seer responded to my questions by saying she had seen the deceased together with Gemma and the Most Holy Virgin, and that she had never met her in real life.)

Then in the same trance the girl replied *in writing* to three letters, one of which, with four questions for the Virgin, was mine. Her answers fit the questions EVEN THOUGH THE GIRL HAD NOT READ THEM. She distributed flowers as directed by the Most Holy Virgin, had certain objects blessed, and began to dictate to me the following while not losing sight of the vision.

The Virgin's subsequent message as relayed by Conchita put the vision of Ramona Oyarbide in perspective, for in fact it did not refer to the woman at all. The Virgin told those who still believed in Ezkioga (it was only ten days after the Vatican backed Bishop Múgica's September 1933 decree denying that the visions were supernatural) how lucky they were. Through Conchita the Virgin asked those present if they led better lives since they learned of the apparitions. When they answered that they thought they did, the Virgin praised their loyalty and pointed out that when she first appeared many thousands came by bus, train, and on foot, and "many of the little angels came down from heaven as well."

The Virgin described for the believers the spirit in their little community, a spirit I still felt in the 1980s and 1990s when speaking to its last original members.

> "Look how happy you are together at this moment! How many such happy moments you have had together since I appeared! Above all, how often you get together to tell stories to each other! Even if they are always the same, you never tire of hearing them. You are told them, you are told them, and you always want to hear them. You ask each other if you have more stories. And if you do, you are all happy; and if you don't, then you go back to repeating the previous ones!"

Conchita said to the Virgin, "You must laugh at us, Mother! Because what can we do? We like your things so much! We are always talking about you, so we are always wanting you to come so we can hear your stories. Keep on, keep on, for we do not tire of them!"

Juan Bautista Ayerbe's sister-in-law made an aside to him, "Others from Urnieta would have wanted to be here." Whereupon the Virgin said something to Conchita, who replied, "Yes, Mother, that is true, and many who are nearby do not want to come and hear you. Jesus says, 'I come to you and you reject me.'" Finally, after a vision that lasted forty-five minutes, the Virgin departed.[15]

This account shows us two phases of the presence of the dead at Ezkioga. In the first the dead came down with the Virgin as little angels while the great public visions were taking place, and the angels were one more factor among many that authenticated the visions. In the second, with the visions discredited and the believers on the defensive, heaven was a reward for continued belief. By the end of October 1931 the Catalans knew that those who came from far away believing in the apparitions would go straight to heaven without passing through purgatory. In this phase appearances by the dead helped maintain the morale and loyalty of the living. Believers led lives of heavenly joy, enriched by heavenly stories brought to them by the Virgin. In both phases the dead were benign spectators at the visions.[16]

But there was an obverse, dark side to the believers' assurance: doubters would go to purgatory, unbelievers to hell. Seers saw some people in purgatory for not believing enough—the brother-in-law of a fervent believer in Ormaiztegi, because he was skeptical about the visions and did not attend the local sessions, and Juan José Echezarreta, for giving in to government pressure and removing the image from the holy place. José Garmendia warned a man from Sabadell who had asked for a blessing that the Virgin of Ezkioga had said "they have to believe in her, and if they do not believe now, at the end they will not have time to believe in her. It will be useless to ask for forgiveness at the last hour. He who does not believe in her does not believe in God Our Lord." Hell was considered a sure punishment for those active in suppressing the visions.[17]

The people of the Goiherri at this time took sudden death when not in a state of grace to be divine punishment and almost certain damnation. Writing about Ataun in 1923, the Basque ethnographer Jose Miguel de Barandiarán observed: "We have never had a homicide, but we have had deaths by accident at work. In these cases one of the things that most torments the family is that the deceased was not able to receive the last rites."[18] When the vicar general Justo de Echeguren died in an automobile accident on 16 August 1937 without last rites, Ezkioga believers felt the dire prophecies had come true (as did believers in the visions at Garabandal in Cantabria when the bishop Vicente Puchol died in a traffic accident on Saint Michael's Day 1967). But by the same token others read Patxi's sudden death in a fall from scaffolding as proof that the visions were not authentic. The most frightening aspect of the chastisement seers predicted for unbelievers is that death would be so sudden as to preclude repentance.

But believers could be sure of their place. Conchita Mateos, who had witnessed other believers in heaven, was seen there herself after her death. Esperanza Aranda saw a host of deceased seers and believers in heaven, including Tomás Imaz, Soledad de la Torre, Juana Aguirre, Juliana Ulacia, Patxi, Cruz Lete, and a number of relatives of her followers. In a vision message narrated by Juan Bautista Ayerbe on 8 December 1950 Aranda was given a glimpse of heaven, and at the request of Conchita's mother, who was present, the deceased Conchita even spoke.

> Now [Aranda] feels herself transported to heaven, and she exclaims, "But Mother, where am I, in heaven or on earth? What music! The angels and saints are singing as a choir 'Tota Pulcra est María.'" At this moment something surprising happens, for one of those present, the mother of the former Conchita Mateos (who died in a Franciscan convent as Madre Sor Ana María), exclaims, "Since today is her saint's day, let Conchita speak to us."
>
> And then the seer says, "I see a dwelling where the glorious souls are carrying what seem to be palm fronds, and one of them comes forward. It is Conchita! Now she prostrates herself at the feet of the Mother and Queen of Heaven and kisses her hands and feet. Conchita is now about to speak: 'Two words for my parents. Mother and father, now you see that I am in heaven. I wait for your arrival here soon. So continue to be models of sanctity, setting a good example everywhere . . . The same goes for my brothers. Be holy, which is the only thing you should desire in this world. In heaven I never forget you. I intercede so you will be happy not bodily but spiritually, which is much greater. You will never be in need of bread, and as until now, peace will never be lacking in your household. From heaven I contemplate you and help you, and I see you are happy, for which I give thanks to my Lord and Master. Do not worry. You will get the warning that in due time I will bring to you. You will be protected against all harm by your dear Mother until one day we will be able to see each other and embrace each other for always, dear parents, in the heavenly land.'"[19]

From heaven Conchita could provide a valuable service, a warning of impending death so that her relatives could prepare themselves, and could live in the meantime without anxiety.

This vision, however rudimentary, of a heavenly space was unusual for the Ezkioga seers. Another seer who described heaven was connected only indirectly with Ezkioga. Anna Pou i Prat was a servant about twenty years old on an estate in Tona in the province of Barcelona. From Tona two bus excursions had gone to Ezkioga in November 1931, and two women from nearby Vic had had visions on the Aulina trips.[20]

Pou i Prat was orphaned at a young age. On 31 January 1933 she experienced what seemed to be a miraculous cure of an infected ankle. The cure occurred during a novena to Our Lady of Lourdes and after prayers at a local shrine to the Virgin. An Ezkioga enthusiast described the cure in a local newspaper, possibly enhancing the matter for Anna herself, and she saw the Virgin for the first time a week later.[21]

The Vic enthusiast alerted Cardús, who visited the new seer on February 26. Subsequently Anna's visions became more complex and tortured. Although her employers first believed her, they fired her on March 20, and she went back to her aunt's house, where she claimed to suffer the Passion on Fridays and receive mystical Communion. She also felt the devil was after her. One of her aunts believed that Anna was mentally ill and that reading Galgani's *Letters and Ecstasies,* a gift from Cardús, had made her worse. No one besides Cardús and his friends heeded the girl, and even they stopped coming in June 1933 after threats from Anna's neighbors.

Five days after her first vision Anna claimed to visit heaven. In the presence of other servants she fell on the floor as if her soul had departed and she had died, and later she said the Virgin had taken her up higher than the stars. As Cardús told it:

> She entered heaven, and the Virgin let her see her mother, who was very resplendent, and then the Crucified Jesus, from whose wounds blood dripped. Heaven seemed to her like immense, grandiose vaults, with a very brilliant, slightly bluish, light. After a little while there, the Virgin said to her, "Come, go back to earth, for your body [left behind on earth] will get cold."[22]

Like most of the Ezkioga visionary dead, Anna Pou's mother did not speak. When Conchita Mateos spoke from heaven, Juan Bautista Ayerbe was surprised, because it is virtually the only time that a seer relayed to him a dead person's words.

AMA FELISA, COURIER FOR SOULS

The connection between the living and the dead was especially strong for children whose mothers had died young (the case of Anna Pou), for mothers whose children had died young (the cases of María Agueda and the mother of Conchita Mateos), and for those whose close relatives had died suddenly in accidents (the cases of the girl from Albiztur and the man from Madrid). These deaths came outside the normal pattern of things and interrupted intense relations, which were left unresolved.[23]

After the church banned public vision sessions, people's ongoing desire to maintain contact with the dead permitted some of the seers to work as intermediaries with the other world. In 1944 Juan Bautista Ayerbe described the seer Marcelina Mendívil: "No longer does she beg door-to-door for her house, which burned down in such an unusual fashion, but she does circulate a lot, we have learned, to take messages from the Virgin and from the souls in purgatory with whom, above all, she is much in contact."[24]

Mendívil formed part of an extensive consulting service about the dead which depended largely on the incessant activity of one woman. For many in the Goiherri Felisa Alcorta Goenaga, variously known as the Bread Lady from Zumarraga, Ama Txikixa [Little Mother], or Ama Felisa [Mother Felisa], came to personify the Ezkioga cult from the late 1930s until her death in 1954. Born about 1882, Ama Felisa operated a bakery from a farm to the north of Zumarraga. For four years her family employed as a servant the woman whose children were later the first seers at Ezkioga, so Ama Felisa took a special interest in the visions. We see her in photographs raptly observing and caring for seers and proud at the ground-breaking of the chapel. After the cult went underground, she led prayer sessions at Ezkioga at night. It may have been through her that several other bakers in the zone converted and attended visions in Ordizia and Ormaiztegi.[25]

Believers, including her own family, thought Ama Felisa had a gift of second sight that enabled her to see things happening elsewhere—she saw the youth from Azkoitia who was posted elsewhere in the Civil War, and she saw one of her own sons in Jaca. She also seemed to foresee events—that a farm building would burn down if its owner did not install an image of the Miraculous Mary in a window, that an anti-Ezkioga priest would be deposed (he went crazy in late 1934), or that Spain would once again be a monarchy. But she herself saw neither the Virgin nor the souls in purgatory, and so she had recourse not only to Mendívil but also to Luis Irurzun, Cándida Zunzunegui, Juliana Ulacia, and above all María Recalde.

Ama Felisa circulated among a regular network of clients, gathering questions for the Virgin or the dead, delivering answers from seers, and collecting alms. Leaving the bakery to her family, she would be gone on foot, by bus, or by train for weeks at a time, staying in the homes of believers. Her regular route included the towns adjacent to Zumarraga as well as Azpeitia, San Prudentzio, Legazpi, Oñati, Aranzazu, Durango, Ordizia, Zaldibia, Tolosa, and San Sebastián. Occasionally she went to Bergara and Mondragón. Her son told me that nothing stopped her, including the Civil War. One nonbelieving observer claimed to me that she or the seers she spoke for coerced peasants into giving money with threats that their houses would burn or their cattle would die. Be that as it may, initiative also came from the believers, who had sons missing in action, problems with farming in hard times, and dead who needed care.

Accompanied by her sister-in-law or other friends, Ama Felisa also paid regular visits to the church of Santa María in San Sebastián and the shrines of Our Lady of Liernia in Mutiloa, Saint Martin of Loinaz, and Saint Anthony of Urkiola in Bizkaia. She would enter the shrine of Our Lady of Aranzazu with a lighted candle and leave many lighted candles behind her. A friar of Aranzazu remembered her visits on the first Saturday of each month and said the students referred to her and her friends as "las iluminadas." Women described her to me "lighting rolls of wax [for the souls in purgatory], mortifying herself with prickly holly under her knees as she prayed, and on the orders of the Virgin wearing the Passionist habit of Gemma Galgani."[26]

Ama Felisa also played a prominent role in the vision sessions in Ordizia. A Passionist who attended one of them described her in 1950:

> There is a female apostle, dressed something like a priest, with a shoulder cape and everything, in the old style of rural clergy. She is advanced in years [by then she was in her late sixties], and they call her "La Ama X." She displays a white silk handkerchief, on which are seen big dark-red spots, which she claims is the blood of Christ.[27]

We get a glimpse of how Ama Felisa worked from a local doctor. Curious about her system, he asks her about the afterlife of a brother who, he said, had died in Bizkaia in the war. She returned after several days saying that a seer had learned that the brother was in purgatory and would go to heaven if the doctor received Communion for nine days with Ama Felisa present. The doctor was a daily communicant anyway, so they went together for nine days. She then checked again with the seer, who claimed to have seen the brother leave purgatory and go straight to heaven while the doctor and Ama Felisa were receiving Communion in the ninth mass. In fact, there was no dead brother.[28]

Ama Felisa cannot have had time to sit in on all the believers' masses and novenas. But by all accounts she was dedicated to helping others and kept none of the alms. Antonia Etxezarreta, the milk-lady, told me that once when she was sick Ama Felisa came to visit, predicted that Antonia's son would have the grace of the Virgin, and seemed to have a vision looking out a window. Ama Felisa was like a pastor to the believing community, looking after their physical and spiritual needs and caring for their souls after death.

There was general agreement that the money Ama Felisa collected went to the needy. Her role as collector of alms and votive money corresponds with an ancient one in Basque and European society—that of the questors for shrines. The woman shrine-keeper (*serora*) at the little shrine of Our Lady of Liernia circulated in a wide area. Much of what she collected would have been pledges for prayers that people felt the Virgin had answered. In the years 1928–1929 she gathered about eight hundred pesetas per year in money or in eggs, chickens, or other produce; she could keep half for herself. Questors also circulated for the construction of churches, like that of Urkiola. With portable images that all members of a farm would kiss, questors provided a home delivery of grace probably related, like home delivery of bread, to a multiplicity of sacred places and competition between them. Ama Felisa, the bread-lady, was delivering personalized grace that the Virgin or the holy dead had certified.[29]

Ama Felisa's son and daughter-in-law told me that she sent some of the alms to a convent in Palencia, where masses for the dead were especially cheap and she could liberate more souls. Ama Felisa would redistribute some of the alms to the sick and the poor on her route. But believers could also choose to have their money go to missions; she brought this money to María Recalde, in sums of five hundred to one thousand pesetas. María told Ama Felisa that angels took this money away at night from a bedside table for use in a place where missionaries never went. By one account it was a place where people dug for potatoes with their hands. Another believer told me the money was "for places where there was no religion, for example, for the missions. Away. Like to India. For you know there are many places where there is no religion." In 1983 older Zumarraga believers were wondering whether that remote place might have been the moon. In any case where the Ezkioga money went was a mystery.[30]

María Recalde was secretive about financial matters, even with her husband and children. She would closet herself with three or four women believers to pray in an improvised chapel. The family knew that Ama Felisa came with the alms, but no one knew what María did with them. On different occasions in Madrid and Mexico, however, María's granddaughter, Mariví Jayo, met people who, when she said she was from Durango, remembered her grandmother well. It seems that María, who belonged to a Basque Nationalist family, generously helped the family members of prisoners in the Durango jail for enemies of the Franco regime. The Durango prison may have been "the place where missionaries had never been." Before she died in 1950 María told her husband that she had twenty thousand pesetas still unspent, a fortune at the time. Mortified, her husband told no one, until on his deathbed he had his children give the money to the Durango priests for masses.[31]

Other seers continued to provide news of the dead. As far as I know, the last two of the seers from the 1930s to do so were Luis Irurzun, who settled in San Sebastián, and Rosario Gurruchaga, who settled in Bergara. A believer from Bergara told me, "If they brought a photograph, she would answer where the dead person was." She would also deliver messages or tokens from the dead to the living. In 1980, for instance, she gave flowers to Leonor Castillo from Leonor's deceased brother, Vidal, the operator of the Ezkioga souvenir stand. These semiprofessional intermediaries with the dead were not new with the Ezkioga visions. Specialists in many parts of Spain, known as *ánimas* or *animeros* and in Languedoc as *armièrs*, had long claimed to be able to make such contacts.[32]

OLD GHOSTS AND NEW SPIRITS

For the Basques dying was a communal enterprise—families needed neighbors to help the dead through the afterworld. Just eight years before the Ezkioga visions started, the Eusko-Folklore Society made a survey of death beliefs and rituals. For most of the rural Basque-speaking area, apparitions of the dead were well known and there was a pattern and an etiquette for dealing with them similar to that in use in medieval France. The report by the society's correspondent from Bedia (Bizkaia) laid out the pattern.

> The village believes the apparition of the dead is a real and frequent phenomenon. They appear in the air just above the ground and dressed with the same garments in which they were buried. Their purpose is typically to reveal that they have some unfulfilled promise that keeps them from entering heaven. The dead appear in any place or time, and always to persons they know (*ezagunai*); but those to whom they appear must be in a state of grace.[33]

While other reports for other towns gave instances of apparitions in the more distant past, that for Bedia recounts one whose seer was still alive. The apparition led many in the community, including the parish priest, to go to the shrine of Begoña for a mass to liberate a soul in purgatory. A beggar woman, they believed, had died when a relative had had a mass said in order to kill her. The beggar's spirit had approached a good woman, Francisca de Muguertzu, to request a mass at the shrine of Our Lady of Begoña, near Bilbao. After the mass the spirit offered Francisca her hand. Counseled by the priest, Francisca extended her handkerchief instead, and where the beggar-soul touched it, the cloth was marked with the oily imprint of fingers. "Even today," the report from 1923 concluded, "Francisca de Muguertzu keeps this handkerchief in a little bottle."[34]

The Eusko-Folklore survey uncovered similar patterns elsewhere in the Basque Country: the dead always took the initiative and the living consulted the parish priest about how to respond. As at Ezkioga, what the dead wore varied because different towns had different customs for shrouding—habits of different religious orders for the married, uniforms of sodalities for the unmarried, wedding clothes or simply the deceased's best clothes for adults, and white for children. The dead in hell who wore religious habits appeared to the living to request that their habits be removed, because with them on they suffered more.[35]

Such apparitions did not happen just to Basques. That the dead needed help was church doctrine and that they occasionally asked for it was general knowledge. In the seventeenth century Spanish theologians Onofre Manescal and Juan de Palafox collected similar evidence. And in 1915 the Jesuit from Mallorca Juan Mir wrote: "It is not open to doubt that God permits the souls of purgatory to visit people in order to show their terrible punishment . . . asking for help and thanking for prayers."[36]

The dead had left signs on handkerchiefs and other objects for hundreds of years. In 1894 an enterprising Missionary of the Sacred Heart, Victor Jouët, began to collect instances of these visions and their relics as evidence that purgatory existed and the supernatural could be tangible. In Rome he founded a brotherhood to help the souls in purgatory and a museum for evidence of their marks. In 1904 Pius X went to see an initial group of twelve objects from France, Germany, Belgium, and Italy. Among the many apparitions of the dead Jouët reported in his bulletin was one in Deusto, not far from Bedia, where another spirit left the imprint of a finger on a handkerchief.[37]

The clientele of the bulletin understood two kinds of dead. The first kind, like those in the Basque survey, actively provoked encounters with the living in order to alleviate suffering in the afterlife. These dead needed the help of the living, and for them people prayed and ordered masses. These dead, however, although they might mean well, were considered dangerous. Evarista Galdós fled her first vision of the Virgin, she said, because at first she thought it a soul in purgatory, presumably of the frightening variety. But the bulletin is also filled with news of the beneficent dead, those who on demand interceded for the living. Grateful clients listed their favors—cures, jobs, apartments—in every issue. In Spain it was common for people to pray to the souls of the dead as intercessors, and in prayer manuals there were novenas and prayers not *for* the dead but *to* the dead on behalf of the living.[38] Although the Ezkioga visions include few instances of the dead interceding for the living, the dead that the seers saw were generally this benign kind.

In the Eusko-Folklore survey a Meñaka (Bizkaia) man told of a farmer in the old days who lived near the church and cemetery and witnessed a nocturnal procession of the dead holding candles. In the 1931 visions only child seers in Ormaiztegi and Unanu admitted to seeing processions of the dead. In 1923 the priest of Galarreta, a hamlet in Alava, wrote, "In the old days people commonly believed in the apparitions of the dead; today only children talk about them." It could be that by then people believed in apparitions less in areas like Alava where traditional beliefs were not protected by a special language. In contrast, people in Basque-speaking zones still gave credence to visions of the dead, and most Ezkioga seers who saw the dead were Basque speakers.[39]

Rural people consulted *azti*, diviners, in the larger towns and the cities to find lost animals, objects, and missing persons, as well as to learn the fate of the dead or the outcome of disease.[40] Probably some people in the Goiherri also consulted mediums, who in most Spanish cities were also seeing the dead at this time. Spirit mediums who served rural folk in Spain were a modern form of azti. For the mid-nineteenth-century folk traditions of ghosts and philosophical and religious speculation about reincarnation took a new turn as spiritism progressed from city to city in Western Europe. The new technique offered contact of an active, verbal kind with the dead. In France spiritism promoted "personal immortality, reincarnation on earth, and the transmigration of souls to other planets." In Spain specialized publishing houses put out the works of major French authors. And as in Italy, spiritism became a specialty of the bourgeois commercial class, often in tandem with Freemasonry. The mediums, however, could be from the servant class and, like Eusapia Paladino in Italy, could have relations with promoters similar to those we have seen for the most convincing visionaries at Ezkioga.[41] Whether or not Ramona acted as a medium, as one reporter claimed, there were spiritist sessions at this time in San Sebastián, Pamplona, Bilbao, and Irun.[42]

Spiritist ideas also circulated in the countryside. About 1909 a man from Ataun returning from Argentina tried to spread spiritist doctrines with pamphlets arguing against Catholicism and the clergy. And in 1924 fishermen from Santander brought spiritism to the Basque seaport of Bermeo. There people sat around tables that replied to questions by knocks. Those present would begin with prayers and then call up a deceased person and ask questions like those put to ghosts in the region—how long had they been dead; where were they (almost always in purgatory); did they need alms; did they have promises pending and if so to what shrine; did they want masses and if so how many. Some who went to such séances were not regular churchgoers, and some questions indicated that the procedure, as in France, cut out the established church. When asked, the Bermeo soul said there was no hell and it was not good to give money to priests or order masses. People also asked where to fish, but fishermen following these tips tended to come back empty-handed.[43]

Catholic experts on spiritism disagreed on how to explain the phenomenon. A few thought spiritist phenomena real and the effect of good, but as yet unidentified, spirits. Others thought them outright fraud. Many thought them real but diabolical. This was the position of the parish bulletin of Pamplona, which described for its readers a typical spiritist session. But whatever spiritism was, by the time of the Bermeo outbreak the church had forbidden Catholics to engage in the practice. Printed examinations of conscience might include questions like "Have you consulted diviners, hypnotists, or spiritists?" or "Have you gone to meetings of hypnotists or spiritists?"[44]

The first to compare the Ezkioga visions and spiritism in print was Agapito Millán in *El Liberal* (Bilbao) in September 1931. After a skeptical account of three seers he had watched, he set out his own idea of the spirit world. There were, he said, natural or high apparitions, which were those that occurred at the initiative of ghosts, suffering souls, and "high entities of the astral world," and also artificial or low ones, which humans initiated. The high, natural apparitions, he held, always occurred for a good reason, one important either for the spirit or the visionary. For the spirit they might serve to attain liberty, tranquillity, or even happiness in the other world. For the living they might serve as a warning of imminent danger. Here we see a congruence between the traditional belief in the apparitions of the dead and the new beliefs of the spiritists. Millán merely added to traditional notions the idea that "higher astral bodies" might appear. He claimed that low, artificial apparitions were

> provoked by experimenters by means of hypnotism, magnetism, and som-
> nambulism, who put their subject sensitives to sleep, and once they are pro-

A photograph of Agapito Millán Estefanía pasted on a souvenir of his Masonic lecture, "My childhood, my life, my ideal," 1934. Courtesy Archivo Histórico Nacional, Guerra Civil, Salamanca

foundly so, double them and project their "double," or astral body wherever or as far as they want. In 1918 a good "subject," put to sleep in Bilbao, sent [his or her] double, in a few instants, to Paris and places on the French front, where it talked with soldiers and was visible to them.

This kind of experiment was going on throughout Europe and the Americas in an attempt to apply positivist methods to the spiritual realm. Scientists like the Nobel Prize winner Santiago Ramón y Cajal had participated in Spain, and Millán thought the sessions could explain what was going on at Ezkioga:

> Why could this same result not be produced now, having a "double" with the appearance of a Saint, the Virgin, or a farmer appear in Ezquioga or anywhere else, so that those present would see and even hear them? . . . The Ezquioga events appear to be sessions of low spiritism.[45]

Interest in the afterlife, sensitives, and astral projection was not unusual for republicans. For instance, *El Heraldo de Madrid* reported in August 1931, when it was ignoring the visions at Ezkioga, that a waiter in a Madrid café who was a "seer, astrologer, and a reader of palms" claimed that his body "doubled" while he was asleep or in trance and traveled across the world and into the future. Similarly, the republican *Voz de Giupúzcoa,* which mocked the Ezkioga visions, found a book entitled *Revelation of the Mystery of the Beyond* "impressive" and recommended enthusiastically a "wise professor of occultism and spiritism." The professor, Hadji Agaf, had settled in Irun where he received about two hundred letters a day requesting his help in matters of "luck, health, love, business, etc." Even the *Voz de Navarra* accepted advertisements from a personal magnetist.

Agapito Millán epitomized this cultural experimentation. He was born in 1893 and as a child in the minefields of eastern Bizkaia peddled clothes, made scapulars for sale in religious fiestas, and cleaned ore. A novel by Tolstoy inspired him at age seventeen to join a revolutionary republican party in Bilbao and struggle against "the oppression of the regime and of the sinister clergy." But he soon turned from violence toward "more humane and spiritual" pursuits. During World War I he tried to interest the French and British embassies in his esoteric powers. He became a vegetarian, a Freemason, and a leader of theosophy. In his travels throughout the north as the salesman of heavy machinery, camomile, and postcards, he handed out broadsides about spiritism and against the death penalty and promoted a sideline as professor of occult science who could find buried treasure, locate lost relatives, give business advice, and avoid the attacks of enemies. In June 1931 he was also a leader of the Radical Socialist Republican Party in Bilbao.[46]

In 1934 Spaniards read about the *duende* of Zaragoza, a female voice that answered questions through a stovepipe. From the first days attention centered on a servant girl, Pascuala Alcobet, who observers suggested might be a spiritist medium. Both the head of the Zaragoza insane asylum and the son of Ramón y Cajal gave credence to the capacity of mediums for psychokinesis. For two weeks in late 1934 the press of all stripes, even the *Times* of London and Fox Movietone News, featured the Zaragoza spirit. Famous psychics visited the site; theosophists went from Madrid and Barcelona; priests sprinkled holy water; the residents of the building went to the shrine of El Pilar to confess, just in case; and a whole busload of observers went from Bilbao. The civil governor eventually judged that the servant girl had produced the voice as "unconscious, hysterical ventriloquism." *El Pueblo Vasco* did not fail to compare the Zaragoza duende with the apparitions at Ezkioga. "The spirits in each case take a different form and use a different technique. But almost never does it turn out that the spirit exists."[47]

But just as freethinkers made fun of Catholic apparitions, Catholics mocked the esoterica of the freethinkers. The correspondent of *Euzkadi* from Orio liked the enthusiasm Ezkioga aroused and contrasted the piety of the Basques with the "dissolute ideas, hatred of the church, impiety, and irreligion" of the Spaniards. The impious, he wrote, "pretend not to believe in God or his church, and at the same time lower themselves in their beliefs and practices to the most absurd black magic and the most extravagant monstrosities and aberrations." Similarly, Rafael Picavea in *El Pueblo Vasco* pointed out the inconsistency of an anticlerical who opposed the Ezkioga prayer sessions yet attended the spiritist séances of a barber in Irun.[48]

Both Catholics and spiritists were searching for meaning in death as well as contact with dead relatives and friends. Both believed in apparitions of the dead and both admitted access to higher entities. According to a Spanish Dominican, spiritism was popular because of "the natural desire to explore the mysteries of the afterlife and to communicate with dear ones that death has taken away." The English Jesuit Herbert Thurston pointed to the convergences, citing persons who converted to Catholicism after séances with saints as spirit guides. Spiritist writers held that what passed for seers among Catholics, including Christ himself, were powerful emissaries who came to help the living from the land of the dead. A French spiritist held that Jeanne d'Arc was a medium and a messiah, one of those who "always come at moments of crisis."[49]

The similarity between Catholic and spiritist beliefs meant that spiritism was an easy way either to explain the Ezkioga phenomena or to dismiss them. A priest in rural Catalonia thought that Salvador Cardús and his wife were spiritists, "very bad people" who had "magnetized" Anna Pou i Prat. Villagers vandalized their automobile for provoking the girl's madness. Another priest lumped spiritists and Masons together with Ezkioga and Soledad de la Torre as part of a conspiracy. When Padre Burguera was forced to address the question, he distinguished the willful tapping of the devil's powers in spiritist or Masonic sessions from the almost routine, unbidden tempting of the seers by the devil in the course of their visions. He invited those who believed that Ezkioga was spiritism to compare the spiritist sessions at the Club Náutico in San Sebastián with an Ezkioga vision.[50]

The assertion of the Bermeo soul in 1924 that there was no hell points up a basic change in ideas about the other world. In the nineteenth and early twentieth century on both sides of the Atlantic there was a concerted challenge to rigorist notions of a vengeful God. The spiritists denied that hell existed at all. Generous Catholic theologians argued that God was merciful and good and sent very few people to hell. The Sacred Heart of Jesus itself was at its origin a message that God was merciful. Marie Thérèse Desandais, "Sulamitis," placed mercy and love at the center of her revelations.[51]

Liberal commentators reacted sharply to the dire and grim side of the visions at Ezkioga. And the people of the Goiherri had radically differing reactions when told by child seers that so-and-so was in hell or would go there. A split between followers of a relatively severe deity and followers of a relatively benign deity seems to have run right through Catholic society from top to bottom. A disposition toward mercy or justice, generosity or rigor, was probably one of the key ways people were (and are) different from one another. Juan de Olazábal of *La Constancia* published a notorious editorial explaining the disastrous floods of 1934 as God's punishment on farmers who worked on Sunday. He was a kind of captain of the rigorist side; Rafael Picavea of *El Pueblo Vasco* could not believe that "his" Virgin would frighten people in visions. He was a leader of the more liberal contingent. Antonio Amundarain was on the former side, his assistant Miguel Lasa on the latter. Padre Burguera was clearly a rigorist, but Raymond de Rigné and Marie-Geneviève Thirouin, who advertised her poems as "dedicated to all the souls who seek God in love and not in fear," were on the generous side.[52]

14. THE END OF THE WORLD

HE FUTURE of mankind as a whole, the end of the human adventure, and the merging of heaven and earth greatly preoccupied elderly believers in the Ezkioga apparitions in the 1980s, but these themes were entirely absent from the visions in July 1931. The ancient apocalyptic tradition entered the Basque visions only gradually. The vision messages at Ezkioga seemed to evolve according to four principles: (1) they became more universal and less local; (2) they became less fixed in time; (3) they became more dire as the visions became less popular; and (4) they converged on preexisting prophecies.

The apocalypse was the vision theme linked least to time and place. This theme emerged at the end of a sequence that had begun with meanings bound to the social and political climate of the Basque Country and the summer of 1931. The same process occurred at Limpias, where people understood the Christ's motions first as the sign for a shrine for Cantabria, then as a Lourdes for Spain, and then briefly as a new Jerusalem that heralded the social reign of Christ. In both cases, as time passed and people came from farther and farther away, messages and meanings had to accommodate timelessness and serve distant believers.

For all its dark drama, the apocalypse emerged at Ezkioga only after the church and the great majority of Basques had rejected the visions. In the balance of human hopes and fears among supplicants to the Virgin of Ezkioga in 1931, the healing of a retarded boy, the danger of a civil war, the peaceful afterlife of a sinful father, and the excitement of new movements of piety outweighed notions of catastrophic divine punishment or the imminent arrival of heaven on earth. By isolating apocalyptic messages in this chapter I necessarily distort the variety in any particular vision session. The indications seers provided about last times came along with others about the here-and-now.

Experts at Ezkioga influenced the content of the apocalyptic messages. They did so by asking questions, by giving the seers books, and by transcribing in their own way what the seers said. We can determine when the messages began, which seers produced them, and which believers influenced them. What emerges is a pattern for one particular way people recycle and renew high traditions.[1] Believers induced millenarian projects in seers who at first felt they had substantially different missions. The inquisitors of the Early Modern period inculcated the peasants in Gipuzkoa and Navarra with learned ideas and converted these people into denouncers and confessants of lascivious, flying witchcraft. In both cases the intelligentsia transmitted their ideas unwittingly. In neither case, however, were those who absorbed the ideas passive. Consciously or not, children and subordinate adults quickly took advantage of the opportunities the new patterns offered.

In both apparitions and witchcraft absorption of learned concepts was facilitated by prior beliefs in the receiving rural society. In the seventeenth century rural folk already had knowledge of the ways they could use sorcery to harm or to help one another, and the learned model of witches in covens who served the devil was an extension of that system. At Ezkioga the seers moved from the idea of chastisement of those opposed to the visions to the kind of chastisement of sinners throughout the world that they had learned in catechism and then on to details of the last times.

APOCALYPTIC TRADITION AT THE TIME OF THE EZKIOGA VISIONS

The Last Judgment is a notion Catholics reaffirm in every mass: "I believe that Jesus Christ rose up to Heaven and is seated on the right hand of God the Father Almighty. I believe that from there he will come to judge the living and the dead." The catechism in use in the diocese of Vitoria provided a reason for the Last Judgment and distinguished it from the judgment of individuals

"He will come to judge the living and the dead." Catechism poster by Ramón
Llimona, Barcelona, 1919. Courtesy parish of Taganana, Tenerife

after death, but it provided no specifics about when the Last Judgment would occur.

143. Q. When will Jesus Christ come to judge the living and the dead?
A. Jesus Christ will come to judge the living and the dead at the end of the world.

144. Q. What is the trial called in which Jesus Christ will judge all men at the end of the world?
A. The trial in which Jesus Christ will judge all men at the end of the world is called the universal judgment.

145. Q. Will there be, then, more than one judgment?
A. Yes, there will be two judgments: one individual, right after the death of every person, and another universal, at the end of the world.

146. Q. Why will there be a universal judgment?
A. The universal judgment will be to confound the bad and glorify the good, and show the triumph of the justice of God.[2]

This vagueness about the timing of the Last Judgment, the sensible result of centuries of mistaken predictions, has been difficult for some Christians to accept. They have tried to reconcile the many references in the Old and New Testaments and assemble them into a program for the future. Additional prophecies by "holy" persons have complicated an already confusing task. Prophetic literature proliferated especially in periods of religious trial, political or social revolt, and military defeat.[3]

In the wake of the French Revolution, prophets in nineteenth-century France like Mlle. Le Normand, the farmer Thomas Martin, Eugène Vintras, the children of La Salette, and Joseph Antoine Bouillan revived medieval traditions of the coming of a great monarch, thus comforting ultraroyalists looking for a return to the Old Regime and ultra-Catholics looking to the pope as a temporal power. Visionaries from other countries like the Lithuanian Pole Andrzej Towianski, the Italian David Lazzaretti, and the Spaniard José Domingo Corbató found comfort and inspiration in France.[4]

The *Voix prophétiques* of the Abbé J.-M. Curicque had great success in France because of the fall of the Papal States and the French loss of the Franco-Prussian War in 1870. The prophecies in this book were the main source for similar collections in Spanish by Corbató in 1904 and the Chilean priest Julio Echeverría in 1932. Padre Burguera used Corbató, and Antonio Amundarain used Echeverría. The Corbató work in turn was the basis for Enrique López Galuá's in 1939, which in turn provided material for the work of Benjamín Martín Sánchez in 1968.[5]

One strain of this prophetic tradition, the reign of the Sacred Heart, was particularly respectable in twentieth-century Spain, perhaps because the Jesuits promoted it. Its origin lay in "promises" the French nun Marguerite-Marie Alacoque had received in vision between 1672 and 1675, especially: "This Sacred Heart will reign in spite of Satan and of all those whom he convokes to oppose it." The "social reign of the Sacred Heart of Jesus" became a central theme of the pilgrimages to Paray-le-Monial in Burgundy in the last quarter of the nineteenth century. The idea of this reign spread through international Eucharistic congresses. Padre Bernardo de Hoyos in 1733 had connected this expected reign more specifically to Spain. At the time of the visions of the Christ of Limpias in 1919, commentators inside and outside the country speculated that the Christ's movements were a sign that the reign was approaching. In the twenties and thirties the notion gave a sharp focus to the phrase in the Our Father "thy kingdom come." Amado de Cristo Burguera was counting on the arrival of the reign of the Sacred Heart; he had received the idea for his great work at Alacoque's vision site at Paray-le-Monial. And the reign of the Sacred Heart played a central role in the false prophecies of María Rafols. In the prophecy that María Naya discovered in January 1932 the Sacred Heart himself told Rafols that the document would be found "when the hour of my Reign in Spain approaches." So it is not surprising that Christ's reign—just what that meant was unclear—became part of the Ezkioga visions and the scenarios the seers described for the end of time.[6]

The end of the world was of particular interest for many Integrists or Carlists. *La Semana Católica* of Madrid recalled that the energetic archbishop and founder of the Claretian order Antonio María Claret had said the world would end around 1930. The magazine also cited an alleged apparition of Pius X in which he said there would be calamities within ten years. In 1923 a canon of Jaén, who agreed with Claret, thought the growing ascendancy of the devil and the apostasy of nations, including wise men, politicians, writers, spiritists, and "twenty million socialists and communists in international collusion," were signs the end was near. He speculated on the different phases that would take place after the coming of Christ—his reign, the millennium, the Last Judgment. And he hoped the dictatorship of Primo de Rivera would delay the apocalyptic catastrophe so that the rest of the world felt its effects first. Writing in January 1931 about an impending worldwide cataclysm, Antonio Amundarain saw the Aliadas as victims who offered themselves to God to avoid the end.[7]

Short-term prophecies came in tracts, broadsides, and leaflets, such as the prophecies related to World War I and the Spanish military setbacks in Morocco. This literature—the Rafols prophecies are prime examples—received a fresh impetus in 1931 with the burning of convents and the separation of church and state. Apparitions of the Virgin, however, provided a more direct way to know the future. The Integrist newspaper *El Siglo Futuro* thought that the Virgin appeared at Ezkioga as at La Salette to warn of a civil war that was a chastisement from God: "Here too the Most Holy Virgin prophesied catastrophes, here too, by means of her faithful servants, male and female, she preached penance to the Spaniards."[8]

The supposed secrets of Mélanie of La Salette, first published in 1871, circulated widely in Spain. The Ezkioga apocalyptic visions eventually converged on this text. The most relevant passage is as follows:

> Paris will be burned and Marseilles swallowed by the sea. Many great cities will be leveled and swallowed by earthquakes. It will seem that all is lost, you will see only murders and hear only the sounds of weapons and blasphemies. The just will suffer greatly; their prayers, their penance, and their tears will rise to heaven, and all the people of God will ask for pardon and pity and will ask for my aid and intercession.
>
> Then Jesus Christ, through a miracle of his justice and his great mercy for the just, will order his angels that all my enemies be put to death. Suddenly, the persecutors of the church of Jesus Christ and all the men given over to sin will perish, and the Earth will become like a desert.
>
> Then peace will be made, the reconciliation of God with men. Jesus Christ will be served, adored, and glorified. Charity will flower everywhere. The new kings will be the right arm of the Holy Church, which will be strong, humble, pious, poor, zealous, and imitate the virtues of Jesus Christ. The Gospel will be preached everywhere, and men will make great advances in faith because there will be unity among the workers of Jesus Christ and men will live in the fear of God.[9]

These macrothemes filtered into the Ezkioga messages in the following sequence: (1) a great miracle; (2) a chastisement, which seers predicted first as local, then as universal; (3) an ever more elaborate program for the end of times that subsumed both miracle and chastisement.

THE MIRACLE

Some observers associated the first visions with the apocalypse because of the bright light around the Virgin and the number of stars around her head. Many seers saw twelve. In October some witnesses mentioned a moon under her feet. The relevant passage is Revelation 12:1: "A great sign appeared in the sky, a woman clothed in the sun, with the moon beneath her feet and a crown of twelve stars above her head." But the resemblance with the woman in Revelation went no farther than this. The woman the seers described at Ezkioga was not pregnant and crying out with the pains of childbirth. The elements they saw were widely available, especially in prints derived from the paintings of Murillo.

Nevertheless, republicans presumed very early that the visions would take an apocalyptic turn. In this assumption they turned out to be better prophets than many of the seers. Writing in his national column for July 19, Antonio Zozaya pointed out that in order to be credible the visions at Ezkioga would have to develop a general message, as at La Salette or Lourdes. Three days later the deputy for Logroño, Isaac Abeytua, warned that the clergy would manipulate apocalyptic imagery to rouse the peasants:

> If we pay heed the preaching of contemporary prophets—Jeremiases and Isaiahs . . . the end of Spain and the end of the world are at hand. Every day the terrified "rubes" [*jebos*] claim this in their pulpits, the Basque social center, or the street. We must be prepared for the day of the apocalypse. The Antichrist is already, now, on the way to the Basque Country, and you have to be armed against him, or against his allies, who are the civil governors, the town councillors, the provincial deputies or those of the Cortes, and all the authorities of the Republic.
> The Basque-Navarrese prophets place little trust in the traumatic effects of the angelic trumpet. They need and ask for the protection of fanaticized country folk, the grandsons of those who fought on the Carlist side.[10]

In late July and August at Ezkioga the visions of angelic hosts holding bloody swords or fighting on the mountain ridges toward Castile did indeed have an apocalyptic flavor. But as Abeytua suggested, this was an apocalypse of a local variety for the benefit of Spanish and Basque Catholics; the seers mentioned no consequences wider or more lasting than the reconquest of Spain from the Second Republic. Nor was there any hint of the end of time in the miracle the seers announced for July. What people expected on July 12, 16, and 18 and into August was the Virgin's sign that the visions were real, a "proof of her power" for all those present. The alternatives people suggested were a vision of the Virgin that everyone could see, some act of God that was counter to nature, or a miracle through a given person.[11]

Not until early October did the seers offer a more complete scenario for the miracle. Patxi Goicoechea explained the scene first about October 1, and the girl from Ataun repeated it to the Catalan Salvador Cardús four days later.

> The Virgin will appear with three angels and with a half moon at her feet and an extraordinary light that will light up everything around, the entire mountain. Twenty meters away will appear walls and from all four sides (or directions) the Virgin will be seen. Saint Michael will come down on a white horse and explain the reason for the appearance in this place. The miracle will begin at a quarter to five in the afternoon and will end at eleven at night. The walls will remain as a sign for what has to be done in this place.[12]

In *El Pueblo Vasco* Rafael Picavea made fun of the white horse, suggesting that Patxi had confused Saint Michael, patron of Basque Nationalists, generally depicted on foot, with Saint James the Moorslayer, the aggressive equestrian version of the patron of Spain, a disquieting thought for Basque patriots. Raymond de Rigné pointed to another alternative, the first of the four horsemen of the Apocalypse: "I saw, and behold, a white horse, and its rider had a bow; and a crown was given to him, and he went out conquering and to conquer" (Rev. 6:2). But here too the allusion seems forced, as the seers did not speak of a bow, a crown, or the other three horsemen. Whatever apocalyptic imagery the miracle included was more decorative and dramatic than substantial.[13]

When Patxi began to have overtly political visions at the end of July 1931, he reserved some of what he saw. A Catalan priest at Ezkioga the next week wrote that Patxi "was the keeper of great secrets." Other seers began to have secrets as well, perhaps because after August 1 the priests asked them, "Did she tell you to keep any secrets?" The girl from Ataun "says she speaks with the Virgin, keeping all the secrets to herself." On August 7 Patxi "asserted that he knows many things but will tell them to absolutely nobody." Benita was keeping secrets by mid-August. And by the end of the month the practice was general.[14]

My initial reading of this secretiveness was that the seers' reticence was simply a strategy to avoid having to give vision messages and an easy way to gain importance. Seers at La Salette, Lourdes, and Fatima also had secrets, and by August at least some of the Ezkioga seers would have known this. But secrets in visions starting with La Salette were not only "a locus of power" but also "carriers of apocalyptic expectations." It could be that some of the seers were already incubating more apocalyptic themes in the summer of 1931. In any case the mere existence of secrets whetted the appetites of those who hoped to find out about the proximity and dimensions of eternity, and their questions alone would have pushed the seers along.[15]

Patxi Goicoechea of Ataun was the chief innovator in 1931 for political messages, for physical behavior in visions, and in creating a sacred landscape. He was also the first to put into words the divine chastisement implicit in the vision tableaux. After all, the blood he saw on the swords of the angels belonged to somebody, presumably the wicked people who burned churches. But by early August he was predicting "great calamities for the sins of mankind." A writer for the Pamplona Integrist newspaper was the first to tease this statement from him. The title of the article, "The seers of Ezquioga; are we approaching the beginning of the end?" left ambiguous whether the end was that of the visions or that of the end of the world. Other seers, however, did not follow up this theme immediately. What chastisement they foresaw in the first month seems to have been divine punishment in the form of a civil war or the striking down of individual sinners, not some great winnowing at the twilight of mankind.

Patxi does seem to have been edging toward the larger theme. In his vision on September 5 he saw the Virgin with a sword in one hand drop a ball from the other "that struck against the earth, throwing up sparks when it broke; the angels shuddered when they saw that the Virgin let the ball drop."[16] He told a reporter in late August or early September that within six months some people would be burned to a crisp (*carbonizados*) at Ezkioga. Cardús was quick to pick up on this, and when Ramona Olazábal told him people "should have their bags packed" (*tener la maleta preparada*, in this case meaning be spiritually prepared) at the time of the great miracle, he deduced that the great miracle would involve some kind of punishment for those disbelievers present. In her vision of September 20 María Agueda Aguirre understood that some more general signs—the darkening of the sky, the spinning of towns, and earthquakes—were a part of the miracle, proof of the reality of the apparitions.[17]

Particular, specific chastisement would befall diocesan and government opponents. Some seers also used these threats against disbelievers in their towns. The town secretary Pedro Balda gave me a rundown of people killed or injured in and around Iraneta in what he considered chastisements for opposing the local seer Luis Irurzun. It included the parish priest, family members of two Iraneta seminarians, and the parish priest of Ihabar.[18]

But, especially after the church rejected Ramona's miracle, some seers began privately to announce a more general punishment. The Catalan García Cascón wrote on October 31:

Some female seer has said that the Most Holy Virgin has announced a tremendous chastisement of three important cities in Spain, if they do not change their ways. It will consist in the total disappearance of the three cities. That is, they will be reduced to ashes in a moment, in an instant, in a flash. One of these cities appears to be improving, and there is the impression that it may be freed from the punishment. But for now the others will not escape.[19]

When the Aulina/Gemma group went to Ezkioga in mid-December 1931, virtually all the seers they talked to predicted a more general chastisement. For instance, they found Rosario Gurruchaga pleading to the Virgin in Basque to spare her town, Urrestilla. Cruz Lete was the most insistent.

He told us that the chastisement was imminent; that it hangs by a thread. He told me that it could even begin at that very moment, and he and I could be designated to die. But that for those in the grace of God it will not be a chastisement, but rather a reward, because to go to heaven is always a reward.

Lete pleaded to the Virgin to allow people time to repent and confess, but he implied they would not be so lucky. This lack of a sign was in line with a shift to a chastisement that would come before rather than after the great miracle.[20]

Lete also said that the entire earth would wear mourning. This was the first hint of another shift: the chastisement would now be worldwide, and hence the

Virgin meant her messages for the world, not just the Basque Country or Spain. There will come a day, Lete reported the Virgin as telling him,

> if we do not want to hear her voice, that we will find corpses and more corpses, and I say to you that what makes me most sad is when I think that so very many souls will be damned. As on a day when the snow is falling hard, so will the souls fall into hell.[21]

Circumstances that favored this dire message included the worsening relations between church and state, the discrediting of the seers in the general public and the church hierarchy, and the presence of a more homogeneous Integrist or Carlist following with a taste for cataclysm.

But the idea was hardly new. Basque verses of the nineteenth-century poet Xenpelar and others about the terrors of the Last Judgment provided a resonance with and perhaps a source for some of the seers' imagery of destruction. People sang these verses during the shucking of corn in the winter. Missioners in sermons described God's chastisement and judgment vividly. There was also a certain amount of loose apocalyptic language in devotional literature, even that destined for children. Writing in March 1931 in the children's magazine that later reported the Mendigorría visions, an educator warned of a chastisement because of lipstick and close dancing:

> If these boys do not become more manly and these girls do not make themselves more virginal . . . to cure and redeem them God has at his disposal fire, plague, famine, and bolshevism, which are scourges to welt the flesh of these wild virgins and to make the eyes pop out of so many degenerate males.[22]

Moreover, there were Basque traditions about the end of the world. The accepted signs were that there would be a store in every house, the roads would all cross, and the threshing board would be in the oven. That is, everything would be out of place. No doubt this is how some people felt things were after the burning of religious houses and the expulsion of the Jesuits. During the Carlist Wars there was a prophet named Hilario de Intxausti in the town of Mendata (Bizkaia). A mysterious old lady revealed the future to him: a victory of the Liberals, a war with the Moors, a civil war, a subsequent war with the Moors, the river of Bilbao red with blood, Bilbao destroyed, the general abandon of Christian doctrine, and then the re-Christianization by rural people led by the pope. Intxausti also announced that the end of the world was at hand with the Second Coming. In 1877 a prophet in Durango proclaimed the Last Judgment imminent and told people to abandon worldly goods and do penance. He said he was Saint Joseph, his wife was Mary, and his boy the child Jesus and he had frequent communication with the angels. His substantial following accompanied him in rosary processions. All of these sources prepared people for the messages of chastisement at Ezkioga in the winter of 1931–1932. The Catalans quickly matched the messages with the prophecies of Madre Rafols, which said that 1932 would be a year of persecution and 1933 a year of triumph.[23]

In December and January seers began to see particular ways the chastisement would occur. Not surprisingly, it was Benita Aguirre who first drew these elements together. She did so in a matter-of-fact conversation after dinner with a Catalan expedition in the Hotel Urola of Zumarraga on 8 February 1932. When those present pointed out the gravity of her words, she "declared solemnly that the Mother of God expressly authorized her to make this statement."

THE CHASTISEMENT
DECLARATIONS OF BENITA AGUIRRE

Viva Jesús

The Virgin does not send the chastisement; rather Jesus does. There will be earthquakes, beginning abroad and then occurring in Spain. During the earthquake in Santiago de Cuba seven persons were martyrs, that is, they offered up their lives. This does not mean that the rest were not saved, but they were not martyrs. Fire will destroy the crops. In the first year, that is, the first stage, there will be famine, in the second year, more famine, and in the third year many people will die of hunger and many will be damned. In the fourth year, that is, in the fourth stage, there will begin to be harvests, and then things will begin to get better.

The smallest children will die in their mothers' arms before the famine. The bad people who do an act of repentance in the moment of death will not be helped—it will not be an act of contrition because it will not be done out of repentance but because of fear of eternal punishment, and if previously they would have gone to purgatory, then they will go to hell and be damned eternally, because in another period which was not the chastisement, that act would have been one of contrition, but now it will be one of attrition [atrición].

The Virgin has said she will concede everything asked of her, except [that she will not stop] the chastisement, because without chastisement the world cannot be saved.

The day will come in which when we take a step we find a corpse, and when we take another, another corpse, so that they will make paths among cadavers as they make paths when there is snow.

This is the last century.

Paris will be carbonized, Marseilles swallowed by the sea, Barcelona has upon it charges [cargo, here meaning indictments for crimes against God] worse than San Sebastián, so that if the Catalans had not gone to Ezquioga, now the inhabitants of Barcelona would be in heaven, hell, or purgatory, because Barcelona would already be leveled. Catalonia has upon it many charges, Madrid, Barcelona, San Sebastián, and Málaga are those with the most charges. The smallest towns are those that have fewer charges than the big ones.

There will be a war bigger than the European one, in which Saint Michael will cut off the heads of the wicked.

The chastisement is for the good of the good people and the punishment of the bad ones. During the chastisement, the rich will be poor, and the poor richer than before, but no one will be very rich.

There will be a great disease, like a plague, and many people will die, and many friars will take care of the sick and some will die. We should ask to die in the first chastisement.

There will be less than half the number of people that there are now. During the chastisement men will be very bad, will forget God, and the few who are good can be easily counted. Then Christ will reign.

During the chastisement there will be no purgatory.

There will be three chastisements and three great miracles.

The Virgin said, after the chastisement the first sword that pierces my heart will make the earth tremble.

Benita says, "He who dies in the first chastisement will be lucky, and I hope to be one of them."[24]

A Catalan present wrote that her "grandiose revelations were in sharp contrast with the learning that a girl nine years old could have, so ingenuous, innocent, and simple." By then it should have been clear that Benita was not to be underestimated. But even for her this was a new turn. This was not a message delivered in trance but a kind of prophecy quite like those in published collections. Benita said to give this message only to believers. Nevertheless, a one-sheet printed version was circulating during Lent. The Jesuit Laburu received one from a family member, who wrote, "I send you this sheet so you can see how they try to frighten the fools who are stupefied by what goes on at Ezquioga."[25]

With its emphasis on the Catalans, Catalonia, and Barcelona, Benita's prophecy reflects her audience. In it the notion of a miracle was almost vestigial. The potpourri of chastisements was made especially grim by sudden death. According to Benita, Jesus, not the Virgin, sent the chastisement. In the Rafols prophecies, spoken by the Sacred Heart of Jesus, it was not Christ who chastised but his Eternal Father. The principle was the same: the divine spokesperson was benevolent; someone else did the punishing.

The secret of La Salette was the source of Benita's phrase "Paris will be burned, Marseilles swallowed by the sea." If the seers did not know about La Salette already, they would have learned about it from pilgrims, such as those from France who in 1932 asked Benita and Evarista if the Virgin had really dictated Mélanie's secret. (Benita said that the Virgin did not respond; Evarista said the Virgin said yes.) There must have been other sources, particularly for the notion of four years or stages. The analogy of corpses with snow reappears in the visions of other seers and may derive from a common origin.[26]

The message clearly referred to the world as a whole. A world war, not a Spanish civil war, was to be part of this chastisement, and the earthquakes would begin elsewhere and only later hit Spain, in accord with the idea that Spain had earned a reprieve. The Santiago de Cuba earthquake had occurred six days earlier (2 February 1932), leaving twelve dead. The notion that some of these were martyrs fit the seers' stance as sacrificial volunteers atoning for the sins of the world and preventing the deaths of others.

Benita's prophecy had great impact, and other seers in February, March, and April 1932 began giving specifics of the chastisement as well. Luis Irurzun offered a variety of chastisements. Most included a military battle led by a sanguinary Saint Michael. One of Luis's versions will stand for many. In this one it appears that the Virgin is speaking.

> First there will come darkness, which will last for three days. . . . People will wear mourning these days . . . Following the darkness a terrifying hurricane will blow out of the northwest, [and] an image of Jesus will appear with a great splendor that will light up all the earth, and great gusts of wind will knock against each other, bringing a storm that will lift people up in the air. That day will be desperate for the bad people, while for my people it will be happy. I will come down with many followers to repent [sic] those who do not believe and settle things. The hurricane will ravage the earth. People will come out of their houses and go from one place to another as if lost. What will become of those who mock and persecute the faith? The power of Jesus with the sword of Michael will smite the evil and the persecutors of religion. The earth will open for many kilometers to cover and bury the persecutors. Millions will fall crushed like snowflakes in the burning hole. Afterward, the world will be in peace, the people content and blessed, because prayer will reign.[27]

As the predictions increased in number and variety, listeners and patrons rewarded some and ignored others. Some motifs appeared only once, like this resplendent image of Jesus in a storm, much like that on the masthead of *El Siglo Futuro*. The hurricane itself was relatively rare as punishment. Conversely, the three days of darkness, which derived from the La Salette secret, the wider apocalyptic tradition, and the Bible itself, became standard content for the chastisement. A rent earth that engulfs the wicked showed up in the visions of other seers; it corresponds to contemporary lithographs.[28]

One of Irurzun's sources was a French seer known as Bug de Milhas (d. 1848). He had predicted an apocalyptic battle along the Tajo river in Spain, a prediction that Irurzun repeated in February 1932. Luis also had access to a Bible in Spanish. One night in September 1933 a bearded man (barefoot, with red cloak, cold and tired, about sixty years old) supposedly dictated a letter to him. The letter turned out to be the Epistle of Saint Jude, lifted from a Bible complete with the commentaries of the translator, Félix Torres Amat.[29]

Ezkioga seers singled out Paris and Marseilles for special punishment, but also San Sebastián, Madrid, Barcelona, Catalonia, Seville, and Málaga. Here we

1 = EL DEMONIO TENTADOR DEL HOMBRE. 2 = EL ÚNICO AFAN DEL DEMONIO ES LLEVAR ALMAS AL INFIERNO. 3 = CASTIGO DE LOS PRINCIPALES PECADOS CAPITALES: ENVIDIA, PEREZA, AVARICIA, SOBERBIA, GULA Y LUJURIA.

"Suffering in hell." Catechism poster by Ramón Llimona, Barcelona, 1919. Courtesy parish of Taganana, Tenerife

hear the voice of the rural people of Gipuzkoa, particularly the Carlist or Integrist variety. Theirs would be the notion of the virtue of the smaller towns and the damnation of cities. For the Carlists Paris was Babylon, the "scourge of France." Paris was not just a mythic place. Basques went there. Dolores Nieto's parents bought her bicycle there, and the freethinking neighbor of the first seers worked as a waiter there. Paris was the quintessential city. Much of the chastisement Benita detailed was from a rural perspective. Like that of La Salette, it had to do with famine and harvests. Her reference to healing friars was particularly appropriate coming from a rural culture that produced friars and felt even closer to them than to the priests it also produced. As in the Vendée rebellion in 1793, these antiurban themes were sharpest at the boundaries between the rural area and newly prosperous towns. In the 1930s the reactionary editorials of the Integrist Juan de Olazábal in *La Constancia* fueled the same antagonisms.[30]

For the Ezkioga seers the local equivalent of Paris was, without doubt, San Sebastián, "focus of evils," epitome of "a life of corruption, vice, and luxury." The seers saw foreigners with red banners invade it, fire ravage it, the sea sweep it away, and a hurricane cleanse it of corpses. Within the generic evil city certain places were especially evil. First and foremost were the beaches. One seer saw Saint Michael "searching the beaches for souls; he has come back without finding a single one." Luis Irurzun accorded special treatment to theaters and cinemas; he saw Saint Michael destroy them with his sword. The Pamplona seer Pilar Ciordia saw the casino of San Sebastián, "cradle of vices and sins . . . swept out by the water to the angry sea." Another woman saw a dance hall on Mount Igeldo burn ("What screams! Look what is going on there!"). But seers also saw the elegant church of Buen Pastor collapsing in flames at high mass, "because it is nothing but a lot of luxury, and people do not go to mass for God, but for show."[31]

Seers also singled out Soviet Russia. Even respected churchmen like Canon Carles Cardó in Catalonia were speculating at this time on the role of Russian communism as an agent of divine chastisement of Spain's frivolous and selfish capitalists. María Recalde said the Virgin told her the bad people of France and Russia wanted to destroy the faith of Spain. And in May 1933 both Benita and a seer in Tolosa foretold Red armies invading the country. But the Soviet Union would fall. Saint Michael took Luis to the "immense plains of very fine grass" of the USSR to see it destroyed.[32]

Benita asked for prayers for the conversion of the Jews, but she (or her version of the Virgin) seemed to consider that atheists were the enemy, not Jews.[33] The seers barely mentioned Freemasons, the other bugaboo of the clergy. Jews and Freemasons seem to have been far from the experience of our rural seers and do not seem to have struck their imagination, as the USSR did. The United Kingdom and the United States appear to have been completely off their mental map.

The last Rafols prophecy said that entire cities would be eliminated but did not say which (at least, the Vatican did not release the names). Many believers badly wanted to know which cities were doomed and asked the Ezkioga seers. Burguera wrote disparagingly of their fascination.

> All questions come back to the chastisement—which, and how many, and how, and when, and where they will take place. We laughed at a certain wealthy Catholic of a northern city who, when he asked about the chastisements, was told that the Virgin had announced that the city would be flooded and swallowed by the sea. With deep sorrow he replied, "Now that I've just bought a chalet on the Concha!"

In 1932 worry about the chastisement may have kept people coming to Ezkioga and kept the visions going.[34]

News of the coming chastisement did not reach the newspapers. The notion was too unlikely for the general public, so believers were discreet. Only in May 1932, after the last Rafols prophecy had rendered chastisement more plausible, did Cardús, for instance, begin to spread the idea in his letters. As he wrote to his Jesuit friend in India: "All this [the chastisement of Spanish cities, Paris, and Russia] we have almost not been able to speak about, because the people would have been scandalized and would have believed even less in the apparitions of the Virgin."[35]

THE REIGN OF CHRIST

At first the chastisement was an incidental aspect of the great miracle. Seers gradually elaborated more and more on the divine punishment as people showed interest. In the same manner notions of what would happen after the chastisement gradually evolved. The first such statement came from the student seer Cruz Lete when, in late December 1931, almost as an aside, he introduced the notion of an eventual holy regime, telling a Catalan: "The only flag there will be after the chastisement will be the banner you have in your hand [a crucifix]."[36] In Benita's and Luis's statements of February and March 1932, the notion went little farther: Christ or prayer would reign.

But when Evarista Galdós delivered her "finished" version of the chastisement to the Catalans on April 5, she had clear ideas of an apocalyptic sequence, including the arrival of the Antichrist, which would lead by a given date to the end of time. Unlike Benita or Luis, she was also able to include in the sequence the great miracle the seers had predicted since the summer of 1931, which she adapted to follow the chastisement. Her audience, like Benita's, was a Catalan expedition in the Hotel Urola.

> The day of the great miracle, at five in the afternoon, the Virgin will appear on the mountain with a half moon at her feet that gives off light

Evarista Galdós in vision at Ezkioga, early 1932. Photo by Raymond de Rigné,
all rights reserved

in all four directions. Saint Michael will appear as well and will explain why the world is so lost, who the seers have been, and what it is they have seen. And this vision which began at five o'clock will last until eleven at night. And Saint Michael will appear on a white horse, though people laugh when they hear this. The Virgin told me that four walls will remain on the mountain, which will be those of the basilica, which will have four towers, and this wooden cross that is on the mountainside will be at the altar.

Of those who are at Ezquioga on the day of the miracle, some will see the Virgin, others only her shadow, and others nothing at all. All will see Saint Michael. In the moment that Saint Michael appears, the Virgin told me, everyone will fall down in terror. The miracle will be seen at Ezquioga but will be noted in the entire world.

On the day of this prodigy Saint Michael will bring a statue of the Sorrowing Virgin, which I have seen and which is about one meter high, and will leave it at the place I will show you this afternoon so it will be venerated in the basilica.

The chastisement, the Virgin told me, will be before the miracle. There will be a rain of fire and a cloud of snakes and sudden deaths. The wicked will be as if carbonized, there will be many dead, and the more one walks, the more one will find. This will be in the entire world, and in Spain less than other places. Saint Michael will cut off many heads. He usually carries two swords, one of fire and the other of blood. What a voice he has! It scares me to hear it.

Many of the wicked will die. Between the chastisement and the miracle there will be little time. The Virgin has told me which day the chastisement will be and which day the miracle, and I have declared it in writing to my confessor in sealed letters that he keeps, and on the envelope is indicated the day he may open them. I have permission from the Virgin to tell people eight days in advance. The Virgin told me that in Barcelona there are many people who believe in her apparitions, and in Madrid the chastisement will be terrible.

The Virgin told me how I will die, but not when. She told me that a person will come from Madrid who has already been here once and will kill me right on the platform. This person will also kill María Recalde and other seers, many of whom will die in María Recalde's arms, and when he kills us, a light will appear above the platform, and as a result of this prodigy he and many other souls will be converted. The Virgin told me that almost all of the seers would die martyred.

She also told me that there will be two hundred fifty seers. There are priests who are seers, although they keep quiet about it. The Virgin told me that here in Zumárraga there is one who has seen her, and there are two in Navarra. The Virgin has said that she appears in fourteen places in Spain. In Navarra she appears in four: Bacaicoa, Iturmendi, Lacunza, and Echarri-Aranaz.

The Virgin also told me that there are twenty-six years left until the end of the world and that the Antichrist is at present eight years and eight months old. That is approximate because she told me about two months ago and I do not remember the exact date. The Antichrist will live for thirty-three years and when he is twenty-six he will begin to work miracles. The Virgin told me where he is from, where he lives, and who he is the son of.

The Virgin says that she has come to convert people and give signs that the end of the world is coming. The end of the world will happen after the miracle. And after the miracle Christ will reign until the end of the world.

The text concludes: "Listening to this statement, in addition to about twenty-five people, were the seers Jesús de Elcoro and the child Benita Aguirre, who added, 'The chastisement of Russia and Paris will be more severe than in other places, and in Spain, that of Madrid.'"[37]

In Evarista's statement there are five themes: the miracle; the chastisement; the martyrdom of the seers; the number of seers and vision sites; and events leading to the end of the world. She laid out a chronology perhaps too precise. The world would end in 1958. But before that there would be a chastisement, which would include the martyrdom of the seers; then the miracle, which would confirm the visions, identify the true seers, and leave an image and the walls and tower of a basilica; then Christ would reign; then in about August 1949 the Antichrist, by then twenty-six, would start working miracles. He would die at age thirty-three, that is, about 1956, or two years before the world ended.

Note the similarity between Evarista's chronology for the Antichrist and that which a canon of Mallorca, Rafael Pijoán, and others deduced from the secret of La Salette:

I do not want to recall here all of the revelations of the Most Holy Virgin, which have been coming true, just that which pertains to the end of time. The revelations of La Salette have the Antichrist born about 1924; and as we know that the Antichrist will start his conquest of the world aged about twenty, and that he will take six years to subdue the earth, and that the persecution of the infernal monster should last three and one-half years, it gives us the total of 1953 [and] one-half, the approximate era of the end of the world, and almost exactly the same as Saint Malachy.[38]

Evarista adopted most of the themes in Benita's prophecy but included original aspects like a cloud of snakes, an assassin from Madrid who would kill seers, and María Recalde's care for the martyrs. She continued in this vein with her visions of black corpses and serpents strangling people.[39]

The radical expansion of the Ezkioga message to foretell events ever more portentous and grandiose seems to obey an inner dynamic common to other apparitions. The messages at Fatima and Garabandal were a graduated sequence of ever more consequential and terrible outcomes. At Ezkioga the seers accompanied ever more frightening messages with ever more heartrending and lengthy crucifixions in a kind of emotional escalation; ever stronger feelings seemed necessary to hold onto believers. And a kind of plot tension depended on the Virgin revealing ever more of her program.

By terrorizing people with the prospect of death without the sacraments, by acting out the crucifixion and provoking their compassion and tears, by predicting massive chastisements, Evarista, Benita, and the other seers also performed a service time-honored in Catholicism: they stimulated the feelings required for repentance. In the Early Modern period public flagellants and penitential processions aroused these feelings in a kind of purposeful sacred theater that onlookers welcomed. The seers at Ezkioga did the same thing for their believers. They evoked changes of heart and love of God, and priests heard the results in confessionals throughout the region. If the seers strayed into calculated theatrics, they may have done so in the belief that the cause was good. While they were elaborating scenarios for the end of time, the Jesuit José Antonio Laburu was gathering material to discredit the vision. But although he had a copy of Benita's statement, he never spoke of the psychology of terror or the apocalypse. The apocalyptic predictions of the seers would have given him powerful arguments against them.

THE GREAT MONARCH AND THE CRUCÍFEROS

From Girona in the summer of 1933 Benita Aguirre revealed new aspects of the end of the world. By that time she too was speaking of the Antichrist (she too said he was born in 1923). But she introduced elements from the prophecies of José Domingo Corbató. Some Spaniards thought that the Great Monarch of the apocalyptic tradition would be the pretender Carlos VII. In Paris around 1900 Corbató, who had fought in the last Carlist War, became certain that he himself was the Gran Monarca and that his court should be in Valencia. While still in Paris, he and his cousin formed a secret society of priests and laymen, the Hermanos de la Milicia de la Cruz, or the Crucíferos. This group was to be a kind of militia for the struggle against the Antichrist. Mélanie of La Salette had her order of "apostles for the last times," the Italian prophet David Lazzaretti proposed the Milizie Crocifere in 1868, the French ultraroyalists had the Chevaliers de la Foi, and most especially San Francesco di Paola (1436–1507), the founder of the Minims, wrote about the Holy Crucifers. Based on the rules of Third Order Dominicans and that of the Minims, Corbató drew up a detailed rule for his order. When he arrived in Valencia, he published the rule in Latin and Spanish. He also issued an organ, *Luz Católica,* for the order.[40]

Corbató soon ran into trouble with the archdiocese, which placed his book *El Inmaculado San José* on the Index in February 1907 and suspended him from saying mass in January 1908. It also banned two other of Corbató's journals, *La Señal de la Victoria* and *Tradición y Progreso*. When Corbató died on 23 May 1913 at age fifty-one he had numerous followers. They included parish priests in the provinces of Huesca, Castellón, and Girona, some of whom believed, I think mistakenly, that he would rise from the dead. They studied and restudied the apocryphal Fourth Book of Esdra; for three more years those in Blanes (Girona) published another journal, *Cruz y Españolismo*.[41] Benita may have met Crucíferos, read their literature in Girona, or obtained Corbató's books from Burguera.

At any rate, in July Benita began to refer to the Great Monarch and in early August to the Crucíferos. She was in some confusion as to when they would become active. She said that at the time of the chastisement the believers would go into the desert, where they would meet a great man who would be the king-general of the world. He would be the Great Monarch and would impose the reign of Jesus. The Antichrist, however, would interrupt this reign. Then there would be another period of the faithful in the desert, followed by the end of the world, which would be at hand, she said, "when women cannot be distinguished from men by their manner of dress." After the end of time would come a period of a thousand years of peace in which the saints would live with the just on the earth. In this period there would be no sin, a kind of paradise on earth.[42]

She introduced the Crucíferos into this program as follows:

> After the chastisements have passed, there will be a single religious order, called the Crucíferos, which will save the entire world by preaching the true faith and conquering souls. The head of the Crucíferos will be a very holy man who, after his apostolate, will die crucified at the gates of Bethlehem. In the last times everyone will speak the same language.

The Crucíferos were the militia of the Great Monarch.

> O Holy Crucíferos, you will destroy the damnable Mohammedan sect, you will put an end to all kinds of heresies and sects in the world, and you will be the end of all tyrants; you will impose silence with perpetual peace for the entire universe world; you will make men holy by force or by will. O holy people! O people blessed by the Holy Trinity! The head-founder will be the great captain of holy people, called the Crucíferos of Jesus Christ. They will obtain dominion over the entire world, temporal as well as spiritual. These servants of God will cleanse the world with the death of an infinite number of rebels. The Chief and Founder of this militia will be the great Reformer of the Church of God.

The first members of the order, she said, would come from the city of Seville, "in which there is much iniquity, vices, and sins." Benita's vision of 20 August 1933, much of it bearing on the Crucíferos, betrays her debt to Corbató. She lifted one section from a prophecy made in 1849 by the Catalan Franciscan, Jacinto Comà, which Curicque published in 1872 and which Corbató took from Curicque.[43]

None of the other Ezkioga seers mentioned the Crucíferos. But Juan Bautista Ayerbe circulated to the Ezkioga believers messages sent to the Crucíferos from Hermano Pedro, the "Jefe-Fundador" of the order. The earliest date on the messages I have is December 1932 and the last is October 1936. They announce chastisements like those the Ezkioga seers predicted. In one message from September 1934 a visionary addresses "Dear brothers in the Sacred Hearts of Jesus and Mary": "As this enterprise [*Obra*] is all very spiritual and secret, you will have to do it in spirit. All under this oath of agreement (which is the equivalent to solemn vows) will be blessed, and if you do not fulfill what you promised, you will be HORRIBLY PUNISHED."[44]

Some sort of group apparently existed. In one message Hermano Pedro reported that he had been enlisting soldiers under the banner of Christ the King at Calle Murrieta in San Sebastián. On 16 October 1933, in terms similar to those of the Ezkioga seers, the Chief-Founder announced that the chastisement had begun. He was in correspondence with Ayerbe, who was sending him the vision messages of Luis Irurzun and doubtless those of others as well. There may have been a female seer who guided the group and passed on orders from Christ to the Chief.[45]

Before the Civil War Hermano Pedro lived in Barcelona, where he acted as a kind of inspired spiritual director among the same kind of people who believed in Magdalena Aulina and the Catalan mystic Enriqueta Tomás. He induced at least one follower, a woman, to give away her belongings and lead an ascetic life.[46] Ayerbe obtained photographs of Hermano Pedro from a Sister of Charity in 1949 and sent one to Sebastián López de Lerena. In this correspondence Ayerbe called himself Hermano Buenaventura and López de Lerena Hermano Nicodemus. It is possible that they had become Crucíferos.[47]

A secret group with a Traditionalist slant or base may have continued after Corbató's death under prophetic leadership in Barcelona through the 1940s. Or, given that Hermano Pedro styled himself the "founder," he may simply have borrowed the name from Corbató and started a new group. The women who cared for Benita in Girona knew about Enriqueta Tomás and may well have known about Hermano Pedro.

In 1984 I asked Pedro Balda who the Crucíferos were. He said he had some of their messages, but he did not know who Hermano Pedro was. He understood that the organization was secret. But he and Luis Irurzun both knew the Crucíferos were a kind of apocalyptic force.

> The Crucíferos are those who are ready when the time comes, with
> the angelic hosts, to confront the major enemies of God and the church.
> Where are they?

Well, I do not know where they are. Personally, I do not place great importance in this. But in an ecstasy in 1933 in Huarte Araquil, the seer [Luis Irurzun] took my hand and said to me, "Crucífero. Today you do not have [power]. But the day will come when you will have power not against one nor a hundred, but against many more." And now, I do not even know where they are.[48]

CONSUMERS AND INTERPRETERS OF PROPHECIES

It is hard to know how many Basque country people were interested in the visions of the end of the world. But people like Padre Burguera, Juan Bautista Ayerbe, and Tomás Imaz dwelled more in the realm of prophecy than in the everyday. We can follow their interest in letters and see how they placed the Ezkioga prophecies in the wider and older tradition, on the one hand, and continually speculated about their applicability to current events, on the other.

Sebastián López de Lerena, the wealthy electrical engineer from Bilbao, wrote a defense of the apparitions in the summer of 1933. For him they announced the end of time:

There [at Ezkioga] and in various other places, the Most Holy Virgin truly appears with the main purpose of preparing the world for the Reign of the Sacred Heart of Jesus, which is imminent and will not come without *enormous universal chastisements,* apparently inevitable. . . . Ezkioga is the confirmation of innumerable ancient and modern prophecies of the greatest authority, and in consequence, it is the precursor . . . of the most transcendental and most moving events of human History. . . . Hence the unlimited variety of material in the visions: . . . [including] announcements of great chastisements, of miracles, of what they call the "Great Miracle," of universal application and which will be the occasion for a general conversion, the Great Monarch, an era of peace before the Antichrist, his reign, the end of the world.[49]

A man in Madrid who was "a fervent devotee of the holy apparitions" wrote a long letter to Ayerbe, which I include in the appendix. It shows how these semiprofessional vision consumers, like modern semiologists, could organize into an apparently coherent pattern whatever ideas came down the pike. The letter reveals the subculture of religious excitement that maintained continuity and gave meaning to religious apparitions and linked them with the mysticism of the convents. This kind of audience needed specific dates connecting the general pattern to the here and now. One seer led Ayerbe to believe, for instance, that the Sacred Heart of Jesus would begin his reign on 25 April 1934.[50] So our seers and their patrons returned to the specific political-historical visions of the first summer of the visions, now rerouted through the complex chronology of the end of times.

Some of the Ezkioga seers delivered a professional level of prophecy. Ayerbe circulated a prophetic update of the Chilean priest Echeverría Larrain, who was touring Europe spreading apocalyptic warnings and spoke at a church school in San Sebastián about 1933. It reads much like the output of Benita.

> He said that the renovation is coming very soon, is imminent. He did not give the date, but he did say that by the year 1935 the world would be completely reformed, within two years or before. A third of the world will die. The Virgin will come with a legion of angels and many priests at her side will absolve those who want to convert.
>
> That then only the good would remain in the world and there would be peace until the end of time. That the church would triumph more than ever. He said that soon there would be a war or a revolution and that in a moment all the communists and soviets would come out to destroy all the nations, trying to triumph by any means, and then would occur the chastisement that God has prepared for us, and in an instant the world would be transformed in peace with the good people until the end of the world.
>
> He said that there is a prince in the desert doing penance who is the descendant of the ancient Bourbons. No one will know where he comes from and he will live and rule from France, but not from Paris, because Paris will no longer exist. It will be destroyed and burned for its great sins and crimes, and more cities as well. It will be a horrible chastisement never been known before, and it will be terrifying. France and Germany are going to get caught up in a war very soon, and soon after will come the terrible chastisement of this unfortunate mankind for the great sins it has committed.[51]

The similarity of Echeverría's conclusions to those the prophets of the Basque uplands reached deserves attention. López de Lerena contrasted the elevated concepts in the Ezkioga visions and the background of the seers:

> These and other transcendent themes are the subject of the daily conversations of the Most Holy Virgin with the seers, very humble country people, all of them honorable, simple, sincere, and with no learning. God loves and takes pleasure in the humble. Nowhere is this so clear as in Ezkioga, and for us it is a new and evident "criterion of certitude."

Such wonder that a peasant or a child knows what she or he could not be expected to know is an ancient commonplace. Thomas Martin, Catherine Labouré, Mélanie, and Bernadette in France and David Lazzaretti and Eusapia Paladino in Italy were recent examples. With the high rates of literacy in contemporary Europe the wonder is often unjustified. Enthusiasts tend to present these adults and children as less tutored, less well-read, and less intelligent than they really were. In my experience persons who have religious visions have a great hunger to understand what is happening to them and they have to respond to insatiable demands from those around them for more and more heavenly material. Those with little background in these matters can receive a rapid and substantial education by carefully reading the books and pamphlets that enthusiasts or spiritual directors inevitably give them.[52] At Ezkioga quick studies like Benita, Evarista, Cruz Lete, Luis Irurzun/Pedro Balda, Pilar Ciordia, and Patxi were the seers who could best satisfy those needing to know about the end of time.

These messages of crusader-like crucifers and apocalyptic battles might seem to be guarded ways of talking belligerently about the internal enemy in Spain and preparing for a civil war. But the emphasis on the Soviet Union and international communism in the contemporary literature about Ezkioga and even a dozen years earlier in that about Limpias points to the deeper perception that a cataclysm was shaking the very roots of civilization. For many Catholics the Cold War began with the Russian Revolution. For them the threat of communism was nothing less than the devil's dominion of the world. This threat was on a different order of magnitude than that posed by Freemasonry or liberalism. Apocalyptic scenarios existed before, but communism gave them actuality on a global scale. For the Ezkioga believers the chastisement was not, in fact, the Spanish Civil War, and the reign of the Sacred Heart did not begin in 1939 with Franco. Indeed, even after the fall of communism the Ezkioga believers still wait for the chastisement of the immorality they see around them.

This prophetic tradition is the basis on which many people make decisions. Thus it is as important for a statesperson, political scientist, or historian to know this line of belief as it is for an economist to understand unlikely economic theories—not because they correctly predict or represent reality but because others use this tradition to take actions of lasting consequence.

For believers in the visions, especially those who stuck with the seers into 1932 and thereafter, these prophecies were deadly serious. I spoke to families of believers in Ormaiztegi, Urretxu, and Portugalete who for many years had special candles and matches ready for the days of darkness, and two families showed me typed or hand-copied instructions for what to do when the chastisement began. The instructions appear to have come from the Barcelona followers of Enriqueta Tomás, who through the 1930s and 1940s developed the cult of the Virgin of the Twelve Stars—alas, another story. Note the open involvement of Saint James as well as Saint Michael:

ON THE DARK AND STORMY NIGHT
(OBSERVATIONS OF ANOTHER [FEMALE] SEER)

1. Daniel Clairin is the devil.
2. About eleven in the morning it will begin to get dark as if there were an eclipse of the sun.
3. In one or two hours the devils will go out.
4. Shut the doors and windows tight, and whoever gets caught in the street must stay outside. For the devil will take advantage of good

people, like family members who call at the door. If the door is opened the devil will come in with them, and all in the house will be lost. So that, without compassion, once the door is shut, open it for no one. The devil will even imitate the voices of people to gain entrance.

5. There will be sounds like an army on patrol, and it will be San Miguel and Santiago who will come down to earth.

6. With the blood of the dead Santiago will mark the doors that he finds closed, so that the infernal enemy may not enter, as with Moses and the Israelites on the mountain of the forefathers.

7. Prepare five candles and five pictures [estampas] of the Virgin of the Twelve Stars, and keep them lit for the forty-eight hours that the slaughter, the screams, and the gases produced by the collision of stars that makes fire in the clouds will last.

8. On Sunday the sun will come out brightly, but because of so much death produced by the collision of the stars, one will not be able to go out.

9. On Monday there will be a strong wind that will clear the atmosphere, and on Tuesday people can go out, and they will see a great many dead.[53]

Many people I talked to recalled that seers predicted the worldwide triumph of communism. An older woman told me, "Our milk-woman said that there would be a river of blood from Izaga to Ezkioga, and that the Russians would be in control." Those witnessing the visions of chastisements remember them vividly:

They saw balls of fire; they wept; it was a spectacle.

They said there would be fire; they screamed; terrible things. We went away terrified.

They were always promising macabre, lugubrious, apocalyptic things . . . The Jehovah's Witnesses say the same things.[54]

Persons in Zaldibia and Urretxu told the same story, which may be apocryphal. Once when seers announced a date for the Last Judgment, a farmer counted up his hens and ate them one by one, so that on the fatal day none would be wasted. The real-estate broker Tomás Imaz gave away all he had. The children of Juan Bautista Ayerbe grew up in Urnieta thinking the end of time could come at any moment. An uncle converted all his money into silver and buried it under a tree. Their mother expected an exodus of Catholics to the desert and had all her valuables in two suitcases ready to leave at a moment's notice. During the Civil War a thief walked off with them.[55]

JUST THREE weeks before the Civil War began, Bishop Mateo Múgica of Vitoria sent a letter to the woman who tended the statue of the Virgin of Ezkioga. In it he condemned with characteristic energy the continuance of the cult:

> As if the bitter tribulations that the Holy Church suffers from the impious were not enough, the so-called Ezquiogista Catholics, who think themselves better than others, year after year . . . continue to violate and scorn sacred dispositions and encourage by all means the presence of believers at the well-known field, theater of "visionaries," of superstitions, of rebellion against the Church. . . .
>
> Now more than ever many go to the field; perform devotions in imitation of those at Lourdes with crucifix and lighted candle; drink and carry away water from a nearby spring, calling it miraculous; carry the crucifix and lighted candles in procession down from the field to the "schismatic" chapel on the highway; make processions in the field with hymns; and pray, sing, and hold their rituals.

He went on to forbid the woman the sacraments, holy burial, or entry into any church as long as she cared for or went into the chapel or went to the field. He threatened to have the decree read in all the churches of the diocese and to excommunicate her if she persisted.[1]

After June 1934, when the Holy Office had backed up the bishop in condemning the cult, groups of believers continued to meet on the hillside, in the house where the image was, at the store in Ordizia, and in private homes. The priest Sinforoso de Ibarguren kept a sharp eye on the activities in his parish and reported all to the bishop. Believers hoped for a reversal. Against the advice of the Catalans, Sebastián López de Lerena, the wealthy engineer from Bizkaia, gathered 1,300 names that he sent to the Vatican in September 1934 in support of a protest he had sent in July. In the spring of 1935 he drew up plans for a basilica at the site; these plans were probably those the believers later showed to the Passionists.[2]

During this period a handful of new seers emerged. Among his trusted friends the Urnieta town secretary Juan Bautista Ayerbe continued to circulate texts of visions. Whenever *L'Enigme d'Ezkioga* arrived by mail, the director of *La Voz de Guipúzcoa* protested indignantly; he blamed Raymond de Rigné for maintaining the cult and eventually precipitated Rigné's expulsion from Spain.[3]

THE CIVIL WAR

From April 1936 on the seer Luis Irurzun of Iraneta had been warning of an imminent military uprising. At the outbreak of the Civil War on 18 July 1936 Gipuzkoa and Bizkaia remained loyal to the Second Republic, but Navarra supported Franco. Luis was visiting believers in Gipuzkoa, but in late August or early September when republican militia began searching houses, Luis decided, allegedly on the advice of the Virgin, to leave Urnieta and cross the battle lines to safety in Navarra. A family accompanied him. Luis described to me how they walked by night and hid in farmhouses by day. They were most in danger after they crossed the front above Ataun and an officer ordered them shot. Luckily the parish priest of Lezaun, who was himself an officer, recognized Luis and vouched for him. Before these troops reached Urnieta, republican militia took Juan Bautista Ayerbe off to a prison ship in Bilbao.

Luis then had to report to Franco's army for conscription and explain where he had been. He told me he went to Pamplona and consulted with a friend, the priest Fermín Yzurdiaga, who was the head of propaganda for the paramilitary Falange. Yzurdiaga signed him up right away, and Luis eventually became aide to the Falangist military commander of Zarautz, José María Huarte. Huarte was a descendant of Iraneta people and believed in Luis's visions; every night at midnight they said the rosary. Luis was in Gipuzkoa in Zarautz (25 kilometers west of San Sebastián) seven months, approximately from early April to November 1937.

Luis told me that after two months together, Huarte put the visions to work. I recount Luis's story here with the warning that I have no other authority for it. It has value at least as legend, for Irurzun had also told the Ezkioga cuadrillas. Franco's forces were having difficulty breaching the carefully constructed complex known as the Iron Belt that defended Bilbao. Huarte told the general staff of the army that maybe the Lord or the Virgin could point where to attack. Luis told me he agreed to ask the Virgin as a measure to save lives:

> The preparations were made. One was General [José López] Pinto, another General [José] Solchaga, I think another was General [José Enrique] Varela, and one more also . . . And [Huarte] introduced me . . . They were there with their wives as well. We prayed the rosary. And indeed, Our Lady came. I know nothing of what goes on around me when I am in ecstasy. And the Virgin indicates to them, "At this point, at that, at that," They had secretaries there . . . When this was all over, four or five days later, just as she had indicated, they broke through all they had to break through; and that was it. It all fell; they took all Bizkaia, all Bilbao, everything.

After six months in Zarautz, Irurzun said, he was arrested by Francoist police in San Sebastián for being a seer. He was about to be taken away and shot when a believer intervened with a general to save him.[4]

There does seem to have been a crackdown on seers and believers in the first months of the Franco government in Gipuzkoa. Raymond de Rigné and Marie-Geneviève Thirouin had returned in July 1936, just as the Civil War got under way, but the Franco regime arrested them after Gipuzkoa fell. They spent forty-five days in the San Sebastián prison of Ondarreta in January and February of 1937, then the government expelled them once more to France. From France Rigné indignantly denounced Bishop Múgica and diocesan officials as Basque separatists and the Spanish episcopate as responsible for the war for not heeding the prophecies of Madre Rafols and the seers of Ezkioga.[5]

The war affected a San Sebastián taxi driver in a different way. He had seen the Virgin twice at Ezkioga in July of 1931 and had had his photograph in the newspaper. When the Civil War started in 1936 he was a marked man among his fellow taxi drivers in Republican San Sebastián. There taxi drivers were generally working-class leftists who were in favor of the Republic and against the church. Anyone who saw the Virgin, they reasoned, would be a Catholic, a rightist, and on the side of the Francoist military that started the Civil War. At a meeting of the transport union, the seer-driver stood up and announced, "What I saw was nothing, and I will demonstrate it now." He fought bravely against the invading Franco troops and escaped to Gijón, going from there to Valencia.[6] The working-class seer from Guadamur, Nicanor Patiño, died fighting for the Republic.

In Republican zones about 4,000 secular priests, 2,000 male religious, and 300 female religious were hunted down and killed under the automatic assumption that as clergy they were subversive. Among them, inevitably, were some of those who figure in our story, both those in favor of the visions and those opposed. The Capuchin Andrés de Palazuelo, who wrote favorably about Limpias and Ezkioga, was shot in Madrid on 31 July 1936, just twelve days after the uprising began. The canon of Lleida Juan Bautista Altisent was killed the same month in Lleida. Gregorio Martín, the parish priest at Guadamur during the apparitions in 1931, was killed in Ocaña on 14 August 1936. Luis Urbano, who opposed the visions of Limpias and Ezkioga, survived only a month in hiding in Valencia and was killed on August 21. On the night of August 22 militia executed seventy clergy and religious by the walls of the the the city slaughterhouse of Toledo. Among them was the dean of the cathedral, José Polo Benito, who had written of Ezkioga as God's offensive. Many of Cruz Lete's companions at Ciempozuelos were shot at Paracuellos del Jarama on November 28. Bishop Manuel Irurita administered the diocese of Barcelona clandestinely from the house of a jeweler until he was found. He was shot on December 12. The archbishop of Barcelona has recently reactivated Irurita's cause of beatification.[7]

On 28 October 1931 Franco's troops, not the republicans, shot the priest Celestino Onaindía as a Basque nationalist. He was a believer in the Ezkioga visions and had been present at Ramona's wounding. The Republic had sent Bishop Mateo Múgica into exile for being a monarchist; now the fascist regime forced him into exile for being a separatist. He remained abroad until 1947 and never regained control of the Vitoria diocese. Among the priests the new military regime jailed or forced into exile and those the diocese reassigned for their Basque nationalist sympathies were some opposed to the visions, like Sinforoso de Ibarguren of Ezkioga, Miguel Lasa of Zumarraga, and the seminary professor Juan Thalamas Landibar, and others who believed in them, like the curate of Itsaso, Joaquín Aguirre.[8]

In Catalonia the Ezkioga enthusiasts who were followers of Magdalena Aulina survived the war fairly well. Aulina benefited from the opposition of the diocese of Girona, and her brother was a prominent republican. Her group sheltered Rafael García Cascón. Leftists in Terrassa considered Salvador Cardús an apolitical historian and archivist and perhaps remembered him as a class victim. He survived the war with all his papers intact. As secretary of the board of the public library and a member of the council of museums, he was able to save the town's notarial archives, most of the parish archives, and works of art in churches and in private hands. He helped many in danger, and priests hid in his house and said mass there. On occasion, he himself had to go into hiding. But leftists killed several prominent Catholics who had taken part in the trips from Terrassa and Sabadell to Ezkioga. As Francisco de Paula Vallet had hoped, many veterans of his spiritual exercises died as martyrs. One was Miquel Marcet, the mill owner who had caused the suicide of Salvador Cardús's father. Marcet had been a local officer of the Parish Exercises movement. The left had long identified him as an enemy; he was killed after being tortured and forced to watch two of his sons die before him.[9]

THE POST–CIVIL WAR PERIOD IN THE BASQUE COUNTRY

The war barely interrupted the day-to-day devotions of believers. Ama Felisa was detained briefly on her rounds on the day rebel troops took Urretxu. And as we saw above, María Recalde was able to use alms from believers for prisoners in the Durango prison.

In November 1941 the Franco government made one last crackdown on the cult, exiling one female seer to Mallorca and ordering an elderly woman from Zaldibia to go to the Burgos town of Villarcayo (although she never actually went). Other believers were to go elsewhere:

> The order is curious. . . . It says, "meetings take place in which mysticism is mixed with politics and things are done that are pernicious for public order even if they are not generally known." Then that it seeks to "cut short all political activity that is forbidden by the law, like Basque nationalism, which is at the root of these meetings."[10]

The government ordered the incorrigible Juan Bautista Ayerbe of Urnieta to Alcaraz in Albacete. His son Daniel, then a priest in a village of Alava, went to police headquarters in Madrid to protest, for his father was being exiled as "an enthusiastic defender and publicist of Ezkioga, which has a clear separatist slant," and his father was anything but a separatist. In Madrid Daniel Ayerbe learned that the initiative had come from the diocesan administrator, Francisco Javier Lauzurica, and that to reverse the order he should go to Vitoria. He did, and the government rescinded the exile fifteen days later.[11]

Throughout the 1940s, in addition to meeting in private houses, believers went to the store in Ordizia on Wednesdays and to the annual mass on the anniversary of the visions in the Passionist church in Urretxu. There the preacher routinely condemned the visions, but the believers were glad to have any mass at all. Numbers were small. For instance, only fifty persons attended the anniversary mass in 1944. On this day the believers held prayers at the vision site and then in a home in Ormaiztegi.[12] The regular seers in this period included Esperanza Aranda, Luis Irurzun, Marcelina Mendívil, and María Recalde. The elderly seer Juana Aguirre of Rentería had died on 4 June 1939. Conchita Mateos entered a Poor Clare convent in 1942 and died there on 10 June 1945. Juliana Ulacia died in Astigarraga on 28 January 1949 and María Recalde in Durango on 10 October 1950. José Garmendia held periodic private visions in San Sebastián in the house of his stepsister; his niece thought some Catalans gave him money. He died about 1961. A few new seers emerged—a man in Bergara who married a seer, and children or adults from Vitoria, Antzuola, Aramaio, Legorreta, and Plasencia de las Armas.

In the mid-1940s a group of believers asked the Passionist Basilio Iraola, who had written a biography of Gemma Galgani, if he would go to Rome to prepare himself to evaluate visions. Strong, ruddy, authoritarian, Iraola was famous for his mission sermons on the Last Judgment. The believers told him they had a mass of material, including vision messages, cures, and photographs. He told Bishop Carmelo Ballester of Vitoria, who agreed to evaluate the material, and Iraola took it in a truck from Legazpi (where, Iraola recollected in 1982, Garmendia was keeping it) to Vitoria on condition that the diocese return it to the believers. Later Ballester told Iraola the verdict of his advisors: "There is one apparition of the devil with an admixture of communism, and no apparition that is true."[13]

When Jaime Font y Andreu became the first bishop of the new diocese of San Sebastián, believers found him slightly more sympathetic. On 17 March 1952 Sebastián and Julián López de Lerena, Juan Bautista Ayerbe, Izmael Mateos (Conchita's father), and Felisa Sarasqueta (a witness to Ramona's wounding) took him twelve notebooks containing photographs of seers and more than eight hundred vision messages. Their six-page statement said that they spoke on behalf of the Virgin. They briefly described the history of the apparitions and mentioned in particular the good deaths of Cruz Lete and Conchita Mateos as religious. And they named fourteen Gipuzkoan companions whom Conchita had drawn to the convent by her example. The statement went into detail about Ramona's wounding, about a seer from Pamplona who had received a medal from heaven, and about the seer in Tolosa who had supernatural Communions. In closing it mentioned the tests of the seers by Carmelites and by doctors and asked that the diocese call for proofs of the visions and permit Catholics to go to the site.[14]

Sebastián López de Lerena described the interview:

> We did not read [the letter] because what our friend [Juan Bautista]
> Ayerbe did was indescribable. He grabbed the papers out of my hands
> and against the will of all of us, he violently jabbered out the text, throw-
> ing in comments of his own that even he did not understand, not ceasing to
> speak in the two and one-half hours that the meeting lasted.
>
> Nevertheless, to judge from the patience and the dizzied interest with
> which the bishop listened to everything that was said and his amiability
> when saying good-bye, we gained a very good impression; he was very dif-
> ferent from what we were used to in the visits with Don Mateo [Múgica].

López de Lerena hoped for a positive result "because otherwise, the catastrophes that we seek to avoid will happen first." By then believers knew that
neither the Spanish Civil War nor World War II was the catastrophe that seers

predicted in the 1930s; no longer did they consider, if they ever had, that Franco was the Great Monarch. Seers learned that Franco would die before the war of chastisement. López de Lerena wrote a friend, "'After the death of [here a blank space, for Franco] will come the world war' appeared in writing twice, and this means that the war will wait a long while because this gentleman is in excellent health, although there may always be unpleasant surprises."[15] Although the bishop did not reopen the case, Font y Andreu allowed seers and believers to pray at the vision site and receive Communion.

Juan Bautista Ayerbe's mad excitement when he met the bishop was not surprising. For twenty years he had put heart and soul into this unearthly enterprise, traveling around the province to transcribe repetitive, rambling vision messages. He dwelt in a secret, enclosed world of Providence and grace, but all the time he was one invisible step away from heaven or worldwide catastrophe. Civil and religious authorities had reprimanded him time and again. Finally, he could speak to the bishop, who could fulfill the Virgin's urgent instructions. At that time Ayerbe was sixty-five years old. Five years later, at age seventy, he died. He fell on ice when going out to mail letters about the visions.

After the war Luis Irurzun married and moved to San Sebastián, where he worked in a factory. But in sessions with local believers he continued to have visions, and gradually in the 1950s and 1960s, as the others died, he became the main seer. A younger generation that could understand Spanish gradually replaced the Basque-speaking country people in the cuadrillas. And as the older Basque-speaking seers died out, their cuadrillas shifted their attention to Luis, who, though he understood Basque, had his visions in Spanish.[16] He was the last of the original seers who kept up semipublic visions, and he died on 5 February 1990.

From Iraneta Pedro Balda continued to send letters about the visions around the world. At the annual dinner of town secretaries of Navarra, he succeeded in recruiting two other colleagues, Santiago Simón Orta of Berrioplano in 1953 and José Javier Martínez Sarrasa of Artajona. Both became dedicated followers of the visions. In their modest ways these men carried on the work that Burguera, Ayerbe, and others had started.

Widowed in 1954, Santiago Simón met his second wife, Juana Urcelay, a believer from Oñati, at the Ordizia vision store about 1956. He recorded the monthly visions of Esperanza Aranda in Ormaiztegi in 1956 and 1957. When I visited him in 1984, he was translating the visions of the Italian seer Maria Valtorta into Spanish.[17]

I went to see José Javier Martínez Sarrasa, known among believers as "the Pilgrim," in 1985 in Barcelona, where he was living with his daughter. He was then eighty-seven years old. During the visions and the riots in May and June 1931 he was the town secretary in Mendigorría, and he later went to Ezkioga as a curious spectator. In 1954 he started a series of pilgrimages on foot to major shrines, first Zaragoza and then Lourdes. Santiago Simón put him in touch with Pedro Balda and Luis Irurzun. A kind of lay missionary, Valerio Babace Hernandorena, himself married to the daughter of a seer, took Martínez Sarrasa to a farm near an industrial town of Gipuzkoa where seven out of twelve children were seers and over thirty different celestial beings appeared. For many years Simón, Balda, Martínez Sarrasa, and five others had regular meetings in Pamplona to pray and to talk of the visions. Babace's brother, Eugenio, was one of the last priests the Ezkioguistas could count on, and when in 1973 Luis Irurzun called for a new picture of the Virgin at the Ezkioga vision site, Eugenio Babace blessed it.

Martínez Sarrasa told me that people built shrines on mountains because mountains are closer to God and that people living in the mountains had visions for the same reason; people in the valley towns were closer to the flesh. He had walked tens of thousands of miles on systematic pilgrimages—first to seven shrines in each diocese in the peninsula, then to a shrine in each village of Navarra, and then to every parish in Barcelona. And he had documented each trip with careful maps and typed accounts. At age eighty-seven he was still walking ten kilometers every day. Had it not been for the apparitions, he told me, there would not be a tree left on the earth. A direct, honest man with luminous eyes, he reminded me of Pedro Balda.

Alberto, a new recruit to the visions, visited these three men in Navarra. He worked in the factory of a small town ten kilometers from Ezkioga. There he met a group of rural believers, and in 1957 after a spiritual crisis he became interested in Ezkioga and attended sessions in San Sebastián with Luis Irurzun. His friends looked askance, as though he had adopted a new religion.

In the mid-1970s there was a bitter strike at Alberto's factory. At first Alberto joined the strikers, and the company fired him with everyone else. But through Luis Irurzun, the Virgin ("La Madre") recommended that he return to work. Eventually the management called him back to work and he went to the factory with two or three other believers, but the strikers stopped them. The management called again and said it would pick him up outside his house. Fortified by the Virgin's promise that he would come through unharmed, Alberto went out to wait in the street. He counted more than eighty persons, many of them longtime neighbors, some on the balconies of nearby apartments, who had turned out to call him names ("awful things that cannot be put in a book") and mock his belief in the Ezkioga visions. When the factory director did not come, Alberto walked his children to school and then continued to wait, peeling and eating two oranges and reading a newspaper under the hail of insults. When after forty-five minutes the boss finally came, women blocked Alberto's way to the car, and one who fell to the ground subsequently charged him with assault. The director had a toy pistol, but the people grabbed it, and civil guards in a Land Rover had to rescue him. Eventually the company broke the strike, and for months afterward the townspeople ostracized and reviled Alberto and his family.

Alberto's is an extreme case of how devotion to Ezkioga could separate people from their neighbors. When he began to know believers and identify with them, he told his wife, "Either we are idiots, we are crazy, or it is everyone else who is crazy."[18] But the converse of this gulf between believers and nonbelievers was the unity that existed among the believers. The notions of family boundaries broke down. The wider believing community had virtually become one big *auzoa*, the unit of rural neighborhood within which Basques help each other in work and prayer.[19] The elderly seer Juana Aguirre died in the care of a wealthy family, one of whose members she had helped to cure. Two poor women seers stayed for varying periods at the farm of other seers in Zaldibia. Marcelina Eraso, desperately poor, passed from house to house, stayed for a while in the family of a seer in Albiztur, and lived for six years with the help of believers in a chapel in Legorreta. And during the war José Garmendia spent nine months in María Recalde's house in Durango. I know of at least three couples who thought that the Virgin arranged their marriages. And warmth and affection shine through the letters that the more literate believers sent one another.

FORGETTING, REMEMBERING, EXPLAINING

Other seers who stayed in the area did not keep up contacts with the believing community; instead, with varying success, they attempted to regain a measure of anonymity. In my progress from town to town I learned not to disturb them. In the Goiherri in the 1980s older people knew perfectly well which persons in their town had been seers, and they respected their privacy and silence scrupulously. In one place, at the start of my study, I asked if any of the seers were now living and people sent me to a man who was a seer's son-in-law. He was quite interested and took me to his wife, the seer's daughter. She was even more interested; it turned out that she had had no idea that her mother, who had been famous throughout the Basque Country in 1931, had been a seer at all. The entire echelon of older persons in the town knew this, but the younger generation, in this case even including the child of a seer, did not. Someone had told her husband once, and he had asked his wife about it, but knowing nothing, she had denied it. I told her what I knew about her mother, and we agreed to keep the mother's secret. I am sure I would have found similar situations elsewhere.

A kind of shame about the visions was general in the region. Before I visited my friend Joseba Zulaika in Itziar, he mentioned to his parents that I was studying Ezkioga. But it was only when I asked them directly that they said they had attended the visions and had known Ramona Olazábal. When in the 1970s I began to look into the matter, the shame had led to a kind of historical amnesia. Joseba, who had attended the Passionist school in Urretxu, next to Ezkioga, had never heard of the apparitions, even though some of his teachers had initially been enthusiasts. Local monographs on the history of Ezkioga and the dozens of other towns where visions took place do not mention the events that made the places famous and drew a million visitors in 1931.[20]

After the first general enthusiasm, people remained perplexed or ambivalent. Belief or disbelief is rarely absolute. More common are degrees of belief, degrees of disbelief. I asked older friends whether Ormaiztegi had been split between believers and nonbelievers. They said no, that the great majority of people were ambivalent—that at first everyone believed, and then people believed and did not believe simultaneously. I often found persons who began by dismissing the matter and by the end of a conversation were ticking off the prophecies that had come true. Most of the nonbelievers, after they relaxed with the subject, wondered out loud, "¿Qué era eso? [What was that, really?]"

Some people found ways to overcome their ambivalence and exorcise the memory of their own enthusiasm. One of the ways they did this was to invent simple, if improbable, "explanations" that cut through the complexity and doubt to a clear conclusion. (This kind of person found similar explanations for the unusual vision states.) Some of the more fetching, if far-fetched, explanations are technological. A contemporary anticlerical writer quite seriously charged that the apparitions at Knock in Ireland in the 1890s were magic-lantern slides that the parish priest projected on the church wall. So for the visions at Guadamur, *El Liberal* of Madrid proposed that the visions were "some apparatus of television which permitted from some secret place the projection over a long distance, by means of waves, the image in question." Similarly for Ezkioga a columnist in *El Día* reported:

> There were those who say that with a great light placed far away, people make the Virgin seem to appear as in a movie. One of these inveterate film buffs said the other day, "How many fools, primitive and innocent, there are in these places. It is incredible that they cannot realize that they can do this with a great spotlight placed elsewhere on the mountains, and do not realize that these days electric power is very advanced and all these things can be done very effectively."[21]

Pedro Balda told me that a general who stopped in the Iraneta tavern told the locals gravely that "they could do all those things by pushing a button in Madrid." And several people wondered to me whether it had been done with lights or was the effect of optical illusions, passing automobiles, or trains.

Other explanations people gave me in the 1980s ran toward "why" someone did it. The "why" explanations seemed to satisfy as well as the "how." The crudest version was that people cooked up the affair to make money. Suspects included local tavern-keepers, the landowner, the photographers, or the Catalans, who would build hotels. ("In my opinion there were some Catalans who wanted to get involved so it would be a success and they could set up hotels and exploit Ezkioga; there was money involved, in my opinion, eh.") The republican press abounded in this explanation in 1931. A more inventive idea came from a local intellectual who wondered whether the visions had been a front so that Catalans could smuggle money out to France. The presence of certain priests led another observer to suspect that it had been "to advance the church, or so that the religion would not collapse." This explanation, with its mite of truth, was made immediately on 8 July 1931 by *El Liberal* of Madrid, which claimed the apparitions were set up by "the priest, of Ezquioga, of Ormáiztegui, or of whatever." This explanation shades into the idea of a monarchist political plot. Believers too created their own reduction of a political nature to explain why the visions failed. Seizing on the explanation published in the magazine *María Mensajera* in 1970, they argue that because the Virgin spoke to Spain as a whole, the Basque nationalists and the diocese rejected what she said.[22]

One way to dismiss the events without bothering to explain them was to refer to immoral behavior among the pilgrims and the seers. Older nonbelievers in the uplands in the 1980s made veiled references to seer pregnancies and couples who would take off into the woods. The saying, derived from a 1930s verse broadside, was still common: "Whether the Virgin Mary appeared at Ezkioga we cannot say, but it is certain along the way there appeared numerous virgins and later Baby Jesuses."[23]

But the quickest way to dismiss the topic, the one most frequent among the less lettered, was to label the apparitions as a whole witch-stuff. *Sorginkeriak*, of course, explained nothing; in fact it was the vernacular way of saying the subject was taboo, a verbal mechanism for repression that left no room for argument. It may be that this mechanism goes right back to 1617, when by an edict of silence the Inquisition ended the witch craze in Gipuzkoa and Navarra.[24]

Bishop Mateo Múgica did essentially the same thing. The final argument by Laburu in his lectures was that the Ezkioga visions were not true because the bishop said so, and who was anyone else to have an opinion: "[Padre Laburu] ended asking that in matters of God people not have private opinions or reservations." A dialogue in Basque printed in *La Cruz* and *Argia* ended similarly:

[Martín:] In the last analysis I do not know what to do.

No Martin, there can be no doubt what you should do. Our Lord Bishop has spoken clearly on the subject. Our duty as Catholics is to follow what he says.[25]

The imposition of silence in 1617 ended public witchcraft accusations. In 1933 it ended public discussion of the visions. But it did nothing to explain either phenomenon and Basques went right on wondering what witchcraft and the visions really were.

A year after withdrawing from involvement in the visions in the fall of 1931, Antonio Amundarain stepped down from his parish in Zumarraga; thereafter he dedicated his life to the Alianza. He died in San Sebastián in 1954. The initial phase of his cause for beatification was completed 19 April 1986.

Francisco de Paula Vallet had more difficulty founding his order for parish spiritual exercises. After returning from Uruguay, he settled in the diocese of Valence in France, and then, when threatened by the French Resistance, he moved to Madrid. There, to the serious detriment of his order, he attempted in vain to convince Cardinal Pedro Segura that the Rafols documents were false. He died in 1947 without returning to the Catalonia where he had been such a powerful leader.[26]

Carmen Medina met Magdalena Aulina around 1935. Carmen became one of Magdalena's patrons, spent long spells at the house, and in 1936 she brought the educator Manuel Siurot to visit. Aulina had even more trouble than Vallet. Manuel Irurita, the bishop of Barcelona, publicly reprimanded her movement, and in 1933 the bishop of Girona, José Cartanyà e Inglés, started investigating it. Because the Spanish republic allowed the organization at a time when there was wholesale killing of priests in the same area, rightists after the war accused the members of being Reds. One pro-Franco clergyman even charged that Aulina was part of a spiritist-Masonic plot to subvert the state:

> At the start of our Movement [that is, at the start of the Civil War], Free-masonry kept a low profile; but the announcements and spiritist groups did not totally stop. The same occurs in Italy and Germany. We raised the alarm. We raised the alarm. Ezkioga and Banyoles have not yet lost their followers. They were not rejected by leftist intellectuals and politicians. These people sneak in through the walls. They are not noticed. First, they spread a false mysticism; then rumors; then, a lack of trust; and finally, rebellion. They sustain, with economic benefits, innumerable secret cells that are like gangrene in the social body and prepare the revolution.[27]

Matters came to a head when between August 1939 and 1941 Bishop Cartanyà denied Aulina and her followers the sacraments. During this period José María Boada died in Banyoles. On his deathbed he refused to renounce Aulina. The diocese would not allow his burial in hallowed ground, in spite of Aulina's appeal to the Falange (Boada's brother Tomás was a high official) and the Franco government. Eventually Bishop Marcelino Olaechea of Navarra became an intermediary between Aulina's Obra and the diocese, which lifted the ban after Aulina publicly admitted her mistakes. Aulina established the first houses of her institute in Navarra in 1943. She founded more houses in Huesca (under Bishop Lino Rodrígo), La Rioja, and then in Valencia after Olaechea became archbishop there. Eventually Rome, in spite of resistance from the Catalan dioceses, approved the order as an all-female secular institute on 6 November 1962.[28]

The fierce opposition Aulina aroused in Catalonia was akin to that Soledad de la Torre provoked in Pamplona. A Barcelona priest said squarely in *El Matí*: "The church never authorized women to act as directors of conscience." Hence the church limited both Madre Soledad's and Aulina's spheres of influence to women. The Aulinas identify their founder more with the battling Jeanne d'Arc than with Bernadette of Lourdes.[29]

Vicenta Marcet had trouble retrieving her husband, Rafael García Cascón, from Aulina's Obra when the war was over. According to family members, it took another holy woman to do it. When the couple went to visit relatives in Bejar, Rafael's aged uncle, a Jesuit, spoke to a saintly nun, Madre Elvira, who people believed subsisted only on the host. He convinced her that the Banyoles Obra was the work of the devil. She told this to García Cascón and he subsequently left the movement. In later years he regularly paid for spiritual exercises run by Vallet's order.

Magdalena Aulina died in 1956 and controversy accompanied her even in death. Vicenta Marcet, who considered that Aulina had divided her family and turned her husband against her, insisted on going to the funeral. When the coffin passed, this normally placid woman stepped forward and shouted, "Witch! Witch! Witch!" For others Aulina was a saint. Anyone attempting a dispassionate biography faces a daunting task. In Catalonia in the 1990s Aulina's institution is just beginning to outlive its long fight for respect and the bitter memory of divided families.

Maria Maddalena Marcucci, the Passionist nun who corresponded with Evarista Galdós and Magdalena Aulina, spent the years 1935 to 1941 directing the construction of a shrine to Gemma Galgani in Lucca. She returned to Spain in 1941, stayed briefly with Magdalena Aulina in Banyoles, and went on to found the Passionist house in Madrid. After her death people learned she was the writer J. Pastor. The Dominicans of Salamanca have published her autobiography and letters. Her beatification is under examination.[30]

The Sisters of Charity of Santa Ana purged the cause for the beatification of Madre Rafols of its spurious aspects and, with the assistance of the historian José Ignacio Tellechea, reintroduced it on a sound historical basis. Pope John Paul II beatified Rafols on 16 October 1994. The complex at Vilafranca is just to the right of the superhighway linking Barcelona and Tarragona.

The bland revelations of Marie Thérèse Desandais (known as Sulamitis) were relatively successful. Rome never condemned them. Based on Desandais's devotion of Merciful Love, the Spanish nun María Josefa Alhama Valera (b. Santomera, Murcia, 1893, d. Collevalenza, Italy, 1983) founded an order of nuns in 1927 and of priests in 1953. Alhama Valera started her religious life as a nun in a small order in Villena which was absorbed by the Claretians. While she was a Claretian, she experienced a miraculous cure and began to have visions. The Claretians brought her to Madrid, and there with some of her companions in 1927 she founded the new order, the Slaves of Merciful Love, in which she took the name Madre Esperanza de Jesús. Because of a vision, she had a large crucifix made, which people immediately considered miraculous. In the early 1930s she set up four houses in Bizkaia and Gipuzkoa. In 1941 the Holy Office called her to Rome for observation. There she stayed on, opening a soup kitchen at the end of the war. People consulted Madre Esperanza as a holy woman and sent her over three hundred thousand letters asking for prayer and counsel. The church is considering her beatification. Pilar Arratia, the wealthy Bilbao supporter of the Ezkioga visions who visited Thérèse Neumann, gave the order all she had and moved in with the founder in Rome, where she died during World War II. The optimistic message of Merciful Love found more appeal in the 1960s, and Pope John XXIII himself visited the shrine at Collevalenza.[31]

The Belgian Catholic activist Léon Degrelle went on to win notoriety as a commander in the Waffen SS on the Russian front. On the last day of the war he escaped by airplane to Spain, where he became a citizen. Though the Belgian government condemned him to death as a traitor, he led a relatively peaceful life in Fuengirola. He was periodically in the news for denying that the Holocaust ever occurred. He did not answer my letter about his trip to Ezkioga—surely a minor episode in a life filled with headlines; he died 2 April 1994.

Fernand Remisch and his friend Ennemond Boniface, the vision aficionados who in the mid-1930s centered their interest on Ezkioga, continued to visit the German mystic Thérèse Neumann until she died in 1962. Remisch died the following year. In 1983 his widow, dying of cancer in a Dijon hospital, gave me photographs by Raymond de Rigné of the Ezkioga seers, her husband's copies of Burguera's and Rigné's books, and the complete set of L'Enigme d'Ezkioga. She told me about her husband's life and asked why I had not come years earlier. No one else cared, she said.[32]

Raymond de Rigné left hundreds of glass plates of the Ezkioga seers in the attic of the house he had rented in France and told his neighbor and friend Simone Duro to look out for them because some day someone would come for them. When I did come it was too late, for they had been broken up and carted off. But Mme. Duro gave me many of the couple's books, which would otherwise have been impossible to locate.

After the Rignés' imprisonment and expulsion from Spain in 1937, they had gone to a receiving center for Spanish refugees in Bayonne. The center placed them in Bidache, about thirty kilometers inland from Bayonne and an equal distance from the Spanish border. There, on the eve of World War II, Marie-Geneviève Thirouin distinguished herself by publishing patriotic verse against appeasement of the Nazis in the national organ of Action Nationale. In 1942 she published a similar poem, reworked, in an anthology of miserable verses praising Marshall Pétain. The couple returned to the Ezkioga area in 1944 and then lived in Madrid from 1945 to 1947. Back at Ezkioga Thirouin completed a movie script and Rigné spent much of his time drawing and making sculptures. He claimed that the president of the United States was very interested in his Mutual Credit scheme and was sure to call him to test it in one of the states.[33] They returned to France around 1950, going first to the French Basque seaside town of Guéthary.

Tracing Rigné and Thirouin in southern France was an adventure. In Guéthary I could find no notice in the town records. Finally I located a retired town employee who recalled that they had caused a lot of trouble. In 1952 he had identified Rigné by his handwriting as the person who had sent an anonymous letter to the town council at the time of the elections. He said Rigné was "twisted," not a bad person, but bad-natured. He sent me on to the Rignés' landlady and to a woman whose daughter had run errands for them in Bayonne, where Rigné had laid out large sums to print photographs.

The landlady thought that from Guéthary the couple had gone to Bidache. There I found the house where they had lived, Mme. Duro, their neighbor, her cache of books, and the sad tale of the glass plates. She said that when the Rignés first arrived, during the Spanish Civil War, people had pitied them. Rigné took a job as assistant to the notary public and Thirouin helped in the nursery school. But they were difficult people. Rigné got into trouble by leaking the notary's secrets—a rich family was secretly paying to maintain some children through the notary and Rigné let the secret out, so the notary fired him. It may have been at that point that the couple went back to Spain.

When they returned to Bidache in the early 1950s to live in a big house behind the church, they were a cross that the town became resigned to bearing. Thirouin spent spells in depression in various mental homes. Neither would stoop to working, so they were very poor. Mme. Duro, who had a kind of exasperated affection for them, says Thirouin did not even know how to sew a button. This impoverished couple nonetheless considered themselves superior to the villagers who were their only source of help, and this attitude did not endear them to the village.

Rigné died near Dax, on 20 September 1956, at age seventy-three. Thirouin wrote news of his death to her friends at Ezkioga.

> On September 8 we had celebrated the twenty-sixth anniversary of our wedding. Twenty-six years . . . and twelve days! But, more than ever, I feel myself his wife, more than ever I must work for him, just for him, making

sure he survives in his work. It was his only ambition, and I must fulfill it. . . . This way this soul so beautiful will begin to shine on a world that is fast falling apart.

She had him buried in his family tomb in Touraine and then went back to Bidache. When she died sometime after 1958, an acquaintance from Bordeaux collected their goods. He was, however, totally uninterested in the Ezkioga material. Mme. Duro threw out the plates and cases of copies of the renamed version of Rigné's book about Ramona.[34]

During the Spanish Civil War the Valladolid priest Baudilio Sedano maintained Padre Burguera in Rome with money from a woman supporter. Sometime after the war Sedano recovered the copies of Burguera's Ezkioga book *Los Hechos de Ezquioga* from its hiding place in Elorrio and stashed it in the convent where he lived. In Valladolid the center of Ezkioga enthusiasm was the house of the organist of the cathedral, and Padre Burguera visited frequently. In the early 1950s, always alert to new visions and visionaries, Sedano took under his wing an eleven-year-old girl seer and her family and with money from wealthy contributors in Bilbao bought them an estate that was the basis for a new religious institute. This new project absorbed Sedano's allegiance and his small salary; once the Bilbao patrons withdrew he begged money from all and sundry and lived miserably himself in order to maintain it. One of his sources of income, however slight, was Burguera's book, which he supplied to a Catholic bookstore in Barcelona. He refused to enter a hospice until his papers were safely in the hands of another believing priest. He died a pauper on 12 January 1986.

After waiting in Rome for a response from the Vatican to his book, Burguera returned to Sueca in Valencia. In 1944 he wrote to the owner of the Hotel Urola in Zumarraga:

> Believe me, María, as you would believe the Symbol of the Faith, that from mid-November 1931, when for the first time I was there and in your house, up to the present, I have done nothing but dedicate myself to the Virgin of Ezquioga. It has been thirteen years of intense work and I have written ten volumes. For the one I wrote there, they tried to offer me *sixty* thousand pesetas *to destroy it*. How horrible! And in October 1933 when I left your hotel, it was because I was persecuted and hunted to be killed, a death the Virgin saved me from, saves me from (for I am still persecuted), and will save me from (I am seeing and I will see the persecutors of the Virgin of Ezquioga go down disastrously to their graves).
>
> I have been twice to Rome, and spent the war there, and the pope, to whom I declared the truth of everything, BELIEVES in the apparitions of the Virgin of Ezquioga, because he sees that everything the Virgin said has come true and is coming true. And to finish: Ezquioga will triumph. My book, which is that of the Virgin, will be approved. In Ezquioga a great shrine

will be built for the entire Catholic world. When? Soon. I know the date. You will see that I am right, and the enemies will be swept away.[35]

That Padre Burguera "knew" the date of the approval of his book suggests that he was still in contact with seers. I confirmed this supposition with his disciple Juan Castells in Sueca in 1983. Castells moved into Burguera's chalet/seminary in 1946. There he helped Burguera to guide a small circle of like-minded persons in the ways of "prayer and penance," as instructed by the Virgin of Ezkioga. By their example and prayers, they hoped to convince others of the truth of the apparitions. Castells asked me if I wanted to be a saint, "because if you want to be a saint, I can show you how; you will live better with fewer things."

His eyes glistened with tears as he told me that Padre Burguera, who had been like a father for him, died on 27 December 1960, at the age of eighty-eight. We were sitting in a prayer room; there were about a dozen chairs along the walls. When Burguera was in Rome, the republicans had burned the books in the house and used it as a school for children evacuated from Madrid. Castells told me there were prayer groups in several towns. After Padre Amado died, they had had other priest directors and priests had come to visit from elsewhere. They continued under visionary guidance.

Until her death Benita Aguirre continued to provide divine information to the group. After studying with women in Girona, she was also cared for by a noblewoman, "her godmother." This lady had houses in Toroella de Montgrí, Barcelona, and elsewhere and took her to see Magdalena Aulina and to visit Lourdes. Benita Aguirre also spent time at Padre Burguera's estate in Sueca and a few months at a school in La Laguna (Tenerife) where a priest from Legorreta was a chaplain.[36]

In 1942 when Benita, about nineteen years old, decided to go to Paris, Burguera opposed the idea, even though she told him the Virgin wanted her to go. In her visions Benita had always emphasized that Paris was a place of perdition. This dispute caused a falling-out between them, at least according to Baudilio Sedano, who concluded that the devil had confused her.[37] In Paris she attended classes at the Sorbonne and eventually married an architect and interior decorator, with whom in the early 1950s she had a child. Around 1955 she separated from her husband and moved to Madrid, found a nanny-companion to live with her, and settled into a comfortable apartment on the Paseo del Castellano. She received financial help and oranges, rice, and vegetables from Burguera's estate in Sueca after her husband died in 1964, and the little household led a quiet, pleasant life. Known as María, Benita took vacations in La Coruña, Vigo, Santander, Salou, and three times in Marbella. Several times she went to Fatima, once to Limpias, and occasionally to Sueca and Valladolid.

From what Benita's younger brother and her female companion said, Ezkioga marked Benita for life. She was devoted to the Virgin and knew a lot about religion. She enjoyed the *Confessions* of Saint Augustine and the works of Teresa de Avila. She went to mass, sometimes at the shrine of Santa Gemma, but not regularly. She did not go to the new apparition sites like Garabandal or Cerdanyola, but once, talking about people who doubted the El Escorial seer Amparo Cuevas, she said, "That always happens; why should she be saying lies?" Benita's brother and her companion agreed that she did not like the church or priests.

> [Her companion]: About priests and the church she would say, "God did not say that. Jesus Christ did not send that. They are men like everyone else. They make mistakes as well."
>
> [Benita's brother]: I heard her say many times: "I have known and I know priests who are authentic saints, who are setting an example wherever they are. And I have known others who with the example they have given and are giving have made it so the Church is where it is now."

She preferred direct contact with God and the Virgin and would sometimes stay up late talking learnedly and obsessively with her companion and a neighbor on the subject. She was also knowledgeable about art and literature.

All this time, according to Juan Castells, Benita supplied the Valencia believers with divine communiqués. When I said this, her companion was perplexed. Benita-María's remarkable self-control was such that in twenty-seven years with her companion she never mentioned anything about her past as a seer. One of her obsessions was the telephone: she always insisted on answering it herself, especially on her deathbed in the hospital. She explained the money from Sueca as coming from her father and godmother. Her companion remembers that one day, years before her death, she burned all her papers in the incinerator of the apartment building and watched to see that the fire consumed them all.

Benita spent some of her time painting, a pastime she picked up from her husband. But she also took a deep and continued interest in those around her. She helped the civil guards in Madrid just as her family had cleaned the clothes of the soldiers in a field hospital in Legazpi. From her window Benita-María could see the pair of guards stationed in front of the Soviet embassy, outdoors in sun, rain, or snow for hours on end. So she started taking them thermos bottles of coffee every day, and she wrote to *ABC* and *El Alcazar* (the latter printed the letter) around 1980, protesting that the men had no shelter in bad weather. The embassy finally put up a shelter.

On the night of the attempted coup of 23 February 1981, Benita was very upset because she was sure the Civil Guard would not do such a thing. The next day she took one of her paintings and asked to see the head of the force, Aramburu Topete. When she was finally allowed in, she explained that she felt bad for the guards, both because of what people were doing to them in her own Basque Country and because of their current predicament, and she wanted to leave the painting as a testimony of her respect. When Aramburu later found what she had done at the embassy, he sent her a moving letter of thanks.

Benita was not afraid of death; many times she said she looked forward to it. On 2 June 1982 she died a painful death of leukemia. She thought she contracted the disease in the many times she donated blood by a primitive vein-to-vein method, for which she was on call at Madrid hospitals. No longer incognito, Benita once more, she was buried in Legazpi. Her mother had accompanied her day in and day out to Ezkioga and was present in many photographs taken during the visions but had let her escape to anonymity when the opposition of the diocese and the force of public opinion became too strong for the family to bear; she died just four months before her daughter.

16. QUESTIONS WITHOUT ANSWERS

THE QUESTIONS

WHAT WILL HAPPEN to me when I die? Why did disaster strike me? What will occur tomorrow? next week? in a thousand years? How did everything begin? How will it all end?

We all want to know more than we can know. From the moment the seers at Ezkioga connected with heavenly beings, people used the new circuit to ask questions. The questions they asked point to problems that the design of the Catholic religion, the political economy of Western society, and the human condition itself raise but cannot resolve. My father committed suicide; is he now in heaven, purgatory, or hell? My husband does not go to church; is he in a state of grace? My son is retarded; can he be cured? My sister is blind; can she regain her sight? Is God angry or pleased with me and my family?

The internal logic of Catholicism governed how people put these questions. And people asked them only after addressing prior doubts: Do the Virgin, the saints, the devil, and God exist? Is the Virgin here? or is this the devil in disguise? Does the Virgin speak to humans? Is this seer really talking to her?

Religion gives order to people's emotions and meaning to their lives. The way any religion does so raises problems even as it solves others. This is the nature of a dynamic system. Normal procedures have unsettling by-products.

Like most religions, Catholicism left unclear where individuals went after death. The partial solution—a purgatory from which most people eventually went to heaven—was not solution enough. For those whose dear ones died suddenly or without absolution or in a dubious state of grace or totally out of the church, it was no solution at all. Survivors yearned for news about loved ones who were in danger of damnation. The apostasy of much of Europe in the Reformation and in the age of progress strained purgatory to the limit. The living knew they had to put the dead to rest. For the living purgatory raised as many worries as it resolved. The living could shorten the suffering of loved ones in purgatory, but only if they knew for sure that loved ones were there and only if they found out what to do. Ghosts came only rarely with this kind of news. Contact with the Virgin Mary was more efficient: she could answer questions about many different souls and could even intervene to help them.

Yet this uncertainty in final destination was to the immense advantage of the church. It could direct behavior by establishing rewards and disincentives with indulgences and jubilees in much the way modern states use tax codes. And uncertainty had an emotional and moral logic. The despair of a living relative at the sure condemnation of a loved one would be too much to bear, and theologians avoided stating categorically that any particular person was damned.[1] Conversely, the salvation of egregious sinners, were it to be known, might reward or encourage sin. So the stipulation of an afterlife organized in thus-and-such a way without certainty of destination served the organization and helped maintain an ethical order.

This gap between what people knew and what they wanted to know was especially troubling for rural Basques. Members of a Basque household were responsible not just for the family dead but also for the household dead. Neighbors had obligations to the dead of neighbors. The living formed a web of collective responsibility for the eternal repose of souls they might not even have known. But the problem is not just Basque, not just from the 1930s, and not just Catholic. People depend on one another and this dependency continues after one of them dies. We find it especially difficult to part with those who die before their time. Writing about a woman she knows, a Galician physician put it this way: "The official explanations about life after death do not satisfy her, and she continually wants to know about the destination and the state of the spirits of her dead."[2]

There are other dilemmas. The scrupulous can never rest easy. Was my confession complete? What did I forget, repress, silence, or half-explain? Was a transgression major? Or was it minor? While priests can give absolution for sins, the possibility of new sins begins the moment you leave the confessional. Priests have various answers to these questions; it depends on which clergyman you consult. And the scrupulous worry that priests make mistakes. So finding peace with God can be hard for the living as well as the dead. Those for whom grace is a minute-to-minute struggle search for relief, and we find the devout wanting to know how they stand straight from the divine.

Is Spain, Catalonia, the Basque Country, San Sebastián, Zumarraga in a state of sin or a state of grace? It is even harder for groups to determine their spiritual standing than it is for individuals. For social bodies there is no sacrament of confession and no absolution. Yet the rhetoric of Catholicism, like that of many other religions, constantly refers to polities as responsible moral units. Since ancient times town governments have made vows, sacred contracts of obligation and allegiance, to particular sacred figures on behalf of inhabitants. The consecration of households, towns, and even nations to the Sacred Heart of Jesus revived this procedure. At El Cerro de los Angeles outside Madrid in 1919 King Alfonso XIII unilaterally consecrated Spain to the Sacred Heart. Some city governments erected oversize statues of Jesus in prominent locations. Non-Catholics and liberal Catholics hotly contested the revival. In 1932 and 1933 non-Catholic town councils removed these statues, most notably in Bilbao. In other places people bombed and defaced them.[3]

In the long history of religious apparitions, saints addressed towns, cities, and nations as moral bodies, offering protection in exchange for devotion. In some apparitions the divinity made it clear that it was punishing the town for its immorality. But there were other visions in times of disease or battle in which the holy figure seemed simply to be providing celestial help and sharing in the travail of the human group. In the eighteenth century Bernardo de Hoyos heard the Sacred Heart voice a preference for Spain; in the nineteenth century Catherine Labouré heard Mary prefer France. Such appearances were rewards rather than punishments. Some Italians took the apparitions in the Papal States in 1796 and 1797 as a reward for massive public penitential processions. The apparitions started in Ancona when the troops of Napoleon were on the point of invading. Subsequently in over fifty towns people saw celestial signs of support—images opening eyes or smiling, candles lighting themselves, holy bodies revolving in their coffins to turn and face the town—all usually after prayers at mass.[4] Given the recurrence of apparitions as warning and as moral support, it is clear that at least in times of trouble many Catholics want to know the attitude of the divine toward human groups as moral bodies.

Was the Virgin appearing to a virtuous Basque Country or to a sinful Spain? Were there sins enough in the Basque Country, with its working-class indifference and sybaritic beaches, to provoke her tears? Engracio de Aranzadi, a devout Nationalist, was sure that the apparitions were signs of divine support for

Euskadi. But the signs were ambiguous: after all, it was the Sorrowing Mother who appeared, and she was in evident distress. Hence the essential, anguished question Ramona Olazábal put to the Virgin on 23 July 1931: "Do you appear because we are good or because we are sinners?"[5] Where do *we* stand?

This yearning for certainty about the intrinsically uncertain applies to grace in another sense.[6] Some people obtain more grace than others. Like the grace from a bishop giving a blessing or offering his ring to be kissed, the blessing from the pope for a well-connected wedding, the *baraka* available in holy bones or special sacred images, or the touch of holy water, holy earth, or a holy twig or leaf, this kind of grace is there for the asking. You can accumulate it. And there is no end to the enterprise: the cup is never full. Visions immediately become a way to garner personalized grace. Many of the Catalan pilgrims to Limpias returned to Barcelona with some kind of glance from the Christ; so too many returned from Ezkioga with a divine smile or a cryptic phrase a seer passed on from the Virgin. Every member of a seer's entourage in every session hoped for some heavenly attention. Those without reward experienced their exclusion with anguish. In daily life there was no way to know if you were accumulating blessings, but at Ezkioga you could know.

Groups seek to know they have God's blessing as much as individuals do. Surely the Aliadas, the Parish Exercises movement, and the Obra of Magdalena Aulina were not the only organizations convinced they had found a special grace from the Virgin on the Ezkioga hillside. Other religious orders claimed a special relation to other apparitions: some Claretians and Dominicans to Fatima, some Jesuits to Paray-le-Monial, and some Capuchins to Limpias.

How will my illness turn out? On which day should I take a trip? Should I leave in the morning or in the afternoon? Some believers also wanted guidance in secular matters. For those of a providentialist turn, the kind that predominated at Ezkioga from 1932, every event, act, and sensation had deeper meaning. Providentialism was one of the main currents among Basque seminarians and priests in the 1930s.[7] The bishop Manuel Irurita and the parish priest Amundarain were prime examples. And Magdalena Aulina led her Catalan followers into a system in which Gemma governed every turn and might reward any act with perfume. Followers wrote Aulina for advice on the most trivial matters. So this was yet another dilemma: if all is providential, how can the individual discover what providence wants him/her to do? Such persons needed not just spiritual direction but secular direction as well. Through the seers, it seemed they could get such guidance directly from heaven.

Some questions were more philosophical. Why do the wicked often prosper and the righteous often fail? Why is there injustice and inequality? Why is there sin? For those believing the apocalyptic visions the seers brought a solution to the existence of evil. The reign of the Sacred Heart would right the age-old signs of a bad world. The wicked would perish in the great chastisement, there would be no more sin, all would speak the same language, and the dead would rejoin the living.

No human agency seemed to be concerned with these questions: the reigning rationalism could not bless or forgive social groups; it left chance, progress, and contingency in charge. And the church sometimes hindered more than it helped. For it stood between people and their dead and people and their gods, and it told people what they could or could not see or hear. At Ezkioga women and children challenged the male priests' tight control over the distribution of grace and access to the other world. With flowers, messages, and blessed rosaries the seers gave absolution, distributed grace, and answered the unanswered questions.

The apparitions were in part a rebellion by an agrarian world still close to the spirits against a system of explanation, a distribution of blessings, and an access to heaven people found unfair. In effect, seers and believers were rejecting the city and the world of commerce that devalued rural sharing and mutual help.[8] But the mass response to visions in the twentieth century throughout the Catholic world demonstrates that the essential issues are not just rural. While Medjugorje and other prominent vision sites are in rural locations, the tens of millions of pilgrims who have gone there are largely urban residents who share a need for answers that their parishes and societies do not provide.

HOPE AND ANGUISH

For many people the apparitions at Ezkioga were simply a great divine event. These people went to the site as they might go to see a solar eclipse. For them Ezkioga was part of a skein of divine intervention that ran back for centuries. In this skein trances, messages, and prophecies repeated and adapted themselves. Seers heard and read what had gone on in the past and what was going on elsewhere; they knew the religious orders and shrines that visions had inspired in the past and present, in Spain and elsewhere.

The skein took on meaning and maintained coherence in a more practical way. "Carriers" were at work before Ezkioga, persons dedicated to receiving, understanding, and propagating communications from the divine. In the last years of sixteenth-century Madrid connoisseurs quite like Padre Burguera elicited the political dreams of Lucrecia de León. The French prophet Thomas Martin had his expert Louis Silvy, Catherine Labouré had Père Aladel, the Italian David Lazzaretti had two priests of the Congregation of San Felipe Neri and the monarchist Le Vachat, and Anna Katerina Emmerich had Clemens Brentano. The type is entirely recognizable and surely goes back to the time of Moses.[9]

These carriers passed on meaning and enthusiasm like a torch, from one set of visions to another. Several of our protagonists connected Limpias with Ezkioga. Both Juan Bautista Ayerbe and Catholic activist María de Echarri had previously interpreted the visions of the Christ of Limpias. Juan José Echezarreta,

The Virgin of Fatima enters Terrassa on García Cascón's car, 13 October 1951. Courtesy Arxiu Salvador Cardús i Florensa, Terrassa

owner of the Ezkioga field, had gone to Limpias, had a vision, and wept there. Joaquín Sicart, chief photographer at Ezkioga, had been cured after a vision at Limpias in 1919, as had the priest Francisco Aguirre, who took down Evarista Galdós's messages. Remigio Gandásegui, the archbishop of Valladolid who encouraged Baudilio Sedano's interest in Ezkioga, had been the most assiduous episcopal visitor to Limpias. Raimundo Galdeano was a Navarrese farmer who linked Ezkioga both to Limpias and Piedramillera. By paying for parish missions by the Capuchins who stimulated the visions at Limpias, he unwittingly prepared a zone of Navarra for visions in 1920. He paid for a mission in the Barranca in 1931, when he accompanied a seer from Lizarraga to Ezkioga.

The skein runs forward as well as backward. Many of the major propagandists took their agendas from Ezkioga to subsequent visions in other parts of Spain and Europe. Raymond de Rigné wrote about the apparitions of Assisi and La Codosera. Several of the seers from Torralba de Aragón in 1931 went to Cuevas de Vinromà in 1947 for the great miracle, and Padre Burguera talked to the seer there. Salvador Cardús was in Solsona when to enormous excitement a traveling image of the Virgin of Fatima entered the town. He immediately bought an image to install in Terrassa. On 13 October 1951 the statue entered the city on top of Rafael García Cascón's car. Three children dressed as the shepherd seers met it in the town square. García Cascón himself never ceased his frenetic visits to apparition sites, whether Fatima, Lourdes, La Codosera, Garabandal, Monte Umbe, or Cerdanyola. He always wanted the cars to go fast and he opposed rest stops. He brought the Utrera seer María Marín to his house in Terrassa and almost had a heart attack when a woman seer at El Palmar de Troya told him he held the Baby Jesus in his arms.[10]

José Javier Martínez Sarrasa hunted out seers all over Spain. In particular, he made friends with those who had visions in La Codosera in 1945, but he also was acquainted with seers of Garabandal (Cantabria) in the 1960s. José Martínez Cajigas, a devout photographer who lived in Santander, took pictures for postcards at Limpias and Ezkioga; some of his descendants befriended the seers at Garabandal. Several seers from Gipuzkoa and many of their followers went to Garabandal in the 1960s. In turn busloads of Garabandal devotees visited the Ezkioga seer Rosario Gurruchaga in Bergara. I first heard of the Ezkioga visions in 1968 from my friend Jon Leemans, a Dutch devotee of Garabandal. He knew a Spanish diplomat who had been a correspondent of Juan Bautista Ayerbe and Pedro Balda and owned what was then, in 1968, one of the few copies of Burguera's book in circulation. In the 1950s and 1960s Padre Pio, the Italian Capuchin, served for many of these people as the same kind of spiritual fulcrum as Thérèse Neumann did in the 1930s.[11] Some of the older surviving devotees in Gipuzkoa and Navarra went to the visions that started at Monte Umbe near Bilbao in the 1970s. The Basque believers are in touch with newer Catalan groups, like one in Barcelona called the White Army.[12] Juan Roig Gironella, a Jesuit who counseled the seers on the outskirts of Barcelona in the 1970s, told me his mother had been one of the Catalan pilgrims to Ezkioga in the 1930s. His opinion was that all apparitions start out being authentic and then because of a lack of spiritual direction almost all get on the wrong track.

Visions spawn devotions. Devotions lead to cures. Cures elicit visions. Some persons cured miraculously feel they have special grace, much as survivors of lightning bolts are thought to have a gift for healing. Thérèse Neumann, Magdalena Aulina, La Madre Esperanza, Anna Pou i Prat, and María Agueda Aguirre began their visions after cures. Pepita Pugés, a visionary who started a shrine in Cerdanyola del Vallès, near Barcelona, in the 1970s, had been cured at Lourdes.

Starting in the early 1970s a specialized magazine, *Maria Mensajera,* and a publishing house, Editorial Círculo, have brought seers and believers of different Spanish visions in contact. The owner of both, Francisco Sánchez-Ventura y Pascual, has promoted certain apparition sites—to the point of buying land and erecting chapels. Since the end of compulsory church approval of religious literature, similar publishing houses and magazines have sprung up throughout the Catholic world. A growing body of Catholics consumes this literature avidly.

The ephemeral nature of any particular event should not distract us from the vital, routine way grace makes credible and freshens ideals, dogmas, and rules. Any organization that is highly adaptive continually renews itself. Each of the Catholic church's established holy places, persons, times, and institutions was once fresh and exciting. The church depends on successive layers of creativity. In the constant process of renewal, grace plays a role similar to that of oxygen in the bloodstream or new water in a tide pool. For many Catholics grace is an energy that reawakens interest and provides hope and direction.

Contact with new grace in heavy concentrations can be intoxicating. The Spanish Jesuit Carlos María Staehlin judged it unhealthy and called it marvellism.[13] Visions, stigmatics, prophets, new devotions, new institutes, and new sources of grace in trees, soil, stones, and water make up a kind of ever-changing (yet never changing) world. It is a world unto itself, and some devout persons like Burguera and Ayerbe dwell almost entirely within it, moving from one hot spot to another.

For those who are a part of this inspired environment, a kind of luminous community develops.[14] I experienced this gentle, generous mood vicariously when I lived in the town of San Sebastián de Garabandal in the late 1960s. The remote mountain village was then paradoxically a crossroads for Catholic enthusiasm in the Western world. Many of the pilgrims who turned up there in search of divine help and love were open and vulnerable. They shared their experiences and their sorrows and listened well to those of others. The cuadrillas of Ezkioga believers were rather more intense, but we have seen the joy they found in penitential prayer.

Sacralization is a process, but institutional religions like to understand the sacred as inherent. A place is either sacred or profane; it cannot be part-sacred, part-profane. Such an attitude toward places applies as well to persons, doctrines, visions, and organizations.[15] Because this attitude limits what evidence the public can have access to, it affects the thinking even of outsiders. Traditional church history—until recently the *only* history of these matters—tends to exclude the outer margin of enthusiasm. We have many documents for apparitions to which the church has granted credence, but few for those the church shunned. It discreetly files away its careful compilations about persons it judges insufficiently saintly, places it deems unworthy of cult, devotions it holds dubious, stigmatics it considers to be fakes, prophecies it judges spurious. Virtually all we know from the church about persons, visions, and orders are success stories. The failures and half-saints, the orders and obras and institutes the church culled—and these are surely the vast majority—are unavailable.

Yet, as at Ezkioga, much religious excitement occurs precisely during the ambiguous period prior to church action, in the margins of what people know and what the church approves, around persons whose works, visions, or organizations the church has not yet judged, at places that are in doubt.[16] Part of the attraction of the not-yet-approved is precisely its novelty, its dynamic, changing nature, its very fragility. The believer can add little to approved, official devotions. By praying at new places, by venerating uncanonized holy people, by joining groups not yet approved, Catholics make a statement about the way heaven ought to be.

The church channels and domesticates religious enthusiasm by organizing memory. Here I understand the church to be a decentralized, collective, articulated process that serves the spiritual needs of Catholics and perpetuates itself, a community of memory with a particular purpose. The mass is a remembrance of the Passion of Christ, a remembrance in the body that entire societies learn by bending knees, by making the sign of the cross with the hands, by hearing a solemn story at the moment of consecration thousands of times over a lifetime, by ingesting the body and blood of Christ. Holy Week brings this memory alive. Those carrying the crosses and floats carry the weight of the cross to Calvary, and still in places there are those who flay themselves and prolong the physical memory of the flaying of Christ.[17]

This exaltation of memory applies to the lives of saints. Religious orders, dioceses, and sodalities all depend on the enthusiasm of their members and their clients for survival and fruitfulness. By remembering particular people these societies define their mission. For the believer holy acts in the present show that God is inspiring individuals now; historical holy lives and holy acts demonstrate that God's wisdom and the Holy Spirit dwell in the organization and its rule.

My inquiries in dioceses and in religious orders about persons involved in the Ezkioga apparitions revealed a certain sensitivity and reticence. I found this difficulty to a lesser or greater extent in regard to memories about Amundarain, Aulina, Degrelle, Vallet, de la Torre, Irurita, Corbató, and Naya. Some—like Corbató, Naya, and Degrelle—their dioceses or orders would prefer to forget. Others had an involvement with Ezkioga that their communities now consider embarrassing.

But these people's stories, and that of Ezkioga as a whole, are necessary and useful. The selective memory that removed this story from church history, Spanish history, and Basque history removed the opportunity for us to learn from the phenomenon. Only through reflection on historical events in all their human detail can we understand a process and avoid the same tragic result. In 1931 Basques, Catalans, and Spaniards seized on people to voice collective hopes. For some of the children especially, the episode hopelessly distorted their lives and confused their family relations. Some lived with fear until their death.

Tens of thousands of older people in the Basque Country were left perplexed by what they saw and heard. The silence the bishop imposed left them ashamed of their own enthusiasm. They too need a historical explanation that makes these events understandable. Hundreds of families of the seers throughout Navarra and Gipuzkoa, especially the rural and small-town families who have not moved, have borne the stigma of Ezkioga in total silence for sixty years. Whatever variations the seers themselves introduced, the visions at Ezkioga were a collaborative enterprise of hundreds of thousands of people in search of meaning and direction. At the turn of the century psychologists suggested that crowds responded to skilled persons who manipulated them, the *meneurs*. At Ezkioga the press, the religious and civic elites, and in the last analysis the general public were the meneurs. How else can we explain an entire Catholic society that delegated its direction to its children and to some of its least prestigious members? These seers gave voice to the society's hope.

Selective memory is a problem not just for the Basques, the church, churches, or institutions. Remembering and forgetting are equally important for all of us. But we generally conceal the way we accumulate, discard, and distribute meaning. In the rush of grace in time of upset—in the visions of Ezkioga as in the cargo cults of New Guinea or in the ghost dances of the American West—we can see the process at work more easily.[18] The process works by trial and error. From an immense range of alternatives we reject some material even before we know it. By the nature of awareness itself, we are never aware of the alternatives. By the very way we know and perceive, we block out information that we cannot use. What remains as information, news, fact, is the recognizable and believable item.

Before the church even starts to confer or deny holiness, people have been at work, consciously or unconsciously eliminating persons, times, places, and messages they consider inappropriate. At Ezkioga the public never saw certain seers and quickly dismissed others. There were vision sites the press in hundreds of articles never mentioned. Seers did not tell about certain supernatural figures—devils or witches, for example. People ridiculed certain visions and locations. Photographers did not portray bizarre visionary poses. People rejected some messages as demonic or invented. In short, there was a constant, intensive weeding out, the elimination of cultural material that did not fit. Conversely, there were rewards for seers who addressed certain problems—the collective predicament of Catholic Basques, Catalans, or Spaniards or the everyday problems of the dead, the missing, the unforgiven, the unabsolved. Wittingly or not, every person who went to see the visions or merely read a newspaper about them was doing this kind of evaluating and rewarding. Certain selectors and patrons played a powerful role in determining which visions and seers prevailed.

It must also be obvious by now, however, that the seers were not puppets of these forces or these guides. We have seen that some of them were better than others at understanding and serving the needs of the society, the general public, and the promoters. The seers who became famous were those who were most alert, sensitive to human feelings and needs, open to strangers, and able to absorb written material. These kinds of skills must also serve seers in other times and places.

After her husband's death, Marie de Rigné wrote that what he most wanted was for people to remember him. Some of the seers simply wanted people to know them while they were alive. But the events at Ezkioga had an internal dynamic and momentum that carried forward seers, believers, and disbelievers alike. This maelstrom of hope and anguish swept along many who had no thought of fame. Now, if not totally forgotten, they are all well on their way to oblivion. Let this work be a memorial to their spiritual adventure.

*Questionnaire about the manifesta-
tions of the Most Holy Virgin at Ezquioga* ("Hoja interrogatorio de las manifestaciones de la Santísma Virgen en
Ezquioga," 1 page, 2 sides, [August
1931], collection of author)

1. What form [*advocación*] did the
   Virgin take?
   (Immaculate Conception, Miraculous Mary, Sorrowing Mary, etc.)
2. Details of her exterior mantle
   (color, length, decorations)
   1) From where does the exterior
      garment hang? (from the head,
      the neck, or the back)
   2) Size, color, width, how it is gath-
      ered or belted.
3. Crown
   1) Its color
   2) Dimensions
   If it had stars:
      Their color?
      How many?
   On the crown was there a cross?
      Or a sword?
      (color and dimensions)
4. Face
   1) Happy? When?
   2) Sad? When?

5. Hands. In what position?
   1) Praying?
   2) Crossed on her breast?
   3) With fingers clasped?
   4) Extended?
   If she had some object in her hands:
       In the right one?
       In the left one?
       Was she doing something with the object?
6. Arms
   Was she holding some image?
   Or some object?
   Of what size?
   In what position?
7. Vision
   Moment of the apparition
   1) Before the Rosary?
   2) During the Rosary?
   3) In which Mystery?
   4) After the Rosary?
   5) During the singing?
   6) Later? How long after the end of the Holy Rosary?
   7) Approximately how long did the vision last?
   How did it first appear?
       The image?
       Or the brightness?
       Or both at the same time?
   Was the brightness in the form of
       A frame?
       An oval?
       A chapel or an altar?
   Did it light only the Virgin?
       Or the atmosphere?
   Was the light intense?
       Or weak?
8. Did it appear with a complete body or only from the waist up?
9. Did it speak, with voice or with gestures?
   If it was heard to speak:
       What did it say?
       Did it say to keep a secret?

10. In the apparitions is the Virgin seen alone?
    Or accompanied by angels?
    Or by doves?
11. What other details did the person favored by the manifestations observe?
12. During the manifestations did she/he feel pleasure, sadness, terror, or awe?
    After the manifestations?
13. The person who had the vision or manifestation
    1) What had been his/her attitude toward what is going on at Ezquioga
       with the visions?
    2) With what intention did she/he come to Ezquioga?
       a) devotion?
       b) diversion?
       c) to laugh?

Name of seer, birthplace, age, current home, parish, street, date of declara-
    tion, witnesses. Do not want name to be given out?
Information about the person
Parents (family antecedents), general knowledge/education, house, social or re-
    ligious background [*ambiente*], demeanor [*desparpajo*], character, prior be-
    havior
Medical observations

Vision of Cruz Lete, 8 February 1932 (signed, private archive)

Thursday
After I got to the vision deck and when I was praying the rosary I saw
the Most Holy Virgin and speaking with her she told me I was going to suffer the Passion. She came to where I was with three silver nails and a square
hammer; all this the Virgin carried in her hands and thus I had the vision of
the Prayer in the Garden, where Jesus was praying on his knees with his gaze
fixed on the firmament; he was dressed in a long tunic the color of straw,
gathered by a belt at the waist. His hair was long down to his shoulders and
dark brown. . . . While in this vision I saw that a group of men advanced,
who by their dress appeared to me to be soldiers, as they wore a kind of Roman soldier's helmet. From this group four came forward with a threatening
attitude and bound me. Then after a few moments they began to crucify me;
first the left hand with three blows, and then the right, later the feet, which
in order to nail they pulled very hard, doubtless so my feet would reach the
hole into which they had to put the nail. They raised the cross, and then I
felt how by the weight of my body little by little the nails advanced from my

palms to my fingers, leaving my hands split, and in that moment my body fell toward the foot of the cross. If in all the Passion my suffering was great, in that moment it was horrible. A few moments later I felt something sharp enter my left side, increasing the pain, which was so great that I lost consciousness.

with all humility, I am poor Cruz de Lete

To my dear seers and friends of the apparitions of the Most Holy Virgin of Ezquioga and nearby places: Health and Peace in Jesus and Mary ("A mis caros videntes y amigos de las apariciones de la Santísima Virgen de Ezquioga y lugares comarcanos: Salud y Paz en Jesús y María," 2 pages typewritten, undated [early 1933], with Fr. Amado de C. Burguera typed at end, and, in his handwriting, "es copia" written beneath, private archive)

Most dear brethren: Far from you in body, but close in spirit, I do not forget you for a moment. Your difficult mission, given over to my care, nourishes my work, which thereby becomes more easy. In response to your countless letters, which I have received joyfully, letters that inform me in minute detail about the progress of our matters, which are those of the Virgin and mine as well, letters that I have answered individually, I write this general one for all of you.

In the first place, I am glad to know that you go forward with love in the paths that your Mother has marked out for you, which are the holy paths of righteousness, however unusual. But precisely because they are unusual, they are full of brambles and false turns. And in the absence of a spiritual director who understands and guides you, I send you here some misgivings and advice, in virtue of the ministry that you all know has been entrusted to me.

I know your sincerity and your zeal; but you do not consider fully enough that our common enemy, who sows discord and corrupts souls, is always alert to what is happening to you in order to imitate it and fool you. I know for sure that the devil has tricked and taken over some seers, causing countless, almost irreparable, evils. Because believing that their vision and revelation is from Our Lord or the Virgin (because they have not had it tested), right away they proclaim what they have seen and heard, even though sometimes it comes from the devil. By so doing they fool others and damage the cause they defend.

That is why you must observe the precautions that previously, in this respect, I gave you and those that I will give you in the future, so that everything is done with truth and charity. And summarizing them again, I say to you:

1. You must make sure of the origin of the apparitions, asking them to say: "Blessed be God," "Blessed be Jesus," "Blessed be the Virgin Mother of God." If the apparition does not respond positively, then it is not divine. Or also by asking it mentally something that it must answer directly. If it does not reply it is the devil.

2. Do not transmit the revelation to anyone until you verify the authenticity of the apparition, using the procedure of a separate revelation made to another or other seers.

3. Check with your personal spiritual director.

4. In the case of general revelations or revelations for the general public, tell no one until they have been screened by your general director.

5. An apparition is good, as a rule, when it serves or tends to the glory of God, when it sanctifies and saves humans, and when it leaves in the soul of the seer a residue of perfect peace, joy in the Holy Spirit, and great stimulus to advance on the road to Christian perfection. When it leaves trouble in the soul it is diabolical.

The second matter I wish to draw to your attention is mutual charity. Saint John says: "God is charity and he who resides in charity resides in God and God in him." (I John 4:16). Saint Paul adds: "We should love the charity of mutual brotherhood (Romans 12:10). Therefore, my brethren, the more love we have in God, the closer we are to God and the better we keep his commandments. But I know that among you there is envy and quarreling, and some of you do not speak well of others, saying that "they do not see." And as the devil sees and hears, he hears this, and sometimes, for the reasons I have mentioned, he imitates divine apparitions and tempts you, making you see defects in other seers or convincing you that they do not see. This too causes numberless evils, like doubts, suspicion, jealousy, and mutual envy, and, above all, reflecting the deceit engendered by the devil, the belief that the vision is of Jesus or the Virgin.

That is why you must take the following precautions:

1. Each of you must humble yourself in the presence of God and reflect on the fact that the graces you receive, undeservedly, are freely given, and may be taken away because of vainglory or other sins.

2. Hold the other seers to be better than you, and love them in God and for God, considering that they may be more acceptable to Him.

3. Never speak badly of anyone.

4. Speak well and with great respect of your fellow seers and with the greatest respect of priests, even of those who may be mistaken, letting God be the judge of all things.

5. Do not let your photograph be taken, except in cases when your spiritual director considers it necessary.

The last matter on which I want to instruct you is to urge you to act always with righteous intent, with reverence and assiduity in prayer, and with the divine will, which is to the greater glory of God and the Virgin and the sanctification of men; this without regard to the acceptance of other people and remembering that the unusual graces you have received merit your gratitude and cooperation if you wish to obtain the eternal reward.

And while you put all this in practice, my dearest ones, I commend you, and my soul as well, to Our Lord God, to the Most Holy Virgin, our sweet Mother, and to Gemma, the very effective protector of our Work: and, by the same token, I commend myself to your fervent prayers, that Jesus and Mary may grant us peace, now, and henceforth in their eternal glory.

These are graces always desired for you by your devoted brother,

Fr. AMADO DE C. BURGUERA

María Maddalena [Marcucci] to Evarista Galdós, Madres Pasionistas, Bilbao-Deusto, 20 March 1932 (handwritten, private collection)

Evarista most dear in the love of the Crucified Jesus and the Sorrowful Mother:

Since I had the pleasure of knowing you, and remembering the graces that the Virgin Mary has promised you for this week, I take the liberty of asking you the favor of remembering this community.

The first grace that we ask of the Most Holy Virgin is that she engrave on our hearts the Passion and death of Jesus and his Sorrows so that we may be in *mind, heart,* and *habit* Passionists and worthy daughters of Our Lord Father Pablo de la Cruz.

Second, if it is not opposed to the will of God, we would like the cure of a nun called María Margarita del Niño Jesús.

For the miserable person who writes you ask that she may perfectly fulfill the will of God and then die and go straight to heaven without going through purgatory. I too will pray for you in a special way before the Monument.

In the Wounds of Jesus, yours truly,
María Maddalena

Future Events (from a letter from Madrid sent by a fervent devotee of the holy apparitions and related to the interpretation of the predictions of the seers) ["Los Acontecimientos Futuros (de una carta de Madrid dirigida por un fervoroso devoto de las santas apariciones y relacionada con la interpretación de las predicciones de los videntes)," 1 page, dittoed, unsigned, n.d. [summer of 1933 to summer of 1934], AC 407, my paragraphs]. The author is probably Juan

Bautista Ayerbe's correspondent, Alfredo Renshaw. The holy lady may be the wealthy Madrid woman Renshaw worked for; she spread the cult of Merciful Love and closely followed the predictions of nuns.

I deduce from the prophecies that I know, and there are a lot of them, that the time of world purification will last until around 1940, although in Spain the Reign of Christ will come sooner while communism spreads over the rest of the world. Only in this way can one explain the child Benita's revelations that speak of the era of famine and of the Great Monarch in which we Catholics will have to emigrate from Spain. That is when the three days of darkness will come as a just punishment for the sins of mankind, perhaps after an era of great persecutions and crimes. I think it will be something worldwide. The seer from Irañeta [Luis Irurzun] has written to a priest who is a friend of mine that it will still be a while before the time of darkness, which confirms my belief.

It is possible that even during the Reign of Our Lord Jesus Christ there will be fateful days, until the Great Monarch appears who will restore his Reign in the whole world. I deduce that after the world war, when the armies are subverted by indiscipline and rebellion and they see the great mortality caused in their ranks by the new and modern means of destruction, they will revolt and proclaim communism. That will be when the dictatorship of Mussolini will fall, as a female seer of Irun [Evarista Galdós?] told me this summer, and the persecution of the pope will begin, which according to her would last from 1936 to 1939.

Here in Madrid there is a very holy lady who one day received a visit from a nun in about 1928, announcing to her that communism would spread all over the world but that Spain providentially would be saved. Also an Andalusian nun, around 1928, announced the fall of the monarchy, the coming of the enemies of Christ, and the restoration of Christ's Reign. She said that all the monarchies would fall within thirteen to fifteen years, being followed by revolution or subversion . . . [sic]

That is to say that judging by all this, the Reign of the Sacred Heart that is announced seems, in my humble opinion, to be a parenthesis of peace, in the midst of chaos and convulsion in the rest of the world, which may well be affected in some way, for as I recall the nun said that some of the flames of the world conflagration would reach Spain. That is, more or less, what I remember, and what seems to be in accord with what I have heard from these seers.

On the other hand, the prophecies of the Franciscan Padre Comà, made many years ago, which have been coming true exactly, when they refer to the current regime, after announcing its fall when it undertook a new confiscation of church [property], add, "Providence retains an unexpected way to do in a single stroke what in the course of things would take a long time." This, evidently, seems to confirm some great chastisement that will get rid of the obstacles to the Reign of the Heart of Jesus that we so desire. Our friend the Padre [Burguera] has this document and it is included in the book entitled "La Apología del Gran Monarca."

In short, we can clearly deduce that the era of definitive world peace will not arrive until about 1940, although in Spain it may happen sooner in a climate of relative peace, but still passing through a period of expiation and purification until the Great Monarch, around 1937, begins his campaign to restore that so desired Reign worldwide.

According to what a priest told me, a nun predicted three years of this regime, three of confusion, and three of restoration. That agrees with all the rest, exactly up to 1940.

Place-names that have changed since 1931

OFFICIAL NAME 1931	OFFICIAL NAME 1994
GUIPÚZCOA	GIPUZKOA
Alegría de Oria	Alegia
Alquiza	Alkiza
Alzo	Altzo
Anzuola	Antzuola
Aya	Aia
Azcoitia	Azkoitia
Cegama	Zegama
Cestona	Zestoa
Cirzurquil	Zizurkil
Deva	Deba
Elduayan	Elduain
Escoriaza	Eskoriatza
Ezquioga	Ezkioga
Gaviria	Gabiria
Icasteguieta	Ikastagieta
Isasondo	Itsasondo
Lazcano	Lazkao
Legazpia	Legazpi
Lizarza	Lizartza
Oñate	Oñati
Ormáiztegui	Ormaiztegi
Oyarzun	Oiartzun

Pasajes	Pasaia
Regil	Errezil
Vergara	Bergara
Vidania	Bidegoyan
Villafranca de Oria	Ordizia
Villarreal de Urrechua	Urretxu
Zaldivia	Zaldibia
Zarauz	Zarautz
Zumaya	Zumaia
Zumárraga	Zumarraga
Aránzazu	Aranzazu
VIZCAYA	BIZKAIA
Abadiano	Abadiño
Ceánuri	Zeanuri
Ceberio	Zeberio
Guernica	Gernika
Larrebezúa	Larrebetzu
Lequeitio	Lekeitio
Marquina	Markina
Santurce	Santurtzi
Urquiola	Urkiola
NAVARRA	NAVARRA
Alcoz	Alkotz
Alsasua	Altsasu
Bacaicoa	Bakaiku
Cilveti	Zilbeti
Echarri-Aranaz	Etxarri-Aranatz
Errazquin	Errazkin
Erroz	Errotz
Gainza	Gaintza
Huarte Araquil	Uharte-Arakil
Irañeta	Iraneta
Irún	Irun
Irurzun	Irurtzun
Lacunza	Lakuntza
Lecumberri	Lekunberri
Torrano	Dorrao
Unanua	Unanu
Uztegui	Uztegi
Yabar	Ihabar

Bañolas	Banyoles
GERONA	GIRONA
LÉRIDA	LLEIDA
Tarrasa	Terrassa
Vich	Vic

NOTES

More complete citations of signed newspaper articles and all other printed material can be found in the bibliography. Unless otherwise noted, letters to and from Salvador Cardús are in the archive of Salvador Cardús, Terrassa, those to Laburu are in the annex of the Jesuit provincial archive at Loyola, Rigné letters to Olaizola are in the papers of José Olaizola, San Sebastián. Unless otherwise noted, letters from Cardús and García Cascón were sent from Terrassa, those from Ayerbe from Urnieta, and those from López de Lerena are from Castillo-Elejabeitia. I have photocopies and in some cases originals of virtually all published and unpublished materials I cite. The complete text of all of the interviews, most of which I tape-recorded, are in my files. If I do not give a source for a photo, it is from my collection.

ABBREVIATIONS

A	*Argia,* San Sebastián
AAJM	Archivo de la Alianza con Jesús por María, Madrid
AC	Ayerbe Collection, author's archive
ADP	Archivo Diocesano de Pamplona
ADV	Archivo Diocesano de Vitoria

AEF	*Anuario de Eusko-Folklore,* San Sebastián
AHCPCR	Archivo Histórico Cooperadores Parroquiales de Cristo Rey, Rome
AHN GC	Archivo Histórico Nacional, Guerra Civil, Salamanca
ARB	Rodes, "Els fets d'Ezkioga"
ASC	Arxiu Salvador Cardús i Florensa, Terrassa
B	Burguera, *Los Hechos de Ezquioga*
B II	Burguera, *De la Creación al Arte*
BOEP	*Boletín oficial eclesiástico de Pamplona*
BOOV	*Boletín oficial del Obispado de Vitoria*
CC	*El Correo Catalán,* Barcelona
DHEE	*Diccionario de Historia Ecclesiástica de España*
DN	*Diario de Navarra,* Pamplona
DS	*Dictionnaire de Spiritualité*
DSS	*Diario de Sesiones de las Cortes Constituyentes*
ED	*El Día,* San Sebastián
EE	*L'Enigme d'Ezkioga,* Bruxelles and Lyon
ELB	*El Liberal,* Bilbao
ELM	*El Liberal,* Madrid
EM	*El Matí,* Barcelona
EZ	*Euzkadi,* Bilbao
FL	Fondo Laburu, Archivo de la Provincia de Loyola, SSJJ
FS	Foto Sicart, author's archive
GN	*La Gaceta del Norte,* Bilbao
HM	*Heraldo de Madrid*
HMM	Hemeroteca Municipal de Madrid
L	Laburu, "Ezquioga"
LC	*La Constancia,* San Sebastián
LIS	*Lilium inter Spinas,* San Sebastián
PN	*El Pensamiento Navarro,* Pamplona
PV	*El Pueblo Vasco,* San Sebastián
R	Rigné, *Une Nouvelle Affaire Jeanne d'Arc*
S	Starkie, *Spanish Raggle-Taggle*
SC D	Cardús, "Declaracions"

SC E   Cardús, "Engrunes"

VG   *La Voz de Guipúzcoa,* San Sebastián

VN   *La Voz de Navarra,* Pamplona

VS   *Vida Sobrenatural,* Salmanca

CHAPTER I. INTRODUCTION

1. Christian, "Santos a María" and *Apparitions;* Niccoli, *Prophecy.*

2. Christian, *Religiosidad local,* 234–241, and "Francisco Martínez."

3. Cholvy and Hilaire, *Histoire religieuse,* 2:19–64, 347–349.

4. Taves, *Household of Faith,* 89–111; Larkin, "Devotional Revolution"; Lynch, "Church in Latin America."

5. For examples of visions see Delpal, *Entre paroisse et commune;* Commission, *N-D de Dimanche;* and Heigel, "Les Apparitions." See also Hamon, *N-D de France,* for Domjevin (Nancy) 1799–1803 (6:59), Scey (Besançon) 1803 (6:273–275), Saint-Cyprien (Périgueux) 1813 (4:137), Lescouët (St. Brieuc) 1821 (4:545), and Montoussé (Tarbes) 1848 (3:450).

6. Aladel-Nieto, *Sor Catalina,* 62–63, 70–71, 93.

7. Zimdars-Swartz, *Encountering Mary,* 43.

8. Niccoli, *Prophecy,* 61–88.

9. Callahan, *Church, Politics,* 128–158, 161, 194, 212, 232–237; see esp. p. 235: "Scruples that led some eighteenth-century bishops to restrain cults were set aside in favor of an effort to spread them like seeds thrown upon the fields."

10. Pérez, *Historia Mariana,* 5:115.

11. Pérez, *Historia Mariana,* 4:221–222, cites *La Voz de María Santísima de la Saleta.* For cult in Spain, see Christian, *Moving Crucifixes,* 10, 160 n. 5.

12. Christian, *Moving Crucifixes,* 6–16, 149–151.

13. Christian, *Moving Crucifixes.*

14. Mateos, "Ntra. Sra. del Rosario de Fátima," 711. For Fatima, ten articles, most by Mateos or Vélez, in *El Santísimo Rosario* (Bergara), 1927–1931; *Mensajero de Corazón de Jesús* (Bilbao), 1928, pp. 181–183, and 1929, pp. 374–375; Jáuregi, *Jaungoiko-zale,* 1929 and 1931; and *Rosas y Espinas,* 15 April 1931. Stimulated by Ezkioga, there was a new spate of interest in Fatima in July 1931: see Efrén, *GN,* 15 July, and *PV,* 17 July; Aldabe, *LC,* 25 July; Arribiribiltzu, *A,* 26 July; and *ED,* 28 July.

15. I refer especially to Perry and Echeverría, *Heel of Mary,* despite its pleasing scope and detail, and de Sède, *Fatima.*

CHAPTER 2. MARY, THE REPUBLIC, AND THE BASQUES

An earlier draft of portions of this chapter appeared as "Tapping and Defining New Power: The First Month of Visions at Ezquioga, July 1931," *American Ethnologist* 14, no. 1 (February 1987): 140–166.

1. The original story about the Torralba visions was in *La Voz de Aragón* (Lacasa, 26 April 1931). Newspapers mostly copied the version in *El Debate,* 29 April 1931 (*ED* and *LC,* 30 April 1931), which reached many children directly in Orzanco, "Las apariciones." The child seers of Ezkioga allegedly read the Basque version in *Argia,* 5 May 1931 (Masmelene,

EZ, 15 July 1931). In 1975 I spoke to one of the Torralba seers, by then somewhat tentative and sheepish, in Zaragoza.

2. Elderly priest present at Vitoria meeting, 10 September 1983, p. 5; on expulsion of Bishop Múgica see Rodríguez de Coro, *Catolicismo vasco,* 51–55; Buonaiuti, *Spagna 1931,* 82; and Arbeloa, "La expulsión."

3. *DN,* 9 June 1931, p. 7. What follows is a best-guess composite of printed reports and oral testimony of villagers of Mendigorría, including one of the seers, on 9 April 1983 and 31 July 1988.

4. All 1931: *PN,* 6 June, p. 7; *DN,* 7 June, p. 7; *VG,* 7 June, p. 5.

5. *PN,* 9 June 1931, p. 3.

6. Orzanco, "Las apariciones," 123.

7. On July 18, at the height of the Ezkioga visions, someone from Pamplona paid for a bus to take the Mendigorría girls to Ezkioga. The woman I talked to said, "They lined us up in a row to see if we saw anything. But we saw nothing." She dismissed the Ezkioga visions as "a lie to make money."

8. All 1931: for train, *VG* and *El Debate,* 16 June; for Mendigorría, *PN,* 19–23 June, *DN,* 20–25 June, and *VG,* 20 June; also Martínez Sarrasa, Barcelona, 17 February 1985.

9. R, "¡¡Aquí No!!" *Adelante* (Bilbao), 27 June 1931; *ED,* 30 June 1931.

10. María Angeles Montoya, 11 September 1983. A priest from Zaldibia corroborated her; if they are correct, the Ezkioga visions began on 29 June 1931. At Mendigorría the authorities used the presence of children who saw nothing as an argument against the visions (*PN,* 9 June 1931, p. 3). At Ezkioga it was a measure of the eagerness with which people received the visions that a child who saw nothing was totally left out of the story (Felipa Aramburu, Zumarraga, 7 February 1986).

11. Norms in *Gaceta,* 22 May 1931, and *El Debate,* 23 May 1931, p. 2. In June, July, and August 1931 there was a rash of articles in Catholic newspapers on schools without crucifixes. In early 1932 women rebelled in Murchante, Estella, Lezaun, Viana, and Salinas de Oro in Navarra and Yécora in Alava (*LC,* 2, 7, and 9 February; *PN,* 20 April; *CC,* 27 April; Francisco Argandoña, Lezaun, February 1991); also towns in Palencia, Pontevedra, Almería, and Cuenca (*El Debate,* 23 March and 13 April; *LC,* 30 April). Women and children wore crucifixes that year after the Carta Circular of the exiled Bishop Múgica of March 12. See *Heraldo Alavés,* 21 April, p. 1; *LC,* 27 April, p. 8 (Zumarraga); *LC,* 29 April, p. 5. For Ezkioga, Manuela Lasa Múgica, 10 September 1983.

12. "Ezquioga," *Enciclopedia general ilustrado del país vasco,* 12:581–585.

13. Micaela Aramburu, Legazpi, 18 August 1982. For the industrial development see Castells, *Modernización,* and Greenwood, *Unrewarding Wealth.*

14. *LC,* 9 and 10 July 1931; *ED,* 9, 11, and 15 July 1931.

15. For apparition legends see Lizarralde, *Andra Mari de Guipúzcoa* and *Andra Mari Vizcaya;* Arregi, *Ermitas de Bizkaia;* López de Guereñu, *Andra Mari en Alava;* Peña Santiago, *Fiestas;* and Facultad de Teología, *Santuarios.* For Lourdes see Christian, *Moving Crucifixes,* 150, factoring in those who did not go on organized pilgrimages.

16. S 145.

17. Ferrer Muñoz, *Elecciones y partidos,* 55.

18. For the press see Cillán, *Sociología electoral,* 147–153, and Saiz, *Triunfo;* for Carlists and Integrists see Blinkhorn, *Carlism and Crisis,* 11 (quote), 46–67; for *El Día* especially interview with Pío Montoya, San Sebastián, 11 September 1983.

19. Teresa Michelena, Oiartzun, 29 March 1983, said another woman spoke to her about the witch in the sky.

20. *Easo,* 17 October 1931; *PV* and *LC,* 18 October 1931; Rodríguez Ramos, *Yo sé,* 16–22.

21. S 129.

22. Miguel Zulaika, Itziar, 18 August 1982; J. M. de Barandiarán, Ataun, 9 September 1983; and P. Dositeo Alday, Urretxu, 15 August 1982: all reported the argument in 1931 against the visions. Masmelene, *EZ,* 15 July 1931, and Larraitz, *ED,* 28 July 1931, made it in print. Masmelene was a student of Barandiarán, and Larraitz one of the founders of the prorepublican Acción Nacionalista Vasca.

23. *LC,* 7 July 1931; *PV,* 10 July 1931.

24. All 1931: for nuns, *La Tarde, ELB,* and *PV,* 11 July; "Ormáiztegui," *PV,* 17 July; priest in *PV,* 18 July.

25. All 1931: seer, aged 16, *ED,* 18 July; predictions on the eighteenth, *ED* and *PV,* 19 July; Ramona, *PV,* 24 July; nun, *LC,* 24 July; servant, *ED,* 26 July.

26. *ED,* 31 July 1931.

27. Junípero, "Oración y penitencia," *LC,* 15 May 1931; *LC,* 5 June 1931, p. 8.

28. *A,* 12 and 19 July 1931, and for Navarrese Nationalists see Apez-bat, *Amayur,* 24 July 1931.

29. *ED* and *PV,* 15 July 1931; *LC* and *PV,* 17 July 1931.

30. All 1931: *PV,* 18 July; *ED,* 19 July; *PV,* 23 July; Lassalle, *PN,* 4 August.

31. All 1931: Abeytua, *ELM,* 22 July, like Uriarte, *ELB,* 19 July; *ED,* 26 and 29 July.

32. S 135; Estornés Zubizarreta, "Las apariciones de Ezkioga," points out the significance of Patxi's prediction; the Madrid edition of 1937 omitted it. Ibarguren vision in Elías, *CC,* 19 August 1931.

33. The priest Masmelene, *EZ,* 15 July 1931, and response, *EZ,* 23 July 1931; Amundarain note against vivas, 28 July 1931, in all Catholic newspapers; Lassalle, *PN,* 4 August 1931, mentions vivas.

34. Egurza, *LC,* 24 July 1931; Echarri, *Heraldo Alavés,* 24 July 1931; for Echarrin see Christian, *Moving Crucifixes,* 61, 89, 99.

35. Echarri, *Heraldo Alavés,* 24 July 1931; Mendigorría children, *PN,* 19 July 1931; Basque seers, *ED,* 28 July 1931.

36. De la Villa, *DSS,* 13 August 1931; Ciriaco, *La Tradición Navarra,* 16 August 1931; Blinkhorn, *Carlism and Crisis,* 62–64; Granja, *Nacionalismo,* 257–263.

37. My thinking here has been helped by Wolf, *Europe,* and del Valle, "Mujer vasca."

38. "Catholic ambience" quote from Guridi, *AEF,* 1924, p. 101; for *La Constancia,* Cillán, *Sociología electoral,* 151.

39. Barandiarán, *AEF,* 1924, pp. 201–202, 168.

40. Liberty quote, *VG,* 16 June 1931; the priest Iriarte, "Estado religioso," 408.

41. *PV,* 10 July 1931, and *ED,* 11 July 1931. The connection between the visions and the Angelus was an embellishment. A woman present as a girl at the first vision, while she believes the children saw something, does not remember them kneeling, praying, or initially giving the vision much thought (Felipa Aramburu, Zumarraga, 7 February and 14 May 1986).

42. On Ramona, *PV,* 21 October 1931, and L 12; rebuttal in R 15, 63, 87. On local distinctions see *AEF,* 1924, pp. 80, 90–91, 102–103.

43. Guridi, 100–101, and Barandiarán, 202–204, in *AEF,* 1924; see S 120, for waiter.

44. Ramona Salamero and José María Busca Isusi, born ca. 1905–1915, interviewed in Zumarraga, 9 May 1984, p. 7.

45. For Markina, *VG,* 13 and 16 June 1931; Zeanuri, *BOOV,* 15 April 1931, p. 321.

46. *VG,* 30 June and 1 July 1932; *VG,* 10 June 1933.

47. Sukia, "El ambiente religioso," 369–370; Ezkioga priest Ibarguren to vicar general (Vitoria) Echeguren, 14 February 1932, ADV. For "pornography" in Urretxu theater, *LC,* 17 April 1934.

48. *AEF,* 1924, pp. 30, 70–73, 92, 124–125, 203. In Zeanuri, one of the most devout towns in the diocese, there were 430 members of the Hijas de María and only 110 Luises.

49. *AEF,* 1924, pp. 10, 57, 92; *A,* 19 July 1931; E. G., "En torno a los sucesos," *Aranzazu,* 15 August 1931, p. 239.

50. Pío Montoya asked Antonio Pildain why he got so carried away in a speech at Gernika on 12 July 1931; Pildain answered he was unused to speaking to applause and was especially pleased at getting it from the young Nationalists, who Aranzadi had said were leaning toward the Republic (15 December 1983). S 100–101, 266–267, 308.

51. See Niccoli, *Prophecy.*

52. Echaide, *Comunicaciones,* and *ED,* 14 July 1931, p. 3. Casilda Arcelus (Ormaiztegi, 9 September 1983), the telephone operator in her town in 1931, worked late for months, and the company had to install a bigger switchboard. San Sebastián's two radio stations, founded in 1924 and 1928, may have spread news of the visions, but in 1931 few country folk owned sets; see Garitaonandía, "La radiodifusión."

53. Reporter, *ED,* 16 July 1931; skeptic, Millán, *ELB,* 9 September 1931.

CHAPTER 3. PROMOTERS AND SEERS I

1. *La Constancia* resumed publication on September 22 and *El Día* on October 25.

2. For Limpias see Christian, *Moving Crucifixes,* 82–118.

3. On St. Francis see Kleinberg, *Prophets.*

4. For the critical role of the parish priest at Oliveto Citra (a vision site in southern Italy) see Apolito, *Dice,* 1–175 and 57: "Tutto evidentemente si gioca nei primissimi giorni."

5. Antonia Etxezarreta, Ezkioga, 1 June 1984 and 6 February 1986; Etxezarreta, *Eup!* April 1994; and Felipa Aramburu, Zumarraga, 7 February and 14 May 1986.

6. Juan María Amundarain Legorburu (Amundarain's nephew), San Sebastián, 3 June 1984. Antonio Amundarain and the priests of his movement were opposed to the subsequent Basque Nationalist alliance with the Republic. In the 1980s this fact colored the attitude toward him of many men in Zumarraga and of the many priests sympathetic to the Nationalist cause.

7. Pérez Ormazábal, *Aquel monaguillo,* 73.

8. *LIS* 50 (September 1932): 246–261. Amundarain eventually wrote a history of the order. He was also favorable to the installation of the Passionists, Artola, *Martín Elorza,* 37 n. 3.

9. *LIS* 17 (February 1929): 6; *LIS* 50 (September 1932): 238–239. Basque Aliadas: San Sebastián (174), Eibar (44), Zumarraga (34), Pasaia (34), Zumaia (33), Mondragón (21), Bilbao (125), Baracaldo (41), Vitoria (156).

10. Amundarain, *LIS* 19 (May–June 1929): 57; Sobrino, *Amundarain,* 275–291.

11. Pérez Ormazábal, *Aquel monaguillo,* 83–84; Amundarain, *LIS* 6 (January–February 1931): 9–10.

12. *BOOV,* 1930, p. 372; Pérez Ormazábal, *Aquel monaguillo,* 93–108.

13. Sobrino, *Amundarain,* 86. The cross was erected 1 May 1900 and again in 1926; for the cross in 1932 see *La Cruz,* 24 April; *LC,* 27 April, p. 8; and *A,* 12 May, p. 1.

14. On Amundarain's credulity see Pérez Ormazábal, *Aquel monaguillo,* 110; Pérez Ormazábal, *Así fue,* 83; on Limpias see Amundarain, *Vida congregación mercedarias,* 329; on Fa-

tima see Salvador Cardús to the Piarist Rimblas, 21 April 1932; on Rafols see Juan María Amundarain, San Sebastián, 23 June 1984; on the French mystic nun, Sulamitis, see Amundarain, *LIS* 35 (June 1931): 1–11.

15. The beatification proceedings opened 27 November 1982.

16. All 1931: *LC*, 7 and 9 July; *GN*, 17 July; *PV*, 18 July; *ED* and *LC*, 28 July.

17. Amundarain to Ozores, Zumarraga, 6 July 1931, and to A. Pérez Ormazábal, 25 July 1931, AAJM. I thank the then director general of the Alianza, Andrea Marcos, for her help. For September pilgrimage see Amundarain, *LIS* 39 (October 1931): 24–27. To this message he added, "Can this be true, my little Sisters?"

18. S 127.

19. S 126; for Ezkioga priest see L 24; the San Sebastián writer, Lassalle in *PN*, 6 August 1931.

20. Delás, *CC*, 20 September 1931; R 8; *EE* 2 (February–March 1934): 6; Rigné, *Ciel ouvert*, p. C.

21. Antonia Etxezarreta, Ezkioga, 1 June 1984, p. 16.

22. Amundarain to A. Pérez Ormazábal, Zumarraga, 10 October 1931, AAJM.

23. R 8 gives Ramona's birthdate as 13 August 1915; *PV*, 18 October 1931, p. 5; Juan de Urumea, *El Nervión*, 22 October 1931; R 11.

24. All 1931: *LC*, 17 July, p. 2; *ED*, 18 July, p. 12; and 31 July, p. 7. Also reports in *ED*, 24 and 26 July, and *PV*, 24 July. Delás, *CC*, 20 September 1931.

25. On Ramona's shopping see Juan María Amundarain, San Sebastián, 3 June 1984, p. 3. Otaegui was certain the miracle would occur, according to Pío Montoya, San Sebastián, 7 April 1983; B 212. Ramona informed the San Sebastián family of Luis Zulueta, a Republican deputy in the Cortes on good terms with Múgica and Echeguren: *LC*, 17 October 1931, p. 2, and 17 May 1932, p. 1.

26. Amundarain to Ozores, Zumarraga, 14 October 1931, AAJM; one of the Aliadas, María Angeles Montoya, San Sebastián, 28 April 1984, p. 7, who was with Dolores Ayestarán, the sister of a priest who worked with Amundarain; for family lunch: Juan María Amundarain, San Sebastián, 3 June 1984, p. 4.

27. R 17–18; L 13. See SC E 83–94 for eyewitness. News on 16 October 1931 in *PV* (San Sebastián), *PV* (Bilbao), *DN*, *Easo*, and *LC*, and on 17 October 1931 in *PV*, *VN*; for excitement that night: Casilda Arcelus, Ormaiztegi, 9 September 1983, p. 3.

28. For Echeguren's involvement: Pío Montoya, San Sebastián, 7 April 1983, pp. 4–8.

29. Montoya's detailed recollection of the hearing coincides with what Echeguren wrote José Antonio Laburu, Vitoria, 13 April 1932.

30. Amundarain to Ozores, Zumarraga, 4 November 1931, AAJM.

31. Gratacós, "Lo de Esquioga," 14–16. ARB 9–10 also mentions the visit. Suspicion of Freemason plots to make the church look ridiculous may derive from the Leo Taxil affair, in which an anticlerical freethinker feigned conversion to Catholicism, got church leaders to believe preposterous stories, and then revealed the hoax (Ferrer Benimeli, *El Contubernio*).

32. Sobrino, *Amundarain*, 93–94. Echeverría Larrain, *Predicciones*, 62. Amundarain loaned his copy to a fellow priest, Juan Ayerbe, whose niece kindly showed it to me. See also below, chap. 14, "The End of the World."

33. *EZ* and *PV* of 18 July 1931; Christian, *Moving Crucifixes*, 52, 126; *ED* and *PV*, 29 July 1931; Echeguren wrote to Rigné, 22 December 1932 (typed copy in private archive), that it was on his instructions that the Aliadas watched Ramona on the day of the miracle. Amundarain may have told him about Ramona's letter, and he must have let Amundarain choose the women.

34. Sevilla, 23 October 1989; Medina, *Memorias*.

35. Carmen Medina had over fifty nieces and nephews and provided them with swimming pools and tennis courts. On 18 March 1932 Luis Irurzun had a vision of the sea wiping out San Sebastián (B 657).

36. S 121–122.

37. S 124–125.

38. For the Carlist past see the biography of Carmen's sister, *Padron de Superioras*, 17–18. For the Sanjurjo affair see S 125; Esteban Infantes, *La Sublevación*; Arrarás, *Segunda República*, 1:505–515; and Rafael Medina, *Memorias*, 131–135. For arrest of her brother Luis see *VG*, 19 November 1932.

39. *PV*, 14 July 1931, p. 7; S 141–142, 145–150.

40. S 130; Moreda, "Mateo Múgica," 222; L 10; R 56, 4 December 1931.

41. Lassalle, *PN*, 9 August 1931.

42. Picavea, *PV*, 6 and 11 November 1931; *ED*, 17, 26, and 29 July 1931; *PN*, 22 July 1931.

43. Elías, *CC*, 19 August 1931; Farre, *EM*, 8 October 1931; Cardús to Rafael García Cascón, 13 October 1931; *PV*, 20 October 1931.

44. Detailed accounts of events on October 15 in *Easo*, 16 October 1931; and in my interview with Pío Montoya, San Sebastián, 7 April 1983, p. 7.

45. R 60; *PV*, 17 October 1931.

46. The pickpocket was Isidoro Arpón Jaime; suspicious reporter: Juan de Urumea, in *PV*, 20 and 21 October 1931, p. 2, and in *El Nervión*, 22 and 23 October 1931.

47. SC E 94–97, 101–104; *LC*, *PV*, *Easo*, and *DN*, 17 October 1931.

48. Teresa Michelena, Oiartzun, 28 March 1983; SC E 101–106, 169; Castellano, *PV*, 20 October 1931; Rigné photography of crowd, plates 33, 261, 262, collection of author; *PV* and *LC*, 18 and 20 October 1931; *Easo*, 19 October 1931; for Medina's interest in the Ataun girl see L 14.

49. S 130; Picavea, *PV*, 13 November 1931. Except for the two-day parenthesis of Ramona's wounds, the press treated Patxi as the central figure from late July to mid-November.

50. Construction, ARB 19–21; miracle predictions, *ED*, 23 July 1931, p. 8; SC E 13; García Cascón to Francisco de Paula Vallet, 31 October 1931, AHCPCR 10-A-27/2; Picavea, *PV*, 6 and 8 November 1931.

51. L 14. Arratia gave 3,000 pesetas to the seminary fund in 1931 (*BOOV*, 1931, p. 354) and provided a house for the Ave Maria schools in Bilbao whose director, Doroteo Irízar, was also an Ezkioga sympathizer. She visited the German mystic Thérèse Neumann in the winter of 1931–1932. María Recalde had a vision in Bilbao at the house of "P. A.," 18 January 1932, allegedly in the presence of the brother of Cardinal Segura, B 601–602.

52. Ormaiztegi (August 31): *Easo*, 17 October 1931. Navarra (Bakaiku): Picavea, *PV*, 6 November 1931. Guadamur: Cardús to García Cascón, 5 October 1931, and Picavea above. Patxi traveled to Bilbao, SC E 111, and in 1933 observed Luis Irurzun in Iraneta (Navarra), according to Pedro Balda, Alkotz, 8 April 1983, pp. 21–22.

53. On deputies, Picavea, *PV*, 8 November 1931; on rumored trip to France, J. R. Echezarreta to Cardús SC E 249, and Clotilde Moreno Eguiguren to a correspondent at Ezkioga, Bilbao, 15 January 1932.

54. ARB 44; R 29; B 290, 320, 717; Múgica, "Declarando," 242, 244; Echezarreta to Cardús, 24 December 1931 (SC E 263–264), and 7 January 1932. Declaration by Ramona to Rodríguez Dranguet, 18 November 1932, from private archive. Sources give the fifth seer as Juana Ibarguren of Azpeitia or María Luisa of Zaldibia.

55. For levitations see chap. 10 below, "The Vision States"; correspondence, Rodríguez Ramos, *Yo sé*, 15; bus excursions, Rafael Medina y Vilallonga, Sevilla, 23 October 1989.

56. Lassalle, *PN,* 9 August 1931.

57. García Cascón to family in Bejar, September 1931, in García Cascón, "Algo más"; Picavea, *PV,* 3 November 1931; Ducrot, *VU,* 30 August 1933, p. 1365.

58. Goicoechea, *ED,* 12 November 1931; Picavea, *PV,* 13 November 1931; vision of Benita Aguirre, date not given, B 568.

59. For prophecy and investigation: Cardús to Ramona, 16 and 30 December 1931; Múgica, "Declarando," 241; and R 41–42. For Patxi in Mondragón: Burguera to Cardús, 22 October 1931; B 380; ARB 163; R 32–33. He was released 13 November 1932.

60. Gil Bare, *PV,* 16 March 1935. For 1934 uprising see Fusi, "Nacionalismo y revolución," and Granja, *Nacionalismo,* 491–505.

61. Her employer, Díaz Alberdi, alleged that she claimed she too would see the Virgin at Ezkioga: Juan de Urumea, *El Nervión,* 23 October 1931. First visions, *ED* and *PV,* 14 and 15 July 1931; also B 32, 714–715; Boué, 23–24. For October 1931 see SC E on 4 October, Rigné photo 261 on 17 October, *PV* and *Easo,* 20 October, and *LC,* 21 October.

62. Hermano Rafael Beloqui, Urretxu, 15 August 1982; *Easo,* 20 October 1931, p. 8; L 10.

63. R 55; B 717.

64. For exercises see SC E 278, citing letter from J. R. Echezarreta of 18 January 1932; for Dolores see the anonymous biography *Padrón de Superioras,* 173–185. Carmen's sister Concepción and a niece were also in the order. On Amundarain see the chronicles in *LIS,* passim. In Vitoria the Aliadas used the Reparadora house for ceremonies in 1929 and 1931. For Loyola exercises see SC E 278. Amundarain did exercises there in early 1920s: Pérez Ormazábal, *Aquel monaguillo,* 73–74, 85–86. Quote is from Édouard Glotin, "Réparation," *DS* 13 (1988), col. 385. Émilie d'Oultremont founded the Reparadoras in Strasbourg in 1857.

65. On Evarista's trouble with Ramona see SC E 279, 434–435; on José Atín, the male convert, see Surcouf, *L'Intransigeant,* 19 November 1932; Rigné to Olaizola, 2 October 1932; Rigné to Ezkioga believer, 29 January 1933. For Evarista in Irun and priest, B 312, 726; García Cascón visited her there 7 December 1933. For community visions, B 714–717.

66. Ayerbe to Cardús, 18 January 1934. She and Carmen lived at Calle Alfonso XII 32, 3° (López de Lerena to Ezkioga believer, 19 April 1934, private collection). More on Evarista and Tedeschini below in chap. 6, "Suppression by Church and State."

67. When Burguera referred to her he often called her C. M.; Picavea wrote obliquely about a "dama aristocrática"; and Laburu even in his private lecture script wrote C. Med., though he spelled out all other names (e.g., L 14).

68. Amundarain, *LIS* 35 (June 1931): 1–11.

CHAPTER 4. PROMOTORS AND SEERS II

1. Christian, *Moving Crucifixes,* 6–16, 86–87, 150, 191.

2. Christian, *Moving Crucifixes,* 151. For Irunta's election as bishop of Lleida in 1926, Cárcel Ortí, "Iglesia y estado," 236.

3. Ricart, *Un Obispo,* 40–41. In Valencia Irurita had been a member of the devotional Escuela de Cristo along with the bishop of Segorbe, who I think was sympathetic to the Ezkioga visions. F. Sánchez Castañer, "Escuelas de Cristo," *DHEE* 5:254.

4. N., "Anduaga-mendiko agerpenak [The Apparitions of Mount Anduaga]." Amundarain told the Catalans about the Baztán seer on 14 December 1931 (Gratacós, "Lo de Esquioga," 15–16); a bus from the Baztán valley went to Ezkioga on July 21: *PV,* 22 July.

5. The photo in my text, without a caption identifying Irurita, appeared in Antigüedad, *Nuevo Mundo,* 21 October 1931, and *El Nervión,* 22 October 1931.

6. For the historic Rafols see Tellechea Idígoras, "Rafols Bruna, Marie," *DS* 13 (1988), cols. 36–38.

7. Manuel Graña, "La Madre Rafols," *El Debate,* 24 May 1932, p. 8; *Vida de Pabla Bescós.*

8. "La Venerable Mare María Rafols," *EM,* 16 September 1931, p. 2; "La imatge del Crist Desemparat exposada a la Capella de Palau Episcopal," *EM,* 15, 16, and 17 September 1931, p. 2; and "La imagen del Cristo Desamparado; Piedad consoladora," *CC,* 17 September 1931, p. 1. Cardinal Pedro Segura dedicated the Vilafranca shrine with three days of prayer in late October 1941, and Esteban Bilbao, minister of justice, said that Irurita had told him about the revelations personally (*La Vanguardia Española,* 28 October 1941, p. 5). Bilbao said that during his captivity in the Civil War the Rafols prophecies, which presaged "the victory of the sword of Franco," always comforted him. Pamphlet by Barcelona canon is Boada y Camps, *Los Crucifijos.*

9. The Roman nihil obstats are 1 December 1931 and 27 April 1932. Demetrio Zurbitu (b. Betelu 1886–d. Barcelona 1936) had been director of Marian Congregations in Barcelona: Mècle, "Deux victimes," 6 (I thank Jacques Mècle for letting me consult this unpublished paper). Arrese, *Profecías;* also López Galuá, *Futura grandeza,* first ed., 1939.

10. There was an article ridiculing the Rafols prophecies in *EM* by P.D., 8 July 1932. Lambert's critical "Los 'escritos póstumos'" was also published in *El Bon Pastor,* April 1933. I do not know if Eugenio Ferrer published "Los escritos," his rebuttal of Lambert. For Pildain: Juan Bautista Ayerbe to Alfredo Renshaw, 6 October 1933, ASC. Manuel Lecuona, in hiding in a convent of Brígidas in Lasarte, found a source for the forgeries and wrote "Escritos de la M. Rafols." He had been suspicious of their pro-Spanish slant. The Dominican Luis Urbano wrote "Neumann, Rafols" and published Josep Tarré's "Crítica interna." According to Lecuona (Oiartzun, 29 March 1983), Tarré wrote an exposé in several volumes but could not publish it. Francisco de Paula Vallet alerted his friend Josep Pou i Martí in Rome against the prophecies in the summer of 1932. Cardinal Pedro Segura was a prime defender of the prophecies; others included Olegario Corral, *Autenticidad,* first in *Sal Terrae,* January 1933, and Castor Montoto, *En los escritos.* The Zaragoza panel (Mècle, "Deux victimes," 8) consisted of Lambert, the Jesuit scholar Zacarías García Villada, and the director of the Archivo Nacional, Miguel Gómez del Campillo, who later participated in the inauguration of the Vilafranca complex.

11. Mècle, "Deux victimes," 13, cites *Caesaraugustan: Beatificationis ac canonizationis Servae Dei Maria Rafols: Inquisitio super dubio an constat de autenticitate scriptorum* (Roma: Polyglotte Vaticane, 1943). For a more recent work see Becker, *Tiempo profético.*

12. Naya had the Sacred Heart say he wanted the Jesuits to be in charge of all the seminaries in Spain and Pius XI to establish the Feast of Christ the King in the Church Universal (Zurbitu, *Escritos,* 59–60). Quote from "La Venerable Mare María Rafols," *EM,* 16 September 1931, p. 2.

13. Zurbitu, *Escritos,* 24, message found 2 October 1931.

14. The Gipuzkoan priest Pío Montoya, who accompanied Irurita to the vision site, remembered that Irurita was at the time seduced by the Rafols prophecies and emphasized their Spanish aspect (San Sebastián, 7 April 1983, p. 16). Quotes from Zurbitu, *Escritos,* 37, and Cardús to Ramona, 9 March 1932, enclosing Rafols booklets.

15. Zurbitu, *Escritos,* 56.

16. Zurbitu, *Escritos,* 68; Cardús wrote an article relating Ezkioga and Rafols, "Els fets," by 27 May 1932; both *El Matí* and *Revista Franciscana* of Vic rejected the article.

17. Long quote, Bordas Flaquer, *La Verdad,* 37; for Naya see Boué, 60, 78–79; for Rome see Cardús to Paulí Subirà, Terrassa, 12 July 1932.

18. ARB 104–105; on 25 February 1932 Cardús sent Ramona excerpts from the Rafols October 1931 message and soon after he sent the full message. Ramona replied on March 10: "When I saw these beautiful booklets I showed them to my confessor and he said that everything in them is related to my [vision] declarations." Ramona was reading the Rafols biography by Guallar when she saw Cardús a week later. On May 10 he sent her excerpts from the new, final prophecy and ten days later several copies of the complete text for her and her confessor. Ramona had passed the brochure to Garmendia by June 6, when she wrote Cardús asking for more pictures of Rafols as "everyone wants one." Visions of Rafols in early 1932 included those by Micaela Goicoechea, April 17 (SC D 76–77); Evarista Galdós, April 29 (Rafols reading letter with date of chastisement, B 719); José Garmendia, May 1 (Virgin confirms congruence of revelations and Ezkioga visions, says more documents will appear and that Rafols knew a chapel would be built and the seers persecuted for it, B 634); a Catalan pilgrim, Antonia Quiñonero, in May (ARB 102); and Benita Aguirre, sometime before June 2 (SC D 112). At that time G.-L. Boué was writing both about Rafols and Ezkioga.

19. Andueza, "Luz de lo Alto" and "Las estupendas profecías"; LC, 10 April 1932, p. 1. El Debate made the connection on 23 April 1932: "Se dice que . . . prueban algunas condiciones que adornan al prelado que rige hoy la diócesis de Barcelona."

20. Zurbitu, Escritos, 34; LC, 11 March 1932, reprinted in Revista Franciscana (Vic), April 1932, pp. 83–84. This article by Andueza was challenged by Txindor and Or Dago in ED, sparking a polemic with Tomás de Arritoquieta.

21. Andueza, LC, 10 April 1932, p. 1; for distribution, LC, 3 June 1932, p. 1. The Rafols prophecies were printed as well in the Mensajero del Corazón de Jesús.

22. LC, 17 May 1932, pp. 1–2, and 26 June 1932, p. 10.

23. Arrese, Profecías, 10. Arrese was secretary to the Basque-Navarrese deputies in the Constituent Cortes.

24. Montserrat García Cascón Marcet, Terrassa, 19 October 1985.

25. Cardús, Espiritualitat Monserratina.

26. Sospedra Buyé, Fa cinquanta anys, 72, and Per carrers, 365.

27. García Cascón to Vallet, 10 October 1931, AHCPCR 10-A-27/3. García Cascón had clients in Legazpi, Mondragón, Tolosa, Rentería, Bergara, and Zumarraga.

28. Salvador Cardús i Florensa (1900–1958) married Rosa Grau, October 1924. Biographical information from his sons Oriol, 19 October 1985, and Josep, 27 November 1993, both in Terrassa, and Cardús, "Context biogràfic." For the 1910 funeral of Antonio José Toroella and the suicide, see Heraldo de Tarrasa, 24 December 1910, p. 2, and 15 July 1911, pp. 1, 4.

29. SC E 26, 30–34, 51–57.

30. SC E 58–82. On October 13 Ramona had a sad vision, which Cardús attributed to the Virgin's sorrow for the upcoming vote in the Cortes to separate church and state.

31. SC E 83–93, 98–105, quotes from p. 92.

32. Garmendia in newspapers, 1931: LC, 25 and 28 July, 2 August; PV, 25 July, 4 August; ED, 28 and 29 July; EM, 8 October. García Cascón to Vallet, 31 October 1931, AHCPCR 10-A-27/2.

33. SC E 117; García Cascón to Vallet, 31 October 1931.

34. Cardús's account in SC E 115–138. El Noticiero Universal, 26 October 1931, p. 7, mentions Macià's close contact with Marcet at Montserrat. See also EM, 21 December 1931.

35. SC E 196–198. For a third visit to Macià, see chap. 6 below.

36. SC E 205–206, 230–235, 261–263. Undated note [April 1932?] in handwriting of Justo de Echeguren in Laburu papers.

37. Garmendia to Cardús, Legazpi, 18 June and 28 October 1933.

38. "Los casos observados en Ezquioga por un médico," *ED,* 21 July 1931, p. 8.

39. *PV,* 31 July 1931, p. 4.

40. Vision of Benita Aguirre on 6 August 1931 in F. D., *CC,* 16 August 1931, p. 2.

41. Elías, *CC,* 15 August 1931, vision around 6 August 1931; Altisent, *CC,* 8 September 1931.

42. Altisent, *CC,* 10 September 1931.

43. Marc Llirò to Cardús, Barcelona, 10 October 1932. The anthropologist Paolo Apolito, glossing a similar comment about an Italian girl, remarks, "If she were [a great actress] nobody would know it" (*Dice,* 292).

44. Delás, *CC,* 20 September 1931.

45. García Cascón to Vallet, 31 October 1931, AHCPCR 10-A-27/2.

46. García Cascón to Vallet, 12 November 1931, AHCPCR 10-A-27/1; Benita Aguirre to García Cascón, 24 October 1931, copy in ASC.

47. García Cascón gave lectures about Ezkioga in the textile town of Sabadell, SC E 239, and Barcelona. García Cascón wrote Vallet on 12 November 1931 that he was going to visit Irurita. *Vida Interior* (Revista Mensual, Organo de la Obra de los Retiros Parroquiales y de las Ligas Parroquiales de Perseverancia, Salto, Uruguay), 2, no. 21 (November 1931): 12–13, and 2, no. 22 (December 1931): 3–4.

48. For Galgani see Boada, "Flors de santedat"; for the Casal see Sospedra Buyé, *Per carrers,* 348–359, 423–448, and *EM,* 1 July 1930.

49. Information on Magdalena Aulina i Saurina (b. Banyoles, 12 December 1897–d. Barcelona, 15 May 1956), unless otherwise noted, is from her successor, Filomena Crous, Barcelona, 25 and 27 February 1985, and ephemeral literature she kindly provided, particularly "Discurso de la directora general, bodas de oro del instituto y décimo aniversario de nuestra madre fundadora . . . 24 mayo 1966," 17-page typescript.

50. Christian, *Moving Crucifixes,* 13, 163.

51. In 1922 Aulina was at Montserrat representing "Patronat d'Obreres de Banyoles" (*La IIIª Assemblea de la federació de patronats d'obreres de Catalunya a Monserrat, 1, 2 i 3 d'abril de 1922* [Barcelona: Impremta Editorial Barcelonesa, 1922]).

52. Boada, "Flors de santedat," 225.

53. Aulina's spiritual directors included Angel Soquer, the parish priest of Banyoles; José María Carbó, a canon of Girona; Fulgencio Albareda, a Benedictine of Montserrat; and finally Marcelino Olaechea, a Salesian who was bishop of Pamplona in 1935 and in 1946 archbishop of Valencia.

54. SC E 193, 230, 236; Gratacós, "Lo de Esquioga." Gemma Galgani articles, all 1931: *EM* and *CC,* 2 December; *CC,* 11 December; *Hormiga de Oro,* 17 December; *EM,* 18 December.

55. *LC,* 11 March 1932.

56. I have not seen the documents, now presumably in the Aulina archives. But Burguera included many of them in his book. My other main sources are the manuscript of Arturo Rodes, the diary of Cardús, and the account of the first trip by Luis Gratacós (and José María Boada), "Lo de Esquioga."

57. Marc Lliró to Cardús, Barcelona, 10 October 1932.

58. Lourdes Rodes, Barcelona, 29 November 1993; B 373–376.

59. On Cruz Lete see ARB 79, 214. Other visions of Gemma by seers in 1931: Benita Aguirre, December 14, ARB 10; Cruz Lete, December 15, ARB 12–13; María Recalde, December 29. In 1932: Luis Irurzun, February 25; Jesús Elcoro, March 14; Loreto Albo, April 5, ARB 109; Benita Aguirre daily in March and June (Benita to García Cascón, 22 May, and

SC D 111–112); Luisa Sabaté in bus, August 24, ARB 115. There were many others from 1933 to 1935. Quote is from Cardús to J. B. Ayerbe, 11 October 1933.

60. B 630–635; ARB; SC D. For Visa, SC D 145–174; ARB 114–117; B 635; copy of expedition document, "Visions de Carme Visa de Dios, tingudes els dies 21 y 22 de juny de 1932," 8-page typescript, ASC. Visa had had an earlier vision in Terrassa on 24 October 1931 while her employers were at Ezkioga, and when she returned she had more in the house. She died 10 October 1932.

61. Gratacós, "Lo de Esquioga," 17–18, 14.

62. ARB 45–46, 245–247; letter from García Cascón to female seer, probably María Recalde, 24 August 1933, private archive; Vitoria Aguirre, Legazpi, 6 February 1986, p. 13. For more on Benita and the Catalans, ARB 48, 89–90, 97–98, 134.

63. Lourdes Rodes, Barcelona, 29 November 1993, p. 2.

64. Lliró to Cardús, Barcelona, 10 October 1932.

65. ARB 7.

66. Otherwise unattributed information on Recalde is from Lorenzo Jayo in Durango, 31 December 1984, and in Tafira Baja, 15 June 1985.

67. Castillo, *ED,* 28 November 1931. Francisco Ezcurdia, Ataun, 9 September 1983, pp. 4–5; ARB 57–59, 173; and B 750–751 describe conversions of an Ezkioga cattle dealer, a Catalan pilgrim, and a Barcelona worker; see Surcouf, *L'Intransigeant,* 19 November 1932: "She has the gift of seeing beings in a state of sin."

68. For Arturo Rodes, ARB 72–73; vision of 28 June 1932, ARB 144–145; for Cardús, SC E 410–413, 442–444 (18 and 19 April 1932); for García Cascón, Cardús, "El Sant Crist de la galeria," 8 pages, ASC, with visions of the servant Carmen Visa from 24 June to 1 July 1932 in Terrassa.

69. ARB 16–18, 143.

70. For buried treasure see SC D 78–79; Cardús makes no mention of anyone finding the jewels and image. The contemporary Catalan mystic Enriqueta Tomás also sent followers to dig for treasure, following an old Mediterranean tradition of prophecy; Barcelona trip, 8–11 June 1932, ARB 76; May 23 vision, ARB 143; Sacred Heart vision on June 14, B 603–604.

71. SC E 534, citing Germán, *Cartas y éxtasis,* 78.

72. Boada, "Flors de santedat," 225.

73. Sulamitis, "Víctimas de amor," *VS,* May 1923, pp. 402–404; Monsó, *Santidad,* 27.

74. Christian, *Moving Crucifixes,* 107–108; Zurbitu, *Escritos,* 56.

75. Andueza, *LC,* 26 June 1932.

76. Burguera, *De Dios a la Creación,* 30–35. Appropriately, women seers came to control Burguera's life completely.

77. *Anuario Estadístico de España,* 1933, p. 667.

78. From a letter from Benita to García Cascón, Legazpi, 12 February 1932, SC D 110.

79. For Reus family, ARB 60, and, probably, visions of Evarista Galdós, 1 and 15 August 1932, B 719. For deceased husband, ARB 107–108.

80. SC E 402–403.

81. Ramona in SC E 79, 422–424; Evarista on 5 April 1932, SC D 67.

82. Lecuona, *Literatura oral,* 51, and interview, Oiartzun, 29 March 1983.

83. Versions of trip in Sospedra Buyé, *Per carrers,* 578–581; ARB 40–44; Rosa Grau to female religious, Terrassa, 29 April 1933; Cardús, "Els dies 6 i 7 d'abril el Pare Vallet . . . ," 8-page manuscript based on accounts of Aguirre family and J. Sicart, the photographer at Ezkioga from Terrassa who introduced Vallet to the seers, ASC; and B 265.

84. Antoni Sospedra Buyé, Barcelona, 25 February 1985.

85. Visions of Garmendia, 10 and 11 April 1932, ARB 43.

86. Sospedra Buyé, *Fa cinquanta anys.* Quote from Vallet to community in Salto from Cuxà, 5 July 1932, AHCPCR 9-A-16/52, cited in Mècle, "Deux victimes," 9.

87. Vallet, *Epistolario,* 111–114.

88. Declaration by Benita in SC D 64–69 and 106–109; similarly, by Evarista, ARB 241–242.

89. For festival see Cardús to R. Grau, 5 October 1931; for general welcome, Cardús, *La Creuada,* 10 October 1931, p. 479. By contrast relatively few pilgrims went from Madrid or Castile, and by April 1932 Benita and Evarista claimed that God would punish Madrid for this disdain.

90. Cardús to J. R. Echezarreta, 21 November 1931.

91. Altisent, *CC,* 15 September 1931.

92. Cardús to Olazábal, 17 November 1932.

93. Even Canon Altisent cautioned against letting down one's guard because of the visions, Altisent, *CC,* 15 September 1931.

94. Idem.

95. Cardús to a believer in Ezkioga, 8 June 1933, private collection.

CHAPTER 5. PROMOTERS AND SEERS III

1. James, *Varieties,* 24.

2. Charles Jean-Marie Raymond de la Ville de Rigné [Raymond de Rigné, Raymond Vroncourt, Jean d'Arvil, Olivier Raynal, Abbé S. Fort, Bénédicte de Marsay], comte de Morville, b. Langres (Haute Marne), 24 August 1883, d. Lanot-Dax, 20 September 1956. Marie-Geneviève Thirouin [Marie de Rigné, G. Thirouin de Morville, Marie de Morville], b. 1895 (from *Mariage nul*), d. Bidache, sometime after 1958.

3. Raymond de la Ville de Rigné, intendant militaire (1840–1927); see his *Aperçu, Poésies, Roles,* and *Souvenirs.*

4. On his Catholicism see Rigné, *Sous l'oeil,* 1921, p. xxvii; on his father, de la Ville, see *Souvenirs,* 245–247. Rigné's first works were in polemic with J. L. Bretonneau, the director of pilgrimages from the diocese of Tours to Lourdes (see Rigné, *Huysmans* and *Autour*). In *Sous l'oeil,* 1921, introduction, pp. ii–iii, x, Rigné created a life for his pseudonym Vroncourt. For prurience see his *Moralités.*

5. Rigné, *Sous l'oeil,* 1921, "Introduction générale"; *Contes;* and *Dans le style. Disciple* 1 and *Disciple* 3 analyzed the compositions of Jules Massenet.

6. For his wife see Rigné, *Contes,* 57–58, and *Sous l'oeil,* 1921, p. xxiii; when he later revised his past he pasted in a new introduction.

7. For Neumann see Rigné and Rigné, *Mariage nul,* 145–148. He saw Neumann in August 1929: Rigné, "Voyages." Thirouin publications: *Rayons* and *Trois essais.* She published *Les Muses* in 1931. For wedding see *Mariage nul,* 207–226, and Thirouin to believers, 30 November 1956.

8. Rigné, *La Clef,* 25–26, *Jehanne,* and *La Vraye Istoire.* I have not seen Rigné's *Le Traité de Troyes et la vraie mission de Jehanne d'Arc,* ca. 1929, advertised in broadside in FL.

9. Rigné, *La Clef,* 26 n.; Rigné, *Sous l'oeil,* 1921, pp. xx and xxv.

10. Rigné, *La Clef,* 19 n.; Rigné, *Disciple* 3, p. x: "I beg once more the reader not to confuse me with d'Arvil. He has his ideas and I have mine; they are not always the same."

11. Rigné, *Sous l'oeil*, 1921, p. xxxvii. No doubt his absence from World War I was an issue in his family; his pseudonym Vroncourt died in the war, pp. ii–iii. As secretary general, *La Clef*, facing p. 1.

12. Rigné and Rigné, *Encyclique*; Rigné, *Testimonio*, 4. Their encyclical was in part a response to Pius XI, "Casti Connubi," of December 1930.

13. Rigné, *Llamamiento*, 2; Rigné to Laburu, Ormaiztegi, 26 April 1932.

14. Fifty years earlier the novelist Léon Bloy sought similar certainty at La Salette and with the visionary Marie Roulé: Griffiths, *Reactionary Revolution*, 138–140.

15. Visions on August 13 and 26. On 27 December 1934, when Mateo Múgica was putting on the heat, Rigné compiled over twenty vision messages confirming his marriage from eleven seers in a letter to a friend in Ezkioga, private collection; hereafter: Rigné marriage visions.

16. Rigné marriage visions, and R 12. My assessment of the number of photos taken is based on photos published and in collections of Remisch, the diocese of Vitoria, Cardús, and Román Barba. Rigné took the most photographs of Evarista, Ramona, Benita, the girl from Ataun, and Marcelina Mendívil.

17. Daniel Ayerbe, Irun, 13 June 1984, p. 5; Manuela Lasa, San Sebastián, 10 September 1983, pp. 4–5.

18. For vision reconstruction, Rigné to García Cascón, Zumarraga, 3 November 1931, describing that of Micaela Goicoechea the previous day, SC E 171–174; on Ramona see Rigné marriage visions.

19. R 49, 86.

20. For investigation see R 41, and Rigné, *Llamamiento*, 2. For breaking fast, Francisco Ezcurdia, whose parents owned the inn, Ataun, 9 September 1983, p. 2. Rigné claimed a special dispensation.

21. García Cascón put the matter of Rigné's book to Garmendia: Rigné to Ezkioga believer, 27 December 1934; request for publisher, Picavea, *PV,* 7 July 1934.

22. Rigné marriage visions, visions of 9 and 16 March 1932.

23. Rigné, *Testimonio;* copies of letters from Justo de Echeguren to Rigné, Vitoria, 17 and 22 December 1932, private collection; in French translation, R 70–73.

24. Rigné, "Ramona," private collection, a Spanish translation of a draft of Rigné's book, with material left out of the final version; R; Múgica, "Declarando" and "Decreto," 1934; Rigné, *Llamamiento,* 4.

25. For miracle false alarms, SC E 366. The Catalan Cardús, who saved almost everything, did not save Rigné's letters and wrote him a sharp reproof for malicious gossip (SC E 548–550). For the chastisement see R 104–108.

26. Rigné visited Governor Jesús Artola, 19 December 1932; Rigné expresses his political position in letters to Olaizola, Ormaiztegi, 20 October, 4 November, and 21 December 1932. He rejected the progressive Sillon movement and in 1928 and 1930 called for friends to leave Action Française: Rigné, *Sous l'oeil*, 1921, p. xxii; *La Clef,* 4, 11–12, 18, 87–89, 91–94; and *Sous l'oeil*, 1930, p. viii ("Lettre ouverte à M. Ch. Maurras, 21 janvier 1924"). At Ezkioga Evarista Galdós relayed a question about Action Française to the Virgin, who supposedly replied, "[Its members] should drop it altogether and do nothing more; I will fix things myself," R 101, and Ducrot, *VU,* 16 August 1933, p. 1292.

27. Cf. his manifesto against all Spanish bishops in April 1932 for accepting civil marriages under the Republic ("Carta a obispos") and his appeal to Pius XI against Mateo Múgica (*Llamamiento*).

28. Burguera, *Roberta Miralles,* 27, 112, 118–124; Burguera, *Ildefonsa Artal,* 38, 180–181.

29. Andrés Ferri Chulio, Sales, 2 December 1983; for patriotism see Burguera, *Historia de Sueca,* 1:110–117. Fermín Cortés, Sueca, 5 December 1983; B 298–299.

30. Burguera, *De Dios a la Creación,* 41–46. Sarachaga's collaborator Victor Drevon organized the national pilgrimages of 1873–1878: Cinquin, "Paray-le-Monial," 187–196 and, for museum, 248.

31. Burguera, *De Dios a la Creación,* 45–49.

32. Burguera's disciple Juan Castells told me that the revised third volume, in manuscript, which related the Ezkioga visions to all of previous history, was lost in the Civil War. Burguera appears to have visited museums in Rome, Paris, London, Bern, Jerusalem, Nazareth, Cairo, and Tetuán. He would have enjoyed an equivalent work, the two-volume, large-format Rivero San José, *Cantabria, Cuna de la Humanidad,* which with color photographs and an analysis of toponyms demonstrates that the area around the village of San Sebastián de Garabandal, the site of visions of the Mary by four girls in the early 1960s, was originally the Garden of Eden.

33. B 665.

34. Motive for visit, from Juan Castells, Sueca, 6 December 1983, p. 4; B 43; B II 625 n. 53, 627–628, 631–632, 636. Iñaki claimed one hundred visions by the time of this meeting.

35. First proof, B II 633 n. 57; Juan Castells, Sueca, 6 December 1983, p. 5; for Bakaiku, B 40, B II 637, and Castells.

36. B 352, 664; Castells, Sueca, 6 December 1983, p. 4; Burguera also told these proofs to the Navarrese believer Pedro Balda: interview, Alkotz, 8 April 1983, p. 5, and Balda to Guerau de Arellano, 9 November 1937, AC 264.

37. B II 634–635, 637, 694. The book was still in press in mid-1932 (prologue to *La Verdad*).

38. Bordas Flaquer, *La Verdad,* 8–10; ARB 151. The prologue is dated in Ezkioga July 5, the censure July 22. The bishop of Segorbe, Luis Amigó, was a devout Capuchin from the Valencian region. He dedicated his order of Capuchin tertiaries to Our Lady of the Sorrows (see Ramo Latorre, *Mensaje,* 151–152).

39. B 665–667; ARB 119–120, 124, 234. Ciordia thereby claimed her visions began before those of Ezkioga.

40. On 5 August 1969 Lourdes Rodes recorded Sedano's reminiscences in Barcelona; hereafter: Sedano tape.

41. Sedano told me that the archbishop of Valladolid, Remigio Gandásegui, was curious about the visions and told him to take notes. Gandásegui, from Baracaldo, was the Spanish bishop who had gone most often to Limpias and he was also a Lourdes enthusiast. After a near-fatal heart attack in 1932 he summered at the Ordizia estate of the doctor Benigno Oreja, himself an Ezkioga sympathizer. Sometime after the Vatican closed the book on the case, Sedano was forced to proclaim his submission.

42. ARB 12–13; Sedano tape, 11–12; elderly sheepman, Ikastegieta, 4 April 1983. On 15 December 1931 Lete predicted his own death (Gratacós, "Lo de Esquioga"). He said the Virgin confirmed to him Ramona's divine wounds, Evarista's ribbon from heaven, and Rigné's second marriage. I have texts of visions from 25 October 1931 until 8 February 1932. He dictated others to Ramona's friend, the Bilbao artist José de Lecue: Lecue to Cardús, Bilbao, 20 February 1934. According to Lecue's niece in 1984, Lecue eventually gave all his records to the diocese.

43. SC E 278; vision declaration signed in Ezkioga 8 February 1932 by Cruz de Lete, 2 sides, private collection.

44. Sedano tape, 13–16.

45. His verdict alienated him from Lecue and Cardús, but they did not publicly challenge him, R 65; SC E 481/ 25–26 and 35–37; Cardús to Ayerbe, 15 January 1934. Francisco Otaño Odriozola was born in Zizurkil in 1883 and became coadjutor of Beizama in 1910. After Laburu's lecture he forbade Ramona to go to Ezkioga. He soon relented, but Ramona's visions ended anyway on 15 August 1932. He wrote Cardús about twenty letters from October 1932 to December 1935. In late 1933 he was reputedly composing Ramona's biography.

46. B 42; for sculptor, Burguera, *Compendio*, 294; for contest, ARB 98–102: "What was the first miracle wrought by God?" "What is the place on earth that is above heaven?" "What is the distance from heaven to hell?" Answers: "The creation"; "The place where the Virgin Mary is to be found in body and soul"; and "Only the fallen angels know this [distance], for only they have traveled it."

CHAPTER 6. SUPPRESSION BY CHURCH AND STATE

1. Justo Antonino de Echeguren y Aldama, born 1884 into a wealthy family of Amurrio, ordained 1907, doctor at Gregorian University in Rome, *licenciado* in law at the University of Valladolid, *secretario de cámara* under Bishop Leopoldo Eijo y Garay of Vitoria and vicar general under Mateo Múgica from 1928 until becoming bishop of Oviedo in January 1935. Opinions from Pío Montoya, San Sebastián, 7 April 1983, pp. 1, 8–9; G. Insausti, Ormaiztegi, May 1984; Barandiarán, Ataun, 9 September 1983, p. 3.

2. The diocesan press delegate, José María de Sertucha, had the bishop's entire confidence.

3. De la Villa, *DSS*, 13 August 1931; Maura in *El Socialista*, 14 August 1931, p. 4. For Azaña the speech was "muy chabacana" (*Obras* [México: Oasis, 1968], 4:82). On Echeguren's attitude, Pío Montoya, San Sebastián, 7 April 1983, pp. 15–16.

4. On the rosaries the directive was unpublished; see *BOOV*, 1 May 1932, p. 264; Echeguren, notes to Laburu, spring 1932; and L 14. Cardús wrote Ramona, 9 March 1932, that Irurita intervened "hace tiempo" (some time ago).

5. For Sertucha see R 41; Boué, 69; Juan Celaya, Albiztur, 6 June 1984, p. 29. Rigné's private life was at issue as well, perhaps because he was seen as aggravating the situation. *BOOV*, 1 January 1932, p. 6, and 1 May 1932, p. 263; Echeguren to Laburu, Vitoria, 20 January 1932.

6. Profiles in *Estrella del Mar*, 8 November 1931, p. 457, and Caro Baroja, *Los Baroja*, 274–275; oratory description from *El Debate*, 24 March 1933; for his psychology see Laburu, *Psicopatología*; *BOOV*, 1930, p. 372. From April to July 1932, in addition to his Ezkioga lectures he gave at least eight in Bilbao, Vitoria, and San Sebastián on childhood education, the psychology of children, wealth and social justice, and the psychology of Ignacio de Loyola. One in San Sebastián, held outdoors, attracted eleven thousand persons.

7. Laburu's family also went to Ezkioga and his mother wanted to know his opinion (letter to Laburu after 8 February 1932).

8. The priest José Ramón Echezarreta, brother of the owner of the apparition site, thought Sertucha's questions were part of the approval process, whence the prohibition of priests at the site, "a measure used first at Lourdes and lately at Fatima." At Ezkioga he had seen Laburu's films, "which provided us with a most agreeable moment" (to Cardús, Legorreta, 4 January 1932).

9. For activity in early 1932: ARB 20–21; Romero, "Comunicado"; "Vuelve la afluencia de gentes a Ezquioga," *LC*, 9 February 1932, p. 1; Andueza, *LC*, 11 March 1931. The

high point was Holy Week, with buses from Pamplona, *VN,* 24 March 1932, p. 2. Early in April Echeguren succeeded in getting Patxi, through an Ataun priest, to take down the stations of the cross he had put up in February (Echeguren to Laburu, 13 May 1932); note in ADV Varios file, 1927–1934, for Echeguren's measures. Echeguren wrote to Laburu regarding the talk on 3, 13, 15, and 18 April 1932.

10. The seminarian Francisco Ezcurdia (9 September 1983, p. 5) originally had been assigned the task of excluding the seers.

11. As far as I know, Laburu never published the complete lecture. In the archives at Loyola are three texts, one handwritten, undated, with corrections by another hand, possibly that of Mateo Múgica; I use, citing as L, a forty-page, double-spaced typescript of the same text; there is also a French translation. I have listed some newspaper reports under Laburu in the bibliography. The best is that by José Miguel de Barandiarán in the seminary's student magazine, *Gymnasium.* That of *GN* was reprinted in *BOOV, CC,* and *Semanario Católico de Reus.* There were short summaries in *Easo, EM,* and *La Verdad* of Pamplona. The June 20 lecture, which had new details and was more combative, is reported best in *PV.*

12. L 11.

13. L 13.

14. L 15.

15. L 18–19. In Laburu's films at Loyola I did not find those from Ezkioga.

16. Francisco Ezcurdia (1908–1993), Ataun, 9 September 1983, pp. 5–6; for Ramona's spiritual director: Ramona to Cardús, 6 June 1932; for convincing of seminarians: Daniel Ayerbe, Irun, 13 June 1984, pp. 4, 7, who did not, however, support the visions.

17. Basque-language weekly: *Ekin-Jaungoiko-zale,* 30 April 1932, p. 3; *Full Dominical* (Terrassa parish bulletin), 5 June 1932; *La Verdad* (Pamplona parish bulletin), no. 36; Joan Colomer i Carreras to Cardús, Barcelona (Sant Andreu), 10 May 1932; SC E 476–480.

18. For Pasaia rector, Pedro Gurruchaga to Laburu, San Sebastián, 18 June 1932; Rigné to Laburu, Ormaiztegi, 26 June 1932. Three days later Rigné in *Llamamiento* denounced the vicar general for opposing the apparitions, for using Laburu as his pawn, and for presenting the bishop with a fait accompli. Pharmacist Gonzalo Formiguera Hernández to Laburu, Barcelona, 29 April 1932; art restorer Pedro María Lage to Laburu, Vitoria, n.d.

19. Baroja, *Los Visionarios,* 539, and similarly, for Ezkioga and Limpias, *El Cura de Monleón,* chap. 21; Caro Baroja, *Los Baroja,* 275.

20. Sinforoso de Ibarguren to Laburu, Ezkioga, 27 July 1932.

21. For P. Rainaldo see B 137, 288; and the Carmelite provincial Ecequiel del S. C. de Jesús to Echeguren, Bilbao, 20 June 1932; and see chap. 8 below, "Religious Professionals." For Limpias see *Diario Montañés,* 6 November 1920, p. 2.

22. For Garmendia, SC E 421, 17 April 1932; for effect of Laburu lecture: Joan Colomer i Carreras to Cardús, Barcelona (Sant Andreu), 10 May 1932, and Benita to García Cascón, Legazpi, 22 May 1932, in SC D 111.

23. The meeting, described in a letter from Cardús to Pare Rimblas, 17 June 1932, and ARB 73–74, allegedly took place May 5 with Franciscan nuns as witnesses.

24. For Laburu as sinner, Juana Aguirre vision, 28 June 1932, in Boué, 78; for change of mind, Evarista vision, 29 June 1932, in B 334 and 721; on cancer, Boué, 97, and *EE;* dismissed by Múgica in *BOOV,* 15 March 1934, p. 245; Benita Aguirre, n.d, B 592, and 5 June 1933, B 494–495; Pilar Ciordia, 14 July 1933, B 691.

25. Echeguren notes to Laburu, spring 1932; ARB 24–25; Echeguren, *BOOV,* 15 June 1932; the vicar general's note was in *ED, LC,* and *EZ* on June 16. In the summer of 1932 some priests forbade their penitents to go to Ezkioga, but this was not a diocesan policy. Garmendia had a vision on August 19 and 20 in which the Virgin said that priests could not

keep properly dressed people from going, B 636. For image, B 42, 387 n. 1; the artist was Martí Gras; more in chap. 11 below.

26. ARB 151.

27. VG, 17 August 1932, p. 1.

28. Del Pozo press declaration, 21 September 1932, in VG 22 September 1932, p. 5, and widely reported elsewhere. B 268 claimed that the order came from Azaña.

29. FS 53; B 42, 379; ARB 27. An eyewitness to the image's arrival by truck (Surcouf, *L'Intransigeant*, 20 November 1932) wrote that some rural folk expected it to come down from heaven.

30. Marcelina Eraso Muñagorri (b. Arriba [Navarra], ca. 1909–d. ca. 1972). Incident reported on 10 October 1932: VG, p. 7; PV, p. 9; Sol, p. 9; *La Vanguardia;* and B 379 (wrongly dates it October 7). Marcelina supposedly told a doctor at Mondragón that she saw a serpent around his neck, and he stopped questioning her, for he was living in sin (elderly believer, Ikastegieta, 16 August 1982, p. 2). On October 24 del Pozo released the hospital diagnosis that she had a weak memory and little judgment and was very suggestible (VN, 25 October, p. 6).

Bago, jailed for storming the provincial seat in 1930, had been the subject of a nationwide homage by republican doctors. He was a trusted adviser to governors under the Republic. See C. and J., VG, 2 May 1931; Barriola, "La medicina donostiarra," 39; and Estornés Zubizarreta, *La Construcción,* 295–296.

31. Unlabeled clipping, 11 October; VG, 3 November; B 379–380; Sicart to Cardús, Ezkioga, 9 October. Strikes closed all San Sebastián daily newspapers from 10 October until 3 November 1932, which facilitated del Pozo's crackdown. The press of Pamplona, Madrid, and Barcelona reported del Pozo's measures in brief notes.

32. B 379–380; ARB 29–30. One of the workers, Juan Benarrás (Ezkioga, 15 August 1982), said the pressure not to act was intense. *El Noticiero Universal,* 12 October; *Ahora,* 13 October; VG, 3 November; Sol, 13 October; ARB 31; SC E 481/ 14. Cardús's account of these days is untitled and numbered separately; I have treated it as part of "Engrunes," in which it would follow p. 481.

33. SC E 481/ 1–2, 6–7; Cardús to García Cascón, Zaragoza, 13 October 1932. According to Sospedra Buyé, Barcelona, 15 February 1983, García Cascón later gave Macià a replica of the Ezkioga statue. For night vigil see ARB 154.

34. Account of events based on SC E 481/ 8–13; Benarrás, 15 August 1982; R 120; and *El Debate,* 15 October 1932, p. 3. For Ibarguren, DN, 15 October, p. 4. Benita claimed to see the cross falling in a vision in Legazpi (ARB 156). For after dinner, SC E 481/ 16–17.

35. SC E 481/ 20–24; DN, 16 October, p. 4; ARB 155–156; B 380, 405. The weekly *La Cruz* alone questioned the governor, asking on October 16 that the believers be left alone. The house, Kapotegi, belonged to Echezarreta.

36. I do not know if Tedeschini really said this, and if so, to Burguera himself or someone else, like Carmen Medina, who was in touch with him that summer (B 137; SC E 481/ 25–27 (quote); Burguera to Cardús, 21 October 1932). The message would not have been out of character; witness Tedeschini's informal statement at Limpias in 1921 in Christian, *Moving Crucifixes,* 79.

37. SC E 481/ 28–31, 34–35; ARB 156–157.

38. SC E 481/ 32–34.

39. SC E 481/ 37–38; ARB 162.

40. Burguera to Cardús, 21 and 22 October; B 380; DN, 22 October, p. 3, and 26 October, p. 3; Sol, 22 October, p. 5; *Crónica Social,* Terrassa, 26 October.

41. ARB 161; *El Socialista,* 9 July 1932, p. 2, and 29 October 1932, p. 6; Sol, 30 October, p. 7; PN, 30 October, p. 3. Dossiers as Freemasons in AHN GC 211/17 and 214/9.

42. B 388–390, a court officer in Azpeitia who was a friend of an Ezkioga believer may have leaked the interview transcripts. Women fined in Viana (Navarra), *PV,* 9 February; Yécora (Alava), *PV,* 11 February; women jailed in Salinas de Oro (Navarra), *CC,* 27 April; women jailed, from *El Debate,* Casa de Miñán (Cáceres), 27 May, Anna (Valencia), 14 July, San Esteban del Valle (Avila), 30 July, Algemesí (Valencia), 6 November, and Navalperal de Pinares (Avila), 6 December. In Galvez (Toledo) women forced the mayor to carry the Virgin on the annual trip from the parish church to the chapel, *LC,* 3 April 1932.

43. For Evarista, B 380, 722; ARB 159–160; unlabeled note in the folder "La Persecució governativa," ASC. For Rosario, B 381; ARB 158–159. For Benita, Benita to García Cascón, Legazpi, 24 October 1932. ARB 161–162.

44. Francisco Otaño to Cardús, Beizama, 26 November 1932.

45. ARB 159; first two questions and answers from Cardús, "La Persecució," ASC; B 391.

46. For arrest B 68–69, 393–398; *VG,* 3 November 1932, p. 7; and on 4 November 1932: *DN,* p. 3; *VG,* p. 4; *PV,* p. 3; *LC,* p. 3; *Sol,* p. 1. Next day: *La Vanguardia,* and Moya, *El Socialista.* Mariano Bordas interceded with the governor of Gipuzkoa for Burguera, who defended himself in *PV,* 2 December 1932. Azpiazu was accused of holding clandestine meetings in his house.

47. Garmendia's certificate of sanity circulated among believers (AC 409). He and others were let out November 13. Recalde in ARB 162–164. Del Pozo in *Noticiero Bilbaino,* 30 October 1932, p. 3, and *PV,* 4 November 1932, p. 3. His downfall came when civil guards massacred villagers at Casas Viejas in Andalusia. Ezkioga believers noted that Casa Vieja in Spanish means Echezarreta in Basque (ARB 165–166). For the new governor, Jesúus Artola, B 403–404, 710; SC E 504–505; R 31.

48. The vicar general's inactivity was anomalous, given his swift reaction to other images in the past. Múgica entered the diocese 11 April 1933; his denial of a role in del Pozo's campaign in *BOOV,* 9 March 1934, pp. 241, 245.

49. Visions about Burguera, Benita, November, SC D 119; Patxi's declaration, 4 December 1932, ASC; Garmendia, 19 December, B 638; cf. visions of Iñes Igoa and Evarista in B 622–623. Burguera was in Barcelona from 16 to 20 November 1932. He saw a bishop December 12 and March 21 (B 323). Vision to publish anyway, Evarista, 1 May 1933 (B 723); see also Ciordia, 4 April (B 684), Evarista, 4 and 9 May (B 723, 725), and Benita, 3 and 5 June (B 493–494).

50. J. B. Ayerbe (ca. 1865–1957), *Hijos ilustres de Segura,* and *El Siglo Futuro,* 23 August 1919, and *El Debate,* 20 July 1921. Another brother, Felipe, and two brothers of his wife were priests.

51. Ayerbe, "Maravillosas apariciones," AC 1 [p. 6], and Boué, 126–127. From private collections of Ezkioga material I have made a consolidated archive (labeled AC) of original or photocopied documents written or recopied by Ayerbe, consisting of over 450 different items; this is a fraction of his output.

52. Ayerbe to Cardús, 24 October 1933; I have Ayerbe's versions of about eighty sessions with Conchita from 10 December 1932 until 15 March 1942. He circulated messages from at least eighteen different seers.

53. Daniel Ayerbe, Irun, 13 June 1984, p. 1; J. B. Ayerbe to García Cascón, 22 March 1934, AC 416.

54. B 280. On the return trip from Lourdes the seer heard the Virgin explain that she wore colored robes in France because France received her better: "When Spain knows how to answer my call, I will show myself in Spain more splendidly than in France . . . and work more miracles than in France."

55. For the pregnancy, Ducrot, *VU*, 23 August 1933, p. 1332; R 47, 95; and *EE*, April–May 1936, p. 2. Sexual immorality during the night visions was already an issue in the summer of 1931. Amundarain in his note of July 28 referred to "atrevidos desahogos nocturnos"; see also Masmelene, *EZ*, 15 July 1931; E. G., "En torno a los sucesos"; Millán, *ELB*, 9–10 September 1931: "una joven señorita . . . recrimina a un señor que se aprovecha del lugar y del momento explorándola descaradamente"; Romero, "Comunicado"; and Txindor, *ED*, 22 March 1932.

56. For verses about the visions, see below in bibliography Emika, Erauskin Errota, Lujanbio Retegi, Luistar, Urdanpilleta, and Zavala, *Txirrita* and *Erauskin*, 87–95. Verse 8 of Urdanpilleta, *Berso Berriak*, reads: "Euzkaldun neska gastiak / favores aditu / gauza biar bezela / nai det esplikatu / gaurko nere etsanak / goguan ondo artu / mariak beretsat lagun / garbiyak nai ditu" (All Basque girls / please listen / I want to explain this / properly / pay good attention / to what I have to say: / Mary wants for herself / clean friends). In 1984 Pedro Manuel Larrain of Alkiza remembered part of the verse debate in Zarautz (personal communication, Kepa Fernández de Larrinoa).

57. Ayerbe, *Las Apariciones*, obviously required Burguera's collaboration. The diocese privately complained to Ayerbe, who withdrew the leaflet. Burguera came to consider him a careless amateur who, although "active and zealous," did not know how to tell good spirits from bad ones (B 20–21).

58. B 280–82, 409, 711.

59. B 83–84, 282 n. 5. At Lourdes in 1858 Dr. Dozous had watched a candle flame in contact with Bernadette's hand, and doctors tested Patxi this way in 1931. Burguera's detractors argued against the test, citing I. Lenain, "Les Événements de Beauraing," *Nouvelle revue téologique de Louvain* (April 1933): 327–356.

60. Aranda, B 711; Lorenzo Jayo, Durango, December 1984, p. 6; for Garmendia's burned hand, Boué, 116; photograph in *VU*, 23 August 1933, p. 1329; for Albiztur, the witness Juan Celaya, Albiztur, 6 June 1984, p. 26; sixteen tested, B 690; Luis Irurzun, San Sebastián, 5 April 1983, p. 17, took the test later.

61. B 638, 24 May 1933.

62. AC 296, 1 June 1933.

63. B 493–494, 565, 636, 727; López de Lerena to Burguera, 26 July 1933, private collection.

64. B 689–693.

65. For publication of Burguera's book, Benita, 3 and 5 June 1933, B 493–494; for letters, Evarista Galdós, 24 May 1933, B 726; Evarista and Pilar visions, Navarra (Uharte-Arakil), 7 July 1933, B 753, and López de Lerena to Burguera, 26 July. Pedro Balda was at the Uharte-Arakil sessions and warned Echeguren (Alkotz, 7 June 1984, pp. 1–2).

66. Benita, 20 July 1933, B 500, and AC 21, p. 2; Benita and Evarista, 9 May 1933, B 685–686, 725; book content, Garmendia, 28 June 1933, B 639.

67. B 232–233.

68. Given Rigné's lifelong delight in flaunting bishops, this attack on Burguera was a low blow; R 112–114, with Pilar Ciordia's retort.

69. López de Lerena to Burguera, 26 July 1933; for ambush, B 699. Burguera said mass covertly in Benita's house (Victoria Aguirre, Legazpi, 6 February 1986).

70. All 1933: Múgica, "Sobre la supuesta sobrenaturalidad," also in *BOEP*, 1 October, 304–307; *La Croix*, 26 September, p. 1; *Études carmélitaines*, October, 136 ff.; and *Iris de Paz*, 935–936.

71. Dated 7 September 1933, the circular was published in the September 15 diocesan bulletin, which newspapers received the eighteenth or nineteenth (*DN*, 19 September, p. 1; *PV*,

20 September, p. 3; *ED*, 20 September, p. 2; *LC*, 20 September, p. 1; *EM*, 20 September; *El Debate*, 20 September, p. 3; *EM*, 21 September, p. 8; *A*, 24 September, p. 1; *La Cruz*, 24 September, p. 2). *El Debate* carried a short note on 16 September 1933, p. 5.

72. On student days, Dr. Mon de Goeyse, Louvain, 22 July 1983. Robert Brasillach, *Léon Degrelle et l'avenir de "Rex"* (Paris: Plon, 1936), 26–28. For the opportuneness of the apparitions see Étienne, *Mouvement rexiste*, 20–21, and Degrelle, *Persiste et signe*, 73–76.

73. Toussaint and Joset, *Beauraing*, and Joset, *Heylen*. There was strong opposition in *Études carmélitaines*, gathered in *Les Faits mystérieux de Beauraing* (Paris, 1933). For contemporary reactions and reports of other visions see *Annales de Beauraing* (January to 1 April 1933), subsequently *Annales de Beauraing et Banneux*. Bruno de Jésus-Marie listed over twenty sets of visions for 1933 in "Beauraing: Notre réponse; Critique historique," *Études carmélitaines*, December 1934, pp. 313–314.

74. *PV*, "El Ezquioga Belga," 10 December 1932; *VG*, "Un Ezquioga en Bélgica," 21 December 1932, p. 16. No comparison with Ezkioga in *Ahora* (Madrid), 16 December 1932, or Vicente Sánchez Ocaña, "Apariciones en Bélgica," in *Estampa* (Madrid), 21 and 28 October and 4 and 11 November 1933. *El Debate* and *LC* ignored the visions until the visions of Tilman Côme drew huge crowds in August. Quote is from Thurston, "The Apparitions of Our Lady in Belgium," *The Month*, November 1933, pp. 455–457. See also *The Month*, February 1933, pp. 159–169, and Léon Merklen in *La Croix*, 27 September 1933, p. 1. Ezkioga analogy also in *Études carmélitaines*, April 1933, p. 143, and October 1934, pp. 255–261.

75. Cardús to Olazábal, 25 January 1933. Múgica used the caution of the Belgian bishops as support for his actions in *BOOV*, 1 December 1933, pp. 624–625.

76. See Joset, *Sources*, 9–10 and bibliography. Degrelle claimed French and Dutch editions of Maistriaux's pamphlets sold seven hundred thousand copies, but others put the number lower (Degrelle, *Persiste et signe*, 75–76; Toussaint and Joset, *Beauraing*, 98–100; Étienne, *Mouvement rexiste*, 20). Other pamphlets by Gerardin, Saussus, Magain, and Sindic are listed in *Vlan*, 8 February 1934, p. 15, and in Rex pamphlets. Charges of exploitation are in "Après la condamnation de Rex," *Annales de Beauraing et Banneux*, 15 May 1937, p. 4.

77. Ducrot, *VU*, 16, 23, and 30 August 1933, pp. 1289–1293, 1329–1333, 1363–1367. In the August 16 issue there was also a page on the Beauraing visions. Three writers went with Degrelle: Raphaël Sindic, a high-school teacher, later wrote on the summer 1933 visions of Tilman Côme; Abbé Daniel Goens wrote about the group's visit to the Tolosa seer in *EE* (May 1934, pp. 1–3) and about a bleeding crucifix in Asti (Italy); Hubert d'Ydewalle, in Spain for Degrelle's biweekly *Vlan* earlier in 1933, was sympathetic toward Nazi Germany. For Viñals see Sindic, *Apparitions en Flandre*, 1–2; Boué, 102–103; and *EE*, December 1933, pp. 1, 5. For Tolosa seer, *EE*, May 1934, pp. 1–3. For Irurzun, AC 230. A rough draft of the letter believers sent to Múgica, "Al Ilmo. Sr. Obispo de Vitoria," private collection.

78. Degrelle, *Soirées*, 21 September 1933, text copied in *Études carmélitaines*, October 1934, pp. 256–257. Goens mentioned Ezkioga in his pamphlet on a bleeding crucifix in Asti, p. 19.

79. On Múgica's circular, Pérez Ormazábal, "Mandando leer la Circular." For Irurzun, believer to Cardús, Ezkioga, 12 October 1933. On handing in material, Casilda Arcelus and Francisco Ezcurdia, Ormaiztegi, 9 September 1983, p. 2.

80. Rigné to Olaizola, Ormaiztegi, 23 September 1933.

81. B 433–437. On 5 January 1934 the mayor of Durango, allegedly on the behest of the parish priest, detained Recalde for a night. López de Lerena apparently had had to promise his parish priest not to go to Ezkioga (letter to friend, 6 October 1933). The priest of Ormaiztegi spoke to Rigné.

82. Irurzun visions of 22 and 26 September 1933 in J. B. Ayerbe's dittoed "Perora-

ciones del portentoso vidente Luis Irurzun de Irañeta (Navarra)," from Balda's letters, AC 231; Martín Ayerbe in J. B. Ayerbe to Cardús, 8 October 1933; catastrophe, in López de Lerena to Ezkioga believer, 25 October 1933, private collection (seer probably Gloria Viñals); Pilar and Benita in B 701–702, and Victoria Aguirre, Legazpi, 6 February 1986, p. 4.

83. Local elites thought they could get bishops moved. Opponents went to Rome to get López y Mendoza shifted from Pamplona about 1905 and almost succeeded. Aranzadi (*Ereintza*, 312–313) asserted that Basques lobbying in Rome moved the centralist Cadena y Eleta from Vitoria in 1913. For rumors, Ayerbe to Cardús, 16 November 1933: "I know a lot about the new bishop and how he intends to arrange this business"; and 4 January 1934: "We know nothing new about the change in the bishop, although we hope it will be this month." On Medina and Granada, ARB 176, and García Cascón to Arturo Rodes, 20 January 1934. Rodrigo (1885–1973) became bishop of Huesca in 1935, where he helped the Aulinas.

84. B 137; Tedeschini went to San Sebastián by train after the accident and stayed there until September 6, when he left for Avila, see from 24 August to 7 September 1933 *El Debate, Osservatore Romano, LC,* and *ED.* The chaplain of the Hijas de la Providencia, the nuns at the San Ignacio clinic, was Jesús Imaz, who thought himself cured by the Virgin of Ezkioga. Evarista told the crucifix story to García Cascón in Irun on 7 December 1933; García Cascón to Arturo Rodes, Terrassa, 20 January 1934, ARB 175–176.

85. For Tedeschini see Redondo, *Historia,* and Garriga, *El Cardenal Segura,* 86–87. The Madrid believer Alfredo Renshaw knew the nuncio and thought him sympathetic to the visions (Ayerbe to Cardús, 24 October 1933).

86. B 438, 414–421; Cardinal Sbarreti's "Comunicación" reached San Sebastián 8 February 1934 (*ED,* 9 February, p. 1; *LC,* 10 February, p. 4); on danger, B 701–702; on his book, visions of September 29 to October 29, B 613, 701–706.

87. Biographical facts from Remisch's widow in Dijon, 17 December 1983. Remisch, *Mystères de Beauraing,* 23, 139. He went to Konnersreuth with Ennemond Boniface on 8 July 1931 and 31 August 1932, and in 1933 published his translation of Helmut Fahsel, *Thérèse Neumann, la mystique de Konnersreuth* (Lessines: Spes). He went back in September 1934 and August 1952. The year before his death he published another book about Neumann, *Trente-trois ans.* Boniface's first book about her, *La Crucifiée,* appeared under the name Paul Romain.

88. Boniface dedicated a copy of his book to Rigné in Lyon on 29 July 1933. Article in *L'Avenir de Luxembourg,* 17–18 September 1933, mentioned in Remisch, "Comment rébondit l'affaire d'Ezkioga," *EE* 1 (December 1933): 1–2. Not until 1936 did Remisch explicitly denounce Degrelle (*EE* 11–12 [November 1936]: 6).

89. The issues were as follows: 1 (December 1933), 23 rue Ketels, Bruxelles, 46 × 30 cm, 6 pages; 2 (February–March 1934), 8 pages; 3 (May 1934), 37 rue Juliette Récamier, Lyon, 8 pages; 4 (September–October, 1934), 48 × 32 cm, 6 pages; 5 (January 1935), 6 pages; 6 (April–May 1935), 6 pages; 7 (July–August 1935), 6 pages; 8 (October–November 1935), 6 pages; 9 (January–February 1936), 6 pages; 10 (April–May 1936), 6 pages; 11–12 (November–December 1936), 8 pages. The Hemeroteca Municipal of Madrid has a microfilm of the set given to me by Remisch's widow.

90. Balda to Remisch/Dorola, 7 October 1935, AC 252; Irurzun to Remisch/Dorola, 13 October 1935; ARB 251. For Rigné, *EE* 1 (December 1933): 5–6; *EE* 2 (February–March 1934): 5; *EE* 3 (May 1934): 6; *EE* 6 (April–May 1935): 2–3; Rigné, "Les Idées"; Rigné, *Ciel ouvert,* p. B n. 2. For Burguera, B 20, 411, 421–424.

91. The "Avertissement" for Rigné's *Une Nouvelle Affaire Jeanne d'Arc* is signed B. M. and dated 25 July 1933, and a postscriptum of 29 October 1933 comments on the bishop's circular. The "présentation" is signed M. l'abbé S. Fort. The title page gives no author or date. The book was supposedly the first of *Les Cahiers d'Ezkioga,* "publiés sous la direction

de F. Dorola"; it was sold at La Librairie Centrale, 41 rue Jeanne d'Arc, Orléans, vi + 120 pages. The photographer, "M. de Riñé," explains and comments on each of the thirty-four photographs in an appendix, pp. 116–121. Ramon de Riñe, "A mis amigos," is dated "Ormáiztegui, 6 enero 1934," in papers of José Olaizola.

92. The French letter is an enclosure in Múgica to Muniz y Pablos, bishop of Pamplona, 5 March 1934, ADP; French letter written 20 December 1933, ADP.

93. Rigné, "Communicación del escritor Sr. Rigné al nuevo Sr. Fiscal eclesiástico del Obispado de Vitoria," Ormáiztegui, 9 February 1934, copy by Ayerbe, private collection; Múgica to Muniz y Pablos, Vitoria, 12 March 1934, ADP; Rigné to Olaizola, 10 March and 23 April 1934. At least one seer wrote Múgica that Rigné's marriage was legitimate in the eyes of God.

94. Rigné to Muniz y Pablos, 5 March 1934, ADP; Rigné to Olaizola, Ormáiztegui, 10 March 1934; Múgica to Muniz y Pablos, Vitoria, 12 March 1954, ADP; Cardús to Francisco Otaño, 29 March 1934; Rigné to Olaizola, Ormáiztegui, 23 April 1934.

95. Múgica, "Declarando 'ipso iure' prohibidas"; also issued separately as an eight-page pamphlet (Vitoria: Montepío Diocesano, 1934) and reported in ED on March 21, p. 1, and in VG the next day, p. 16. The bishop of Tarbes backed up Múgica on April 16 and condemned Boué's book. The follow-up circular ("Tres disposiciones"), signed by Antonio Pérez Ormazábal, was in ED, 4 April 1934, p. 6. Priests were to proclaim the three works forbidden "**as a mortal sin**" [his boldface] to be purchased, read, or kept.

96. SS. Congregación del Santo Oficio, "Decreto declarando destituidas de todo carácter sobrenatural," BOOV, 1 July 1934, pp. 479–483, was first published in Latin on p. 1 of Osservatore Romano, 18–19 June 1934. ED, VG, and El Debate of Madrid carried the news on June 19 and EM on June 21. The decree was published again in San Sebastián July 6 and 7, in Terrassa, Full Dominical, July 8, and EM and Iris de Paz, July 18.

97. The donor, Ulpiano Rodríguez, born ca. 1905 in Briviesca, was killed on a prison ship in Bilbao by leftists during the Civil War (B 749–751, and Sedano memoir, pp. 30–31). The book cost over twenty thousand pesetas to print.

98. Cardús to Ayerbe, 15 November 1933 and 15 January 1934. For Aulina on Burguera, SC E 732–733.

99. For Benita, B 745–746. The Catholic press of the north treated the Asti events, which began 11 August 1933, respectfully. See La Verdad, 24 May 1934, p. 3, and ED, 3 June 1934, p. 1.

100. Daniel Goens in "Quelques heures," EE 3 (May 1934): 1–3, said this seer gave out crucifixes and medals from heaven.

101. According to Sedano's memoir (p. 31), Juan José Echezarreta paid for their upkeep and donated paper for the book.

102. For this period his "Les Idées," and Rigné to Braulio Corres, Santa Lucía, 8 March 1935, private collection. Quote is from López de Lerena to a believer, 25 January 1935, private archive.

103. Rigné, "Voyages"; Rigné to Olaizola, Orleans, 12 May 1936. He claimed the priests of Ezkioga turned him in to the military governor, León Carrasco. Rigné to Ezkioga believer, Santa Lucía, 19 June 1935, and López de Lerena to Múgica, 21 June 1935, both in private collection.

CHAPTER 7. THE PROLIFERATION OF VISIONS

1. Apolito, Cielo in Terra, 116, usefully distinguishes between vague "weak" visions, as of a flare or light with little content, and "strong" visions, those with clear visual content

or messages. He notes that the weak visions of credible people often serve to "confirm" the strong visions of the less credible. On the cuadrilla as a Basque institution, see del Valle, *Korrika*, 42.

2. On 27 March 1983 I spoke with four people in their seventies. Raimundo Conde and a woman who did not wish to have her name used had been with Ignacio.

3. "¿Las Apariciones de Ezquioga en Alava?" *La Libertad* (Vitoria), 26 October 1931, p. 1; "Gobierno Civil," *El Heraldo Alavés,* 26 October 1931, p. 2; and note in *ELB,* 27 October, p. 5.

4. Ezkioga material was reprinted in *El Castellano* in 1931 on 13, 16, 17, 18, 20, 21, 23, and 30 July; 1, 4, 8, 10, 20, and 26 August; 26 September; and 16 and 17 October.

5. *El Debate,* 18 August 1931, p. 2, and *El Imparcial* of 30 August and 6 September 1931—Quero, Menasalbas, Puebla de Montalbán, Mazarambroz, Lucillos, and Alcaudete de la Jara.

6. Marqués, *HM,* 18 August 1931.

7. "Aparición en un pueblo de Toledo," *El Debate,* 18 August 1931, p. 4.

8. For Molina at Ezkioga, Altisent (who met him there), *CC,* 9 September 1931, and Molina, *El Castellano,* 24 August 1931. Molina organized the Eucharistic Congress of 1926. On del Solar see Juan María Amundarain, who served as his altar boy, 3 June 1984, p. 4; an Ezkioga resident, 7 February 1986; R 35–36, 62, 117; and Rigné's photograph 7 in R of del Solar leading the prayers. Polo Benito, *El Castellano,* 11 September 1931.

9. All 1931: "¿Otra aparición en Guadamur?" *El Castellano,* 28 August, p. 4; "Supuestas apariciones en Toledo," *El Debate,* 29 August, p. 5; "Las Apariciones de la Virgen y el calor," *ELM,* 29 August, p. 5.

10. *Ahora,* Madrid, 5 September 1931, p. 16.

11. *El Castellano,* 3 September 1931, p. 4.

12. "Nueva aparición de la Virgen: Ayer fue vista en una torre de la Catedral de Sigüenza," *El Imparcial,* 30 August 1931, p. 1. All 1931: "Otra aparición en Guadalajara como tantas otras," *ELM,* 5 September, p. 5; "La Virgen aparece ahora en Guadalajara," *El Imparcial,* 6 September, p. 3; Cruz Romero, *El Defensor de Granada,* 8 September; Constancio, *El Defensor de Granada,* 11 September; "Apariciones en masa," *Crisol,* 8 September, p. 4; "La Virgen, su marido, San Roque, todo un cortejo se ha aparecido en Orgiva," *ELM,* 9 September, p. 5; cartoons by Bagaria, *Crisol,* 1 September, and Menda, *ELM,* 6 September; and in the anticlerical *La Traca,* 5 and 26 September, "Otra vez se nos ha aparecido la Virgen de Villabrutos" and "Se acabaron los milagros—la Virgen de Guadamur."

13. The final reference in *El Castellano* was a letter by Martín Ruíz on October 3. The other Meseta site I know of that fall was near Palencia (see below).

14. Millán, *ELB,* 9–10 September 1931.

15. José Miguel de Barandiarán, Ataun, 9 September 1983, p. 2.

16. On August 18 in Altisent, *CC,* 6 September 1931.

17. Francisco Mendieta Araña and friends, Arbizu, 15 June 1984.

18. Felipe Rezano (b. 1911) and Felisa Lizarraga (b. 1922), Dorrao, 15 June 1984.

19. B 621–623.

20. Interview with villagers, Iturmendi, 17 June 1984. There were already *bandos* (factions) in many of these towns, probably based on lineages, and in some places opposing attitudes toward the visions probably formed along these cleavages. See Olabarri, "Documentos." Don Juan Estanga Armendáriz, from Iraneta, was part of a set of local professionals opposed to the visions; the group included his niece, the schoolteacher in Urdiain; the Urdiain parish priest, from Etxarri-Aranatz; and the parish priest of Bakaiku, a village native

(Santiago Simón, town secretary of Iturmendi and Bakaiku from 1932 to 1938, Pamplona, 18 June 1984).

21. *PV*, 18 October 1931, p. 5, named a ten-year-old girl seer at Ezkioga who had already had visions in Etxarri-Aranatz; on Juaristi see Ceballos Vizcarret, *Victoriano Juaristi;* Blasco Salas, *Recuerdos*, 159, 203–205; Carlos Juaristi Acevedo, Pamplona, 17 June 1984; Juaristi, *DN*, 25 October 1931.

22. José Maiza Auzmendi, Etxarri-Aranatz, 17 June 1984. He also went to Fatima and the more recent apparitions at Monte Umbe near Bilbao. For Holy Family see Francisco Argandoña, "Apariciones de Lizarraga," citing his cousin from Etxarri-Aranatz, Leopoldo Quintana.

23. Millán, *ELB*, 9–10 September 1931.

24. B 663–664. Burguera used Celaya's notebook when preparing his book; the notebook is probably with his papers in Sueca. B II 628, 636–637.

25. Child sodalities were founded to the Infant Jesus of Prague in Vitoria in 1905, San Sebastián and Pamplona in 1908, Villafranca in 1910, Elizondo in 1917, and a number of villages in Navarra in 1922 and 1923 (Doroteo, *Historia prodigiosa*, 168–229). Arte Cristiana of Olot, a major factory for religious images, started making the Infant Jesus of Prague in 1905 (company records).

26. B II 634–637. The teacher was the village representative for the children's religious magazine, *La Obra Máxima* (January 1931, p. vi).

27. B 664.

28. Francisco Argandoña (b. 1924), "Apariciones de Lizarraga," 4–5.

29. B II 628; quote from Pedro Balda, the Iraneta town secretary, to Guerau de Arellano, 9 November 1937, AC 264; Burguera (B 662) mentions a *redondel* in which seers prayed; for delivery van, Pedro Balda, Alkotz, 8 April 1983, pp. 8–9.

30. B II 635 n. 59, 632 n. 55; B 662–663; Juaristi, *DN*, 25 October 1931.

31. Balda to Gerau de Arellano, [Iraneta], 9 November 1937, AC 264.

32. Emilio Andueza (b. 1902), Lakuntza, 15 June 1984.

33. B 650 gives the Huarte vision as Iraneta's first, but Irurzun (San Sebastián, 5 April 1983, p. 2) and Balda (Alkotz, 8 April 1983, pp. 17–18) were firm that Inocencia started everything. I base my account of Iraneta on these interviews in addition to the other citations.

34. The other youth was Francisco Diego Jamós, B 650.

35. B 651–652.

36. Virto, *Elecciones*, 157–214. For politics in these towns also Ferrer Muñoz, *Elecciones y partidos*, 92, 98, 161–163, 507–508.

37. Maritxu Güller, San Sebastián, 4 February 1986, p. 10.

38. "A un vecino de Irañeta se le prohibe ver visiones," *PV*, 27 March 1932, p. 2; advertisements for bus trips on Good Friday, 25 March 1932, in *VN*, 24 March, p. 2; for Barranca, Andueza, *LC*, 11 March 1931.

39. Muniz y Pablos circular of March 23. B 267–268, 365–369. Díaz Sintes, "Tomás Muniz de Pablos," makes no mention of the visions or the bishop's attitude.

40. Ducrot, *VU*, 30 August 1933.

41. Pedro Balda (distributed by J. B. Ayerbe), "Visión del joven labrador Luis Irurzun . . . 12 de octubre, 1933 a las 17:15," AC 233. By then Balda had recorded over four hundred vision sermons. [Pedro Balda to Juan Bautista Ayerbe], "Dos cartas interesantes de Irañeta," 18 May 1934, AC 246.

42. Maritxu Güller (maiden name, Erlanz), San Sebastián, 4 February 1986, pp. 1–6. "There were many things which I later realized that I added myself": Pedro Balda, Alkotz, 7 June 1984, p. 8.

43. Variants of this poem, entitled "Voces en el desierto" or "Avisos de la Santísima Virgen de Ezkioga," are on four of J. B. Ayerbe's circulars. The only dated one is 5 January 1934, AC 235, 235 a, b, c.

44. For Luis's predictions of deaths: Maritxu Güller, 4 February 1986, p. 12, and Pedro Balda, Alkotz, 7 June 1984, pp. 2, 14. For varieties of malevolent power: Barandiarán, "En Ataun," *AEF,* 1923, p. 114; Barandiarán, "En Orozco," *AEF,* 1923, p. 5; in Zegama, Gorrochategui and Aracama, *AEF,* 1923, p. 107. Evarista Galdós claimed to predict the dates of death of the sister of a believer, a priest, and a boy from Azkoitia (B 715, 719, 721). She thought of this as a kind of holy knowledge, like that of nuns who announced the date and time of their own deaths; but some people I talked to saw it as a bad kind of knowledge. Gábor Klaniczáy discusses the danger of charisma for women in "Ambivalence of Charisma."

45. Boniface, *Genèse d'Ezkioga.* ADP Fondo Parroquias: Izurdiaga. Marcelo Celigueta, presbítero, al Provisor y Vicario General, Pamplona, 1 folio, 2 sides, manuscript, dated "Aibar, Fiesta de San Xavier [3 December] de 1931." This folio has holes punched in it and may have come loose from a binder relating to the 1931 events. It was the only item relating to the 1931 visions in the parish correspondence files for all villages where I knew there had been visions.

46. Tomás Muniz y Pablos, "A los Rvdos. Sres. párrocos y sacerdotes de los valles de Araquil y Burundi," 23 de Marzo de 1933 (in B 366–367).

47. Pedro Balda, Alkotz, 8 April 1983, p. 8; *La Obra Máxima,* September 1931, p. 281, and October 1931, p. 312.

48. *La Obra Máxima,* May 1932, p. 150, and September 1931, p. 281.

49. B 167–169.

50. María Teresa Beraza, Hernani, 2 May 1984; Justa Ormazábal, Zumarraga, 10 May 1984, who was older, went twice.

51. See Luistar, "Albiztur," in *A:* 19 and 26 July; 2, 9, 16, 23, and 30 August; 6 and 27 September; and 22 November 1931. His personal collection of *Argia* with handwritten corrections is in Instituto Labayru, Derio.

52. *LC,* 24 March 1932, p. 6, and 20 May 1932, p. 6.

53. Luistar, *A,* 2 October 1932. He went on to write twenty pieces against the visions, the last on 1 October 1933.

54. For May 1933, Ducrot, *VU,* 30 August 1933; and for after that, relatives of girl seers from two houses, Albiztur, June 1984.

55. *El Día* of Palencia had given ample coverage to Ezkioga and by mid-November 1931 the fourteen-year-old daughter of a building constructor was having daily visions of the Virgin, who arrived as at a séance preceded by loud knocks. The girl announced an apparition in the chapel of Our Lady of the Sorrows in Palencia for 10 A.M. on Sunday, November 22, just one hour before a public meeting of the anticlerical Radical Socialists, but the bishop refused to open the chapel and issued a statement dismissing the visions. All 1931: *ELM,* 20 November, p. 9; *HM,* 20 November, p. 4; *El Día* (Palencia), 24 November, p. 1; *El Debate,* 24 November, p. 1; *ELM,* 24 November, p. 9. At a vision session in or near Palencia in mid-May of the next year, an Ezkioga believer saw a girl, perhaps the same one, divide among the thirty or so persons present an apple she had received from the Holy Family. "Apariciones en Palencia," letter from Florentino Sánchez, Hornillos, 16 May 1932, typed excerpt, 1 page, private collection. For Tolosa, elderly male eyewitness, San Sebastián, 13 May 1986.

56. Ducrot, *VU,* 23 August 1933. Strictly speaking, seers and believers were not excommunicated.

57. Schoolteacher of Zaldibia in *La Voz de Gipuzkoa,* 11 November 1933; "Desde Zaldivia," *PV,* 5 December 1933, p. 7, and similarly 19 December, p. 9.

58. *LC,* 4 January 1933, listed seven seminarians from Zaldibia. One in early 1935 wrote about the stubborn devotion of many families to the apparitions: Sukia, "El Ambiente religioso," 371.

59. Elderly male believer, Zaldibia, 31 March 1983, pp. 5–11.

60. All 1935: *La Noticia,* 22 January, and *ED,* 23 January; *ED* and *VG,* 24 February; Sarasqueta, *VG,* 28 February.

61. The son of one of those arrested gave the date of the raid as 7 January 1937. In the parliamentary elections of 1933 the Basque Nationalists received 210 votes, the Carlists 350, and the Republicans 6 (*PV,* 21 November 1933). These proportions held for almost all of the rural towns in Gipuzkoa with important groups of believers, with the exception of Ataun, Legazpi, and Ezkioga, which in 1933 swung to the Nationalists. The rural towns with industries had more Republican votes, but not many (see also Granja, *Nacionalismo,* 415–439). Zaldibia had been further polarized by the open partisanship of Elorza, who on occasion displayed the Carlist flag in church. On 5 June 1933 Carlists in Zaldibia and Ordizia clashed violently with Nationalists and Republicans (*ED,* 6 June). On competing piety: Sukia, "El Ambiente religioso," 367. For political arrests: son of seer, Zaldibia, 20 August 1982, p. 2; for town council: elderly priest, 10 September 1983, pp. 2–3.

62. Interviews, Zaldibia, 31 March 1983, p. 10, and 10 September 1983, p. 5.

63. The seers included Cándida Zunzunegui, Juliana Ulacia, Luis Irurzun, Marcelina Mendívil, and José Garmendia.

64. *VU,* 23 August 1933.

65. Elderly male believer, Zaldibia, 31 March 1983, pp. 15–16.

66. Ormaiztegi nonbeliever, 9 September 1983, pp. 3, 10.

67. A composite account from three witnesses: Dionisio Oñatibia, Urretxu, 7 April 1983, pp. 2–3, 5; elderly woman, Zumarraga, 29 May 1984, p. 2; and Ormaiztegi nonbeliever, see n. 66 above. In a magazine of the Passionists of Bilbao a former believer in the visions described an Ordizia session in which Gemma Galgani appeared (see P. Beaga, "O locos o endemoniados").

68. Boué, 60, 78–79; Ducrot, *VU,* 23 August 1933; B 561, 711; Benita to García Cascón, 28 June 1932, in SC D 113–114. Garmendia vision in SC D 52–53 and ARB 216.

69. For J. Imaz, *BOOV, Guía Diocesana,* 1931, p. 116, and B 301. For garage, Ducrot, *VU,* 23 August 1933, p. 1331. The devil appeared by the bus just beyond Tudela in the Ribera, the domain of the left.

70. For Imaz fearlessness, Ayerbe to Cardús, 5 May 1934; Garmendia's vision against Imaz, 24 June 1933, B 639; also one of Esperanza Aranda, 20 April 1933, to halt trips to Zaragoza and Aralar, B 711, B 282 n. 1.

71. Seers also went to Limpias and Lourdes, possibly with Imaz.

72. Pedro Balda, Alkotz, 7 June 1984, p. 7; Lidia Salomé, Betelu, 7 June 1984, pp. 2–3; Barandiarán, *AEF,* 1924, pp. 165, 168; and Etxeberria, *AEF,* 1924, p. 71.

73. Múgica, "San Miguel"; Mugueta, *PN,* 17 July 1931.

74. Aranzadi, *EZ,* 20 August 1931. At the Nationalist fiesta at Aralar on 20 August 1933 about a third of the eighteen thousand persons were from Navarra; *PV,* 25 August, p. 8.

75. Bilbao: "La Policía descubre un Ezquioga establecido en un quinto piso," *VG,* 12 February 1933, p. 5; San Sebastián: Sarasqueta, *VG,* 10 April 1934, refers to "a certain San Sebastián gathering-place for the pious"; Portugalete: lifetime servant of the López de Lerenas, interviewed by telephone, 7 May 1984; Juana Urcelay, Pamplona, 18 June 1984, p. 4.

76. The poet José Azurmendi, San Sebastián, 4 February 1986; Gorrochategui, *AEF*, 1922; and Gorrochategui and Aracama, *AEF*, 1924, pp. 108–109.

77. Gorrochategui and Aracama, *AEF*, 1924, p. 103. For Aranzazu see Guridi, *AEF*, 1924, pp. 99–100; and Gorrochategui, *AEF*, 1922, p. 51.

78. For Marcelina Mendívil, Boué, 60, who cites a vision in Zegama on Easter Sunday, 1932, and R 59. Ducrot in *VU*, 16 August 1933, p. 1289 (photograph). For rest on Martín Ayerbe, B 624–628. Francisco Otaño, curate of Beizama, wrote Cardús from Beizama, 25 March 1933, "The priests of Cegama received orders from Vitoria prohibiting access to the place, but then a counter-order a few days later permitted access and asked that the bishop be informed of whatever occurred."

79. Kale'tar bat [a man from the street, or town center], *PV*, 1 and 2 December 1934.

80. J. B. Ayerbe, *LC*, 5 December 1934.

81. Kale'tar bat, *PV*, 12 December 1934.

82. *PV*, 15 December 1934, p. 1 (also *LC*, p. 8, and *ED*, p. 1); *PV*, 16 December 1934, p. 1.

83. J. B. Ayerbe, "Visión de Asunción Balboa, 23 Dicbre. 1934—En Tolosa," 2 pages, typewritten, AC 213: "No quieren que reine el Rey Alfonso pero Tú dices que ha de reinar en España . . . Pero sí reinará. No tardará mucho tiempo."

84. For Zegama man: Francisco Ezcurdia, 10 September 1983, p. 3.

85. For Legorreta: José María Celaya, OFM, from Legorreta, Aranzazu, 1 June 1984; his father carried the torch.

86. Elderly Zaldibia believers, 31 March 1983, pp. 10–12.

87. For children as accusers of witchcraft see Henningsen, *Witches' Advocate*, 117–119, 129, 140, 209, 254, 301, 326, and Monter, "Les Enfants au sabbat." Both witchcraft persecutions in the 1607–1617 period and apparitions in 1931–1936 occurred in the Barranca. See Staehlin, *Apariciones*, 86–90, 389–390, for provoked collective visions in children. I am grateful to Gábor Klaniczáy for pushing me to make this comparison.

88. Barandiarán, *Mitología vasca*. The Virgin Mary seemed at Lourdes to control the local spirits in the river Gave de Pau. During her fourth vision of 19 February 1858 (according to Estrade, *Les Apparitions de Lourdes*, chapter 9 [Tours: Mame, 1899]), Bernadette, kneeling with her back to the river, "heard a tumult of voices that seem to come out of the depths of the earth and break out on the waters of the Gave; they called one another, intersected, and clashed noisily as if a multitude in struggle. One voice, imposing itself on the others, called out stridently and angrily, 'Go away! Go away!' To this shout, which seemed to be a threat, the Lady had raised her head and wrinkled her brow, looking toward the river. With this simple gesture, the voices panicked and fled in all directions."

CHAPTER 8. RELIGIOUS PROFESSIONALS

1. I extrapolated the number of religious vocations from the number of diocesan priest vocations using the ratio of 4 to 1 that holds for Ataun, Zeanuri, and Navarra as a whole. For the Franciscan Conceptionist: Urquizu, "Sor María Paz." Esnal (b. 1888) wrote Patxi from San Sebastián on 31 December 1932 to pray for him and come to see him but not to tell anyone (private collection).

2. *Zeanuri'ko abade* (Priests from Zeanuri). I thank Ander Manterola for this reference. For 1923 see Gorostiaga, *AEF*, 1924, p. 124. For the specialization of Dima in Trinitarians see Irukoistar, *Dima*.

3. Duocastella, *Sociología y pastoral,* chap. 6; Ricart, "Bruno Lezaun"; Cipriano Lezaun, *Don Bruno;* Pazos, *Clero navarro.*

4. Controlling for size of town, the most vocations came from the adjoining Duranguesado and Villarreal sectors of Bizkaia and Alava, the mountainous band of Gipuzkoa from Zegama to Oiartzun, the southeastern corner of Alava, and the Campezo area of Alava. In the 1931 directory of the diocese of Vitoria I counted the diocesan priests born in each town, then calculated the number of inhabitants per priest for those towns that were the birthplaces of five or more priests. Conversely, for towns of six hundred inhabitants or more, I made a list of those towns producing the fewest diocesan priests. Since I measure vocations by all priests living in 1931, to some extent the results reflect population distributions prior to that year.

5. Derived from Arín, *Clero de Atáun.* For Zeanuri in 1935 the equivalent figures are 136 houses with one vocation, 23 houses with 2 (total = 46), 9 houses with 3 (27), 4 houses with 4 (16), 7 houses with 5 (35), and 1 house with 7 (7) (from *Zeanuri'ko abade,* 19).

6. Out of 123 Ataun vocations in 1931, 47 had sibling clerics, 25 had near relatives on the father's side, and 20 had both kinds. Figures for the 13,000 vocations in Navarra in 1980 show similar proportions. Slightly more than one-third had siblings as religious or priests; see Imízcoz, *Una Emigración particular,* 462, citing figures from J. A. Marcellán Eigorri, *Cierzo y bochorno: Fenómeno vocacional de la Iglesia en Navarra (1936 y 1986)* (Pamplona: Ed. Verbo Divino, 1988). For vocations of secular priests see Pazos, *Clero navarro.*

7. Houses with most vocations: Larrazea, Lauspelz, Orlaza-aundia, Telleri-aundia, Arin-aundia, Arratibel-azpikoa, Geaziñe-zarra, and Itzate-berri.

8. Imízcoz, *Una Emigración particular,* 470. For Durango's missionaries see Anitua, *Nuestro misionero 1932.* Perea, *El Modelo,* 2:881–1142, describes the organization of the mission effort.

9. See Benita's vision of 23 October 1932, in SC D 118. On the previous day she heard the Virgin ask for prayers for the Jews.

10. Imízcoz, *Una Emigración particular,* 493–495; Ruíz de Gauna, *Catálogo,* includes fourteen different mission magazines published in Gipuzkoa, Bizkaia, Alava, and Navarra in the 1931–1936 period; other magazines, like *La Milagrosa y Los Niños* (Vincentians, Madrid) and *El Siglo de las Misiones* (Jesuits, Burgos), circulated in the area.

11. Based on extensive testimony 1982–1984 from Zumarraga residents, fellow priests, and religious. For Otaegui, *ED* and *EZ,* 11 July 1931; for Lasa quote, Pío Montoya, San Sebastián, 11 September 1983.

12. Casares to Echeguren, Santa Lucía, 18 March 1932, ADV, Ezkioga. The Itsaso priest claimed that Echeguren gave him "the express command to inform him of what was going on in this matter."

13. Masmelene, *EZ,* 15 July 1931; José Miguel de Barandiarán, Ataun, 9 September 1983; Manuel Lecuona, Oiartzun, 29 March 1983; cf. for an enthusiastic Nationalist, Apezbat [a priest], *Amayur,* 24 July 1931.

14. In 1934 the Basque archbishop of Valladolid launched a drive to raise money to build the church of the Great Promise. The promise of the Sacred Heart of Jesus to the Jesuit Bernardo de Hoyos—that Christ would reign in Spain with more devotion than in other nations—naturally raised the hackles of Basque Nationalists, who did not consider Spain their country. *La Constancia* collected contributions, and the printed lists of contributors were a way for the Carlists and Integrists to stand up and be counted on an issue that bore the approval of Bishop Mateo Múgica of Vitoria himself. Juan Bautista Ayerbe was one of the first contributors, and Conchita Mateos, Tomás Imaz, Juana Usabiaga, and several priests

who had been or continued to be sympathetic to the Ezkioga cause proclaimed their Spanishness in this way.

15. On Oyarbide and sister, Rigné to Olaizola, Ormáiztegui, 4 September 1932; R 59; and B 624–628. The other curate was José Cruz Beldarrain (b. 1889, Oiartzun), Oiartzun, 29 March 1983.

16. On 3 August 1919 Francisco Aguirre led another pilgrimage to Limpias. *Diario Montañés,* 5 August 1919 and 11 October 1919; see also Leopoldo Trenor, *¿Qué Pasa en Limpias?* (Valencia: Tipografía Moderna, 1920), 293–295; for Evarista, B 308–312, 726, 739–740.

17. J. J. Aracama spent a month with his uncle at the height of the Albiztur visions in the summer of 1932; *A,* 31 July 1932, p. 3. For Irízar: B 316; R 19, 74–75; Echeguren to Laburu, Vitoria, 20 January 1932; and López de Lerena to Echeguren, 21 December 1932, private collection. For Ormazábal: B 316; R 18, 71; Echeguren to Rigné, 22 December 1932, private collection.

18. Tusquets, *Masonería,* 65–66 (thirty thousand copies were printed).

19. See Soledad del Santísimo Sacramento [Soledad de la Torre], "Respuesta al Cuestionario [del Obispo de Pamplona]" (hereafter Cuestionario), Betelu, 15 December 1928, 8 pages, handwritten, ADP, Betelu. Antonio Matute of Durango ceded the house to her in 1922 on the condition that her order be canonically approved. For the papal permission see Presbítero, *LC,* 27 December 1933.

20. Torre, *Constituciones,* 3 (in ADP, Betelu); A. Brou, "Associations pour la sanctification du clergé," *DS* 1 (1937), cols. 1038–1045.

21. Lidia Salomé, María Salomé, and Juanita Lazcano, Betelu, 7 June 1984.

22. Examination by Dr. Bienvenido Solabre and Lic. Nestor Zubeldia, Pamplona, 11 May 1920, in Torre, *Constituciones,* 46.

23. Torre, *Libro de las casitas,* 274–276.

24. Torre, *Constituciones,* 6; for priest-sons and spiritual mothers, Ciammitti, "One Saint Less"; for *jauntxos,* "Lecumberri" in *VG* 1932 on 15 and 31 January, 11 February, 23 and 31 March, 15 April, 19 July, and 17 November; see also complaints about Betelu's priest, Fermín Lasarte, answered in "Desde Betelu," *PV,* 1 July 1933, p. 8.

25. Rodríguez de Prada, *Visiones; BOEP,* 1919, pp. 68–71. For the Obra in the diocese of Vitoria: Perea, *El Modelo,* 2:1005–1008.

26. For Zubeldia: Pazos, *Clero navarro,* 314 n. 40; Goñi, *DHEE,* 4:2813–2814, and Z. M., *Don Nestor Zubeldia.*

27. Pío and Angeles Montoya, San Sebastián, 9 February 1986; Salomé et al., Betelu, see n. 21 above.

28. Torre, *Constituciones,* 45, 48; Carlos Juaristi, Pamplona, 17 June 1984.

29. Mateo Múgica y Urrestarazu, "Nos el Dr. . . . cumpliendo rendida y literalmente . . . ," Pamplona, 23 February 1925, 3 pages, handwritten, ADP, Betelu. The decree of the Congregation of Religious seems to have been on 4 February 1923. *BOEP,* 13 June 1925, p. 328, carries condemnation of the movement by the Holy Office dated 20 February 1924 in a letter sent by Card. Merry del Val to Múgica, 1 June 1925; see Pazos, *Clero navarro,* 314.

30. Cuestionario, 4–6. Postulant: Felicitas Aranzabe y Ormaechea, age 30, Lizartza (Gipuzkoa).

Novices who had professed in private: Juana Arocena y Iturralde, age 29, Almándoz (Navarra); Juana María Ezcurdia Marticorena, 36, Errazkin (Navarra).

Professed nuns: María Solabre y Lazcano, age 27, Los Arcos (Navarra); Rosa Arrizubieta y Otamendi, 32, Uztegi (Navarra); Lorenza Pellejero y Goicoechea, 33, Gaintza (Navarra); Juana Balda y Ezcurdia, 35, Gaintza (Navarra); Beatriz Celaya y Gurruchaga, 38,

Zarautz (Gipuzkoa); Juana Agorreta y Ibarrola, 40, Zilbeti (Navarra); María Luisa Cediel y Angulo, 42, Bogotá; Angelina Rozo y Alarcón, 60, Bogotá; Soledad de la Torre y Ricaurte, 43, Bogotá.

Gaintza, Errazkin, and Uztegi are small villages next to Betelu and Lizartza is the first town in Gipuzkoa on the road from Betelu. Almándoz is also in the same zone. The other places are within a sixty-kilometer radius.

31. Madre Soledad did not convey her enthusiasm for the Ezkioga visions to the villagers. The Betelu women I spoke to had been to Ezkioga only once, when a woman from Pamplona, a summer resident, hired two buses for the townspeople: Lidia Salomé, María Salomé, and Juanita Lazcano, Betelu, p. 4. I know of no visions around Betelu.

32. Juan Celaya, Albiztur, 6 June 1984, pp. 29, 43. Some Navarrese followers took an interest in the visions in the Barranca. The Iraneta group learned about Madre Soledad from her last confessor, Fermín Lasarte, whose brother and sister-in-law often went to watch Luis Irurzun. Other priests who had been followers of Madre Soledad also took an interest in Luis (Pedro Balda, Alkotz, 7 June 1984, pp. 3–4).

33. I verified the date of death in the parish register as December 8, for some villagers claimed that she died on Good Friday at 3 P.M. Some nuns chose to leave the convent, for in November 1935 only five were left, two of them infirm (letter from Sor María Luisa de la Cruz, Beatriz de Jesús María y José, and Rosa de Santa Ana to the bishop of Pamplona, Betelu, 24 November 1935, typewritten, 2 pages, ADP, Betelu).

34. Presbítero, *LC*, 27 December 1933; J. B. Ayerbe, "Visión de Conchita Mateos, en su casa de Beasain, el 30 de Dicbre, 1933," 3 pages, typewritten, signed by Conchita Mateos and J. B. Ayerbe, AC 302.

35. J. B. Ayerbe, "Interesantes revelaciones sobre varias almas, 8 Abril 1949, Festividad de los Dolores," 2 pages, typewritten, AC 74.

36. For Catholic examples, Selke, *El Santo Oficio;* Kagan, *Lucrecia's Dreams;* Zarri, *Finzione;* Zarri, *Le Sante Vive,* 103; and Bilinkoff, "Confessors and Penitents."

37. Egurza, *LC*, 24 July 1931; Salvador Cardús to Ayerbe, 11 October 1933; letter from nun to Cardús, 21 September 1933.

38. For Zarautz, Petra de la Maza, 14 December 1983; for Aldaz, Rodríguez de Prada, *Visiones,* 27–29, 81–82, 104–106, about María de los Dolores de Jesús y Urquía, who began to record her visions in May 1932 and likely had them previously; she died 26 February 1934. See also *Vergel Augustiniano,* October 1934 and 1935, p. 478.

39. From *Anuario estadístico de España,* 1933, p. 664.

Religious living in the Basque Country on 31 December 1930:

	FEMALE	MALE
Gipuzkoa	2,649	1,142
Bizkaia	2,039	810
Alava	762	299
Total	5,450	2,251

Total religious per 10,000 inhabitants and nationwide rank:

	GIPUZKOA	ALAVA	NAVARRA	BIZKAIA	SPAIN
1900	83 (1)	71 (2)	64 (3)	57 (6)	29
1910	145 (1)	83 (2)	74 (3)	62 (4)	30
1920	131 (1)	102 (2)	77 (3)	63 (7)	33
1930	125 (1)	102 (2)	97 (3)	59 (7)	35

40. *Anuario estadístico de España,* 1933, p. 667; *Guía diocesana,* 1931; and *Anuario eclesiástico,* 1919.

41. For Oñati: Petra de la Maza, Zarautz, 14 December 1983, p. 1.

42. Marcucci (1888–1960), *En la cima,* 186.

43. Marcucci to Evarista Galdós, Bilbao-Deusto, 20 March 1932, private collection (text in appendix). For Cardús, SC E 534. Aulina told Cardús on 6 February 1933 that Marcucci was a saint who had had a vision of Gabriele dell'Addolorata in which the saint introduced her to Gemma Galgani.

44. See, for instance, Marcucci, *En la cima,* 288, 335, 348.

45. For Mondragón, SC E 534 (6 February 1933). Aulina visited the Mondragón convent 15 October 1932, SC E 481/ 22; in December 1933 the nuns still believed, ARB 177–178. For Valladolid: Sedano de la Peña, Barcelona, 5 August 1969, p. 15.

46. For tutelary angels, the servant María Nieves Mayoral, 13 October 1932, in J. B. Ayerbe, "Mensajes divinos," n.p., dittoed, ca. 1935, 14 pages, p. 9, AC 6; for Evarista, 21 October 1932, but order, convent, and place are unidentified in B 721; for Viñals, R 50–51; for Benita, J. B. Ayerbe, "Maravillosas apariciones," AC 1, p. 2; Izurdiaga girl, 11 September 1932, in a private house, B 167–168; for deconversion, B 479.

47. For Conchita see J. B. Ayerbe, "18 Enero, 1942, Aparición de la gloriosa religiosa María Angeles, muerta en octubre de 1941 en el convento de . . . ," half-page, typewritten, AC 353; believers were there from Urnieta, Bergara, Anoeta, and Azkoitia (ARB 171). Of the 9 girls who were seers in Mendigorría in 1931, 4 became nuns—2 of them Daughters of Charity, 1 a Dominican, and 1 a Redemptorist Oblate. María Recalde wanted to be a Carmelite nun when she was nineteen (B 598 and L. Jayo). The Izurdiaga girls wanted to be nuns and the boy a priest. Of the 21 girls and 21 boys in the Santa Lucía school in 1932, 1 girl became a Mercedarian, 1 boy a Franciscan and another a parish priest, an overall rate of 1 in 14, not unusual for the Goihierri and lower than for parts of Navarra. Given such rates, 8 of the 120 children and youths who were seers would have taken vows in any case.

48. The first woman from Ataun joined the Daughters of Charity in 1852. In 1931 seventeen from the town were in the order, but only one joined after 1915: Arín, *Clero de Atáun,* 226–237. Their associated male order, the Vincentians, had no houses in Gipuzkoa or Bizkaia. Mercedarian Sisters of Charity attracted to their novitiate in Zumarraga the kind of girls who had earlier joined the Daughters of Charity. The Mercedarian Sisters had eight houses in Gipuzkoa, but despite their close relation with Antonio Amundarain I do not know of any involvement in the Ezkioga visions. Amundarain, *Vida congregación mercedarias,* 187–199, 317–332; Arín, *Clero de Atáun,* 238–243.

49. Photos in Degrelle, *Soirées,* 21 September 1933; cure dated Tolosa, 22 July 1933, signed by, among others, María Recalde's sister-in-law, Victoria Jayo (B 736–737), who was at Ezkioga with another nun in May 1932 (ARB 143). Aranda vision, B 710, apparently 8 December 1932. A children's magazine distributed by the institute printed the fullest report of the visions in Mendigorría: Orzanco, "Nuevas apariciones." And in May 1932 these Sisters of Charity in Madrid were among the first to witness what seemed to be a bleeding statue of the Sacred Heart of Jesus. The news reached Ezkioga believers through the letters of a "Sor Benigna." See J. B. Ayerbe's circular "Cartas de las H. H. de la Caridad del paseo del Cisne en Madrid" (AC 402), which includes letters sent in May and June 1932 about an image in the house of Mercedes Ruíz that the sisters went to see in pairs; see also Rivera, "Sagrado Corazón."

50. Alumnos, "Desde Beasain," *PV,* 26 March 1932.

51. Dossier in ADV Denuncias with letters to Bishop Múgica from the president of the Colegio de Médicos de Vizcaya, Bilbao, 15 August and 13 September 1935, and Sor Sofía Pulpillo, Asistenta, Madrid, 25 August 1935.

52. This devotion spread to Oiartzun in 1920 from Rentería and Irun without the involvement of religious. Within three years the images linked 480 families in Oiartzun: Lecuona, *AEF*, 1924, pp. 21–22.

53. Txibirisko, *PV*, 10 July 1931; "De Ormaíztegui," *PV*, 17 July 1931, p. 8; *PV*, 25 July 1931, p. 2. The girls of Albiztur especially tended to see La Milagrosa, *LC*, 28 July 1931, p. 5, and *A*, 23 August 1931, p. 2. Quote from Pepe Miguel, *PV*, 31 July 1931, p. 4.

54. For Gabiria, Antonio M. Artola with Joseba Zulaika, Bilbao-Deusto, September 1982, p. 4. For life at the school, *Ecos de San Felicísmo*, 1932, pp. 197–199, 230–233, and Artola, *Martín Elorza*, 16–31. Initial Passionist enthusiasm: Basilio Iraola Zabala (b. 1908), Irun, 17 August 1982, p. 1, who said his first mass in Gabiria in 1931, and Dositeo Alday, Ramón Oyarzabal, and Rafael Beloqui, Urretxu, 15 August 1982; confessions, B 51; for Patxi's "levitations," Elías, *CC*, 21 August 1931; for Gabriele dell'Addolorata, ARB 33–34; for I. Galdós, B 755.

55. For mission, Venancio Jáuregui, "En Goizueta," *BOEP*, 1916, p. 154. Basilio de San Pablo, "Manifestaciones de la Pasión." Luistar was the distributor of *El Pasionario* in Albiztur. Another Passionist magazine, *Ecos de San Felicísimo*, printed a report on the visions on 1 September 1931.

56. B 739–740. After the war a few Passionists still believed in the visions; see Beaga, "O locos o endemoniados."

57. B 301 mentions a Franciscan missionary assigned to India who was cured of gout at the shrine. For the plot see Lucas Elizalde, Tolosa, 6 June 1984, p. 2, and for the rumor see Ducrot, *VU*, 23 August 1933, p. 1331.

58. M. Ayerbe died before becoming a friar. A seer from Zaldibia was a novice in 1952. Figures from José A. de Lizarralde, in Guridi, *AEF*, 1924, pp. 97–100.

59. Damaso de Gradafes at Basurto, who had taken his youth group to Limpias, took the members to Ezkioga as well, and Andrés de Palazuelo, who wrote in favor of Limpias, published an article on Ezkioga in *El Mensajero Seráfico*, 16 September 1931. For Ezkioga as plot Enrique de Ventosa, Salamanca, 5 May 1989, and Francisco de Bilbao, Madrid, 6 May 1989. Pedro Balda, Alkotz, 7 June 1984, p. 16: he and Luis had first tried to leave Luis's notebooks at the Jesuit house in France, La Rochefer, but they failed. A sympathetic Capuchin, P. Bernabé, occasionally preached in the Goiherri. The Claretians had been sympathetic to the Limpias visions and printed favorable articles about Ezkioga in their national magazine, *Iris de Paz*. But I know of no Basque Claretian involvement.

60. For Arintero and Merciful Love see Fariñas, "Apostol"; Suárez, *Arintero*, 275–309; and Staehlin, *Padre Rubio*, 247–251. See Gaytán de Ayala obituary in *VS* 40, no. 361 (January–February 1959), pp. 69–70; he gave a speech about the devotion in the Vitoria seminary in February 1932, *Gymnasium*, 1932, p. 124; the Sulamitis leaflets received the nihil obstat in Vitoria by March 1929. P. M. Sulamitis, *España'ko Katolikoai* (To Spanish Catholics), was published in Bergara with the imprimatur of Justo de Echeguren and Manuel Lecuona in 1932. For paintings, see Fariñas Windel, "Apostol," 114, and "Un Cuadro de Ciga," *La Tradición Navarra*, 29 December 1931, pp. 1–2. The Dominicans of Atocha in Madrid published the magazine *Amor Misericordioso*. For Jesús Elcoro, R 8.

61. J. B. Ayerbe claimed to García Cascón, 22 March 1934, 3 pages, typewritten (AC 416), that Conchita Mateos convinced her confessor at Lazkao, Padre Leandro. A seer from Zaldibia entered a Benedictine convent in Oñati: Rigné, *Ciel ouvert*, p. D.

62. B 51–52, 751–752. See the Azpeitia correspondent's passionate reply to de la Villa in *A*, 23 August 1931, p. 2.

63. French visitors at Loyola at end of August, "Les Apparitions d'Ezquioga," *La Croix*,

Paris, 15 October 1931, p. 3, from *Le Semeur,* Tarbes. Pere Pou i Montfort S.J. to Cardús, Sacred Heart College, Shembaganur, Madura District, 18 August 1932.

64. On the expulsion of Jesuits, Cardús cites a vision by a female seer, 1 September 1931, who complained to the Virgin, "What will we do without them?" and Burguera cites one by Benita Aguirre, 30 June 1933 (B 497); at the end of 1932 J. B. Ayerbe claimed the support of Padre Iriarte, "que está considerado en gran santidad" ("Las maravillosas apariciones," AC 2:4). For Viñals (Padre Zabala): Sebastián López de Lerena to Ezkioga believer, 2 September 1934, private collection. For Azkoitia (Padre Imaz): Juan Celaya, Albiztur, 6 June 1984, pp. 27–28.

65. In addition to the small house of Carmelites at Altzo above Tolosa, there were others in Bizkaia at Larrea, Begoña, and Markina and in San Sebastián, Pamplona, and Vitoria.

66. Domingo Onaindía Zuloaga, Saint Jean de Luz, 11 September 1983. Padre Rainaldo had written in *Vida Sobrenatural* about Thérèse de Lisieux, who was canonized in 1925. Pilgrimages went to Lisieux from Pamplona in 1923 and 1926, but by 1931 the first flush of the devotion had passed and Saint Thérèse appeared to the Ezkioga seers infrequently. J. B. Ayerbe recorded her giving blessings cheerfully in visions of Asunción Balboa in Urnieta and Tolosa in 1934 and María Nieves Mayoral in Urnieta in 1935 (AC 209, 210, 213, 372).

67. For Padre Valeriano (b. Amorebieta, 1865), *DN,* 22 December 1933, p. 5, his golden anniversary; Maritxu Güller, San Sebastián, 4 February 1986, p. 15; and R 52. A street urchin converted by a flower from a seer went for confession to the Pamplona Carmelites (Rolando, *DN,* 19 October 1932). For Padre Mamerto: Pío Montoya, San Sebastián, 11 September 1983, p. 4, and 9 February 1986; Domingo Onaindía Zuloaga, Saint Jean de Luz, 11 September 1983; and P. Santiago Onaindía, Larrea, 10 February 1986.

68. Doroteo, *Historia prodigiosa;* in Tolosa, Ezkioga believer to Cardús, 12 October 1933; on Doroteo and Patxi: Ayerbe to Cardús, 24 October 1933; Padre Santiago Onaindía, Larrea, 18 October 1986—"era muy aficionado a esas cosas"; on Doroteo and Ramona on 4 February 1933: Rigné to Ezkioga believer, Santa Lucía, 27 December 1934, private collection; quote from López de Lerena et al. to bishop of San Sebastián, 1952, p. 5.

69. B 351; for Rome trip, Sedano de la Peña with Lourdes Rodes, Barcelona, 5 August 1969, p. 42.

70. In some of the other orders there were one or two religious who pursued an interest in the visions, like Padre Maguncio of the Clérigos of San Viator in Vitoria, or the Redemptorist Padre Mariscal, known within the order for his interest in the marvelous: Christian, *Moving Crucifixes,* 46–50; Balda to Mariscal, Irañeta, 11 October 1934, AC 250.

The Brothers of Christian Schools had at least ten schools in Basque-speaking Spain, including those in Zumarraga and Beasain; they brought students to the site in February 1932 (Surcouf, *L'Intransigeant,* 20 November 1932). The Marist Brothers were expanding and had eight schools in the same zone, including the one Cruz Lete attended. I know of no involvement of the Brothers of the Sacred Heart, who had a novitiate and six schools in Gipuzkoa, or of the Brothers of Christian Instruction, who had six in Bizkaia. These teaching orders were of French origin.

71. J. B. Ayerbe, "Las maravillosas apariciones," AC 2:4.

CHAPTER 9. KINDS OF SEERS AND CONTACT BETWEEN SOCIAL CLASSES

1. Lewis, *Ecstatic Religion,* 23.
2. *PV,* 18 July 1931. For the committee at Oliveto Citra see Apolito, *Cielo in terra,* 49–56, 59, 135–136.

3. F. D., at Ezkioga, August 6, in *CC*, 16 August 1931; Aranzadi in *ED*, 26 July 1931.

4. Lassalle, *PN*, 6 August 1931; S 128.

5. For history of women in visions, Christian, "Visions in Spain"; for quote see Luzear, *ED*, 21 July 1931.

6. Visions before 21 August 1931 reported in the press (excluding the original two seers):

	ALL SEERS REPORTED	2+ VISIONS REPORTED	ALL VISIONS REPORTED	VISIONS PER SEER
Male adults	23	1 (4%)	27	1.2
Female adults	16	3 (19%)	25	1.6
Male *jóvenes*	15	4 (27%)	36	2.4
Female *jóvenes*	20	11 (55%)	79	4.0
Male children	8	4 (50%)	22	2.8
Female children	9	7 (78%)	70	7.8
[Age not known]	[2]			
Total	91	30 (33%)	259	2.8

Seers with visions in this period not reported in the press who later became prominent: four women (M. A. Aguirre, E. Aranda, P. Ciordia, M. Recalde), one young woman (G. Viñals), and one male child.

7. Bishop Mateo Múgica of Vitoria promoted the sodality: Echaniz, *Estrella del Mar* 1931; *LC*, 12 May, p. 4, and 5 June 1931, p. 8. See also Asociación de Hijas de María de la diócesis de Vitoria, *Reglamento*, 9th ed. (Vitoria: Montepío Diocesano, 1929).

8. Romero, *HM*, 5 August 1931.

9. For Galgani see Elías, *CC*, 19 August 1931, and Sans, "Problemática"; a later example of facial transformation in Staehlin, *Apariciones*, 387–389. For Jeanne d'Arc see B 275, 291, 413; for the teenage Virgin see *PV*, 12 July, and *ED*, 19 July 1931.

10. For Estella children: Bienvenida Montoya, San Sebastián, 11 September 1983. All 1931: for San Sebastián city boy, *ED*, 19 July, p. 9, 21 July, p. 8, and 6 August, p. 2; for seven-year-old girl, *ED*, 15 July, p. 8; for de la Villa speech, *DSS*, 13 August; *Crisol*, 27 July.

11. On children in Basque culture: *AEF*, 1924, pp. 71, 85, 148; as intercessors for the dead: Ott, *Circle*, 91; and mission processions: Perea, *El Modelo*, 2:997–1001. For Guy de Fontgalland see Perroy, *La Mission d'un Enfant*. On children as mediators with the supernatural in other contexts, Frijhoff, *Evert Willemsz.*, and Apolito, *Dice*, 141–144.

12. Legaz, "En Navarte," 317.

13. Argandoña, "Apariciones en Lizarraga"; for Torralba connection: Romero in *La Prensa*, 8 July; Masmelene, *EZ*, 15 July; and Amundarain in *PV*, 18 July 1931.

14. *La Obra Máxima*, August 1931, p. 253, letter of April 9. The children could have read about Fatima in the magazine *Jaungoiko-zale*.

15. Tellechea, *Tapices*, 59–60; Basque children still play "church": Manterola, *Juegos*, 580.

16. Blackbourn, *Marpingen*, 47; for Garabandal, García de Pesquera, *Se fue*, 16–21; for Villaesteva, Manuel Moreira, Villaesteva, 6 August 1977.

17. For Ignacio Galdós: Sedano memoir, 5–7, and Elías, *CC*, 15 August 1931. For confirmatory visions of men, Blackbourn, *Marpingen*, 142. The visions of the farm laborer Auguste Arnaud at Saint-Bauzille-de-la-Sylvie in 1873 attracted only local attention (Commission, *N-D de Dimanche*).

18. Evarista Galdós predicted in 1932 there would be 250 seers, SC D 64–69. For some seers I have only fragmentary information; newspaper reports might give the hometown and indicate the age and sex but little else; sometimes reports did not give a seer's name.

19. Seers at Ezkioga proper, date of first mention (in parentheses, number of these seers photographed):

DATE OF FIRST MENTION	ONLY ONE VISION KNOWN	MORE THAN ONE VISION	TOTAL
July 1931	55 (7)	39 (28)	94
August–December 1931	6	31 (17)	37
1932–1936	3 (2)	36 (25)	39
Unknown	4	18 (1)	22
Total	68	124	192

20. In four photographs 15 and 18 October 1931 I could distinguish 495 males and 480 females and in four photos from Lent 1932 I found 262 males and 289 females.

21. Emilia Cantero Llaurado from the convent of the Esposas de la Creu had visions on 7 and 8 March 1932 (Cardús to Rimblas, 10 March 1932); Evarista vision of 5 April 1932, SC D 64–69—clerical seers would have had every reason to keep quiet. Loreto Albo Molins was from a landed family of a village near Vic, the unmarried sister of two priests and a doctor; she had visions 4 and 5 April 1932, ARB 109, B 633, Sicart photos 15, 39. For Iñaki Jaca see B II 625 and ED, 26 July 1931, LC, 28 July 1931, and ED, 29 July 1931.

Haydée de Aguirre talked to Salvador Cardús (SC E 101–102) October 17 about what she had seen the day before: "[The girl] was in ecstasy, and all at once some of us realized that a little above the seer were hanging suspended in the air some rosaries. Some invisible being was holding them with two hands by two upper ends, so that they took the form of an elongated triangle. The child, still in ecstasy, reached out a hand and took it. . . . Today has been the day of my life that I have received Communion with the most devotion." See also R 34, and for Haydée de Aguirre at Ezkioga, Easo, 16 October 1931, p. 10.

22. Niece of Ulacia in Tolosa, 6 June 1984, and Boué, 92.

23. For the very poor see O'Neill, Social Inequality.

24. Non-Basque family names: Aguado, Aranda, Bedoya, Cabezón, Fernández, Miranda, Núñez, Rodríguez, Sánchez, and Taboada.

25. Gentry quote in Santander, ABC (Madrid), 13 August 1931, p. 16. LC, 16 July 1931, p. 8, and 19 July 1931, p. 2; also the pamphlet ¿Qué Pasa en Ezquioga? p. 8, and Lugin, A, 23 August 1931; Molina, El Castellano, 24 August 1931, p. 1; Christian, Moving Crucifixes, 97–99.

26. On class structure see Caro Baroja, Los Baroja, 273; "El Castigo: Declaraciones de Benita Aguirre" (vision of 8 February 1932), printed, in Laburu papers in Loyola. B 488–489 omits these lines.

27. Juan María Amundarain, San Sebastián, 3 June 1984, p. 2. The vicar general Echeguren described José Garmendia to the Jesuit Laburu, "smelling like wine, hardly able to articulate words" (notes in FL). Ciordia vision, B 692–693.

28. B 579, undated.

29. S 125.

30. Tellechea, Tapices, 83, 311, 413.

31. Cf. Blackbourn, Marpingen, 126.

32. Sabean, Power, 25.

33. Picavea, *PV*, 13 November 1931, p. 3.

34. Scott, *Hidden Transcript.*

35. L. Valls and Ll. Millet, "Som germans! [We are Brothers]" in Obra dels Exercicis Parroquials, *Manual de l'Exercitant* (Barcelona: P. Calmell, 1928), 48.

36. For Recalde Laburu accounts, ARB 73–74, and Cardús to Pare Rimblas, 17 June 1932.

CHAPTER 10. THE VISION STATES

1. Two forums for this running debate were *La Revue métapsychique* and *Études carmélitaines mystiques et missionaires.*

2. Orixe (Nicolás de Ormatxea), "Amona," written 1896–1900; farmer seer, March 1983, pp. 18–19; for Durango prophet see Barandiarán, *AEF*, 1924, pp. 178–184. Basque visions of the dead or the vision of the prophet of Mendata in the 1870s seem to have been without trance.

3. Lisón, *Endemoniados;* de Martino, *Terra del rimorso;* Gallini, *Ballerina;* Jansen, "Dansen voor de geesten"; Lewis, *Ecstatic Religion;* Rouget, *Music and Trance.* For therapeutic trance dancing by women throughout North Africa, see Jansen, *Women without Men.*

4. For first days see Justa Ormazábal, Zumarraga, 10 May 1984, p. 2; and *LC*, 7 July 1931. For historical background, Christian, *Apparitions,* passim.

5. *BOOV*, 1930, p. 472.

6. All 1931: *ED* and *LC*, 9 July; *LC*, 10 July; José Garmendia, *EZ* and *ED*, 11 July (quote); *A*, 19 July. For Santa María del Villar (*Época*, 16) Amundarain's account was a translation for those who did not know Basque.

7. All 1931: *LC* and *ED*, 12 July; *ED*, 14 July; and *LC*, 14 July. For "dear melody" see Dunixi, *ED*, 18 July. For the liturgy at Oliveto Citra see Apolito, *Cielo in terra,* 41.

8. *PV*, 14 July 1931.

9. *ED*, 14 July 1931, probably Juana Ibarguren of Azpeitia; for boy see *LC*, 16 July 1931.

10. *PV*, 16 July 1931, and *ED*, 17 July 1931; see also Gatestbi, "Ezkion zer? [What Happens in Ezkioga?]."

11. All 1931: *ED*, 19 July; Luzear, *ED*, 21 July; *PN*, 19 July; Iturbi, *EZ*, 23 July. From these sources the liturgy on July 18 consisted of a rosary led by a priest and two or three youths, a hymn, two Litanies, Salve Regina Gregoriana, Hail Marys to the Seven Sorrows, the hymn "Egizu zuk Maria," then prayers dispersed through the crowd. Over the month of July the order of these elements varied.

12. Martínez Gómez, *VN* and *PN*, 22 July 1931.

13. S 132–133. For this mix at Oliveto Citra see Apolito, *Dice,* 218.

14. Similarly, when Bernadette said the rosary at Lourdes, she saw the Virgin counting beads. *LC*, 22 July 1931, has the first mention of the Agur hymn. The press referred to "Egizu zuk Maria" more frequently, and of the hymn the canon Juan Bautista Altisent of Lleida wrote: "When . . . a shrine is built here that all of Spain visits in enormous pilgrimage, this hymn will without doubt be the equivalent of the 'Ave' of Lourdes" (*CC*, 9 September 1931).

15. *PV*, 24 July 1931, p. 2.

16. Amundarain to A. Pérez Ormazábal, 25 July 1931, in Pérez Ormazábal, *Aquel monaguillo,* 109–110; Echarri, *Heraldo Alavés,* 25 August 1931. María de Echarri was at Ezkioga sometime in the preceding week.

17. For day vision see *LC,* 25 July 1931, p. 2. Patxi tried and failed to have a vision at the same time (*ED,* 24 July 1931, p. 8). Ten days earlier Amundarain had organized a rosary at 6:30 P.M. to see if Patxi and others would have visions in daylight, but they did not. Quote from F. D., *CC,* 16 August, for 6 August. Similarly the canon Altisent, *CC,* 9 September, for 18 August, "It has just got dark . . . the time for deep emotions has come."

18. At Knock in Ireland in 1880 the priest switched to English from Gaelic as pilgrims came from farther afield; see Nold, "The Knock Phenomenon," 45. There were at least two and generally three five-mystery rosaries between July 29 and Ramona's wounding on October 15. I do not know if priests led all of them.

19. Visitor: Cuberes i Costa, *EM,* 5 August 1931; for girl from Bergara: N., "Anduagamendiko agerpenak [The Apparitions of Mount Anduaga]," 708; for Albiztar girl: Luistar, *A,* 23 August 1931.

20. S 148; Millán, *ELB,* 10 September 1931; also Txibirisko, *La Tradición Navarra,* 19 September 1931.

21. Delás, *CC,* 20 September 1931, about her visit September 3–5.

22. SC D 102–103.

23. ARB 122, 139–140.

24. For the language of flowers, of which this seems to be a refraction, Goody, *Culture of Flowers,* 232–253.

25. See ARB, passim, for descriptions of these events, for instance, pp. 110–111. G. Klaniczáy pointed me to an early equivalent in the way the ecstatic boy Henricus distributed kisses in "Legenda S. Emerici Ducis," E. Szentpétery, ed., *Scriptores Rerum Hungaricum* (Budapest, 1938), 2:452.

26. Christian, *Apparitions,* 185–187.

27. Marchetti, "La simulazione."

28. For pulse, all 1931: *LC,* 12 July; *EZ,* 15 July; *ED,* 17 July; *ED,* 19 July; Picavea, *PV,* 6 November.

29. All 1931: *LC,* 7 July; *DN,* 7 July; *PV,* 10 July (Aguado quote); *A,* 12 July (Aguado confession); *GN,* 17 July.

30. All 1931: *LC,* 9 July; *LC,* 12 July; *PV,* 12 July (quote); *A,* 12 July.

31. For Xanti see *ED,* 11 July 1931; Garmendia, *EZ,* 12 July 1931; and Cuberes i Costa, *EM,* 5 August 1931, citing Rvdo. Juan Casares's notebook. According to local people, Xanti stayed converted even though he worked in a factory. For Cabezón, all 1931: *ED,* 12 July; *PV,* 14 July; *ED,* 14 July; *ED,* 19 July.

32. All 1931: factory worker (*LC,* 12 July), taxi driver (*ED,* 17 July; *LC,* 17 July; *PV,* 23 July; S 127–128). Patiño vision, 29 August, in *El Castellano,* 31 August 1931, Martín Ruíz, *El Castellano,* 2 September 1931, and León González Ayuso, Guadamur, 5 November 1976; for Los Arcos youth: Christian, *Moving Crucifixes,* 132–133, 140; see also Bloch, "Réflexions," and Goguel, *La Foi dans la Résurrection,* 419.

33. *PV,* 16 July 1931.

34. *ED,* 15 July 1931.

35. *ED,* 19 July 1931.

36. Campoamor, *DSS,* 1 September 1931.

37. Lassalle, *PN,* 9 August 1931, "Mother, Mother, do not weep! Weep not, kill me, but forgive the others, who do not know what they do. Mother, forgive me, don't cry!"

38. For pulse see *LC,* 9 July; *EZ,* 14 July; S 135; Molina, *El Castellano,* 24 August; Altisent, *CC,* 9 September; B 177. For pricks see *ED,* 19 July; *PV,* 23 July; Lassalle, *PN,* 4 August; for lancet see J. B. Ayerbe, "Maravillosas apariciones," AC 1:2. For burns see Lassalle, *PN,* 4 August, and for pupillary reflex, *ED,* 18 July. For eyelid reflex see *ED,* 23 July;

Molina, *El Castellano,* 24 August; Delás, *CC,* 20 September. For convulsions see *PV,* 23 July, and for morphine see Picavea, *PV,* 6 November. Clean bill of health from Dr. Pinto of Santa Agueda, B 380, and Dr. Carrere, AC 405.

39. "¿Qué ocurrió al joven Goicoechea?" *ED,* 2 August 1931, p. 2; *ED,* 4 August 1931, p. 5; *PV,* 4 August 1931, p. 3; Lassalle, *PN,* 4 August 1931; Rodríguez Ramos, *Yo sé,* 12–14. Micaela Goicoechea, age 24, who worked as a servant in Legorreta, allegedly levitated on September 6 (Boué, 148; R 47; Paul Romain in *EE* [April–May 1935]: 3), but two days later a reporter could find no witnesses (Txibirisko, *La Tradición Navarra,* 19 September 1931). At the end of September the rumor circulated in Bilbao that a boy had risen two meters, "and that because of all this and some other things the doctor was convinced of the truth of everything" (letter from a woman believer, 27 September 1931, private archive). Patxi supposedly levitated again October 17 (*Easo,* 19 October 1931, p. 8). An old-time believer (Ikastegieta, 16 August 1982) told me he himself saw a woman rise two meters in the air and two men grab her and bring her down.

40. Altisent, *CC,* 9 September 1931; Aranzadi quote, *ED,* 14 July 1931; Aranzadi said in *PV,* 23 July 1931: "The reality of his severe excitation and convulsions cannot be open to doubt."

41. For Louvain see Tuya, "¿Apariciones?"; for Galdós, ARB 146; for pulse patterns, B 56–57, 124–134; for Laburu, L 40.

42. "Noticies de Badalona," *EM,* 19 September 1931 (burns); Baudilio Sedano de la Peña with Lourdes Rodes, Barcelona, 5 August 1969, p. 1; for skeptical doctor, Pascal, "Visite"; Antonia Echezarreta, Ezkioga, 1 June 1984, p. 12 (tests on Ignacio Galdós); Pedro Balda, 7 June 1984, p. 13 (French doctors prick Luis Irurzun); old-time believer, Ikastegieta, 16 August 1982 (use of needles in faces); *El Castellano,* 26 September 1931, p. 1 (use of light in eyes); Tuya, "¿Apariciones?" (hand over eyes); Celigueta report, ADP, Izurdiaga.

43. B 57–58, 129–134 (pupils do not react to light); Millán, *ELB,* 9 September 1931 (young man does not blink when lighted match passed before eyes); Altisent, *CC,* 9 September 1931, on Benita Aguirre and again, *CC,* 13 September, on Patxi, who did not blink for half an hour in vision; for similar observations: Farre, *Diari de Sabadell,* 7 October 1931, on teenage girl; Juaristi, *DN,* 25 October 1931, on Unanu girl; and Bernoville, *Études,* 20 November 1931, on woman seer.

44. Tests with interposed objects reported in *PV,* 23 July 1931; *ED,* 22 July 1931 (on girl); S 144 (on Lolita Núñez); F. D., *CC,* 16 August 1931 (on Benita Aguirre). Thérèse Neumann and seers in Belgium saw in spite of interposed objects, so their visions were classed as interior: Pascal, *Hallucinations;* on this test at Medjugorje see Apolito, *Cielo in terra,* 84.

45. *PV,* 17 July 1931; Altisent, *CC,* 9 September 1931; Delás, *CC,* 20 September 1931; SC E 31.

46. Tuya, "¿Apariciones?" 625; Pascal, *Hallucinations,* 34–35, who cites Estrade, *Les Apparitions de Lourdes.*

47. Patxi about 6–8 August 1931 in Lassalle, *PN,* 9 August 1931; interviews in Ormaiztegi, 2 May 1984, p. 2, and with sisters in New York, 3 October 1981.

48. Pedro Balda, Alkotz, 7 June 1984, p. 5, told me that Victoriano Juaristi remarked on the sheen on Luis's face, and Maritxu Güller also mentioned seeing it; for the transformation of faces, "Lo que ha visto un cacereño en Ezquioga," *El Castellano,* 26 September 1931, from *Extremadura;* and ARB 39.

49. Luébanos in Cuberes i Costa, *EM,* 5 August 1931. Gratacós, "Lo de Esquioga," 17. Dr. Tortras Vilella of Barcelona commented: "I confess with perplexity that I never observed the least injury" (B 125).

50. For memoirs of a Basque doctor at Lourdes, Achica-Allende, *Cuadernos.* Asuero (1886–1942) reportedly assured children they would have no more visions. He had achieved world renown in March and April 1929 for his cures by stimulating the trigeminal nerve. See Barriola, "La medicina," 41–45; Sánchez Granjel, *Médicos Vascos,* 36–38; Barbachano, *El Doctor Asuero;* and *ED,* 12 January 1933, p. 12. On Marañón, *ELB,* 23 July 1931, and *PV,* 23 July 1931; S 138; Patxi in Rodríguez Ramos, *Yo sé,* 15. The San Sebastián priest Pío Montoya, 7 June 1983, p. 3, assured me that Marañón had been there.

51. The prominent urologist Benigno Oreja Elósegui (1880–1962) provided Patxi with the use of a car, according to Laburu (L 14). Oreja was a cofounder of the Clínica San Ignacio of San Sebastián and spent weekends and summers at his house in Ordizia, Aurteneche, "Vida y obra," 14–67. Patxi approached Oreja's brother Marcelino, the deputy in the Cortes, without success. The daughter of the doctor of Segura was a seer, as was the maid of the doctor of Ormaiztegi: *PV,* 25 July 1931; *PN,* 22 July 1931; and Luis S. Granjel, Salamanca, 2 November 1994.

52. On Sabel Aranzadi: Mate sisters, Zumarraga, 10 May 1984, p. 2. Vidaur when widowed became a Jesuit and went to China; Barriola, "La medicina," 19.

53. On Iza, *PV,* 18 October 1931. Iza followed the misogyny of his mentor, Novoa Santos, who argued in the Cortes, 2 November 1931, against women's suffrage: "La mujer es eso: histerismo." Heliófilo in *Crisol,* 3 November 1931, quoted from a 1929 Novoa Santos book: "A woman is a child who has achieved full sexual maturity. The guiding force of her morphological and 'spiritual' distinctiveness is her ovary."

54. Nieto, "Sobre el estado," 698. I owe this reference to Thomas Glick.

55. Romanones made the remark to the prominent French writer Gaëtan Bernoville in the summer or early fall of 1931: *Études,* 20 November 1931, p. 464.

56. For the comparison with Ezkioga see Arteche, *ED,* 14 July 1931. Polo Benito, *El Castellano,* 11 September 1931, cited Neumann and Ezkioga, along with Lourdes, Fatima, and Guadamur, as elements of an "ofensiva de Dios." Tuya in "¿Apariciones?" suggested waiting for the truth of Ezkioga to come clear as a cardinal suggested waiting in the case of Neumann. Bishop Mateo Múgica contrasted Neumann's obedience with the seers' rebellion (Sebastián López de Lerena, "Relación de la visita que la vidente Gloria Viñals hizo al Sr Obispo de Vitoria el día 6 de septiembre de 1933," private archive).

For local news of Neumann see Basilio de San Pablo, "Manifestaciones de la Pasión"; "El caso asombroso de Teresa Neumann," *ED,* 3 April 1931, p. 12; Farges, *Easo,* 19, 20, and 21 October 1931; Bay, *PV,* 27 October 1931; "Un caso inexplicado, Teresa Neumann, la estigmatizada de Konnersreuth," *Easo,* ten-part series from 25 November to 8 December 1931; *EM,* 12 January 1932, p. 8; *A,* 9 October 1932, p. 2; for *Informaciones* Neumann article distributed at Ezkioga see Juan de Urumea, *El Nervión,* 23 October 1931.

57. Spanish devotion to Padre Pio in Christian, *Moving Crucifixes,* 91–92; and *Diario Montañés,* 13 June 1922, p. 1. Basilio de San Pablo, "Manifestaciones de la Pasión," 1930, pp. 58–62, cites articles in *El Debate* in September 1927 by "Danubio," in *El Debate* in September 1928 by Bruno Ibeas, in *El Siglo Futuro* in October 1928, and in *ABC* (Madrid) on 3 July 1929 by Polo Benito. Warnings about gullibility: Tarré in *La Hormiga de Oro,* 6 October 1927, and *Gazeta de Vich,* 15 October 1931, and Urbano, "Neumann, Rafols." Martínez de Muñeca, *El Debate,* 26 July 1932. *El Pasionario* held off reporting on Neumann because of the false miracles at Gandía in Valencia in 1918, the exaggerations at Limpias starting in 1919, and the case of P. Pio.

58. Spirago, *La Doncella estigmatizada;* Lama, *Una Estigmatizada;* and Alujas, *Teresa Neumann.* Herder published Waitz, *Mensaje,* in 1929, and "Els Fets de Konnersreuth" began ap-

pearing in *La Veu de l'Angel de la Guardia* in October 1930. For Neumann's popularity see M. Lecloux, "Une Conférence sur Thérèse Neumann," *La Croix,* 27 November 1931, p. 2.

59. There was a woman who supposedly lived only on the host in Montecillo, near Espinosa de los Monteros (Burgos) in the 1930s (Baroja, *El Cura de Monleón,* 146). In 1977 I heard of a similar young girl in the province of Orense, considered a saint for not eating, who had people lining up to visit her and leave alms until a doctor from Vigo administered a drug and she vomited octopus. Apart from the better known cases of holy abstinence in saints, studied by Imbert-Gourbeyre, C. Bynum, and R. Bell, there appears to have been a long and continuous folk tradition of "living saints" of this nature in peasant Europe. See, for example, the Austrian woman in Bourneville, *Louise Lateau,* 86, and for Asturias, Cátedra, *This World, Other Worlds,* 264–268.

60. For Arratia see Echeguren to Laburu, Vitoria, 20 January 1932; Azkue, *La Estigmatizada,* first published in *Reseña Eclesiástica.* See R 51, "an eminent priest who has seen Thérèse Neumann, assures that the revelations of Gloria Viñals will be more important"; he mentions Azcue a few pages later.

61. *VN,* 3 August 1932, p. 8; *LC* and *ED,* 16 December 1932, and *PV,* the next day; J. B. Ayerbe, "Las maravillosas apariciones," AC 2:5.

62. J. B. Ayerbe to Alfredo Renshaw, 6 October 1933, ASC; Antonio Gil Ulacia, a priest in Zaragoza, "Un caso inédito: A modo de prólogo," in Vallejo Najera, *El Caso.* Neumann was also used as an almanac. *Diari di Vich,* 10 September 1931, p. 3, said she predicted flooding from a great storm that month. In October 1931 she was said to have confirmed the apparitions at Marpingen; as in 1877 Louise Lateau also was thought to have backed these visions: Blackbourn, *Marpingen,* 167, 368.

63. Picavea, *PV,* 20 November 1931.

64. Perales, *Supernaturalismo,* defended Teresa de Avila's visions, locutions, and divine raptures against naturalists like Maury but nevertheless diagnosed her as suffering from grand mal of Charcot (270, 338) and cited as certainties phenomena of spiritism and magnetism (285–297), which he attributed to the devil. Brenier de Montmorant, *Psychologie des mystiques,* 237 n. 1, gives other participants in the controversy.

65. Novoa, *Patografía;* he raised the angina issue in a lecture at the Madrid Atheneum, 20 November 1931. For French background see Herman, *Trauma and Recovery,* 7–28; Hilgard, *Divided Consciousness,* 1–14; Duchenne, *Mécanisme de la physionomie,* 145–154; Maury, *Le Sommeil,* 229–255; Godfernaux, *Le Sentiment,* 48–59; Charcot, *La Foi qui guérit;* Charcot and Richer, *Les Démoniaques;* Didi-Huberman, *Invention de l'hysterie;* Didi-Huberman, "Charcot, l'histoire et l'art"; Murisier, *Maladies,* 7–72; and Ribot, *The Diseases,* 94–103. Richet's *Tratado de Metapsíquica* was published in Barcelona by Editorial Araluz in 1923. For Catholic defense see Brenier de Montmorant, *Psychologie des mystiques,* 103–205; Mir, *El Milagro,* 2:712–13, 3:295–315, 361–400; Antonino de Caparroso, *Verdad y caridad,* 1932; and for a good bibliography see Gratton, *DS.*

66. See, for instance, Robert van der Elst, "Autour d'une stigmatisation," *La Croix,* 24 December 1931, p. 3, and his "Stigmates" in *Dictionnaire apologétique* (Paris: Beauchesne). For Lateau see Imbert-Gourbeyre, *Les Stigmatisés,* vol. 1, and Curicque, *Voces proféticas,* 367–399. Bourneville, *Louise Lateau,* cites other works.

67. Mir, *El Milagro,* 3:399–400.

68. Pascal, "Visite" and *Hallucinations.* He also wrote "Une explication naturelle des faits d'Ezkioga est-elle possible?" *EE* 8 (October–November 1935). Pascal had already written *Le Sommeil hypnotique produit par le scopochloralose* (1928); *Un Révélateur du subconscient: Le Hachich* (1930); and *La Question de l'hynoptisme* (1930). Under the name Pascal Brotteaux he published *Hachich, herbe de folie et de rêve* (Paris: Editions Vega, 1934).

69. Pascal, *Hallucinations,* 42–43; Juaristi, *DN,* 25 October 1931, p. 12; Picavea, *PV,* 14 and 20 November 1931. The treatise on crowd psychology by Rossi, *Sugestionadores,* 113–135, gave examples of group suggestion, including some Italian religious visions.

70. Pascal, *Hallucinations,* 45. See the similar, if cruder, analysis by Millán, *ELB,* 10 September 1931: "They 'see' their own thoughts, they 'speak' with the mental figure that their brain has lodged and given form, and they 'hear' words that their own 'ego' pronounces, according to the beliefs, feelings, or physical circumstances of the seer-sensitive."

71. Pascal, *Hallucinations,* 48, citing Coué; B 89–115.

72. Pascal, *Hallucinations,* 54–73.

73. The shift in seer behavior may reflect in part the smaller audiences of the seers and their adaptation to the reserve of the urbane Catalans (B 131; Pascal, *Hallucinations,* 27).

74. J. B. Ayerbe, "Maravillosas apariciones," AC 1:2.

75. Gratacós, "Lo de Esquioga," 17–18.

76. Dr. Tortras Vilella's report, 25 November 1932, B 128. Luis in Ducrot, *VU,* 30 August 1933, p. 1365. Joan Colomer, the parish priest of Sant Andreu in Barcelona, wrote to Salvador Cardús, 10 May 1932, describing "un vident que despres del rapte encenia tranquilament un pitillo com si res hagues passat."

77. Gallini, "Lourdes"; also Staehlin, *Apariciones.* Use of a written *interrogatorio* had for centuries been normal practice in both civil and religious investigations involving multiple witnesses. Sinforoso de Ibarguren would have abstracted many of the questions, posed as alternatives, on his two-side printed sheet from what earlier seers told him. He had participated in Jose Miguel de Barandiarán's surveys. We are left wondering just how much of what the seers said they saw was an artifact of the questions, or vice versa. The general patterns, I think, preceded the questionnaire. They certainly persisted long after it was in use.

78. Light: in trees, *LC,* 7 July; as cross, ARB 123; as flash, *LC,* 25 July 1931, and Luis Irurzun, San Sebastián, 5 April 1983, p. 2. Ramona quote in Delás, *CC,* 20 September 1931. Elderly seer, 31 March 1983, p. 18. Rafael García Cascón in *La Creuada,* 12 October 1931, pp. 424–425.

79. Vision on 7 July 1931, B 714–715.

80. Vision de María Nieves Mayoral (of Beizama) in Ciudad Rodrigo, 2 February 1932, AC 369; Benita vision, 6 August 1931, in F. D., *CC,* 16 August 1931, full text in chap. 4 above.

81. Some descriptive phrases: nimbado por un aro, alrededor de la cabeza una corona difundiendo una luz, bajo un arco de luz, unas luces y entre ellas la Virgen, envuelta en resplandores, envuelta en una ráfaga de luz, luz que envuelve la Aparición, rodeada de luz. For light from hands see María Fernández, 18 July 1931, *ED,* 19 July; the model would be the rays from the Miraculous Mary. For Bustos on 19 July 1931, Luzear, *ED,* 21 July.

82. Vision, 4 December 1931, B 717. Some seers saw the Virgin heading for Ezkioga on horizontal, unlighted routes. The cattle buyers from La Rioja saw her in the road, and then thought they had run over her (7 July 1931 in *ED,* 10 July, p. 3, and *PV,* 18 July, p. 2). And from a hotel window in Zumarraga María Huerva saw her passing through the sky (2 August 1932 in ARB 123, 125).

83. Light increasing: Badalona, *EM,* 19 September 1931; light related to prayers: Evarista Galdós, 7 July 1931, private collection; yellow light: 31 March 1983, p. 18; reddish light: *ED,* 8 July 1931. *PV,* 8 November 1931, cites Patxi.

84. Pascal, *Hallucinations,* 31. No seers complained that their eyes had been injured. Patxi quote, August 16 or 18, in Molina, *El Castellano,* 24 August 1931. For end of light: Ricardo Fernández, age 17, 19 July 1931, and Carmen Visa on 22 June 1932.

85. Zumarraga boys, July 26: *ED,* 28 July 1931, p. 3; Iraneta youth: Pedro Balda, Alkotz,

8 April 1983, p. 17; similar ribbons hung by the improvised altar in Luis Irurzun's house. Conchita González at Garabandal in the 1960s predicted a banner in the sky with words that would vindicate her visions. For Benita: Pepe Miguel, *PV*, 31 July 1931, B 486; Benita vision label, 5 August 1932, at the shrine of the Christ of Lezo (SC D 115). The contemporary holy card appeared in *El Mensajero Seráfico* in late 1931, p. 718.

86. Luistar, *A*, 16 August 1931.

87. Ramona visions around 30 September 1931, SC E 11–12; later ones in J. B. Ayerbe, "Maravillosas apariciones," AC 1:6. The French writer Gaëtan Bernoville, who had a detailed account, refers to similar tableaux in Patxi's visions: *Études*, 20 November 1931, p. 460.

88. J. B. Ayerbe, "Maravillosas apariciones," AC 1:6. Galdós vision, 1 September 1932, · B 719.

89. B 718–719.

90. For I. Galdós, SC D 96–97. Along with song recitals and short plays, theatrical tableaux were staples of the evenings organized by mission societies, church groups, and seminaries. Descriptions: in Pamplona, *VN*, 29 December 1933, p. 6; in San Sebastián, *ED*, 2 April 1933, p. 4; in the Vitoria seminary, *Gymnasium*, passim; in Zumarraga, *PV*, 22 January 1932, p. 4; and in the Gabiria Passionist seminary, *Ecos de San Felicísimo*, 1 May 1932, pp. 197–198. For Ramona summaries: J. B. Ayerbe, "Maravillosas apariciones," AC 1:6.

91. For the Zumarraga boy, ARB 46–47; Evarista vision, 4 October 1932 (B 715, SC E 10–11).

92. For convergence of pose as seen in photos see Christian, "The Mind's Eye." For a contemporary set of rules for religious discernment, see Mir, *El Milagro*, 1:612–613, 2:696–713, 3:342–360.

93. Burguera, undated letter to seers, spring 1932, private archive. See also his description of a "perfect ecstasy," hedged with exceptions, which reflects the style of the last seers he believed; B 146–147.

94. Bernoville, *Études*, 20 November 1931, p. 465. Maurice Goguel in *La Foi dans la Résurrection*, 417, challenged this distinction.

95. Germán, *Vida*; Germán, *Cartas y éxtasis*; Basilio de San Pablo, *Lo Sobrenatural*.

96. Germán, *Cartas y éxtasis*; 240: "Look Jesus, many people come to me hoping for a divine favor."

97. Schmitt, *Raison des gestes*, 319; R 45. Catholic experts like Padre Mir took this variety for granted: "The truth of the raptures can be known more for the things discovered in them than from their exterior signs" (Mir, *El Milagro*, 2:706, citing Lapuente, *Guía espiritual*, book 3, chap. 8, par. 8).

98. Christian, "Apparitions and the Cold War."

99. Braude, *Radical Spirits*.

100. Atxabalt, *La Cruz*, 8 October 1933. Larraitz wrote, "Rather than believe what is said by those that are bent over [*makurtu*] or unconscious [*korderik gabe*] we have believed the church hierarchy," again placing a central emphasis on the altered state of the seers (*A*, 3 September 1933). Araxes observed in *La Constancia*: "Those alleged ecstasies had for the crowd aspects of something beyond human capability."

101. Beasain woman: Zumarraga, 9 May 1984, pp. 2, 6.

102. José Cruz Beldarrain, Oiartzun, 29 March 1983.

103. My ideas have been clarified by the works of I. M. Lewis, Gilbert Rouget, Erika Bourguignon, and Barbara Lex (see bibliography). Already in 1894 André Godfernaux held that the tendency toward dissociation manifest in extreme form as ecstasy "exists in different de-

grees, although often imperceptibly, in normal individuals," and he noted the return to normal after the ecstatic crisis: *Le Sentiment*, 49, 58. Maury, *Le Sommeil*, 229–231, cites J. Braid, *Observations on Trance* (London, 1850).

104. Goodman et al., *Trance, Healing, and Hallucination;* for the effect of repeated rosaries see Apolito, *Cielo in terra*, 149.

105. María Teresa Beraza Zabaleta, Hernani, 2 May 1984, pp. 3, 7.

106. *Vida*, chap. 20, cited by Mir, *El Milagro*, 2:707.

107. Cather, *Death Comes to the Archbishop*, 50–51.

CHAPTER 11. SACRED LANDSCAPES

1. Shrine images of Christ in Spain are usually in chapels on the fringes of towns, in parish churches, or in cathedrals. Few are associated with natural features. About a fifth of all the Spanish district shrines are in towns and have no association with natural attributes. All figures are from Christian, "Santos a María," a census made from 1966 to 1972 of shrines in peninsular Spain which draw the devotion of three or more towns. See also Nolan and Nolan, *Christian Pilgrimage*. A version of this chapter was published in Gajano and Scaraffia, *Luoghi sacri*, and is informed by the other papers in the volume.

2. Of thirteen cases of visions in Spain before 1520, one was associated with a hill, five involved springs or other sources of water, three involved trees, and two involved stones. Two were outside preexisting rural chapels, and three were in towns (Christian, *Apparitions*). Of twenty-five public vision sequences in the 1931–1934 period, eleven were associated with trees, seven were on hills or mountains, three by rivers or springs, and one in a cave. Of eleven well-known vision sequences in the years 1945–1962, six were associated with trees, three with hills or mountains, and two each with springs, caves, and stones (Christian, "Apparitions and the Cold War"). Each of the major vision sites in the 1980s was associated with at least one of those natural features.

3. *LC*, 7 July 1931, p. 1; Felipa Aramburu, Zumarraga, 7 May 1986.

4. *PV*, 10 July 1931, p. 3.

5. *ED*, 12 July 1931, p. 12; *ED*, 14 July 1931, p. 12.

6. *LC*, 7 July 1931, p. 1; photographs in *ED*, 15 July 1931, and *GN*, 18 July 1931, p. 2. For downhill location see Felipa Aramburu, Zumarraga, 14 May 1986, and photograph reconstruction by Joaquín Sicart (my files).

7. *ED*, 17 July 1931.

8. *GN*, 17 July 1931; E. G., "En torno a los sucesos," 238.

9. *ED*, 19 July 1931, p. 9.

10. For the Franciscan's report, E. G., "En torno a los sucesos," 238; *ED*, 21 July 1931, p. 10.

11. Lugin, *A*, 23 August 1931 (from the town of Matxinbenta); Amundarain in *LC*, 28 July 1931. See also E. G., "En torno a los sucesos," describing crowd on 16 July: "no todos los que asisten llevan los mismos sentimientos." On October 14 a priest interrupted the rosary to berate a judge and his wife for smoking; *ELB*, 15 October 1931, p. 7.

12. *PV*, 14 July 1931, p. 7. Comparisons to Lourdes abound in the articles written about the visions, with the suggestion frequently expressed that Ezkioga would be the Basque Lourdes; see, for example, Abeytua, *ELM*, 22 July 1931, and N., "*Anduaga-mendiko agerpenak*," 707 (N. was there on 30 July 1931). Inza in *PV*, 18 July 1931; Adrián Lizarralde, *Aránzazu* (Oñate, 1950).

13. Rvdo. Pedro Agote, San Sebastián, 15 December 1983.

14. Shrine visions in B 600–601 and *ED*, 23 July 1931, p. 8; duke of Infantado and four trees in S 118–119; quote from Delás, *CC*, 20 September 1931.

15. S 126; cross in Lassalle, *PN*, 6 August 1931.

16. Erection of cross: Molina, *El Castellano*, 24 August 1931, and Altisent, *CC*, 6 September 1931; diocesan reaction: *PV*, 6 September 1931, and Echeguren to Laburu, 13 April 1932. *La Croix* (Paris), 15 October 1931, p. 3.

17. Delás, *CC*, 20 September 1931; *LC*, 18 October 1931, p. 10.

18. Pepe Miguel, *PV*, 17 October 1931, p. 3, and *PV*, 31 July 1931.

19. *La Hormiga de Oro*, 13 August, p. 2; Larraitz, *ED*, 28 July 1931.

20. Juaristi, *DN*, 25 October 1931, and Carlos Juaristi, Pamplona, 17 June 1984; Santander, *ABC* (Madrid), 13 August 1931.

21. ARB 20–21; photo Sicart, "Trazando un Via Crucis" (my files).

22. Ibarguren to Echeguren, 18 February and 19 March 1932, ADV; ARB 21; Echeguren to Laburu, 13 April 1932; Echeguren handwritten note, ADV Varios 1927–1934. Patxi apparently thought the diocese would put up a canonically approved set of stations of the cross.

23. ARB 21–25; B 634–635; ARB 137–138.

24. Surcouf, *L'Intransigeant*, 19 November 1932; Cardús to Rimblas, 17 June 1932; also Rigné, *Llamamiento*, dated 29 June 1932.

25. ARB 26–27; B 32–33. Salvador Cardús wrote to Pare Rimblas, 17 June 1932: "Això fa pensar amb Fàtima i Lourdes [That makes one think of Fatima and Lourdes]." From the vision platform the trees and the cross were in front of the chapel and the image pedestal was on an axis with them. Thus while the center of gravity of the visions shifted to the pedestal-with-spring, it did so retaining the cross and the trees.

26. Ibarguren to Laburu, 27 June 1932; ARB 27; unsigned, typewritten declaration by site owner Juan José Echezarreta, dated 10 January 1936 (AC 418), who believed that María Celaya saw the ceremony in vision from Bakaiku and sent word that the Virgin blessed the fountain.

27. For basilica plans: letters of Sebastián López de Lerena and Pilar Domingo, private collections, and Basilio Iraola, Irun, 17 August 1982.

28. Alberto, factory town, 13 June 1984.

29. In parts of Bizkaia people still erect may poles (*donienatxak*); they used to be oaks or poplars but are now generally pines, with branches and bark removed, and at the top are tied ears of corn and vegetables, laurel and flowers (Gurutzi Arregi, doctoral thesis, University of Deusto). For cows see S 127 and *GN*, 17 July 1931.

30. ARB 25.

31. S.B. in *ED*, 7 November 1931, suggested as parallels to Ezkioga not only Lourdes and Fatima but also Mount Carmel.

32. Picard, "Chemin de la Croix," *DS* 2 (1953), cols. 2576–2606; Leatherbarrow, "The Image and Its Setting," and Christian, "Provoked Religious Weeping."

33. Froeschlé-Chopard, *La Religion populaire* and "Les Saints."

34. Delpal, *Entre paroisse et commune*, 155–169.

CHAPTER 12. PETITIONS FROM BELIEVERS

1. All 1931: boy, *LC* and *ED*, 16 July; girl relays woman's request in *LC*, 22 July; Patxi in *ED*, 23 July; Lolita Núñez in S 146; for airplane crash see F. Santander, *ABC* (Madrid), 13 August—the vision was on July 25. S 131, ca. 29 July. Molina noted the sick present for healing on August 16 in *El Castellano*, 24 August 1931.

2. Christian, "Secular and Religious Responses"; Douglass, *Death in Murelaga;* Tellechea, *Tapices.*

3. Claverie, "Voir apparaître," and now, Bax, *Medjugorje,* 43–50.

4. Elías, CC, 19 August 1931.

5. Pascal, "Visite," 11. He was at Ezkioga sometime in the spring of 1932. For Patxi see Rodríguez Ramos, *Yo sé,* 15.

6. From October 1931 to September 1935 Cardús sent at least 47 letters to Ramona Olazábal and 12 others to her confessor, Francisco Otaño, receiving in return 14 letters from her and 8 from her confessor. From December 1931 to May 1934 he sent at least 22 letters to José Garmendia and received 15. His archive (see Notes headnote, p. 413 above) contains copies of or references to over 400 letters from 1931 to 1939 dealing with Ezkioga and related apparitions.

7. *El Día* (Terrassa), 5 October 1931, p. 2.

8. SC E 15–18, 29–35.

9. Cardús to García Cascón, Ezkioga, 5 October 1931, for crowd the preceding day.

10. SC E 53–57, 11 October 1931.

11. García Cascón to Vallet, 31 October 1931, AHCPCR 10-A-27/2.

12. Four of the persons on whose behalf Cardús wrote to the seers were clergy or religious. In addition to his friend the Piarist in Tàrrega and the nun who had been his wife's teacher, there was a Jesuit missionary from Terrassa in India and the well-known Barcelona priest and historian of Marian shrines, Fortià Solà. All four asked him to be discreet, for by the time of their petitions Ezkioga was controversial and clerical opinion in Catalonia had swung against it.

13. Garmendia to Cardús, Legazpi, 4 December 1932.

14. Sources of each petition quotation, in order: Cardús to Ramona Olazábal, 31 October 1931; Cardús to Garmendia, 7 December 1931; Rosa Grau to Olazábal, 7 December 1931; Cardús to Olazábal, late July 1932; Cardús to Olazábal, 31 March 1932; Cardús to Garmendia, 18 February 1932.

15. Letter from a friend to Rosa Grau, 27 March 1932.

16. On Benita's writing: Pepe Miguel, *PV,* 31 July 1931, "esta nena de nueve años escribe sus impresiones sobre la aparición al llegar a su casa"; and ARB 162.

17. Request for outcomes: Garmendia to Cardús, Legazpi, 15 February 1932; declaration (SC E 544–546) sent 8 January 1933; García Cascón wrote Garmendia 28 January 1933.

18. SC E 207–209. For the favor, M. C. C., in *Manantial de Vida,* (Vic), June 1932.

19. Benita to Cardús, Legazpi, 27 November 1932; SC E 448–451, quote from the seer Joan Guiteras i Roca, 23 April 1932. His visions occurred shortly after the communist uprising in Alt Llobregat and shortly before an anarchist one in Terrassa itself in which dozens of workers were killed.

20. SC E 389–396; the couple saw light 8 April 1932.

21. Garmendia to Cardús, Legazpi, 15 February 1932; SC E 322–325.

CHAPTER 13. THE LIVING AND THE DEAD

1. Dead persons seen or learned about in Ezkioga visions, 1931–1950:

Relatives of seers: 19 (grandparents: 3; aunts: 2; parents: 4; spouse: 1; siblings: 6; children: 2; others: 2)

Relatives of believers: 22 (parents: 7; spouses: 2; siblings: 4; children: 3; in-law: 1; other or unspecified: 5)

Other: 30 (members of village: 13; someone connected with an onlooker: 6; seer's associates: 3; deceased seers: 4; deceased believers: 2; deceased notables: 2)

Gender of the dead seen: total males: 42; total females: 26; males and females together: 4; gender not specified: 6. Women and children tended to see children; men tended to see (or be asked about) adults.

Ezkioga seers who learned about the dead, 1931–1950, by gender and age:

	FEMALE	NUMBER OF VISIONS	MALE	NUMBER OF VISIONS
Child (up to age 14)	10	16 (Benita 6)	3	5 (M. Ayerbe 3)
Youth	4	8	2	2
Adults	9	20 (Aranda 5, Recalde 4)	4	8 (Garmendia 4)
Total seers	23		9	
Total visions about dead		44		15

2. All 1931: Madrid man: Manuel Sánchez del Río, *ED,* 21 July, p. 8; Bergara girl: N., "Anduaga-mendiko"; Benita: B 486–487, and *LC* and *PV,* 31 July; Garmendia: *PV,* 4 August; Zumarraga boy: García Cascón, "Algo más"; Albiztur girl: Luistar, *A,* 23 August.

3. AC 22: "Relato por la interesada de la curación prodigiosa y primeras visiones de Doña María Agueda Antonia Aguirre Aramendía, domiciliada en la casería 'Berantegui' de la villa de Vidania" (4 pages, written after 20 September 1931, possibly typed and titled by J. B. Ayerbe after fall 1932 from an account written down in 1931), p. 3.

4. Ibid., p. 4, sixth vision, 15 September 1931.

5. Mendizábal, *AEF,* 1923, pp. 104–105. Martín Ayerbe gained credibility from his detailed descriptions of five dead Zegama children as angels. He also saw his baby sister and, exceptionally, she spoke to him, telling him that he would see her often and she would help him (visions, 13 and 15 October 1931, B 624–625).

6. Visions of about 1 September 1931, as told to Matilde's parents and Luisa Arriola and recounted by them to Rodríguez Ramos, *Yo sé,* 21.

7. Juaristi, *DN,* 25 October 1931.

8. Vision for Terrassa woman: 5 October 1931, SC E 14–15; for Cardús, SC E 53–57.

9. Gratacós, "Lo de Esquioga," 13–14.

10. Jesús Aguirre, Madrid, 4 April 1994.

11. Ducrot, *VU,* 16 August 1933, p. 1292.

12. ARB 144; Olazábal, *Santa Cruz.*

13. Bordas Flaquer, *La Verdad,* 35.

14. B 491. Boué, 143, gives a more complex version.

15. Juan Bautista Ayerbe, "Visión de la Niña Conchita Mateos, en Beasain 10 Fbro. 1934," 2 pages, dittoed, signed by Conchita Mateos, AC 307 and 308.

16. For Catalans see García Cascón to Vallet, 31 October 1931, AHCPCR 10-A-27/2. Garmendia told García Cascón, José María Boada, and Manuel Esquisabel on 9 December 1931 that if they kept on as they were then [leading a good life], they would not go to purgatory (SC E 237).

17. Garmendia in SC E 241–242. Condemnation of nonbelievers: López de Lerena to Burguera, 26 July 1933, private archive; B 690–693; Albiztur girls told Gregorio Aracama, Juan Celaya, Albiztur, 6 June 1984, pp. 29–30; Pío Montoya, San Sebastián, 7 April 1983, p. 13; of governor of Gipuzkoa, *PV,* 4 November 1932.

18. Barandiarán, *AEF,* 1923, p. 113; Patxi Goicoechea of Ataun claimed to see in hell a worker who had once been his friend and who had died suddenly (Boué, 143). For long history see Schmitt, *Les Revenants,* 257.

19. "Mensaje de la Stma. Virgen. 8 Dic. 1950 ¡La Inmaculada! Grandiosa vision. Consoladoras manifestaciones de nuestra amorosísima Madre del Cielo. Al final, sorprendente mensaje familiar de una alma gloriosa, que fué vidente y murió en un convento en olor de santidad," 2 pages, AC 159.

20. A salesman from Vic happened on the crowd at Ezkioga 17 October 1931: Vigatà, *Gazeta de Vich,* 22 October. The first trip from Tona and Vic went October 19–23 and another was planned for a week later (*Gazeta de Vich,* 24 October; *EM,* 8 November). There was a favorable lecture in Vic by Joaquim Soler i Tures on 11 April 1932 (*Gazeta de Vich,* 9 and 13 April; *EM,* 13 April).

21. SC E 555–777 (22 February to 10 June 1933) and Cardús's correspondence with the enthusiast Paulí Subirà of Vic, the Galobart family of Mas Riambau, and Miguel Fort of Santa Eulàlia de Riuprimer (21 February 1933 to 5 October 1933, ASC). Subirà, *Gazeta de Vich,* 6 February 1933; there was a Lourdes chapel next to the estate; Anna Pou had prayed at Our Lady of La Gleva.

22. SC E 581–583.

23. This kind of vision has many parallels elsewhere, from the dream visions of Giovanni Pagolo Morelli in fifteenth-century Florence (Trexler, *Public Life,* 161–186) to my acquaintances in the present day.

24. J. B. Ayerbe to an abadesa, 1 July 1944, 10 pages, p. 3, AC 423.

25. The first seers' mother was the niece of a neighbor in Ama Felisa's hamlet. For Ama Felisa see her son Domingo Plazaola Goenaga and wife, Zumarraga, 8 April 1983.

26. For visits to San Sebastián, Juan María Amundarain, San Sebastián, 3 June 1984, p. 4; for her route, Juana Urcelay, Pamplona, 18 June 1984, p. 2; for Aranzazu, Franciscan keeper of San Martintxu, Beasain, 4 April 1983; older women, Zumarraga, 29 May 1984, p. 8.

27. Beaga, "O locos o endemoniados," 155. He may be describing a session Juan Bautista Ayerbe attended on 29 October 1947: Ayerbe to "Felipe" (probably his brother in Bergara), Urnieta, 27 November 1947, AC 424.

28. Dionisio Oñatibia, Urretxu, 7 April 1983, p. 1.

29. For Our Lady of Liernia see ADV Denuncias, Mutiloa, 1928–1929; for questor visits see Sukia, "El ambiente religioso," 364.

30. For the place of potatoes see Juliana Urcelay, Pamplona, 18 June 1984, p. 1; for India: elderly woman, Zumarraga, 10 May 1984, p. 8; for moon: older believers, Zumarraga, April 1983.

31. Lorenzo and Mariví Jayo, Durango, 31 December 1984 and 23 July 1986, and Tafira Baja, 15 June 1985 and 8 December 1989.

32. Bergara believer, 12 June 1984, p. 8; Leonor Castillo, Bermeo, 7 May 1984, p. 5; for similar specialists Bethencourt, *Costumbres populares,* 285–288, at the turn of the century describes a man in Icod de los Vinos (Tenerife) and a woman on the island of Hierro; for Asturias see Cátedra, *This World, Other Worlds,* 264–268, and for the *armièrs* of Languedoc see Kselman, *Death and the Afterlife,* 60.

33. William Douglass has carefully described the communal aspect of death in rural Bizkaia in *Death in Murelaga.* For Bedia see Ispitzua, *AEF,* 1923, pp. 17–22.

34. A girl saw a ghost who left burn marks on a handkerchief in Itziar in the mid-1940s, according to Rodríguez Ramos, *PV,* Bilbao, 12 May 1949, and Joseba Zulaika, personal communication.

35. Gorrochategui and Aracama, *AEF*, 1923, p. 111; Sáez de Adana, *AEF*, 1923, pp. 59–60.

36. Manescal, *Miscellanea*, 160–187; Palafox, *Luz;* and Mir, *El Milagro,* 2:692.

37. Koch, *I Contabili dell'Aldilà,* 132. The Deusto apparition was reported in the August 1909 issue of *Il Purgatorio visitato dalla pietà dei fedeli.* The bulletin had a Spanish as well as French and English editions, but there were few members of the brotherhood in Spain.

38. Koch, *I Contabili dell'Aldilà,* 80. In 1969 three out of the fourteen villages I surveyed in Cantabria had as their active patron saints the souls in purgatory: see Christian, *Person and God,* 68, 93–96, 142.

39. For Meñaka see Marcaida, *AEF,* 1923, pp. 35–36; for Galarreta in Alava see Sáez de Adana, *AEF,* 1923, p. 59. For antecedents of these ghost processions, see Schmitt, *Les Revenants,* 115–145, Kselman, *Death and the Afterlife,* 58–60, and Redondo, "La Mesnie Hellequin." People remembered such processions at Oliveto Citra in 1985: Apolito, *Cielo in terra,* 71–73. In Galicia in the 1960s adults as well as children saw the dead in processions; there language protected the belief as well (Christian, "Apparitions and the Cold War").

40. Etxeberria, *AEF,* 1923, pp. 94, 98. In the 1930s there was a woman from Girona operating in Irun (*VG,* 21 December 1934, p. 8) and a famous woman diviner in Mundaka (see Erkoreka, *Medicina popular,* 302).

41. There is no good history of spiritism in Spain. For spiritism: at origin, Braude, *Radical Spirits;* in France, Kselman, *Death and the Afterlife,* 143–162; in Italy, Gallini, "Eusapia."

42. On Ramona as a medium (she denied the charge), see Juan de Urumea, *El Nervión,* 21 October 1931. Maritxu Güller and others told me about spiritism in Pamplona: one middle-class commercial family held small, private séances; a butcher woman from Sangüesa did divining at night; adepts set up ad hoc sessions for visiting mediums. Even after the war priests and prominent citizens held experiments in thought transmission in the residence of a new religious institute.

43. Barandiarán, *AEF,* 1924: for Ataun, pp. 216–217, for Bermeo, pp. 197–199.

44. For positive opinion of spiritism see Thurston, *Spiritualism,* and his "Communicating with the Dead"; for a measure of the confusion in France, see the exchange between Louis Gérold and O. Kardec, *La Croix,* 25 October 1931, p. 3, and 29 December 1931, p. 3. For fakery see Heredia, *Los Fraudes.* For devilry see Mir, *El Milagro,* 3:473–514, and *La Verdad,* 13 March 1932, p. 2; Ugarte de Ercilla suspended judgment on spiritism in *Razón y fe,* 1923, pp. 105–108. For church prohibitions see Koch, *I Contabili dell'Aldilà,* 98, and M. D. Griffin, "Spiritism," *New Catholic Encyclopedia* 13 (1981): 576–577; the Congregation of Inquisition on 30 July 1856 condemned the evocation of departed spirits. On 24 April 1917, the Holy Office (and two days later Benedict XV) forbade attendance at sessions even if no medium was present. Questions in *Rayos de sol,* n.d., nos. 148–149.

45. Millán, *ELB,* 9–10 September 1931; J. V. Ibarz Serrat, "La Psicología en la obra de Santiago Ramón y Cajal," doctoral thesis, Facultat de Psicologia, Universitat de Barcelona, 1988 (I thank Antonio Cano for this reference).

46. Marqués, *HM,* 18 August 1931; Meromar, *Revelación,* reviewed in *VG,* 17 May 1933, p. 6; for Hadji Agaf, who came from South America, see *VG,* 13 September 1934, p. 4. Millán moved from Bilbao to Eibar in the early 1930s. For his letters, broadsides, and essays, see AHN GC Teosofía 25/851 and Masonería 174/A/27 (pseudonym Tolstoi), wherein the 1934 speech, "Mi niñez, mi vida, mi idea," I cite in text. In 1943 a Franco court sentenced him in absentia to twelve years in prison for Freemasonry.

47. All 1934: the *duende* was fully reported in *PV, VG,* and *ED* from November 23 until December 8; for psychokinesis see *PV,* 24 November, p. 3; for visitors in November see

VG, 25 November, p. 5, and *PV,* 27 November, p. 3, and 30 November, p. 3; for governor see *VG,* 4 December, p. 5. *La Voz de Aragón* and the flat's owner thought the servant girl was not involved at all (*PV,* 8 December, p. 2); for *duende* and Ezkioga see Axari-Beltx, *PV,* 15 December. For similar poltergeist in Italy, see Gallini, "Storie di case."

48. *EZ,* 19 July 1931, p. 9; Picavea, *PV,* 11 November 1931.

49. For Catholic attitudes, Koch, *I Contabili dell'Aldilà,* 100; Dominican quote from Barbado, "Boletín de psicología"; Thurston, *Spiritualism,* 16, 54–55, 368–384; Denis, *Joan of Arc,* 214, citing one of his spirit guides, "John, disciple of Peter," June 1909.

50. On accusation of spiritism see Cardús notes, 27 June 1933; for spiritism and Masonry see Tusquets, *Masonería,* 65–66. B 105–107.

51. For the appeal of spiritism to the more optimistic American Protestants, see Braude, *Radical Spirits,* 34–55. For the shift toward optimism in France, from Paris in the 1830s to the countryside in the second half of the century, see Kselman, *Death and the Afterlife,* 82–83; for a generous theologian, Alonso Getino, *Del gran número,* first published by Urbano in *Rosas y espinas* and *Contemporánea.*

52. Olazábal, *LC,* 17 June 1934, and subsequent polemic, especially *LC,* 24 and 28 June, 1 and 2 July; *VG,* 18 June; *ED,* 20 June; and *PV,* passim.

CHAPTER 14. THE END OF THE WORLD

1. Apolito, *Cielo in terra,* 139, noted a similar process at Oliveto Citra near Salerno (Campania).

2. Múgica, *Catecismo,* 22.

3. Carbonero, "Prólogo," vi; Thurston, *The War,* 189.

4. For late medieval and Early Modern prophets: Niccoli, *Prophecy;* Frijhoff, "Prophétie et société"; for nineteenth-century prophets: Caffiero, *La Nuova era;* Griffiths, *Reactionary Revolution;* Kselman, *Miracles and Prophecies;* Boutry and Nassif, *Martin l'Archange;* Lazzareschi, *David Lazzaretti;* Peterkiewicz, *Third Adam,* 63–66. Thurston, *The War,* lists prophetic literature from the 1870s.

5. Corbató, *Apología;* Echeverría Larrain, *Predicciones;* López Galuá, *Futura grandeza;* and Martín Sánchez, *Los Últimos Tiempos.* Curicque himself used the collection *Recueil des prophéties les plus authentiques.* A Spanish translation of *Voix prophétiques* with some additional material was published in 1874. For Spanish background on Antichrist see Caro Baroja, *Formas complejas,* 247–265. Raymond de Rigné used Elie Daniel, *Serait-ce vraiment la fin des temps?* (Paris: Téqui); for Rigné's other reading see R 104–108, and for that of Burguera see B 469–471.

6. Alacoque was beatified in 1864. Pius XI considered the feast of the Sacred Heart a bulwark against liberalism and made it universal in 1856. On the promises see Ladame, *Paray-le-Monial,* 237–266. On the reign of the Sacred Heart see Cinquin, "Paray-le-Monial," 269–273; and Christian, *Moving Crucifixes,* 109–116. For prophecy, Zurbitu, *Escritos,* 56.

7. Predictions in Sarrablo, "Verdades," and *La Semana Católica,* 4 August 1923, pp. 142–143, and 8 March 1924, p. 306; Morrondo (the canon of Jaen), *Proximidad* and *Jesús no viene;* citation from Morrondo's article in *La Semana Católica,* 8 September 1923, pp. 302–303; on Primo de Rivera see *La Semana Católica,* 29 March 1924, pp. 402–404. After more on the end of the world in July and August 1924, readers of the magazine were told to disregard the predictions on 6 September 1924, p. 299. Burguera read Morrondo (*De Dios a la Creación,* 83). Amundarain, *LIS,* 1931, pp. 9–10.

8. On World War I prophecies see Christian, *Moving Crucifixes,* 185 n. 102. *La Semana Católica,* 26 July 1924, p. 111, cites a pamphlet by Gil Zarco, *Los Milagros y profecías en el momento presente,* about the seer/prophet/healer Bernardo Carboneras, who operated in Valencia and Cuenca, and his success in finding soldiers lost in Morocco, *El Siglo Futuro,* Madrid, 16 January 1934.

9. Texts in: Corbato; Curicque, *Voces proféticas,* 82; R 105; López Galuá, *Futura grandeza,* 70; and Martín Sánchez, *Los Últimos Tiempos,* 42–43. For critical issues regarding Mélanie's secret, see Zimdars-Swartz, *Encountering Mary,* 183.

10. Abeytua, *ELM,* 22 July 1931.

11. All 1931: quote is from two girl seers July 17: *PV,* 18 July; group vision: *PV,* 14 July, *ED,* 21 July; act of God: *PV,* 18 July; miracle through person according to a female seer on July 25 (in Santander, *ABC* [Madrid], 13 August) and José Garmendia on August 15: autograph, private collection.

12. R 14; SC E 13; García Cascón to Vallet, 31 October 1931, AHCPCR 10-A-27/2.

13. Picavea, *PV,* 6 and 8 November; R 14n.

14. All 1931: for Patxi, *ED,* 29 July, and Elías, *CC,* 21 August; Ataun seer, August 6 to 8 in Elías, *CC,* 19 August; Patxi, *ED,* 8 August; Altisent, *CC,* 9 September, with Benita, August 18; García Cascón, *La Creuada,* 12 September; other children with secrets, *PV,* 18 October.

15. Zimdars-Swartz, *Encountering Mary,* 165–244; for one priest the very fact that the seers had and kept secrets, given recent apparitions, was enough; J. B. Ayerbe, "Las maravillosas apariciones," AC 2:6.

16. Lassalle, *PN,* 9 August 1931, at Ezkioga August 6 to 8.

17. Patxi in Delás, *CC,* 20 September 1931; for bag packed, Rodríguez Ramos, *Yo sé.* Cardús had heard the rumor of predicted chastisement by October 13 (SC E 72). For María Agueda Aguirre, "Relato por la interesada . . . ," p. 4, AC 22: "el girar los pueblos en su derredor."

18. Pedro Balda, Alkotz, 7 June 1984, p. 11.

19. García Cascón to Vallet, 31 October 1931, AHCPCR 10-A-27/2. See also visions in Lizarraga, late November, B II 628.

20. Gurruchaga vision of 14 December 1931, ARB 11; Gratacós, "Lo de Esquioga," 18; Lete vision, 15 December 1931, ARB 12–13.

21. On mourning, Lete vision, 28 December 1931, SC D 22; quote from Lete vision, December 1931, ARB 64, SC D 11.

22. For quote, Siurot, "La Inmaculada," 34. For Xenpelar see Lecuona, *Literatura oral,* 53–54; Lecuona, *AEF,* 1924, p. 21; for missions and especially Capuchins see Christian, *Moving Crucifixes,* 29–50, 142–143, 194 n. 9.

23. For Basque traditions see Barandiarán, *AEF,* 1924, pp. 178–183; for Rafols see Pare Rimblas to Cardús, Tàrrega, 25 January 1932, in SC E 286.

24. ARB 243 gives the circumstances of Benita's declaration. These versions are virtually identical: ARB 243–244; SC D 106–111; and the undated printed page "El Castigo" in the papers of Laburu; B 489 is a shortened version. Conchita Mateos memorized the declaration and repeated it verbatim in a vision on 11 December 1932, AC 6, AC 292. Cardús first cited it 2 March 1932 to Pare Rimblas, "One of the seers has said that the chastisement has already begun."

25. ARB 243; handwritten note to Laburu undated, unsigned, accompanying vision page in FL.

26. For French pilgrims see Boué, 67; one suspects in the conversion of years to "stages" a scribe trying to head off disprovable propositions.

27. Vision of Luis Irurzun, 11 March 1932, B 657 (ellipses in B).

28. For hurricane see B 243. The candles were specified by Inés Igoa, 3 December 1932, B 622; poster in Balcells Maso, *Manual de la enseñanza gráfica*.

29. For Tajo battle see visions of Luis Irurzun in February 1932, B 658. For Bug see López Galuá, *Futura grandeza*, 199–221. J. B. Ayerbe later circulated the Bug de Milhas prophecy. José Luis Manzano García (b. Toledo, 1972), who says his visions began in Palma de Mallorca in 1985, claims to be the "Great Warrior of the Tajo." He has established a shrine in Talavera de la Reina (Toledo); see Carrión, *El Lado oscuro*, 78–100. For bearded man see [Juan Bautista Ayerbe], "Un Caso ináudito," 1 folio, dittoed, n.d., AC 234. Burguera, B 247–248, gave the date of the dictation as 20 November 1933, pointed out the Torres Amat connection, and indignantly asserted that Christ never appeared old or with a red cloak. He concluded that the old man was the devil in disguise. Balda wrote to Ayerbe 21 May 1934: "San Juan in his Apocalypse, what does he say? Many times Luis has repeated in his visions, 'Let them look well at the Gospels and the prophecies and there they will find these warnings'" (AC 247).

30. Garmendia, *Ideología carlista*, 39–40, 191, 215, 246, 259, 453–459; Blinkhorn, *Carlism and Crisis*, 17–18.

31. On San Sebastián see vision of Luis Irurzun, 24 February and 12 March 1933, B 657, 659. For beaches see vision of Asunción Balboa, Urnieta, 10 September 1934, 2 pages, AC 211. For theaters see Irurzun vision, 12 March 1932, B 657; for casino see Ciordia vision poem, ca. June 1933, AC 218. For Mount Igeldo see vision of Asunción Balboa, Tolosa, 23 December 1934, 2 pages, AC 213. For Buen Pastor Cathedral: conversation with Ezkioguista women on train recalled by María Angeles Montoya, San Sebastián, 11 September 1983, p. 2.

32. Rimblas to Cardús, Tàrrega, 14 March 1932, reported a talk by Cardó a week before. For Recalde, 8 May 1932, SC D 81; Benita, 22 September 1933, B 516 and B 587–589; Tolosa seer, 30 November 1933, AC 278; Irurzun, 19 March 1932, B 657–658, and Pedro Balda, Alkotz, 7 June 1984, p. 6.

33. Benita visions, 22 and 23 October 1932, SC D 116–118. Unlike *La Constancia*, which carried anti-Semitic articles by Emilio Ruíz Muñoz and others, the seers mentioned Jews infrequently. José Garmendia's vision of 14 January 1934 is an exception ("Yes Mother, why are they so strong? Take them away Mother, take away those Jews. Why not, Mother?") ("Visión del Vidente José Garmendia . . . ," 1 page, typed, private collection).

34. B 480.

35. Cardús to Pou i Montfort, 13 May 1932.

36. Cruz Lete vision, 29 December 1931, SC D 22.

37. ARB 241 gives the setting. I have used the text from SC D 64–69. Not surprisingly, Burguera left this prediction, far too specific and disprovable, out of his book.

38. Pijoán, *El Siglo XX*, 194–195. Burguera used the second (1920) edition of *El Siglo XX* in *De Dios a la Creación*, 85. Pijoán's pamphlet, "El Gran Triunfo de Leo Taxil" (Biblioteca Antimasónica, Cuaderno XIV, Barcelona, Tip. y Lib. de la Inmaculada Concepción, 1889, 30 pages), ended: "Tu nombre, ¡Oh Taxil! / se cubre de gloria / tu hermosa memoria / eterna será."

39. Visions of 15 and 17 April 1932, B 718–719.

40. For the Carlist Great Monarch, Garmendia, *Ideología carlista*, 506, 631, mentions the prophecies of a nun, Sor María Antonia del Señor, and gives references published in 1869. For Mélanie see Zimdars-Swartz, *Encountering Mary*, 184; for Lazzaretti see Lazzareschi, *David Lazzaretti*, 59, 83, 119, 181–196; for Martin, Boutry and Nassif, *Martin*

l'Archange, 214. For Corbató see his *Regla de la milicia de la cruz, Regla Galatea,* and *Apología,* 2:214–18, and García Miralles, "El Padre Corbató," 361–400.

41. For archdiocesan ban: *Boletín eclesiástico de Valencia,* 15 March 1907. García Miralles, "El Padre Corbató," 454, 472–487. Corbató may have influenced the La Salle Brother Estanislao José (Olimpio Fernández Cordero, 1903–1926), who had revelations that he himself would be pope and that there would be a Eucharistic kingdom based in Spain with a Eucharistic army. His superiors did not allow him to deliver a secret message for Alfonso XIII, and only his close friends took his visions seriously: Rodríguez, *Un Joven heróico,* 100–111.

42. Visions of Benita Aguirre, 23 to 28 July, 7 and 8 September 1933, B 488, 502–503, 513.

43.

Benita Aguirre	P. Comà, from Curicque
La Italia, regada con la sangre de tantos mártires, es la esclava de una demagogia diabólica, que ha llegado a constituirse en consejera del Poder.	L'Italie, arrosée du sang de tant de généreux martyrs, est l'esclave d'une démagogie diabolique, qui est arrivée à se constituer la conseillère du pouvoir. . . .
Y la pobre España, que, palmo a palmo, ha sido conquistada por la Cruz, se ha convertido en un pueblo de ilotas, que corre al precipicio y lucha por romper con sus tradiciones y su propia manera de ser.	Et notre pauvre Espagne, qui a été conquise pied à pied par la Croix, est devenue un peuple d'ilotes, qui court au précipice et lutte pour briser avec ses traditions, son histoire et sa propre manière d'être.

Visions of Benita Aguirre 6, 20, 30 August 1933, B 504, 508, 511; Curicque, *Voix prophétiques,* 2:383. See Staehlin, *Apariciones,* 109–120, for similar borrowing by Gemma Galgani in 1902 and by the Madrid mystic Josefa Menéndez (1890–1923) in 1920.

44. Ayerbe distributed "¡Cuanto nos ama Jesús! (Relaciones del hermano Crucífero Serafín)," excerpts of four letters from Serafín to Hermano Pedro dated from December 1932 to July 1933 (AC 373–375); another letter to "Mi querido P. from Serafín de Jesús," 5 September 1933 (2 sides, AC 377); and two undated texts (AC 383). The citation is from a page copied by Ayerbe, 18 September 1934, AC 378, beginning "Queridos hermanos en los Sagrados Corazones de Jesús y María" and is part of a message on 1 September 1934 from "el Divino Maestro" via a seer for Hermano Pedro.

45. Recruiting on 27 August 1935, from "Extracto de una carta a los crucíferos" in ARB 253, with another message dated 13 October 1936; for chastisement see "J. M. J. De una carta del fundador-jefe de los crucíferos 16 octubre, 1935," 1 page, dittoed, AC 380 and ARB 253; and "De Una carta del Hno. Pedro 29 abril 1936" 1 folio, dittoed, AC 381; for female seer María, see "Mensaje de Jesús a sus predilectos Crucíferos" 2 sides, n.d., AC 383.

46. According to Josefina Romà, personal communication.

47. Ayerbe to nun, 15 November 1949, AC 427. López de Lerena began his letters with a symbol associated with the Crucíferos, a C with a cross inside it, in mid-1941.

48. Pedro Balda, Alkotz, 7 June 1984, pp. 1, 9.

49. López de Lerena, "A propósito de Ezquioga."

50. Ayerbe to Cardús, 9 November 1933.

51. "Fragmentos de una Carta—Terribles predicciones" and "Profecías de Bug de Milhas," 2 sheets, dittoed, unsigned, n.d., AC 458. After the date 1935 there is a handwritten note: "It appears the chastisement has been delayed."

52. López de Lerena, "A propósito de Ezquioga." Staehlin, *Padre Rubio,* 109–110, for the voracious reading of the seamstress Josefa Menéndez.

53. "Sobre la noche obscura y de tempestad," 1 page, dittoed, n.d., AC 14.

54. For river of blood: woman about age seventy in Zumarraga, May 1984. Izaga, the section of Zumarraga closest to Ezkioga, was partial to the visions, and the seer Marcelina Men-

dívil spent her last years there. Quotes from (1) woman from believing household in Ezkioga, age about fifty, August 1982; (2) woman from Ordizia, age seventy-two, December 1983; (3) man from believing household, Urnieta, June 1984. The overlap of predictions with those of the Jehovah's Witnesses led at least one Ezkioga cuadrilla to defect. Arrinda and Albisu draw the comparison in *Jehovatarrak* (Jehovah's Witnesses), 11.

55. Daniel Ayerbe, Irun, 13 June 1984, confirmed by his sister Matilde, in San Sebastián the next day.

CHAPTER 15. AFTERMATH

1. Copy of letter from Mateo Múgica, bishop of Vitoria, 26 June 1936, in private collection.

2. López de Lerena correspondence, private collection; for cathedral plans, Basilio Iraola, Irun, 17 August 1982.

3. Pedro Sarasqueta in *VG* 1934: 20 February, 22 March, 10 April, 11 July; in *VG* 1935: 24 January, 28 February, 15 October.

4. Luis Irurzun, San Sebastián, 5 April 1983. Since the Cinturón de Hierro was broken in 1937 on June 12, with Bilbao falling June 19, by Luis's account this session would have taken place about June 7. Casilda Ampuero, who married the general Varela after the war, knew nothing of the episode but did not rule it out (Cádiz, 21 August 1986). A skeptical José Solchaga had visited Ezkioga in the summer of 1931 (Teresa Michelena, Oiartzun, 29 March 1983). Luis said it was a General Quintanilla who saved him.

5. Believers in Zaldibia remember a set of arrests about 21 January 1937. Rigné, "Mes voyages," and Rigné, *Verdaderos asesinos,* 3.

6. Interview with a retired taxi driver who was an official of the transport union and present when the seer spoke, San Sebastián, 19 June 1984.

7. Montero, *Historia,* 242, 309–310, 330–331, 340–346, 416–421, 762, 834; for Urbano see Christian, *Moving Crucifixes,* 177; for Andrés de Palazuelo see Buenaventura de Carrocera, *Mártires Capuchinos de la Provincia Castilla en la revolución de 1936* (Madrid: El Mensajero Seráfico, 1944), 17–40.

8. Talde, *Archivo.*

9. Oriol Cardús, Terrassa, 19 October 1985, and letter to author with copies of confirming documents, 15 January 1994; among those killed who had gone to Ezkioga were Joan Salvans Piera, Antoni Barata Rocafort, and Montserrat Subirach Cunill; see Navarro, "La repressió."

10. Letter from López de Lerena to Ezkioga believer, Bilbao, 14 November 1941, private archive.

11. Daniel Ayerbe, Irun, 13 June 1984, pp. 2–3, 7. It appears the government withdrew the other exile orders as well. Ayerbe remembered that the order was signed by Caballero, Director General de Seguridad, who had been the civil governor of Gipuzkoa.

12. Basilio Iraola, Irun, 17 August 1982, p. 2; J. B. Ayerbe to abbess of Clarisas, 1 July 1944, AC 423.

13. Basilio Iraola, Irun, 17 August 1982, pp. 1–2. I found no trace of the documents in Legazpi, and José Garmendia's niece there thought it unlikely he would have kept the collection.

14. Sebastián López de Lerena, "Al Ilmo. Sr. Obispo de San Sebastián."

15. López de Lerena to an Ezkioga believer, Bilbao, 26 March 1952, private collection.

16. New believer and worker Alberto, factory town, 13 June 1984, p. 1.

17. Santiago Simón and Juana Urcelay, Pamplona, 18 June 1984.

18. Alberto, factory town, 13 June 1984.

19. Douglass, *Death in Murelaga*, chap. 4.

20. Silvan, *Los Pueblos,* and other books in the series Pueblos Guipuzcoanos.

21. McCarthy, *Priests and People,* 228–252; see also Nold, "The Knock Phenomenon"; Donnelly, "Knock," 55–57; *ELM,* 28 August 1931, p. 5; Larraitz, *ED,* 28 July 1931.

22. For *María Mensajera* see Sánchez-Ventura, "Las Apariciones."

23. Rev. Andoni Eizaguirre Galarraga, of Andoain, San Sebastián, 26 June 1984: Ama Birjiña Ezkio'n azaldu zan edo ez, iñork garbi ez dakigu; bañan bai bide baztarretan ama birjin ugari agertu zirala, eta ondoren amaika niño Jesus.

24. Henningsen, *Witches' Advocate,* 378–381.

25. *LC,* 22 June 1932, account of Laburu speech in San Sebastián; Atxabalt, *La Cruz,* 8 October 1933.

26. Mècle, "Deux victimes."

27. Irurita, "Sobre ciertos hechos"; for Red-baiting, Auguet Tort, *Bañolas,* and interview, Barcelona, 8 November 1984; for Medina, Siurfat, and general postwar history of Aulinas, F. Crous, Barcelona, 25 February 1985, pp. 3–4; quote is from Tusquets, *Masones y pacifistas,* 72–73, as cited in Ricart, *Desviación,* 380–381.

28. Ricart, *Desviación.* The denial of the sacraments to Aulina and her followers was decreed 5 August 1939; See also *Arxiu Vidal i Barraquer,* vol. 3, parts 1 and 2, pp. 928–930. The institute issued booklets commemorating the founding ceremonies at Funes (1946), Zaragoza in the diocese of Huesca (1948), and Aldeanueva de Ebro (1949).

29. Balcells, *EM,* 19 January 1934.

30. María Magdalena de Jesús Sacramentado to Sabino Lozano, Girona, 9 August 1941, in Marcucci, *En la cima,* 369. Marcucci may have visited Aulina again in Barcelona in 1957 (*En la cima,* 645). In San Sebastián in 1941 she stayed with a wealthy woman who had taken a great interest in the visions of Ezkioga, Sofía Olaso de Chalbaud (*En la cima,* 372, and Marcucci, *Autobiografía,* 531).

31. For origins of Esclavas, Mondrone, "Madre Speranza," Pujades, *Padre Postius,* 336–342; for Pilar Arratia, Josefa Akesolo, Bilbao, 15 June 1993. Madre Esperanza unsuccessfully tried to get Doroteo Irízar, who had supported the Ezkioga visions, to found her order of priests. In 1941, after the archbishop of La Habana decided against the distribution of the Sulamitis leaflets in his diocese, many bishops got the idea that the devotion had been condemned; *Arxiu Vidal i Barraquer,* vol. 2, part 3, pp. 633–634, and Sáenz de Tejada, *Bibliografía,* 25. As late as 1950, however, there were six monthly masses dedicated to the devotion in six different churches in San Sebastián.

32. Widow of Fernand Remisch, Dijon, 17 December 1983.

33. Thirouin poem in *L'Indépendant,* 5 November 1938; poem, "L'Appel des Morts," 1942; for Mutual Credit scheme, letter from Rigné to a friend in Melilla, Ezkioga, 17 May 1949, private collection.

34. Martin Halsouet and Mme. Estaló, Guéthary, and Simone Duro, Bidache, all 6 April 1983; and Simone Duro, Bidache, 28 June 1990. Quote from Maria Genoveva de la Ville de Rigné, Condesa de Morville, to friends at Ezkioga, Lanot-Dax, 30 November 1956, and Bidache, 27 December 1958.

35. Burguera to María Josefa Maté, Sueca, 29 March 1944.

36. On Benita's later years see Juan Castells, Sueca, 6 December 1983; Benita's companion and her brother Jesús Aguirre, Madrid, 19 May 1984; her sister Victoria Aguirre, Le-

gazpi, 6 February 1986. Her "godmother" appears to have been in touch with Cardinal Segura in Rome in 1933 (Cardús to Ayerbe, 11 October 1933).

37. Baudilio Sedano de la Peña, Valladolid, 12 December 1983.

CHAPTER 16. QUESTIONS WITHOUT ANSWERS

1. Alonso Getino, *Del gran número*, 35–48.

2. Personal communication, Ana González Vázquez, Santiago de Compostela, May 1993.

3. For Bilbao see *BOOV*, 1 March 1933, pp. 103–108; vivid description of destruction of image in a village in Jaén during carnival 1932 in *La Verdad* (Pamplona), 8 May 1932, p. 4, from *Pueblo Católico*, Jaén, 23 February 1932. When the Second Republic was proclaimed in 1931 some men allegedly tried to place a phrygian hat and republican banner on the Sacred Heart at El Cerro de los Angeles, according to *Semanario Católico de Reus*, 6 June 1931, p. 391.

4. Christian, *Local Religion* and *Apparitions*; Cattaneo, "Gli Occhi di Maria."

5. "The Virgin did not answer, but the angels smiled" (*PV*, 24 July 1931).

6. Pitt-Rivers, "Grace in Anthropology."

7. Baroja, *El Cura de Monleón*, 46–47; Apolito, *Cielo in terra*, 216.

8. Schneider, "Spirits and the Spirit of Capitalism." Estornés Zubizarreta, "Las Apariciones de Ezkioga," 590, calls the Ezkioga phenomenon "one of the last gasps of Basque preindustrial society."

9. Kagan, *Lucrecia's Dreams*, 86–113; Boutry and Nassif, *Martin l'Archange*, 69–70, 93–94; Lazzareschi, *David Lazzaretti*, 102, 190; Staehlin, *Apariciones*, 347–349.

10. Rigné to director of *ABC* (Madrid), Zumarraga, 27 February 1948, carbon copy, private collection. Cardús described the Fatima entry at length in an unpublished manuscript, ASC. For García Cascón: family member, Terrassa, 19 October 1985.

11. McKevitt, "San Giovanni Rotondo," and his doctoral thesis at the London School of Economics. For the worldwide aspect of the modern phenomena, see Stirrat, *Power and Religiosity*.

12. Basque believers in Ezkioga showed me a number of mimeographed sheets, for example, Felix Sesma, "Ejército Blanco de María Madre, Circular," Barcelona, 6 January 1970, 1 page, announcing special grace for a select few who resist the devil's dominion over the world as apocalyptic events approach, and Félix Sesma, "Consideraciones, Marzo 1971: El Ejército Blanco como tremendo anuncio de Dios y como llamada de la Reina de Cielos y Tierra," 5 pages, mimeo.

13. Staehlin, *Apariciones*, 72–91. Carlos Maria Staehlin and the English Jesuit Herbert Thurston were exceptional in their careful attention to contemporary "marginal" religious enthusiasms and devotions in Catholicism. Kenneth L. Woodward's *Making Saints* is a more recent, sensitive study.

14. Turner and Turner, *Image and Pilgrimage*.

15. See Christian, Sr., *Doctrines of Religious Communities*.

16. Zarri, *Finzione*; Kleinberg, *Prophets*.

17. Connerton, *How Societies Remember*; Mitchell, *Passional Culture*.

18. See Fernandez, *Bwiti*.

BIBLIOGRAPHY

This bibliography includes signed newspaper articles and both signed and unsigned magazine articles. For each author the items are in order of date of publication. See introduction to notes for abbreviations.

UNSIGNED WORKS

A la Madre Dolorosa de Ezquioga. 4-page printed prayer. N.p., n.d.

Anuario eclesiástico, 1919. Barcelona: E. Subirana, 1919.

Anuario estadístico de España. Madrid: Sucesores de Rivadeneyra, 1933.

"Las Apariciones de Ezkioga." *La Baskonia,* 30 August 1931, p. 526.

"Las Apariciones en Ezkioga." *La Baskonia,* 20 August 1931, pp. 504–505.

Argia'ren egutegia 1932 (Argia almanac 1932). Vol. 11. Donostia: Iñaki Deunaren Irarkola, 1932.

El *Avance de la provincia de Guipúzcoa desde 13 de septiembre de 1923 a 31 de marzo de 1929: Memoria.* San Sebastián: Imp. de la Diputación de Guipúzcoa, 1929.

"Un Caso inexplicado: Teresa Neumann, la estigmatizada de Konnersreuth: 1. Estudio objetivo sobre los hechos; 2, 3. Exposición de los hechos; 4, 5. La Actitud de la Iglesia sobre los hechos; 6, 7. El Ayuno absoluto; 8. El Ayuno del bienaventurado Nicolas de Fleuwe; 9, 10. Las Comuniones extáticas." *Easo,* 25, 26, 27,

28, 30 November 1931, and 1, 2, 3, 4, 5, 8 December 1931.

"De la aparición de la Virgen en Guadamur." *La Semana Católica*, 1931, pp. 229–230.

"Ecos de Fátima." *El Santísimo Rosario*, September 1930, pp. 526–529.

"En San Sebastián-Donosti." *La Baskonia*, 10 September 1931.

"Ezkioga: Faut-il étouffer l'affaire?" *Annales de Beauraing et Banneux*, 1 November 1933, p. 3.

Un Fruto de Ezquioga: Hermano Cruz de Lete y Sarasola: Religioso de la Orden Hospitalaria de San Juan de Dios: Una nota biográfica con su glosa. [Barcelona]: Patrici Arnau, 1933.

Guía de Guipúzcoa. San Sebastián: Diputación de Guipúzcoa, 1930.

Guía diocesana de Vitoria. Vitoria: Montepío Diocesano, 1931, 1933, 1935.

"Hermano Cruz de Lete." *Caridad y Ciencia* 59 (1933): 699–704.

Hoja interrogatorio de las manifestaciones de la Santísima Virgen en Ezquioga. 2-sided printed sheet. N.p., n.d. [1931].

"Lo que ha visto un cacereño en Ezquioga." *El Castellano* (from *Extremadura*, Cáceres), 26 September 1931, p. 1.

"Los Milagros de Ezkioga." *La Baskonia*, 10 August 1931, p. 494.

"Noticies de Badalona: La visita d'uns Badalonins a Ezquioga." *El Matí*, 19 September 1931.

Padrón de Superioras: Dolores Medina y Garvey, en religión M. María del Corazón de Jesús, religiosa del Instituto de María Reparadora. Cádiz: Establecimientos Cerón, Librería Cervantes, 1944.

"Pastoral sobre Ntra. Sra. de Fátima." *El Santísimo Rosario*, May, June 1931, pp. 263–269, 321–327.

¿Qué pasa en Ezquioga? Resumen de hechos y exposición de actitudes. Pasajes: Artes Gráficas Pasajes, 1931.

El Santo Cristo de Lezo: Breve reseña de algunos datos referentes a esta prodigiosa imagen. San Sebastián: Tipografía Joaquín Muñoz Baroja, 1924.

"Los Sucesos de Ezquioga." *Ecos de San Felicísimo*, 1 September 1931, pp. 358–360.

"Las Supuestas Apariciones de la Virgen en Ezquioga." *Mundo Gráfico*, 21 October 1931, p. 23 (3 photos).

"Vich: Impressions d'Ezkioga." *El Matí*, 13 April 1932, p. 11.

Vida de la sierva de Dios Pabla Bescós Espiérrez, superiora general del Instituto de Hermanas de la Caridad de Santa Ana, de Zaragoza. Tarazona: Luis Martínez Moreno, 1935.

Los Videntes de Ezkioga: A la opinión pública creyente. San Sebastián: Artes Gráficas Pasajes; Depósito en "La Constancia," 1931.

Zeanuri'ko abade, lekaide eta lekaimeen izenak: 1935-gn, bagila 28-an yainko-yai aintzgarriak (The names of priests, and male and female religious from Zeanuri: The blessed festivities of the Lord on June 28, 1935). Bermeo: Gaubeka, 1935.

SIGNED WORKS

A. "Sobre los fenómenos de Ezquioga: Interesante referencia de un médico. El orden y la compostura de la muchedumbre. Ayer percibieron la visión varias personas." *LC*, 12 July 1931, p. 1.

A. B. "Desde la ciudad del Vaticano: El prodigio de la Sagrada Espina de Andría ha tenido lugar." *LC*, 10 April 1932, p. 5.

A. L. "L'Évêque de Vitoria et les 'apparitions' d'Ezquioga." *La Croix*, 24–25 September 1933.

Abaurrea, P. de. "Los Escritos de la Madre María Rafols." *El Pensamiento Navarro*, 27, 28, 29 July 1932; 3, 10 August 1932.

Abeletxe. *See* Ciarsolo Gironella, Manuel.

Abeytua, Isaac. "La Virgen de Guipúzcoa y el diablo en Navarra: Ineficacia de los milagros políticos." *El Liberal* (Madrid), 22 July 1931, p. 1.

Achica-Allende, Alberto de. *Cuadernos de Lourdes: Cuaderno primero*. Bermeo: Tipografía de Pedro Ruíz, 1918.

Aladel, Jean Marie. *Sor Catalina Labouré y la Medalla Milagrosa*. 3d ed., rev. and augmented by Ponciano Nieto. Madrid: Imp. Cleto Vallinas, 1922.

Aldabe. "La Virgen del Rosario del Fátima." *LC*, 25 July 1931, p. 4.

Aldea Vaquero, Quintín; Tomás Marín Martínez; and José Vives Gatall, eds. *Diccionario de historia eclesiástica de España*. 4 vols. Madrid: Instituto Enrique Flórez, Consejo Superior de Investigaciones Científicas, 1972–1975.

Algorri. *See* Zuatzaga, Jon.

Alonso Getino, Luis G. *Del gran número de los que se salvan y de la mitigación de las penas eternas: Diálogos teológicas*. Madrid: Editorial F. E. D. A., 1934.

Alonso Lobo, Arturo. *El P. Arintero, precursor clarividente del Vaticano II*. Salamanca: San Esteban, 1970.

Altisent, Juan Bautista. "De mi carnet: Las apariciones de Ezquioga. 1. El Monte de las apariciones; 2. Lo que me han contado; 3, 4, 5. Lo que yo he visto; 6. Conclusión." *CC*, 6, 8, 9, 10, 13, 15 September 1931.

———. "De mi carnet: Los restos de la M. Rafols." *LC*, 28 April 1934, p. 3.

Alujas, Moisés. *Teresa Neumann o la favorecida de Santa Teresa del Niño Jesús: Relación completa de los prodigios de Konnersreuth*. Barcelona: Editorial Litúrgica Española, 1929.

Alumnos de la escuela de párvulos, un grupo de antiguos. "Desde Beasain, Sor Antonia Garayalde Mendizábal." *PV*, 26 March 1932, p. 6.

Amigó y Ferrer, Luís. *Obras completas*. Ed. Agripino González and Juan A. Vives. Madrid: Biblioteca de Autores Cristianos, 1986.

Amundarain Garmendia, Antonio. "Estáis en peligro." *Lilium inter Spinas* 19 (May–June 1929): 47–48.

———. "Fugite fornicationem." *Lilium inter Spinas* 19 (May–June 1929): 57.

———. "Nuestra modesta voz." *Lilium inter Spinas* 25 (September 1930): 10–15.

———. "Cruzada urgente." *Lilium inter Spinas* 30 (February 1931): 9–10.

———. "Mensaje divino: Sulamitis." *Lilium inter Spinas* 35 (June 1931): 1–11.

———. "Sobre las apariciones de Ezquioga: Algo que conviene tener en cuenta." *PV*, 15 July 1931, p. 5.

——— ("Comisión Eclesiástica"). "Estampas y medallas: Piedad y respeto." *ED* and *LC*, 28 July 1931.

——— (unsigned). "Nuestra visita a Ezquioga." *Lilium inter Spinas* 39 (October 1931): 24–27.

———. *Vida, espíritu y hechos de la congregación de Religiosas Hermanas Mercedarias de la Caridad*. Madrid: Imp. Avilista, 1954.

Andrés de Palazuelo. "Las Apariciones de Ezquioga." *El Mensajero Seráfico*, 16 September 1931, pp. 597–598.

Andueza, Bartolomé de. "Luz de lo alto: Las estupendas Profecías de la Madre María Ráfols." *LC*, 25 February 1932; 5, 11 March 1932.

———. "Las Estupendas Profecías de la Madre Ráfols." *LC*, 26, 30 March 1932; 10, 23 April 1932; 8, 12, 17 May 1932; 3, 17, 26 June 1932.

Anitua, Pedro de. "Durango." *Nuestro Misionero Gure Mixiolaria*, 1932, pp. 105–119.

Antigüedad, Daniel R. "Las Supuestas Apariciones de la Virgen en Ezquioga." *El Nuevo Mundo,* 17 July 1931, [2 pages].

———. "Emoción y espectáculo de las apariciones de Ezquioga." *El Nuevo Mundo,* 21 October 1931, [2 pages].

Antón, Pedro. "Notas de actualidad: El Señor de la Villa y Ezquioga." *LC,* 12 November 1931, p. 5.

Antonino de Caparroso. "Los fenómenos místicos." *Verdad y Caridad* 8 (1931): 402–404; 9 (1932): 18–20, 50–52, 83–85, 114–116, 146–147, 205–207, 237–239.

Apez-bat (A priest). "Ezkioga." *Amayur,* 24 July 1931, p. 1.

Apolito, Paolo. *"Dice che hanno visto la Madonna": Un caso di apparizioni in Campania.* Bologna: Il Mulino, 1990.

———. *Il Cielo in terra: Construzioni simboliche di un'apparizione mariana.* Bologna: Il Mulino, 1992.

Aranzadi y Etxeberría, Engracio de. *La Nación vasca.* Bilbao: Grijielme, 1923.

———. "La Aparición de Ezquioga." *ED,* 11 July 1931, p. 3; also *CC,* 18 July 1931, p. 5.

———. "Por San Miguel de Aralar." *EZ,* 20 August 1931, p. 1.

———. *Ereintza: Siembra de nacionalismo vasco 1894–1912.* San Sebastián: Editorial Auñamendi Argitaldaria, 1980.

Araxes. "Algo acerca de lo de Ezquioga." *LC,* 26 June 1932, p. 10.

Arbeloa, Victor Manuel. *La Semana trágica de la iglesia en España (octubre de 1931).* Barcelona: Galba Edicions, 1976.

Arbeloa, Victor Manuel, and Miquel Batllori, eds. *Arxiu Vidal i Barraquer.* Vol. 2, part 3. Barcelona: Abadia de Montserrat, 1975.

Arcaya, Alejandro de. *See* Pildain, Antonio.

Arcelus, Andrés ("Luzear"). "Ezkio'ko gertaerak dirala ta . . . Guk ikusi ta entzundakoa" (About the events at Ezkioga . . . what we saw and heard). *ED,* 21 July 1931, p. 10.

Areitioaurtena, Luis ("Larraitz"). "Ezkioga'ko mirariak" (The miracles of Ezkioga). *ED,* 28 July 1931, p. 10.

———. "Ezkio'tzaz" (Against Ezkioga). *A,* 3 September 1933, p. 3.

Argandoña, Francisco. "Las Apariciones de Lizarraga." 8 pages. Lezaun, 1991.

Arín Donorronsoro, Juan de. *Clero y religiosos de Atáun.* Vitoria: Montepío Diocesano, 1964.

Aristi, Pako. *Irene, tempo di adagio.* Donostia: Erein, 1989.

Arnal, C. "Trucs que no fallen: Preparant l'aparició d'una nova verge." Cartoon in *L'Esquella de la Torratxa,* 9 October 1931, p. 653.

Arraiza. "Preparando otra guerra civil." *VG,* 9 June 1931, p. 3.

Arrarás, Joaquín. *Historia de la Segunda República.* 4th rev. ed. Vol. 1. Madrid: Editora Nacional, 1969.

Arregi Azpeitia, Gurutzi. *Ermitas de Bizkaia.* Bilbao: Instituto Labayru, 1987.

Arrese, Domingo de. *El País vasco y las constituyentes de la Segunda República.* Madrid: Gráficas Modelo, 1931.

———. *Profecías de la Madre Rafols.* Barcelona: Eugenio Subirana, 1939.

Arribiribiltzu. "Fatima'ko gertaerak: Ama Birjiñaren agerpena" (The events at Fatima: The apparition of the Virgin Mother). *A,* 26 July 1931, p. 1.

Arrinda, Donato, and Anastasio Albisu. *Jehovatarrak: Testigos de Jehova,* Berriz: Colegio Vera Cruz, 1977.

Arritoquieta, Tomás de. "Contestando ¿Ezquiogan zer?" (What happened in Ezkioga?). *LC,* 24 March 1932, p. 7.

———. "Ezquiogan'zer." *LC,* 3 April 1932, p. 6.

Arrue, Ramón ("Baserritarra" [A farmer]). "Albiztur." *A,* 14 May 1933, p. 3.

Arteche, José. "En torno a lo de Ezquioga: La mano de Dios." *ED,* 12 July 1931, p. 5.

———. "Insistiendo sobre el caso de Ezquioga: La mano de Dios." *ED,* 14 July 1931, p. 12.

Artola, Antonio María. *Monseñor Martín Elorza, C. P.: Obispo misionero pasionista.* Bilbao: PP. Pasionistas, 1978.

Atxabalt. "Alkarrizeta Ezquioga'ko gora beratzaz" (Conversation about the Ezkioga affair). *La Cruz,* 8 October 1933, p. 6.

Atxelai. "Bizkaitik Gipuzkoara: Ezkioga" (From Bizkaia to Gipuzkoa: Ezkioga). *EZ,* 2 August 1931, p. 6.

Auguet Tort, Gabriel (Marqués de Monteviñedo). *Bañolas ¿Retracción o ficción?* Madrid: Horta, 1950.

Aurteneche Goiriena, Juan José. "Vida y obra del doctor Oreja." Doctoral thesis, Facultad de Medicina, Universidad de Salamanca, 1984.

Axari-Beltx. "Consejos: Duendes enanos y fantasmas gigantescos." *PV,* 15 December 1934, p. 1.

Ayerbe, Juan Bautista. *Hijos ilustres de Segura.* San Sebastián, 1912.

———. "El Santo Cristo de Limpias, relato de un testigo." *El Siglo Futuro,* 23 August 1919, p. 1.

———. "Los Acontecimientos de Limpias." *El Debate,* 20 July 1921, p. 3.

———. *Maravillosas apariciones de la Sma. Virgen en Ezkioga.* Dittoed, corrected by hand. [Urnieta], December 1932.

———. *Las Apariciones de la Sma. Virgen en Ezkioga: Una personalidad científico-religioso en Guipúzcoa (Urnieta, Abril 1933).* 1933.

———. *Las Maravillosas Apariciones de Ezkioga: Algunas observaciones a un escritor madrileño que ha calificado de superchería tan portentosas apariciones.* Dittoed ["tirada 200 ejemplares"]. [Urnieta], 1933.

——— ("Felipe"). "Desde Urnieta: Buruntza-Urnieta." *LC,* 5 December 1934, p. 5.

Azaña, Manuel. *Obras completas.* Vol. 4. Mexico City: Oasis, 1968.

Azcue Arregui, Dionisio de ("Dunixi"). "Verá a la Virgen." *ED,* 18 July 1931, p. 12.

Azkue, Resurrección María de. *La Estigmatizada de Konnersreuth.* Barcelona: E. Subirana, 1929.

Bagaria. "Niños precoces." Cartoon in *Crisol,* 1 September 1931, p. 1.

Balcells Masó, Ramón. "Desviacions de la pietat." *El Matí,* 19 January 1934.

———. *Manual de la enseñanza gráfica del catecismo de la doctrina cristiana.* 9th ed. Barcelona: Editorial Vilamala, 1963.

Barandiarán, José Miguel de. "Las Montañas y los bosques: Los aparecidos." *Eusko-Folklore* 2, no. 16 (1922): 13–16.

———. "En Ataun." *AEF* 3 (1923): 112–26.

———. "En Orozko." *AEF* 3 (1923): 5–12.

———. *Fragmentos folklóricos—Paletnografía Vasca.* San Sebastián, 1923.

———. "Nacimiento y expansión de los fenómenos sociales." *AEF* 4 (1924): 151–229.

———. *Mitología vasca.* 5th ed., augmented and corrected. San Sebastián: Txertoa, 1983.

Barbachano, José María de. *El Doctor Asuero mago de la medicina.* 2d ed. San Sebastián: Editorial Leizola, [1929?].

Barbado, M. "Boletín de psicología: Metapsíquica." *Ciencia Tomista,* 1923, pp. 71–101.

Baroja, Pío. *Los Visionarios.* Vol. 6 of *Obras completas.* Madrid: Biblioteca Nueva, 1948 (orig. ed., 1932).

————. *El Cura de Monleón.* 3d ed. San Sebastián: Editorial Txertoa, 1972 (orig. ed., 1936).

Barriola, Ignacio María. "La Medicina donostiarra en el primer tercio de este siglo." *Cuadernos de Historia de la Medicine Vasca* 5 (1987): 9–45.

Baserritarra. *See* Arrue, Ramón.

Basilio de San Pablo. "Manifestaciones de la Pasión: La estigmatizada Teresa Neumann, de Konnersreuth." *El Pasionario,* February 1930 to February 1932.

————. *Lo Sobrenatural en la historia: Vida abreviada de la venerable Gema Galgani.* Santander: Administración de *El Pasionario,* 1932.

Bax, Mart. "Popular Devotions, Power, and Religious Regimes in Catholic Dutch Brabant." *Ethnology* 24 (1985): 215–220.

————. "The Seers of Medjugorje: Professionalization and Management Problems in a Yugoslav Pilgrimage Centre." *Ethnologia Europaea* 20 (1990): 167–176.

————. "Marian Apparitions in Medjugorje: Rivalling Religious Regimes and State Formation in Yugoslavia." In *Religious Regimes and State Formation: Perspectives from European Ethnology,* ed. Eric R. Wolf, pp. 29–53. Albany: State University of New York Press, 1991.

————. *Medjugorje: Religion, Politics and Violence in Rural Bosnia.* Amsterdam: VU Uitgeverij, 1995.

Bay, Alberto. "La Estigmatizada de Konnersreuth, una mujer alemana que llora lágrimas de sangre." *PV,* 27 October 1931, p. 2.

Beaga, P. "O Locos o endemoniados." *Redención,* May 1950, pp. 153–156.

Bearak, Barry. "Visions of Holiness in Lubbock: Divine or Imagined?" *Los Angeles Times,* 9 April 1989, pp. 1, 36–38, 40.

————. "Lubbock Visions: 'Miracles' Are Explained but Not Forgotten." *Los Angeles Times,* 10 April 1989, pp. 1, 19–21.

Becker, Gerhard. *Tiempo profético de María Rafols.* Zaragoza: Editorial Círculo, [1974?].

Beguiristain, Santos. *Por esos pueblos de Dios . . .* 4th ed. Madrid: Euramerica, 1959.

Benz, Ernst. *Die Vision: Erfahrungsformen und Bilderwelt.* Stuttgart: Ernst Klett Verlag, 1969.

Bergamín, José. "El Laburismo español y nueva paradoja del comediante." *Diablo Mundo,* 28 April 1934, p. 3.

Bernoville, Gaëtan. "Les Faits étranges d'Ezquioga." *Études,* 20 November 1931, pp. 456–476.

————. "Les Faits étranges d'Ezquioga." *La Croix,* 3 December 1931, p. 4.

Bethencourt Alfonso, Juan. *Costumbres populares canarias de nacimiento, matrimonio, y muerte.* Ed. Manuel A. Fariña González. Santa Cruz de Tenerife: Aula de Cultura de Tenerife, Museo Etnográfico, Cabildo Insular de Tenerife, 1985.

Bilinkoff, Jodi. "Confessors, Penitents, and the Construction of Identities in Early Modern Avila." In *Culture and Identity in Early Modern Europe (1500–1800): Essays in Honor of Natalie Zemon Davis,* eds. Barbara B. Diefendorf and Carla Hesse, pp. 83–100. Ann Arbor: University of Michigan Press, 1993.

Billet, Bernard. "Apparitions ou prodiges attribués à la Vierge et non reconnues par l'Église." In *Vraies et Fausses Apparitions dans l'Église.* Paris: Letheilleux, 1976.

Blackbourn, David. *Marpingen: Apparitions of the Virgin Mary in Bismarckian Germany.* Oxford: Clarendon Press, 1993.

Blasco Salas, Simón. *Recuerdos de un médico navarro: Aspectos retrospectivos de la época y médicos durante más de medio siglo.* Pamplona: Editorial Gómez, 1958.

Blinkhorn, Martin. *Carlism and Crisis in Spain 1931–1939.* Cambridge: Cambridge University Press, 1975.

———. "Right-wing Utopianism and Harsh Reality." In *Spain in Conflict 1931–1939: Democracy and Its Enemies,* ed. M. Blinkhorn, pp. 183–205. London: Sage, 1986.

Bloch, Marc. "Réflexions d'un historien sur les fausses nouvelles de la guerre." *Revue de Synthèse Historique* (1921).

Boada, Josep María. "Flors de santedat: Gema Galgani." *Germanor,* 1 May 1930, pp. 223–225.

Boada y Camps, Juan. *Los Crucifijos y las profecías de la Madre Rafols: Relación histórica.* 3d ed. Barcelona: Llibreria La Bona Parla, 1932.

Boniface, Ennemond ("Paul Romain"). *La Crucifiée de Konnersreuth, Thérèse Neumann.* Paris: Bloud et Gay, 1932.

——— ("Paul Romain"). "Genèse d'Ezkioga." *L'Enigme d'Ezkioga,* July-August 1935, p. 3.

———. *Thérèse Neumann, la crucifiée de Konnersreuth devant l'histoire et la science: Essai d'introduction à la étude de la phenomenologie mystique.* Paris: P. Lethielleux, 1979.

Bordas Flaquer, Mariano. *La Verdad de "Lo de Ezkioga": Estudio filosófico-teológico.* Barcelona: Vda. de Mariano Blasi, 1932.

Boué, G.-L. *La Mére Rafols et ses écrits posthumes.* Tarbes: Imp. Lesbordes, 1932 [not seen].

———. *Merveilles et prodiges d'Ezquioga: 1. Coup d'oeil historique, 2. Voyants et visions.* Tarbes: Imp. Lesbordes, 1933.

Bourguignon, Erika. "Dreams and Altered States of Consciousness in Anthropological Research." In *Psychological Anthropology,* ed. F. K. L. Hsu. Homewood, Ill.: Dorsey, 1972.

Bourneville, Désiré Magloire. *Louise Lateau, ou la stigmatisée belge: Science et miracle.* 2d ed. Paris: Delahaye, 1878.

Boutry, Philippe. "Marie, la grande consolatrice de la France au XIXe siècle." *L'Histoire* 50 (November 1982): 30–39.

———. *Prêtres et paroisses au pays du curé d'Ars.* Paris: Les Éditions du Cerf, 1986.

Boutry, Philippe, and Michel Cinquin. *Deux pèlerinages au XIXe siècle: Ars et Paray-le-Monial.* Paris: Éditions Beauchesne, 1980.

Boutry, Philippe, and Jacques Nassif. *Martin l'Archange.* Paris: Gallimard, 1985.

Braude, Ann. *Radical Spirits: Spiritualism and Women's Rights in Nineteenth-century America.* Boston: Beacon Press, 1989.

Brenier de Montmorant, Maxime. *Psychologie des mystiques catholiques orthodoxes.* Paris: Librairie Félix Alcan, 1920.

Brotteaux, Pascal. *See* Pascal, Émile.

Buonaiuti, Cesare Marongiu. *Spagna 1931: La Seconda Repubblica e la Chiesa.* Roma: Bulzoni Editore, 1976.

Burguera y Serrano, Amado de Cristo. *Enciclopedia de la Eucaristía.* 7 vols. Estepa: Antonio Hermoso, 1905–1906.

———. *Reglamento del catequismo católico ostipense para uso de la Congregación vulgarmente llamada de la Doctrina Cristiana.* Estepa: Antonio Hermoso, 1906.

———. *Compendio de la Enciclopedia Eucarística o el misterio de la fe universalmente considerado.* Valencia: Domenech y Taroncher, 1908.

———. *Musas armónicas: Poesias originales.* Sueca: Máximo Juan, 1915.

———. *Memoria sobre la Venerable Orden Tercera de Penitencia . . . presentada al congreso nacional de Terciarios Franciscanos de Madrid.* Madrid: Antonio López, 1916.

———. *La Extática Sierva de Dios Roberta Miralles y Sales, natural de Sueca: Biografía documentada: Norma de vida de la obrera de la aguja.* Madrid: Tipografía del Sagrado Corazón, 1917.

————. *Los Terciarios franciscanos regulares en Fontilles.* Madrid: Tip. Sagrado Corazón, 1917.

————. *La Venerable Ildefonsa Artal de Sueca.* Madrid: Máximo Juan, 1918.

————. *La Milagrosa Imagen de Nuestra Señora la Virgen de Sales y su magnífico santuario.* Madrid: Antonio López, 1920.

————. *El Smo. Cristo del Hospital y su devota capilla: Los santos mártires Abdón y Senén.* Madrid: Antonio López, 1920.

————. *Historia fundamental documentada de Sueca y sus alrededores.* Vol. 1. Madrid: Antonio López, 1921.

————. *Historia fundamental documentada de Sueca y sus alrededores (1500–1925).* Vol. 2. Valencia: Renovación Tipográfica, 1925.

————. *De Dios a la creación: De la creación al arte: Del arte a Dios: Estudios superiores, en tres volúmenes, de reconstitución científica, histórica, artística y social, o de reintegración de lo sobrenatural en el saber humano.* Vol. 1: *De Dios a la creación.* Valencia: Tipografía del Carmen, 1931. Vol. 2: *De la creación al arte.* Valencia: Tipografía del Carmen, 1931 (appeared 1932).

————. "Apariciones: Surge Fray Amado de C. de Burguera: y dice." *PV,* 2 December 1932, p. 2.

————. *Los Hechos de Ezquioga ante la razón y la fe.* Valladolid: Imprenta y Librería Casa Martín, 1934.

C. "Ormáiztegui: Fervor Republicano." *VG,* 20 September 1932, p. 12.

————. "Ormáiztegui: Viles artimañas." *VG,* 20 November 1932, p. 12.

C. y J. "Los Hombres de la República, perfiles locales: Pepe Bago." *VG,* 2 May 1931, p. 16.

Cabecerán, Manuel. "Oportunidades." *Semanario Católico de Reus,* 29 August 1931, p. 584.

Cadoret-Abeles, Anne. "Les Apparitions du Palmar de Troya: Analyse antropologique d'un phénomène religieux." *Mélanges de la Casa de Velazquez* 17 (1981): 369–391.

Caffiero, Marina. *La Nuova Era: Miti e profezie dell'Italia in rivoluzione.* Genoa: Marietti, 1991.

Callahan, William J. *Church, Politics, and Society in Spain, 1750–1874.* Cambridge: Harvard University Press, 1984.

Campoamor, Clara. (Speech) *Diario de Sesiones de Cortes Constituyentes* 1 (1 September 1931): 698–701.

Carasatorre Vidaurre, Rafael. *Barranca Burunda.* Pamplona: Gráficas Pamplona, 1993.

Carbonero y Sol y Merás, Manuel. "Prólogo del traductor." In M. G. Rougeyron, *El Anticristo, su persona, su reinado, y consideraciones sobre su venida, según las señales de la época presente.* Madrid: Imprenta de "La Esperanza," 1872.

Cárcel Ortí, Vicente. "Iglesia y estado durante la dictadura de Primo de Rivera 1923–1930." *Revista Española de Derecho Canónico* 45, no. 124 (1988): 209–248.

————. *La Persecución religiosa en España durante la Segunda República (1931–1939).* Madrid: Rialp, 1990.

Cardús i Florensa, Salvador. "Apunts d'Ezquioga." *La Creuada,* 10 October 1931, p. 479.

———— [?]. "Ezquioga." *La Creuada,* 10 October 1931, pp. 473–474.

———— ("Un que hi és"). "Les Apariciones de la Verge a Ezquioga." *La Creuada,* 17 October 1931, p. 489.

————. "Engrunes de Cel (Intims records)" (Crumbs of heaven, intimate memoirs). Terrassa, 1931–1933. ASC.

————. "Els Fets d'Ezquioga i les profecies de la Mare Rafols." Typescript. Terrassa, 1932. ASC.

————. *Espiritualitat Monserratina de Terrassa.* Terrassa: Joan Morral, 1947.

Cardús i Grau, Josep. "Context biogràfic de Salvador Cardús i Florensa." In Salvador Cardús i Florensa, *L'Escultor Arnau Cadell i el seu claustre de Sant Cugat,* 11–17. Sabadell: Fundació Bosch i Cardellach, 1993.

Caro Baroja, Julio. *Los Baroja: Memorias familiares.* Madrid: Taurus, 1972.

————. *Las Formas complejas de la vida religiosa.* Madrid: Akal, 1978.

Carrión López, Gabriel. *El Lado oscuro de María (el gran fraude de las apariciones marianas).* Alicante: Editorial Aguaclara, 1992.

Carroll, Michael P. *The Cult of the Virgin Mary: Psychological Origins.* Princeton: Princeton University Press, 1986.

Castellano y Mazarredo, José Luis. "Un testimonio (carta)." *PV,* 20 October 1931, p. 2.

Castells, Luis. *Modernización y dinámica política en la sociedad guipuzcoana de la Restauración 1876–1915.* Madrid: Siglo XXI, 1987.

Castillo, Vidal. "Los Sucesos de Ezquioga toman un nuevo sesgo: Una carta." *ED,* 28 November 1931, p. 3; also *El Matí,* 8 December 1931.

Cátedra, María. *This World, Other Worlds: Sickness, Suicide, Death, and the Afterlife among the Vaqueiros de Alzada of Spain.* Trans. William A. Christian, Jr. Chicago: University of Chicago Press, 1992.

Cather, Willa. *Death Comes to the Archbishop.* New York: Knopf, 1927.

Cattaneo, Massimo. "Gli Occhi di Maria sulla Rivoluzione: I miracoli del 1796–1797 nello Stato della Chiesa." Rome, 1993. Files of William Christian Jr.

Ceballos Vizcarret, Rose María. *Vida y obra del Dr. Victoriano Juaristi.* Temas Donostiarras 19. San Sebastián: Sociedad Guipuzcoana de Ediciones y Publicaciones, 1992.

Charcot, J. M. "La Foi qui guérit." In *Les Démoniaques dans l'art, suivi de La Foi qui guérit,* 111–123. Paris: Macula, 1984 (orig. ed., 1892).

Charcot, J. M., and Paul Richer. *Les Démoniaques dans l'art.* Paris: Macula, 1984.

Chidester, David. *Salvation and Suicide: An Interpretation of Jim Jones, the Peoples Temple, and Jonestown.* Bloomington: Indiana University Press, 1988.

Cholvy, Gérard, and Yves-Marie Hilaire. *Histoire religieuse de la France contemporaine: 1880–1930.* Vol. 2. Paris: Privat, 1986.

Christian, William A., Jr. "De los santos a María: Panorama de las devociones a santuarios españoles desde el principio de la edad media hasta nuestros días." In *Temas de antropología española,* ed. Carmelo Lisón Tolosana, pp. 49–105. Madrid: Akal, 1976.

————. *Apparitions in Late Medieval and Renaissance Spain.* Princeton: Princeton University Press, 1981.

————. *Local Religion in Sixteenth-Century Spain.* Princeton: Princeton University Press, 1981.

————. "Provoked Religious Weeping in Early Modern Spain." In *Religious Organization and Religious Experience,* ed. John H. R. Davis, pp. 97–114. London: Academic Press, 1982.

————. "Religious Apparitions and the Cold War in Southern Europe." In *Religion, Power and Protest in Local Communities: The Northern Shore of the Mediterranean,* ed. Eric R. Wolf, pp. 239–266. Berlin: Mouton, 1984.

————. "Tapping and Defining New Power: The First Month of Visions at Ezquioga, July 1931." *American Ethnologist* 14, no. 1 (1987): 140–166.

———. "Francisco Martínez quiere ser santero: Nuevas imágenes milagrosas y su control en la España del siglo XVIII." *El Folklore Andaluz* (Homenaje Andaluz a Julian Pitt-Rivers, vol. 2) 4 (1989): 103–114.

———. *Person and God in a Spanish Valley.* Rev. ed. Princeton: Princeton University Press, 1989.

———. "The Mind's Eye: Basque Visionaries in Trance, 1931." Malinowski Memorial Lecture, London School of Economics, 17 May 1990.

———. *Apariciones en Castilla y Cataluña (siglos XIV–XVI).* Rev. ed. Trans. Eloy Fuente. Madrid: Nerea, 1990.

———. *Religiosidad local en la España de Felipe II.* Rev. ed. Trans. Javier Calzada and José Luis Gil Aristu. Madrid: Nerea, 1991.

———. "Secular and Religious Responses to a Child's Potentially Fatal Illness." In *Religious Regimes and State Formation: Perspectives from European Ethnology,* ed. Eric R. Wolf, pp. 163–180. Albany: State University of New York Press, 1991.

———. *Moving Crucifixes in Modern Spain.* Princeton: Princeton University Press, 1992.

———. "Visions in Spain: The Seers the Authorities Believe and Those We Do Not Hear About." Lecture, Conference on Structure, Identity, and Power, Amsterdam, 3 June 1995.

Christian, William A., Sr. *Doctrines of Religious Communities: A Philosophical Study.* New Haven: Yale University Press, 1987.

Ciammitti, Luisa. "One Saint Less: The Story of Angela Mellini, a Bolognese Seamstress (1677–17[?])." In *Sex and Gender in Historical Perspective,* ed. Edward Miur and Guido Ruggiero, pp. 141–176. Baltimore: Johns Hopkins University Press, 1990.

Ciarsolo Gironella, Manuel ("Abeletxe"). "Bilbo-Ezquioga." *EZ,* 23 July 1931, p. 5.

Cillan Apalategui, Antonio. *Sociología electoral de Guipúzcoa (1900–1936).* San Sebastián: Sociedad Guipuzcoana de Ediciones y Publicaciones, 1975.

Cinquin, Michel. "Paray-le-Monial." In *Deux pèlerinages au XIXe siècle: Ars et Paray-le-Monial,* ed. Philippe Boutry and Michel Cinquin, pp. 171–305. Paris: Beauchesne, 1980.

Ciriaco. "El Señor de la Villa tiene miedo." *La Tradición Navarra,* 16 August 1931, p. 2.

Claverie, Elisabeth. "La Vierge, le désordre, la critique." *Terrain* 14 (March 1990): 60–75.

———. "Voir apparaître: Les Apparitions de la Vierge à Medjugorje." *Raisons Pratiques* 2 (1991): 1–19.

Commission Historique du Centenaire 1873–1973. *Notre-Dame du Dimanche: Les Apparitions à Saint-Bauzille-de-la-Sylvie.* Paris: Beauchesne, 1973.

Connerton, Paul. *How Societies Remember.* Cambridge: Cambridge University Press, 1989.

Constancio. "Silueta del día—Apariciones." *El Defensor de Granada,* 11 September 1931, p. 1.

Corbató Chillida, José Domingo María. *Regla Galatea de los Hermanos de la Milicia de la Cruz o forma de vida religiosa y política de la nueva Orden de los Crucíferos.* Valencia: Biblioteca Españolista, 1903.

———. *Revelación de un secreto o Introducción a la regla de la milicia de la cruz.* Valencia: Biblioteca Españolista, 1903.

———. *Apología del Gran Monarca: primera parte, Racionalidad de la cuestión: segunda parte, Temas capitales sobre el Gran Monarca y su imperio.* Valencia: Biblioteca Españolista, 1904.

Corral, Olegario. *Autenticidad de los escritos de la M. Rafols.* Barcelona: Talleres Gráficos Núñez, 1933.

Cousin, Bernard. *Notre Dame de Lumières: Trois siècles de dévotion populaire en Lubéron.* N.p.: Desclée de Brouwer, 1981.

Cruz Romero, Manuel. "Las Apariciones milagrosas." *El Defensor de Granada*, 8 September 1931, p. 3.

Cuberes i Costa, Isidre. "Sis hores a Ezquioga." *El Matí*, 5 August 1931.

Curicque, J.-M. *Voix prophétiques ou Signes, apparitions et prédictions modernes touchant les grands événements de la Chrétienté au XIXe siècle et vers l'approche de la fin des temps*. 5th rev. and enl. ed. Paris: Victor Palmé, 1872.

———. *Voces proféticas ó Signos, apariciones y predicciones modernas concernentes á los grandes acontecimientos de la cristiandad en el siglo XIX y hacia la apoximación del fin de los tiempos*. Spanish ed. (from 5th French ed.), with additions by translator. Trans. Pedro González de Villaumbrosia. Barcelona: Imp. y Lib. Religiosa y Científica, 1874.

Degrelle, Léon. "Les Deux-tiers des hommes vont mourir." *Soirées* (Belgium), 21 September 1933, 3 pages.

———. *Léon Degrelle, Persiste et Signe*. Paris: Jean Picollec, 1985.

Delás, María de los Angeles de. "Tres tardes en Ezquioga." *CC*, 20 September 1931, p. 2.

De la Villa, Antonio. [Speech about Ezkioga]. *Diario de Sesiones de Cortes Constituyentes* 1 (13 August 1931): 392–394.

———. [Speech about Ezkioga]. *Diario de Sesiones de Cortes Constituyentes* 2 (23 October 1931): 1927–1928, 1930.

Delpal, Bernard. *Entre paroisse et commune: Les catholiques de la Drôme au milieu du XIXe siècle*. Valence: Editions Peuple Libre, 1989.

Del Valle, Teresa. "La Mujer vasca a través del análisis del espacio: Utilización y significado." *Lurralde* 6 (1983): 251–269.

———. *Korrika: Basque Ritual for Ethnic Identity*. Trans. Linda White. Reno: University of Nevada Press, 1994.

De Martino, Ernesto. *La Terra del rimorso*. Milano, 1961.

Denis, Léon. *The Mystery of Joan of Arc*. Trans. Arthur Conan Doyle. London: John Murray, 1924.

De Sède, Gérard. *Fatima: Enquête sur une imposture*. Paris: Alain Moreau, 1977.

Díaz Sintes, F. "El Gobierno de la diócesis de Pamplona por el Excmo. Sr. D. Tomás Muniz de Pablos 1928–1935." Ph.D. diss., Theology, Universidad de Navarra, 1973.

Didi-Huberman, Georges. *Invention de l'hysterie: Charcot et l'iconographie photographique de la Salpêtrière*. Paris: Macula, 1982.

———. "Charcot, l'histoire et l'art." In *Les Démoniaques dans l'art, suivi de La Foi qui guérit*, 125–215. Paris: Macula, 1984.

Di Febo, Giuliana. *La Santa de la raza, Teresa de Avila: Un culto barroco en la España franquista (1937–1962)*. Trans. Angel Sánchez-Gijón. Barcelona: Icaria, 1988.

Donnelly, James S., Jr. "The Marian Shrine of Knock: The First Decade." *Éire-Ireland* 28, no. 2 (1993): 54–99.

Dorola, F. *See* Remisch, Fernand.

Doroteo de la Sagrada Familia. *Historia prodigiosa del milagroso Niño Jesús de Praga (1617–1924)*. Barcelona: Luis Gili, 1924.

Douglass, William A. *Death in Murelaga: Funerary Ritual in a Spanish Basque Village*. American Ethnological Society, monograph no. 49. Seattle: University of Washington Press, 1969.

Doyle, Arthur Conan. *The History of Spiritualism*. Vol. 2. London: Cassell, 1926.

Duchenne, Guillaume Benjamin. *Mécanisme de la physionomie humaine ou Analyse électro-physiologique de l'expression des passions*. Paris: Veuve Jules Renouard, 1862.

Ducrot, J.-A. "Le Grand Chatiment: La fin du monde est-elle proche? 1. Visions diaboliques ou divines? 2. La Vierge aux pattes de coq; 3. Comment j'ai fait le portrait du diable." *VU*, 16, 23, 30 August 1933, pp. 1289–1293, 1329–1333, 1363–1367.

Dunixi. *See* Azcue Arregui, Dionisio de.

Duocastella, Rogelio; Juan Lorca; and Salvador Misser. *Sociología y pastoral: Estudio de sociología religiosa de la diócesis de Vitoria.* Madrid and Barcelona: I. S. P. A., 1965.

Eade, John, and Michael J. Sallnow, eds. *Contesting the Sacred: The Anthropology of Christian Pilgrimage.* London: Routledge, 1991.

Echaide, Ignacio María. *Comunicaciones de Guipúzcoa.* Publicaciones de la Red Telefónica de Guipúzcoa. Burgos: Rafael Ibáñez de Aldecoa, 1924.

Echaniz, Cipriano. "Juventudes marianas guipuzcoanas, 1860–1930." *La Estrella del Mar,* February 1931, p. 75.

Echarri, María de. "¡Ama Virgiña!" *Heraldo Alavés,* 24 July 1931, p. 4.

———. "Lourdes, Santa Juana de Arco, Ezquioga . . . Santa Teresa de Jesús." *Heraldo Alavés,* 25 August 1931.

Echeguren, Justo de ("Vicaría general del Obispado"). "Sobre las misteriosas apariciones de Ezquioga: Una nota de la . . ." *ED, PV,* 29 July 1931; *Gaceta del Norte,* 30 July 1931; *El Matí,* 1 August 1931; *CC,* 2 August 1931.

———. "Para orientar a la opinion . . ." *Easo, Heraldo Alavés,* and *El Nervión,* 17 October 1931; *El Debate, DN, Imparcial, LC, El Liberal* (Madrid and Bilbao), and *PV,* 18 October 1931; *El Castellano, Crisol,* 19 October 1931; *El Socialista,* 20 October 1931; *La Creuada,* 24 October 1931.

———. "Vetitum pro sacerdotibus accedendi ad locum vulgo 'Ezquioga.'" *BOOV* 68 (1 January 1932): 6.

———. "Ha sido prohibido la edificación de una capilla en Ezquioga." *BOOV* 68 (15 June 1932): 324.

Echeverría Larrain, Julio. *Predicciones privadas acerca de algunos acontecimientos modernos.* Santiago de Chile: Carnet Social, 1932.

Efrén. "Las Apariciones de Iria." *La Gaceta del Norte,* 15 July 1931.

Egurza, Pedro de. "Algunas observaciones en torno a las apariciones de Ezquioga." *LC,* 24 July 1931, p. 5.

———. "En torno a las apariciones de Ezquioga." *LC,* 25 July 1931, p. 2.

Elías, Martín. "Cuatro días en Ezquioga: Impresiones." *CC,* 15, 19, 21 August 1931, p. 1.

Emika. (Poem) "Ezkio'ko Ama, lagun iguzu!" (Help us, Mother of Ezkioga!). *A,* 23 August 1931, p. 1; also 21 May 1933, p. 5.

Erauskin Garmendia, José Francisco. "Bertso Berriak Ezkioga'ko Ama Birjiñari" (New verses to the Virgin Mother of Ezkioga). *A,* 8 November 1931.

——— (Poem) *Ezkio'ko Agermenari* (To the apparition of Ezkioga). 1931 or 1932.

——— ("Erauskin Errotari"). "Ordizia: Ezkon deya" (Ordizia: The wedding announcement). *A,* 23 April 1933, p. 5.

———. "Ordizia: Mujika'tar Juan'eri" (Ordizia: To Juan Múgica). *A,* 14 May 1933, p. 5.

———. "Ezkio'ko ama lagun eiguzu" (Help us, Mother of Ezkioga). *A,* 21 May 1933, p. 5.

Erkoreka, Anton. *Análisis de la medicina popular vasca.* Bilbao: Labayru Ikastegia, 1985.

Erniazu. "Deun Mikel Goi-Aingerua ta Aralar'ko mendia" (Saint Michael the Archangel and Mount Aralar). *Argia'ren Egutegia* 11 (1932): 109–111.

Erriko-seme. "Elorrio: La Verdad en su sitio." *EZ,* 7 August 1931, p. 10.

Erromerieta. "Irun: Albiztur'ko 'Luistar' eri" (Irun: To Luistar of Albiztur). *A,* 14 May 1933, p. 4.

————. "Irun: 'Luistar' Entzat" (Irun: For Luistar). *A*, 27 August 1933, p. 4.

Esteban, Salvador. "¿Qué pasa en Ezquioga?" *La Ilustración del Clero*, 16 November 1931, pp. 306–309.

Esteban Infantes, Emilio. *La Sublevación del general Sanjurjo, relatada por su ayudante.* Madrid: José Sánchez de Ocaña, 1933.

Estornés Zubizarreta, Idoia. "Un Episodio molesto: Las apariciones de Ezkioga." *Muga: Revista Trimestral*, 1979, pp. 70–77.

————. "Las Apariciones de Ezkioga." *Enciclopedia General Ilustrado del País Vasco* 12 (1981): 586–591.

————. *La Constitución de una nacionalidad vasca: El autonomismo de Eusko-Ikaskuntza (1918–1931).* Cuadernos de Sección Historia-Geografía 14. San Sebastián: Editorial Eusko Ikaskuntza, 1990.

Étienne, Jean-Michel. *Le Movement Rexiste jusqu'en 1940.* Cahiers de la Fondation National des Sciences Politiques. Paris: Armand Colin, 1968.

Etxarri, Tonia. "Echarri Aranaz, un pequeño 'Belfast' en Navarra." *El País*, 29 April 1983, p. 23.

Etxeberria, Francisco de. "En Altza." *AEF* 3 (1923): 93–97.

————. "Andoain." *AEF* 4 (1924): 48–78.

Etxezarreta, Antonia ("Lierni"). "Andua: Ama Birjiñaren agerpenak" (Anduaga: Apparitions of the Virgin Mother). *A*, 6 December 1931, p. 6.

————. "Gure herriko agerpenen alde" (In favor of the apparition of our village). *Eup! Ezkio-Itsasoko Herri Aldizkaria* (Hey There! The magazine of the township of Ezkio-Itsaso), April 1994, p. 14.

Ezeizabarrena. "Ezkioga'n" (At Ezkioga). *PV*, 1 August 1931, p. 9.

F. D. "Una Visita a Ezquioga." *CC*, 16 August 1931, p. 2.

Facultad de Teología, Vitoria. "Santuarios del país vasco y religiosidad popular." In *II Semana de historia eclesiástica del país vasco in Vitoria*. Caja Provincial de Alava, 1982.

Farges, Dr. "Al margen de los hechos de Ezquioga: Unas cuartillas sobre estigmatizaciones desde el punto de vista científico." *Easo*, 19, 20, 21 October 1931.

Fariñas Windel, M. L. "Apóstol del Amor Misericordioso." *Vida Sobrenatural* 17 (February 1929): 103–122.

Farre, Manuel. "De Col.laboració: Impressions d'Ezquioga." *Diari de Sabadell*, 7 October 1931, p. 1.

————. "Les Reals o suposadas apariciones de la Verge Maria: Impressions d'Ezquioga." *El Matí*, 8 October 1931, p. 2.

Federico dell'Addolorata. "Gemma Galgani (sainte)." *Dictionnaire de Spiritualité* 6 (1967): 184–187.

Feliu Corcuera, Alfredo. *"Baga, Biga, Higa . . .": Una etnología de lo insólito vasco.* Bilbao: Ediciones Mensajero, 1991.

Fernandez, James W. *Bwiti: An Ethnography of the Religious Imagination in Africa.* Princeton: Princeton University Press, 1982.

Ferrer Benimeli, J. A. *El Contubernio judeo-masónico-comunista: Del satanismo al escándalo del P-2.* Madrid: Istmo, 1982.

Ferrer i Dalmau, Eugeni. "Los Escritos póstumos de la Madre Rafols: Réplica." Ca. 1933. ASC.

Ferrer Muñoz, Manuel. *Elecciones y partidos políticos en Navarra durante la Segunda República.* Pamplona: Gobierno de Navarra, 1992.

Foix, Jordi de. "L'Acció Catòlica i el quietisme des visionaris." *El Matí*. 22 February 1933.

Frijhoff, Willem. "Prophétie et société dans les Provinces-Unies aux XVIIe et XVIIIe siècles." In *Prophètes et sorciers dans le Pays-Bas XVIe–XVIIIe siècle,* ed. Willem Frijhoff, Marie-Sylvie Dupont-Bouchat, and Robert Muchembled, pp. 263–362. Paris: Hachette, 1978.

———. *Wegen van Evert Willemsz.; Een Hollands weeskind uit de zeventiende eeuw op zoek naar zichzelf.* Nijmegen: SUN, 1994.

Froeschlé-Chopard, Marie-Hélène. *La Religion populaire en Provence orientale au XVIIe siècle.* Paris: Beauchesne, 1980.

———. "Les Saints du dedans et dehors en Provence orientale." In *Luoghi sacri e spazi della santità,* ed. Sofia Boesch Gajano and Lucetta Scaraffia, pp. 609–629. Torino: Rosenberg and Sellier, 1990.

Fusi Aizpurua, Juan Pablo. "Nacionalismo y revolución: Octubre de 1934 en el país vasco." In *Octubre 1934,* ed. Gabriel Jackson, pp. 177–196. Madrid: Siglo XXI, 1985.

G., E. "En torno a los sucesos de Ezquioga." *Aranzazu,* 15 August 1931, pp. 237–239.

Gaite, Carmen María. *El Conde de Guadalhorce, su época y su labor.* Madrid: Colegio de Ingenieros de Caminos, Canales, y Puertos, 1977.

Gajano, Sofia Boesch, and Lucetta Scaraffia, eds. *Luoghi sacri e spazi della santità.* Torino: Rosenberg and Sellier, 1990.

Gallini, Clara. *La Sonnambula meravigliosa: Magnetismo e ipnotismo nell'ottocento italiano.* Milano: Feltrinelli, 1983.

———. "Storie di case 'dove ci si sente.'" *Il Piccolo Hans* 45 (April–June 1985): 109–133.

———. *La Ballerina variopinta.* Napoli: Liguori Editore, 1988.

———. "Eusapia e il professore: Lo spiritismo nella Napoli di fine '800." *Quaderni* (Istituto Universitario Orientale), 3d new ser., nos. 3/4 (1989): 17–54.

———. "Lourdes e *Lourdes.*" Rome, 1993. Files of William Christian Jr.

García Cascón, Rafael (unsigned). "Els Fets meravellosos d'Ezquioga." *La Creuada* (Terrassa), 12 September 1931, pp. 424–425.

———. "Algo más sobre las maravillosas apariciones de la Virgen en Ezquioga (Guipúzcoa, España): Párrafos de la carta de un perseverante de Cataluña." *Vida Interior* (Salto, Uruguay) 2 (December 1931): 3.

García de Pesquera, Eusebio. *"Se fue con prisas a la montaña": Los Hechos de Garabandal.* Pamplona: Litografía G. Huarte, 1979.

García Miralles, Manuel. "El Padre Corbató o las pasiones políticas del siglo XIX." Valencia, 1969. Dominican Fathers, Valencia.

García Morales, Juan. "Las Apariciones de Ezquioga." *Heraldo de Madrid,* 22 October 1931, p. 16.

García Onaindía, Rainaldo (Rainaldo María de San Justo). "La Infancia espiritual." *Vida Sobrenatural* 10, nos. 55, 57, 60 (1925).

Garitaonandía Garnacho, Carmelo. "La Radiodifusión durante la dictadura de Primo de Rivera: Los orígenes." In *La crisis de la restauración: España entre la I guerra mundial y la II República,* ed. J. L. García Delgado, pp. 361–401. Madrid: Siglo XXI, 1986.

Garmendia, Vicente. *La Ideología carlista (1868–1876) en los orígenes del nacionalismo vasco.* Zarautz: Diputación Foral de Guipúzcoa, 1984.

Garmendia Cortadi, José ("Zeleta"). "Mirarizko Ama Neketsua'ren agertuna Gipukoa'ko Santa Luzia unguruan Bertan Ikusi deguna eta esan digutena" (The miraculous apparition of the Sorrowing Mother near Santa Lucía in Gipuzkoa: What we saw and were told there). *EZ,* 11 July 1931, p. 5; also *ED,* 11 July 1931.

———. "Ezkio'ko Ama Neskutza'ren mirarizko agerkunak" (The miraculous apparitions of the Virgin Mother of Ezkioga). *ED,* 15 July 1931, p. 8.

Garrán. "Como en Ezquioga." Cartoon in *El Imparcial,* 19 August 1931, p. 1.

Garriga, Ramón. *El Cardenal Segura y el Nacional-Catolicismo.* Barcelona: Planeta, 1977.

Gatestbi, A. "Ezkion zer?" (What happens at Ezkioga?). *Aranzazu,* 15 August 1931, pp. 250–251.

Germán de San Estanislao, ed. *Cartas y éxtasis de la sierva de Dios Gema Galgani.* Colección "Los Santos," vol. 14. Barcelona: Herederos de Juan Gili Editores, 1914.

———. *Vida de Gema Galgani Virgen de Luca.* 2d ed. Trans. Modesto H. Villaescusa. Colección "Los Santos," vol. 10. Barcelona: Herederos de Juan Gili, 1918.

Gil Bare. "El Vidente que nada ha visto." *PV,* 16 March 1935.

Godfernaux, André. *Le Sentiment et la pensée et leurs principaux aspects physiologiques: Essaie de psychologie expérimentale et comparée.* Paris: Félix Alcan, 1894.

Goens, Daniel. *Un Crucifix qui saigne: Reportage.* Bruxelles: Imp. J. Remy-Saimpain, 1934.

Goguel, Maurice. *La Foi dans la résurrection de Jesús dans le Christianisme primitif: Étude d'histoire et de psychologie religieuses.* Paris: Librairie Ernest Leroux, 1933.

Goicoechea, Francisco. "Más sobre Ezquioga: El de Ataún contesta a Alcibar." *ED,* 12 November 1931, p. 12; also "Una Carta de Francisco Goicoechea," *LC,* 12 November, p. 4, and "Mes sobre Ezquioga," *La Creuada,* 28 November, p. 561.

Goiko. "¡¡Aquí, No!!" Cartoon in *¡Adelante!* Semanario Católico, 27 June 1931, p. 1.

Gómez, Victor. "Trágicos resultados del clericalismo: Un obrero condenado a seis años de presidio por no descubrirse al paso de una procesión." *El Socialista.* 24 October 1931, p. 1.

Goñi, J. "Zubeldia Inda, Néstor." *DHEE* 4 (1975): 2813–2814.

González-Ruano, César. "La Medalla religiosa de Ezquioga tiene anverso, reverso y canto." *El Nuevo Mundo,* 19 November 1931, 2 pages.

González Ruíz, Nicolas. "Fátima, centro de devoción portuguesa, está en plena actividad constructiva." *El Debate.* 24 February 1935, supplement.

Goodman, Felicitas D.; Jeannette H. Henney; and Esther Pressel. *Trance, Healing, and Hallucination: Three Field Studies in Religious Experience.* New York: John Wiley, 1974.

Gorce, M.-M. "Arintero (Juan-Gonzales)." *DS* 1 (1937): 855–859.

Gorostiaga Extebarria, Eulogio de. "Zeanuri." *AEF* 4 (1924): 118–133.

——— ("Masmelene"). "¿Euzkadi-n Andra Mari agerpenak?" (Apparitions of Our Lady in Euskadi?). *EZ,* 15 July 1931, p. 6.

Gorrocha. "Desde Ormáiztegui: Mirando al viaducto." *VG,* 24 September 1932, p. 7.

Gorrochategui, José Andrés. "Zegama." *AEF* 2 (1922): 50–53.

Gorrochategui, José Andrés, and José Antonio Aracama. "En Zegama." *AEF* 3 (1923): 107–112.

———. "Zegama." *AEF* (1924): 102–109.

Granja, José Luis de la. *Nacionalismo y II República en el País Vasco.* Madrid: CIS, 1986.

Gratacós, Luis. "Lo de Esquioga." *La Cruzada Eucharística* (México), April 1933, pp. 8–20.

Gratton, Henri. "Psychologie et extase." *Dictionnaire de Spiritualité* 4 bis (1961): 2171–2182.

Greenwood, Davyd J. *Unrewarding Wealth: The Commercialization and Collapse of Agriculture in a Spanish Basque Town.* Cambridge: Cambridge University Press, 1976.

Griffiths, Richard. *The Reactionary Revolution: The Catholic Revival in French Literature, 1870–1914.* London: Constable, 1966.

Guallar Poza, Santiago. *De la vida, gracias y virtudes de la sierva de Dios Madre María Rafols, fundadora del Instituto de Hermanas de la Caridad de Santa Ana.* Zaragoza: Gambón, 1931.

Guridi, Leonardo de. "Oñate." *AEF* 4 (1924): 90–101.

Hamon, André. *Notre-Dame de France.* 7 vols. Paris: Plon, 1861–1866.

Heiberg, Marianne. *The Making of the Basque Nation.* Cambridge: Cambridge University Press, 1989.

Heigel, Henri. "Les Apparitions de la Sainte Vierge en Lorraine de langue allemande en 1800 et 1873." *Les Cahiers Lorrains,* no. 4 (1957): 68–74.

Henningsen, Gustav. *The Witches' Advocate: Basque Witchcraft and the Spanish Inquisition (1609–1614).* Reno: University of Nevada Press, 1980.

Heredia, Carlos María de. *Los Fraudes Espiritistas y los fenómenos metapsíquicos.* 1931.

Herman, Judith Lewis. *Trauma and Recovery.* New York: Basic Books, 1992.

Higinio de Santa Teresa. *Apuntes para la historia de la Venerable Orden Tercera del Carmen en España, Portugal, y America.* Vitoria: Ediciones "El Carmen," 1954.

Hilgard, Ernest R. *Divided Consciousness: Multiple Controls in Human Thought and Action.* New York: John Wiley, 1977.

Ibarguren, Sinforoso de. "Pueblo de Ezquioga." *AEF* 7 (1927): 27–57.

Imbert-Gourbeyre, A. *Les Stigmatisés.* 2d ed. Paris: Victor Palmé, 1873.

Imízcoz, José María. "Una Emigración particular: Misioneros navarros en América." In *Navarra y América,* ed. José Andrés-Gallego, pp. 457–495. Madrid: Editorial Mapfre, 1992.

Iriarte, Mateo de. "Estado religioso de Eibar." *Idearium* 2 (1935): 399–410.

Irigarai, Fermín. *Guía médica del intérprete de milagros y favores.* Madrid: Espasa-Calpe, 1949.

Irukoistar Batzuk [Some Trinitarians]. *Dima trinitario y sacerdotal: Apuntes biográficos de los trinitarios, sacerdotes, y religiosos de este municipio de Vizcaya.* Madrid: Padres Trinitarios, 1972.

Irurita Almándoz, Manuel. "Sobre ciertos hechos a los que se atribuye carácter sobrenatural." *Boletín Oficial del Obispado de Barcelona* 76 (16 August 1933): 264–265; also in *Hormiga de Oro,* and the *Boletines* of Tarragona and Vitoria.

Ispitzua, Tiburcio de. "En Bedia (Bizkaya)." *AEF* 3 (1923): 13–22.

Iturbi. "Abadino'tik; Ezkioga'rantza" (From Abadiano: Going to Ezkioga). *EZ,* 23 July 1931, p. 5.

Ixaka. "Desde Elgoibar: En torno a lo de Ezquioga: Relato personal." *LC,* 20 October 1931, p. 8.

Jakinzale. "Actitudes diversas." *ED,* 18 July 1931, p. 12.

———. "La "Aparición" subjetivamente considerada: Fraude y sugestión." *ED,* 21 July 1931, p. 8.

———. "En torno a las apariciones de Ezquioga: La "aparición" subjetivamente considerada." *ED,* 22 July 1931, p. 12.

———. "En torno a Ezquioga: La alucinación." *ED,* 23 July 1931.

———. "En torno a los sucesos de Ezquioga: Milagros y milagros." *ED,* 24 July 1931, p. 8.

James, William. *The Varieties of Religious Experience: A Study in Human Nature.* New York: Longmans, Green, 1929.

Janet, Pierre. *Névroses et idées fixes.* 3d ed. Vol. 2. Paris: Librairie Félix Alcan, 1924 (orig. ed., 1898).

———. *Névroses et idées fixes.* 4th ed. Vol. 1. Paris: Librairie Félix Alcan, 1925 (orig. ed., 1898).

———. *De l'angoisse à l'extase.* Paris: Société Pierre Janet, 1975 (orig. ed., 1925).

Jansen, Willy. *Women without Men: Gender and Marginality in an Algerian Town.* Leiden: Brill, 1987.

———. "Dansen voor de geesten: Bezetenheid in multidisciplinair perspectief." In *Waanzin en vrouwen*, ed. W. Jansen and C. Brinkgreve, pp. 191–222. Lisse: Swets and Zeitlinger, 1991.

Jáuregi, Angelo. "Fatima, Portugal'ko Lourdes" (Fatima, the Lourdes of Portugal). *Jaungoiko-zale* (Friend of God), 15 August 1929, pp. 251–258.

———. "Fatima'ko Andra Maria'ren agerkunak egiazkoak dira" (The apparitions of Our Lady of Fatima are true). *Jaungoiko-zale*, 15 February 1931, pp. 52–56.

Joset, Camille-Jean. *Thomas-Louis Heylen, vingt-sixième évêque de Namur (1899–1941) confronté aux apparitions de Beauraing*. Dossiers de Beauraing 1. Beauraing: Pro Maria, 1981.

———. *André Marie Charue, vingt-septième évêque de Namur (1941–1974) reconnaît les apparitions: Documents*. Dossiers de Beauraing 2. Beauraing: Pro Maria, 1981.

———, ed. *Sources et documents primitifs inédits antérieurs à la mi-mars 1933*. Dossiers de Beauraing 4. Beauraing: Pro Maria, 1982.

Juan de Urumea. "Las Multitudes de Ezquioga." *El Nervión*, 19 October 1931, p. 1.

———. "Ezquioga: Lo que se dice, lo que vemos, lo que vamos averiguando." *El Nervión*, 21 October 1931, p. 1.

———. "Ezquioga: Un paso más, casual, pero lleno de posibilidades." *El Nervión*, 22 October 1931, p. 1.

———. "Ezquioga: En busca del carterista." *El Nervión*, 23 October 1931, pp. 1, 3.

Juaristi, Victoriano. "Apariciones en la Barranca." *Diario de Navarra*, 25 October 1931, p. 12.

Junípero, Fray. "Mesa revuelta: Oración y penitencia." *LC*, 15 May 1931, p. 4.

Kagan, Richard L. *Lucrecia's Dreams: Politics and Prophecy in Sixteenth-Century Spain*. Berkeley, Los Angeles, and London: University of California Press, 1990.

Kale'tar bat (A man from the village center) (unsigned). "Desde Urnieta." *PV*, 1 December 1934, p. 4.

——— (unsigned). "En Urnieta: Precisando una noticia muy comentada." *PV*, 2 December 1934, p. 2.

———. "Desde Urnieta: Precisando lo de las visiones." *PV*, 12 December 1934, p. 4.

Kardin. "Elorrio: La Virgen de Ezquioga y su significado local." *El Liberal*, 29 July 1931, p. 3.

Klaniczáy, Gábor. "The Ambivalence of Charisma: Late Medieval Female Sainthood and Witchcraft." Lecture at the Getty Center for the History of Art and the Humanities, Santa Monica, spring 1992.

Kleinberg, Aviad M. *Prophets in Their Own Country: Living Saints and the Making of Sainthood in the Later Middle Ages*. Chicago: University of Chicago Press, 1992.

Koch, Francesca Romana. *I Contabili dell'Aldilà: La devozione alle anime del purgatorio nella Roma postunitaria*. Torino: Rosenberg and Sellier, 1992.

Kselman, T., and S. Avella. "Marian Piety and the Cold War in the United States." *Catholic Historical Review* 73, no. 3 (1986): 403–424.

Kselman, Thomas A. *Miracles and Prophecies in Nineteenth-Century France*. New Brunswick: Rutgers University Press, 1983.

———. *Death and the Afterlife in Modern France*. Princeton: Princeton University Press, 1993.

L. "Ráfagas: El milagro de Ezquioga." *El Pensamiento Navarro*, 2 August 1931, p. 1.

La Barre, Weston. "Materials for a History of Studies of Crisis Cults." *Current Anthropology* 12 (1971): 3–44.

Laburu, José Antonio. "Ezquioga." Typescript. 1932. Archives of the Jesuit province of Loyola.

———. "En el seminario diocesano: Magnífica disertación del P. Laburu sobre lo de Ezquioga." *Heraldo Alavés,* 21 April 1932, p. 3.

———. "Dice el P. Laburu: En Ezquioga no hay indicios de sobrenaturalidad." *PV,* 22 April 1932, p. 1.

———. "La Verdadera Base de la religión." *Gaceta del Norte,* 22 April 1932, p. 1.

———. "Crítica documental: Lo de Ezquioga ante datos experimentales y las ciencias médico-místicas: Una conferencia del P. Laburu." *CC,* 27 April 1932, p. 1.

———. "Notabilísima conferencia del P. Laburu sobre lo de Ezquioga." *BOOV* 68 (1 May 1932): 260–264.

———. "Conferencia del P. Laburu." *Gymnasium* 6 (May–June 1932): 181–187.

———. "Ayer, en el Victoria Eugenia: Lo de Ezquioga, visto por el Padre Laburu, a través de Santa Teresa." *LC,* 22 June 1932, p. 2.

———. "Conferencia de P. Laburu en el Victoria Eugenia sobre 'lo de Ezquioga.'" *ED,* 22 June 1932, p. 5.

———. "En el Victoria Eugenia: La conferencia del P. Laburu sobre 'lo de Ezquioga.'" *PV,* 22 June 1932, p. 3.

———. *Problemas de psicopatología: Anormalidades del carácter.* Montevideo: Editorial Mosca Hermanos, 1941.

———. *Psicología médica: Curso oficializado por la Facultad de Ciencias Médicas de Buenos Aires.* 2d ed. Montevideo: Editorial Mosca Hermanos, 1942 (1st ed., 1940).

Lacasa, José María. "¿Qué ha ocurrido en Torralba de Aragón? Unos vecinos aseguran que la imagen de la Dolorosa ha dirigido unas palabras al pueblo." *La Voz de Aragón,* 26 April 1931; *Heraldo Alavés and El Debate,* 29 April 1931; *A,* 3 May 1931.

Ladame, Jean. *Les Faits de Paray-le-Monial.* Paris: Éditions Saint-Paul, 1970.

Lafora, Gonzalo R. *Don Juan: Los milagros, y otros ensayos.* Madrid: Alianza, 1975 (orig. ed., 1927).

Lage, Pedro María. "Curiosidades: Las apariciones de Ezquioga." *Heraldo Alavés,* 2 September 1931.

Lama, Federico Ritter de. *Una Estigmatizada de nuestros días: Teresa Neumann de Konnersreuth: Relato de un testigo presencial.* Trans. Moisés Alujas. Barcelona: Editorial Litúrgica Española, 1930.

———. *Die Muttergottes-Erscheinungen in Marpingen (Saar).* Karlsruhe: Badenia, 1934.

Lambert, Aimé. "Sur les "Escritos póstumos" de la V. M. Rafols." *Revue d'Histoire Écclésiastique* 29 (January 1933): 96–107.

———. "Sobre los "Escritos póstumos" de la V. M. Rafols." *El Bon Pastor* 76 (April 1933): 388–405.

Lancre, Pierre de. *Tableau de l'inconstance des mauvais anges et demons.* Rev. ed. Paris: Nicolas Buon, 1613.

Langlois, Claude. *Le Catholicisme au feminin: Les congrégations françaises à supérieure générale au XIXᵉ siècle.* Paris: Les Editions du Cerf, 1984.

Larkin, Emmet. "The Devotional Revolution in Ireland." *American Historical Review* 77 (1972): 625–652.

Larraitz. *See* Areitioaurtena, Luis.

Lassalle, Javier de. "Un Viaje a Ezquioga: ¿Apariciones?" *El Pensamiento Navarro,* 4 August 1931, p. 8.

———. "Más sobre los fenómenos de Ezquioga." *El Pensamiento Navarro,* 6 August 1931, p. 8.

————. "Los Videntes de Ezquioga: ¿Abordamos al principio del fin?" *El Pensamiento Navarro,* 9 August 1931, p. 4; also *El Castellano,* 20 August, p. 3.

Laurentin, René, ed. *Lourdes, dossier des documents authentiques.* 2d ed. 2 vols. Paris: Lethielleux, 1962.

————, ed. *Lourdes, histoire authentique.* 4 vols. Paris: Lethielleux, 1962–1963.

Lazzareschi, Eugenio. *David Lazzaretti: Il messia dell'Amiata.* Bergamo: Morcelliana, 1945.

Leatherbarrow, David. "The Image and Its Setting: A Study of the Sacro Monte at Varallo." *Res* 14 (1987): 107–122.

Lecuona, Manuel. "Oyartzun." *AEF* 4 (1924): 1–47.

————. *Literatura oral euskérica.* San Sebastián: Beñat Idaztiak, 1936.

———— ("R. S."). "Escritos de la M. Rafols: Sus fuentes." *Ciencia Tomista* 59, no. 185 (1941): 452–462.

Lefebvre, F. *Louise Lateau de Bois-d'Haine, sa vie, ses extases, ses stigmates: Étude médicale.* 2d ed. Louvain: Peeters, 1873.

Legaz, Robustiano. "En Navarte." *Boletín Oficial Eclesiástico de Pamplona* 59 (1920): 317.

Le Gouvello, Hippolyte. *Apparitions d'une âme du purgatoire en Bretagne,* 5th ed. Paris: Pierre Téqui, 1934.

Leuba, James H. *The Psychology of Religious Mysticism.* New York: Harcourt, Brace, 1925.

Lewis, I. M. *Ecstatic Religion: A Study of Shamanism and Spirit Possession.* 2d ed. London: Routledge, 1989.

Lex, Barbara W. "Neurological Bases of Revitalization Movements." *Zygon* 13 (December 1978): 276–312.

————. "The Neurobiology of Ritual Trance." In *The Spectrum of Ritual: A Biogenetic Structural Analysis,* ed. Charles D. Laughlin, Eugene G. d'Aquili, Jr., and John McManus, pp. 117–151. New York: Columbia University Press, 1979.

————. "Recent Contributions to the Study of Ritual Trance." *Reviews in Anthropology* 11, no. 1 (1984): 44–51.

Lezaun, Cipriano. *Don Bruno: Forjador de vocaciones.* Pamplona: Editorial Gómez, 1963.

Lisón Tolosana, Carmelo. *Endemoniados en Galicia hoy.* Madrid: Akal, 1990.

Lizarralde, Adrián M. *Andra Mari de Guipúzcoa.* Bilbao: Dochao de Urigüen, 1926.

————. *Andra Mari, reseña histórica del culto de la Virgen en la provincia de Vizcaya.* Bilbao: Dochao de Urigüen, 1934.

López de Guereñu, Gerardo. *Andra Mari en Alava: Iconografía mariana de la diócesis de Vitoria.* Vitoria: Diputación Foral de Alava, 1982.

López de Lerena, Sebastián. "A propósito de Ezquioga: Al P. Luis Urbano, O. P. Valencia." 1933. Private collection.

López de Lerena, Sebastián; Julian López de Lerena; Juan Bautista Ayerbe; Ismael Mateos; and Felisa Sarasqueta. "Al Ilmo. Sr. Obispo de San Sebastián." Typescript. San Sebastián, 17 March 1952. Private collection.

López Galuá, Enrique. *Futura grandeza de España según notables profecías.* Augmented ed. La Coruña: Moret, 1941.

Lugin. "Matxinbenta." *A,* 23 August 1931, p. 3.

Luistar. *See* Múgica, Juan.

Lujanbio Retegi, José Manuel ("Txirrita"). "Bertso Berriyak Txirritak Jarriyak" (New verses by Txirrita). *Bertsolariya,* 4 October 1931.

————. "Ezkioga'ko agermenari Txirritak jarriyak" (Txirrita's verses to the apparition of Ezkioga). *Bertsolariya,* 8 November 1931.

————. *Bertso Berriak Ordaintzat Jarriak* (New verses for sale). 1933.

Luzear. *See* Arcelus, Andrés.

Lynch, John. "The Catholic Church in Latin America 1830–1930." In *The Cambridge History of Latin America*, ed. Leslie Bethell, 4:541–546. Cambridge: Cambridge University Press, 1986.

Manescal, Honofre. *Miscellanea de tres tratados, de las apariciones de los espiritvs el vno, donde se trata como dios habla à los hombres, y si las almas del purgatorio bueluen* . . . Barcelona: Geronymo Genoves, 1611.

Manterola, Ander, ed. *Juegos infantiles en Vasconia*. Atlas Etnográfico de Vasconia 2. Bilbao: Etniker Euskalerria, 1993.

Marcaida, Manuel de. "En Meñaka (Bizkaya)." *AEF* 3 (1923): 30–36.

Marchetti, Valerio. "La Simulazione di santità nella riflessione medico-legale del sec. XVII." In *Finzione e santità tra medioevo ed età moderna*, ed. Gabriella Zarri, pp. 202–227. Torino: Rosenberg and Sellier, 1991.

Marcucci, Maria Maddalena (María Magdalena de Jesús Sacramentado). *Apostol de amor: Autobiografía de J. Pastor*. Ed. Arturo Alonso Lobo. Salamanca: Vida Sobrenatural, 1971.

———. *En la cima del Monte Santo*. Ed. Arturo Alonso Lobo. Salamanca: Vida Sobrenatural, 1972.

Marín, Benito. *Dios me va cercando: Biografía de Fray Benito Mateos, O. P.* Villalva-Pamplona: Editorial OPE, 1967.

Marqués, Florencia M. "Un Camarero vidente, astrólogo y quiromante predice grandes disturbios en el porvenir de España." *Heraldo de Madrid*, 18 August 1931, p. 9.

Marsay, Bénédicte de. *See* Rigné, Raymond de.

Martínez de Muñeca, Laureano. "Impresiones personales de Konnevsreuth [*sic*]." *El Debate*, 26 July 1932, p. 8.

Martínez Gómez, Pedro. "Las Maravillas de Ezkioga." *La Voz de Navarra*, 22 July 1931, p. 4, and *El Pensamiento Navarro*, 22 July 1931, p. 4.

Martín Ruíz, Gregorio. "Unas Cuartillas del señor cura ecónomo de Guadamur." *El Castellano*, 2 September 1931, p. 4.

———. "De Guadamur: Las apariciones y el clamor del naturalismo." *El Castellano*, 1 October 1931, p. 4.

Martín Sánchez, Benjamín. *Los Últimos Tiempos: Profecías públicas y privadas sobre los últimos tiempos: Se avecinan grandes acontecimientos*. Zamora: Ediciones Monte Casino, Benedictinas, 1968.

Masmelene. *See* Gorostiaga Etxebarria, Eulogio.

Mateos, Benito. "Ntra. Sra. del Rosario de Fátima." *El Santísimo Rosario*, December 1927, pp. 711–714.

———. "Nuestra Señora del Rosario de Fátima." *El Santísimo Rosario*, December 1928, pp. 738–742.

———. "Los Videntes de Fátima." *El Santísimo Rosario*, February 1929, pp. 101–106, 113–116.

Maury, L.-F.-Alfred. *Le Sommeil et les rêves: Études psychologiques sur ces phénomènes et les divers états qui s'y rattachent; suivis de recherches sur le développement de l'instinct et de l'intelligence dans leurs rapports avec le phénomène du sommeil*. 3d ed. Paris: Didier, 1865.

McCarthy, Michael J. F. *Priests and People in Ireland*. Dublin: Hodges, Figgis, 1902.

McKevitt, Christopher. "San Giovanni Rotondo and the Shrine of Padre Pio." In *Contesting the Sacred: The Anthropology of Christian Pilgrimage*, ed. John Eade and Michael J. Sallnow, pp. 77–97. London: Routledge, 1991.

Mècle, Jacques. "Deux victimes de 'Luc-Verus' dans la lettre du Père Vallet au Cardinal Segura (14 juillet 1943)." 15 pages. Roma, 1984. Archives of Cooperadores Parroquiales de Cristo Rey.

Medina y Vilallonga, Rafael de. *Memorias de una vida: Luis de Medina y Garvey (1870–1952)*. Sevilla: Gráficas Sevillanas, 1975.

Menda. "Revolución clerical por motivo estomacal." Cartoon in *El Liberal* (Madrid), 23 August 1931, p. 3.

————. "Teatro de verano." Cartoon in *El Liberal* (Madrid), 6 September 1931, p. 6.

Mendive, Tomás. "Los Encantos del viernes santo." In *La Linterna mágica*, 113–118. Bilbao: Editorial Bilbaino, 1919.

————. "Linterna mágica: La santa de Conqueiros." *El Liberal* (Madrid), 11 July 1931, p. 1.

————. "De Don Diego a la Cibeles: La Virgen de Ezquioga y los niños." *Crisol*, 27 July 1931, p. 10.

————. "Linterna mágica: El coloquio virginal." *El Liberal* (Madrid), 17 October 1931, p. 1.

Mendizábal, Ramón. "En Bidania." *AEF* 3 (1923): 104–107.

Menoa. "Desilusiones." Cartoon in *El Liberal* (Madrid), 11 December 1931, p. 3.

Meromar, E. *Revelación del misterio del más allá*. Madrid: Biblioteca Más Allá, 1933.

Mesa, Carlos E. *El Padre Pueyo, obispo de Pasto*. Medellín: Editorial Zuluaga, 1984.

Meyer, Jean. *La Cristiada*. Mexico, D.F.: Siglo Veintiuno Editores, 1973.

Millán, Agapito. "Apariciones: Fe, fanatismo, y farándula." *El Liberal* (Bilbao), 9 September 1931, p. 6; 10 September 1931, pp. 6–7.

Mira, Pere. "Marginal als fets d'Ezkioga." *El Matí*, 14 May 1932.

Mir y Noguera, Juan. *El Milagro*. Augmented ed. 3 vols. Barcelona: Librería Católica de Hijo de Miguel Casals, 1915.

Mitchell, Timothy. *Passional Culture: Emotion, Religion, and Society in Southern Spain*. Philadelphia: University of Pennsylvania Press, 1990.

Mitis, Fr. "Maravillas." *Semanario Católico de Reus*, 8 August 1931, p. 530.

Molina, Ramón. "Las Apariciones de Ezkioga: Lo que yo he visto." *El Castellano*, 24 August 1931, p. 1.

Mondrone, D. "Madre Speranza Alhama di Gesù, apostola dell'Amore Misericordioso." *La Civiltà Cattolica* 135, no. 3206 (1984): 140–154.

Monsó y Vigo, José. *Santidad en el mundo: Vida admirable de la sierva de Dios Carmen de Sojo de Anguera*. Barcelona: La Hormiga de Oro, 1933.

Monter, William. "Les Enfants au sabbat: Bilan provisoire." In *Le Sabbat des sorciers, XVe–XVIIIe siècles*, ed. N. Jacques-Chaquin and M. Préaud, pp. 383–388. Grenoble: Jérome Millon, 1993.

Montero Moreno, Antonio. *Historia de la persecución religiosa en España 1936–1939*. Madrid: Biblioteca de Autores Cristianos, 1961.

Montoto, Castor ("Gustavo Luis"). *En los escritos de la madre Rafols ¿Hay anacronismos? ¿Hay plagios?* 2d ed. Sevilla: Impr. San Antonio, 1967 (1st ed., 1941).

Moreda de Lecea, C. "Don Mateo Múgica Urrestarazu: Antecedentes, pontificado en Pamplona y algunos aspectos de su pontificado en Vitoria." Ph. D. diss., Universidad de Navarra, 1978.

Morrondo Rodríguez, Cristino. *La Proximidad de la catástrofe del mundo y el advenimiento de la regeneración universal: Estudios bíblico-milenarios*. Jaén: Mora y Alvarez, 1922.

————. *Jesús no viene, Jesús vendrá: Catástrofe y renovación*. Jaén: El Pueblo Católico, 1924.

Mounereau, Guy. "Le Diable en Espagne." *Voilà*, 31 March 1934.

Moya, Jorge. "Romance efímero: ¡Qué compañías!" *El Socialista*, 20 October 1931, p. 1.

————. "Romance efímero: El último milagrero." *El Socialista*, 5 November 1932, p. 6.

Múgica, Juan ("Luistar" [Member of Luis Gonzaga sodality]). "Ezkioga'n" (At Ezkioga). *A*, 19 July 1931, p. 2; also *La Cruz*, 19 July 1931, p. 6.

————. "Albiztur." *A*, 26 July 1931, p. 2; also *EZ*, 26 July 1931, and *ED*, 28 July 1931.

————. "Albiztur: Andua Auzoa'n" (In the hamlet of Anduaga). *A*, 2 August 1931, p. 2.

————. "Albiztur." *A*, 9 August 1931, p. 2.

————. "Albiztur: Edurretako Andra Maria'n egunean, au da il onen bostean" (On the day of Our Lady of the Snows, that is, the fifth of this month). *A*, 16 August 1931, p. 2.

————. "Albiztur: ¡Irakurle!" (Reader!). *A*, 23 August 1931, p. 2; also *La Cruz*, 25 August 1931, pp. 7–8.

————. "Albiztur: Ezkioga'n" (At Ezkioga). *A* and *La Cruz*, 30 August 1931.

————. "Albiztur." *A* and *La Cruz*, 6 September 1931.

————. "Albiztur: Ezkioga'n izaten gera" (We go to Ezkioga). *A*, 27 September 1931, p. 2.

————. "Ezkioga'ko Ama" (The Mother of Ezkioga). *A*, 1 November 1931, p. 2.

————. "Alcibar Juanari" (To Señor Alcibar). *A*, 22 November 1931, p. 1.

————. "Albiztur: Agurtza edo errosarioa" (The rosary). *La Cruz*, 10 April 1932, p. 6.

————. "Ezkio-ko gertakerak Azkoiti'ko 'Norbait' eri" (The events at Ezkioga for Norbait of Azkoitia). *A*, 2 October 1932, pp. 1–2.

————. "Albiztur: Erantzun bearra" (The need to respond). *A*, 5 February 1933, p. 4.

———— ("Aralar"). "Ezkio-ko agermenari bertsoak" (Verses to the apparition of Ezkioga). *A*, 16 April 1933, p. 2.

———— ("Luistar"). "Ezkio'ko gaiaz . . . ara besteak" (More about the Ezkioga matter). *A*, 30 April 1933, p. 2.

————. "Albiztur: 'Erauskin Errotaria'-ri, Irun'go 'Erromerieta'-ri, Erri ontako 'Baserritarra'-r" (To Erauskin Errotaria, to Erromerieta of Irun, and to Baserritarra of this village). *A*, 21 May 1933, p. 3.

————. "Albiztur: Bertso berriak: Ezkio'ko gaiaz egiak esanaz eta iritziak agertuaz" (New verses: Speaking truths and giving opinions about the Ezkioga matter). *A*, 2, 9, 16, 23, 30 July 1933; 6, 13 August 1933.

————. "Albiztur: Irun'go 'Erromerieta'-rena" (Albiztur: About Erromerieta of Irun). *A*, 3 September 1933, p. 3.

————. "Albiztur: 'Larraitz'ek; Altzo'ko 'Otxabio'ri" (Larraitz; for Otxabio from Altzo). *A*, 10 September 1933, p. 3.

————. "Albiztur: Eskio'ko gaiaz" (On the Ezkioga matter). *A*, 17 September 1933, p. 3.

————. "Albiztur: Ezkio'ko gaiaz" (On the Ezkioga matter). *A*, 1 October 1933, p. 3.

Múgica y Urrestarazu, Mateo. *Carta pastoral [Sobre la blasfemia]*. Burgo de Osma: Imprenta y Librería de Jiménez, 1920.

————. "Carta pastoral [Sobre San Miguel Arcángel]." *Boletín oficial eclesiástico de Pamplona* 66 (1927): 441–476.

————. *Catecismo de la doctrina cristiana: Texto oficial de la diócesis de Vitoria arreglado por una comisión de teólogos bajo la dirección del reverendísimo prelado en tres grados*. New ed., corrected and augmented. Vitoria: Montepío Diocesano, n.d. (ca. 1932).

————. "Sobre la supuesta sobrenaturalidad de lo que ocurre en Ezquioga." *BOOV* 69 (15 September 1933): 525–530.

———. "Declarando 'ipso iure' prohibidas varias publicaciones sobre las supuestas apariciones de Ezquioga editadas sin censura [circular num. 181]." *BOOV* 70 (15 March 1934): 239–246.

———. "Campaña por la moralidad de nuestras playas [circular num. 195]." *BOOV* 70 (15 June 1934): 416–420.

———. "Decreto declarando destituidas de todo carácter sobrenatural las supuestas apariciones y revelaciones de la B. Virgen María en el lugar de EZQUIOGA y prohibidos ipso iure tres libros que tratan de ellas." *BOOV* 70 (1 July 1934): 479–483.

———. "El Itmo. y Rvdmo. Sr. Dr. D. Justo A. de Echeguren y Aldama Obispo preconizado de Oviedo." *BOOV* 71 (15 February 1935): 122–127.

Mugueta, Juan. "Lo que espera de Navarra la España católica." *El Pensamiento Navarro,* 17 July 1931, p. 1.

Murisier, E. *Les Maladies du sentiment religieux.* 19th ed. Paris: Félix Alcan, 1903.

N. "Anduaga-mendiko agerpenak" (The apparitions of Mount Anduaga). *Euzkerea,* 15 August 1931, pp. 707–708.

Napolitano, Rafael. *Superstición y espiritismo: Vulgarizaciones.* Trans. "un padre pasionista." Bilbao: Pía Sociedad de San Pablo, 1943.

Navarro, Xavier. "La Repressió juliol-desembre 1936." *Terme* (Terrassa) 1 (November 1986): 47–61.

Niccoli, Ottavia. *Prophecy and People in Renaissance Italy* [*Profeti e Popolo nell'Italia del Rinascimento* (Roma: Laterza, 1987)]. Trans. Lydia G. Cochrane. Princeton: Princeton University Press, 1990.

Nieto, Gregorio. "Sobre el estado de enajenación mental del procesado M. G. D." *El Siglo Médico* 93 (1934): 660–665, 694–698.

Nolan, Mary Lee, and Sydney Nolan. *Christian Pilgrimage in Modern Western Europe.* Chapel Hill: University of North Carolina Press, 1989.

Nold, Patrick. "The Knock Phenomenon: Popular Piety and Politics in 'Modern' Ireland." Honors thesis, History, University of Michigan, 1993.

Norbait. "Azkoiti: Albiztur'ko 'Luistar'-i" (Azkoitia: To Luistar from Albiztur). *A,* 25 September 1932, p. 4.

Novoa Santos, Roberto. *Patografía de Santa Teresa de Jesús y el instinto de la muerte.* Madrid: Prensa Moderna, 1932.

Olabarri Gortázar, Ignacio. "Documentos sobre la preparación de las elecciones por los partidos del turno en Navarra, 1916–1918." *Boletín de la Real Academia de la Historia* 187, no. 1 (1990): 99–116.

Olaizola, José. [Letter]. *PV,* 20 October 1931, p. 2.

Olazábal y Ramery, Juan de. "De Dios nadie se rie." *LC,* 17 June 1934, p. 1.

———. *El Cura Santa Cruz, guerillero.* San Sebastián: Hordago, 1979.

Onaindía, Alberto de. "Auras regeneradoras: La emoción religiosa de Ondarroa." *EZ,* 14 August 1931, p. 6.

O'Neill, Brian Juan. *Social Inequality in a Portuguese Hamlet: Land, Late Marriage, and Bastardy, 1870–1978.* Cambridge: Cambridge University Press, 1987.

Or Dago. "¿Ezkioga'n zer? Arritokieta'tar Tomas'eri" (What happens in Ezkioga? For Tomas Arritokieta). *ED,* 2 April 1932.

———. "¿Ezkioga'n zer?" *ED,* 15 April 1932, p. 8.

Ormatxea, Nicolás de ("Orixe"). "Amona" (Grandmother). In *Euskaldunak poema eta olerki gutziak* (Collected Basque poems), 577–578. San Sebastián: Auñamendi, Estornés, Lasa, Hnos, 1972.

Orzanco, Hilario. "Las Apariciones de la Virgen Dolorosa a unas niñas de Torralba de Aragón y de Mendigorría (Navarra)." *La Milagrosa y los Niños,* 1 July 1931, pp. 121–123.

———. "Nuevas apariciones de la Virgen." *La Milagrosa y los Niños,* 1 October 1931, pp. 137–138.

Ott, Sandra. *The Circle of Mountains.* Oxford: Clarendon Press, 1981.

Otxabio. "Altzo: Argia'ko zuzendari jauna" (Altzo: The director of Argia). *A,* 27 August 1933, p. 3.

——— (?). "Altzo." *A,* 3 September 1933, p. 3.

———. "Altzo: Altzotar batek Ezkiogaz itz egiten du" (A man from Altzo has spoken about Ezkioga). *A,* 17 September 1933, p. 3.

P. D. "Les Desviacions de la pietat." *El Matí,* 15 April 1932, p. 2.

Palafox y Mendoza, Juan de. *Luz a los vivos y escarmiento en los muertos.* Madrid: Bernardo de Villa-diego, 1668.

Pascal, Émile. "Une Visite à Ezquioga." *Revue Métapsychique,* April 1933; also Étampes: Ternier Frères, 1933.

——— ("Pascal Brotteaux"). *Hallucinations ou miracles? Les apparitions d'Ezquioga et de Beauraing: La prophétie du moine de Padoue.* Paris: Les Éditions Véga, 1934.

Pazos, Antón M. *El Clero navarro (1900–1936): Origen social, procedencia geográfica y formación sacerdotal.* Pamplona: Ediciones Universidad de Navarra, 1990.

Peña Santiago, L. P. *Fiestas tradicionales y romerías de Guipúzcoa.* San Sebastián: Txertoa, 1973.

Pepe Miguel. "Ayer dijeron que la Virgen no quería una ermita." *PV,* 31 July 1931, p. 4.

Perales y Gutiérrez, Arturo. *El Supernaturalismo de Santa Teresa y la filosofía médica, o sea, los éxtasis, raptos y enfermedades de la santa ante las ciencias médicas.* Madrid: Librería Católica de Gregorio del Amo, 1894.

Perea, Joaquín. *El Modelo de la iglesia subyacente en la pastoral del clero vasco (1918–1936).* 4 vols. Bilbao: Instituto Diocesano de Teología y Pastoral, 1991.

Pérez, Nazario. *Historia Mariana de España.* Vols. 4 and 5. Valladolid: Impresos Gerper, 1947, 1949.

Pérez Ferrero, Miguel. "El Lenguaje de los fusiles enrobinados: La Virgen de Ezquioga y el demonio en Lecumberri." *Heraldo de Madrid,* 28 August 1931.

Pérez Ormazábal, Antonio María. "Mandado leer la circular sobre lo de Ezquioga." *BOOV* 69 (1 October 1933): 562.

———. "Tres disposiciones sobre lo de Ezquioga." *BOOV* 70 (1 April 1934): 270–271.

———. *Así fue el padre.* Vitoria: Ediciones AJM, 1954.

———. *Aquel monaguillo de Elduayen.* Vitoria: Ediciones AJM, 1955.

Pérez y Pando, Joaquín. "La Santísima Virgen en Ezquioga." *El Santísimo Rosario,* November 1931, pp. 674–679.

Perroy, Henry. *La Mission d'un enfant (Guy de Fontgalland 1913–1925).* Lyon: Librairie Catholique Emmanuel Vitte, 1931.

Perry, Nicholas, and Loreto Echeverría. *Under the Heel of Mary.* London: Routledge, 1988.

Peterkiewicz, Jerzy. *The Third Adam.* London: Oxford University Press, 1975.

Picavea, Rafael. "Actualidad permanente: Hablemos también de Ezquioga." *PV,* 31 October 1931, p. 1.

———. "Lo de Ezquioga: Fondas, tinglados, damas y videntes." *PV,* 3 November 1931, p. 1.

———. "Lo de Ezquioga: Siguen el examen objetivo y el relato imparcial." *PV,* 4 November 1931, p. 1.

————. "Lo de Ezquioga: Hablemos hoy de los 'videntes' más favorecidos." *PV*, 6 November 1931, p. 1.

————. "Lo de Ezquioga: Visiones y vaticinios de extraño vidente Patxi." *PV*, 8 November 1931, p. 1.

————. "Lo de Ezquioga: Hablan los videntes que se dicen estigmatizados." *PV*, 11 November 1931, p. 1.

————. "Lo de Ezquioga: Diálogos campechanos: El vidente se nos ha engreído." *PV*, 13 November 1931, p. 3.

————. "Lo de Ezquioga: ¿Y en definitiva, qué se deduce de todo ello?" *PV*, 14 November 1931, p. 1.

————. "Lo de Ezquioga: Paseando por los misterios de la psicopatía . . ." *PV*, 18 November 1931, p. 1.

————. "Lo de Ezquioga: Recordando los estigmas de Teresita Neumann." *PV*, 20 November 1931, p. 1.

————. "Amenamente: Hablamos, hoy de reverencias y de irreverencias." *PV*, 24 April 1932, p. 1.

————. "Apariciones: Surge Fray Amado: Dos palabras." *PV*, 2 December 1932, p. 2.

————. "Recordando: Roma y las visiones de Ezquioga." *PV*, 7 July 1934, p. 1.

Pijoán, Rafael. *El Siglo XX y el fin del mundo según la profecía de San Malaquías.* 1st ed. Barcelona: La Hormiga de Oro, 1914.

Pildain, Antonio; Manuel Lecuona; Leoncio Aravio-torre; and José Miguel de Barandiarán ("Alejandro de Arcaya"). *Unas Observaciones al Dr. Lafora acerca de su estudio "Milagros curativos, laicos, y religiosos."* Vitoria: Gymnasium, Seminario Conciliar, 1928.

Pirala, Angel. *Santuarios guipuzcoanos.* Madrid: Sucesores de Rivadeneyra, 1895.

Pitt-Rivers, Julian. "Postscript: The Place of Grace in Anthropology." In *Honor and Grace in Anthropology,* ed. J. G. Peristany and Julian Pitt-Rivers, pp. 215–246. Cambridge: Cambridge University Press, 1992.

Polo Benito, José. "La Ofensiva de Dios." *El Castellano,* 11 September 1931, p. 1.

Postius, Juan. "Miscelanea mariana: La iglesia ante Ezquioga." *Iris de Paz,* 1933, pp. 935–936.

Pou y Martí, José. "De Roma: El milagro de Andria." *CC,* 2 April 1932, p. 1; also *Voz de Navarra,* 5 April 1931.

Presbítero, Un. "Una Angelical Criatura: La Rvdma. Madre Soledad del Santísimo Sacramento." *LC,* 27 December 1933, p. 1.

Prieto, Indalecio. (Reply to de la Villa about Ezkioga) *Diario de Sesiones de Cortes Constituyentes* 1 (23 October 1931): 1929–1931.

Prior de Roncesvalles. "El Pesimismo." *La Avalancha,* 25 April 1932, pp. 116–117.

Pujadas, Tomás Luis. *El Padre Postius: Un hombre para la iglesia.* Barcelona: Editorial Claret, 1981.

R. "¡¡Aquí, No!!" *¡Adelante!* Semanario Católico, 27 June 1931, p. 1.

Ramo Latorre, Mariano. *Mensaje de amor y de redención: El siervo de Dios P. Luis Amigó Ferrer.* Valencia: J. Domenech, 1973.

Ramos, José. "En torno al milenarismo sano." *La Ilustración del Clero,* 1 June 1923, pp. 165–167; 1 July 1923, pp. 196–199; 1 August 1923, pp. 218–220; 1 October 1923, pp. 230–232; 16 October 1923, pp. 293–296; 1 November 1923, pp. 314–316, 324–326.

Redondo, Augustin. "La 'Mesnie Hellequin' et la 'Estantigua': Les traditions hispaniques de la 'chasse sauvage' et leur resurgence dans le 'Don Quichotte.'" In *Traditions populaires et diffusion de la culture en Espagne (XVIᵉ–XVIIᵉ siècles)*, 1–27. Bordeaux: Presses Universitaires, 1983.

Redondo, Gonzalo. *Historia de la Iglesia en España 1931–1939.* Vol. 1. *La Segunda República (1931–1936).* Madrid: Rialp, 1993.

Remisch, Fernand ("F. Dorola"). *Les Mystères de Beauraing: Reportage critique.* Paris and Lessines: Spes, Rex, 1933.

——————. *Trente-trois ans avec Thérèse Neumann.* Paris: A. Fayard, 1962.

Rentería Uralde, Julen. *Pueblo vasco e iglesia: Reencuento o ruptura definitiva.* Bilbao, 1982.

Ribelles, José. "Las Apariciones de Ezquioga Guipúzcoa." *Semanario Católico de Reus,* 1 August 1931, pp. 520–521.

Ribera, Andreu. "Impressions d'un palamosí que anà a Ezkioga, I y II." *El Matí,* 4 November 1931, p. 10, and 5 November 1931, p. 10.

Ribera, Montserrat. "Sabadellencs a Ezquioga." *Diari de Sabadell,* 8 October 1931, p. 2.

Ribot, Th. *The Diseases of the Will.* Trans. Marwin-Marie Snell. Chicago: Open Court, 1915.

Ricart Torrens, José. *Desviación de un apostolado: El caso de Bañolas con apostillas al proceso canónico judicial de la Srta. Magdalena Aulina.* Barcelona: Gráfica Industrial, 1941.

——————. "Don Bruno Lezaun, sacerdote navarro, apóstol de las vocaciones sacerdotales y religiosas (1877–1961)." *Vida Sobrenatural* 65 (May–July 1964): 223–232.

——————. *Un Obispo de antes del Concilio: Biografía del Excmo, y Rdmo, doctor don Manuel Irurita Almándoz, obispo de Barcelona.* Madrid: Religión y Patria, 1973.

Rigné, Marie. *See also* Thirouin, Marie-Geneviève.

Rigné, Marie, and Raymond de Rigné. *Encyclique de S.S. Innocent XIV sur la morale conjugale (29 Juin 1941): Oeuvres de Supplien Costecèque (Innocent XIV).* Paris: La Renaissance Universelle, 1931.

——————. *Mariage nul: Oeuvres d'Olivier Raynal.* Paris: La Renaissance Universelle, 1931.

——————. "Lo de Ezquioga: Dice monsieur de Rigné." *PV,* 28 October 1931, p. 3; also as "Els Fets de Ezquioga" in *La Creuada,* 7 November 1931, pp. 526–527, and in *El Matí,* 8 November 1931, pp. 18.

Rigné, Raymond de. "Mes voyages." Manuscript notebook, 31 pages plus 4 maps. 1887–1947. Collection of William Christian Jr.

—————— ("Raymond Vroncourt"). *Autour de Huysmans.* Tours: E. Menard, 1910.

—————— ("Raymond Vroncourt"). *Huysmans et l'Ame des Foules de Lourdes: Notes de critique suivies d'un répertoire de l'oeuvre catholique de Huysmans.* Tours: E. Menard, 1910.

——————. *Moralités gauloises: Tout est pur pour les purs . . .* Corbeil: Crété, 1917.

——————. *Les Contes du Bel-Amour.* Paris: La Renaissance Universelle, 1921.

——————. *Le Disciple de Massenet.* Vol. 1. Paris: La Renaissance Universelle, 1921.

——————. *Sous l'oeil vivant des morts: 1. Le Martyr de la victoire; 2. Un Coeur de sainte.* 1st ed. Paris: La Renaissance Universelle, 1921.

——————. *Dans le style de Huysmans, Conan Doyle, Paul Bourget: Oeuvres de Jean d'Arvil.* Paris: La Renaissance Universelle, 1922.

——————. *Le Disciple de Massenet.* Vol. 3. Paris: La Renaissance Universelle, 1923.

——————. *La Clef de l'erreur judiciare de Pierre Cauchon.* Paris: Editions Valp, 1928.

——————. *Jehanne d'Arc heroïne du droit: Les véritables causes de son abandon et de sa condemnation.* Paris: Chez Picart, 1929.

——————. *La Vraye Istoire de Jehanne-la-Pucelle.* Paris: La Renaissance Universelle, 1929.

——————. *Sous l'oeil vivant des morts: 1. Le Martyr de la victoire; 2. Les Coeurs dans la tourmente.* Rev. ed. Paris: La Renaissance Universelle, 1930.

———— ("Juan d'Arvil"). "Carta dirigida a todos los obispos de España en abril 1932." Type-script, 2 pages.

————. *Llamamiento a S.S. el Papa Pio XI a propósito de los hechos de Ezquioga (29 Junio 1932).* 1932.

————. *Un Testimonio histórico: Los hechos milagrosos de Ezkioga: Ormáiztegui 8 de Diciembre de 1932.* Ormáiztegui, 1932.

———— ("B. M."). *Une Nouvelle Affaire Jeanne d'Arc.* Orléans: La Librairie Centrale, 1933.

————. "Ramona de Olazábal, estigmatizada de la Virgen de Ezkioga." Typescript. 30 June 1933. Private collection.

———— ("Ramon de Riñé"). *A los videntes de Ezkioga.* Leaflet. Ormáiztegui, 25 July 1933. Collection of William Christian Jr.

———— ("Ramon de Riñe"). *A mis amigos.* Ormáiztegui, 6 January 1934.

———— ("Jean d'Arvil"). "Les Idées de Jean d'Arvil." *L'Enigme d'Ezkioga.* April-May 1935, pp. 2–3.

———— ("Bénédicte de Marsay"). *Le Ciel ouvert sur l'abîme: Témoinage historique et appel au Pape.* Orléans: Librairie Jeanne-d'Arc, 1936.

————. *Los Verdaderos Asesinos del pueblo español: Carta abierta al episcopado español.* 24 August 1937. Collection of William Christian Jr.

Rivera, Ramón. "Sagrado Corazón de Jesús que derrama sangre." *San José de la Montaña,* March 1933.

Rivero San José, Jorge María. *Cantabria, cuna de la humanidad.* Valladolid: Ediciones de Cámara, 1985.

Rodes Buxados, Arturo. "Los Hechos prodigiosos de Ezquioga" [Els Fets prodigiosos d'Ezkioga (1932)]. Trans. Lourdes Rodes de Lafuente. Barcelona, 1983. Papers of Lourdes Rodes de Lafuente.

Rodríguez, Ginés de María. *Hermano Estanislao José, un joven heróico desconocido.* Fuenlabrada: Talleres Gráficas Peñalara, 1983.

Rodríguez de Coro, Francisco. *Colonización política del catolicismo: La experiencia española de Posguerra (1941–1945).* San Sebastián: Caja de Ahorros Provincial de Guipúzcoa, 1979.

————. *Catolicismo vasco entre el furor y la furia (1931–1936).* Cuadernos de Sección Historia-Geografía 9. San Sebastián: Editorial Eusko-Ikaskuntza, 1984.

Rodríguez de Prada, A. *Visiones sobrenaturales de la R. M. María de los Dolores de Jesús y Urquía, religiosa del convento de agustinas de Aldaz (Navarra).* El Escorial: Imprenta del Monasterio, 1935.

Rodríguez Ramos, Juan. *Yo sé lo que pasa en Ezquioga . . . Notas de un reporter.* San Sebastián: Imp. Martín y Mena, 1931.

———— ("Juan de Hernani"). "En Trucios como en Icíar los fantasmas sufren mucho si se les toma a broma." *PV-Correo Español,* 12 May 1949, p. 6.

———— ("Juan de Hernani"). "Yo no hablaba de patología: Estaba hablando de brujas, que es tema más divertido." *PV-Correo Español,* 13 May 1949, p. 6.

Rolando. "Cosas de Ezquioga." *Diario de Navarra,* 19 October 1932, p. 3.

————. "Ecos de Ezquioga." *Diario de Navarra,* 26 October 1932, p. 3.

Roldán, Pepe. "Apariciones de la Virgen en Ezquioga (a título de información)." *El Santísimo Rosario,* August 1931, pp. 489–492.

Romain, Paul. *See* Boniface, Ennemond.

Romero, Epifanio. "En serio y en broma: En torno al 'camelo' milagroso de Ezquioga." *Heraldo de Madrid,* 5 August 1931, p. 4.

———. "Comunicado para el señor gobernador: En Ezquioga no se cumple la Constitución." [*La Prensa?*], ca. 4 February 1932.

Rossi, Pascual. *Los Sugestionadores y la muchedumbre.* Trans. Félix Limendoux. Barcelona: Henrich, 1906.

Rouget, Gilbert. *Music and Trance: A Theory of the Relations between Music and Possession.* Trans. Brunhilde Biebuyck. Chicago: University of Chicago Press, 1985.

Rubio López, Julián. *Guía de Navarra.* Pamplona: Editorial Navarra, 1952.

Ruíz, Ladislao. "El Alcalde de Marquina y las jóvenes 'delincuentes' que bailan." *VG,* 13 June 1931, p. 6.

Ruíz de Gauna, Adolfo. *Catálogo de publicaciones periódicas vascas de los siglos XIX y XX.* San Sebastián: Euzko Ikaskuntza, 1991, and Vitoria: Eusko Jaulauritza; Kultura eta Turismo Saila, 1991.

S. B. "Sobre Ezquioga: Comentando a Alcíbar." *ED,* 7 November 1931, p. 10.

S. Officii, Suprema Sacra Congregatio. "Decretum assertae beatae Mariae Virginis apparitiones et revelationes in loco 'Ezquioga' . . . 13 June 1934." *Acta SS. Congregationum* 1, no. 10 (1934): 433.

Sabean, David Warren. *Power in the Blood: Popular Culture and Village Discourse in Early Modern Germany.* Cambridge: Cambridge University Press, 1984.

Sáenz de Tejada, José María. *Bibliografía de la devoción al Corazón de Jesús.* Bilbao: Editorial el Mensajero del Corazón de Jesús, 1952.

Sáez de Adana, Asunción. "En Galarreta." *AEF* 3 (1923): 53–62.

Saiz Valdevielso, Alfonso Carlos. *Triunfo y tragedia del periodismo vasco (prensa y política) 1900–1939.* Madrid: Editora Nacional, 1977.

Salido, Cruz. "Glosas ingenuas: La niña de las llagas." *El Socialista,* 20 October 1931, p. 1.

Sallnow, Michael J. *Pilgrims of the Andes: Regional Cults in Cusco.* Smithsonian Series in Ethnographic Inquiry, ed. Ivan Karp and William L. Merrill. Washington, D.C.: Smithsonian Institution Press, 1987.

Sanabre, Josep. "Darrera fase d'Ezkioga." *El Matí,* 26 April 1932, p. 9.

———. "Entorn dels fets d'Ezkioga." *El Matí,* 5 May 1932.

Sánchez Granjel, Luis, ed. *Diccionario histórico de médicos vascos.* Bilbao: Seminario de Historia de la Medicina Vasca, Universidad del País Vasco, 1993.

Sánchez-Ventura y Pascual, José. "Las Apariciones como fenómeno universal: Ezquioga (1931)." *María Mensajera,* 27 November 1970, pp. 3–4.

Sangrán y González, Joaquín [Marqués de los Ríos]. *La Profecía del Apocalipsis y los tiempos actuales.* Madrid: Voluntad, 1929.

Sans, Lluis. "Problemática del mecanismo de las visiones y audiciones en las experiencias de un vidente de Ezquioga." *Estudios Franciscanos* 74, no. 347 (1973): 113–161.

San Sebastián, Koldo. "'Apariciones' de muchachas muertas en el Lea-Artibai." *Deia,* 24 February 1985, p. 21.

Santa María de Villar, El Marqués de. "Los Fenómenos maravillosos de Ezquioga." *La Época,* 16 July 1931, p. 1.

———. "Por tierras vasco-navarras." *La Época,* 31 August 1931, p. 3.

———. "Camino de Aranzazu." *La Época,* 17 October 1931, p. 2.

Santander, Federico. "Las Apariciones de Ezquioga." *ABC* (Madrid), 13 August 1931, p. 16.

Sarasqueta, Pedro. "L'Enigme d'Ezkioga." *VG,* 20 February 1934, p. 16.

———. "Croniquilla vasca: Los explotadores de Ezquioga." *VG,* 22 March 1934, p. 16.

———. "Croniquilla vasca: Feligreses en rebeldía." *VG,* 10 April 1934, p. 16.

———. "Croniquilla indígena: El epílogo de Ezquioga." *VG,* 11 July 1934, p. 16.

———— ("Pedro Gorri"). "Ezquioga: La 'indigna farsa.'" *VG*, 24 January 1935, p. 16.

———— ("Pedro Gorri"). "Sobre la indigna farsa: Uno de los extranjeros explotadores de Ezquioga insulta a nuestra ciudad." *VG*, 28 February 1935, p. 2.

————. "La Cuestión es vivir: Los milagros de Ezquioga." *VG*, 15 October 1935, p. 16.

Sarrablo y Palacio, Alfonso. "Verdades eternas." *La Semana Católica*, 17 March 1923, pp. 336–337.

Sbarreti, Cardinal. "Communicación aprobando el proceder del Ecmo. Sr. Obispo Diocesano en lo referente a Ezquioga y sometiendo a su vigilancia la opinión favorable a las supuestas apariciones." *BOOV* 70 (1 February 1934): 41–42.

Schmitt, Jean-Claude. *La Raison des gestes dans l'Occident médiéval*. Paris: Gallimard, 1990.

————. *Les Revenants: Les vivants et les morts dans la société médiévale*. Paris: Gallimard, 1994.

Schneider, Jane. "Spirits and the Spirit of Capitalism." In *Religious Regimes and State Formation: Perspectives from European Ethnology*, ed. Eric R. Wolf, pp. 181–219. Albany: State University of New York Press, 1991.

Scott, James C. *Hidden Transcripts: Domination and the Arts of Resistance*. New Haven: Yale University Press, 1990.

Sedano de la Peña, Baudilio. Unpublished memoir. Valladolid.

Selke, Angela. *El Santo Oficio de la Inquisición: Proceso de Fr. Francisco Ortiz*. Madrid: Ediciones Guadarrama, 1968.

Silvan, Leandro. *Los Pueblos de la alcaldía mayor de Areria: Arriarán, Itxaso, Ezquioga, Gaviria, Olaberría, Gudugarreta, Astigarreta, Garín*. San Sebastián: Caja de Ahorros Municipal de San Sebastián, 1974.

Sindic, Raphaël. *Des Apparitions en Flandre?* Louvain: Rex, 1933.

Siurot, Manuel. "La Inmaculada y el pudor." *La Milagrosa y los Niños*, 1 March 1931, pp. 33–34.

Sobrino, José Antonio de. *Antonio Amundarain: Desafío y esperanza*. Madrid: Biblioteca de Autores Cristianos, 1990.

Sociedad de Estudios Vascos. "Fiestas Populares." *AEF* 2 (1922).

————. "Creencias y ritos funerarios." *AEF* 3 (1923): 139.

————. "La Religiosidad del pueblo." *AEF* 4 (1924).

————. "Establecimientos humanos y casa rural-1." *AEF* 5 (1925).

Sospedra Buyé, Antoni. *Fa cinquanta anys: Assaig històric sobre el naixement de l'Obra dels Exercices Parroquials del P. Vallet*. Barcelona: Editorial Balmes, 1975.

————. *Per carrers i places: La premsa de Catalunya i l'Obra dels Exercicis Parroquials del P. Vallet*. Barcelona: Bibliograf, 1977.

Spirago, Francisco. *La Doncella estigmatizada de Konnersreuth, Teresa Neumann*. Trans. Moisés Alujas. Barcelona: Editorial Litúrgico Español, 1930 [not seen].

Staehlin, Carlos María. *Apariciones: Ensayo crítico*. Madrid: Razón y Fe, 1954.

————. *El Padre Rubio: Vida del apóstol de Madrid*. 3d rev. ed. Madrid: Egda, 1974.

Starkie, Walter. *Spanish Raggle-Taggle: Adventures with a Fiddle in Northern Spain*. New York: E. P. Dutton, 1935.

————. *Aventuras de un irlandés en España*. Trans. Antonio Espina. Madrid: Espasa-Calpe, 1937.

Stern, Jean, ed. *La Salette: Documents authentiques*. 2 vols. Paris: Desclée de Brouwer, 1980; Cerf, 1984.

Stirrat, R. L. *Power and Religiosity in a Post-Colonial Setting: Sinhala Catholics in Contemporary Sri Lanka*. Cambridge: Cambridge University Press, 1992.

Suárez, Adriano. *Vida del M. R. P. Fr. Juan G. Arintero, Maestro en Sagrada Teología, de la Orden de Predicadores*. Vol. 2. Cádiz: Salvador Repeto, 1936.

Subirá, Paulí. "Una Curació prodigiosa?" *Gazeta de Vich*, 6 February 1933, p. 2.

Sukia, José María de. "El Ambiente religioso de Zaldibia." In *Homenaje a Eduardo de Ezcarzaga*, 355–374. Vitoria: Montepío Diocesano, 1935.

Sundén, Hjalmar. *Religionen och Rollerna: Ett psykologist studium av fromheten*. Stockholm: Svenska Kyrkans Diakonistyrelses Bokförlag, 1959.

Surcouf, Baronne Marie. "Apparitions: Au mont sacré d'Eskioga où tous voient la Vierge . . ." *L'Intransigeant*, 18 November 1932, pp. 1–2.

———. "Au mont sacré d'Eskioga 2: L'aventure de Patzi [sic] qui avait parié d'emporter la Vierge." *L'Intransigeant*, 19 November 1932, pp. 1–2.

———. "Au mont sacré d'Eskioga 3: En quittant le village où règne la sérénité." *L'Intransigeant*, 20 November 1932, pp. 1–2.

T. "A Ezquioga." *Ausetania*, 7 November 1931, p. 2.

Talde, E. A. *Archivo Clero Vasco I: Año 1936 . . . En la persecución*. Usurbil: Gráficas Izarra, 1978.

Tarré, Josep. "El Caso de Teresa Neumann la 'estigmatizada.'" *La Hormiga de Oro*, 6 October 1927.

———. "Encara sobre el cas de Teresa Neumann." *Gazeta de Vich*, 15 October 1931, pp. 1–2.

———. "Crítica interna de los manuscritos atribuidos a la M. Ráfols." *Contemporánea*, February 1933, pp. 187–203.

Taves, Ann. *The Household of Faith: Roman Catholic Devotions in Mid-Nineteenth-Century America*. Notre Dame: University of Notre Dame Press, 1986.

Tejada, Alfonso. "En Legazpia: Un homenaje de los obreros a su patrón." *PV*, 8 January 1932, p. 8.

Tellechea Idígoras, Juan Ignacio. *Tapices de la memoria: Historia clínica 279,952*. Donostia-San Sebastián: Gipuzkoa Donostia Kutxa, 1991.

Thirouin, Marie-Geneviève. *Des rayons dans la nuit*. Paris: Les Gémeaux, 1922.

———. *Trois essais pour la scène: Pages de douleur et de gloire; Fantaisies allégoriques [Le Dernier Jour de Jeanne d'Arc, Noël de France, Les Deux Beautés]*. Paris: Les Gémeaux, 1924.

——— (G. Thirouin de Morville). *Les Muses aux fontaines*. Paris: Editions de la Jeune Acadèmie, 1931.

——— (Marie de Rigné). (Poem) "L'Appel des morts." *L'Indépendant: Organe d'Action Nationale*, 5 November 1938, p. 2.

——— (Marie de Rigné). (Poem) "L'Appel des morts." In Les Poètes de chez nous, *Credo à la France*, 4th ed., p. 162. Paris: Les Autographes de la Revue Moderne des Arts et de la Vie, 1942.

——— (Marie de Morville). "Trois frères abbés." Typescript with handwritten emendations, iii plus 173 fols. Santa Lucía, 1948. "Avertissement" by R. de Rigné dated 12 May 1946. Collection of William Christian Jr.

Thurston, Herbert. *The War and the Prophets: Notes on Certain Popular Predictions Current on This Latter Age*. London: Burns and Oates, 1915.

———. "Communicating with the Dead." *The Month* 129 (1917): 134–144.

———. *The Church and Spiritualism*. Milwaukee: Bruce, 1933.

———. *Beauraing and Other Apparitions*. London: Burns and Oates, 1934.

Torre Ricaurte, Soledad de la. *Constituciones de la Obra de Sacerdotes Niños*. Pamplona: Imprenta y Librería García, 1920.

————. *Libro de las Casitas para los que pertenecen a la Obra de Sacerdotes Niños*. Pamplona: Imprenta y Librería García, 1921.

Toussaint, F., and Camille-Jean Joset. *Beauraing, les Apparitions: Le livre du cinquantenaire*. N.p.: Desclé de Brouwer, 1981.

Trexler, Richard C. *Public Life in Renaissance Florence*. New York: Academic Press, 1980.

Turner, Victor, and and Edith Turner. *Image and Pilgrimage in Christian Culture: Anthropological Perspectives*. Oxford: Basil Blackwell, 1978.

Tusquets, Juan. *Masonería y separatismo*. Ediciones Antisectarias, ed. J. Tusquets. Burgos: Ediciones Antisectarias, 1937.

Tuya, Manuel de. "¿Apariciones de la Virgen? Impresiones de un viaje a 'Ezquioga.'" *El Santísimo Rosario*, October 1931, pp. 623–626.

Txibirisko. "Lo que vio y oyó el reporter: Las apariciones de la Virgen en Ezquioga." *PV*, 10 July 1931, p. 3.

————. "En Ezquioga: Para mañana se espera un gran acontecimiento." *PV*, 11 July 1931, p. 3.

————. "Fe y supersticiones: Las supuestas apariciones de la Virgen en Ezquioga." *Ahora*, 12 July 1931, p. 22.

————. "Las Famosas Apariciones: Sigue la afluencia de visitantes a Ezquioga: Ya llegan hasta de Lérida." *La Tradición Navarra*, 19 September 1931, pp. 1–2.

Txindor. "¿Ezkiogan zer?" (What happens in Ezkioga?). *ED*, 22 March 1932, p. 10.

————. "¿Ezkioga'n zer?" *ED*, 30 March 1932, p. 8.

Txirrita. *See* Lujanbio Retegi, José Manuel.

Urbano, Luis. "Apariciones de la Virgen por tierras vascongadas." *Rosas y Espinas: Revista mensual ilustrada hispano-americana de literatura y de arte*, August 1931, [pp. 1–2].

————. "Todavía lo de Ezquioga." *Contemporánea*, January 1933, pp. 66–70.

————. "El Mercantilismo en Ezquioga." *Contemporánea*, June 1933, pp. 232–234.

————. "Teresa Neumann. La Madre Rafols." *Contemporánea*, October 1935, pp. 59–62.

Urdanpilleta, José. *Berso Berriak José Urdanpilletak jarriak* (New verses by José Urdanpilleta). 1933.

———— (unsigned). *El Gran Milagro de la Virgen de Ezquioga*. 1933.

Uriarte. "Elgoibar: La Virgen de Ezquioga." *El Liberal*. 19 July 1931, p. 6.

Urquizu, María del Stmo. Sacramento. "Sor María Paz de la Sagrada Familia Esnal Lasa Garmendia Urquizu, Concepcionista Franciscana (1909–1955)." *Vida Sobrenatural* 56 (January–February 1976): 122–131.

Vallejo Najera, A. "El Caso de Teresa Neumann." *BOOV* 72 (1 January 1936): 18–21.

————. *El Caso de Teresa Neumann a la luz de la ciencia médica*. 2d ed. Valladolid: Librería Santaren, 1939.

Vallet Arnau, Francisco de Paula. *Epistolario: Part A, Colección [Juan] Guinart [Roig]*. Documentos de Historia, vol. 2, ed. Antonio Sospedra Buyé. Pamplona: C.P.C.R., 1975.

Vélez, Urbano. "Nuestra Señora del Rosario de Fátima: Aprobación oficial de su culto." *El Santísimo Rosario*, November 1930, pp. 654–661.

————. "Nuestra Señora del Rosario de Fátima." *El Santísimo Rosario*, March 1931, pp. 174–178.

————. "En el Santuario del Rosario de Fátima: Grandiosa apoteosis mariana." *El Santísimo Rosario*, August 1931, pp. 486–488.

Vigatà, Un. "Una Impresió viscuda d'Ezquioga." *Gazeta de Vich*, 22 October 1931, p. 3.

Ville de Rigné, Raymond de la. *Aperçu sur le présent et l'avenir de l'Espagne*. Tours: Paul Bousrez, 1902.

————. *Poésies: 1877–1905*. Cannes: G. Cruvès, 1906.

————. *Roles de l'ame et du cerveau dans le sommeil magnétique*. Vichy: Wallon Frères, 1907.

————. *Souvenirs et campagnes*. Cannes: G. Cruvès, 1908.

Virto Ibáñez, Juan Jesús. *Las Elecciones municipales de 1931 en Navarra*. Pamplona: Institución Principe de Viana, Gobierno de Navarra, Departamento de Educación y Cultura, 1987.

Vivero, Augusto. "De la España castiza: El demonio se presenta en Navarra." *Heraldo de Madrid*, 21 July 1931, p. 1.

————. "El Vals de Ezquioga: Ramona y su dulce aparición." *Heraldo de Madrid*, 19 October 1931.

Waitz, Segismundo. *El Mensaje de Konnersreuth*. Trans. Juan Llauró. Barcelona: Herder, 1929.

Winston, Colin M. *Workers on the Right in Spain, 1900–1936*. Princeton: Princeton University Press, 1985.

Wolf, Eric R. *Europe and the People without History*. Berkeley, Los Angeles, and London: University of California Press, 1982.

Woodward, Kenneth L. *Making Saints: How the Catholic Church Determines Who Becomes a Saint, Who Doesn't, and Why*. New York: Simon and Schuster, 1991.

X. "Los Sucesos de Ormáiztegui: Lo que yo he visto en Ezquioga . . ." *La Gaceta del Norte*, 17 July 1931, p. 2.

Z. M., I. *El Muy Iltre, Sr. Don Nestor Zubeldia: Notas biográficas y sucesos sorprendentes*. Pamplona: Editorial Gómez, 1966.

Zarri, Gabriella. *Le Sante Vive: Profezie di corte e devozione femminile tra '400 e '500*. Torino: Rosenberg and Sellier, 1990.

————, ed. *Finzione e santità tra medioevo ed età moderna*. Torino: Rosenberg and Sellier, 1991.

Zavala, Antonio. *Xenpelar bersolaria* (The poet Xenpelar). Tolosa: Auspoa, 1969.

————. *Txirrita (José Manuel Lujanbio Retegi, 1860–1936): Bizitza eta bertsoak* (Life and verses). 2 vols. Tolosa: Auspoa, 1971.

————. *Patxi Erauskin bertsolaria* [The poet Patxi Erauskin] *(1874–1945)*. Vol. 3. Tolosa: Auspoa, 1978.

Zelai Txiki. "Albiztur-tik." *LC*, 6 January 1933, p. 8.

Zeleta. *See* Garmendia Cortadi, José.

Zimdars-Swartz, Sandra. "Popular Devotion to the Virgin: The Marian Phenomena at Melleray, Republic of Ireland." *Archives de Sciences Sociales des Religions* 67, no. 1 (1989): 125–144.

————. "Religious Experience and Public Cult: The Case of Mary Ann Van Hoof." *Journal of Religion and Health* 28, no. 4 (1989): 36–57.

————. *Encountering Mary: From La Salette to Medjugorje*. Princeton: Princeton University Press, 1991.

Zozaya, Antonio. "Cartera de un solitario: ¿Qué querrá?" *VG*, 19 July 1931.

Zuatzaga, Jon ("Algorri"). "Galdakano: 'Zeleta'-ri" (Galdakano: For Zeleta). *EZ*, 18 July 1931, p. 5.

Zurbitu, D. *Escritos póstumos de la sierva de Dios Madre María Rafols: Documentos hallados el primer viernes de octubre de 1931 y el día 29 de enero de 1932*. Zaragoza: Gambón, 1932.

SUBJECT INDEX

Page references to visual evidence and maps are in **bold**. The provinces of Bizkaia, Gipuzkoa, and Navarra are abbreviated by the initials B, G, and N, respectively, for example, Durango (B).

Acción Nacionalista Party, 39
accordion (devil's bellows), 181
Action Française, 427n26
active vs contemplative religion, 234–235
Adelante (Bilbao), **17**
Adrian, Saint, 177
adultery, 204
adults: and child seers, 212, 250, 257, 259; as seers, 250, 251. *See also* age; men; women
age: of dead in visions, 459n1; of seers, 176, 177, 448n6
"Agur Jesusen Ama" (hymn), 264, 267
Aitzkorri, Mount, 173
Alava, 165, 211–212, 218, 230
Albiztur (G), **23**, **164**, 219; removal of Sacred Heart, 193; seers at Ezkioga, 192, 291; visions in, 148, 192–195, 381. *See also* Aracama Aguirre, Gregorio; Luistar
Alcaraz (Albacete), 377
Alcaudete de la Jara (Toledo), 437n5

Alcazar, El (Madrid), 390
alcoholism, 78, 131, 204, 244, 449n27
Alcoz (N). *See* Alkotz
Aldaz (N), 227, 230
Aldeanueva de Ebro (Rioja), 468n28
Alegia (barrio of Itsaso, G), 223
Alegia (G), 51
Alegría de Oria (G). *See* Alegia (G)
Algemesí (Valencia), 432n42
Aliadas: Basque, in 1932, 418n9; at Ezkioga, 47; origin and practices of, 44–45; and Reparadoras, 64; seer among, 49; as victims, 351; watch Ramona, 50
Alkotz (N), **23**, 181
Alliance in Jesus through Mary (La Alianza en Jesús por María). *See* Aliadas
Almándoz (N), 227, 444n30
Alsasua (N). *See* Altsasu
altars: in child play, 249; church, visions on, 15, 189, 208; home, of seer, **183**; outdoor, in Barranca, 173, 174, 175, 177, 178, 179, 184; visions of, 289
Alt Llobregat (Barcelona), 459n18
Altsasu (N), **23**, 172
Altzo (G), 233, 241
Alzo (G). *See* Altzo
Amor Misericordioso. *See* Merciful Love

Amurrio (Alava), 429n1
anarchists, 7, 14, 16, 244, 257
Ancona (Italy), 394
Andalusia, 14, 19
Andoain (G), and Saint Michael, 204, **205**
Angeles de las Missiones (Berriz), 222
angels: activities of, 91, 272, 293, 335; attributes of, 82–83, 293; like children, 271, 292; children dressed as, 247, **248**, **249**; children shrouded as, 327–328; child seers like, 47, 84, 124, 145, 281; cult of, 204; dead children as, 81, 95, 326, 327, 329, 460n5; in early visions, 333, 334; exterminating, **349**, 352; good and bad, 150; helpers at Dorrao as, 174; and Prophet of Durango, 263; in questionnaire, 405; take money, 339; warlike, 31–32, 83, 293, 353. *See also* Michael, Saint
angelus, 36, **36**, 417n41
animal magnetism, 274
animals in visions. *See* donkey; dove; dragon; horse; monkey; oxen; pigeon; serpent; sheep; snakes
ánimas or *animeros*, 339
Anna (Valencia), 432n42
Annales de Beauraing et Banneux, 155
Annales de Notre Dame de Lourdes, 86

Anoeta (G), 445n47
anonymity, 43, 165, 381, 389
Ansota (Arbizu, N), 172
Antichrist, 353, 365–367
anticlericalism: Bilbao, 344; in Civil War, 376; in nineteenth century, 3, 5; press, 33; regional Catholics and, 106; rural Basques and, 18; spiritist, 342, 345; Sueca, 120; Terrassa, 76
anticlerical riots: 1835, 5; 1909, 106; 1931, 14, 17, 32, 119
anticommunism, 6, 151
anti-Semitism, 197, 286
Antzuola (G), seer from, 378
Anzuola (G). See Antzuola
apocalypse: and Carlists and Integrists, 356; in Ezkioga visions, 347–372; horsemen in, 353–354; as solution to evil, 395–396. See also chastisement; end of world; Last Judgment; reign of Christ; reign of Sacred Heart
apostasy, 205, 351
Apostles for the Last Times, 366
apparitions: in church history, 399; divine purpose, 38, 394–395; history in Spain, 1–2, 5–6; legends of, 21, 260; nocturnal, 2; to politics, 394–395; Spain 1900–1931, 22–23; Spain 1965–1995, 317. See also visions
Aralar, Mount, 204–206
Aramaio (Alava), seer from, 378
Aranzazu (shrine, G), 23, 237; and Ezkioga, 206, 237, 306, 312, 337; and Zegama, 207
Arbizu (N), 23, 164, 172–173, 184, 330
Argentina, 129, 342
Argia (San Sebastián), 25; in Albiztur, 192, 193, 439n51; in Santa Lucía, 43; sympathy for visions, 31

arguments against visions: the dead, 314; death of seer, 334; fraud, 282; immorality at site, 147, 383; of Laburu, 130–133; Navarra, 173, 180–181, 183, 189; peasant seers, 252; seer behavior, 146, 191, 259–260, 288; too scary, 223; visions at will, 300; witch-stuff, 27, 173, 298, 383. See also proof of visions; retiro; witch-stuff
aristocrats: Andalusian, 54, 65; and Benita, 389; and church, 218; control vision precinct, 306–307; interest in visions, 74, 254; seers serve, 49. See also Medina y Garvey, Carmen
Arlon (Belgium), 155
armièrs, 339
arms in form of cross, 20, 37, 46, 72, 264, 266
army: French, 109; Red, invades Spain, 361; sent to North, 33. See also soldiers
Arrasate (G). See Mondragón
Artajona (N), 379
Arte Cristiana (Olot), 438n25
artisans, as seers, 253
art restorer, 133
Assisi (Italy), apparitions at, 397
Asti (Italy), bleeding crucifix in, 159, 434n77
Astigarraga (G), 196, 222
astral projection, 342–343, 344
Asturias, 1934 uprising in, 62
Ataun (G), 23, 35, 374; clergy, 313; devotions, 204; doctor, 278; seer of devil, 27; spiritism, 342; vocations, 219–220. See also Ataun, girl from; Goicoechea Urrestarazu, Francisco
Ataun, girl from, 57–58, 59; and Catalans, 75, 76, 319, 321; predictions, 353; medal from heaven, 58; and Medina, 131, 259; and other

seers, 50, 58, 60; and Rigné, 111; secrets, 354; spiritual exercises, 64; spiritual services, 318, 319, 330; stigmata, 58, 78, 113
atheism, 324
athletes of God, 296
atonement: for beach sins, 45; crucifix display as, 70; in crucifixions, 99; of Daughters of Charity, 235; for disbelievers, 99; in Ezkioga prayers, 47, 267; for 1931 riots, 46; in spiritual exercises, 64; of voluntary victims, 359
attributes in question: of Christ, 131, 465n29; of Joseph, 83; of Mary, 30, 31, 33, 131, 167; of Saint Michael, 353–354
audience, affects vision content, 358
Augustinian friars, 228
Augustinian nuns: Aldaz, 227; Oñati, 231
Aulinas (Señoritas Operarias Parroquiales), 86, 87
autism, 319, 323
automobiles: bishops in accidents in, 154, 326, 334; driver seers, 244, 258, 275, 375; lights and visions, 382; seer privilege, 131, 176; visions on, 177
autonomy: statute of Basque, 25, 30, 137; statute of Catalan, 137
awareness in vision, 288, 300–301; Aguado, 274; La Cruz, on 297; Evarista, 294; Irurzun, 375; Pascal on, 286; Patxi, 275
Azcoitia (G). See Azkoitia
Azkoitia (G), 23, 64, 204, 240
Azkorte, Santa Cruz de (chapel, Urnieta), 209
Azpeitia (G), 23, 265, 337; court at, 141, 432n42
azti (diviners), 341, 342

Bacaicoa (N). See Bakaiku
Bachicabo (Alava) visions, 164, 165–167

Badalona (Barcelona), 86, 106
Bakaiku (N), 23, 119–120, 164, 176–177, 180–181
bakers, believing, 138, 337
banishment of seers and believers, 377
bank director, 200
banner, embroidered, 206
Banneux (Belgium) visions, 152
Bañolas (Girona). *See* Banyoles
Banyoles (Girona), 22, 86–87
Baracaldo (B), 30
barber, 192
Barcelona, 164; Burguera in, 143; buried treasure, 95; Casal Donya Dorotea, 86, 92, 104; cathedral clergy, 70; chastisement, 105, 357, 364; diocese of, censor, 67; doctors from, 282, 452n49; Ezkioga seers from, 423n18, 455n82; Ezkioga seers visit, 79, 92, 95–96, 138; and Limpias, 66, 134; local holy folk, 282, 368, 371–372, 425n70; observers from, 58, 84, 90, 92, 318, 430n18; piety, 70, 96; promoters from, 67, 70, 87–88, 134; and Rafols crucifixes, 70; religious conflicts, 5; shrines, 94, 461n21
barefoot, as penance, 176, 209
Barrio (Alava), 166
basilica at Ezkioga, 307, 312, 364, 374, 388–389
Basque: in ceremonies, 105, 165; and cuadrillas, 147, 203, 379; geography, 7, 164, 171; and ghost beliefs, 341; pilgrims learn, 169; in visions, 20, 26, 93, 332; and vision spread, 20, 164, 212
Basque autonomy, 25, 30, 32, 137
Basque Country, 7, 22–23, 24, 30, 164
Basque folklore, 26, 212–213, 309, 339–341

Basque nationalism, 7; and Ezkioga, 30–33, 104–106, 161, 225; in visions, 290
Basque Nationalist Party, 19, 25, 30, 206, 209; club (*batzoki*), 260, 353
Basque nationalists: against Carlist-Integrists, 193, 198–199; Echeguren and, 128; against Ezkioga, 383; and Great Promise, 442n14; and Jeanne d'Arc, 246; against Republic, 33, 62, 78; with Republic, 209, 210; seers, 60, 63, 196, 253, 339
Basques: and the dead, 393; and Mary, 29–33, 104; piety, 5, 6, 21, 30, 33–39, 105–106; as "race," 30; and Rafols forgeries, 71, 73–74; and Republic, 14, 16–19, 39, 62, 105–106, 374; seers ethnic, 254
batzoki, 260, 353
Bayonne (Pyrénées-Atlantiques), 386
Baztán, Valle de (N), 67
beaches: and morality, 35, 45, 97, 129; and rural folk, 256; in visions, 26, 149, 361
Beasain (G), 23, 164; active nun in, 233–234; seers, 145, 275; shrine, 337
beatas, 45
beatification: of Amundarain, 47; of Gemma, 88; of López de Maturana, 222; of Madre Esperanza, 386; of Madre Soledad, 229; of Marcucci, 385; of Rafols, 68–70, 385
Beauraing visions, 152, 153, 155, 163, 286
beauty: Burguera on, 120; Rigné on, 109; in seers, 147, 246
Bedia (B), 22, 340
beggar woman, 336, 340
Beizama (G), 23, 49, 290
Bejar (Salamanca), 22, 74, 385
Belgium: and Basque visions, 152, 153, 155–

156, 196; visions, 152, 155, 157, 159, 163, 286
belief, as cumulative process, 122
believers: fraternity, 381; guide visions, 40; intercessors, 207; kiss seers, 84, 131; marriages of, 381; and seers, 42, 84, 260, 272 (*see also* petitions); study of, 8; as subversives, 384
Beloki, cross of (Zumarraga), 46
Benedictines: Lazkao, 14, 219, 220, 239. *See also* Montserrat
Bergara (G), 23, 164; Ama Felisa in, 337; cuadrilla held in, 198; seers from, 245, 326, 378; tension in, 17, 29, 245
Bermeo (B), 22, 342
Berrioplano (N), 379
Berriz (B), 22, 221, 222
bertsolari, 146–147
Betelu (N), 23, 164, 204, 225–229, 422n9
Bethlehem, 367
Bible, Irurzun uses, 359
bicycle, almost hits Virgin, 169
bicycles, and girls, 35, 37, 191
Bidache (Pyrénées-Atlantiques), 386–388
Bidegoyan (G), 327–328
Bilbao, 22, 164; crucifix, 206; patrons in, 58, 95, 149, 388; politics, 19, 248, 344, 394; prison ship, 374; religious, 28, 134, 230; seers in, 64, 152, 182, 420n51; shrine, 340; spiritism, 342–343; visions and, 182, 356, 375
bilberries for healing, 179
births by unwed seers, 147, 383
Bizkaia: Colegio de Médicos, 234; vs Gipuzkoa, 165; shrine, 337
blackmail, 157, 158
Blanes (Girona), 367
blasphemy, 4, 5, 204, 292; and vision, 166, 275
blessing of objects, 92, 200, 333; by seers, 187; by Virgin, 188, 323

blind, 317
blood: on Christ, 31, 336; of devil, 202–203; on doors, 372; and Gemma, 296; on images, 159, 200, 445n49 (see also crucifixes, bleeding); Mary's tears, 182, 292, 319; Mary with, 83; Neumann's tears, 283, 284; as relic, 50, 183, 200, 308, 338; river of, 32, 356, 372; on seer hands, 50, 182, 201, 273; of seer-martyrs, 154; as sins, 83; on Spain, 135; on swords, 32, 55, 83, 354; tableau of, 293
Bogotá, 444n30
bolshevism, 356
books: angels with, 293; inspiration from, 86; visions about, 114, 208; vision sources, 73, 336, 359, 366, 371, 466n43
boys. See child seers; teenagers
brothel, 182
Brothers Hospitallers, 103, 124, 376
Brothers of Christian Instruction, 447n70
Brothers of Christian Schools, 447n70
Brothers of the Sacred Heart, 447n70
Brussels, 155
bulls, psychology of, 129
Burgos, 39, 317
burial clothes, 327–330, 332, 340
burning bush, 313
Buruntza, Mount (Urnieta), 209
buses: to Ezkioga, 51, 89, 165, 172, 192; pick up seers, 61, 95, 182; visions on, 90–91, 131, 202–203, 314

cabarets, women in, 97
Cáceres, 280
Cádiz, province of, 143
Calahorra, diocese of, 385
Calatayud (Zaragoza), 297
Calella (Barcelona), 86
Calvary, 313–314
Cambo-les-Bains (Pyrénées-Atlantiques), 22

Canary Islands, 94, 123, 317, 389, 461n32
candles: blessed, for end of world, 207, 371, 372, 373; miraculous, 395; during visions, 191, 200, 264
candy, mystical, 173
canonical inquiry, and cult, 307
Cantabria, devotion to souls, 462n38
Capuchins, 15, 172, 237–238, 376, 395
Carlists and Carlist-Integrists: ideology, 32, 255, 351, 361; promoter background, 44, 55–56, 116; roots, 18–19, 25, 33; in villages, 198–199, 207; and visions, 32, 191, 224, 353, 361, 440n61, 442n14
Carlist Wars: First, 18; Third, 19, 44, 55–56, 255, 366
Carmel, Mount, 313, 458n31
Carmelite fathers, 134, 160, 234, 240–241
Carmelite nuns, 67, 86, 256
carriers, in vision sequences, 396–399
cartoons, 16, 17, 34, 167, 171
Casa de Miñán (Cáceres), 432n42
Casal Donya Dorotea (Barcelona), 86, 92, 104
Casas Viejas (Cádiz), 432n47
casino, washed to sea, 361
Castejón (N), 16
Castellano, El (Toledo), 167, 168, 171
Castellón de la Plana, 367
Castile, republican enthusiasm, 39
catacombs, 141, 146
Catalan, in parish exercises, 74
Catalan nationalism, and Ezkioga, 104–107
Catalan pilgrims: Aulina trips, 87–90, 89, 107, 311, 331; and Basques, 104–106; and Benita, 80, 82–85, 85, 91, 92, 93, 103, 272; bring

devotions, 73, 90; and chastisements, 105, 355, 357, 358, 362; in Civil War, 376; convert, 99, 100, 319, 324; defend visions, 133, 138, 143; and Evarista, 89, 319; and Garmendia, 78–80, 84–85, 322–323; at Lourdes, 5, 86; petitions, 318–324, 395; and Rafols, 72–73; and Ramona, 76–78, 318; and Recalde, 95–96; as seers, 90, 134, 259; suspected, 141, 382–383; visit promoters, 52, 121
catalepsy, 174, 278, 295
Catalonia, 7, 19, 76, 106–107; and apparitions, 5, 66, 86; salvation, 78, 104–105, 357; seers suffer for, 96
catatonia, 274, 278
catechism, 86, 119, 348–350; posters, 349, 360; visions during, 207–208
cathedral, vision on, 169
Catholic Action movement, 151
Catholic church: definition, 400–401; reform in last times, 367; and state relations, and visions, 128, 356; and visions, 8
Catholicism: history, 399; internal logic and problems, 392–396; novelty in, 399–400
cattle dealer, 132
caves, 212, 302
Ceánuri (B). See Zeanuri
Cegama (G). See Zegama
Cerdanyola del Vallès (Barcelona) visions, 398
Cerro de los Angeles, El (Madrid), 394
Cestona (G). See Zestoa
chalice: for shrine, 207; in visions, 292
chapel: at Albiztur, 193, 193; at Bachicabo, 166; on highway, 373–374; in Legorreta, 381; of light, 289; Zegama vision site, 208
chapel at Ezkioga: Burguera helps with, 125; construction, 94, 135–136, 136, 310–311, 311;

civil war *(cont'd)*
list Wars; Spanish Civil
War
clairvoyance, 134, 192. *See
also* sins
Claretians, and Madre Es-
peranza, 386, 395,
446n59
clergy, parish: Amundarain
group, 45, 224; anti-
Ezkioga, 223, 224, 242;
atonement for, 99; au-
thority, 35, 227, 315,
330; and Bachicabo vi-
sions, 166, 167; Baran-
diarán group, 34–36,
224; and Barranca vi-
sions, 173, 175, 179–
180, 182, 187–188, 194;
blamed for visions, 383;
Catalan, 90, 319; chas-
tisement of, 255; deaths
in Civil War, 376; de-
pendence on seers, 242;
in divided towns, 222–
223; duties regarding
seers, 151, 153, 155,
158–159; and Ezkioga
liturgy, 264–268; and
fire tests, 148; forbidden
at site, 128, 129; geography of vocations, 18,
217–223; and Gipuzkoa
mini-Ezkiogas, 192–193,
195, 197–200, 207–208;
Gipuzkoa vs Vitoria,
133; guerrilla, 31–32,
34, 331–332; keep
bloody handkerchiefs,
309; link classes, 255;
Madre Soledad group,
225–229; and Mendig-
orría visions, 15; with
opinion unknown, 222–
223; parish, 217–229,
241–242, 315, 330;
Patxi and, 61, 61–62;
police youth, 37–38;
politics, 19, 45, 65,
196–199, 207, 224–225;
pro-Ezkioga, 38, 122,
130, 193, 223, 224–225,
229, 242, 259, 309; ru-
ral ethnographers, 34;
and sacred landscaping,
313; sanctification of,
226–229; seers, 253,
364; seers act like, 180,
187, 201, 351, 396;
serve seers, 259; and

social class, 218; take
declarations, 53, **247**;
testify to judge, 143; and
visions of afterlife, 314,
340; Zegama group,
224–225. *See also indi-
vidual priests*
clothes. *See* burial clothes;
dress; habit; mourning
clothes
Cold War, 371
Collevalenza (Italy), 386
Colombia, 225, 241
commerce, and appari-
tions, 128, 176, 382–
383, 416n7
commission at Ezkioga,
25–26, 53, 119, 122,
243–244. *See also* ques-
tionnaire
commons, sale of, 19
communal work, 166
Communion, first, 190,
249
Communion, Holy: daily,
132; denial, 151, 158,
196, 198–200, 374,
384; to free soul, 338;
mystic, 159–160, 201,
258, 336, 378; Rigné
and, 114, 157, 158,
160, 427n20
communists: agents of
apocalypse, 351, 356,
370–372, 409; and vi-
sions, 7, 378. *See also*
Soviet Russia
company towns, 34
Concha, La (beach, San
Sebastián), 26, 362
confession: of believers,
Pamplona, 241; bishop
cannot control, 242; as
child play, 249; direct
through seers, 201; fruit
of visions, 52, 223, 236,
239, 366; Rigné and,
114; of seers, 242, 257.
See also conversion
Congregation of San Felipe
Neri, 396
consciences, gift of reading. *See* sins
Constancia, La (San Sebastián): defends visions,
209; ideology, 25, 32,
346, 361, 442n14; pro-
motes Rafols, 73–74;
subsidized, 34
Constituent Cortes: clergy

in, 25, 70, 169, 277;
and Ezkioga, 33, 128,
240, 246; Gipuzkoa can-
didates, 25; and Guada-
mur, 169; women's suf-
frage, 277
contest, seer-run, 125
contraception, 111
convents, as vision sites,
191, 203
conversion: of heathens,
98, 190; of Laburu, 260;
in last times, 364, 370;
at Lourdes, 33; of male
seers, 244, 274–277; pe-
titions for, 319, 323, 324;
proof of visions, 134,
147; by reaction, 166,
181, 274–277, **276**, 287;
when seers know sins,
95, 132, 159, 182, 192;
of skeptical pilgrims, 90,
192, 273; of urchin by
flower, 447n67
convulsions, 278, 295
co-optation of observers in
visions, 84
Córdoba, 234, 282
Corpiño, El (Pontevedra),
263
corpses: fall like snow to
hell, 356, 357; prepara-
tion of, 234, 356
Corpus Christi, in Oñati,
204
Correo Catalán (Barce-
lona), 66, 84, 132, 134
counting, of prayers and
visions, 45, 93
Creuada, La (Terrassa),
318
Cristero rebellion, Mexico,
151
Cristo de la Pureza y
Desconsuelo, 69
Cristo Desamparado, 70,
202
Croix, La (Paris), 307
cross: arms in form of,
20, 37, 46, 72, 264,
266; Etxarri-Aranatz,
176; Patxi installs, 62,
307, 308, 312; Rex
group's, 152–153, 312;
sawed down, 139, 312;
dispels devil, 26, 27;
trees and, 307–308, **308**,
312; as vision focus,
269, 308
Crucíferos, 366–368

crucifixes: locus of grace in visions, 91, 95, **185**, 200, 272–273; miraculous, 206, 386; moving, in northern Spain, 6, 15, 396–397 (*see also* Limpias; Piedramillera); Rafols, 68–71, 73–74, **183**, 202; removals, 14, 18, 70, 97, 130, 416n11; women wear, 416n11. *See also* crucifixes, bleeding

crucifixes, bleeding: Europe-wide, 156, 159, 195, 434n77; of Evarista, 155; of García Cascón, 95; of Rafols, 70; in Zegama, 208

crucifixions, seer, 101, 102; Lete text, 124, 405–406; mystic models, 285, 295–296; in Navarra, 174, 191, 195; at Oiartzun, 102; after rejection, 100, 130, 295, 366; and spiritual exercises, 64, 366; spiritual purpose, 97–99, 366. *See also* Passion

Cruz, La (San Sebastián), 25, 297, 431n35

Cruz y Españolismo (Blanes), 367

cuadrillas: at Ezkioga, 42, 62, 195, 327, **328**; in Gipuzkoa from 1932 on, 198–199, 201, 203, 210–211, 379

Cuevas de Vinromà (Castellón), 297, 397

cures: agent in dispute, 323; at Beauraing, 152; by berries, 179; of cancer, 233, 381; certification of, 90, 322; Ezkioga, and doctors, 90, 282, 322; by Ezkioga water, 200, 207, 311, 381; at La Salette, 4; lead to enthusiasm, 110, 155, 397; lead to visions, 86–87, 335, 386, 398; at Limpias, 224–225, 397; at Lourdes, 5, 86, 110, 155; of Passionist with vision, 237; petitions for, 232, 317, 318, 323, 408; by roses, 200; of seer in first vi-

sion, 237, 327; spiritist, 117; at Urretxu, 191

curses, power of, 187

damnation, 76, 392–393

dance hall, 204, 361

dancing: close, 35, 36, 37, 38; by Múgica, 113; Ramona, 131; and trance, 263

Danzig, 197

Daughters of Charity of Saint Vincent de Paul: and Ezkioga, 233–235; in Gipuzkoa, 99, 220, 233–235; outside Gipuzkoa, 3–5, 16, 368, 445n49

Daughters of Mary sodality: in Gipuzkoa, 37, 38, 192, 245; in Mendigorría, 15; piety and morality, 26, **36**, 37, 38, 245–246; and visions, 38, 58, 179, 246

Dax (Landes), 387

dead: children contact, 247, 207; diviners and the, 341; gender and age in visions, 459n1; mute in visions, 336; nuns appear, 233; petitions regarding, 77, 134, 192, 323, 324, 330–333, 336–339; phases in visions of, 334; the premature, 326, 336, 393; processions of, 330, 341; to rejoin living, 396; relation to seers, 330; spiritists and the, 341–342, 345; traditional apparitions, 339–342; visions of household, 326–332; in vision tableau, 293

death: in mortal sin, 100; of opponents foretold, 187, 334, 388; reward for believers, 207, 332–336, 355; as sacrifice, 99, 100, 357, 359; of seers, 103, 124, 296, 297, 334; seers ask for, 62, 100; seers know date of, 95, 99, 100, 335; sudden, anxiety about, 77, 319, 326, 330, 334, 358. *See also* chastisement; murder of seers

deathbed, prophecies on, 230

death penalty, opposition to, 344

déjà-vu, visions as reverse, 300

democracy, subverts family, 35

desert, and last times, 367, 370

Detentes, 45

Deusto (Bilbao), 341

devil: appearance, 27, 55, 178–179, 205; besets female mystics, 87, 116; blood on bus, 202–203; in chastisement, 371–372; in disguise, 26, 55, 150, 465n29; as dragon or serpent, 149, 202–206; and false book, 150; fights Saint Michael, 177, 178, 184, 187, 202–203; fools seers, 55, 84, 103, 294–296; at Garabandal, 250; Garmendia and, 78, 90, 140; judge like, 141–142; makes faces, 131; runs modern world, 120; and spiritism, 342; takes opponents, 103–104, 143, 150, 360; tests against, 144, 406–407; visions caused by, 189, 378. *See also* discernment

devotional objects: blessed in visions, 92, 178, 188, 270, 270–273; gift exchange, 272; seers fix on, 95. *See also* crucifixes; holy cards; medals; rosaries

devotional religion, 21, 316

devotions: "active" vs "contemplative," 234–235; French, in Spain, 5, 230, 234–235; of religious orders, 2, 231; in visions and religious orders, 231

Día, El (San Sebastián), 25, 28, 41, 128, 242

diagnoses for altered states, 274, 275, 298

Dima (B), 441n2

diocesan magistrate (*fiscal*). *See* Sertucha

diplomats, 118, 253, 398
disappearance of vision: flash of gold, 304; into hole, 83; slow fade, 27
disbelief, matter of degree, 382
discernment of seers: Bordas, 134; Burguera, 119, 126, 147–148; by fire, 147–148; Gemma as model, 296; Laburu, 130–132; local criteria, 35–37; petitions for, 323–324; rules for auto-, 144, 149, 407; by seers, 149. *See also* testing seers
diviners (*azti*), 341, 342
divorce, 110, 111
doctors: allies of seers, 87, 278, 279; and Aulina, 87; at Beauraing, 152; chastisement of, 255; and famous mystics, 285–286; French and Belgian, 156, 279, 282; link social classes, 255; and Navarrese seers, 175, **175**, 178–180, 182; protest healer-nun, 234; and Rafols cult, 74; rule some seers out, 51, 243–244; seer at Guadamur, 169; and vision states, 278–283, 285–287. *See also* Aranzadi, Sabel; Juaristi, Victoriano
documents, 112, 122, 123, 139, 378
doll: Baby Jesus as, 226; Baby Jesus like, 177; for Benita, 92
domestic service, 44, 253. *See also* chauffeurs; servants
Dominicans, 238, 366, 395, 446n60
Domjevin (Meurthe-et-Moselle) visions 1799–1803, 415n5
donkey, spirit, 176
Donostia–San Sebastián (G). *See* San Sebastián
Dorrao (N), **164**, 173–174
doughnut man (*churrero*) seer, 176
dove: becomes horse, 293; in questionnaire, 405; in vision, 290, 291, 293, 307

dowries for religious, 218
dragon, devil as, 149, 202–203, 204, **205**, 206
dress: Aliadas, 44; chastisement for, 97; immodest, 35, 97, 204, 305; of Mary, 28, 30, 313, 403, 432n54; unisex, and apocalypse, 299
Dreux-Vouvant (Vendée), convent of, 238
Drôme (France), outdoor visions 1848–1849 at, 315
drugs, as explanation, 298
duende de Zaragoza, and Ezkioga, 344
Durango (B), **22**, **164**; believers visit, 93–95, 123, 337, 381; opponents visit, 134–135, 154; prison, 339; Prophet of, 263, 356; Recalde in, 93–95, 339

Ea (B), girls of, 248–249
earth: opens for sinners, 359, **360**; relic of chapel site, 310
earthquakes, 352, 355, 357, 359
eau-de-cologne, mystical, 160
Echarri-Aranaz (N). *See* Etxarri-Aranatz
Echternach (Luxembourg), 263
École Bardique, 118
"ecstasy," 274
ecstatic religion, 143. *See also* vision states
Eden, Garden of, 118, 428n32
Éditions Rex, 151
Editorial Círculo (Zaragoza), 398
Editorial Litúrgica Española (Barcelona), 284
"Egizu zuk Maria" (hymn), 265, 268, 450n11, 450n14
Egypt, seers enact flight to, 210
Eibar (G), 23, 35, 258, 462n46
Elduain (G), 44
Elduayan (G). *See* Elduain
elections: April 1931, 14; June 1931, 16–17, 24–

25, 30; November 1933, 440n61
Elgoibar (G), 23, 29, 30, 277
Elizondo (N), 438n25
Elorrio (B), **22**, 160, 234, 388
emotions: of Benita in vision, 82, 84, 91; of crowd at Ezkioga, 264–266, 296; and discernment, 144, 294–295, 407; intensify in child play, 250; of Izurdiaga seers, 188; of Mary in visions, 27–28, 188, 265, 291; of observers, 77, 84; of seers at Ezkioga, 244, 280, 287–288, 372, 405; of those holding seers, 21, 93. *See also* fear; fright; shame; weeping
end of world: in Basque folklore, 356; dates for, 350, 351, 356–357, 362–365; preparations for, 371–372; scenarios, 367–368, 370. *See also* apocalypse; chastisement; Last Judgment; reign of Christ; reign of Sacred Heart
Enigme d'Ezkioga, l' (Brussels and Lyon), 156, **156**, 374, 386
enthusiasm, and church history, 399
epilepsy, 274, 298
Errazkin (N), 227, 444n30
Errazquin (N). *See* Errazkin
Errotz (N), boy seer from, 172
Erroz (N). *See* Errotz
Escorial, El (Madrid), apparitions at, 390
Escoriaza (G). *See* Eskoriatza
Escuela de Cristo, 421n3
Esdra, Fourth Book of, 367
Eskoriatza (G), 241
Espejo (Alava), 166
Espluga Calba, l' (Lleida), 86
Espluga de Francolí, l' (Tarragona), 119, 122
Esquella de la Torraxa, L' (Barcelona), 106

Estella (N), 23, 172, 246
ETA, 172
ethnography, Basque, 34, 339–342
Etichove (Belgium) visions, 152
etiquette, with ghosts, 340
Études Carmélitaines Mystiques et Missionaires, 450n1
Etxarri-Aranatz (N), **164**, 174, 175–176, 438n21
Eucharistic adoration, 187, 226
Eucharistic Congresses, 351, 437n8
Eucharistic studies, 116, 117–118
Eusko-Folklore group, 34, 224, 339–342
Euzkadi, 25, 32
evil, apocalypse solution to, 395–396
existence of God, proofs for, 3, 6, 86–87
exorcism, of bewitched houses, 230
expiation vs good works, 98–99
exploiters of workers, 204–205
Exuperio, Saint, 170
eyes, during vision, 188, 201, 263, 278–279, 282, 285, 290
Ezkioga (G), 17–19, 23, **164**; Ezpeleta fonda, 18; officials, 25, 139; parish church, **205**. *See also* chapel at Ezkioga
Ezkioga visions: area of attraction, 20, **22**–23, 163, 165; and Basque nationalists, 30–33, 104–106, 161, 225, 290, 383; Beauraing and, 152–153, **153**; and Carlist-Integrists, 32, 191, 224, 353, 361, 440n61, 442n14; and Catalan nationalists, 104–107; collective etiology, 29–40, 401–402; and earlier prophecies, 356, 369; and Fatima, 32, 46, 389, 398; as Freemason plot, 225, 237, 384; and La Salette, 351, 352, 358; and Lourdes visions, 5, 32, 146, 196, 240, 306

(*see also* Lourdes); and Mendigorría, 33, 416n7; as mission sessions, 265, 266, 296, 366, 397; and moving crucifixes, 28, 396–397 (*see also* Limpias; Piedramillera); and Rafols forgeries, 71–73, 422n18; site, **24**, **51**, 302–315; as spiritism, 342–343; and Torralba de Aragón, 248, 415n1. *See also* seers; visions; vision states
Ezquioga (G). *See* Ezkioga

factories, rural vs urban, 257
factory owner, 34, 76
factory work, and mores, 36
factoryworker seers, 180–181, 254, 275. *See also* Garmendia, José
"fainting spells," 265, 276, 295
fairy tales, 173
faith, reasoned or emotional, 132
faking visions and trances, 265, 274, 294
Falange, 374, 384
fame, and seers, 40, 49, 58, 100, 114
families, 35, 207, 218, 317
famine, 357, 358, 409
farmers. *See* peasants
farm laborers, 169, 172, 181
farms: teenage seers from, 245; tenant, 19
fast, before Communion, 114
fasting, women, 283, 284, 285, 384
fathers, 327
Fatima (Portugal) visions, 6, **22**; Basques and, 6, 21, 25, 46, 248–249, 415n14; children and, 248–249; escalation in, 365–366; and Ezkioga, 32, 46, 389, 398; as model, 8, 312; and religious orders, 6, 395; replications, 163; traveling images, 397, 397–398
fear: in crowd, 266, 268; provokes visions, 287; of

saints, 346, 364; in seers, 276, 280, 287, 290; of sudden death, 77, 319, 326, 330, 334, 358. *See also* fright
female religious. *See* nuns
fiestas, and visions, 166, 181
film. *See* cinema
filtering, 24–33, 39–40, 126, 243–251; by promoters, 105, 126, 143–144, 146–151; of seers, 24–27, 105, 143–151, 243–251; of text by visions, 150, 160; of visions, 27–40, 407
fines, 143, 198, 199, 209, 338
fire: in chastisement, 293, 361, 364, 372; in hell, 360; test of seers, 147–150, **148**, 278, 296, 433n59
fireballs, 173
fireflies, and visions, 245
fires, house, preternatural, 336, 337
First Fridays, 15
first seer boy, 48, 103, 140, 280–281, 300, 308. *See also* first seers
first seer girl, 43, 48, 264, 304. *See also* first seers
first seers, 48; bolstered by Aguado, 274; as cowherds, 312; origin of visions, 286; parents of, 18, 20, 48, 253, 461n25; and promoters, 48, 56, 75, 264; site of vision, 303, 304; vision content, 47, 264, 291; vision states, 274, 295. *See also* first seer boy; first seer girl
fishing towns, 14, 218, 254, 342
"fits," 265, 287
flagellation, as sacred theater, 196, 400
floods of 1934, 346
Florence, 461n23
flowers: adorn exiled image, 139; adorn vision sites, 136, 179, 307; blessed in visions, **185**, 191, 200, 271, 272; blessed roses, 191, **271**; as connection to land-

flowers (cont'd)
scape, 194; convert,
447n67; and devil, Izur-
diaga, 189; gifts for
seers, 141; gifts from
dead, 339; heal, 200;
language of, 451n24; at
La Salette, 249; Mary
vision attribute, 28, 226,
304; May, 18; paper,
179; and Priest-children,
226; seen as Mary, 166,
191; seers arrange, in
vision, 188; seers distribute, in vision, 188, 192,
333, 339; as virtues of
Mary, 226; visions in-
clude, 82–83, 189, 290
folklore, Basque, 26, 212–
213, 309, 339–341
folk religion, and urban
Catholics, 36, 36
forgery, of Rafols docu-
ments, 68–74
fortune-tellers, 167
Fox Movietone News, 344
frames, 289, 304
France: and apocalypse,
370; Basque religious in,
221; Catholicism, 3,
463n51; devotions, 5,
230, 234–235; divine
preference for, 394;
ghosts and spiritism,
340, 341; orders in
Spain, 230, 447n70; pol-
itics, 427n26; seer from,
296; visionaries, 3–5,
159, 300, 350–351; vi-
sions and witch-hunts,
211; war with Germany,
370
Franciscan nuns: house in
Castile, 233; Santa Isa-
bel of Mondragón, 232;
Santa Isabel of Valla-
dolid, 232; Villasana de
Mena, 218
Franciscans, 44, 237;
Aranzazu, 206, 237,
306, 312, 337. See also
Burguera y Serrano,
Amado de Cristo
Franco government, 375,
377, 384
Franco-Prussian War, 350
fraud: seers accused of,
131, 141, 187, 295,
297, 299; and spiritism,
342

Freemasons: and Aulina,
384; and anticlerical
measures, 70; Ezkioga
opponents, 52, 141,
237, 343; and Integrists,
34; in visions, 174, 361;
visions plot of, 225,
237, 384
freethinkers, 37, 124, 344
friendships among believ-
ers, 146
fright, 167, 245, 372. See
also fear
Fuengirola (Málaga), 386
fueros, 18, 30, 34
funeral, civil, 76
Funes (N), 468n28
furniture maker, 26

Gabiria (G), 23, 63, 236–
237, 275
Gaintza (N), 227, 444n30
Gainza (G), teenage girl
from, 198
Gainza (N). See Gaintza
Galarreta (Alava), 341
Galvez (Toledo), 432n42
games in visions, 191, 194,
249–250
Garabandal (Cantabria)
visions, 365–366, 398,
399, 428n32
Garín (G), 233
Gaviria (G). See Gabiria
gender: of Basque reli-
gious, 217, 219,
444n39; of dead in vi-
sions, 459n1; at end of
world, 367; of Ezkioga
seers, 243–254, 448n6;
mixing, 203, 228; and
models of sacrifice, 96–
103; and number of vi-
sions, 448n6; of persons
at visions, 449n20; and
piety in Zegama, 207;
and reactions to visions,
276–277; and religious
belief, 168; of seers in
mini-Ezkiogas, 194; of
seers of dead, 459n1; of
spectators, 252, 252,
449n20; and vision
states, 299
gentry, Basque urban, 74,
123, 130, 254
Germany, 144, 370
Gernika, mission pageant
at, 220
Gerona. See Girona

Gethsemane, 288
ghosts, and spiritism, 342
Gijón (Asturias), 375
Gipuzkoa: elections, 14,
17, 24–25, 30, 440n61;
Irurzun visions through-
out, 182; postwar crack-
down, 377; priests of,
133; religious in, 217,
219, 230, 444n39;
shrines, 337, 338; tele-
phone network, 40; vi-
sion cuadrillas 1932 on,
210–211; visions spread
in, 164, 191–213; and
witchcraft, 211–212
Gipuzkoan dialect, 171,
165
girls. See child seers; teenagers
Girona, 22, 164, 462n40;
Benita in, 150, 159, 361,
366–368, 389; diocese
of, 87, 384
God: acting directly, 189;
justice, 33; severe or benign, 345–346; speaking
with, 263
Goiherri (upland Gipuz-
koa): burial customs,
327–330; habitual seers
from, 165; politics, 25,
440n61; vocations, 219–
222
Good Friday processions,
204
gossipers, 205
Gota de Leche, La, 233
governors, civil, 137, 353.
See also Artola, Jesús;
Bandrés; Del Pozo Ro-
dríguez, Pedro
grace: accumulation of,
395; allotment of, 188,
192, 195, 272–273,
395–396; appeals for,
266; through crucifixes,
91, 95, 185, 200, 272–
273; through flowers,
272; home delivery, 232,
234, 338; intoxication
from, 399; for polities,
394–395; of seers of
ghosts, 340
Granada, 154, 227, 282
Gran Promesa subscrip-
tion, 442n14
grass, eating, 296
Great Monarch, 350, 366–
367, 370, 409

Grenoble, 4
Guadalajara, **164**, 169, 282
Guadamur (Toledo), **164**; Patxi and Medina visit, 60, 105; priest killed, 376; seers, 169, **170**, 276; visions 1931, 167, 169–171, 240, 275, 382
Guernica (B). *See* Gernika
Guéthary (Pyrénées-Atlantiques), 387
Guipúzcoa. *See* Gipuzkoa

habits: Franciscan, as burial clothes, 332; as ghosts' clothes, 340
hallucination, 31, 244, 286, 295
halo, angel places, 332
handkerchiefs: with blood of Christ, 338; ghost marks on, 340, 341, 461n34; Mary attribute, **329**; Mary carries bloody, 83; messages on, 81; and Ramona's blood, 49, 132, 308
hands: bleeding, 49–51, **52**, 83, 273, **284**; clasped shut, 142, 273; fixed as a cross, 273; juice as sign on, 176; light from Mary's, 3, 178, **235**, **248**, 290; of Mary, in questionnaire, 404
headlights, and visions, 167
healer: Daughter of Charity, 234; Padre Mamerto, 241; seer as, 182
healing: by blessed flowers, 200; by blessed ribbons, 204; by water and dirt, 303
heart, changes of, 366
heaven: dead in, 77, 131, 173; families reunited in, 335; kin in, 326–332; kin of others in, 327–332; for publicists, 114; request to go directly to, 232; for seers and believers, 99, 293, 327–332, 334–335; visions of, 189, 335–336
heavenly gifts: on beams of light, 290; Laburu on,

131; medals, 58, **63**, 64, 246, 271, 378, 436n100; religious picture, 187; rosaries, 50, 78, 253, 436n100; statue, 432n29. *See also* flowers, blessed
heaviness, as sign, 198, 273
Hechos de Ezquioga, Los: and devil, 150; financing, 159, 436n101; imprimatur, 143–144, 159–160; money to destroy, 388; preparation, 143, 149–150, 155, 159–160; storage, 160, 388, 398; visions relating to, 144, 208
hell: for active opponents, 143, 150, 334; dead in, 131, 173, 174, 461n18; for nonbelievers, 186, 207, 232; people thrown to, **349**, 356, **360**; reactions to visions of, 346; spirits deny existence of, 342
Hendaye (Basses Pyrénées), 282
Heraldo Alavés (Vitoria), 32
Heraldo de Madrid, 344
herder seers, 165, 166, 172, 302–303, 309, 312, 324, 398
heresies and sects, extermination of, 367
Hernani (G), 49
Herri Batasuna, 172
"hidden transcript," 260
Hierro, El (Santa Cruz de Tenerife), 461n32
Hijas de la Providencia (San Sebastián), 435n84
hills. *See* mountains
holy cards, 95, 96, 205, **291**, 372
holy family, 176, 210
Holy Land, 74, 104, 118
Holy Office: and Claire Ferchaud, 284; and Ezkioga, 151, 159; and Madre Esperanza, 386; and Madre Soledad, 228; and Padre Pio, 284
holy war, 30–33, 78, 260
Holy Week, 236, 313, 400

Hormiga de Oro, La (Barcelona), 309
horse: dove changes into, 293; white, of Saint Michael, 177, 353–354, 364
hotels, visions to build, 383
Hotel Urola (Zumarraga): Burguera at, 150, 155, 388–389; and Catalan expeditions, 84, 90, 357, 362; owners, 134, 388–389; seers at, 84, 357, 362
house, unit of identity, 172, 181
houses. *See* vision sites, houses
Huarte Araquil (N). *See* Uharte-Arakil
Huesca, 367, 385, 435n83
Huici (N), 263
humor about visions, 166–167, 170, 171, 174, 210–211, 362, 383. *See also* ridicule
hymns: "Agur Jesusen Ama," 264, 267; in Barranca, 179, 182–183; on deathbed, 124; "Egizu zuk Maria," 265, 268, 450n11, 450n14; at Ezkioga, 46–47, 151, 265, 267, 268, 299; "Izar Bat," 46–47; at Lourdes, 264; in visions, 267, 335
hypnotism, 113, 274, 279, 286–287, 298
hypnotists, 113, 342
hysteria, 130, 180, 245, 282, 285, 295, 344

Ibdes (Zaragoza), 297
Icasteguieta (G). *See* Ikastegieta
Icod de los Vinos (Santa Cruz de Tenerife), 461n32
iconoclasm, 5, 14, 16, 26
Igeldo, Mount (G), 361
Ihabar (N), 183, 355
image of Virgin of Ezkioga, **329**; arrival in miracle, 364; commission, 136; copy for Macià, 431n33; installed and removed, 137–139, 311–312; in Kapotegi,

165, 212. *See also*
Basque; Catalan; Spanish
Languedoc, 339
La Puye (Vienne), 60
La Salette vision, 4, 163,
249; and Ezkioga, 352,
358; in Spain, 4, 5, 8,
25, 365
Lasarte (G): Brigida nuns,
219; mission tableau,
248
Las Palmas de Gran Canarias, 94
Last Judgment: in catechism, 348–350, **349**;
dates for, 350, 351,
356–357, 362–365; Goiherri anecdotes, 210,
372; in poetry, 356; in
vision, 283, 330
Latin America, Basques in,
44, 68, 129, 221, 224,
256
Lauspelz (house, Ataun),
220
lawsuit, over Lizarraga
visions, 178
lawyer believers, 87, 253
Lazcano (G). *See* Lazkao
Lazkao, Benedictines at,
14, 219, 220, 239
leaves, relics of visions,
305
Lecumberri (N). *See*
Lekunberri
Legazpi (G), 19, 23; Ama
Felisa in, 337; boy seer
from, 246; Múgica visits, 158; rector, 148–
149, 154, 224; sinners,
99; turns on seers, 134.
See also Aguirre Odria,
Benita; Garmendia, José
Legazpia (G). *See* Legazpi
legends, shrine, 166, 195,
302, 309
Legorreta (G), 23, 138,
164, 219, 389; Communion denied, 242;
image in, 312; Saint
Michael appears in, 210;
seers, **276**, 378, 381. *See
also* Echezarreta Urquiola, Juan José
Lekunberri (N), 23, 172,
181
Lequeitio (B). *See* Lekeitio
Lérida. *See* Lleida
Lescoüet (Côtes-du-Nord)
visions 1821, 415n5

letters, secrets in sealed,
49, 50, 60, 91, 176, 364
levitation, alleged, 25, 61,
278, 295, 452n39
Lezaun (N), 23, 177, 248,
374
Lezo (G), witness from, 51
Liberal, El (Bilbao), 24,
30, 171, 342
Liberal, El (Madrid), 31–
32, 171, 352
liberal Catholics, 97, 345–
346
liberal professions, few
seers in, 254
Liberals, 34, 255, 267
Librería Ignaciana (San
Sebastián), 73
Libro de las Casitas, El,
226, 228
lies, and seers, 50, 60, 173,
297, 331
light: divinities want, 200;
around Mary, 56, 289–
290, 352; Mary emanates, 3, 83, 178, 235,
248, 290; moving like
UFO, 324; precedes visions, 15, 168, 289,
327; in questionnaire,
404
lily, scent of, 189
Limpias, Christ of: bleeds
in Ordizia, 159, 200;
image in Zumarraga, 46;
picture in Aldaz, 230
Limpias (Cantabria) visions, 6, 22; Catalan
pilgrimages, 66; and
Catholic movements, 42;
and communism, 371;
Ezkioga compared to,
28, 254; Ezkioga enthusiasts at, 33, 91, 134,
144, 224–225, 236, 376,
396–397; Ezkioga opponents at, 238; Ezkioga
seers at, 160, 389,
440n71; meaning, 97,
161, 347; other seers
and cult of, 230, 285;
personal grace at, 395;
replications, 163; role of
parish priest, 53; social
class and, 252, 254
Lisieux, Navarrese pilgrimages to, 447n66
Litany: arms as cross, 20,
37, 46, 72, 264, 266; in
vision liturgy, 178, 264–

265, 267; and vision
states, 15, 299
literacy, 24, 87, 226
liturgy: Amundarain and,
264–269; heavenly figure
joins in, 27–28, 266;
order of, at vision sessions, 200–201, 450n11;
ornaments for Ezkioga
shrine, 207; seers give
instructions on, 232–
233, 265, 268; traditional, and apparitions,
264; and vision states,
263–272
Lizarraga (N), **164**, 177–
178, 181, 248, 397
Lizartza (G), 227, 444n30
Lizarza (G). *See* Lizartza
Lleida, 86, 159, **164**, 376
Llívia (Girona), 91
Longwy (Meurthe-et-
Moselle), 155
Lorenzo, San, migrating
image of, 166
Los Arcos (N), 275,
443n30
lottery, 123
Lourdes, 22; Basques at,
21, 192, 197, 264, 314;
in Belgium, 152; and
Catalans, 66, 335; cult,
3, 5; cures, 5, 86, 155,
274, 335, 398; Ezkioga
compared to, 5, 32, 146,
196, 240, 306; Ezkioga
enthusiasts at, 33, 110,
111, 133, 155, 185,
264, 398; and Huysmans, 109; Irurita and,
67; liturgy at, 314;
model for Ezkioga, 8,
28, 264, 273, 306, 312,
314, 373; profitability,
128; replications, 163;
in Spain, 5–6, 25, 146,
237; Spanish seers at,
146, 398, 440n71; in
Spanish visions, 192,
291; visions and trances,
4, 263, 273, 287. *See
also* Soubirous, Bernadette
Louvain (Belgium), 151,
279
lowland-upland cultural
divide, 212
Loyola (G), 23, 105–106,
124, 239–240
Lucca, 231

Lucillos (Toledo), 437n5
Luises sodality, 36, 38,
  192, 326
Luxembourg, 156
Luz Católica, 366
Lyon, 155

Madonna dell'Arco shrine
  (Campania, Italy), 263
Madrid, **164**; anticlericalism, 5, 14, 18, 32, 376;
  assassin from, 364; be-
  lievers in, 56, 385, 410–
  411; chastisement, 357,
  364, 365, 426n89;
  clergy killed, 376; devotions, 5, 238, 394,
  446n60; image bleeds in,
  445n49; Merciful Love
  center, 238, 446n60;
  promoters in, 65, 387;
  seers from, 169, 326,
  460n2; seers in, 65, 258,
  344, 389, 390, 466n43;
  Vallet in, 384
magazines, women in, 97
magic, black, 187, 345
magnetist, 344, 345
Málaga, chastisement, 357
males. *See* child seers—
  boys; gender; men
Mallorca, 118, 365, 377
Mañeru (N), 15
mania, 274
Marcha Real, as royalist
  anthem, 141, 143
Marcilla (N), 16
Mari, as mountain spirit,
  213
Mariage Nul, 110, 111
María Mensajera (Zara-
  goza), 383, 398
Marist Brothers, schools,
  447n70
market gardener, 94
Markina (B), **23**, 37
Marpingen (Saarland, Ger-
  many) visions, 8, 163,
  454n62
Marquina (B). *See* Mar-
  kina
marriage, civil, Rignés oppose, 111
Marseillaise, 5, 39
Marseilles, chastisement,
  352, 357
martial law, 160, 198
martyrs: believers to be,
  143, 169, 467n9; and
  earthquakes, 357, 359;

in Last Judgment, **349**;
  men as, 96; seers as,
  100, 140, 141, 154, 364
marvellism, 399
Mary: and Aliadas, 47;
  asks for prayers, 20,
  275, 327; assists in seer
  crucifixions, 149, 407;
  attributes, 28, 32, 358,
  403–404; attributes in
  doubt, 30, 31, 33, 131,
  167; aura, 188; avatars,
  28, 194, 291, 403; bap-
  tismal names, 192; and
  Basques, 29–33, 104;
  benign or stern, 346;
  and blood, 83; and Cat-
  alans, 104–105; celestial
  rank, 199; and chastisement, 104–105, 354,
  357; condemns clergy,
  79; and the dead, 331;
  devotion in Albiztur,
  192; dress, 28, 30, 313,
  403, 432n54; emotions
  of, in visions, 27–28,
  188, 265, 291; and
  flowers, 28, 166, 191,
  226, 304; gestures of, in
  questionnaire, 404; gifts
  for angels, 271; as girl
  or teenager, 246; girl
  seers compared to, 246,
  280; as healer, 31, **292**;
  heavenly court, 272;
  kisses objects, 91; and
  light, 56, 289–290, 352
  (*see also* light); marks
  shrine site, 310, 312;
  mute in visions, 27, 48,
  291; at night, 314; par-
  ticipates in prayers, 266,
  267; picture on tree,
  195; reveals Bilbao de-
  fenses, 375; and rivers,
  441n88; and Spain, 16,
  33, **292** ; and trees, 302,
  304; wants clear peti-
  tions, 321. *See also*
  Mary Sorrowing; Mirac-
  ulous Mary; *and names
  of individual Marian
  shrines (by place)*
Mary Sorrowing: in Ez-
  kioga visions, 27, 31,
  84, 139, 235, 313; im-
  ages, 307, 313, **329**,
  364; Mendigorría, 15–
  16; in mini-Ezkiogas,
  194

Masons. *See* Freemasons
mass: to kill, 340; to release the dead, 331, 340;
  to show off, 361
Mataró (Barcelona), 86,
  106
matches, blessed, for end
  of world, 371
Matí, El (Barcelona), 66,
  132
Matxinbenta (G), 254
may poles, 458n29
Mazarambroz (Toledo),
  437n5
medals: blessed in visions,
  91; of Daughters of
  Mary, 38, 58, 63; divine
  gifts, 58, 63, **64**, 246,
  271, 290, 378,
  436n100; miraculous,
  3–5, 234; touched to
  tree, 308
media, and vision mes-
  sages, 39–40
Medjugorje (former Yugo-
  slavia), 8, 163, 396
memory: in Catholicism,
  399–401; immediate, of
  vision, 285, 286, 288; as
  vision, 300; visions retained and lost, 177;
  wishful, and vision site,
  303
men: Catalan vs Basque,
  106; as converts, 244;
  exercises for, 106; Mary
  on, 228
Meñaka (B), 341
Menasalbas (Toledo),
  437n5
Mendata (B), 356, 450n2
Mendigorría (N), **23**; electoral violence, 16; seers
  at Ezkioga, 33, 416n7;
  town secretary, 379; visions, 14–16
meneurs, general public as,
  401
men seers, 26, 243–244,
  250–251; as confirmers,
  250, 274; humbled by
  visions, 274–277, **276**;
  hysterical, 277–278; not
  initiators, 250; and vision states, 299
mental command, as test
  of seers, 241
mental hospital at Mon-
  dragón, 138, 142, 143,
  145

mental illness: of seers, 61, 130, 187, 274, 336; seers because of, 282–283; and vision states, 299
mentally retarded, 179
mental patients, and seers, 283
Mercedarian Sisters of Charity, 44, 45, 222
merchant-client ties, 200
Merciful Love, Jesus of, 238, **239**, 386, 409
mercy vs chastisement, 238
mesmerism, 286
messages: dictated in vision, 333; omitted or rejected, 401; private from divine [*encargos*], 144, 195, 200, 210; rewarded, 401
metamorphosis: horse to dove, 293; flower to Mary, 166; monkey to witch, 26
Mexico, 151, 339
Michael, Saint: and Basque Nationalists, 206; in Basque processions, 204, **205**; to bring statue, 364; description, 177–178, 205, 293, **349**, 353–354, 364; to explain apparitions, 353, 364; in Ezkioga church, 21, 204, **205**; fights devil in Navarra, 178, 181, 184, 187, 195, 202–203, **205**; fights on mountains, 32; in Last Judgment, 204, **349**; motto in vision sessions, 201; past apparitions, 21, 204; and reign of Sacred Heart, 204, **205**; in world war, 358. *See also* San Miguel de Aralar
Milagrosa y los Niños, La, 16
military exercises, 41
military service, and mores, 36
militias against Antichrist, 366–367
Milizie Crocifere, 366
millennium, 351, 367
mill towns, 106
mini-Ezkiogas, general features of, 194–195

Minims, 366
miracles: enemies of, 137, 286; of Ezkioga spring and soldier, 133; the great, 49, 206, 353–354, 355, 369; invisible candy, 173; Mary saves oxcart, 250; preparation for, 206; Ramona asks about, 49; seers become, 271
miracles predicted: 10 July 1931 on, 28; 12 July 1931, 20, 28, 353; 16 July 1931, 20, 28, 60, 353; 18 July 1931, 20, 28, 78, 353; for fall 1931, 51; for mid-October 1931, 60, 76; 15 October 1931, 49–51, 77, 113, 114; 16 October 1931, 20; 17 October 1931, 113; 18 October 1931, 78; 20 October 1931, 63; 1 November 1931, 63; 4 December 1931, 63; 8 December 1931, 182; 26 December 1931, 60, 62, 113, 129; for January 1932, 62, 129; in Cuevas de Vinromà, 297; disappointment, 268; García Cascón and, 76; on height above Urretxu, 191; Laburu on, 131; in Rafols forgery, 70, 71–72; Rigné spreads word, 114; unpunished, 297; when stage completed, 77
Miraculous Mary: circulating image, **235**; in Gipuzkoa, 234–235, 248, 337, 446n52; girl as, **248**; in Navarra, 16, 179; original vision, 3–4; in visions, 234–235, 282, 291, 455n81. *See also* Labouré, Catherine; miraculous medal
miraculous medal, 3–5, 234
Miranda del Ebro (Burgos), 154, 166
misogyny, 453n53
missing persons, 341, 344, 464n8
mission, divine: of Aliadas, 47, 52; of Ayerbe, 144;

of Basque deputies, 60; of Boada, 87; of Burguera, 119–120, 121–122, 143, 146, 149; of Franco, 74; of Irurita, 71–72; of Jesuits, 71; of Macià, 79; of Pius XI, 71; of Rigné, 111, 114, 133; of Vallet, 84–85
missionaries: female, 221–222, **221**, **222**, 226; male, 44, 98, 203, 220–221
Missionaries of the Sacred Heart, 340–341
Missionary Sisters of the Holy Eucharist (Betelu), 225–229
mission magazines, 442n10; Carmelite, 190, 248–249
missions, overseas: Ama Felisa and, 339; Carmelite, 241; children and, 190–191, 220, 221, **222**, **248**; prayers for, 36
missions, parish: Barranca, 172; and children, 247; and collective vows, 37; defensive, 19; and gender, 244, 245; and the Passion, 236, 397; vision sessions like, 265, 266, 296, 366, 397
Miss República and Miss Spain, 98
Mollerussa (Lleida), 86
monarchists, 32, 383
monarchy, predicted return, 210, 337
Mondragón (G), 23, 337; asylum, 138, 142, 143, 145, 452n38; convent of Santa Isabel, 232
money: for chapel, 166; for masses, 99, 331; for prisoners, 339; visions for, 181, 382–383
monkey, in Ormaiztegi visions, 26
Montecillo (Burgos), 454n59
Monte Gargano (Puglia, Italy), 21, 204
Montesclaros (Dominican house, Cantabria), 238
Monte Umbe (B) visions, 398, 438n22

Month of Mary (devotion), 86, 192
Month of May (devotion), 18
Montoussé (Hautes-Pyrénées) visions 1848, 415n5
Montserrat (shrine, monastery), 74, 79, 87, 92
moon: cult, 179; destination of alms, 339; at feet of Mary, 353, 362
"Moors," in prophecies, 356, 367
Morocco, war in, 351
morphine, 278
mortifications, 45, 226, 337
Morzine (Haute-Savoie), 286
mothers: children of seer, 95; pressure children to see, 248; and seer children, 56, 83, 180, 391; seers see dead, 78, 327, 336
mountains: shrines on, 302, 380; spirits of, 212; visionary fighting on, 32, 206. See also vision sites: mountainside
mourning clothes, in chastisement, 359
mouth, cannot open as sign, 273
mulberries, and Infant Jesus, 176
Mundaka (B), 462n40
Murchante (N), 416n11
murder, of seers, 26, 100, 364
music: Amundarain and, 43; clergy and, 123; at death, 124; stimulates visions, 404; vision command, 56. See also hymns
Muslims, in visions, 353, 367
Mutiloa (shrine, G), 337, 338
mysticism, conventual, and apparitions, 369

narration: of heaven by seers, 330; of mystic mass by seers, 201; of tableaux by saints, 293–294; of visions by

Amundarain, 264; of visions by seers, 173
Narvaja (Alava), Cistercian convent at, 231
national decadence, 97
nationalism, 7, 19, 104–107. See also Basque nationalism; Catalan nationalism; Spanish nationalism
Navalperal de Pinares (Avila), 432n42
Navarra, 7, 181; Basque language in, 7, 171, 212; children identify dead, 330; and Euskadi, 206; and Limpias, 6; literacy 1931, 24; and Lourdes, 5; pilgrims from, 165, 268, 380; politics, 16, 25, 137, 374; religious in, 230, 444n39; visions in, 171–191; vocations in, 15; and witchcraft, 211–212
needles, seers pierced by, 149, 278, 296
neighbors, 142, 257, 317, 339, 393
Netherlands, 156
"neurotic contagions," 179, 180, 286, 295
newspapers. See press
night, retiro by, 9, 27, 35, 36, 37, 131
night visions: in Barranca, 175; prime time, 267–268, 451n17; suspect, 2, 27, 131, 264, 314
noisy army at night, 372
novenas, 86, 90, 323
nudism, 97, 109, 126
Nuestra Señora de Angosto shrine (Valdegovia, Alava), 165–166
nuns: active, 98–99, 230, 233–234; and Aliadas, 45; Basque, 217; in Basque Country, 99, 230, 444n39; contemplative, 99, 227, 230, 231–233, 242; corrupted, 147; deaths in Civil War, 376; and diocesan priests, 225–229; at Ezkioga, 121, 234; Llívia, 91; in mental hospital 143; Pamplona, disbelievers, 191; predict Ezkioga visions, 28, 29;

prophetic, 230, 409–410; seers at Ezkioga, 232, 252; seers become contemplative, 196, 233; seers see in visions, 266; seers work to convince, 143, 231–233; spiritual direction, 44, 231, 233; as spiritual directors, 226, 232; visionary, and Ezkioga, 228, 229–231; as writers, 238. See also religious orders; and convents (by town); individual nuns; individual orders

Obra de la Santa Infancia, 227
Obra Maxima, La (Carmelite mission magazine, San Sebastián)
obsession, 274
Ocaña (Toledo), 376
Oiartzun (G), 23, 100
Oliveto Citra (Campania, Italy) visions, 8; escalation, 463n1; liturgy, 450n7, 450n13; processions of dead, 462n39; role of parish priest, 418n4; vision committee, 447n2
Olot (Girona), 438n25
Oña (Burgos), Jesuit school at, 129
Oñate (G). See Oñati
Oñati (G), 23, 164; believers at Ordizia, 200; Ezkioga rosary group, 206, 337; religious, 231, 237; Saint Michael in procession, 204; seers, 251, 306; youth transgressions, 36
Ondarreta jail (San Sebastián), 198, 199, 375
Onkerzele (Belgium) visions, 152
Opus Dei, 45
oracles, 229
oral history, biases of, 177
Ordizia (G), 23, 58, 124, 164, 200, 337; cinema and dances, 38; clandestine visions, 160, 196, 199, 200–201, 377, 379; seer excursions from, 201, 203; seers in, 196; vocations, 219

Orense (province), 454n59
Orgiva (Granada), 164, 170
original sin, 111
Orio (G), 344
Orlaza-aundia (house, Ataun), 220
Orléans, 160
Ormaiztegi (G), 23, 164; dancing in, 38; politics, 38, 330; public opinion, 382; rector, on Ezkioga, 222; Rignés in, 112, 132; vision house, 29, 207, 377, 379; visions in, 26, 131, 330; vocations, 219
Ormaiztegi seers: servant, 29; teenage girl, 267; young girls, 7, 20, 26, 58, 119, 241, 246
Ormáiztegui (G). See Ormaiztegi
Our Lady of Begoña shrine (Bilbao), 340
Our Lady of El Pilar (Zaragoza): Basque antipathy to, 193; and duende, 344; and mental patient, 283; seers visit, 202; and Spain, 33, 189
Our Lady of La Gleva shrine (Vic, Barcelona), 461n21
Our Lady of Liernia shrine (Mutiloa, G), 337, 338
Our Lady of Mount Carmel, 210, 234
oxen, and vision, 166
Oyarzun (G). See Oiartzun

paganism, 217, 303, 313
pagans, conversion of, 190, 191, 221
pageants, mission, 220, 221, 221
pain: insensitivity to, in seers, 147–150, 148, 278, 279, 285, 288, 296, 433n59; taste for, 96; in vision crucifixion, 406
paintings, seers like, 280
Palamós (Girona), 86
Palencia, 164; bishop of, 194; convent in province, cheap masses, 338–339; visions near, 194, 439n55
Palermo, 263

Palmar de Troya, El (Sevilla), García Cascón at, 398
Pamplona (N), 23, 164; cathedral canons, 206, 227, 374; diocese and Barranca visions, 175, 184, 189, 190; diocese and Madre Soledad, 226–229; diocese and press, 6; first Communion, 249; Infant Jesus in, 241; and Iraneta visions, 182; normal school, 124; politics, 16; postwar prayer meetings, 380; religious and visions, 28, 191, 238, 241; Rignéin, 158; rural seers in, 124, 182, 191; spiritists, 462n42; vision sites, 191, 194; young women seers, 121–122
Papal States, apparitions 1796–1797, 163, 394
paper mills, 19, 138
Paracuellos del Jarama (Madrid), 376
Paray-le-Monial (Saô-et-Loire), 2, 117–118, 351
Paris: Benita in, 389; Burguera in, 117; chastisement, 352, 357, 361, 365, 370; Corbató in, 366; and 1830 visions, 3–4; Rigné and Thirouin in, 157; rural Basques in, 37, 361
parish church: attendance, 36; image not allowed in, 139; keeper, 192; seers reject, 167, 180, 194, 351; as vision site, 6, 14, 15, 182, 187–190, 192, 315; vision site like, 305–307
Parish Exercises movement, 74–76; and class mixing, 260; and Ezkioga prayers, 107; martyrs, 96, 376
parish missions. See missions, parish
parish priests. See clergy, parish
Pasaia (G), 14, 23, 164; servant girl seer from, 31, 245
Pasai Donibane (G), rector of, 133

Pasajes (G). See Pasaia
Pasionario, El, 236
Passion: of Ciordia and Galdós, 149, 294; of Gemma, 296; Mary at, at Ezkioga, 231; model for self-abnegation, 259; Pou i Prat suffers, 336; replication of landscape, 313–314; and spiritual exercises, 64; visions of, by Neumann, 283. See also crucifixions, seer
Passionist Fathers: anniversary mass, 377; and basilica, 374; circulate images, 234; Deusto-Bilbao, 231–232; Gabiria, and visions, 236–237; and Limpias, 236; later silence, 382; missions, 236; and victim terminology, 96
pathology, and vision states, 299
patron-client patterns, and visions, 255–257
Paul, Saint, and attributes, 208
peasants, 19–20, 255; pope will lead, 356; and visions, 209, 253, 353, 396
peddler, 344
penance, 176, 209, 267
Pensamiento Navarro, El (Pamplona), 15, 25
perception, structuring of, 8
perfume, of saints, 90, 91, 189
Perpetual Help, Mary of, 312
Peter, Saint, in tableau, 293
petitions: ambiguous responses, 323; to avoid purgatory, 408; for blessings, 111, 294, 318, 408; for conversions, 319, 323, 324; for cures, 232, 317, 318, 323, 408; for discernment, 323–324; estimated number, 319; for dead, 77, 134, 192, 323, 324, 330–333, 336–339; Gemma and, 296; importance for seers, 322; make visions habitual,

sciousness, 274–275. *See also* arguments against visions
prophecies: in Bizkaia, 356; danger for seers, 187; experts in, 369–371, 408–410; fascination, 382; in France, 4, 350; importance, 371; responses to petitions as, 322; short-term, 351; in times of trouble, 350
prostitutes, 54
Protestants, 4, 109, 111
providence, 90, 395
psychiatrist, 175
psychokinesis, 344
psychologists, 129, 285–286
Puebla de Montalbán (Toledo), 437n5
Pueblo Vasco, El (San Sebastián), 25; in Urnieta, 209; in Zaldibia, 196
puerility: as spiritual discipline, 227; of visions, 130–131, 134; of women, 97
pulse rates, 201, 274–275, 278–279
pupillary reflex, 188, 201, 278, 282
purgatory: anxiety about, 392–393, 408; communion to free soul, 338; crucifixions free souls, 99; hell in chastisement, 357; live people seen in, 131, 134, 338; Mary takes man from, 332; neighbors in, 176, 192; pilgrims avoid, 85, 460n16; prayers get souls out, 192, 210, 331–332, 341; relatives in, 78, 130–131, 332; for skeptics, 334; souls as intercessors, 328–329, 341, 462n38
purification of Spain, 72, 410
purity, 45, 109, 245

quarrels: among promoters, 150; among seers, 64, 107, 144, 406–407
quarry worker, 192
Quero (Toledo), 437n5
questionnaire, 26, 403–405, 455n77; and con-

versions by reaction, 277; light, 289; Mary's gestures, 291; seer reactions, 295
questions: captious, for seers, 103, 188, 338; guide visions, 26, 40, 82
quietism, visions as, 107

racism, 197, 286
Radical Socialist Republican Party, 344, 439n55
radio, 74, 129, 418n52
Rafols crucifixes, 68–71, 73–74, 183, 202
Rafols forgeries, 67–74; and Basque gentry, 73–74; and Civil War, 375; and Ezkioga enthusiasm, 73, 130; and Ezkioga messages, 71–73, 422n18; and Franco, 74, 422n8; Irurita and, 71–73, 422n14; Jesuits and, 71, 422n9, 422n12; opponents of, 70–71, 422n10; Pius XI and, 70, 71, 422n12; Segura and, 384, 422n8, 422n10; Vallet and, 104, 384, 422n10
railroads: access to vision sites, 3, 194; Andalusian, 109; assaults on, 16; in Basque country, 22–23, 165; lights cause visions, 382; republican employees, 7; vision on train, 138; visions along tracks, 176, 180; visions at stations, 67, 119
rape, 146
rationalism: and contingency, 396; cures refute, 5, 6; and mystical phenomena, 286, 296
razor blade, 51
real-estate broker, 201
reciprocity, in Iberian society, 320
reflexes, in visions, 282
Regil (G). *See* Errezil
reign of Christ: association, 118; in Balda poem, 186; in Benita's scenario, 358; until end of world, 365; and Great Monarch, 367; in Morrondo, 351. *See also* reign of Sacred Heart

reign of Jesus and Mary, in Inés Igoa's visions, 174
reign of Sacred Heart: Alacoque visions, 2, 350–351; Bernardo de Hoyos, 351; and Burguera, 351; and Franco in 1940, 74; imminent in 1932, 351; Jesuits promote, 350–351; and Limpias, 347, 351; in 1934, 369; in 1940, 74, 409–410; in Rafols forgeries, 71, 351; and Saint Michael, 204, 205; and Sarachaga, 117–118; solution to evil, 395–396; visions prepare, 369. *See also* reign of Christ
reincarnation, 341
relics: blood from picture, 200; blood on cloth, 50, 183, 308, 338; earth from chapel site, 310; fragments of cross, 139, 312; of Gemma, 95; from trees, 305, 307–309
religiosity, local, 1–2
religious, female. *See* nuns; religious orders; *and individual orders*
religious, male: and chastisement, 358; deaths in Civil War, 376; from diocese of Vitoria, 217; and Ezkioga, 236–241; and rural folk, 361. *See also* religious orders; *and individual orders*
religious orders: active vs contemplative, 219, 220; and Carlism, 18; and French devotions, 5; members of, in Basque Country, 230; recruitment, 218, 231; and Republic, 231; social class within, 219; as subcultures, 231; and urban migration, 230; visions bless, 395. *See also* nuns; religious, male; *and individual orders*
Reparadoras, 64, 96, 99
repentance, 236, 355, 357, 366
replication, of visions and messages, 163, 396

reporters, 40, 47, 84, **276**
repression, intensifies belief, 199–200
Republic: Amundarain prayer, 65; as Antichrist, 353; and Barranca visions, 182, 183; and Basques, 19, 30–33; and diocese of Vitoria, 14, 142, 143, 209–210; as dragon of Aralar, 206; Ezkioga and, 18; and Medina, 55–56; 1932 crackdown, 137–143; 1934–1935 crackdown, 198, 209–210; and nuncio, 155; and regional Catholics, 105; and religious, 231; and removal of crucifixes, 14, 18, 70, 97, 130, 416n11; removes images, 193, 394; and rural children, 191; and Sanjurjo rebellion, 136–137; seers on, 78, 120; separation of church and state, 128; should promote visions, 115; and social relations, 14, 33–40; youth support, 39. *See also* civil governors; Constituent Cortes
republicans: assault trains, 16; explain visions, 383; and Ezkioga apocalypse, 352–353; like spiritism, 344; urban immigrants, 19, 30; in villages, 227, 330, 443n24
retiro (curfew for women), 27, 35, 36, 37, 131
Reus (Tarragona), 86, 99
revival meetings, American, 286
Revue Métapsychique, La, 450n1
Rex group, 152–153, 160, 434n77
ribbons, **183**, 204, 291
ridicule: of Aranda, 228; Balda addresses, 186; of Burguera, 143; of Ezkioga and *duende*, 344; of Michael on horse, 353, 364; of occultism, 344–345; of Orgiva visions, 170; of pilgrims in Barranca, 184; of Recalde, 95; of seers and

believers in Goiherri, 30, 60, 78, 193, 196, 210, 381; by seers before visions, 274–275, 405; of seers by Laburu, 133; by seers of devil, 189; of vision sites, 304, 314
Rielves (Toledo), **164**
right-left imagery, 83, 150, 330
rigorism, 109, 192, 199, 345–346
Rinconcito, El (vision site, Ordizia), 196, 199, 200–201, 377, 379
rituals, quasi-religious, 187
river: Infant Jesus walks on, 176; red with blood, 356; spirits and Bernadette, 441n88; visions by, Bakaiku, 119, 176, 180; visions by, Goiherri, 26, 172, 195
rivers, and *lamiak*, 212
road, visions in the, 169, 177–178, 314, 455n82
roads, and access to visions, 194
Rochefer, La (Jesuit house in France), 446n59
Roman soldiers, 124, 405
Rome: Burguera and Sedano in, 160, 388; Madre Esperanza in, 386; Madre Soledad visits, 228; modern world like pagan, 97; purgatory museum, 340–341
rosaries (beads): blessed in visions, 91, 178, 270–272, **270**; consecrated or not, 188; from heaven, 49, 50, 58, 78, 131, 253, 271
rosary (prayer): Aliadas count, 45; Amundarain leads, 46, 47, 264; apparitions to restore, 38; at Bachicabo, 166, 167; in Barranca, 172, 173, 174, 181, 184; as curse, 138; decline, 36, 38; exhilarating effect, 300; at Ezkioga, 27, 264–265, 267, 268, 269, 404; at Goiherri sites, 193, 196, 200–201, 206, 209; at Guadamur, 170; Imaz leads, 203; impulse to attend, 167; at

Lourdes, 4, 264; Mary requests, 20, 38, 268, 275, 327; Mary says, in vision, 267, 450n14; at Mendigorría, 15; priests cannot lead, at Ezkioga, 51; in school, 18; during statue removal, 139; and vision states, 299
Rosas y Espinas, 238
roses, **272**, 292
Rotary Club, Tusquets on, 225
rural landless, as seers, 253–254
rural life, idealization of, 260
rural sharing, visions support, 396
rural to urban migration, 3, 165, 230
rural-urban alliance at Ezkioga, 33, 260

Sabadell (Barcelona), 86, 106, 321, 423n47
Sacerdotes Niños, Obra de los, 225–229
Sacrament, Blessed, prayers to, 187
sacraments, denial of, 374, 379, 384
Sacred Heart of Jesus: amulets, 45; bleeds, **135**, 445n49; in boy's vision, 266; children and, 247; consecration of Spain, 394; Detentes, 45; Great Promise campaign, 442n14; in houses, 207; and Integrism, 19; and Labouré, 4; Mary gives girl picture, 187; in Mendigorría, 15; in nineteenth-century Spain, 5; original visions, 2; in public, contested, 193, 394; in Rafols forgeries, 68–74; repels break-in, 120; Saint Michael fights for, 204, **205**; and Spain's salvation, 189; statues, 39; in Sueca, 119; in textile mill, 76; wounds Recalde, 96. *See also* reign of Sacred Heart
Sacred Heart of Mary, and Labouré, 4
sacrifice, 96–103, 207

seers *(cont'd)*

ers, 42, 260, 272; Catalan at Ezkioga, 90, 134, 259, 423n18, 455n82; and Catalan trips, 75–96, 99–107; as Christ, 99 (*see also* crucifixions, seer); control wealthy believers, 260; after cures, 86–87, 335, 386, 398; of dead, 459n1; death of, 103, 124, 296, 297, 334; demands on, 316–325, 370–371; direct liturgy, 232–233, 265, 268; "distinguished," 252–253; ethnic Basques, 254; excursions, 147, 202–204, 206; families stigmatized, 94, 100, 193, 400; female, and cloistered nuns, 231–233; female, welcome visions, 277; as frauds, 131, 141, 187, 295, 297, 299; friends with reporters, 40, 84; gifts to, 92, 131, 141, 297; habitual, 165, 251–254; hold court, 272; hometowns, 20, 22–23, **164**; as intermediaries with dead, 336; as intermediaries with heaven, 320; "invisible," 78, 93, 250–252; kinds of, 243–254; know owners of objects, 188; as martyrs, 100, 140, 141, 154, 364; as mentally ill, 61, 130, 187,274, 336; as missioners, 296; number, 26, 250–251, 364; piety scrutinized, 36–37, 131; poor rural, 162, 381; not puppets, 85, 401; and reporters, 40, 84, **276**; rural, 147, 370; against seers, 149; skills of successful, 371, 401; as sorcerers, 187; spectators become, 250; sudden social importance, 320, 325; symbiosis with promoters, 42, 109, 114, 126, 161–162; as underdogs, 115, 162; unmarried, pregnancies, 93, 146; vet book, 150; as victims, 26, 96–103,

364; and visionary nuns, 228, 229–231; visit other visions, 33, 60, 397. *See also* child seers; herder seers; men seers; servant seers; teenage seers; women seers; *and individual seers*

Segorbe (Castellón), 22, 120, 143

Segura (G), 78, 144, 228, 453n51

self-deception by Ramona and Neumann, 285

Semana Católica, La (Madrid), 351

seminarians, 132, 198

seminary of Vitoria, 14, 130

Señal de la Victoria, La (Valencia), 367

Señoritas Operarias Parroquiales, 86, 87

separatists, seers as, 199

sermons, 192, 356; against Ezkioga, 197; seers give, 173, 182, 184, **185**, 186

serora of Liernia, 338

serpent, 149, 204, 432n30

servants: as cultural mediators, 255, 259; spread visions, 171; teenage women as, 36; ties with employers, 200, 256; in visions and witch-scare, 212; Zaragoza medium, 344. *See also* servant seers

servant seers, 253, 258–259; in Catalonia, 91, 259, 332, 335–336; employers and, 257, 337; from Goiherri, 29, 49, 57–58, 63, 192, 196, 207, 245; in 1980s, 259

Sestao (B), 30, 165

settlement patterns, 171, 212

Seven Sorrows of Mary, 265, 323

Seville: anticlerical riots 1931, 32; Casa Blanca (palace), 56; Casa de Pilatos (palace), 53; Crucíferos in, 367; Irlandesas convent, 53; Sanjurjo coup, 136–137

sex: attitudes toward, 37–38, 109, 111; and female charismatics, 228;

at vision site, 131, 146–147

sextons, 181, 192

shame, after Ezkioga visions, 94, 381–382, 400

sheep, 192, 291, 292, 297

shepherds, 302–303, 309, 324, 398. *See also* herder seers

shopkeepers, as believers, 207

shrines, 46, 166, 302–303, 308. *See also* pilgrimages; *and individual shrines*

Siglo Futuro, El (Madrid), 351, 359

signs: altered states, 273–274; for end of world, 356, 367; in Ezkioga visions, 273; hoped for, 28; mean trouble, 324; in medieval visions, 273; moving light, 324; preternatural heaviness, 198; scents as, 90; of souls in purgatory, 340–341; towns spinning, 355; walls after miracle, 353, 364

Sigüenza (Guadalajara), 123, **164**, 169

silence, ecclesiastically imposed, 211, 383

Sillon movement, 427n26

Sinai, Mount, 313

sinners, 99, 204–205

sins: Benita knows, 95, 123; capital, catechism poster and, **360**; Evarista knows, 90; Laburu on knowledge of, 132; Lete knows, 124; Luis knows, 182, 186–187; Madre Soledad knows, 227; of modernity, 37; Recalde knows, 95, 132; seers know, 134; Sueca seers know, 116

Siracusa (Sicily) visions, 163

Sisters of Charity of Saint Anne, 67–74, 323, 385

skeptics at visions, 273

Slaves of Merciful Love, 386

sleeplessness after vision, 56, 275, 277

snakes, and chastisement, 293, 364

snow, 28, 356, 357, 358, 359

social class: in clergy, 219, 255; contact between, 203, 254–261; in La Mancha, 167; and the right, 260–261; and visions, 252, 325

Socialista, El (Madrid), 143

socialists: and apocalypse, 351; Basque, 7; horizontal bonds, 257; La Mancha, 167, 168; and 1934 uprising, 62; seers, 244

Social Reign of Jesus Christ (association), 118

social work, 86–87, 227, 230, 233–234

sociocentrism, Iberian, 116

sodalities, 192 *See also* Daughters of Mary sodality; Luises sodality

Soirées (Brussels), 153, 158

soldiers, 133, 182, 337, 464n8

Soledad, Virgen de la, at Guadamur, 169

Solsona (Lleida), 397

somnambulism, 274

Sorbonne, 389

sorginkeriak (witch-stuff), 27, 173, 298, 383

Soria, mental patient in, 282

Sorrowing Mother. *See* Mary Sorrowing

souls in purgatory. *See* purgatory

souvenirs, **69**, 73, 91, 138, 240

Soviet Russia, 361, 365, 371, 390

Spain: apparitions in, 1–2, 5–6, **22–23**, 317; blood on, **135**; chastisement, 33, 97, 361; consecrated to Sacred Heart, 394; divine preference for, 364, 394; Ezkioga visions for, 32; Gemma cult in, 295; literacy 1931, 24; news of European visions in, 5–6, 25, 152, 230, 234–235, 248–249; news of Neumann in, 284; prayers for, 15, 16, 32, 33, 56, 72, 188, 189, 267; puri-

fication of, 72, 410; as wounded sinner, **292**

Spanish, in visions, 26

Spanish Civil War: clergy killed, 376; not chastisement, 371; Rafols forgeries and, 375, 422n8; religious mobilization for, 107, 261, 371; seers and believers in, 374–377; in Zaldibia, 198

spas, 119, 226, 254

spectators, **252**, 449n20

Spirit, Holy, pigeon as, 201

spiritism: American, 297, 320; Catholic church and, 117, 206, 342, 345; and de la Villa, 109; and Ezkioga, 225, 298, 342–345; Sueca, 117; at time of visions, 341–342, 343–345, 462n42; Tusquets charge, 225, 384; and visions, Laburu on, 279

spirits, and literature, 110–111

spiritual direction: by Amundarain, 44; by Arintero, 231, 238; by Aulina, 385, 395; by Burguera, 144, 151, 407; by Madre Soledad, 226, 227, 385; by seers, 201, 395–396; of seers, 124, 241, 398, 424n53

spiritual exercises: deconvert convents, 233; feelings in, 64, 314; imagery in visions, 64, 124; in San Sebastián, 46, 64, 129; seers attend, 64; for textile workers, 76; in Zumarraga, 46. *See also* Parish Exercises movement

spring: at Ezkioga, 310–312; hoped for, 28, 306; shrine and, 302, 313; and unbelieving soldier, 133

stage, Patxi's, 58, 60, 77, 101, 236, 308; effect on audience, 269, **269**; Laburu on, 131

stages: in Barranca, **174**, 175, 184; in Passionist missions, 236

stairway, celestial, 267, 293

star, distributed in vision, 236

stars: collision of, 372; around Mary, 135, 182, 352; staring at, 174

stations of the cross: at Ezkioga, 99, 130, 223, 271, 310; in Navarra, 263; at Ordizia, 200; in Ormaiztegi, 207; in Urnieta, 209. *See also* Way of the Cross

statue. *See* image

steel mill, 95

stereotypes, 243–250

stigmatics: contemporary, 25, 98, 156; Ezkioga female seers, 50, 58, 96; Gemma, 295–296; Neumann, 283, 284; Padre Pio, 284; suggestion in, 287

stockbrokers from Bilbao, 95, **123**

Strasbourg, 4

strikes, 14, 76, 141, 431n31; Mary intervenes, 380–381

strolls: sinful by couple, 37, 38; visions on, 169

Studium Catholicum, break-in at, 120, 389

Sueca (Valencia), 22, 116, 121–122, 388–389

suggestion: at Ezkioga, 42, 150, 266, 279, 286; and stigmata, 285, 287

suicide, 76

summer people, 167, 253, 254

Sunday, work on, 4, 5, 204, 346

"superstitions," 309, 373

sweating, of Mary in visions, 28

sword: of God, Balda on, 186; Mary holds, 31–33, 83

swords: angels with, **205**, 349; bloody, 32, 55, 83, 354; of fire and blood, 364

tableaux: of chastisement, 293; children in, **36**, 248, 456n90; vision, 27, 31–32, 291–294

Tabor, Mount, 288, 313

Tajo River, apocalypse battle by, 359
Talavera de la Reina (Toledo), 465n29
Tarbes (Hautes-Pyrénées), 5, 157, 240, 436n95
Tarrasa (Barcelona). *See* Terrassa
Tàrrega (Lleida), 320
taxi drivers, 134, 244, 275, 375
tears. *See* weeping
teenage boys, 38, 46
teenage boy seers: Bachicabo, 165–166; Barranca, 180–187; Dorrao, 173. *See also* Cabezón, Aurelio; Lete Sarasola, Cruz
teenage girls, 46, 245
teenage girl seers, 245–246, 251; Bakaiku, 176–177; Dorrao, 173–174; later nuns, 196, 233; Rielves, 168; Zaldibia, 196. *See also* Ataun, girl from; Celaya, María; Galdós Eguiguren, Evarista; María Luisa; Núñez, María Dolores; Olazábal, Ramona; Soubirous, Bernadette; Viñals Laquidain, Gloria
teenagers, in visions and witchcraft, 211–212
teenage seers, as models, 38
telephones, in Gipuzkoa, 40, 50
television, at Guadamur, 382
telluric symbol-signs, 118
Tenerife, 123
Terrassa (Barcelona), 22, 164; in Civil War, 376, 467n9; devotion to Montserrat, 74; Fatima image enters, 397, 397–398; parish bulletin, 132; Parish Exercises,74; pilgrims at Ezkioga, 78, 86, 318–320; political tensions, 76, 106
testing seers: by fire, 147–150, 148, 278, 296, 433n59; by mental command, 241; by mental request, 144. *See also* discernment

textile industry, 74, 76, 256
theater: Amundarain writes for parish, 43; Ezkioga liturgy as emotional, 265–266, 296, 366; Navarrese visions like, 330; parish missions as emotional, 247; seers more convincing than actors, 84; visions dismissed as, 171, 295, 298, 373
theaters, 130, 133, 149, 204, 256, 361. *See also* cinemas
theosophy, 344
Tibadabo shrine (Barcelona), 96
Times (London), 344
Tobalina (Alava), 166
Toledo, 164, 167, 169, 376; executions of clergy, 376; interest in Ezkioga, 167, 169; interest in Guadamur, 169
Tolosa (G), 19, 23, 164; cure in hospital, 233; doctors, 51; Ezkioga cult in, 242, 254, 337; mystic Communion, 152, 159–160, 241; teenage girl seers in, 56, 58, 114, 258; visions of Asunción Balboa, 210; visions near, 194
Tona (Barcelona), 86, 164, 335
Torelló (Barcelona), 86
Toroella de Montgrí (Girona), 389
Torralba de Aragón (Huesca) visions, 14, 22, 248, 397, 415n11
Torrano (N). *See* Dorrao
Torrente de Cinca (Huesca), 91
tourism, and mores, 33–38. *See also* summer people
Tours, 109
town centers (*kaleak*) vs farms, 45
town councillors, seers at Guadamur, 169
town council meetings, seers in, 199
town secretaries, 144, 146, 181, 186, 379
Traca, La (Valencia), 33

Tradición Navarra, La (Carlist, Pamplona), 25
Tradición y Progreso (Valencia), 367
Traditionalists. *See* Carlists and Carlist-Integrists
Tragic Week of 1909, 106
trains. *See* railroads
"trance," 87, 110, 263, 265, 275. *See also* vision state
transhumance, 172
treasure, buried, 95, 344, 425n70
trees: apparitions save, 380; inside basilica, 307; as bleachers, 167; and crosses, 307–308, 308, 312; frame vision, 327; medals touched to, 308; rejected as vision sites, 314; relics from, 305, 307–309; as *reredos*, 306, 310; seers in, 166; shrines and, 302; symbolize Basque provinces, 307. *See also* trees, visions near
trees, visions near, 194; apple, 49, 140, 303; ash, 173; holm oak, 306; oaks, 180, 304–310, 311, 312–314; olive, 169, 170; pine, 166, 174, 178, 179; poplar, 176, 180; walnut, 173, 174
Trent, Council of, 303
Trinitarians, 441n2
tuberculosis, 103, 317
Tudela (N), 202, 203, 227
typhoid fever, 234

Uharte-Arakil (N), 164, 368–369
Unanu (N), 164, 178–180, 179
Unanua (N). *See* Unanu
United Kingdom, 361
United States of America, 221, 361, 387
urban migration, 3, 165, 230. *See also* immigrants
urban-rural cultural divide, 33–36, 212, 253–260, 359–362
Urdiain (N), 437n20
Urkiola (B), 22, 203, 337, 338

Urnieta (G), **164**; believers in, 144, 333; Irurzun escapes, 374; visions in, 145, 208–209
Urquiola (B). *See* Urkiola
Urrestilla (G), 142, 225, 355
Urretxu (G), 23; anniversary mass, 377; boy seer from, 28, 32; mother of seers, 253; religious, 233, 377, 381–382; visions in, 191, 314
Uruguay, 74, 86, 129
usury, 204
Utrera (Sevilla), 398
Uztegi (N), 444n30
Uztegui (N). *See* Uztegi

Valdegovia (Alava), 165; shrine, 165–166
Valence (Drôme), 104, 384
Valencia, 19, 376, 385, 421n3; archdiocese and Burguera, 116, 140; Corbató in, 366–367
Valladolid, 22, **164**; convent of Santa Isabel, 122, 232; Ezkioga enthusiasts, 388; Great Promise shrine, 442n14; Lete visits, 124; printer for Burguera, 159
Vallmanya (Lleida), 138–139
Vascones, 179
Vatican, 70, 228, 385. *See also* Holy Office; Pius XI; *and individual popes*
vegetarians, 344
Vendée Rebellion, 361
Vergara (G). *See* Bergara
verse broadsides (*bertsoak*), 100, 146–147
Viana (N), 416n11
Vic (Barcelona), 86, 253, 335, 461n21
vicar general of Vitoria. *See* Echeguren y Aldama, Justo de
Vich. *See* Vic
victims: cloistered nuns as God's, 96; for father's conversion, 99; seers as God's, 96–103; women transcend role of, 141
Vidania (G). *See* Bidegoyan
Vida Sobrenatural (Salamanca), 231
Vilabona (G), 256

Vilafranca del Penedès (Barcelona): Rafols birthplace, 67; Rafols complex, 70, 71, 385, 422n8; seer, 324
Villaesteva (Lugo) visions, 250
Villafranca (N), 438n25
Villafranca de Oria (G). *See* Ordizia
Villanañe (Alava), 237
Villarcayo (Burgos), 377
Villarreal de Urrechua (G). *See* Urretxu
Villasana de Mena (Burgos), 218
Villaseca (Soria), Last Judgment, 283
Villena (Alicante), 386
Vincentians, 3–4, 282
Virgin. *See* Mary
Virgin of the Twelve Stars, 371
vision content and messages: distortions, 186; evolution, 347–348; incorrect, 131; many facets, 333, 348; predictable, 300; texts, 122
vision leaders in mini-Ezkiogas, 179, 194
visions: counter-church, 167, 180, 194; cyclical dynamic, 8, 163; daytime, 267, 451n17; decorum at, 47, 268, 289–290, 305–306, 457n11; on demand, 129–130, 187; devil's work, 187, 189, 378; evolving motifs, 195; and external enemy, 7; for family, 176, 194, 196; and fiestas, 166, 181; gift of God, 144, 407; interpretation of, 240, 242, 246; legends of, 166, 195, 302, 309; "mental contagion," 130–132; minor, smoked out, 168, 169; monopolies attempted, 150, 322–323; new power, 20–21, 24; political, 31–33, 39, 55, 210, 337; private sessions, 195–203, 206–211; replications, 163–213; sacred theater, 171, 236, 265–266, 296, 366; Spanish after 1945, 380,

397–399, 457n2; Spanish before 1520, 2, 272–273, 457n2; spread by contact, 171–194; spread by persecution, 195–211; spread by press, 165–171; "strong" vs "weak," 165, 437n1; study of, through believers, 40; "subjective" or "objective," 279; success of, 194; towns with, **164**; "truth" of, 9; undermine faith, 8, 38, 133, 189–190; unorthodox, 25–27; vague to definite, 289; vindicate powerless, 260; and witchcraft, 163, 180, 187, 211–213. *See also* arguments against visions; Ezkioga visions; night visions; proof of visions; seers; vision states
vision sites: blackberry bushes, 304; building exteriors, 169, 178, 194, 314; on bus, car, or truck, 91, 177, 202–203, 314; caves or grottos, 4, 152, 170, 302, 306, 457n2; in chapel, 191, 208, 209, 315, 457n2; church porch, 192–193; houses, Bizkaia, 206; houses, Gipuzkoa, 131, 141, 145, 191, 194, 198, 207, 209; houses, Navarra, 173, 176, 177, 178, 184, **185**, 191, 196; insane asylum, 143; mountainside, Barranca, 177, 178, 187, 191; mountainside, Catalonia, 324; mountainside, France, 4, 315; mountainside, Gipuzkoa, 193, 194, 212–213, 302, 303, 305, 313, 315; office, 141–142; in parish church, 6, 14, 15, 182, 187–190, 315; railroad tracks, 67, 119, 176, 178; rectory, 199; rejected, 314, 401; religious houses, 3, 124, 191, 203, 232–233; return to landscape, 315; rivers, Barranca, 119,

INDEX OF PERSONS

280; and Gemma, 90, 424n59; and chastisement, 355; and holy regime, 362; vision text, 405–406; predicts death, 428n42; and Sedano, 124; death as religious, 103, 378; pamphlet about, prohibited, 158; "in heaven," 334

Le Vachat (French royalist), 396

Lewis, I. M., 456n103

Lex, Barbara W., 456n103

Lezaun, Bruno (rector, Abárzuza), 218

Lizarraga, Felisa (Dorrao), 173–174

Lizarraga, José (seer, Dorrao), 173

Llanza i de Montoliu, Ignasi (Aulina supporter, Barcelona), 139–141

Lliró, Marc (Piarist, Barcelona), 84, 90, 92

Llull, Ramon (theologian, mystic, Mallorca), 118

Lolita. See Núñez, María Dolores

López de Lerena, José María (Portugalete), 206

López de Lerena, Julián, sees bishop in 1952, 378–379

López de Lerena, Sebastián (electrical engineer, Bizkaia): and Viñals 1933, 149; rebukes Burguera, 150; defends visions, 369, 370; and Degrelle, 153; petition to pope 1934, 374; possibly Crucífero 1940s, 368; sees bishop in 1952, 378–379

López de Maturana, Margarita María (founder, Berriz), 221

López Galuá, Enrique (priest, writer), 350

López Pinto, General José, 375

López y Mendoza, José (Augustinian bishop of Pamplona 1899–1923), 204, 226, 227

Loyola, Ignacio de (founder, canonized 1622), 46, 429n6; celebrates vision mass, 201;

seer poses like images, 240

Lucio (boy seer, Mendigorría), 15–16

Luébanos, Consuelo (seer from Sevilla), 281

Luis. See Irurzun, Luis

Luis de Santa Teresita (bishop, Carmelite), 241

Luistar (Juan Múgica Iturrioz, barber, poet, Albiztur), 147, 192, 193

Lujanbio Retegi, José Manuel ("Txirrita," poet), 146–147

Macià, Francesc (president, autonomous government of Catalonia): Garmendia involves, 79, 138–139, 141; at Montserrat, 79, 80; Ezkioga image for, 431n33

Maguncio, Padre (Clérigo de San Viator, Vitoria), 447n70

Maiza Auzmendi, José (Etxarri-Aranatz), 175, 184

Malachy, Saint, 365

Mamerto, Padre (Carmelite, Altzo), 241

Manescal, Onofre (theologian), 340

Manjón, Andrés (Catholic educator, Granada), 119

Manterola, Ander, 441n2

Manzano García, José Luis (seer, Talavera), 465n29

Marañón, Gregorio (medical eminence), 282

Marcelino, Padre (Passionist), 237

Marcet, Antonio María (Benedictine, abbot of Montserrat), 74, 79, 80

Marcet, Miquel (mill owner, Terrassa), 76, 376–377

Marcet, Vicenta (member, textile family, Terrassa), 74, 385

Marcos, Andrea (Aliada, Madrid), 419n17

Marcucci, Maria Giuseppina Teresa. See Marcucci, Maria Maddalena

Marcucci, Maria Maddalena (Passionist mystic, Bilbao): vision of

Gemma, 445n43; knows Aulina, 232, 385; and Ezkioga, 231–232; believes Evarista, 408; later life and beatification, 385

María Antonia del Señor, Sor (prophet), 465n40

María Luisa (teenage seer, Zaldibia), 141, 196, 203, 420n54

Maria Maddalena de Gesú. See Marcucci, Maria Maddalena

María Margarita del Niño Jesús (Passionist, Deusto), 408

Marín, María (seer at El Palmar de Troya), 398

Mariscal, Padre (Redemptorist), 447n70

Marsay, Bénédicte de. See Rigné, Raymond de; Thirouin, Marie-Geneviève

Martin, Thomas (French prophet), 350, 370, 396

Martínez Cajigas, José (photographer from Santander), 280, 398

Martínez de Muñecas, Laureano (Capuchin), 284

Martínez Sarrasa, José Javier (town secretary, Mendigorría), 379–380, 398

Martín Ruíz, Gregorio (rector, Guadamur), 171, 376

Martín Sánchez, Benjamín (priest, writer), 350

Masmelene (Eulogio Gorostiaga Etxebarria, priest, writer), 32, 417n22

Massenet, Jules (composer), 426n5

Mateos, Izmael (father of seer, Beasain), 378

Mateos Ayesta, Conchita (child seer, Beasain): background, 145; Imaz scribe, 145, 203; interrogation, fall 1932, 141; in mental hospital, 145; and Ayerbe, 145, 432n52; experts evaluate, 144, 149, 285; Burguera excludes, 149; and

Pius XII (pope 1939–
1958), alleged belief in
Ezkioga, 388
Polo Benito, José (dean,
Toledo), 169, 376
Ponsoda, José María
(sculptor), 125, 136
Porsat, Madeleine (French
nun, mystic, nineteenth
century), 53
Pou i Martí, Josep (Cata-
lan Franciscan, Rome),
71
Pou i Montfort, Pere
(Jesuit in India), 240,
447n63
Pou i Prat, Anna (seer, servant, Tona), 335–336,
345
Primo de Rivera, Miguel
(military dictator 1923–
1930), 7, 14, 74, 351
Puchol Montis, Vicente
(bishop of Santander
1965–1967), 334
Pugés, Pepita (seer, Cer-
danyola), 398
Puig-Ràfols, Teresa (seer,
Vilafranca del Penedès),
324

Quiñonero, Antonia
(cleaning lady, seer, Barcelona), 423n18
Quintanilla, General,
467n4

Rafols y Bruna, María
(founder, Daughters of
Charity of Santa Ana,
Zaragoza, 1781–1853):
founds order, 67; litera-
ture on, 68–71, 75, 157;
devotion to, 46, 73;
Neumann on, 285; vi-
sions of, 73, 293,
423n18; cause for beati-
fication, 68–70, 385. See
also Rafols forgeries in
subject index
Rainaldo de San Justo
(Carmelite from Mar-
kina), 134, 241
Ramona. See Olazábal,
Ramona
Ramón y Cajal, Santiago
(histologist, Madrid),
343, 344
Recalde, María (seer, Du-
rango), iii; background

and character, 93–94,
142; early visions, 93,
95; Sedano is scribe,
123; knows sins and
converts, 95, 132, 134,
159; and Catalans, 95–
96, 273, 324, 332,
424n59; activity in
vision, 270; Bilbao
supporters, 95, 259,
420n51; martyrdom in
chastisement, 364; re-
bukes Laburu, 134–135,
260; chapel and spring,
94, 310; questioned and
remanded, 141, 142,
143; and Burguera, 122,
148, 149, 150; with
Múgica in Durango,
154; detained in Du-
rango, 434n81; mission
money, 337, 339; in war
and after, 93, 339, 377,
381
Remisch, Fernand (writer,
steel company employee,
Lyon), 155–156, 386
Renshaw, Alfredo (private
secretary, Madrid), 409–
410
Reyes, Pedro de los (teenage witch-tester, Oiart-
zun), 212
Rezano, Felipe (Dorrao),
173–174
Rigné, Raymond de
(French writer and art-
ist): background and
works, 109; character,
110–111, 113, 126,
157–158, 160–162;
Catholicism, 115, 133,
346, 353–354; crisis and
second marriage, 110;
divine mission at
Lourdes, 111, 133; at
Ezkioga, summer 1931,
111–113; vision photog-
raphy, 111–112; Ra-
mona and wounds, 113;
defense of Ramona, 113,
114, 115, 157, 158,
160, 388; Sertucha in-
vestigates, 113–114,
129; and Laburu, 133;
attracts foreign journal-
ists, 156, 158, 184; and
Múgica's circular, 154;
and Burguera, 126, 148,
150; Múgica exposes,

157–158; defense against
diocese, 158, 160,
430n18; denied com-
munion, 158, 160; ex-
pelled 1935, 160; jailed
and expelled 1937, 375,
386, 387; return after
war, 387, 397; enduring
friendships, 115–116;
death in France, 387;
Cité Vivant, Le, 109;
"Encyclical on Conjugal
Morality," 111; Nou-
velle Affaire Jeanne
d'Arc, Une, 114–115,
115, 157. See also Thir-
ouin, Marie-Geneviève
Rita, Santa (seer in
Etxarri-Aranatz), 176
Rivero San José, Jorge
María (writer), 118
Roch, Saint, 170
Rodes Bagant, Lourdes
(teenager, Barcelona), 92
Rodes Buxados, Arturo
(Barcelona clerk, writer),
90, 92, 93, 93, 95, 273
Rodrigo Ruesca, Lino
(auxiliary bishop of
Granada 1929–1935),
154, 385
Rodríguez, Ulpiano
(worker, Bilbao),
436n97
Rodríguez Dranguet,
Alfonso (republican
magistrate), 141–143
Roig Gironella, Juan (Je-
suit, San Cugat), 398
Romain, Paul. See Boni-
face, Ennemond
Romanones, Count of
(Liberal leader), 283
Romero, Epifanio (Ezkioga
schoolteacher, republi-
can), 245
Rouget, Gilbert, 456n103
Roulé, Marie (French seer),
427n14
Rozo y Alarcón, Angelina
(nun, Betelu), 443n31
Ruíz, Mercedes (owned
image, Madrid), 445n49
Ruíz Muñoz, Emilio ("Fa-
bio," Integrist canon,
Málaga), 465n33

Sabaté, Luisa (seer, Reus),
425n59
Sabean, David, 259

Tomás, Enriqueta (cont'd)
lona), 282, 371–372,
425n70
Toroella, Antonio José
(politician from Te-
rrassa), 76, 423n28
Torras y Bages, José
(bishop of Vic 1846–
1916), 105
Torre Ricaurte, Soledad de
la (founder of convent,
Betelu), 225–229, 334,
345, 385
Torres Amat, Félix (bishop
of Astorga 1835–1847),
359
Tortras Vilella, Antonio
(doctor, Barcelona),
452n49
Touchet, Stanislas (cardinal of Paris), 110
Towianski, Andrzej (Lith-
uanian prophet), 350
T'serclaes, Duke of
(Madrid), 56
Tusquets, Juan (crusader
against Freemasons),
225, 345, 384
Tuya, Manuel de, 453n56
Tximue. See Imaz Lete,
Tomás
Txindor (writer, El Día),
423n20
Txirrita. See Lujanbio Re-
tegi, José Manuel

Ulacia Odriozola, Juliana
(seer from Tolosa and
Zaldibia), 198, 210,
253, 334, 337, 377
Unamuno, Miguel de (phi-
losopher, deputy in Cor-
tes), 128
Urbano Lanaspe, Luis (Do-
minican writer, Valen-
cia), 71, 238, 376
Urdanpilleta, José (poet),
147
Uribe, Matilde (wealthy
protector of seers, Elo-
rrio and Bilbao), 95, 160
Urquía, María de los Do-
lores de Jesús y (Augus-
tinian seer, Aldaz),
444n38

Urquijo, Julio (deputy in
Cortes), 25
Usabiaga, Juana (shop-
keeper, Ordizia), 199,
200, 442n14

Valeriano de Santa Teresa
(Carmelite, Pamplona),
241, 447n67
Vallet, Francisco de Paula
(preacher, founder of
order): Parish Exercises
movement, 74–75, 87,
96, 106–107; forced to
Uruguay, 75; news of
Ezkioga, 76, 79; Ezkioga
seers report blessing,
84–85, 87; against Ez-
kioga, 103, 113; holds
Naya fraud, 103, 104,
384; seers and believers
abandon, 103–104; to
Valence, 104, 384; death
in Madrid, 384
Valtorta, Maria (Italian
mystic), 379
Varela, General José En-
rique, 375
Vianney, Jean ("Curé
d'Ars," canonized 1925),
133
Vidal i Barraquer,
Francesc de Asís (arch-
bishop of Tarragona,
1919–1943, cardinal
from 1921), 74, 104,
143
Vidaur, Miguel (opthamol-
ogist, San Sebastián),
282
Vilallonga, José (industrialist, Bilbao), 54
Villa, Antonio de la (journalist, Radical Socialist
deputy in Cortes): pro-
tests in Cortes, 33, 128,
240, 246; rebuttal to,
169; Burguera on, 120
Villafranca de Gaytán de
Ayala, Count of (Ber-
gara), 238
Ville, Raymond de la
(French general), 109
Viñals Laquidain, Gloria
(teenage seer, Pam-

plona): meets Burguera,
121–122; visions in con-
vents, 232; demand for
retraction, 148; and Rex
group, 152; and Rigné
marriage, 158
Vincent de Paul (founder
of Vincentians, canon-
ized 1737), 98
Vintras, Eugène (cult
leader), 350
Visa de Dios, Carmen
(seer, servant in Te-
rrassa), 91, 95, **259**,
332
Vroncourt, Raymond de.
See Rigné, Raymond de

Xanti from Gabiria, con-
version of, 275
Xenpelar (poet), 100,
356

Ydewalle, Hubert d'
(Belgian journalist),
434n77
Yzurdiaga, Fermín
(Falangist canon, Pam-
plona), 374

Zabala, Padre (Jesuit,
Bilbao), 447n64
Zabaleta, León (farmer
seer, Oñati), 251
Zacchia, Paolo (Italian
physician), 274
Zozaya, Antonio (colum-
nist), 352–353
Zubeldia, Nestor (rector,
Pamplona seminary),
227
Zulaika, Joseba, 381
Zulueta, Luis (deputy in
Cortes, diplomat), 49,
419n25
Zumalcarregui, Tomás
(Carlist military hero),
207
Zunzunegui, Cándida
(seer, farm in Zaldibia),
196, **197**, 198–199,
337
Zurbitu, Demetrio (Navar-
rese Jesuit), 70, 240,
422n9

Designer: Seventeenth Street Studios
Text: 9.5/13 Sabon
Display: Sabon
Compositor: Braun-Brumfield, Inc.
Printer/Binder: Edwards Brothers, Inc.